GLOSSARY

Abbaye	Abbey
Baie	Bay
Barrage	Dam
Boucle	Meander
Butte	Mount, hill
Calvaire	Calvary
Cap	Cape
Chau	Château
Ecluse	Canal lock
Haras	Stud farm
Forêt	Forest
Ile	Island
Marais	Wetlands, marsh
Mont, Mt	Mount, mountain
Pays	Region
Plage	Beach
Pointe	Headland, point
Pont	Bridge
Presqui'île	Peninsula
Rocher, roche	Rock
Vallée	Valley

THE GREEN GUIDE

Normandy

Rainbow over Normandy farmland, A. de Valroger/MICHELIN

MICHELIN

General Manager Cynthia Clayton Ochterbeck

THEGREENGUIDE **NORMANDY**

Editor Alison Coupe
Principal Writer Margaret LeMay
Production Manager Natasha G. George
Cartography Stéphane Anton, John Dear
Photo Editor Yoshimi Kanazawa
Photo Researcher Claudia Tate
Proofreader Karolin Thomas
Interior Design Chris Bell
Layout Alison Rayner
Cover Design Chris Bell, Christelle Le Déan
Cover Layout Michelin Apa Publications Ltd.

Contact Us

The Green Guide
Michelin Maps and Guides
One Parkway South
Greenville, SC 29615
USA
www.michelintravel.com

Michelin Maps and Guides
Hannay House
39 Clarendon Road
Watford, Herts WD17 1JA
UK
☏01923 205240
www.ViaMichelin.com

Special Sales

For information regarding bulk sales, customized editions and premium sales, please contact our Customer Service Departments:
USA 1-800-432-6277
UK 01923 205240
Canada 1-800-361-8236

HOW TO USE THIS GUIDE

PLANNING YOUR TRIP

The blue-tabbed PLANNING YOUR TRIP section at the front of the guide gives you **ideas for your trip** and **practical information** to help you organise it. You'll find tours, practical information, a host of outdoor activities, a calendar of events, information on shopping, sightseeing, kids' activities and more.

INTRODUCTION

The orange-tabbed INTRODUCTION section explores Normandy's **Nature** and geology. The **History** section spans Roman times through William the Conqueror to the modern day. The **Art and Culture** section covers architecture, art, literature and music, while the **Country Today** delves into modern Normandy.

DISCOVERING

The green-tabbed DISCOVERING section features Principal Sights by region, featuring the most interesting local **Sights**, **Walking Tours**, nearby **Excursions**, and detailed **Driving Tours**. Admission prices shown are normally for a single adult.

ADDRESSES

We've selected the best hotels, restaurants, cafés shops, nightlife and entertainment to fit all budgets. See the Legend on the cover flap for an explanation of the price categories. See the back of the guide for an index of where to find hotels and restaurants.

Sidebars

Throughout the guide you will find blue, peach and green-coloured text boxes with lively anecdotes, detailed history and background information.

A Bit of Advice

Green advice boxes found in this guide contain practical tips and handy information relevant to the sight in the Discovering section.

STAR RATINGS★★★

Michelin has given star ratings for more than 100 years. If you're pressed for time, we recommend you visit the ★★★, or ★★ sights first:

★★★ **Highly recommended**
★★ **Recommended**
★ **Interesting**

MAPS

- National Driving Tours map, Places to Stay map and Sights map.
- Region maps.
- Maps for major cities and villages.
- Local tour maps.

All maps in this guide are oriented north, unless otherwise indicated by a directional arrow. The term "Local Map" refers to a map within the chapter or Tourism Region. A complete list of the maps found in the guide appears at the back of this book.

PLANNING YOUR TRIP

INTRODUCTION TO NORMANDY

DISCOVERING NORMANDY

Welcome to Normandy

This former dukedom today incorporates all or part of seven French *départements*, **with Rouen as the capital; to the west lie the British Channel Islands. The coast offers elegant resorts, while cows, orchards and hedgerows provide rural charm. Castles and abbeys such as Mont-St-Michel evoke history, which includes the June 1944 Normandy Landings. The cuisine, favouring cream, is justly celebrated.**

CALVADOS *(pp80–151)*

Lying along the English Channel, Calvados offers sandy beaches under rugged cliffs and elegant resorts such as Deauville. The Normandy Landing Beaches provide sombre memories. Inland lie ancient hedgerows, apple orchards and pretty half-timbered houses. Castles and abbeys recall Duke William, whose conquest of England is illustrated by the tapestry at Bayeux. Pause to savour cheese, cider and "Calva".

Deauville, Calvados

© Veni/iStockphoto

PRESQU'ÎLE DU COTENTIN *(pp152–161)*

Shaped like a snail's head, this rocky peninsula extends into the English Channel with the port of Cherbourg-Octeville at its tip. Lighthouses, bays and splendid views line the coast. A national park offers excellent bird-watching.

EURE *(p162–193)*

Medieval villages and beautiful gardens draw visitors to this eastern portion of Normandy, site

Le Bec-Hellouin, Eure

© Peter Rees/Dreamstime.com

of the famed home and garden of Impressionist painter Claude Monet at Giverny. The ruined abbey of Le Bec-Hellouin, as well as châteaux and manor houses galore, provide glimpses of great beauty and tumultuous history, while the Forêt de Lyons to the northeast reigns as France's greatest beech forest.

EURE-ET-LOIR *(pp194–201)*

The Perche, the Norman corner of this inland *département*, lures visitors from nearby Paris with its wooded hills and picturesque villages. Dreux, the area's principal city, houses the remarkable 19C funerary monuments of the Orléans family, while the splendid Château d'Anet recalls a 16C royal mistress, Diane de Poitiers. The Parc naturel régional de Perche offers woodland drives and the surprising town of Nogent-le-Rotrou, with its massive 12C–13C castle and late Gothic city centre.

MANCHE *(pp202–249)*

Extending into the English Channel, for which "Manche" is the French name, this *département*'s greatest monument is the abbey of Mont-St-Michel, which has drawn visitors since medieval times. The long coastline lures holidaymakers to charming seaside villages, while inland towns such as Ste-Mère-Église and St-Lô recall the fierce battles of the Normandy Landings.

MAYENNE *(pp250–263)*

The portion of of this *département* that extends into Normandy includes the cities of Laval, with its medieval centre and terraced Perrine Gardens, and Mayenne, with its 8C castle. Ruins of the Roman town of Jublains recall Julius Caesar's Gaul, while the countryside offers forests, castles, and fields where horses graze. Along the River Mayenne, visitors can bathe and rent watercraft.

ORNE *(pp264–299)*

This inland portion of Normandy is renowned for stud farms, including the Haras du Pin, on the grounds of an 18C château. Sturdy Percheron horses are found around Bellême; farms offer shows and rides. Local products include Camembert cheese.

PLAGES DU DÉBARQUEMENT *(pp300–309)*

Three suggested driving itineraries take you around the beaches and battlefields of the 6 June 1944 so-called D-Day Landings, when Allied forces stormed ashore in an attempt to reclaim Europe from the Nazis.

SEINE MARITIME *(pp310–79)*

The richest and most commercial part of Normandy stretches north of the River Seine from Rouen to the great port of Le Havre. Its long seacoast takes in the delightful resorts of Dieppe and Étretat, while the interior offers woodland, prosperous farmland, and the quirky geology of the Bray Buttonhole. Ruins of Jumièges Abbey, on a bend of the Seine, provide a pensive interlude.

Étretat, Seine-Maritime

LA SUISSE NORMANDE *(pp380–383)*

Pack sturdy walking shoes for a trip through the "Norman Switzerland", where pleasant hikes along valleys and escarpments tempt even adepts of low-impact travel. Watercourses rushing through the wooded landscape have created opportunities for canoeists, kayakers, anglers, hikers, climbers and base-jumpers (people who plunge off cliffs on artificial wings!), as well as for those who only wish to observe.

THE CHANNEL ISLANDS *(pp384–417)*

Off the west coast of Normandy, much closer to France than to Britain, the Channel Islands offer English charm, extensive tourist amenities, bathing beaches, and delightful rambles along country lanes. Principal islands are Alderney, Guernsey and Jersey, as well as little Sark, where there are no cars.

Cliffs at Etretat
© Moemrik/iStockphoto

Michelin Driving Tours

1 NATURAL DELIGHTS

290km/180mi from St-Lô and back

Part of the northwestern edge of France, off the main tourist routes, the Cotentin Peninsula (also known as the Cherbourg Peninsula) faces the sea on three sides. Where the countryside is lush and green, cows graze placidly. In the regional nature park, canals, rivers and ponds provide a cool resting place for tourists and migratory birds alike. Sandy beaches are protected by cliffs and promontories. The towns and villages are picturesque and the cities have been built (or rebuilt after World War II) in local granite. Pack good walking shoes and a bathing suit.

2 MARVELLOUS MONT-ST-MICHEL

210km/130mi from Granville and back

The tour starts in Granville, a town proud of its maritime heritage. The route takes you through quiet hamlets and lively small towns, mostly rebuilt after World War II, using the typical regional granite blocks. The most unforgettable spot is, of course, Mont-St-Michel, a pinnacle of art, architecture, spirituality and European culture. You can walk across the bay from Genêts or Courtils.

3 THE LANDING BEACHES ON THE CÔTE DE NACRE

180km/112mi from Caen and back

This tour takes you along the lovely coast known as the Mother-of-Pearl, and also inland through a landscape steeped in memories of the momentous D-Day Landings. Caen, at the centre of the Battle of Normandy (6 June–1 Sept 1944), is well worth a visit for its art collections, abbeys, lively town centre, and the emotive Museum for Peace just outside the town. Bayeux is known for its precious tapestry and also as the only town in the region to have survived the war relatively unscathed. Arromanches-sur-Mer was the site chosen for the famous artificial or mulberry ports towed across from Great Britain to assist the Allied landing. The coast is also full of family-style resorts.

4 SUISSE NORMANDE

210km/130mi from Alençon and back

Perhaps you have to live in Normandy to appreciate why this area is likened to Switzerland. The hills here rise no higher than 360m/1 181ft, but that is enough for them to form a landscape of steep cliffs, deep valleys with rivers winding through them, and hairpin bends; meadows and woods alternate with the slopes.

5 THE MAYENNE COUNTRYSIDE AND THE ALPES MANCELLES

210km/130mi from Laval and back

The Mayenne Valley is quite different from the popular tourist areas of the coast. The charm of this hidden corner of Normandy lies in its many ponds, lakes and streams, and the hills of the Sarthe Valley. The granite houses with slate roofs echo the neighbouring region of Brittany, and the mild climate and gracious lifestyle are reminiscent of the Loire. An especially enjoyable section of this drive is through the Nomandie-Maine Regional Nature Park, where traditional agriculture and crafts are still practised, and you can enjoy cycling, climbing or rambling on one of the many way-marked paths.

6 THE CÔTE FLEURIE AND THE AUGE COUNTRYSIDE

200km/124mi from the Pont de Normandie and back

After admiring the graceful span of the Normandy Bridge, take this drive to the charming town of Honfleur, on the Seine estuary, and continue to the popular beach resorts of Trouville, Deauville, Houlgate and Cabourg. When you leave the coast, you enter the Auge country (Pays d'Auge), a land of green pastures and half-timbered houses, famous for its fine aged Calvados and savoury cheeses. The route winds through Lisieux, home of St Theresa, then on to Camembert, Vimoutiers and the Vie Valley. The Valley de la Risle leads back to the Seine estuary by way of the Bec-Hellouin Abbey, Pont-Audemer and the Vernier wetlands.

7 THE HEART OF TRADITIONAL NORMANDY

300km/186mi

This tour carries you through the heartland of historic, rural and culinary Normandy. Visit the site of the Battle of Ivry, the Château d'Anet, the Perch Nature Park; keep an eye out for Percheron horses; enjoy blood sausage in Mortagne or *rillettes* in Mamers. The gentle hills are wooded and serene.

8 THE LANDSCAPES OF NORMANDY: RIVERSIDE, WOODS, COAST

400km/249mi from Les Andelys and back

This drive follows the north bank of the River Seine, winding along past many spectacular sights: Les Andelys and Château-Gaillard, the Fontaine-Guérard Abbey, the Roman city of Rouen, Duclair, the monasteries of St-Martin-de-Boscherville, Jumièges and St-Wandrille, Caudebec-en-Caux, Villequier, Ételan Castle and the Roman amphitheatre at Lillebonne. Across the Pont de Normandie lies the major port of Le Havre, which merits a visit for its many museums and modern architecture (the city was almost obliterated during the war). The suggested tour next follows the shore known as the Alabaster Coast (Côte d'Albâtre), with its striking chalk cliffs and shingle beaches.

The arch and needle, two unique rock formations off the coast of Étretat, are emblematic of this area; Fécamp and Dieppe are typical fishing ports with many interesting things to see and do. The route turns inland, crossing the Eawy Forest, and passing through the picturesque town of Forges-les-Eaux, continues along the Andelle Valley and into the lovely Lyons Forest. The tour finishes in the delightful village of Lyons-la-Forêt.

9 LOWER REACHES OF THE RIVER SEINE

300km/186mi from Vernon and back

Vernon is the starting point for a trip to Bizy Castle and Monet's famous house and garden in Giverny. Follow the north bank of the Seine through the gentle meanders of the Gaillon Valley to Les Andelys; the remains of the formidable Château-Gaillard rise above the river. On the road to Rouen, you can stop and admire the statues at Notre-Dame d'Écouis, the regional art centre in Vascœuil, and the château-museum in Martainville. After touring the historic city of Rouen and its famous cathedral, carry on as far as the estuary and the Pont de Normandie. Here you can cross the estuary to enjoy the beaches at Trouville and Deauville before discovering the delights of the south bank. The first stop is Pont-l'Évêque, home of the eponymous cheese. After the pretty village of Pont-Audemer, the road leads into the Brotonne Regional Nature Park, with its traditional crafts museums and recreational facilities. The château of Champ de Bataille illustrates a more refined way of life with its elegant rooms and formal French gardens. From here, the route offers splendid views from the castle of Robert le Diable, the rocks at Orival and the Amfreville canal locks.

10 DISCOVERING THE EURE

200km/124mi.

After a tour of Rouen, take a trip into the *département* of the Eure. You can see the châteaux of Robert le Diable and Champ de Bataille on the way. Drive along the Charentonne Valley as far as St-Évroult, then head northeast towards Évreux. The tour meets up with the River Eure at Pacy-sur-Eure and follows the valley back north. Between Elbeuf and Rouen, the Roches d'Orival appear on the horizon.

When and Where to Go

SEASONS

The most pleasant time of year here is July to September, although the mildness of the coastal climate makes it possible to visit Normandy at any time of the year. In spring the blossoming of the apple trees transforms the Normandy countryside. Apples flower last, after the Gaillon cherries and the Domfront pears. Apple blossom time is really without equal, and this would therefore be the ideal time to explore the countryside by driving through the Pays d'Auge and along the Seine Valley.

In summer the hot weather comes earlier inland than on the coast. The beach season does not begin before June, when the last storms have died away. From Le Tréport to Mont-St-Michel, the coast is taken over by the people in search of sea air, relaxation and amusement. The sky remains hazy, and the sunshine has a special quality, filtered through the light clouds. Inland, the fine weather inspires long rambles through the picturesque countryside, and the many recreational areas along the winding rivers provide opportunities to cool off in bucolic surroundings.

The autumn months are the wettest of the year but as soon as November approaches there are many magnificent days. It is the time of year to enjoy the wonderful changing colours of the forest trees. The light is incomparably soft, making the stone buildings appear all the more substantial. It is never very cold.

THEMED TOURS

HERITAGE TRAILS

To help tourists discover France's national heritage in its historical context, municipalities, recently aided by the **Fédération nationale des Routes Historiques**, have set up a number of routes focussing on a given theme. Each itinerary is clearly signposted by panels laid out along the roads and is described in leaflets available from the tourist offices for each *département* or locality. In Calvados, for example, you could choose the Route of the Old Mills, through Fontaine-Henry and Creully; in Orne you could explore the land of Sir Lancelot, around Domfront, Lassay and La Ferté-Macé, or perhaps the Forest Route, taking in the countryside between Essay and Domfront.

Plan Your Itinerary

The website www.normandy-tourism.org, produced by the Normandy Tourist Board, offers a few itineraries (Impressionists, 3 days; Cathedrals, 5 days; a listing of rose gardens) as well as detailed bilingual (English/French) downloadable booklets, ordered by post or consulted online, so you can plan a personalised itinerary. One booklet covers parks and gardens; another describes 46 historical sites and monuments. A linked website (www.normandiememoire.com) describes the **Normandy Landings** (*see Battle of Normandy Itineraries p16*).

THEMATIC ITINERARIES

Driving tours have been prepared for you throughout this guide. Others, on more specific themes, have been mapped out for you by French specialists.

Following in William the Conqueror's Footsteps

A suggested 7-day itinerary, with supporting information and links, follows the career of the Conqueror from Fécamp through 20 towns and sites. You can also write for information to: President of the Route, 5 pl. du Chauchix-St-Léonard, 22510 Moncontour-de-Bretagne. Or call ☎02 96 73 50 28 or ☎06 81 87 33 40.

Route des Colombiers Cauchois

Visit Normandy's famous dovecotes nestling along the valleys of the Durdent, Valmont or Gonzeville.

A website gives a detailed itinerary, in English, as well as photos and links: www.francerama.com/escapade/colombiers cauchois.

Route de la Pomme et du Cidre

The countryside stretching from the Pays de Caux and the Pays de Bray is dotted with *cour-masures* planted with venerable apple trees. Leaflets about apples and cider making are available from local tourist offices or http://routeducidre.free.fr.
There is also a Route du Poiré, a sparkling drink made from pears, around the town of Domfront: Maison du Parc, BP 05, 61320 Carrouges. ✆02 33 81 75 75. www.parc-naturel-normandie-maine.fr.

Route Historique des Abbayes Normandes

This route takes you to 33 abbeys and priories (of 60 surviving in Normandy) as well as 24 châteaux and museums along the valley of the Seine, around Caen and in Basse-Normandie.
Contact Route Historique des Abbayes Normandes at 6 r. Couronné, BP 60, 76420 Bihorel. ✆02 35 12 41 60. www.abbayes-normandes.com.

Route Historique du Patrimoine Cultural Québécois

Three circuits have been developed especially for French Canadians seeking to learn about the land of their ancestors.
Comité Chomedey de Maisonneuve, Centre Culturel Maisonneuve, 10190 Neuville-sur-Vanne, Aube, France. http://perso.orange.fr/comite.maisonneuve.

MUSEUMS OF NORMANDY

The extraordinary cultural heritage of Normandy is reflected in museums of all types: art, traditional industry and crafts, natural history, etc., many tucked into out-of-the way villages you might easily miss. The website www.normandie-tourisme.fr lists museums (including those devoted

Visiting Mont-St-Michel Bay

The bay surrounding Mont-St-Michel, which features on UNESCO's list of World Nature and Culture Heritage Sites, is also an exceptional place on account of its tidal range – the greatest in continental Europe. During spring tides, the sea level can rise up to 15m/49ft between low and high tide. The water recedes 15km/9mi from the coast, then rushes back, accelerating in pace towards the end.

Throughout the year, the **Maisons de la Baie** welcome tourists, organise tours of the bay, provide information and stage exhibits aimed at promoting the heritage of the bay. The Maisons are located at Genêts, Vains-St-Léonard, Courtils and Le Vivier-sur-Mer (on the Breton side). The Maisons and local tour guides organise visits, crossings (5–6hr), walks, hikes (2hr30min–4hr) and even horseback and bicycle tours (25–30km/15.5–18.5mi; you can hire bicycles). Most tour agencies are open daily April to October, weekdays only November to March.

To obtain further information, or to make reservations (essential), apply to:
- **Maison de la Baie du Mont-St-Michel**, Relais de Courtils, 21 route de la Roche Torin, 50220 Courtils. ✆02 33 89 66 00. www.baie-mont-saint-michel.fr
- **Maison de la Baie** (Brittany), Pont Le Vivier, Cherrueix, 35960 Le Vivier-sur-Mer. ✆02 99 48 84 38. www.maison-baie.com
- **Chemins de la Baie**, 34 rue de l'Ortillon, 50530 Genêts. ✆02 33 89 80 88. www.cheminsdelabaie.com
- **Découverte de la Baie**, La Maison du Guide, 1 rue Montroise, 50530 Genêts, ✆02 33 70 83 49. www.decouvertebaie.com

to Impressionist art), but for more complete information – lists, maps, and detailed practical information – go to www.musées-basse-normandie.fr (61 museums) and www.musees-haute-normandie.fr (41 museums). Both websites offer English versions.

GARDENS OF NORMANDY

The mild climate has long inspired Normans to cultivate lovely gardens which are the perfect setting for a leisurely stroll.
The **Comité Régional de Tourisme de Normandie** (www.normandy-tourism.org) offers a brochure listing some 60 gardens open to the public.
The **Comité des Parcs and Jardins de France** has regional associations in Normandy. The excellent website, www.parcsetjardins.fr (in French only), lets you locate gardens by type, region, name or on interactive maps. Local garden organisations, under the umbrella of the national Comité, are:

- **Union des Parcs et Jardins de Basse-Normandie**
  Maison des Quatrans,
  25 r. de Geôle, 14000 Caen.
  ✆02 31 15 57 35.
- **Union des Parcs et Jardins de Haute-Normandie**
  7 r. de Trianon, 76100 Rouen.
  ✆02 32 18 76 18.

Claude Monet's garden at Giverny
© Anyka/iStockphoto

Here is a selection of gardens and parks described in this guide:

- Jardin des Plantes in Avranches.
- Gardens of the Château de Brécy.
- Park and gardens of Thury-Harcourt.
- Botanical gardens in Vauville.
- Parc Emmanuel-Liais and its greenhouses in Cherbourg.
- Jardin des Plantes Quesnel-Morinière in Coutances.
- Jardin Christian-Dior in Granville.
- Park of the Château de Nacqueville.
- Floral park of the Bois des Moustiers at Varengeville-sur-Mer.
- Jardin des Plantes at Rouen.
- Park of the Château de Miromesnil.
- Gardens and terraces of the Château de Sassy.
- Park of the Château d'Acquigny.
- Park of the Château de Beaumesnil.
- Parc zoologique Jean-Delacour at Clères.
- Claude Monet's garden at Giverny.
- Park of the Château de Launay.

BATTLE OF NORMANDY ITINERARIES

Eight themed itineraries, under the general title The Historical Area of the Battle of Normandy (signposted in French along the routes as Normandie: Terre-Liberté) take in the sites, museums and memorials relating to the events of June 1944 in the Manche, Calvados and Orne *départements*. The symbol to follow along the roads is a seagull. For detailed maps and descriptions of the sights, contact the Tourism Office, Maison du Département, 50008 St-Lô, ✆02 33 05 98 70 or go to www.manchetourisme.com.

- **Overlord-L'Assaut** *(70km/43.5mi)* from Pegasus Bridge to Bayeux via Sword, Juno and Gold beaches.
- **D-Day-Le Choc** *(130km/81mi)* from Bayeux to Carentan taking in Omaha Beach and St-Lô.

- **Objectif-Un Port** *(95km/59mi)* from Carentan to Cherbourg via Ste-Mère-Église and Valognes.
- **L'Affrontement** *(207km/128.6mi)* This itinerary completes the Overlord-L'Assault one and carries on from Bénouville to Vire coming back by Caen.
- **Cobra-La Percée** *(155km/96mi)* from Cherbourg to Avranches via Coutances.
- **La Contre-Attaque** *(162km/100mi)* from Avranches to Alençon via Mortain.
- **L'Encerclement** *(145km/90mi)* from Alençon to L'Aigle via Chambois and Montormel.
- **Le Dénouement** *(122km/76mi)* from Caen to L'Aigle via Montormel and Vimoutiers.

An entry ticket purchased full price at any of the museums of the Espace historique de la bataille de Normandie entitles the holder to a pass (1€) giving reduced fares at all other museums on the tour.

D-Day Tours

Normandy Sightseeing Tours *(6 r. Saint-Jean, 14400 Bayeux; ✆02 31 51 70 52; www.normandywebguide.com)* offer D-Day Tours departing from Bayeux. You can take a half- or full-day tour, taking in such historic sites as Omaha Beach, Ste-Mère-Église, Dead Man's Corner Museum, Canadian Cemetery and Ardenne Abbey. Half-day 50€; full-day 80€.

Normandy Campaign
For a day-by-day account of the Normandy Campaign, from the landings on 6 June 1944 to the liberation of Paris on 25 August, with detailed maps, go to the website of the American Battle Monuments Commission, at www.abmc.gov.

What to See and Do

OUTDOOR FUN

CANOEING/KAYAKING

The fast-flowing rivers in the Suisse Normande are particularly good for canoes and kayaks.
Notable sites in Normandy are Pont-d'Ouilly, Clécy, Sillé-le-Guillaume and St-Léonard-des-Bois. The rivers **Eure** (around Dreux-Louviers) and **Risle** (around L'Aigle-Seine estuary) have excellent sites; contact clubs in **Rouen** or **Belbeuf**. You can also practice sea-kayaking out of major nautical centres such as Le Havre and Fécamp.

- **Comité Départemental de Canoë-Kayak Calvados**, 4 quai Caffarelli, 14000 Caen. ✆02 31 53 92 23 www.calvados-nautisme.com
- **Fédération Française de Canoë-Kayak** 87 quai de la Marne, 94344 Joinville-le-Pont. ✆01 45 11 08 50. www.ffcanoe.asso.fr

The Fédération publishes a map, *Les Rivières de France*, showing all the good canoeing and kayaking watercourses in France.

- **Comité régional de Normandie de Canoë-Kayak** – 40 r. des Mouettes, 76960 Notre-Dame-de-Bondeville. ✆02 35 75 16 10 www.crck.org/normandie

CRUISES ON THE RIVER SEINE

A number of boats able to accommodate between 80 and 350 passengers visit the main harbours (Le Havre, Honfleur, Rouen).
Trips can take half a day or a whole day, including meals on board, or you can opt for luxury cruises between

Paris and Honfleur lasting up to a week, with stops along the way. The following list features the most popular boats offering this type of excursion.

- **CroisiEurope**
  12 r. de la Division-Leclerc, 67000 Strasbourg
  ℘03 88 76 44 44
  www.croisieurope.com
  Cruises between Paris and Honfleur, or the reverse, in 5–7 days.
- **Viking Croisières Fluviales** – Athenaeum, 39 r. de Marbeuf, 75008 Paris
  ℘01 58 36 08 36
  www.athenaeum.fr
  On a luxury boat-hotel, from April–September, 8-day cruises between Paris and Le Havre, with bus excursions.
- **Le Guillaume-le-Conquérant** – Contact Rives de Seine Croisières, 72 r. Scheurer-Kestner, 76320 Caudebec-lès-Elbeuf
  ℘02 35 78 31 70
  www.rives-seine-croisieres.fr
  Shorter cruises, about 4hr with a meal between Poses and Muids.

CLIMBING

Climbers are attracted to the steep rocky slopes of the Alpes Mancelles and Suisse Normande, particularly the vertical walls of the Rochers des Parcs near Clécy or the Fosse-Arthour northwest of Domfront. For information apply to Tourist Information Centres or to:

- **Club Alpin Français**
  92 r. de Geôle, 14000 Caen
  ℘02 31 86 29 55
  www.ffcam.fr
- **Comité Départemental de la montagne et de l'Escalade**
  www.ffme.fr
  M Lebègue,
  25 r. André-Letard, 61600, St-Georges-des-Groseilliers
  ℘02 33 96 13 19

CYCLING

Good cycling country is found in the Brotonne Forest, Lyons Forest, Eure Valley, Seine Valley and along the Caux coast; there are steeper gradients in the Alpes Mancelles, the Suisse Normande and the Cotentin Peninsula. Voies vertes (ecolo-paths for all-terrain bikes) are being developed throughout the region. Consult tourist offices. You can take the train for part of your circuit; your bike travels for free. Certain train stations even rent bikes, which you can turn in at another station. For up-to-date information, consult;

- **Fédération Française de Cyclotourisme**
  12 r. Louis-Bertrand, 94207 Ivry-sur-Seine Cedex
  ℘01 56 20 88 88
  www.ffct.org
  The Fédération supplies itineraries covering most of France, giving mileage, difficult routes and sights to see.
- **Fédération Francaise de Cyclisme**
  5 r. de Rome, 93561 Rosny-sous-Bois, Cedex
  ℘01 49 35 69 24
  www.ffc.fr
  This group produces an annual repertry covering 46 000km/ 28 5901mi of marked trails for all-terrain bicycling.
- **Comité Départemental de Cyclotourisme de l'Eure**
  Mme Monique Loride, Le Clos Tiger, 27170 Beaumonte
  ℘02 32 45 35 06
  www.codep27.fr
- **Comité départemental de Cyclotourisme de Seine-Maritime**
  86 r. Léon-Gambetta, 76320 Caudebed-lès-Elbeuf
  ℘02 35 77 03 37
  www.ffc76.fr
- **Comité Départemental de Cyclotourisme de la Manche**, Maison Tollemer, 50190 Périers
  ℘02 33 47 93 51
  www.cyclisme50.com

FISHING

For those interested in freshwater fishing, it is necessary to know the dates of the *saison de la pêche*: all over France, the second Saturday in March heralds the start of the fishing season for rivers belonging to the first category *(première catégorie)*, ending on the third Sunday in September. In the case of second-category rivers *(deuxième catégorie)*, fishing is permitted all year round, except for pike, which can usually be caught between July and January, depending on the area. Normandy is dotted with a great many lakes, rivers and ponds of astounding variety. This particular type of topography makes it one of France's most treasured regions for fishing. The fast-flowing rivers abound in fario trout, a local variety, and rainbow trout, brought over from America, whereas the various lakes and ponds are the favourite haunt of carnivorous species such as pike, pikeperch and salmon. The most popular rivers among anglers are the **Risle** (fario trout, carnivores), the **Iton** (pike, rainbow trout), the **Charentonne** (fario trout), the **Huisne** (grayling, fario trout), the **Touques** (fario trout), the **Yères** (fario trout), the **Bresle** (sea trout), the **Arques** (salmon and sea trout) and the **Durdent** (fario trout, sea trout).

Wherever you choose to go fishing, make sure you obey the laws on angling and apply for details from the relevant federations and associations. You have to become a member (for the year in progress) of an affiliated angling association in the ***département*** *of your choice, pay the annual angling tax or buy a day card, and obtain permission from the landowner if you wish to fish on private land.*

- **Fédération de Calvados pour la pêche**
  18 r. de la Girafe, 14000 Caen
  02 31 44 63 00
  www.federation-peche14.fr
- **Fédération de la Manche pour la pêche**,
  16 r. du Pont-l'Abbé, 50190 Périers
  02 33 46 96 50
  www.federationpeche.fr/50
- **Fédération de l'Orne pour la pêche**,
  59 r. Julien, BP 91,
  61014 Alençon Cedex
  02 33 26 10 66
  www.federationpeche.fr/61
- **Fédération de l'Eure pour la pêche et la protection du milieu aquatique**
  av. de l'Europe, Immeuble Leipzig, BP 412, 27504 Pont-Audemer Cedex.
  02 32 57 10 73
  www.eure-peche.com
- **Fédération de Seine-Maritime pour la pêche**,
  11 cours Clemenceau,
  76100 Rouen
  02 35 62 01 55
  www.federationpeche.fr/76

A leaflet with a map and information called *La Pêche en France* (Fishing in France) is available from the **Office national de l'eau et des milieux aquatiques (ONEMA)** "Le Nadar" Hall C, 5 sq. Félix Nadar, 94300 Vincennes. 01 45 14 36 00. www.onema.fr.
Anglers are expected to comply with legislation on fishing, in particular concerning the size of their catch. They are expected to throw back certain fish into rivers if their length does not meet the required standards (40cm/16in in the case of pike; 23cm/9in in the case of trout). It is possible to take up sea fishing, both along the coast and on board one of the boats leaving from Trouville, Honfleur, Fécamp, Dieppe, Le Tréport or St-Valery-en-Caux. The waters near Dieppe are said to be teeming with fish and anglers who settle near the piers, often to see their patience rewarded by landing mackerel, pollock, sole or bass. Details are available from regional tourist offices.

GOLF

Normandy has some 35 golf courses; all the major resorts have clubs, many very beautiful. For information about golf in Calvados, la Manche or Orne *départements*, contact:

- **Ligue de Golf de Basse-Normandie**
  Mairie de Varaville, 2 av. du Grand-Hôtel, 143 Le Home Varaville
  ✆02 31 28 31 00
  www.liguedegolfdebasse normandie.fr

For information about courses in the Sarthe and La Mayenne départements, contact www.ligue-golf-paysdelaloire.asso.fr. For the Eure and Seine-Maritime contact:

- **Ligue de Golf de Haute-Normandie**
  94 r. St-Jacques, 76600 Le Havre
  ✆ 02 35 42 71 19. http://liguede golfdehautenormandie.com.
- **Fédération Française de Golf**
  68 r. Anatole-France,
  92309 Levallois-Perret Cedex
  ✆01 41 49 77 00
  www.ffgolf.org.

HIKING

Walking is one of the best ways of discovering the countryside – the superb beech forests and the occasional manor houses on well-kept farms. Throughout the region there are long-distance footpaths (*sentiers de grande randonnée*, or **GR** – one- or two-day hikes) marked with red-and-white lined posts and shorter, local paths (*petite randonnée* or PR) marked on posts with a single yellow line. Detailed topographical guides are available showing the routes and giving good advice to walkers. The Topo-guides are published by the **Fédération Française de la Randonnée Pédestre** (Comité National des Sentiers de Grande Randonnée) and are on sale at 14 r. Riquet, 75019 Paris. ✆01 44 89 93 90. www.ffrandonnee.fr.

Several of these well-marked footpaths cross Normandy.

- The **GR 2** follows the north bank of the Seine and crosses the Londe and Roumare forests.
- The **GR 21** runs up the Lézarde Valley to meet the coast at Étretat.
- The **GR 22** from Paris to Mont-St-Michel crosses the southwest of Normandy up to Mamers.
- The **GR 23** follows the left bank of the Seine and crosses the Forest of Brotonne.
- The **GR 211** leaves from the Seine and reaches the coast passing through the forest of Mauléverier.
- The **GR 221** crosses parts of the Suisse Normande and the Cotentin Peninsula.
- The **GR 222** starts in the Yvelines *département* and then winds its way across the Eure and Calvados *départements* to reach the Côte de Nacre at Deauville.
- The **GR 223** (444km/276mi) runs along the north coast and the Cotentin Peninsula, often following old customs agents' trails with superb views, notably at Cap de la Hague.
- The **GR 225** passes from the Vexin to the Lyons Forest and then the Pays de Bray before reaching the sea near Dieppe.
- The **GR Sur les traces du chasse-marée** (on the trail of the fishmongers) follows the ancient medieval cart-track that, until the arrival of the railway in 1848, brought fish from Dieppe to Rouen and Paris. Information and a topographic map are available from the tourism offices in Dieppe and Rouen and from the tourist office of the *département* of Seine-Maritime.
- The **Chemins de Saint-Michel** follow routes taken by pilgrims in the years when Mont-St-Michel drew penitants from all over France. These trails, long forgotten, have been progressively traced and marked with bright blue posts. Two 200km/124mi trails in the North Cotentin are collectively named the *Chemins aux Anglais*, while the *Chemin de l'Intérieur* leaves from Barfleur and crosses Ste-Mère-l'Église, Carentan, St-Lô, Coutances, La Haye-Pesnel, to arrive in Genêts.

The *Chemin Côtier* links Cherbourg with Genêts following the seacoast. Other trails lead to St-Michel from Caen, Rouen, Chartres and Paris
For information, contact **Les Chemins du Mont-St-Michel**, r. de Picardie, 14500 Vire
✆02 31 66 10 02
www.lescheminsdumontsaint michel.com.

- **Voies vertes, sentiers de découverte and sorties natures** are shorter, less ambitious trails organised locally or in regional parks. Contact tourist offices for information.

HORSE-RIDING

In such a well-known horse-breeding region many riding clubs and centres organise rides on the many miles of bridle paths through the woodlands or exhilarating canters along the shore as well as pony-trekking holidays. There are many local gymkhanas and equestrian events and racegoers are spoiled for choice for a day at the races. From September to Easter, experienced riders can hunt in the forests of Écouves or Andaines to the sound of the horn. Some *gîtes* will even put up both you and your horse! Information is available from:

- **Comité National de Tourisme Équestre**
  9 bd Macdonald, 75019 Paris
  ✆01 53 26 15 50
  www.tourisme-equestre.fr
  The committee publishes an annual brochure listing equestrian events, horseback rides and accommodation welcoming horse and rider.
- **Comité Régional d'Équitation de Normandie**
  www.chevalnormandie.com
- **Comité Départemental de Tourisme Équestre du Calvados**
  Jean-Louis Faucher, Le Haut de la Vallée, 14480 Lantheuil
  ✆02 31 08 23 95
  www.cheval-calvados.fr.st
- **Comité Départemental de Tourisme Équestre de la Manche**
  rue Corbeauville, 50500 Meutis
- **Comité Départemental d'Equitation de l'Orne**
  Centre équestre Sagien, BP 4, route d'Essay, 61500 Sées.
  ✆02 23 27 55 11
  www.equitorne.fr

Horse-drawn Caravans

In the Orne and Calvados *départements* you can hire a horse-drawn caravan *(roulotte)*. Enquire at local tourist information centres.

HUNTING

For all enquiries apply to the various *Fédérations départementales de Chasse*:

- **Calvados**
  r. des Compagnons, 14000 Caen
  ✆02 31 44 24 87
  www.fdc14.fr
- **Manche**
  La Malherbière, 31 r. des Aumônes, 50750 St-Romphaire
  ✆02 33 72 6363
  www.fdc50.com
- **Orne**
  46 r. de Bretagne, BP 177, 61005 Alençon CEDEX
  ✆02 33 80 05 05
  www.fdc61.com
- **Eure**:
  r. de Melleville, 27930 Angerville-la-Campagne
  ✆02 32 23 03 15
  www.fdc27.com
- **Seine-Maritime**
  Maison de la Chasse et de la Nature, r. de l'Étang, 76890 Belleville-en-Caux
  ✆02 35 60 35 97
  www.fdc76.com.
- **Union Nationale des Fédérations Départementales des Chasseurs**
  48 r. d'Alésia, 75014 Paris
  ✆01 43 27 85 76
  www.chasseurdefrance.com

LAND SAILING

The great stretches of sandy beach on the Calvados and Cotentin coasts are ideal for land sailing *(char-à-voile)*, an exhilarating sport performed on a three-wheeled cart equipped with a sail; speeds can reach 100kph/62mph. **Speed sailing**, a form of windsurfing on wheels is also available. Further information may be obtained from:

- **Fédération Française de Char à Voile**
  17 r. Henri-Bocquillon, 75015 Paris.
  ℘01 45 58 75 75
  www.ffcv.org
  The federation offers a list of clubs, guidebooks and calendars.

REGIONAL NATURE PARKS

Normandy's four regional nature parks are a popular destination for hikers and nature lovers alike since they provide countless opportunities for a wide range of open-air activities. In these highly protected areas, extensive facilities have been set up to introduce visitors to local flora and fauna and to increase their awareness of environmental concerns.
There are a great many sports in which to indulge, depending on the time of year. **Boucles de la Seine Normande** *(see Forêt de BROTONNE, p313)* **Perche** *(see MORTAGNE-AU-PERCHE, p290)*, **Normandie-Maine** *(see Château de CARROUGES, p284)* and **Marais du Cotentin et du Bessin** *(see Presqu'île du COTENTIN, p153)*.

SAILING

The Channel coast is a favourite venue for boaters and sailors. Many sailing clubs offer lessons at all levels of skill, and in the bigger coastal towns, annual regattas are a glorious sight. The main moorings and marinas for visiting yachtspeople are indicated on the **Places to Stay map** *(pp37–8)*. They usually provide fuelling facilities, convenient water stands for drinking water and electricity points, WCs, showers and sometimes laundry facilities, handling equipment and repair facilities and a 24-hour guard.

France Stations Nautiques is an association of coastal villages, tourist sites and marinas offering first-rate facilities for nautical sports.

- **France Stations Nautiques**
  17 r. Henri-Bocquillon, 75015 Paris
  ℘01 44 05 96 55
  www.france-nautisme.com

For further information on sailing, contact:

- **Fédération Française de Voile**
  17 r. Henri-Bocquillon, 75015 Paris.
  ℘01 40 60 37 00
  www.ffvoile.net

Foreigners who own or want to rent a boat (with an engine of more than 6hp) in France must take a compulsory test in sailing skills (carte mer).

SKIN DIVING

The right conditions for deep-sea diving are to be found between Dieppe and Le Havre and between Barfleur and Avranches on the Cotentin coast.

- **Fédération Française d'Étude et de Sports sous-marins**
  24 quai de Rive-Neuve,
  13284 Marseille Cedex 07
  ℘04 91 33 99 31
  www.ffessm.fr

SPAS

Normandy has several centres for **thalassotherapy and water cures**. In addition to the bracing climate and vivifying sea air, they rely on the curative virtues of the local waters, mud and algae:

Granville

Le Normandy:

- **Centre de Rééducation et de Réadaptation Fonctionnelles en Milieu Marin**
  1 r. J.-Michelet, BP 619,
  50406 Granvile Cedex
  ℘02 33 90 33 33
  www.lenormandy.com
- **Prévithal Institut de Thalassothérapie**
  3 r. J.-Michelet, BP 618,
  50 406 Granville Cedex

✆02 33 90 31 10
www.previthal.com

Luc-sur-Mer

- **Institut de Cure Marine**
  r. Guynemer, 14530 Luc-sur-Mer
  ✆02 31 97 32 22
  www.thalasso-normandie.com

Deauville

- **Thalsasso-Deauville**
  3 r. de Sem, 14800 Deauville
  ✆02 31 87 72 00
  www.thalasso-normandie.com

Ouistreham

- **Thalazur Ouistreham - Normandie**
  av. du Cmdt-Keiffer,
  14150 Ouistreham
  ✆02 31 96 40 40
  www.thalazur.fr

Bagnoles-de-l'Orne

The Grande Source, **a hot spring** with slightly radioactive mineralised water, is said to provide relief for circulatory problems, especially in the legs, and for arthritis and rheumatism as well as problems of the endocrine glands. The season runs mid-Mar–early Nov.

- **Thermes de Bagnoles-de-l'Orne**
  r. du Prof.-Louvel, BP 33,
  61140 Bagnoles-de-l'Orne
  ✆08 11 90 22 33
  www.thermes-bagnoles.com
  You can take a tour Tue–Fri at 5pm.
- **Centre d'Animation de Bagnoles-de-l'Orne –**
  1 r. du Prof.-Louvel, BP 27, 61140 ,
  Bagnoles-de-l'Orne
  ✆02 33 30 72 70
  www.bagnoles-de-lorne.com

SWIMMING

The Norman beaches are of two types: **sandy** along the Côte Fleurie (Cabourg, Houlgate, Deauville, Trouville, Honfleur, etc.) and **shingle** (stoney) along the Alabaster Coast (Étretat, Yport, Fécamp, St-Valéry-en-Caux, Varengeville, Dieppe, etc.). Guarded beaches have a system of flags to warn bathers of possible risks: **green** – safe bathing; **orange** – dangerous, be careful; **red** – bathing prohibited; **violet** – polluted water. If you want to know the water quality of any beach, check on www.infosplage.com.

WINDSURFING

This sport, which is permitted on lakes and in sports and leisure centres, is subject to certain rules. Apply to local sailing clubs. Boards may be hired on all major beaches. www.ffvoile.net.

ACTIVITIES FOR CHILDREN

In this guide, sights of particular interest to children are indicated with a KIDS symbol (👪). Some attractions may offer discount fees for children.

SHOPPING

In France, the big stores and larger shops are open Mondays to Saturdays from 9am to 6.30 or 7.30pm. Smaller, individual shops may close during the lunch hour, almost universally so in smaller towns. Food shops – grocers, wine merchants and bakeries – are generally open from 7am to 6.30 or 7.30pm; some open on Sunday mornings. Many food shops close between noon and 2pm and on Mondays. Hypermarkets usually remain open non-stop until 9pm or later. People travelling to the USA cannot import plant products or fresh food, including fruit, cheeses and nuts. It is all right to carry tinned products or preserves.

Channel Islands

In Jersey, shops are open from 9am to 5pm, 5.30pm or 6pm, and are closed on Sunday and Thursday afternoon. On Guernsey, shops are open Monday to Saturday from 9am until 5.30pm.

TRADITIONAL MARKETS

All cities and nearly all towns have weekly markets, usually held in the morning. The following are only examples – there are literally hundreds. Check with tourist offices.

Calvados

Bayeux (r. St-Jean Wed, pl. St-Patrice Sat); **Dives-sur-Mer** (Sat year-round, July–Aug Tue); **Honfleur** (Sat; organic produce Wed; antiques 2nd Sun of month; flowers Sat); **St-Pierre-sur-Dives** (Mon); **Trouville** (Wed and Sun).

Eure

Les Andelys (Sat); **Bernay** (Sat); **Évreux** (town centre Wed and Sat, la Madeleine Sun); **Lyons-la-Forêt** (Thu and weekends); **Le Neubourg** (Wed); **Pont-Audemer** (Mon and Fri); **Verneuil-sur-Avre** (Sat).

Manche

Coutances (Sun); **St-Hilaire-du-Harcoët** (Wed in summer, market of artisanal objects); **St-Vaast-la-Hogue** (Sat); **Valognes** (Fri).

Orne

L'Aigle (animal market at 7.30am Tue, followed by traditional market); **Bagnoles-sur-l'Orne** (Tue and Sat).

Seine-Maritime

Caudebec-en-Caux (Sat); **Dieppe** (Sat); **Étretat** (Thu); **Eu** (Fri); **Fécamp** (Sat); **Forges-les-Eaux** (Thu and Sat); **Harfleur** (Sun); **Le Havre** (Les Halles centrales Mon–Sat except holidays; antiques, cours de la République, Fri); **Vieux Rouen** place St-Marc (Sun); **Yvetot** (Wed).

VALUE ADDED TAX

There is a **Value Added Tax** (VAT) in France of 19.6% on almost every purchase. VAT **refunds** are available to visitors from outside the EU only if purchases exceed 175€ on one day in one store; the VAT cannot be refunded for items shipped. The system works in large stores which cater to tourists, in luxury stores and other shops advertising Duty Free. Show your passport, and the store will complete a form which is to be stamped by a customs agent at the airport or at whatever point you are leaving the EU. You may have to show the agent the items purchased, so don't pack them in checked luggage. www.douane.gouv.fr.

Channel Islands

There is no VAT on the Channel Islands, which accounts for the profusion of very busy shops. The most popular purchases are alcohol, tobacco, perfume, cream caramels and the famous Jersey and Guernsey wool.

SIGHTSEEING

GUIDED TOURS

Many sights, such as châteaux, can be visited only on a guided tour. The departure time of the last tour of the morning or afternoon may be up to 1hr before the actual closing time. Most tours are conducted by French-speaking guides; some of the larger and more popular sights may offer guided tours in other languages. Enquire beforehand. Also available are notes, pamphlets or audioguides.

CHURCHES

Churches are usually closed from noon to 2pm. Visitors should refrain from walking about during services. Visitors to chapels are accompanied by the person who keeps the keys. A donation is welcome.

BOOKS

Norman Conquest

The Norman Conquest: A New Introduction
Richard Huscroft (Pearson, 2009)
1066: The Hidden History in the Bayeux Tapestry
Andrew Bridgeford (Walker, 2005)

Mont St-Michel

Mont-Saint-Michel from A to Z
Henry Decaens, Adrien Goetz, Gerard Guiller (Flammarion, 1997)
Tides of Mont St-Michel
Roger Vercel (1938, reissued by Kessinger Publishing, 2005)

Gardens

Gardens in Normandy
Marie-Françoise Valéry (Flammarion, 2000)

The Magic of Monet's Garden
Derek Fell
(Firefly Books Ltd., 2007)

Claude Monet

Monet in Normandy
Richard Bretteil (Rizzoli, 2006)
Claude Monet
Christoph Heinrich (Taschen, revised 2000)

Cuisine

Cuisine Grandmere: Brittany, Normandy, Picardy and Flanders
Jenny Baker (Faber and Faber, 1995)
The Cuisine of Normandy
Princess Marie-Blanche de Broglie (Houghton-Mifflin 1984)

Battle of Normandy

D-Day: the First 24 Hours
Will Fowler (Barnes and Noble, 2006)
The Germans in Normandy
Richard Hargreaves, Pen & Sword, 2006)
The Americans at Normandy, The Americans at D-Day
Two volumes by John C McManus (Tom Doherty, 2004–5)
British Armour in the Normandy Campaign 1944
John Buckley (Frank Cass, 2004)
The D-day Landings
Philip Warner (Pen & Sword, 2004)
Overlord-D-Day and the Battle of Normandy, 1944
Max Hastings (Pan MacMillan, reissued, 2004)
The D-Day Landing Beaches: The Guide
Georges Bernage (Heindal, 2001)
A Traveller's Guide to D-Day
Carl Shilleto, Mike Tolhurst (Interlink, 2000)

FILMS

The Umbrellas of Cherbourg (1964)
Starring Catherine Deneuve: Jacques Demy's charming musical about love and loss in Normandy.
Tess (1979)
Roman Polanski's gorgeous version of Thomas Hardy's novel was shot in the lush Norman countryside.
The Longest Day Fox Video (1962)
Re-creation of the Normandy Landings.
Saving Private Ryan (1998)
Steven Spielberg drama about the Battle of Normandy.
Band of Brothers (2001)
TV drama (HBO) based on the Stephen Ambrose book.
Dunkirk MGM/UA (1958)
Sombre portrait of the Dunkirk evacuation.

Calendar of Events

Especially during summer months, towns and villages throughout Normandy hold fairs, festivals, commemorations of all sorts. You can plan an itinerary to take in these events, whose dates tend to shift from year to year. Consult www.normandie-tourisme.fr for exact dates, and ask at local tourist offices.

MARCH

Caen – Aspects of Contemporary Music – ☎02 31 30 46 86.
Deauville – Festival of Asian Film and Festival of Scientific Film
Rouen – International Festival of Nordic Film.
☎02 32 08 32 40. www.festival-cinema-nordique.asso.fr.

30 APRIL–1 MAY

Rouen – 24-hour motorboat races.
☎02 32 08 32 40.

APRIL–OCTOBER

Le Havre – International regattas

SUNDAY PRECEDING ASH WEDNESDAY

Granville – Carnival.
☎02 33 91 30 03.
www.ville-granville.fr.

1 MAY

Le Marais Vernier – Branding of cows. ✆02 32 57 61 62

MAY

Conches-en-Ouche – Meetings of area farmers (Les Comices Agricoles). ✆02 32 30 20 41.

Coutances – Jazz Festival Under the Apple Trees (Ascension week). ✆02 33 76 78 50. www.jazzsouslespommiers.com.

Deauville – Easter Festival, two weeks of classical music (Easter time)

Le Tréport – Nautical Sports Festival

Mont de Cerisy – Rhododendron Fair (end of month). ✆02 33 65 06 75.

Mont-St-Michel – Rando-Baie du Mont-St-Michel (hike around the bay, 2nd weekend of month). ✆02 33 89 64 00

Pacy-sur-Eure – Stock fair *(Les Foulées pacéennes).* ✆02 32 36 29 38.

Rouen – Joan of Arc Festival, performances in medieval dress (last weekend of May). ✆02 32 08 32 40. www.rouentourisme.com.

Ste-Adresse – Dixie Days Jazz Festival

WHIT SUNDAY AND WHIT MONDAY (PENTECOST)

Bernay – Pilgrimage to Notre-Dame-de-Couture

Honfleur – Seamen's Festival – Sunday: Blessing of the sea; Monday morning: Seamen's Pilgrimage

La Perrière – Art Market. ✆02 33 73 35 49.

MAY–DECEMBER

Montivilliers – *Les Concerts de l'Abbaye*, Music Festival. ✆02 35 30 96 58.

JUNE

Pays d'Auge – Heritage Days. ✆02 31 48 52 16

Cabourg – Cabourg Film Festival. ✆02 31 91 20 00 (mid-June)

Deauville – International Jumping Competitions (Equestrian)

Deauville – International Sailing Week

Évreux – Rock Music Festival

Fécamp – Festival of the Sea and Music (*Les Estivales* – weekend before 21 June)

Le Havre – Biennial Show of Contemporary Art (biennial)

Ste-Mère-Église – Commemoration of the D-Day Landings (6 June). ✆02 33 41 41 35.

Utah Beach – Commemoration of the landings of 6 June 1944. ✆02 33 71 58 00.

JUNE–JULY

Blainville-Crevon – *Archéo-Jazz*, festival of jazz and contemporary music. www.archeojazz.com.

Mortagne-au-Perche – *Les Musicales de Mortagne*, festival of chamber music (last weekend in June and first 2 weekends of July).

Pont-Audemer – Les Mascarets street festival. ✆02 32 36 29 38.

JULY

Barneville-Carteret – Jersey–Carteret Sea Race (last weekend of July). ✆02 33 04 90 58.

Bayeux – Medieval Festival (1st weekend in July). ✆02 31 51 28 28.

Le Bourg-Dun– Festival of Linen Products

Deauville – Swingin' Deauville

Dives-sur-Mer – *Festival de la Marionnette*: Puppet Festival (around 15 July). ✆02 31 28 12 53.

Domfront – Orne Music Festival, lyrical and classical music. ✆02 33 38 56 66.

Haras National du Pin – *Festival Équestre la Équit'Orne*: international equestrian competitions (mid-July). ✆02 33 36 68 68.

Le Haye-de-Routot – St-Clair bonfire night (16 July).

Mont-St-Michel - Pilgrimage from Genêts across the sands at low tide. ✆02 33 60 14 05

Pontmain – Blessing of cars and motorcycles (2nd Sun of July), ✆02 43 05 07 26

Rouen – *Les Terraces du Jeudi*, concerts in front of bars and cafés on Thursdays.

Rouen – Armada of Tall Ships (every 4 years, next date 2012).

St-Christophe-le-Jajolet – Motorists' Pilgrimage (last Sun of July). 02 33 35 34 24.

St-Vaast-la-Hougue – Festival of books about sea adventures (2nd or 3rd weekend of July). 02 33 23 19 32.

Le Tréport – Festival of the Sea

LAST SUNDAY IN JULY OR FIRST SUNDAY OF AUGUST

Granville – Pardon of the Corporations of the Sea: Procession of guilds with their banners; open-air mass and torchlight procession. 02 33 91 30 03.

JULY–AUGUST

Bellême – Perche Terre de Légendes: night-time show (last 3 weekends in July and first 2 of August). 02 33 25 23 23.

Dreux – L'été sous les sharmes, festival of world music, free concerts. 02 37 38 87 00. www.dreux.com.

La Mayenne region – Les Nuits de la Mayenne: entertainment organised in some 15 sites around the region (Ste-Suzanne, Jublains, Laval) from mid-July to mid-August. 02 43 53 34 84. www.nuitsdelamayenne.com.

EARLY AUGUST

Barfleur – Regattas (2nd weekend of August). 02 33 54 02 48.

Carrouges – Festival of hunting and fishing (1st weekend of August). 02 33 37 15 88.

Crèvecoeur-en-Auges – Les Mediévales: Medieval festival (1st 2 weeks of August). 02 31 63 02 45. www.chateau-de-crevecoeur.com.

Jobourg – Foire aux moutons: sheep fair (1st Saturday of August). 02 33 10 00 40

St-Lô – Normandy Horse Show (2nd week of August). 02 33 06 09 72. www.normandie-horse-show.com.

AUGUST

Barfleur – Antiques Show (3rd or 4th weekend of August). 02 33 43 22 09

Blangy-sur-Bresle – Glass Festival

Deauville – Sale of yearlings (3rd or 4th week of August). 02 31 14 40 00

Deauville – Grand Prix: Horse racing events and Polo Championship Cup (last Sun of month). 02 31 14 40 00

Deauville – Musical August, a week of classical music

Dieppe – International Kite Festival (from 2nd to 3rd weekend of August, even-numbered years). 02 32 90 04 95. www.dieppe-cerf-volant.org.

Houlgate – Festijazz (3rd weekend of August).

Laval – The Uburlesques, humour festival (last weekend of August) 02 43 49 19 55

Île de Tatihou – Les Traversées de Tatihou: Music festival on the island, near St Vaast-la-Hougue (2nd or 3rd week of August, depending on tides). www.tatihou.com.

FESTIVALS OF THE VIRGIN, ON OR ABOUT 15 AUGUST

Douvres-la-Délivrande – Feast Day of the Coronation of the Virgin: Procession of the Black Virgin (1st or 2nd Sat after 15 August)

Lisieux – Procession to the Smiling Virgin. 02 31 48 55 08. www.therese-de-lisieux.com.

Pontmain – Pilgrimage to the Virgin. www.sanctuaire-pontmain.com.

Pont d'Ouilly – The Pardon of St-Roche (Sun after 15 August). 02 31 69 80 46.

St-Cyr-la-Rosière – Festival of the Percheron Horse at the Priory of Ste-Gauburge. 02 33 73 48 06.

AUGUST–SEPTEMBER

L'Aigle, **Alençon**, **Argentan**, **Bagnoles-de-l'Orne**, **Mortagne**, **Domfront**, **Croutes**, **Carrouges**, **Ceton**, **Prieuré de Vivoin**, **Flers**, **Mortrée**, **Sées**, **Laval** – Musical

September on the Orne: concert series (end of August, beginning of September). ☎02 33 26 99 99.

IN SEPTEMBER

Deauville – American Film Festival (1st week of September). ☎02 31 14 14 14.

Haras National du Pin – Competition for Percheron horses (last Friday and Saturday of September). ☎02 33 36 68 68

Lessay – Foire de la Ste-Croix: Holy Cross Fair, the largest and most typical fair in Normandy (2nd weekend of September). ☎02 33 76 58 80

Lisieux – Feast of Ste-Thérèse (last weekend of September). ☎02 31 48 55 08

SEPTEMBER–OCTOBER

Bellême – International Mushroom Festival. ☎02 33 73 34 16. www.mycologiades.com.

Fécamp– Multicup 60' Catamaran sailing races, boat salon (4 or 5 days).

OCTOBER

Caen – International Organ Festival ☎02 31 30 46 86.

Deauville – Equi'Days, Festival of Calvados horses and races.

Deauville – Paris–Deauville Rally, with classic cars

Haras national du Pin – Horse racing events; prestigious cross-country race and procession of carriages and stallions. ☎02 33 36 68 68

Mont-St-Michel – Feast of the Archangel Michael: Mass in the abbey church in the presence of the bishops of Bayeux and Coutances (1st Sunday of October). ☎02 33 60 14 05

Pacy-sur-Eure – Pedestrian relay races. ☎02 32 36 29 38.

OCTOBER–NOVEMBER

Caen – Puces Caennaises: Fleamarket (last weekend of November) ☎02 31 29 99 99.

Calvados – Equi' Days: Horse-riding events throughout the region. ☎02 31 27 90 30.

Seine-Maritime and Eure départements – Several cities participate in autumn in Normandy; music, theatre and dance. ☎02 32 20 87 00.

DECEMBER

Sées - Turkey Fair. ☎02 33 28 74 79.

Dreux - Les Flambarts Carnival: Festivities celebrating light. ☎02 37 38 87 00.

St-Hilaire-du Harcouët – Nativity Play (2nd fortnight of December). ☎02 33 79 38 88. www.creche-vivante.org.

GASTRONOMIC FAIRS

Every year a number of fairs and events are held throughout Normandy in connection with local specialities. The following list offers a sample:

MARCH

International *Boudin* (white or blood sausages) Festival in **Mortagne-au-Perche** (3rd weekend of March).

MAY AND JUNE

Saturday-morning foie gras market in **Bernay** in June.

Gastronomic fair and competition in **Cherbourg**, early May.

Festival of local products in **Crèvecoeur-en-Auge**, mid-May

Mussels Fair in **Le Tréport** (1st weekend in May or June). ☎02 35 86 05 69.

Cherry Fair in **Vernon** (4 days over Whit' weekend/Pentecost).

JULY AND AUGUST

Cheese fair in **Pays d'Auge** (1st weekend of August). ☎02 31 63 47 39

Camembert festival in **Camembert** (last Sunday of July).

Carrot Festival in **Créances** (2nd Sat in August).

Fair of cheese and regional products at **Livarot** (1st weekend of August).

SEPTEMBER

Norman pastries competition in **Caudebec-en-Caux** (3rd Sunday of September)

Cheese Fair in **Neufchâtel-en-Bray** (mid-September). ☎02 32 97 53 01

OCTOBER

Cider festival in **Beuvron-en-Auge**, end of October-early November.

Prawn Festival in **Honfleur** (1st weekend of October)

Foie gras market in **Le Neubourg** October–December

Festival of gastronomy (1 weekend) held around Old Market in **Rouen**

Apple Fair in **Vimoutiers** (mid-October)

NOVEMBER

Herring Fairs in **Dieppe**, **Fécamp**, **Le Tréport** and **St-Valery-en-Caux**

Feast of St-Martin autumn festival at **Neufchâtel-en-Bray** (mid-November)

THE CHANNEL ISLANDS

APRIL

Guernsey – Floral Guernsey Spring Festival Week (3rd week of April)

Throughout April, there are springtime gastronomic events as well.

Herm – Garden tours on Tuesdays

Sark – Wildflower Event (last week of April, first week of May.

9 MAY

Guernsey and Jersey – Liberation Day, 9 May, commemorating the liberation of Guernsey during World War II, holiday with a parade and a carnival.

MAY–JUNE

Guernsey and Jersey – Spring Walking Week: guided walks

JUNE–JULY

Guernsey – Carnival at St Peter Port

Jersey – June in Bloom Floral Festival (mid-June)

Sark – Sark's Midsummer Show

Guernsey – Floral Guernsey Summer Festival Week with Battle of Flowers in Saumarez Park (early July). www.visitguernsey.com.

JULY

Guernsey – Second Summer Floral Festival, 1 week, early July

Guernsey and Jersey – *Le Tour des Ports de la Manche* yacht race (mid-July).

Jersey – *Bonne Nuit* Harbour Festival

Sark – Sheep-racing (mid-July)

AUGUST

Alderney – Carnival week (early August)

Jersey and Guernsey – Battle of Flowers Carnivals (mid-August Jersey, late Aug Guernsey). www.battleofflowers.com

Jersey – Samarès Manor Autumn Fair (end of August) www.samaresmanor.com

Sark – Carnival (mid-August)

AUGUST–SEPTEMBER

Jersey and Guernsey – Sea Guernsey regattas (end of August–early September)

SEPTEMBER

Guernsey – Jazz Festival (late September)

Guernsey and Jersey – Commemoration of the Battle of England and Battle of Britain Air Display (mid-September). www.jersey.com.

Guernsey and Jersey – Channel Islands Festival of Arts and Crafts (last 2 weeks of September)

OCTOBER

Guernsey – Floral Guernsey Autumn Festival (2nd week of October)

Jersey – Standard Chartered Jersey Marathon. A run through St Helier and across the island. www.jersey-marathon.com.

Jersey – Autumn, Fruit, Flower and Vegetable Show (mid-October). This also includes a poultry show and the Autumn Cattle Show.

OCTOBER–NOVEMBER

Guernsey–Jersey – Tennerfest, gastronomic festival with meals at reduced prices, throughout October and early November. www.tennerfest.com

DECEMBER

Jersey – *La Fête de Noué* fair from 1 December up to Christmas: moonlight island walks, lighting displays, traditional markets, parades, street theatre.

Know Before You Go

USEFUL WEBSITES

The following selected websites offer information in English and provide links to other useful sites.

www.normandy-tourism.org
This official site of the Normandy Tourist Board provides information about places to visit, maps, suggested itineraries as well as tips for those interested in sports, gastronomy, the travel industry, etc. There are also links to tourist offices, for booking hotels and lodging, transport and other services.

www.francetourism.com
This commercial site offers information about France generally, with a section on each region, including Normandy. Maps, information on tours, places of interest, hotel and transport bookings and lots of links.

www.franceguide.com
The site of the French Government Tourist Office offers information aimed at foreign visitors, with sites adapted for each country. It has a particularly good practical information section, and a list of facilities accessible to people with disabilities.

www.normandie.visite.org
This site is updated daily and provides weather news, schedules for festivals and other events, and tourist information as well as links to websites covering news, education, business, shopping, chat sites, e-cards, etc.

www.abmc.gov
The site of the American Battle Monuments Commission offers information on events at the Normandy American Cemetery and Memorial. There is a link to the World War II database giving the location of individual casualties buried in ABMC cemeteries.

www.info-france-usa.org
The French Embassy's website provides practical information (visa requirements, driving, transport, tipping), a link to the US Embassy website in Paris (www.amb-usa.fr), recent news stories, and links (consulates in the US, regions, cities, ministries, commercial sites).

www.ambafrance-ca.org
The Cultural Service of the French Embassy in Ottawa has a bright and varied site information about travel in France, France–Canada relations, links to consulates, and much more.

www.visiteurope.com
The European Travel Commission provides useful information on travelling in 30 European countries, and includes links to commercial booking services (such as vehicle hire), rail schedules, weather reports and more.

TOURIST OFFICES

For information, brochures, maps and assistance in planning a trip to France, you should apply to the French Tourist Office in your own country.

FRENCH TOURIST OFFICES ABROAD

Australia – New Zealand

Sydney – Level 13, 25 Bligh St, Sydney, New South Wales, Australia.
℘61 (0)2 9231 5244
http://au.franceguide.com

Canada

Montreal – 1800 ave McGill College, Suite 1010, Montreal, Quebec H3A 3J6
℘(514) 288-2026
http://ca-en.franceguide.com

Ireland

Dublin – ℘(1) 560 235 235
http://ie.franceguide.com

South Africa

Johannesburg – ATOUT FRANCE 3rd floor Village Walk Office Tower cnr Maude and Rivonia, Sandton

✆ 00 27 (0) 11 523 82 92
http://za.franceguide.com

United Kingdom

London – Lincoln House, 300 High Holborn, London WC1V 7JH
✆09068 244 123 (60p/min)
http://uk.franceguide.com

United States

Three offices are available, but the quickest way to get a response to any question or request is by phone.
✆514 288 1904
http://us.franceguide.com

East Coast

825 Third Avenue, 29th Floor, New York NY 10022

Mid West

205 N.Michigan Ave, Suite 3770, Chicago 60601, IL

West Coast

9454 Wilshire Bld – Suite 210, Beverly Hills 90212 CA

REGIONAL TOURIST OFFICES

To telephone directly to a local tourist office or *syndicat d'initiative* from within France, even if you don't know the number, dial 3265 (0.34€/min), then pronounce clearly the name of the town that interests you. You will be connected directly.

- **Comité Régional de Tourisme de Normandie**
  14 r. Charles-Corbeau,
  27000 Evreux
  ✆02 32 33 79 00
  www.normandy-tourism.org

Departmental Tourist Offices

- **Calvados**
  8 r. Renoir, 14054 Caen Cedex 4
  ✆02 31 27 90 30
  www.calvados-tourisme.com
- **Eure**
  3 r. du Cdt-Letellier,
  BP 367, 27003 Évreux Cedex
  ✆02 32 62 04 27
  www.cdt-eure.fr
- **Manche**
  Maison du Département
  98 rte de Candol,
  50008 St-Lô Cedex
  ✆02 33 05 98 70
  www.manchetourisme.com
- **Mayenne**
  84 av. Robert Buron,
  BP 0325, 53003 Laval
  ✆02 43 53 18 18
  www.tourisme-mayenne.com
- **Orne**
  86 r. St-Blaise, BP 50, 61002
  Alençon Cedex
  ✆02 33 28 88 71
  www.ornetourism.com
- **Seine-Maritim**
  6 r. Couronné,
  BP 60, 76420 Bihorel
  ✆02 35 12 10 10
  www.seine-maritime-tourisme.com

TOURIST INFORMATION CENTRES

Ccntact details for the local tourist office of each Principal Sight can be found in the green-coloured Orient Panels of the *Discovering Normandy* section of this guide.

INTERNATIONAL VISITORS
DOCUMENTS

Passport

Nationals of countries within the European Union entering France need only a national identity card or, in the case of the British, a passport. Nationals of other countries must be in possession of a valid national passport. In case of loss or theft, report to the embassy or consulate and the local police. You must carry your documents with you at all times; they can be checked anywhere.

Visa

No entry visa is required for Australian, Canadian, New Zealand and US citizens travelling as tourists and staying less than 90 days, except for students planning to study in France. If in doubt, apply to your local French Consulate. **US citizens** should obtain the booklet *Safe Trip Abroad, 2002* ($2.75) from the Government Printing Office. ✆(202) 512-

EMBASSIES AND CONSULATES IN FRANCE		
Australia	Embassy	4 rue Jean-Rey, 75015 Paris ☏01 40 59 33 00. www.france.embassy.gov.au
Canada	Embassy	35 avenue Montaigne, 75008 Paris ☏01 44 43 29 00. www.international.gc.ca
Eire	Embassy	4 rue Rude, 75016 Paris ☏01 44 17 67 00. www.embassyofireland.fr
New Zealand	Embassy	7 rue Léonard-de-Vinci, 75016 Paris ☏01 45 00 24 11. www.nzembassy.com/france
South Africa	Embassy	59 quai d'Orsay, 75007 Paris ☏01 53 59 23 23. www.afriquesud.net
UK	Embassy	35 rue du Faubourg St-Honoré, 75008 Paris ☏01 44 51 31 00. www.ukinfrance.fco.gov.uk/e
	Consulate	16 bis rue d'Anjou, 75008 Paris ☏01 44 51 31 00
	Consulate	353 boulevard du Président Wilson, 33073 Bordeaux ☏05 57 22 21 10
USA	Embassy	2 avenue Gabriel, 75008 Paris ☏01 43 12 22 22. http://france.usembassy.gov
	Consulate	2 rue St-Florentin, 75001 Paris ☏01 43 12 22 22

1800 or order at http://bookstore.gpo.gov, or consult online and download at www.pueblo.gsa.gov (click on travel publications). General passport information is available by phone toll-free from the Federal Information Center (item 5 on the automated menu), ☏800-688-9889. US passport forms can be downloaded from http://travel.state.gov.

CUSTOMS

In the UK, **HM Revenue & Customs** (www.hmrc.gov.uk) publishes *A Customs Guide for Travellers Entering the UK* (download only) on customs regulations and duty-free allowances. **US citizens** should view *Tips for Traveling Abroad* online *(http://travel.state.gov/travel/tips/tips_1232.html)* for general information on visa requirements, customs regulations, medical care, etc. There are no customs formalities when bringing caravans, pleasure boats and outboard motors into France for a stay of less than six months, but a boat's registration certificate should be kept on board.

Canadians can consult and download *I Declare* at www.canadaonline.about.com. For **Australians**, *Know Before You Go* is available at www.customs.gov.au. For **New Zealanders**, *Advice for Travellers* is at www.customs.govt.nz. After an absence of about a week, **Americans** can bring home, tax free, US$800 worth of goods; **Canadians** CDN$750; **Australians** AUS$900 and **New Zealanders** NZ$700. People living in a Member State of the European Union are not restricted in regard to good for private use, but the recommended allowances for alcohol and tobacco can be found at www.taxfreetravel.com/UK%20duty%20free%20allowances.

There are no customs formalities for holidaymakers bringing their cars or caravans into France for a stay of less than six months. No customs document is necessary for pleasure boats and outboard motors for a stay of less than six months but the registration certificate should be kept on board.

HEALTH

First aid and medical advice are available from chemists/drugstores *(pharmacie)* identified by the green cross sign. In every town, a *pharmacie* remains on duty at night, based on a revolving schedule. All prescription drugs must be clearly labelled; it is essential you carry the prescriptions You should take out comprehensive insurance coverage as the recipient of medical treatment in French hospitals or clinics must pay. Nationals of non-EU countries should check with their insurance companies about policy limitations. **Americans and Canadians** can contact the International Association for Medical Assistance to Travelers: for the USA ☎(716)754-4883 or for Canada ☎(416) 652-0137 or ☎(519) 836-0102. www.iamat.org.

British and Irish citizens (and all EU citizens) should apply for a European Health Insurance Card (EHIC), which has replaced the E111. Everyone in the family must have one, even children. **UK subjects** can apply online to www.dh.gov.uk/travellers, or telephone ☎0845 606 2030, or pick up an application at the post office. **Irish citizens** may visit www.ehic.ie. UK subjects travelling to the **Channel Islands** should carry private health insurance, as National Health Service does not cover them.

ACCESSIBILITY

The sights described in this guide which are easily accessible to people of reduced mobility are indicated for the Sights in the *Admission times and charges* by the symbol ♿. For a list of accessible sites, carrying the Tourisme et Handicap designation, go to www.franceguide.com. For Normandy, booklets in English describing disabled access can be downloaded from www.normandie-tourisme.fr. The principal French source for information on facilities is the **Association de Paralysés de France**, 17 bd Auguste-Blanqui, 75013 Paris, www.apf.asso.fr (in French only).

The APF publishes a *Guide vacances* available on the website, or by mail (5.30€ plus postage).

The **Michelin Guide France** and the **Michelin Camping Caravaning France**: Revised every year, these guides indicate where to find facilities accessible to the disabled.

The French railway (SNCF) gives information on travel at www.voyages-sncf.com, as does Air France at www.airfrance.fr.

THE CHANNEL ISLANDS

ENTRY REGULATIONS

Passports are not required for British subjects. The same requirements apply for other tourists as in France.

TRAVEL

By Air

There are flights to **Jersey**, **Guernsey** and **Alderney**:

Jersey, **Guernsey** and **Alderney** airports are served by British Airways, (www.britishairways.com), Flybe (ww.flybe.com), Air Southwest (www.airsouthwest.com), BmiBaby (www.bmibaby.com), Jet2 (www.jet2.com), Blue Islands (www.blueislands.com) as well as Swiss (www.swiss.com) from Zurich and TwinJet (www.twinjet.com) from Paris.

Aurigny Air Services offers flights between Guernsey, Jersey and Alderney and several British airports as well as Dinard in France. www.aurigny.com.

By Sea

Fast catamaran ferries run to the Channel Islands from England (Poole, Weymouth and Portsmouth) and France (Granville, Diélette, Carteret, St-Malo). Contact www.condorferries.co.uk; www.hdferries.org; www.manche-iles-express.com.

Scheduled ferries run among the islands. Note that, for all ferry services, where they land and at what time depends on tides.

Getting There and Getting Around

BY AIR

The principal cities of Normandy are served out of St-Exupéry airport in Lyons.

Brit'Air (Air France) has flights to and from Caen, Rouen and Le Havre daily. Information and reservations: ✆0 820 820 820. www.airfrance.com or www.britair.com.

Twin Jet has flights connecting Paris/Orly and Cherbourg-Jersey. ✆0 892 707 737. www.twinjet.net.

The regional airports are:

Aéroport de Caen-Carpiquet – ✆02 31 71 20 10. www.caen.aeroport.fr.

Aéroport de Cherbourg-Maupertus ✆02 33 88 57 60. www.aeroport-cherbourg.com.

Aéroport Le Havre-Octeville – ✆02 35 54 65 00. www.havre.aeroport.fr.

Aéroport Rouen Vallée de Seine – ✆02 35 79 41 00. www.rouen.aeroport.fr.

BY SEA

There are numerous **cross-Channel passenger and car ferry services**, from the United Kingdom and Ireland.

- **P & O Ferries**, Channel House, Channel View Road, Dover, Kent CT17 9JT. ✆08705 980 333 (in the UK) or ✆0825 120 156 (in France) **www.poferries.com**. Service between Dover and Calais.
- **Norfolk Line**, Norfolk House, Eastern Docks, Dover, Kent CT16 1JA. ✆870 870 10 20 (in the UK) or ✆03 28 59 01 01 (in France). **www.norfolkline.ferries.org**. Service between Dover and Dunkerque.
- **Brittany Ferries**, Millbay Docks, Plymouth, Devon PL1 3EW. ✆0870 9 076 103 (in the UK) or ✆0825 828 828 (in France). **www.brittany-ferries.co.uk**. Service between Portsmouth, Poole, Plymouth and Cork and ports in France and Spain.
- **Irish Ferries**, Ferryport, Alexandra Road, Dublin 1. ✆8705 17 17 17 (UK), ✆0818 300 400 (in N. Ireland), ✆0818 300 400 (ROI), ✆(01) 44 88 54 50 (France). **www.irishferries.com**. Service between Rosslare in Ireland and Cherbourg and Roscoff in France.
- **Seafrance Ferries Ltd**. Whitfield Court, Honeywood Close, Whitfield, Kent CT16 3PX. ✆0871 663 2546 (in the UK). **www.seafrance.com**. Service between Dover and Calais.
- **LD Lines**, Continental Ferry Port, Wharf Road, Portsmouth P02 8OW. ✆0844 576 8836 (in the UK) or **www.ldlines.co.uk**. Service between Dover and Boulogne.

BY RAIL

Eurostar runs via the Channel Tunnel between **London** (St Pancras International) and Paris in 2hr15min. The trip from **London** to **Lille** takes 1hr20min. At present, the only high-speed train serving Normandy connects **Marseilles** and **Le Havre** in 6hr30min.

Bookings and information ✆0345 303 030 in the UK; ✆1-888-EUROSTAR in the USA or **www.eurostar.com**. Or contact the French national railways **www.voyages-sncf.com**. SNCF operates a **telephone information, reservation and prepayment service in English** from 8am to 7pm (French time). In France call ✆0892 33 35 39 (when calling from outside France, drop the initial 0 and add 33). Dial 42 as soon as the connection is made. The **Corail Intercités** network connects Paris with Norman cities: Rouen, Le Havre, Dieppe, Trouville, Dreux, L'Aigle, Beauvais and Le Tréport. Trains run several times daily. **Trains express régionaux (TER)** form an efficient local network, which also makes use of buses.

Eurailpass, **Flexipass**, **Eurailpass Youth**, **EurailDrive Pass** and

Saverpass may be purchased by residents of countries outside the EU. In the Western Hemisphere go to **www.raileurope.com**.
Alternatively, in the **USA**, contact Rail Europe ℘800-622-8600. In **Canada**, contact ℘800-361-7245. **Australians** call ℘1300 555 003, for **New Zealanders**, call ℘649 377 5415.
European residents can buy an individual country pass if not a resident of the country where they plan to use it. In the **UK or Ireland**, contact Rail Europe ltd at www.raileurope.co.uk or ℘0870 848 848.
Tickets bought in France must be validated *(composter)* by using the orange automatic date-stamping machines at the platform entrance. Failure to do so may result in a fine.

BY BUS

Each *département* in Normandy operates local and intercity bus services with inexpensive fares. Information is available, in French, from the website of each *département*.
Calvados: www.cg14.fr;
Eure: www.cg27.fr; **Manche**: http://manche.fr; **Orne**: www.cg61.fr;
Seine-Maritime: or www.seine-maritime.net/fr.
You can also consult local tourist offices once you arrive in Normandy.

DRIVING IN FRANCE

PLANNING YOUR ROUTE

Michelin **Local** maps give a close, detailed look at two or three *départements*, with maps of major towns. For Normandy, you will need **Local 310** (covering the *départements* of Mayenne, Orne, Sarthe), **303** (Calvados, Manche) and **304** (Eure, Seine-Maritime), and may also want the **Regional 513** (Normandy, including maps of Caen and Rouen) and **517** (Pays-de-la-Loire) maps, which list towns, show secondary roads and offer information for tourists.
The map of France 721 offers a view of all Normandy, with major arteries leading from your point of arrival.
The latest Michelin route-planning service is available on the internet, **www.ViaMichelin.com**. Travellers can calculate a precise route using such options as shortest route, route avoiding toll roads, GPS navigation, Michelin-recommended route and gain access to tourist information (hotels, restaurants, attractions).
The roads are very busy during the holiday period (particularly weekends in July and August), and you should consider recommended secondary routes (signposted as *Bison Futé – itinéraires bis*). For information on traffic conditions, call ℘0 892 681 077 or visit **www.autoroutes.fr**.

DOCUMENTS

Travellers from other EU countries or North America can drive in France with a valid national, home-state or provincial **driving licence** for up to a year; you should have a French translation attached. An **international driving licence** is recommended, however. To procure one in the **USA**, contact the National Automobile Club ℘1-800-622-2136, www.nationalautoclub.com, or contact your local branch of the American Automobile Association or go online to www.aaa.com.
In Canada, contact www.caa.ca.
The Australian Automobile Association is at www.aaa.asn.au and the **New Zealand Automobile Association** is at www.aa.co.nz.
For the vehicle, you must have the registration *(carte grise)* and the insurance certificate *(carte verte)*.

INSURANCE

Certain motoring organisations (AAA, CAA, AA, RAC) offer accident insurance and breakdown service schemes for members. Check with your current insurance company in regard to coverage while abroad. If you plan to hire a car using your credit card, you may have liability insurance automatically (and thus save paying for optimum coverage).

ROAD REGULATIONS

The minimum driving age in France is 18. Traffic drives on the right. It is compulsory for all passengers, in front and back seats, to wear **seat belts**. Children under the age of 10 must travel on the back seat of the vehicle. In the case of a **breakdown** a red warning triangle or hazard warning lights are obligatory. In the absence of stop signs at intersections, as in roundabouts, cars must **yield to the right**. Vehicles must stop when the lights turn red at road junctions and may filter to the right only when indicated by an amber arrow. The regulations on **drinking and driving** (limited to 0.05% or 0.50g/l) and **speeding** are strictly enforced – usually by an on-the-spot fine and/or confiscation of the vehicle.

Speed Limits

Speed limits are 50kph (31mph) in towns and built-up areas; 90kph/56mph on ordinary roads; 110kph/68mph on dual carriageways and motorways without tolls; and 130kph/81mph on toll motorways *(autoroutes)*. Check for variations.

Parking

In town there are zones where parking is either restricted or subject to a fee; tickets should be obtained from the ticket machines (*horodateurs* – small change necessary) and displayed inside the windscreen on the driver's side; failure to display may result in a fine, or towing and impoundment. In some towns where you find blue parking zones *(zone bleue)* marked by a blue line on the pavement or road and a P sign, a cardboard disc gives you 1hr30min (2hr30min over lunchtime) free. Discs are sold in supermarkets or gas stations (ask for a *disque de stationnement*) and are sometimes given away free.

Tolls

In France, most motorway sections are subject to a toll *(péage)*. Pay by cash or credit card.

Fuel: Petrol/Gasoline

French service stations dispense *sans plomb* 98 (super unleaded 98), *sans plomb* 95, *diesel/gazole* (diesel) and GPL (LPG). Fuel in France is relatively expensive; is usually cheaper off the motorway, so check the hypermarkets.

CAR RENTAL

There are car rental agencies at airports, railway stations and in all large towns throughout France. Most European cars have manual gearboxes; automatic cars are available only if an advance reservation is made. Drivers must be over 21; between ages 21 and 25, drivers must pay an extra daily fee. Hiring a a car in France is expensive: take advantage of fly-drive offers, or ask a travel agent.

MOTORHOME RENTAL

Several companies offer motorhome rental in France. Caravans are not allowed into the Channel Islands. See: www.motorhomesworldwide.com; www.ukandeuropetravel.com; www.car-rental-hire.co.uk; www.ideamerge.com.

RENTAL CARS – CENTRAL RESERVATION IN FRANCE		
Avis:	✆ 08 20 05 05 05	www.avis.fr
Europcar:	✆ 08 25 35 23 52	www.europcar.fr
Budget France:	✆ 08 00 10 00 01	www.budget.fr
Hertz France:	✆ 01 39 38 38 38	www.hertz.fr
SIXT- Eurorent	✆ 01 40 65 01 00	www.sixt.fr
National-CITER	✆ 01 45 22 88 40	www.citer.fr

Where to Stay and Eat

The *Michelin Green Guide* is pleased to offer a selection of accommodations and restaurants for Normandy. Turn to the **Addresses** sections within the individual Sights for descriptions and prices of typical places to stay **(Stay)** and to eat **(Eat)**. The Legend on the cover flap explains the symbols and abbreviations used in these sections. *Please note: Coin ranges for the Channel Islands are derived from approximate conversions of the euro coin ranges in the same Legend into Pound Sterling (£).*

WHERE TO STAY

FINDING A HOTEL

Turn to the **Addresses** within individual sight listings for descriptions and prices of typical places to stay **(Stay)** with local flair. Use the **Places to Stay** map in the following pages to identify recommended places for overnight stops. It can be used in conjunction with the **Michelin Guide France** – with its well-known star-rating system – which lists an even greater selection of hotels and restaurants. For further assistance, **La Fédération Loisirs Accueil** is a booking service that has offices in most French *départements*: 280 bd St-Germain, 75007 Paris. ℘01 44 11 10 44. http://www.loisirsaccueilfrance.com.
Relais et Châteaux provides information on booking in luxury hotels with character: 15 r. Galvani, 75017 Paris. ℘01 45 72 90 00. www.relaischateaux.com.

ECONOMY CHAIN HOTELS

If you need a place to stop en route, these can be useful, as they are inexpensive (35–45€ for a double room) and generally located near the main road. There may not be a restaurant; rooms are small, with a television and private bathroom. Rather than sort through hotels yourself, you can go to websites that cover several chains, where you can select your hotel and book online:
www.accorhotels.com covers some 1 400 hotels in france, including the Formule 1 chain, at about 35€, as well as Novotel, Mercure, Sofitel, etc.
www.activehotels.com covers a wide range of hotels and reviews.
www.day-tripper.net covers reasonably priced hotels, by location, throughout France.
www.louvrehotels.com covers more expensive hotels (more than 60€) Campanile, Kyriad, and Première Class.
Here are some modestly priced chains:

- **Akena**
  ℘01 69 84 85 17.
  www.hotels-akena.com.
- **B&B**
  ℘02 98 33 75 00.
  www.hotel-bb.com.
- **Etap Hôtel**
  ℘08 92 68 89 00.
  www.etaphotel.com.
- **Best Hôtel**
  ℘03 28 27 46 69.
  www.besthotel.fr.

RURAL ACCOMMODATION

The **Maison des Gîtes de France et du Tourisme Vert** is an information service on self-catering accommodation in the regions of France. *Gîtes* usually take the form of a cottage or apartment decorated in the local style where visitors can make themselves at home. The organisation also covers specialised gîtes, for fishing, camping, hiking, etc.
Contact **Gîtes de France:** 59 r. St-Lazare, 75439 Paris Cedex 09. ℘01 49 70 75 75. www.gites-de-france-normandie.com. You can order five different brochures at no charge; two can be downloaded. In total, the association lists some 2 000 rural gîtes and more than 1 000 bed-and-breakfasts in Normandy.
The publication **Bienvenue à la Ferme** lists some 300 Norman farmers who offer accommodation of varying degrees of comfort on their farms, including meals: Service Agriculture et Tourisme, 9 av. George V, 75008 Paris,

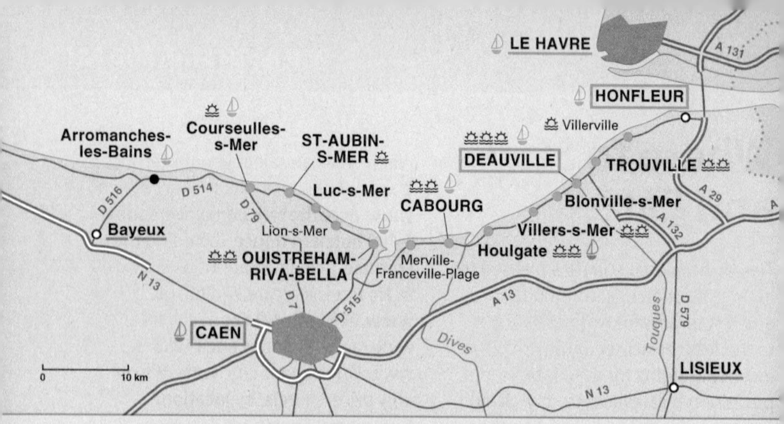
LE HAVRE
A 131
HONFLEUR
Villerville
Arromanches-les-Bains
Courseulles-s-Mer
ST-AUBIN-S-MER
DEAUVILLE
TROUVILLE
A 29
Luc-s-Mer
CABOURG
Blonville-s-Mer
A 132
D 516
D 514
D 79
Bayeux
Lion-s-Mer
Villers-s-Mer
OUISTREHAM-RIVA-BELLA
Merville-Franceville-Plage
Houlgate
N 13
D 7
D 515
A 13
Touques
D 579
CAEN
Dives
LISIEUX
N 13
0
10 km

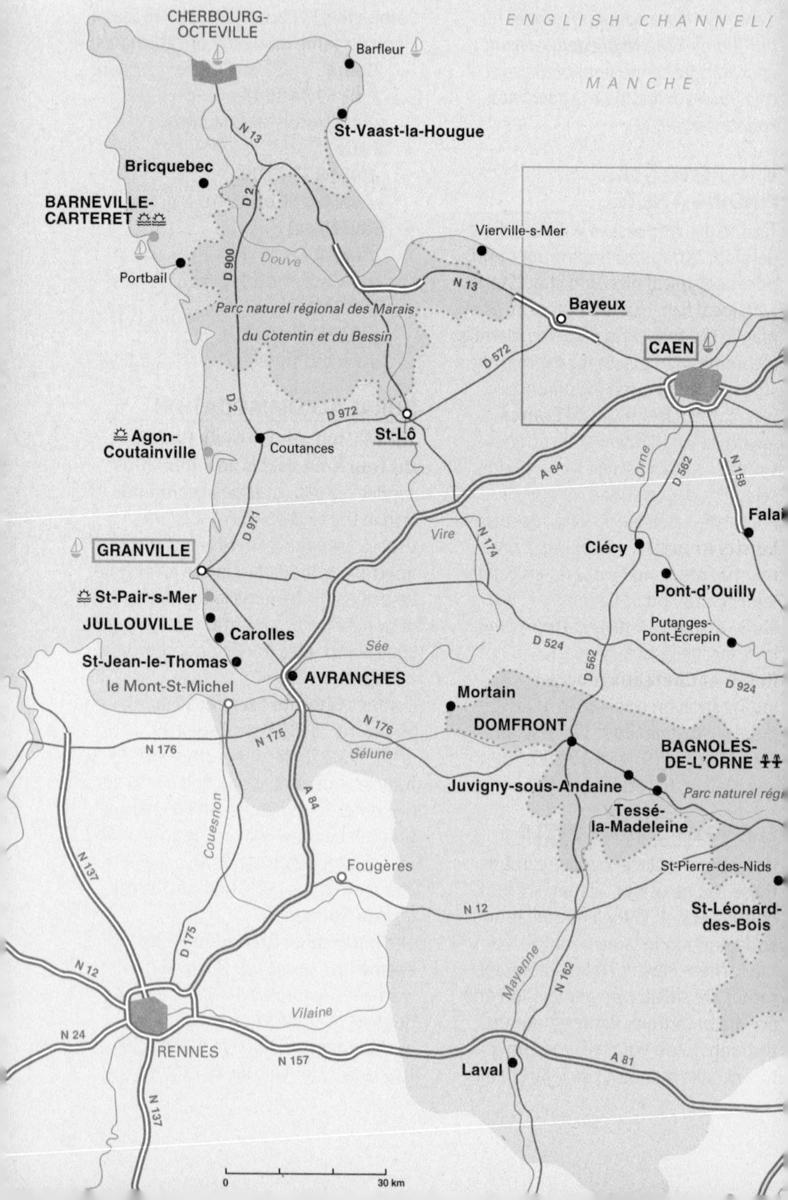
CHERBOURG-OCTEVILLE
ENGLISH CHANNEL/
MANCHE
Barfleur
St-Vaast-la-Hougue
N 13
Bricquebec
D 2
BARNEVILLE-CARTERET
Vierville-s-Mer
Portbail
Douve
D 900
N 13
Bayeux
Parc naturel régional des Marais du Cotentin et du Bessin
CAEN
D 572
D 2
D 972
St-Lô
Agon-Coutainville
Coutances
A 84
Orne
D 562
N 158
Falai
GRANVILLE
D 971
Vire
N 174
Clécy
Pont-d'Ouilly
St-Pair-s-Mer
JULLOUVILLE
Carolles
Putanges-Pont-Ecrepin
Sée
D 524
St-Jean-le-Thomas
AVRANCHES
D 562
D 924
le Mont-St-Michel
Mortain
DOMFRONT
N 176
N 175
N 176
BAGNOLES-DE-L'ORNE
Sélune
Juvigny-sous-Andaine
Parc naturel rég
Tessé-la-Madeleine
A 84
Couesnon
N 137
Fougères
St-Pierre-des-Nids
N 12
St-Léonard-des-Bois
D 175
Mayenne
N 162
N 12
Vilaine
N 24
RENNES
N 157
A 81
Laval
N 137
0
30 km

Places to stay

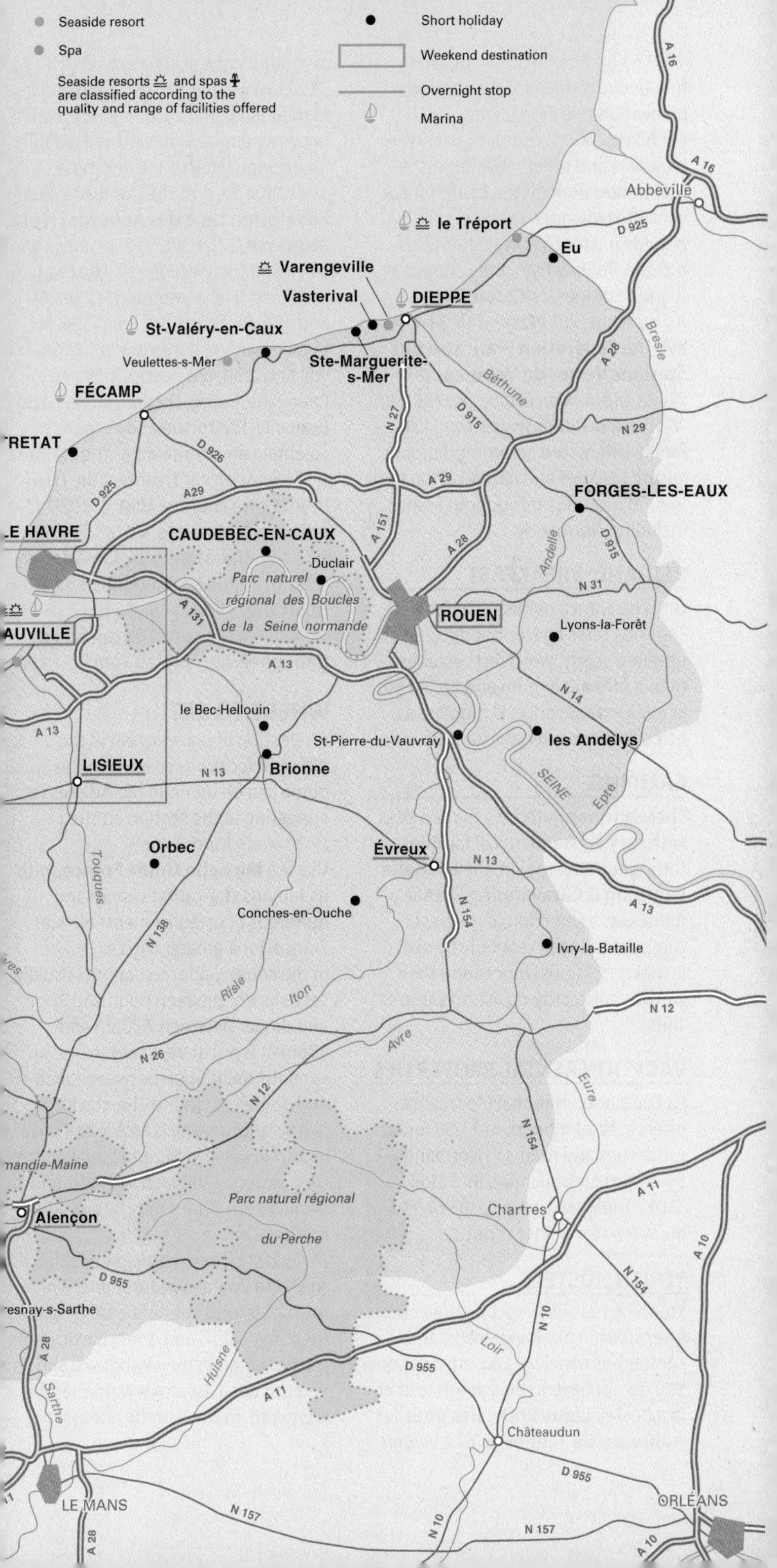

℘01 53 57 11 44. You can order the free book, or download it at www.bienvenue-a-la-ferme.com.

For hikers, skiers, climbers, kayakers, bicyclists and others seeking rustic accommodation off the beaten track, consult www.gites-refuges.com.

A guide in French is available: *Gîtes d'Étape, Refuges* by A and S Mouraret (Rando Éditions, *La Cadole, 74 r. A-Perdreaux, 781 Vézily; ℘01 34 65 11 89*). The **Fédération Française des Stations Vertes de Vacances** *(BP 71698, 21016 Dijon Cedex; ℘03 80 54 10 50, www.stationsvertes.com)* lists family-orientated accommodation, leisure facilities and natural attractions in rural locations throughout France, including Normandy.

BED-AND-BREAKFAST

Gîtes de France publishes a booklet Tous nos Gîtes en Normandie (20€) updated yearly, which lists establishments offering a room and breakfast at a reasonable price. Buy online at http://librairie.gites-de-france.fr.

CAMPING

There are many officially graded sites with varying standards of facilities throughout the region; the **Michelin Camping & Caravanning France** guide lists a selection of the best campsites, visited regularly by our inspectors. Tourist offices and their websites also provide lists of campsites.

VACATION RENTAL PROPERTIES

La Fédération National Clévacances offers a list of more than 1 000 rental properties and rooms in Normandy: 54 bd de l'Embouchure, BP 52166, 31022 Toulouse Cedex. ℘05 61 13 55 66. www.clevacances.com.

YOUTH HOSTELS

Youth hostels *(auberges de jeunesse)* offer spartan but inexpensive and sometimes convivial accommodation. You do not have to be a youth to stay in a hostel. **Ligue Française pour les Auberges de Jeunesse** *(67 r. Vergniaud, Bâtiment K, 75013 Paris; ℘01 44 16 78 78; www.auberges-de-jeunesse.com)*. Membership in the Ligue (LFAJ), which issues a membership card, is available for an annual fee of 11€ for those under age 26, and 16€ for those older. **Fédération Unie des Auberges de la Jeunesse** *(27 r. Pajol, 75018 Paris; ℘01 44 89 87 27; www.fuaj.org)*. The **Fuaj** card costs 11€ a year (under age 26), and 16€ for those older and 23€ for families with children under 14. You will find affiliated hostels in Bayeux, Caen, Cherbourg, Dieppe, Eu, Genêts, Granville, Pontorson and Vernon.

To obtain an International Youth Hostel Federation card, contact the IYHF in your own country: **USA** ℘202-783-6161, www.hiusa.org; **UK** ℘1707-324-170, www.hihostels.com; **Canada** ℘613-237-7884, www.hihostels.ca; **Australia** ℘61-2-9565-1669, www.hihostels.com. You can book through www.hihostels.com.

WHERE TO EAT

A selection of places to eat in the different locations covered in this guide can be found in the **Addresses** appearing in the section entitled *Discovering Normandy*.

Use the **Michelin Guide France**, with its famous star-rating system and hundreds of establishments all over France, for a greater choice.

In the countryside, restaurants usually serve lunch between noon and 2pm and dinner between 7.30pm and 10pm. It is not always easy to find an establishment open between lunch and dinner, as "round-the-clock" restaurants are still scarce in the provinces. However, a hungry traveller can usually get a sandwich in a cafe, and ordinary hot dishes may be available in a brasserie.

Many restaurants participate in the **Assiette de Pays** programme, which promotes local specialities at 6–18€ for a single dish and drink; participants post the logo in their windows, and you can get a list at www.normandie-pays.com, under *Assiette de Pays*.

Useful Words and Phrases

Commonly Useful Words

	Translation
Goodbye	Au revoir
Hello/Good Morning	Bonjour
Excuse Me	Excusez-moi, Pardon
Thank You	Merci
Yes/no	Oui/non
Please	S'ilvous plaît

Sights

	Translation
Abbaye	Abbey
Beffroi	Belfry
Chapelle	Chapel
Cimetière	Cemetery
Cloître	Cloisters
Cour	Courtyard
Couvent	Convent
Écluse	Lock (Canal)
Église	Church
Gothique	Gothic
Halle	Covered market
Jardin	Garden
Mairie	Town Hall
Maison	House
Marché	Market
Monastère	Monastery
Moulin	Windmill
Musée	Museum
Place	Square
Pont	Bridge
Port	Port/harbour
Quai	Quay
Remparts	Ramparts
Romain	Roman
Roman	Romanesque
Tour	Tower

Natural Sites

	Translation
Barrage	Dam
Belvédère	Viewpoint
Cascade	Waterfall
Corniche	Ledge
Côte	Coast, hillside
Étang	Pond
Falaise	Cliff
Forêt	Forest
Grotte	Cave
Lac	Lake
Marais	Marsh
Plage	Beach
Rivière	River
Ruisseau	Stream
Signal	Beacon
Source	Spring
Vallée	Valley

On the Road

	Translation
Car Park	Parking
Diesel	Diesel/Gazole
Driving Licence	Permis de conduire
East	Est
Garage (for repairs)	Garage
Left	Gauche
Motorway/highway	Autoroute
North	Nord
Parking Meter	Horodateur
Petrol/Gas	Essence
Right	Droite
Roundabout	Rond-point
South	Sud
Toll	Péage
Traffic lights	Feu tricolore
Tyre	Pneu
Unleaded	Sans plomb
West	Ouest

Time

	Translation
Today	Aujourd'hui
Tomorrow	Demain
Yesterday	Hier
Week	Semaine
Monday	Lundi
Tuesday	Mardi
Wednesday	Mercredi
Thursday	Jeudi
Friday	Vendredi
Saturday	Samedi
Sunday	Dimanche

Numbers

	Translation
0	Zéro
1	Un
2	Deux
3	Trois
4	Quatre
5	Cinq
6	Six
7	Sept

8	Huit
9	Neuf
10	Dix
11	Onze
20	Vingt
50	Cinquante
60	Soixante
100	Cent
1 000	Mille

Shopping

	Translation
Bakery	Boulangerie
Bank	Banque
Butcher Shop	Boucherie
Chemist's/drugstore	Pharmacie
Closed	Fermé
Cough mixture	Sirop pour la toux
Entrance	Entrée
Exit	Sortie
Fishmonger's	Poissonnerie
Grand	Big
Grocer's	Épicerie
Newsagent/bookshop	Librairie
Open	Ouvert
Painkiller	Analgésique
Plaster (Band-Aid)	Sparadrap
Post office	Bureau de poste
Pound (Half Kilo)	Livre
Pull	Tirer
Push	Pousser
Shop	Magasin
Stamps	Timbres

Food And Drink

	Translation
Beef	Bœuf
Beer	Bière
Butter	Beurre
Bread	Pain
Breakfast	Petit-déjeuner
Cheese	Fromage
Chicken	Poulet
Dessert	Dessert
Dinner	Dîner
Duck	Canard
Fish	Poisson
Fork	Fourchette
Fruit	Fruits
Glass	Verre
Ham	Jambon
Ice cream	Glace
Jug of water	Carafe d'eau
Knife	Couteau
Lamb	Agneau
Lunch	Déjeuner
Meat	Viande
Mineral water	Eau minérale
Mixed salad	Salade composée
Mussels	Moules
Orange juice	Jus d'orange
Oysters	Huîtres
Plate	Assiette
Pork	Porc
Red wine	Vin rouge
Salt	Sel
Sparkling water	Eau gazeuse
Spoon	Cuillère
Sugar	Sucre
Vegetables	Légumes
White Wine	Vin blanc

Personal Documents and Travel

	Translation
Airport	Aéroport
Credit card	Carte de crédit
Customs	Douane
Passport	Passeport
Platform	Voie
Railway station	Gare
Suitcase	Valise
Train/plane ticket	Billet de train/ d'avion
Wallet	Portefeuille

Clothing

	Translation
Coat	Manteau
Dress	Robe
Jumper	Pull
Raincoat	Imperméable
Shirt/blouse	Chemise
Shoes	Chaussures
Trousers	Pantalon

USEFUL PHRASES

Do you speak English?
Parlez-vous anglais?
I don't understand
Je ne comprends pas
Talk slowly, please Parlez lentement, s'il-vous plaît
Where is...? Où est...?
When does the ... leave?
A quelle heure part...?
When does the ... arrive?
A quelle heure arrive...?
When does the museum open?
A quelle heure ouvre le musée?

How much does it cost?
Ça coûte combien?
Where is the nearest petrol/ gas station? Où se trouve la station d'essence la plus proche?
Where can I change traveller's cheques? Où puis-je changer un traveller's chèque?
Where are the toilets?
Où se trouve les toilettes?
Do you accept credit cards?
Acceptez-vous les cartes de crédit?
I have an allergy to nuts/dairy products
J'ai une allergie aux fruits à coque et à l'arachide/aux produits laitières

Basic Information

BUSINESS HOURS

Offices and other businesses are open Mon–Fri, 9am–noon, 2–6pm. Many also open Saturday mornings. Town and village shops are generally open Tue–Fri; there are local variations. Midday breaks may be much longer in the south. However, in cities, tourist centres or resorts, businesses may keep longer hours or stay open all day, seven days a week, especially if they primarily serve the tourist market.

ELECTRICITY

The electric current is 220 volts/50 Hz. Circular two-pin plugs are the rule. Adapters should be bought before you leave home; they are on sale in most airports.

EMERGENCIES

Police (Gendarme) 17
Fire (Pompiers) 18
Ambulance (SAMU) 15

First aid, medical advice and chemists' night-service rotas are available from chemists/drugstores (*pharmacie*, identified by a green cross sign). American Express offers its cardholders a service, "Global Assist", for any medical, legal or personal emergency: ✆01 47 77 70 00.

MAIL/POST

Look for the bright yellow *La Poste* signs. Main post offices are generally open Mon–Fri 9am–7pm, Sat 9am–noon. Smaller branches generally open 9am–noon, 2–4pm weekdays. There are often automatic tellers *(guichets automatiques)* inside which allow you to weigh packages and buy postage and avoid a queue. You may also find that you can use a Minitel, change money, make copies, send faxes and make phone calls in a post office. To mail a letter from the street look for the bright yellow postboxes. Stamps are also sold in newsagents and cafés that sell cigarettes *(tabac)*. www.laposte.fr.

MONEY

CURRENCY

There are no restrictions on the amount of currency visitors can take into France. Visitors wishing to export currency in foreign banknotes in excess of the given allocation from France should complete a currency declaration form on arrival.

Coins and notes – The unit of currency in France is the **euro** (€). One euro is divided into 100 cents or *centimes d'euro*. Old franc notes can still be exchanged by the Banque de France until early 2012.

In the Channel Islands, legal tender is the **Pound Sterling** (£). The local currency issued by the banks of Jersey and Guernsey is not legal tender outside the islands. All the British clearing banks have branches in the Channel Islands.

BANKS AND CURRENCY EXCHANGE

Banks are generally open Mon–Fri 9am–5.30pm. Some branches are open for limited transactions on

Saturday. Banks limit opening hours on the day before a bank holiday.
A passport or other ID may be necessary when cashing cheques (traveller's or ordinary) in banks. Commission charges vary and hotels usually charge considerably more than banks for cashing cheques, especially for non-residents.
By far the most convenient way of obtaining French currency is the **24-hr cash dispenser** or ATM (*distributeur automatique de billets* in French), found outside many banks and post offices and easily recognisable by the CB (Carte Bleue) logo. Most accept international credit cards (don't forget your PIN) and almost all also give instructions in English. Note that American Express cards can be used only in dispensers operated by the Crédit Lyonnais bank or by American Express. Foreign currency can also be exchanged in major banks, post offices, hotels or private exchange offices found in main cities and near popular tourist attractions.

CREDIT CARDS

Major credit and debit cards (Visa, MasterCard, Eurocard, Maestro) are widely accepted in shops, hotels, restaurants and petrol stations. Pay-at-the-pump automatic petrol stations accept most cards (including Maestro debit cards). If your card is lost or stolen call the appropriate 24hr hotlines: **American Express**: ☎01 47 77 72 00. **Visa**: ☎08 36 69 08 80. **MasterCard**: ☎08 00 90 13 87
You must report any loss or theft of credit cards or traveller's cheques to the local police who will issue you with a certificate (useful proof to show the issuing company).

PUBLIC HOLIDAYS

There are 11 public holidays in France. In addition, there are other religious and national festivals days, and a number of local saints' days, etc. On all these days, museums and other monuments may be closed or may vary their hours of admission.

PUBLIC HOLIDAYS	
1 January	New Year's Day *(Jour de l'An)*
Mon after Easter Sun	Easter Monday *(Pâques)*
1 May	Labour Day
8 May	VE Day
Thu 40 days after Easter	Ascension Day *(Ascension catholique)*
7th Sun after Easter	Whit Monday *(Pentecôte)*
14 July	**Fête National** France's National Day **(or Bastille Day)**
15 August	Assumption *(Assomption)*
1 November	All Saints' Day *(Toussaint)*
11 November	Armistice Day
25 December	Christmas Day *(Noël)*

SCHOOL HOLIDAYS

French schools close for holidays five times a year. In these periods, all tourist sites and attractions, hotels, restaurants and roads are busier than usual. These school holidays are one week at the end of October, two weeks at Christmas, two weeks in February, two weeks in spring, and the whole of July and August.

SMOKING REGULATIONS

In February 2007, France banned smoking in public places such as offices, universities and railway stations. The law became effective for restaurants, cafés, bars, nightclubs and casinos in January 2008.

TELEPHONES

The telephone system in France is still operated largely by the former state monopoly France Télécom. They offer an English-language enquiries service on ☎0800 364 775 (within France) or ☎00 33 1 55 78 60 56 (outside France).
The French **ringing tone** is a series of long tones.
To use a **public phone** you need to buy a prepaid phone card *(télécarte)*. Some telephone booths accept credit

cards (Visa, MasterCard/Eurocard). *Télécartes* (50 or 120 units) can be bought in post offices, cafés that sell cigarettes *(tabac)* and newsagents, and can be used to make calls in France and abroad. Calls can be received at phone boxes where the blue bell sign is shown.

MOBILE/CELL PHONES

While in France, all visitors from other European countries should be able to use their mobile phone just as normal. Visitors from some other countries, notably the USA, need to ensure before departure that their phone and service contract are compatible with the European system (GSM).
All the charges are given in the 'welcome' message you will receive on using your phone for the first time in France. The three main mobile phone operators in France are SFR, Orange and Bouygues.
If you do not have your mobile phone with you, or you discovered it would not be compatible with the European system, depending on the length of your visit and on how often you plan on using the phone, it may be wise to consider buying or hiring one with a coverage plan that fits your needs. There are a variety of options you can choose from, making it less expensive than you might imagine.
Bouygues www.bouyguestelecom.fr
Orange www.orange.fr
SFR www.sfr.fr

NATIONAL CALLS

French telephone numbers have ten digits. Numbers begin with 01 in Paris and the Paris region; 02 in northwest France; 03 in northeast France; 04 in southeast France and Corsica; 05 in southwest France. However, all ten numbers must be dialled even in the local region.

INTERNATIONAL CALLS

To call France from abroad, dial the country code 33, omit the initial zero of the French number, and dial the remaining nine-digit number. When calling abroad from France dial 00, followed by the country code, followed by the local area code (usually without any initial zero), and the number of your correspondent.
To use the personal calling card of a telephone company, follow the instructions on the card, dialling the access code for the country you are in. e.g.:
AT&T ✆0800 99 0011
BT ✆0800 99 0244
MCI/Verizon ✆0800 99 0019
Sprint ✆0800 99 0087
Canada Direct ✆0800 99 0016
Cheap rates with 50% extra time are available at various times to the UK, Canada, Australia and the USA.
Toll-free numbers in France begin with 0800.

TIME

WHEN IT IS **NOON IN FRANCE**, IT IS	
3am	in Los Angeles
6am	in New York
11am	in Dublin
11am	in London
7pm	in Perth
9pm	in Sydney
11pm	in Auckland

TIPPING

Under French law, any service charge is included in the prices displayed for meals and accommodation. Any additional tipping in restaurants and hoteessary and is at the visitor's discretion. However, in bars and cafés it is not unusual to leave any small change that remains after paying the bill, but this generally should not be more than 5 per cent. Taxi drivers do not have to be tipped, but it's usual to give a small amount, not more than 10%. Attendants at public toilets should be given a few cents. Tour guides and drivers should be tipped according to the amount of service given: from 2 to 5 euros.

INTRODUCTION TO NORMANDY

Honfleur in the Calvados region

Normandy Today

21ST CENTURY

Normandy today takes pride in its agricultural and fishing traditions as one of the most rural regions of France, while adapting to the wider European economy as a major centre for maritime trade; technology-based industries are also coming to the fore. Today, Basse-Normandie (Lower Normandy) markets its milk, cider and Camembert cheese around the world. Haute-Normandie (Upper Normandy) has continued development as a centre for modern industry, although parts remain quite rural.

POPULATION

Although Lower Normandy (population 1.457 million) remains rural in terms of economy, some 65% of the population lives in and around the urban centres of Alençon, Caen and Cherbourg; in the countryside, demographic decline is a worry, as young people leave. Seaside resorts, on the other hand, have attracted new inhabitants. Upper Normandy (population 1.811 million), with its industrial and service employment and proximity to Paris, has a more evenly distributed population. Normandy has a fairly young population, with about 25% under the age of 20. Life expectancy for men is 75 years, and for women 82 years.

LIFESTYLE

Normandy immediately conjures images of a leisured life along broad beaches, or among verdant pastures and dew-drenched orchards. Curiously, the fact that most inhabitants live in urban areas has left the countryside bucolic. In addition, quite a few of those pretty half-timbered houses and quaint seaside villas, as well as the many flats in buildings along the coast, belong to Parisians who drive up only on holidays, so roads are rarely crowded during the week. But the people who live on the coast or in the countryside, as opposed to visitors on holiday, are famously hard-working.

RELIGION

Normandy's rich heritage of churches and abbeys dates, with very few exceptions, to older times. Today, religion plays a far smaller part in daily life. Some 75% of Normandy residents profess Roman Catholicism, with a light dusting (1–2%) of Protestants and Muslims (1–3%), the latter living in urban areas of Upper Normandy. A quarter of inhabitants profess no religion, about the French average. Churches fill up for traditional festivals, but not for Sunday mass. Yet the buildings, which belong to the French state, are carefully maintained. The ties of the Catholic tradition remain strong.

FOOD

Local Specialities

According to Norman tradition one should eat duck in Rouen, tripe in Caen and La Ferté-Macé, leg of lamb from the salt meadows of Mont-St-Michel Bay and an omelette in Mont-St-Michel; one should also taste Dieppe sole, Duclair duckling, Auge Valley chicken garnished with tiny onions, Vire chitterlings *(andouillette)*, black pudding from Mortagne-au-Perche and white pudding from Avranches. Among the tasty meat dishes, try the *côtes de veau vallée d'Auge*, which are veal cutlets fried in butter and flambéed in Calvados then braised in cider and fresh cream.

As for seafood, there are shrimps and cockles from Honfleur, mussels from Villerville and Isigny, lobsters from La Hague and Barfleur and oysters, Atlantic crabs, spider crabs, winkles and whelks from Courseulles and St-Vaast. Seafood may be accompanied by rye bread, salted butter and a glass of dry cider.

Fish – sole, turbot and mackerel to mention only a few – is often served with a delicious sauce.

Local pastries, all made with butter, include apple turnovers *(chaussons aux pommes)*, flat cakes baked in the oven (*falues* or *fouaces*), biscuits *(galettes)*, shortbread *(sablés)* and buns *(brioches)*. *Douillons* are pears hollowed out and filled with butter, wrapped in pastry and baked.

Cream and Normandy Sauce

Cream, the mainstay of the Normandy kitchen, is at its best in the so-called Normandy Sauce *(sauce normande)*, which elsewhere is just a plain white sauce, but here both looks and tastes quite different.

Cheese

If cream is the queen of Normandy cooking, cheese is the king of all fare. **Pont-l'Évêque** has reigned since the 13C; **Livarot** is quoted in texts of the same period; the world-renowned Camembert probably dates to the 17C, at least.

The Normandy cheeseboard also includes fresh cheese from the Pays de Bray – the **bondons**, *demi-sel* or double cream. Before sweeping France, the **petit-suisse** was a much appreciated farmhouse cheese. **Neufchâtel** cheese can be eaten within 12 days of being made, although a mature Neufchâtel takes up to three months.

CIDER

Apple cider has been made locally since the Middle Ages, and it is still possible to find a farmhouse brew distilled in the traditional way.

The apples are gathered in huge baskets then stored for a short while before being emptied into a circular granite trough, where they are crushed by a round wooden millstone pulled by a horse. The crushed apples (*marc*) are transferred to the press, where they are laid between layers of rye straw and then pressed. The rye straw is then extracted and the apple pulp is put to soak in a vat before being pressed a second time to produce a weaker brew which is kept for use on the farm.

Whether it is *brut* (dry, strongly flavoured with apple with an alcohol content of 4–5%), *demi-sec* or *doux* (made artificially sweet by stalling the fermentation process when the alcohol content reaches 2.5–3%), cider is the perfect accompaniment for pancakes or apple desserts. It should always be served chilled.

Calvados

Calvados, or *calva* as it is better known, is a cider brandy made from a mash of apples fermented with yeast; it is distilled twice and matured in oak for six to ten years. The tradition of the *trou normand* (Norman hole) is still observed; during a heavy meal a small glass of Calvados is swallowed at one go to help the digestion. Restaurants often serve an apple and Calvados sorbet instead. Calvados is usually drunk after coffee; for just a taste, eat a sugar lump dipped in Calvados. A great many distilleries and storehouses are open to the public.

Perry

Perry *(poiré)* is similar to cider but is made from pears and usually comes from the areas around Mortain and Domfront.

Pommeau

This alcoholic beverage is made by mixing two-thirds of apple juice with one-third of Calvados and features an alcohol content of 16–18%. The ageing process is carried out in oak casks for a period of 18 months. It can be drunk chilled as an apéritif (without ice) or be drunk at room temperature to accompany oysters, foie gras, melon or apple pie. It is also appreciated in cooking.

ECONOMY

The two areas of Normandy present very different economic profiles. Upper Normandy, which stretches along the Seine river estuary, possesses a large industrial sector, with Renault auto plants at Elbeuf and Le Havre, oil refineries, petrochemical plants, a big construction industry and many light industries. The principal import is crude oil; principal exports are refined petroleum and petrochemical products, and autos and auto parts. The ports of Le Havre and Rouen are among France's biggest.

In Lower Normandy, three-quarters of the land is agricultural, by far the highest proportion in all France, much of it devoted to dairy cows. Industry occupies only 20% of the workforce, and milk processing is the biggest industry. Many people are employed in small businesses and tourism. Norman farms also produce grain (wheat, maize, barley), oils (linseed, rape), several sorts of fruit, animal feed, sugar beet and potatoes.

Calvados and Manche produce 12% of the French fish catch, much of it shellfish, and nearly all of it sold dockside to wholesellers.

Lower Normandy's agricultural sector sheltered its economy during the 2008–09 recession. Upper Normandy was hit harder, although the combination of low fuel prices and good grain harvests kept ports humming. French holidaymakers, choosing to stay at home, supported the Norman tourist industry.

GOVERNMENT

The area covered by this book corresponds to the former province of Normandy, divided in 1789 into five *départements*, with remaining bits absorbed by the départements of Eure-et-Loire and Mayenne. Eure and Seine-Maritime make up the region of Upper Normandy, while Calvados, Manche and Orne make up Lower Normandy.

There are 26 **regions** in France (22 within French borders, four overseas), governed by elected councils. The regions are composed of **départements** (100 in all of France), each of which is divided into **communes**, governed by municipal councils and mayors. **Cantons** exist only to elect members to the departmental council.

A large *commune*, such as Le Havre, will include several *cantons*. In a rural area, there may be several *communes* in a *canton*. In recent years, the regions have gained more authority over the *départements*. You can tell where people are from by reading the licence plates on their cars: each *département* has its own number.

History

TIMELINE

ROMAN PERIOD

58-51 BC — Roman conquest. New towns appear: Rotomagus (Rouen), Caracotinum (Harfleur), Noviomagus (Lisieux), Juliobona (Lillebonne), Mediolanum (Évreux).

56BC — The Unelli crushed by Sabinius in the Mont Castre area.

1C — Growth of main settlements (Coutances, Rouen, Évreux, etc.).

2C — Nordic (Saxon and Germanic) invasions of the Bessin region. Conversion to Christianity.

260 — Bishopric of Rouen founded by St Nicaise.

284 and 364 — Nordic invasions.

FRANKISH DOMINATION

497 — Rouen and Évreux occupied by Clovis.

511 — Neustria or the Western Kingdom inherited by Clothaire, Clovis's son.

6C — The first monasteries founded.

7C — Monasteries flourish: St-Wandrille, Jumièges.

709 — Mont Tombe consecrated to the cult of St Michael by Aubert, Bishop of Avranches.

VIKING INVASIONS

The Vikings or Norsemen who sailed from Scandinavia harassed western Europe, parts of Africa and even headed into the Mediterranean.

800 — Channel coast invaded by Vikings.

820 — Seine Valley laid waste by Vikings.

836 — Christians persecuted in the Cotentin region.

858 — Bayeux devastated by Vikings.
875 — Further persecution in the west.
885 — Paris besieged by Vikings.
911 — Treaty of St-Clair-sur-Epte: Rollo becomes the first Duke of Normandy.

THE INDEPENDENT DUKEDOM

Under William Longsword the dukedom takes on its final form with the unification of the Avranchin and the Cotentin.
10-11C — Consolidation of ducal powers. Restoration of the abbeys.
1027 — Birth of William, the future conqueror of England, at Falaise.
1066 — Invasion of England by William. King of France threatened by his vassal, the Duke of Normandy, now also King of England.
1087 — Death of William the Conqueror in Rouen.
1087-1135 — William's heirs in dispute; ducal authority restored by Henry Beauclerk who becomes King of England as Henry I (1100–35) after his brother William Rufus.
1120 — The wreck of the White Ship off Barfleur Point with the loss of Henry I's heir, William Atheling, and 300 members of the Anglo-Norman nobility.
1152 — Marriage of Henry II Plantagenet, to Eleanor of Aquitaine, whose dowry included all of southwest France.
1154-89 — Henry II of England.
1195 — Château-Gaillard built by Richard Lionheart.
1202 — Loss of Norman possessions by John Lackland, King of England.
1204 — Normandy united to the French crown

FRENCH DUKEDOM TO THE PROVINCE OF NORMANDY

1315 — Granting of the Norman Charter, symbol of provincial status, which remained in being until the French Revolution.
1346 — Normandy invaded by Edward III of England.
1364-84 — The Battle of Cocherel marks the start of Du Guesclin's campaigns.
1417 — Normandy invaded by Henry V of England.
1424 — English repulsed by Louis d'Estouteville, defender of Mont-St-Michel.
1431 — Trial and torture of Joan of Arc at Rouen.
1437 — Founding of Caen Uni-versity.
1450 — Normandy recovered by the French crown after the victory at Formigny and the recapture of Cherbourg.
1469 — Charles of France, last Duke of Normandy, is dispossessed of his dukedom.
1514 — The Rouen Exchequer becomes the Parliament of Normandy.
1517 — Founding of Le Havre.
1542 — Rouen created as a self-governing city for treasury purposes.
1589 — Henri of Navarre victorious at Arques and the following year at Ivry-la-Bataille.
1625 — Alençon also created as a treasury district.
1639-40 — Revolt of the Barefoot Peasants provoked by the introduction of the salt tax *(gabelle)*.
1692 — Naval battle of La Hougue.
1771-75 — Suppression of the Parliament at Rouen.

LATE 18C TO TODAY

1789 — The Caen Revolt.
1793 — The Girondins' attempted uprising; siege of Granville.

1795-1800 — Insurrection of the Norman royalists, the Chouans.
1843 — Inauguration of the Paris-Caen railway.
1870-71 — Franco-Prussian War; occupation of Haute-Normandie and Le Mans.
June 1940 — Bresle Front breached.
August 1942 — Dieppe Commando raid by Canadian and British troops.
June 1944 — Allied landing on the Calvados coast. Battle of Normandy.
1954 — René Coty, born in Le Havre, is elected President of the Republic.
1959 — Inauguration of the Tancarville Bridge.
1967 — Commissioning of the Atomic Centre at La Hague.
1971 — Launch of the Redoutable, the first French nuclear submarine, at Cherbourg.
1974 — Creation of the Brotonne Regional Nature Park.
1975 — Creation of the Normandie-Maine Regional Nature Park.
1977 — Completion of the Normandy motorway (A 3).
1983-84 — Start-up of Paluel Nuclear Power Station.
Start-up of Flamanville Nuclear Power Station.
1987 — Commemoration of the 900th anniversary of William the Conqueror's death.
1991 — Inauguration of France's 27th regional nature park in the Cotentin and Bessin area.
6 June 1994 — 50th anniversary of the Battle of Normandy.
January 1995 — Inauguration of the Pont de Normandie.
1997 — A violent controversy breaks out between Greenpeace environmentalists and COGEMA over nuclear waste dumped near La Hague.
1999 — Tall Ships Armada of the Century on the Seine, from Rouen to Le Havre.
1999 — Violent windstorms in December uproot innumerable trees and damage buildings.
2000 — Wreck of the *Evoli Sun*, an Italian ship loaded with chemicals, off Cap de la Hague.
2004 — Sixtieth anniversary of the Normandy landings attended, for the first time, by leaders of Germany and Russia.
2005 — The centre of Le Havre is named a UNESCO World Heritage Site.
2006 — Port 2000 at Le Havre opened.
2009 — 65th anniversary of D-Day.

NORMANS THROUGHOUT HISTORY

The story of the Norsemen, or Vikings, who settled in the Frankish kingdom and from there set out on expeditions of conquest to southern Italy and Sicily as well as to England, Wales, Scotland and Ireland, has inspired many tall tales and cinematic extravaganzas.

In the 8C, pagan barbarians from Denmark, Norway and Iceland began their plunder of coastal settlements in Europe and by the 9C they had established a permanent foothold in the region that is now Normandy. In the year 911, **Charles III (The Simple)** signed the treaty of **St-Clair-sur-Epte** with the Viking chief **Rollo**. According to Dudon de St-Quentin, the first historian of Normandy, the Viking simply placed his hands between those of the French king to ratify the agreement creating the dukedom of Normandy: no written treaty was ever drafted.

The Norsemen continued to expand their holdings until well into the 11C, ruling through a succession of ruthless dukes and counts.

Eventually, the Norse converted to Christianity and adopted the French language, but retained a reputation for

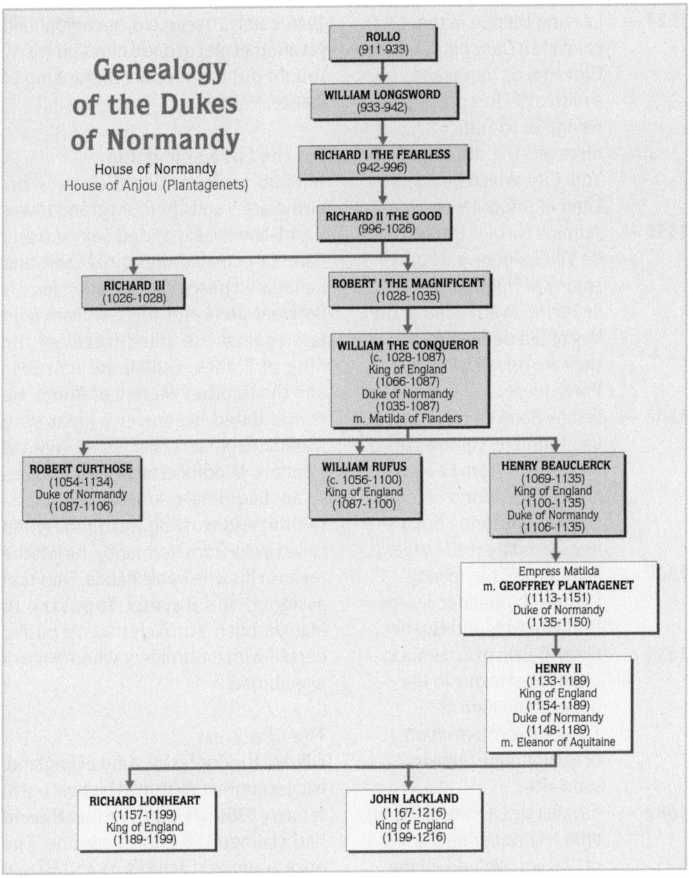

recklessness, love of combat, cunning and outrageous treachery. At the same time, wherever they went, they showed a remarkable capacity for adapting to local customs. William, Duke of Normandy, became King of England in a coup known as the **Norman Conquest** (1066), while the Norman kingdom of Sicily was founded by the descendants of Tancrède de Hauteville. Norman rulers were among the most powerful and successful of their time, and established enduring political institutions.

In Normandy, the Normans quickly adopted the precepts of feudalism, became masters of cavalry warfare and fostered the cult of knighthood. Eventually, their reputation for fierceness and brutality was softened by religion, marked by pilgrimages to Rome and the Holy Land. In England, their rule made the kingdom safer from foreign invasion and brought discipline to church organisations.

Later still, explorers continued to embark from Normandy in search of new lands:

1402 — Jean de Béthencourt, of the Caux region, becomes King of the Canary Islands, but cedes his realm to the King of Castile.

1503 — Paulmier de Gonneville, gentleman of Honfleur, reaches Brazil in the Espoir.

1506 — Jean Denis, a sailor from Honfleur, explores the mouth of the St Lawrence, preparing the way for Jacques Cartier.

1524 — Leaving Dieppe in the caravel *La Dauphine*, Giovanni da Verrazano, a native of Florence and navigator to François I, discovers the site of New York City, which he names Land of Angoulême.

1555 — Admiral Nicolas Durand de Villegaignon sets up a colony of Huguenots from Le Havre on an island in the bay of Rio de Janeiro, but they are driven away by the Portuguese.

1563 — Led by René de la Laudonnière, colonies of Protestants from Le Havre and Dieppe found Fort Caroline in Florida but are massacred by the Spaniards.

1608 — Samuel de Champlain, Dieppe shipbuilder, leaves Honfleur to found Quebec.

1635 — Pierre Belain of Esnambuc claims Martinique in the name of the King of France; the colonisation of Guadeloupe follows soon after.

1682 — Cavalier de La Salle of Rouen, after reconnoitring the site of Chicago, sails down the Mississippi river and takes possession of Louisiana.

WILLIAM THE CONQUEROR

William was the son of Robert the Magnificent and his concubine Herleva (The Beautiful Arlette), from the town of Falaise. A descendant of the great Viking chief Rollo, he was first known as William the Bastard.

In 1035, when his father died on his way back from the Holy Land, William, then eight years old, became the seventh Duke of Normandy. His tutors instructed him in the rudiments of Latin and the fine points of military strategy, and also instilled in him a deep religious faith.

Later, three of his guardians and his tutor were assassinated by parties who objected to the Bastard's succession. In 1046, barely 20 years old, he confounded yet another plot to undo him, and wisely sought out the support of the King of France, Henri I.

For the Love of Matilda

William built castles (Falaise – his birthplace – and Cherbourg) and towns (Saint-James), expanded Saint-Lô and Carentan, created the city of Caen, and negotiated peace with his enemies.

Between 1054 and 1060, William held fast against the allied forces of the King of France, Guillaume d'Arques and the Geoffrey Martell of Anjou. He consolidated his power by marrying Matilda, daughter of Baldwin V, Count of Flanders. Mindful of all he had suffered as an illegitimate son, William was a faithful and trusting husband. When called away from Normandy, he left the realm in his wife's able hands. Tradition assigned the **Bayeux Tapestry** to Matilda, but it is unlikely that she busied herself with embroidery when William was abroad.

The Conquest

Edward the Confessor, King of England, had recognised William as his heir, but in January 1066 news arrived that **Harold** had claimed the English throne. The duke appealed to the Pope and Harold was excommunicated.

Within seven months, William was master of England. On 12 September 1066, protected by the Pope's ensign, about 12 000 knights and soldiers embarked upon 696 ships followed by smaller boats and skiffs bringing the total number of vessels to 3 000. On 28 September, at low tide, the Normans landed at Pevensey, Sussex. William, the last to disembark, stumbled and fell full length. The superstitious Normans were alarmed, but William laughed and, according to the records, retorted: "My Lords, by the glory of God have I seized this land with my own two hands. As long as it exists it is ours alone."

The Normans occupied Hastings. Harold, who had been busy fighting other attackers, rushed to the scene and pitched camp on a hill. On 14 October William launched an assault, and after a terrible struggle the Normans were victorious; Harold died in combat. The history of the invasion is recounted in the Bayeux Tapestry, which shows fascinating details of combat dress and equipment.

While remaining Duke of Normandy, William was crowned King of England on Christmas Day, 1066, at Westminster Abbey, London. He suppressed revolts, brought to heel the corrupt aristocracy, encouraged noble Norman families to settle in England, and overcame the Pope's opposition to his control over church affairs. Norman art flourished in England, as the cathedrals at Canterbury, Winchester and Durham show.

Ruling 52 years in Normandy and 21 years in England, William maintained a large measure of peace and justice in his realm. He died on 9 September 1087 near Rouen and was buried at St-Étienne Church in Caen, as he had requested.

MONASTICISM IN NORMANDY

Normandy, like Champagne and Burgundy, was a centre of monasticism during the religious revival that swept the 11C, as the many abbeys attest.

Under **Benedictine Rule**, which gradually supplanted other religious rules, nuns and monks made vows of obedience, poverty and chastity. They practised fasting, silence and abstinence.

The monks' working day was taken up by divine office (prayers scheduled throughout the day), holy reading and, to a greater extent, manual labour, such as baking bread, weaving cloth for the monastic habits, carrying firewood, sweeping, serving meals, preparing the sacristy, growing vegetables, etc.

Throughout the Middle Ages monasticism played a vital role in society, securing the propagation of Christianity, promoting the authority of the Pope and contributing to the conservation and transmission of learning.

MEDIEVAL MONASTERIES

The monastic buildings surrounded the cloisters as detailed below.

Cloisters

Generally, four galleries corresponding to the compass points surrounded a central courtyard, often laid out as a medicinal herb garden.

Abbey Church

The abbey church was characterised by an extremely long nave; the monks spent long hours in church for mass and other religious offices. In Cistercian churches, a rood screen placed near the high altar separated the monks' choir from that of the lay brothers.

Sacristy

The room in which ecclesiastical garments and altar vessels were stored and in which the priest would don his robes before leading the service.

Chapter House

Used for daily monastic activities, including prayers before the day's work and the reading of a chapter taken from the monastic rule.

Calefactory

The only heated room in the monastery, accessible to all the monks under certain conditions.

Scriptorium

A room reserved for the copying out of manuscripts.

Refectory

A large bare room, endowed with surprisingly good acoustics. During meals, the reader in the elevated pulpit would recite passages from the Bible.

Dormitories

There were generally two: one for the monks above the chapter house and one for the lay brothers above the cellars. In the Cistercian order seven hours were allowed for rest. The monks slept fully dressed in a communal dormitory.

Outbuildings

These included the barns and the porter's lodge, often a grand building with a huge gateway to allow the passage of both carriages and people on foot. The porter's lodge had living quarters on the first floor, where alms were distributed and justice was dispensed to the population.

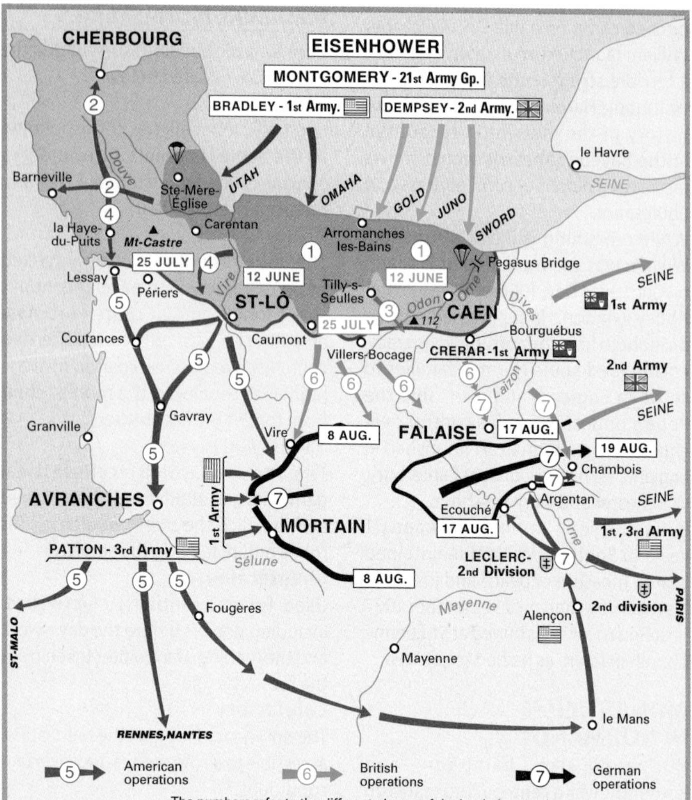

The numbers refer to the different phases of the battle (see text).

THE BATTLE OF NORMANDY

On 6 June 1944 the coast of Normandy was the setting for yet another crucial invasion which would, in its own turn, change the course of history.

From the autumn of 1941 the British authorities had envisaged a landing on the continent of Europe, but it was only after the entry of the United States that offensive action on such a scale could be seriously considered. The COSSAC plan, approved at the Churchill-Roosevelt meetings in Washington and Quebec in May and August 1943, foresaw the landing of invasion troops along the Calvados coast, which was defended by the German 7th Army. This sector was preferred to the Pas-de-Calais (15th German Army) because it meant that the Germans' lines of communication would be more vulnerable: Lower Normandy would be isolated if the bridges over the Seine and Loire were destroyed. It was also known that the enemy was preoccupied by the defence of the Pas-de-Calais.

Preparation

The building of artificial ports – a lesson learned as a result of the costly Dieppe commando raid of 1942 – and the construction of landing craft was carried out with other training in the winter of 1943–44. On 24 December 1943 General Eisenhower was named Chief of the Allied Expeditionary Force and General Montgomery made responsible for tactical coordination of all land forces (21st Army Group) for **Operation Overlord**.

Air raids to paralyse the French railway system began on 6 March 1944. During the spring of 1944 Marshal Rommel had the beaches and their approaches covered with obstacles. It became urgent to find a means of destroying these obstacles by using tanks as bulldozers or sending frogmen to dispose of them.

First Week of the Landing

Circled numbers refer to the map.

① Originally D-Day had been planned for 5 June but it was postponed for 24 hours owing to bad weather.
At dawn on D-Day, 6 June 1944, British and Commonwealth ground forces established beachheads at **Sword**, **Juno** and **Gold** and rapidly linked up with the airborne troops dropped to their east. The Americans, landing on **Omaha** Beach, joined up with their airborne flank only after the capture of Carentan on 12 June.

Layout of the Bridgehead

Advances were substantial but of unequal depth: the Americans threatened Caumont on 13 June; the British and Canadians were held up by very fierce fighting 6km/3.7mi north of Caen in the Tilly-sur-Seulles sector on 7 June and broke through only on the 20th – the village changed hands some 20 times. The Caen sector, as Montgomery had foreseen, became the principal hinge of the whole front.

Isolation of the Cotentin Peninsula and the Capture of Cherbourg

② The Americans attacked across the Cotentin Peninsula on 13 June and secured it, capturing Barneville on 18 June. Turning north they attacked Cherbourg, which fell on 26 June – a victory in the battle to ensure supply lines.

Battle of the Odon and Capture of Caen

③ On 26 June a hard battle, which was to last a month, began for a crossing over the Odon upstream from Caen and the taking of Hill 112. Montgomery decided to outflank Caen to the southwest. The city of Caen on the left bank was attacked in force from the west and northeast and fell on 9 July.

Breakthrough Preparation

In early July General Montgomery laid out his breakthrough strategy: "Keep the greatest possible number of the enemy divisions on our eastern flank, between Caen and Villers-Bocage, and pivot the western flank of the Army Group towards the southeast in a vast sweeping movement in order to threaten the line of retreat of the German division."

War of the Hedgerows

For the American soldiers of 1944 the Cotentin campaign – the advance to Cherbourg and the Battle of St-Lô – was simply "the war of the hedgerows".
Leafy hedges and sunken lanes such as those that divide the Normandy countryside came as an unpleasant surprise for the attackers, but for defensive warfare or guerrilla tactics the terrain offered unending opportunities.
Modern arms were not much help: four-inch shells scarcely shook the tree-covered embankments, which constituted natural anti-tank barriers; only the foot soldier could fight successfully in this hell of hedges.
The effort of fighting against an invisible enemy was exhausting; every field and orchard crossed was a victory in itself; progress was slow and was often estimated by the number of hedges passed. So that the tanks could operate with a maximum of efficiency, an American sergeant devised a system whereby a sharp steel device, not unlike a ploughshare, was attached to the front of each tank.

The Battle for St-Lô

④ On 3 July the American 8th Corps launched its offensive, in the face of fierce German resistance, towards the road centre of St-Lô, thus assuring more favourable positions for the large-scale operations to come. Fighting was fierce for La Haye-du-

Puits and Mount Castre. St-Lô fell on 19 July and the Americans entrenched their position behind the Lessay–Périers–St-Lô stretch of road. Progress at this time was slow in the Caen sector. A breakthrough was attempted towards the southwest of the town but was halted in the Bourguébus sector on 19 July. For one interminable week, from 19 to 25 July, bad weather suspended operations on all fronts.

The Breakthrough (Operation Cobra)

⑤ At midday on 25 July, following intense aerial bombardment, the 7th corps attacked west of St-Lô, the 8th between Périers and Lessay.

By 28 July, Allied armour was driving down the main roads, carrying out vast encircling movements. Coutances fell on 28 July, Granville and Avranches on 31 July. On 1 August General Patton, taking command of the 3rd Army, hurled it into the lightning war. The 8th Corps burst west into Brittany (Rennes fell on 4 August and Nantes on 12 August), while the 15th Corps and the French 2nd Armoured Division under General Leclerc moved east towards Laval and Le Mans (9 August).

The Thrust South of Caen

⑥ Backing up these operations, Montgomery, with the 1st Canadian Army (General Crerar), moved up to the Caen-Falaise road at the eastern end of the front; the British divisions, pushing southeast from Caumont and Villers-Bocage (5 August), overwhelmed the last defences on the west bank of the Orne.

Battle of the Falaise-Mortain Pocket

⑦ When the German 7th Army was threatened by the American 15th Corps to their rear and the British to the north, Hitler himself organised a counter-offensive to cut off the 3rd Army from its supply bases by taking control of the Avranches bottleneck. The German 7th Army began its westerly counter attack on 6–7 August in the Mortain region. The Allied air forces crushed the move at daybreak. After a week of bitter fighting the Germans retreated east (12 August). During this time the French 2nd Division moved northwards from Le Mans, took Alençon on 12 August and on 13 August breached the Paris-Granville road at Écouché.

The Canadians, halted between the 9 and 14 August at the River Laison, entered Falaise on 17 August, thus forming the northern arm of the pincer movement. Meeting with the Americans at Chambois (19 August), they cornered the German 7th Army and forced its surrender at Tournai-sur-Dives. By the night of 21 August the Battle of Normandy was over – it had cost the Germans 640 000 men, killed, wounded or taken prisoner.

Reconstruction

The Scale of Devastation

Normandy, like Britain and unlike many other French and European territories, is not on any European invasion route and so had remained unscathed since the Wars of Religion; towns had scarcely altered since the 16C. The German invasion of 1940 and the air raids and army operations of 1944 caused widespread devastation and nearly all the great towns suffered – Rouen, Le Havre, Caen, Lisieux.

Of the 3 400 Norman *communes*, 586 have been rebuilt to modern standards.

Town Planning and Reconstruction

Modern town planning has altered what were narrow winding main streets into wide straight thoroughfares to accommodate increased traffic, while providing for public gardens, parks and car parks. Houses, flats and offices have been built and an effort has been made to restore individual character to towns and villages; limestone is used for buildings on the Norman sedimentary plain and plateaux, while sandstone, granite and brick are used in the woodland regions. Many historic monuments were damaged but most have been restored and are enhanced by improved settings.

Montgomery explaining troops' dispositions and battle movements to the King

Commanders in the Battle of Normandy

General Dwight Eisenhower (1890–1969) was the Supreme Allied Commander for Overlord. He was present when the German capitulation was signed in Berlin on 8 May 1945. Eisenhower was then to become US president from 1953 to 1961.

General George Patton (1885–1945) commanded the 3rd American Army. After the Avranches breakthrough his units swept across Brittany, the Paris basin, participated in the defence of Bastogne in the Battle of the Bulge then went as far as Bohemia.

General Omar Bradley (1893–1981) commanded the American assault forces during the landing operation. He then led his troops from Brittany across Europe in the Advance to the Elbe.

General Bernard Montgomery (1887–1976) commanded the land forces for the Allied landing operation. Montgomery then led the northern wing of the 21st Army Group through the Netherlands and Denmark in the Drive to the Baltic.

General Philippe de Hauteclocque (1902–47), known as **Leclerc**, commanded the 2nd Armoured Division of Free French Forces. He landed at Utah Beach on 1 August and took the 2nd Armoured Division from Cotentin to Colmar, liberating Paris on the way.

Field Marshal Erwin Rommel (1891–1944) was overall commander of German forces along the North Sea and Atlantic coasts and chief of the armies of the B group. Wounded on 17 June, suspected of having taken part in a plot against Hitler, he committed suicide on 14 October 1944.

Art and Culture

The Norse, a people long considered barbaric, were in fact masters of wood-carving and metalworking, as their sophisticated domestic implements and fine jewellery testify. Over the centuries, their descendants produced the great Norman and Gothic religious architecture of the 11C to 13C, and later proved great innovators in the decorative arts, music (Saint-Saëns, Honegger, Satie), literature (Corneille, de Toqueville, de Maupassant, Flaubert, Maurois), painting (the 19C Impressionists) and, most recently, the cinema.

ARCHITECTURE

NORMAN BUILDING MATERIALS

Rouen and the towns of the Seine are built with chalky limestone from the valley sides. A similar affinity exists between the local materials and the buildings in the Caux region, where pebbles are set in flowing mortar. Clay, in cheap and plentiful local supply, was used for the cob of the timber-framed thatched cottages and for making bricks, which were often ingeniously set to make decorative patterns.

ROMANESQUE (11C–EARLY 12C)

The Benedictines and Romanesque Design

In the 11C, immediately after the period of Viking invasions, the Benedictines returned to their task of clearing the land and constructing churches and other monastic buildings. These architect monks retained the robust building methods employed by the Carolingians and then embellished their constructions with the Oriental dome or the barrel vault used by the Romans for bridges and commemorative arches. This new architectural style, created by the Benedictines, was named Romanesque by Arcisse de Caumont, an archaeologist from Normandy, who in 1840 outlined the theory of regional schools of architecture. Despite its apparent simplicity Romanesque architecture is wonderfully diverse. In England the style is known as Norman.

Norman School and Its Abbey Churches

The Benedictines, supported by the dukes of Normandy, played an immensely important part in the whole life of the province; only their work as architects and creators of the Norman School is described below.

The first religious buildings of importance in Normandy were the churches of the rich abbeys. Early monastic buildings may have disappeared or been altered, particularly after the Reform of St Maur, but examples of the Benedictine flowering have survived – the ruins of Jumièges Abbey and the churches on Mont-St-Michel, in Cerisy-la-Forêt, St-Martin-de-Boscherville as well as Église St-Étienne and Église de la Trinité in Caen.

The **Norman School** is characterised by pure lines, bold proportions, sober decoration and beautiful ashlared stonework. The style spread to England after the Norman Conquest. Durham Cathedral provides the first official example of quadripartite vaulting, erected at the beginning of the 12C. The Norman style is to be seen in Westminster Abbey, which was rebuilt by Edward the Confessor, in the two west towers and the square crossing tower of Canterbury Cathedral and in the cathedrals of Southwell, Winchester and Ely in England.

Norman architecture also appeared in Sicily in the 11C in the wake of noble Norman adventurers; in France it paved the way for the Gothic style.

The abbey churches are characterised by two towers on either side of the west front, giving the west face an H-like appearance, and a square lantern tower above the transept crossing, which also served to increase the light inside.

The towers, bare or decorated only with blind arcades below, get lighter with multiple pierced bays the higher they rise (in the 13C many were crowned by spires quartered by pinnacles).

ABC of architecture

Religious Architecture

ROUEN – Ground plan of the Cathédrale Notre-Dame (12-15C)

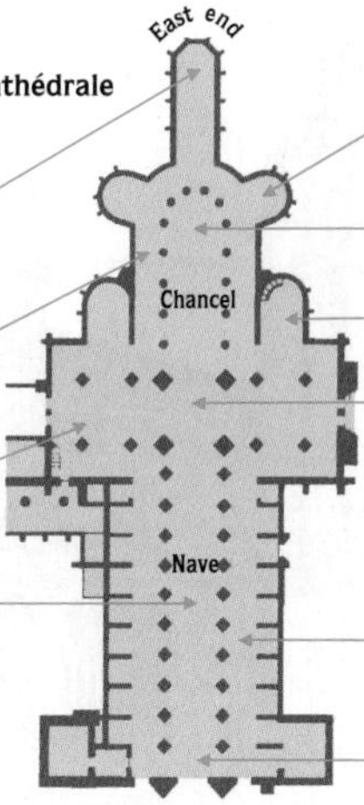

Lady chapel: in churches that are not dedicated to the Virgin, this chapel is often consecrated to Our Lady.

Ambulatory: semicircular or polygonal aisle enclosing the apse, originally used for processional purposes in pilgrimage churches

Arms of the transept: sometimes projecting

Bay: transverse section of the nave between two pairs of pillars

Side aisles, sometimes double

Narthex: enclosed vestibule stretching across the entrance to the church

ROUEN – Cross-section of the Cathédrale Notre-Dame (12-15C)

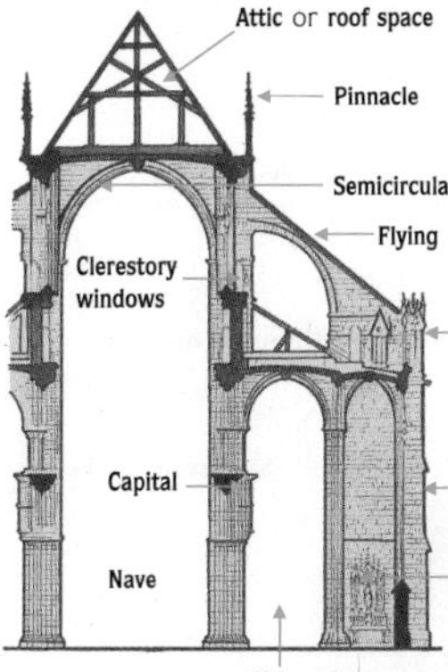

Buttress supporting the base of the wall

CAUDEBEC-EN-CAUX
Vaulting in the Lady Chapel of the Église Notre-Dame (14C)

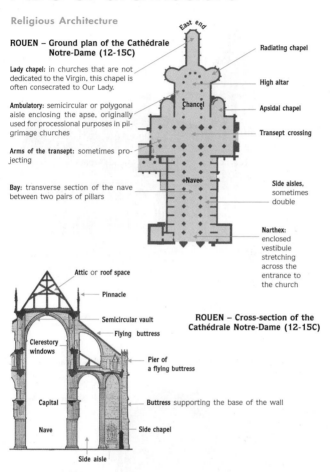

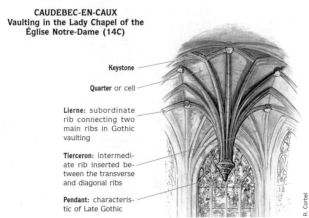

Lierne: subordinate rib connecting two main ribs in Gothic vaulting

Tierceron: intermediate rib inserted between the transverse and diagonal ribs

Pendant: characteristic of Late Gothic

R. Corbel

CAUDEBEC-en-CAUX – Église Notre-Dame (14C)

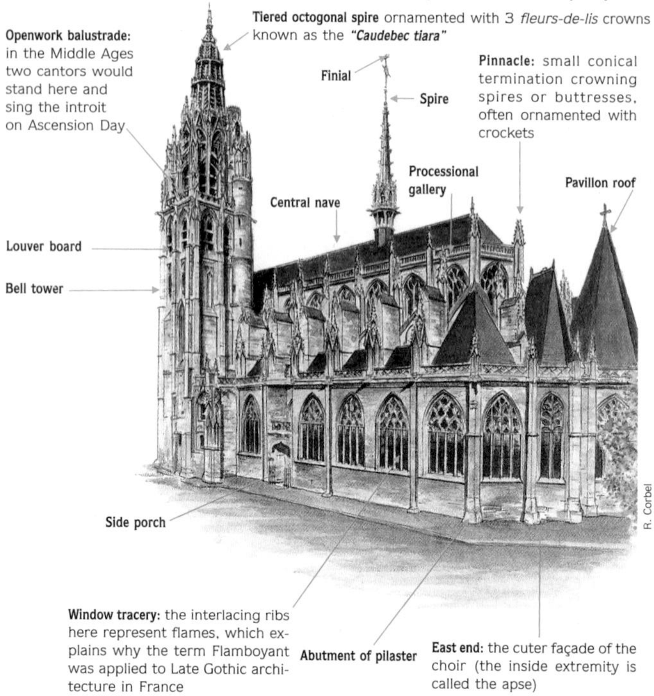
Tiered octogonal spire ornamented with 3 *fleurs-de-lis* crowns known as the ***"Caudebec tiara"***
Openwork balustrade: in the Middle Ages two cantors would stand here and sing the introit on Ascension Day
Finial
Spire
Pinnacle: small conical termination crowning spires or buttresses, often ornamented with crockets
Processional gallery
Pavillon roof
Central nave
Louver board
Bell tower
R. Corbel
Side porch
Window tracery: the interlacing ribs here represent flames, which explains why the term Flamboyant was applied to Late Gothic architecture in France
Abutment of pilaster
East end: the cuter façade of the choir (the inside extremity is called the apse)

ROUEN – Portail des Librairies, Cathédrale Notre-Dame (1482)

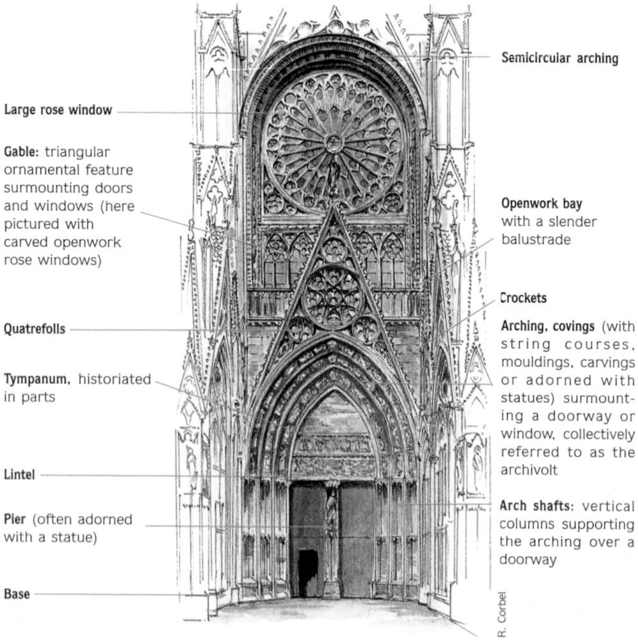
Semicircular arching
Large rose window
Gable: triangular ornamental feature surmounting doors and windows (here pictured with carved openwork rose windows)
Openwork bay with a slender balustrade
Crockets
Quatrefolls
Arching, covings (with string courses, mouldings, carvings or adorned with statues) surmounting a doorway or window, collectively referred to as the archivolt
Tympanum, historiated in parts
Lintel
Arch shafts: vertical columns supporting the arching over a doorway
Pier (often adorned with a statue)
Base
R. Corbel

ROUEN – Chancel and Transept Crossing in the Abbatiale St-Ouen (14C)

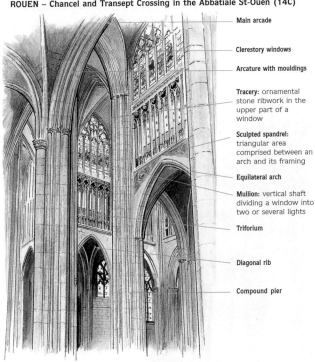

CAUDEBEC-EN-CAUX – Grand Organ in the Église Notre-Dame (1541-1542)

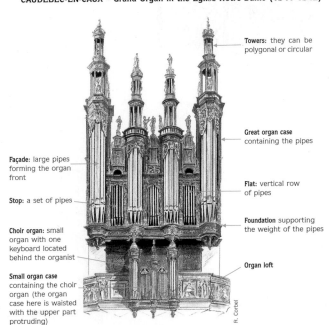

ÉVREUX – Stained glass (early 14C) in the Cathédrale Notre-Dame

The main function of stained glass is to provide a translucent framing for church windows and to regulate the intensity of the light inside the building. "The stained-glass windows in the chancel of Évreux Cathedral are the finest examples of 14C work. They are pure in the extreme, artfully combining light yellows and limpid blues with transparent reds and silvery whites... They are in perfect harmony with the radiant chancel, suffused with dazzling day light", remarked Emile Mâle

Glass edging surrounding the finished panes

French T-bar armature: iron band used between panels to fix them onto the saddle-bar

Ferramenta: iron framework that provides a fixing for the panels within the window

Internal lead: strip of lead used to fit together the pieces of glass in the panel

Silver stain: pigment made of silver nitrate mixed with ochre that produces a lovely yellow after firing in the kiln

Grisaille: pigment made with iron oxide producing a variety of greys and blacks after firing in the kiln

Saddle-bars: iron shafts embedded in the masonry of windows to support the panels

ÉCOUIS – Stalls in the chancel of the Collégiale Notre-Dame (14C)

High back

Elbow rest

Cheek: narrow upright face forming the end of a row of stalls

Separation between two stalls

Misericord: ledge projecting from the underside of a hinged seat which, when the seat is raised, provides support to worshippers or choir singers out of mercy (per misericordiam). 15C and 16C stalls were often sculpted with amusing grotesques or bizarre creatures called **"drolleries"**

Rural Architecture

Thatched Cottage at LYONS-LA-FORÊT

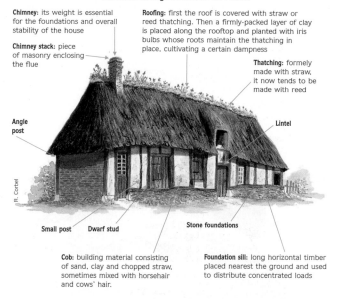

Chimney: its weight is essential for the foundations and overall stability of the house
Chimney stack: piece of masonry enclosing the flue
Roofing: first the roof is covered with straw or reed thatching. Then a firmly-packed layer of clay is placed along the rooftop and planted with iris bulbs whose roots maintain the thatching in place, cultivating a certain dampness
Thatching: formely made with straw, it now tends to be made with reed
Angle post
Lintel
R. Corbel
Small post
Dwarf stud
Stone foundations
Cob: building material consisting of sand, clay and chopped straw, sometimes mixed with horsehair and cows' hair.
Foundation sill: long horizontal timber placed nearest the ground and used to distribute concentrated loads

Military Architecture

Château d'HARCOURT (13C)

Although it has suffered from the ravages of time and history, the **Château d'Harcourt** remains a perfect example of medieval defensive architecture.

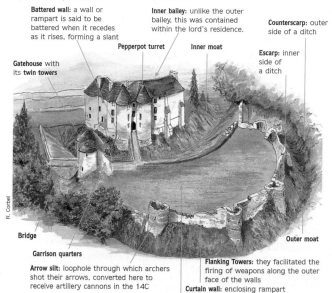

Battered wall: a wall or rampart is said to be battered when it recedes as it rises, forming a slant
Inner bailey: unlike the outer bailey, this was contained within the lord's residence.
Counterscarp: outer side of a ditch
Pepperpot turret
Inner moat
Escarp: inner side of a ditch
Gatehouse with its **twin towers**
R. Corbel
Bridge
Outer moat
Garrison quarters
Flanking Towers: they facilitated the firing of weapons along the outer face of the walls
Arrow silt: loophole through which archers shot their arrows, converted here to receive artillery cannons in the 14C
Curtain wall: enclosing rampart connecting two bastions or towers
Outer bailey: courtyard lying outside the castle perimeter but protected by its ramparts: it was used to accommodate the quartermasters' lodgings and to receive the population in the event of a slege

Seaside Architecture

DEAUVILLE – Villa Strassburger (early 20C)

This villa is a pastiche of the half-timbered mansions typical of the area. Its genuine Norman characteristics are combined with those from Alsace and some other French regions, complemented by a few eccentric touches prompted by the imagination of architect **G. Pichereau:** asymmetrical rooftops, profusion of skylights and dormer windows, projecting eaves.

Civil Engineering

The Pont de NORMANDIE (1988-1994)

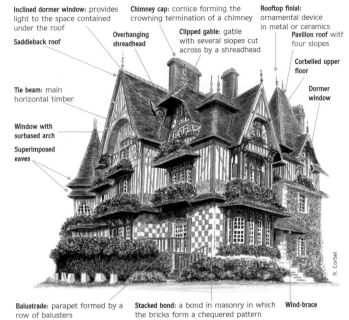

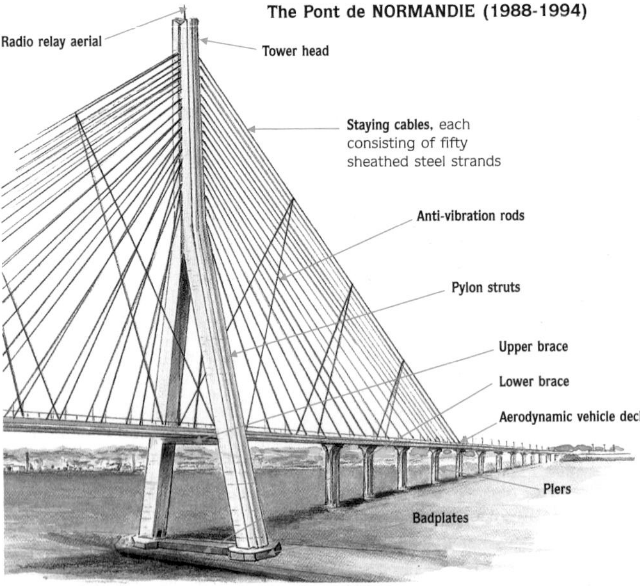

Charming country churches are often surmounted by Romanesque belfries, which are crowned with a saddleback roof or a four-sided squat wood or stone pyramid, the forerunner of the Gothic spire.

The interior light and size of Norman abbeys is very striking. The naves are wide with an elevation consisting of two series of openings above great semicircular arches – an amazingly bold concept for a Romanesque construction. The Norman monks eschewed the heavy barrel vault in favour of a beamed roof spanning the nave and galleries, reserving groined stone vaulting (the crossing of two semicircular arches) for the aisles. The vast galleries on the first level open onto the wide bays of the nave and repeat the design of the aisles. At clerestory level a gallery or passage in the thickness of the wall circles the church. A dome over the transept crossing supports a magnificent lantern tower which lets in the daylight through tall windows.

Norman Decoration

The abbey churches, like all others of Romanesque design, were illuminated on a considerable scale with gilding and bright colours as were the manuscripts of the time. The main themes were those of Byzantine iconography.

Norman sculptural decoration is essentially geometric; different motifs stand out, of which the most common is the key or fret pattern (straight lines meeting at right angles to form crenellated or rectangular designs). The decorative motifs are sometimes accompanied by mouldings, human heads or animal masks emphasising recessed arches, archivolts, cornices and mouldings. Sometimes the monks executed in low-relief motifs copied from cloth, ivories or metalwork brought back from the Orient; this is the origin of the cornerstones in the great arcade in Bayeux.

Capitals are rare and, where they exist, they are carved with gadroons or stylised foliage.

GOTHIC (12C–15C)

The style, conceived in Île-de-France, apart from quadripartite or rib vaulting, which originated in Norman England, was known as French work or French style until the 16C when the Italians of the Renaissance, who were resistant to the Parisian trend, scornfully dubbed it Gothic. The name survived. The French copied the H-shaped façades and great galleries of the Norman abbeys (the west front of Notre-Dame in Paris is based on that of the Église de la Trinité in Caen and its galleries on those of the Église St-Étienne).

The Cathedrals

Gothic is an ideal artistic style for cathedrals, as it symbolises the religious fervour of the people and the growing prosperity of the towns. In an all-embracing enthusiasm, a whole city would participate in the construction of the house of God. Under the enlightened guidance of bishops and master builders, all the guilds contributed to the cathedral's embellishment: stained-glass makers, painters, wood and stone carvers went to work. The doors became the illustrated pages of history.

Gothic Architecture in Normandy

Gradually the national Gothic style percolated into Normandy before the province was seized by Philippe Auguste in 1204.

In the 13C the Gothic and traditional Norman styles merged. The best example of this fusion is Coutances Cathedral, where the pure proportions and the lofty austerity of the Norman style combine with Gothic sophistication as in the lantern tower. This was also the period of the superb belfries of the Caen and Bessin plains, typified by their tall stone spires, often pierced to offer less resistance to the wind, and quartered with pinnacles.

The magnificent Merveille buildings of Mont-St-Michel give an idea of total Norman Gothic ornamentation. Sobriety provides the foundation over which foliated sculpture reigns supreme;

plants of every variety decorate the round capitals, cover the cornerstones and garland the friezes. The three- and four-leafed clover in relief or hollowed out is a frequent motif but statuary is rare. Lisieux Cathedral and the Tour St-Romain of Rouen Cathedral show the degree of French Gothic influence in Normandy by the end of the 12C.

The Flamboyant Style

By the 14C, the period of great cathedral building had come to an end. The Hundred Years War (1337–1453) killed architectural inspiration; bits were added, buildings were touched up, but little created. When the war was over a taste for virtuosity alone remained – and the Flamboyant style was born. Rouen is the true capital of the Flamboyant, which was particularly widespread in Haute-Normandie.

In this new style, the tracery of bays and rose windows resembles wavering flames – the derivation of the term Flamboyant. The Flamboyant style produced such single masterpieces as the Église St-Maclou in Rouen, the Tour de Beurre of Rouen Cathedral, the belfries of Notre-Dame in Caudebec and La Madeleine in Verneuil-sur-Avre. Civil architecture developed in importance and passed from Flamboyant to Renaissance – a change symbolised in the gables, pinnacles and balustrades of the Palais de Justice in Rouen.

Feudal Architecture

In medieval Normandy permission to build a castle was granted to the barons by the ruling duke, who, prudent as well as powerful, reserved the right to billet his own garrison inside and forbade all private wars. Over the years the building of castles along the duchy's frontiers was encouraged – Richard Lionheart secured the Seine with the most formidable fortress of the period, Château-Gaillard.

Originally only the austere keeps were inhabited, but from the 14C a courtyard and more pleasing quarters were constructed within the fortifications. This evolution can be seen in the castles at Alençon, and Dieppe and some of the Perche manor houses.

A taste for comfort and adornment appeared in civil architecture; wealthy merchants and burgesses built tall houses where wide eaves protected half-timbered upper storeys that overhung stone-walled ground floors. The results were as capricious as they were picturesque: corner posts, corbels and beams were decorated with lively and fantastic carvings.

THE RENAISSANCE (16C)

Georges I d'Amboise, Archbishop of Rouen and patron of the arts, introduced Italian taste and usage to Normandy. The new motifs – arabesques, foliated scrollwork, medallions, shells, urns, etc. – were combined with Flamboyant art. Among the outstanding works of this period is the chevet of the Église St-Pierre in Caen, a masterpiece of exuberance.

Castles, Manor Houses and Old Mansions

The Renaissance style reached its fullest grace in domestic architecture. At first, older buildings were ornamented in the current taste or a new and delicately decorated wing was added (Château d'O and the château at Fontaine-Henry); fortifications were replaced by parks and gardens.

The Classicism rediscovered by humanists took hold so that architects aimed for correct proportion and the imposition of the three Classical Orders of Antiquity.

Imperceptibly the search for symmetry and correctness produced aridity; fantasy was stifled by pomposity.

In Normandy, the Gothic spirit survived, appearing most successfully in small manor houses and innumerable country houses with sham feudal moats, turrets and battlements incorporated in either half timbering or stone and brick.

Norman towns contain many large stone Renaissance mansions. The outer façade is always plain and one must enter the courtyard to see the architectural design and the rich

decoration (Hôtel d'Escoville, Caen; Hôtel de Bourgtheroulde, Rouen).
In the 16C decoration became richer and less impulsive but the half-timbered construction technique remained the same. Many of these old houses have been carefully restored and there are good examples in Alençon, Bayeux, Bernay, Caen, Domfront, Honfleur, Pont-Audemer, Verneuil-sur-Avre and Rouen.

CLASSICAL (17C–18C)

In this period, French architectural style, now a single concept and no longer an amalgam of individual techniques, imposed its rationalism on many countries beyond its borders.

Louis XIII and the "Jesuit Style"

The reign of Henri IV marked an artistic rebirth. An economical method of construction was adopted in which bricks played an important part: it was a time of beautiful châteaux with plain rose and white façades and steep grey-blue slate roofs.
The first decades of the 17C coincided with the Counter-Reformation. The Jesuits built many colleges and chapels – cold and formal edifices, their façades characterised by superimposed columns, a pediment and upturned consoles or small pavilions joining the front of the main building to the sides.

The Grand Siècle in Normandy

The symmetrical façades of the Classical style demanded space for their appreciation as in the châteaux at Cany, Beaumesnil, Balleroy and elsewhere. The Benedictine abbeys, which had adopted the **Maurist Reform** (the Benedictine Congregation of St Maur was founded in 1621), rediscovered their former inspiration. At the beginning of the 18C, the monastery buildings of the Abbaye-aux-Hommes in Caen and at Le Bec-Hellouin were remodelled by a brother architect and sculptor, **Guillaume de la Tremblaye**. The original plan was conserved but the design and decoration were given an austere nobility.
The urban scene was transformed by the construction of magnificent bishops' palaces, town halls with wide façades and large private houses.

CONTEMPORARY (19C–20C)

Following the extensive destruction caused by World War II many towns and villages in Normandy were rebuilt in the mid-20C in accordance with the precepts of modern town planning. A good example of successful reconstruction is Aunay-sur-Odon, with its large and imposing church.
Auguste Perret (1874–1954), the architect who pioneered the use of reinforced concrete construction, was appointed Chief Architect for the reconstruction of Le Havre; his works include the modern district of Le Havre and the Église St-Joseph. His work makes use of textured concrete and is designed to take the best advantage of natural light.
Normandy is a region of innovation as well; in Le Havre, note the **Espace Oscar-Niemeyer**, named after the Brazilian architect as an example. Two surprising white structures evoke a volcano, and stand out in contrast to the buildings designed by Perret. The Musée des Beaux-Arts André-Malraux, also in Le Havre, resembles a glass ship at anchor. In Rouen, the renovation of place du Vieux-Marché in the 1970s included the construction of the Église Ste-Jeanne-d'Arc, based on a design by Louis Arretche. The roof of the church is in the shape of a boat hull (upside down).
Three of Normandy's bridges are also noteworthy examples of modern architecture: the **Tancarville bridge** was inaugurated in 1959, the **Brotonne bridge** in 1977, and the colossal **Pont de Normandie**, spanning the Seine estuary, opened in 1995. The most recent bridge is not only a boon to travellers, it is also a work of art and a technological feat, a milestone of civil engineering. It is a cable-stayed bridge, more elegant and cheaper to build than a suspension bridge, made of steel and

concrete, able to withstand winds of 440kph/274mph.

POPULAR ARCHITECTURE

Normandy is often associated with **half-timbered** houses. The basic box frame is essentially composed of horizontal and vertical beams, but there are very often different local methods of construction. Footings or a base of some solid material is laid to prevent damp from rising. A wooden sill or horizontal beam is laid along this base to ensure the correct spacing of the upright posts or studs. It is divided into as many sections as there are intervals between the vertical posts. The upper horizontal beam, sometimes known as a summer or bressumer, consists of a single beam. Along the gable ends it is known as a tie-beam. Bricks are often ingeniously used to make attractive patterns between the timbers.

Roofing materials such as thatch, which is so vulnerable to fire, and shingles of sweet chestnut, are becoming increasingly rare. The schist slabs of the Cotentin are a typical part of the landscape. The slate which has been used since the 18C for houses and outbuildings alike has a silver tinge. A watertight roof depends on the correct hanging of the slates. The appearance of the villages is conditioned by the local materials used and the trades of the various villagers. One well-known building material, **Caen stone**, is quarried from the Jurassic deposits. It can be either friable or durable and varies in colour through grey and off-white to its more characteristic light creamy colour. The ashlar blocks are divided into two groups, one with the grain running vertically for façades, corner stones and gables and the second with a horizontal grain for courses and cornices.

Farms

In the open landscape of the **Caen plain** the typical courtyard farms are surrounded by high walls. A gateway gives access to the courtyard with the one- or two-storeyed farmhouse at the far end. The smaller crofts usually consist of two buildings, one long house for the living quarters and cowshed or barn and another for the stable or byre.

The farm buildings of the **Bessin** stand round a large courtyard that has two entrances, side by side, one for wheeled vehicles and a second for people. The house stands at the far end with the service and outbuildings to the right and left. There is usually a well in the middle. Built of limestone or Jurassic marls, the house has a pristine appearance. The windows are tall and wide; the roofing is either tiles or slates.

The small flat-tiled houses in the **Argentan** area have symmetrical façades. The buildings are usually a harmonious mixture of schist, brick (chimneys and window surrounds) and limestone (the walls). Some are surrounded by walls or a screen of vegetation. Large barns are frequently adjoined by sheds.

Brick and small laminated schist tiles predominate in the **Sées** countryside. Sometimes the buildings fit snugly one against the other, creating a jumble of roofs of varying pitch.

The farms in the region of **Alençon** are built around an open courtyard. The infinitely varied architecture reflects the wide range of rocks: granite, schist, flint, clay and kaolin.

The most common house type in the **Falaise** countryside is akin to those found in the Caen region. The walled courtyard predominates. The brick chimney replaces the rubblework one and tiles are used for roofs in the area bordering the Auge region.

The houses in the **Suisse Normande** are built of schist known as Pont-de-la-Mousse slate quarried near Thury-Harcourt and the settlements often have the rugged appearance of mountain villages. In the Orne Valley the houses huddle closely together on the flats whereas those on the slopes are scattered, even isolated.

The farm courtyard in the **Vire** *bocage* is often planted with apple and pear trees. On either side of the farmhouse are the barns, cattle sheds and outbuildings for

Dovecotes of Normandy

Château de Crèvecoeur-en-Auge

Manoir de Caudemonde

Dovecote in the hamlet of Petit Veauville, Héricourt-en-Caux

Manoir d'Auffray, Oherville

M. Dewynter/MICHELIN

Château de Betteville

the cider press. Brown or red schist is the main building stone.

Seaside Architecture

In the 19C, the coast became a popular destination and bathing in the sea a novel pastime. Wealthy patrons ordered quirky houses for their holiday pleasures. Sometimes they were built in or near existing fishing villages, and in other places whole resort communities sprang up. Many of these villas are still standing along the coast at Cabourg, Houlgate, Villers, Deauville, Trouville, Villerville, Ste-Adresse, Étretat, Dieppe, Le Tréport, Mers-les-Bains etc. Generally, they are remarkable for their multicoloured façades, busy with balconies, bow windows, railings, gables and other decorative elements.

A profusion of skylights, projecting eaves and rooftop finials adds to the exuberance. Other models are more reserved and even stately, recalling the Renaissance style. Some are more modestly termed chalets, and are said to be in the Swiss, Spanish or Persian style, depending on their features.

NORMAN DOVECOTES

The practice of keeping pigeons, formerly known as doves, dates back to the earliest civilisations. Although domestication is believed to have originated around 4500 BC, the practice became widespread some 2 000 years later, in ancient Egypt, where pigeon was appreciated for its succulent flesh, a fact evidenced by the many frescoes of feasts and banquets.

THE CARRIER PIGEON

The carrier pigeon is mostly known for its military role in times of war. News of the conquest of Gaul by Julius Caesar was relayed to the capital by means of pigeons, as was Napoleon's defeat at Waterloo. During the Siege of Paris in 1870, 400 birds helped defend the city by carrying tiny strips of film attached to their claws.

More recently, during World War I, English troops entrusted some 10 000 messages to their feathered friends. Several warrior birds became legendary figures and some were even awarded a military decoration: The Mocker, Lord Adelaide, Burma Queen etc. The cities of Brussels and Lille have erected memorials to these worthy messengers.

THE HOMING PIGEON

In the early 19C, a new sport appeared in Belgium – pigeon racing, in which birds are trained to return to their home loft after being released in the wild. The first long-distance race (160km/99.4mi) was held in 1818 and the sport gradually gained prominence in Great Britain, France and the United States. Today, many French villages have their own Pigeon-Fanciers Club *(Société Colombophile)* and organise races regularly.

FOR THE BIRDS

A familiar sight in Normandy, especially in the Pays de Caux, is the dovecote *(colombier)*. Norman dovecotes are square, polygonal or round; the last type is the most common. The door is at ground level, usually rectangular but sometimes rounded at the top and often surmounted by the arms of the owner. The projecting ledge halfway up *(larmier)* is designed to prevent the entry of rodents. There are openings for the pigeons all round. The roofs, conical on circular dovecotes and faceted on square or polygonal dovecotes, are often covered with slates. The lead finial may be in the shape of a pigeon or a weathervane.

The interior is lined with pigeon-holes *(boulins)* – one hole for each pair of pigeons – and the number varies according to the wealth of the owner. They are reached by a ladder fixed to an arm attached to a central post which pivots on a hard stone. In some dovecotes only the upper part is intended for pigeons; the lower part may be used as a hen house or a sheep pen. When the two parts are separated by a wooden floor, the door to the upper part is above the stone rat ledge and reached by an external detachable ladder.

There are two kinds of dovecote. The standard or classic type is built of ashlar stone (not common), in an attractive contrast to black flint and white stone (north and northeast of Le Havre), in brick, black flint and ashlar stone (brick tended to replace black flint after the 17C), or in brick and stone (fairly common). The type of dovecote called secondary includes buildings in light coloured flint (a similar shade to ashlar stone), in flint and stone, or in flint, brick and stone.

The first known laws on pigeon breeding were instituted in the Middle Ages. In Normandy, the owners of fiefs were the only ones entitled to build dovecotes. This right, known as the *droit de colombier*, was abolished on 4 August 1789 and very few new dovecotes were built after the French Revolution.

A total of 535 were officially registered in the Seine-Maritime in the early 20C. However, many have been abandoned and are now in a state of neglect. The French government and local authorities have recently taken measures to finance the restoration of these charming buildings, which are an essential part of Normandy's rural heritage.

DECORATIVE ARTS

CERAMICS AND POTTERY

The glazed pavement in the chapter house of St-Pierre-sur-Dives (13C) demonstrates the long tradition of ceramic art in Normandy. In the mid-16C Masséot Abaquesne was making decorated tiles, which were greatly prized in Rouen, whereas potteries in Le Pré-d'Auge and Manerbe (near Lisieux) were producing "earthenware more beautiful than is made elsewhere".

In 1644 **Rouen faïence** made its name with blue decoration on a white ground and white on blue.

By the end of the century production had increased so that when the royal plate was melted down to replenish the Treasury, "the Court changed to chinaware in a week" (Saint-Simon). The so-called radiant style is reminiscent of the wrought-iron work and embroidery for which the town was well known. The desire for novelty brought in the vogue for chinoiserie. In the middle of the 18C came the Rococo style with its quiver decoration and the famous Rouen cornucopia, a horn of plenty overflowing with flowers, birds and insects. This industry was ruined by the 1786 trade treaty, which allowed the import of English chinaware into France.

NORMAN FURNITURE

Sideboards, longcase clocks and wardrobes – the three most characteristic and traditional pieces of furniture in Normandy – are valued for their elegance, solidity and generous proportions. The wardrobe, which gradually replaced the medieval chest, first appeared in the 13C; by the beginning of the 17C the sideboard was already in existence and in the 18C longcase clocks became widespread.

The golden age of furniture making in Normandy produced well-proportioned and delicately carved sideboards or kitchen dressers; coffin clocks (broader at the top than at the bottom); longcase clocks characterised by carved baskets of fruit and flowers round the clockface; tall pendulum clocks, with delicately chased dials in gilt bronze, copper, pewter or enamel; majestic oak wardrobes, ornamented with finely worked fittings, in brass or other metals, or with medallions, surmounted with carved cornices of doves, birds' nests, ears of corn, flowers and fruit or Cupid's quiver, etc.

The wardrobe was often part of a young woman's dowry and contained her trousseau; its transfer from her parents' house to her new home was the occasion for traditional celebrations.

PAINTING

Painting took first place among the arts in 19C France. Landscape totally eclipsed historical and stylised painting and Normandy was to become the cradle of Impressionism.

THE OPEN AIR

While the Romantics were discovering inland Normandy, Eugène Isabey, a lover of seascapes, began to work on the still deserted coast. **Richard Bonington** (1801–28), an English painter who went to France as a boy, trained there, and, in his watercolours, captured the wetness of sea beaches.

In the second half of the 19C artistic activity was concentrated on **Eugène Boudin** (1824–98) round the Côte de Grâce. This painter from Honfleur, named King of the Skies by Corot, encouraged a young 15-year-old from Le Havre, **Claude Monet**, to drop caricature for the joys of real painting and urged his Parisian friends to come and stay in his St-Siméon farmstead.

IMPRESSIONISM

The younger painters, nevertheless, were to outstrip their elders in their search for pictorial light. They wanted to portray the vibration of light, hazes, the trembling of reflections and shadows, the depth and tenderness of the sky, the fading of colours in full sunlight. They – Monet, Sisley, Bazille and their Paris friends, Renoir, Pissarro, Cézanne and Guillaumin especially – were about to form the Impressionist School, which gave France a front rank in the history of painting.

From 1862 to 1869 the Impressionists remained faithful to the Normandy coast and the Seine estuary. After the Franco-Prussian War they returned only occasionally – although it was in Normandy, at Giverny, that Claude Monet set up house in 1881 and remained until he died in 1926.

Impressionism, in its turn, gave birth to a new school, **Pointillism**, which divided the tints with little touches of colour, applying the principle of the division of white light into seven basic colours, to get ever closer to a luminous effect. Seurat and Signac, the pioneers of this method, also came to Normandy to study its landscapes.

In the early 20C **Fauvism** was born as a reaction against Impressionism and neo-Impressionism. These brightly coloured linear compositions exploded on the canvas.

For half a century, therefore, the Côte de Grâce, the Pays de Caux, Deauville, Trouville and Rouen were the sources of inspiration of a multitude of paintings.

A PLEIAD OF PAINTERS

Numerous artists still came to Normandy in the first half of the 20C, notably Valloton and Gernez (the latter died in Honfleur); Marquet, who had worked in Gustave Moreau's studio in Paris; Othon Friesz, who particularly enjoyed Honfleur, which he portrayed in its many aspects; and Van Dongen, painter of the worldly and the elegant and a frequent guest at Deauville.

Marquet, Friesz and Van Dongen were strongly influenced by Fauvism, whereas **Raoul Dufy**, a native of Le Havre, soon overthrew accepted convention to associate line drawing and richness of colour in compositions which were full of movement.

LITERATURE

Literature and architecture both sprang from the monasteries. It is therefore hardly surprising that Normandy and its abbeys became rich in literary activity from the 13C. Monks and clergymen with a sound knowledge of history and legend, together with travellers and pilgrims, provided the poets with the inspiration needed to create the Christian epics known as the *chansons de geste*. Such verse appeared chronologically after the early hagiographic literature (lives of saints) but remains one of the first examples of the use of French as a literary mode of expression. In the 12C the Anglo-Norman **Robert Wace**, who was born in Jersey but brought up in Caen, wrote two notable verse chronicles. *Le Roman du Rou* (1160–74) was commissioned by Henry II of England and is a history of the dukes of Normandy.

17C

Pierre Corneille (1606–84) is often called the father of French Classical tragedy. His main works are known

together as the classical tetralogy: (1637), *Horace* (1640), *Cinna* (1641) and *Polyeucte* (1643).
The dramatist enjoyed a happy life with his extended family in Rouen (he married and had seven children; his brother married his wife's sister and their households were very close), and despite occasional brushes with the authorities, his plays were generally well received. Balzac praised him, Molière acknowledged him as his master and the foremost of dramatists, Racine lauded his talent for versification. From the 20C viewpoint, it is clear that Corneille also had a great impact on the rise of comedy, and in the development of drama in general, in particular in regard to his ability to depict personal and moral forces in conflict.

18C

Born in Le Havre, **Bernardin de St-Pierre** (1737–1814) travelled the world to fulfil his dreams, and spent part of his life on the Indian Ocean island of Mauritius. In Paris, he became the disciple of the Romantic philosopher Jean-Jacques Rousseau. His best-known works are *Paul and Virginie* (1787) and *Studies of Nature* (1784).

19C

The founder of Norman regionalism is **Barbey d'Aurevilly** (1808–99), a nobleman from Cotentin, who was born in St-Sauveur-le-Vicomte. In a warm and bright style, illuminated with brilliant imagery and original phrases, he sought, like the Impressionists, to convey the atmosphere, the quality, the uniqueness of his region. Valognes, the town where he spent most of his adolescence, is mentioned in several of his works (*Ce qui ne meurt pas*, *Chevalier des Touches* and *Les Diaboliques*).
Although born in Paris, **Charles Alexis de Tocqueville** (1805–59) was from an old Norman family. It was during stays at the ancestral home, the Château de Tocqueville, not far from Cherbourg, that he wrote many of the works which were to bring him fame. This political scientist, politician and historian is best-known for his timeless classic *Democracy in America*.
Gustave Flaubert (1821–80), a prime mover of the Realist School of French literature, considered art as a means to knowledge. His masterful *Madame Bovary* (1857), a portrait of bourgeois life in the provinces, took him five years to complete. The French government sought to block its publication and have the author condemned for immorality – he narrowly escaped conviction.
Flaubert greatly influenced **Guy de Maupassant** (1850–93), a family friend born in Dieppe who regarded himself as the older author's apprentice. Maupassant's work is thoroughly realistic, the language lucidly pure and the imagery sharp and precise. The author wrote best-selling novels (*Une Vie*, *Bel-Ami*, *Pierre et Jean*), but his greatest achievement lies in his short stories; many of these works are considered among the finest in French literature. Today, he is one of the most widely read French authors in English-speaking countries.
Octave Mirbeau (1848–1917), from Trévières near Bayeux, was an active participant in the literary and political quarrels of his time, speaking out in defence of anarchist ideas. As a novelist, he was fiercely critical of the social conditions of the time, and his work

Detail of On the Beach (1880) by Eugène Boudin

©Imagestate/Tips Images

Journal of a Lady's Maid (*Le Journal d'une femme de chambre*, 1900) is typical of this attitude.

20C

Maurice Leblanc (1864–1941), born in Rouen, created the gentleman burgler Arsène Lupin. A museum in Étretat is devoted to this still-popular author.

André Maurois (1865–1967), born Émile Herzog in Elbeuf, is known for his war memoires, novels, biographies of literary figures such as Disraeli, Shelley, Victor Hugo, Balzac and Proust, and historical works (*History of England*, 1937, *History of the United States*, 1943).

Alain (1868–1951), made a name for himself by his columns in a Rouen newspaper. A professor of philosophy and author of many essays, he revolted against all forms of tyranny. His works *Remarks on Happiness* (1928) and *Remarks on Education* (1932) are noteworthy.

Jean de la Varende (1887–1959), from the Ouche region, evokes in his novels the Normandy of yesteryear. His work *Par Monts et Merveilles de Normandie* is a description of all he saw and admired in the region.

André Breton (1896–1966), from Tinchebray in the Orne, was a poet, essayist and "Pope" of the Surrealist movement. His work, including *Nadja* (1928), *L'Amour Fou* (1937) and two Surrealist manifestos, stirred up, as intended, intense controversy.

Armand Salacrou (1899–1989), born in Rouen, called his dramatic works a "meditation on the human condition". He experimented with different dramatic styles. Two of his popular successes were *Un homme comme les autres* (1926) and *Boulevard Durand* (1961).

Raymond Queneau (1903–76) was born in Le Havre and achieved distinction as the director of the prestigious *Encyclopédie de la Pléiade*, a scholarly edition of past and present authors. As the author of many poems, novels and plays, Queneau stands out for his quirky style and verbal juggling, revealing the absurdity that underlies our everyday world. One of his best-loved works, *Zazie dans le métro* (1959), was made into a charming film.

MUSIC

Composer of operas and comic operas, **François-Adrien Boieldieu** (1775–1834) was born in Rouen. His work *The Caliph of Baghdad* (1800) earned him a glowing reputation throughout Europe. From 1803 to 1810 he was Director of Music at the Imperial Opera of St Petersburg. His talent was universally recognised with his masterpiece *La Dame Blanche* in 1825. **Camille Saint-Saëns** (1835–1921) was born in Paris, but his father was from Normandy. A brilliant pianist, he composed symphonies, operas, concertos and religious works. His most famous works include the *Danse Macabre* (1875) and *Samson et Dalila* (1877).

Arthur Honegger (1892–1955) was born in Le Havre, of Swiss origin. At first he composed melodies to poems by Cocteau, Apollinaire and Paul Fort, then *Pacific 231* (1923) and *King David* (1924). *Joan at the Stake* (1935) and *The Dance of the Dead* (1938) have texts by Paul Claudel.

Born in Honfleur, **Erik Satie** (1866–1925) began as a pianist in the cabarets of Montmartre (The Black Cat), where he met Debussy. Sarcasm and irony permeate his works, his greatest being the symphonic drama *Socrates* (1918) for voice and orchestra based on texts by Plato. Satie exerted an undeniable influence both on his time and on musicians such as Ravel, Debussy and Stravinsky.

Nature

Normandy is not a homogeneous geographical unit, rather it is an old province, formerly a dukedom, embracing two large areas with different geological structures, which become progressively younger from west to east. The sandstone, granite and Precambrian schists of the Armorican Massif in the west give way to strata of clay, limestone and chalk dating from the Triassic (beginning 254 million years ago) to the Tertiary (beginning 65 million years ago) periods, which belong to the geological formation of the Paris basin. Normandy can therefore be conveniently divided into two quite distinct regions: Haute-Normandie, which lies northwest of the Paris basin, and Basse-Normandie, which resembles its neighbour Brittany and consists of an eroded foundation of ancient rocks. The administrative region of Haute-Normandie is made up of the Eure (27) and Seine-Maritime (76) *départements*; Basse-Normandie includes the Calvados (14), Manche (50) and Orne (61) *départements*.

REGIONS OF NORMANDY

The inland areas can be divided into two types of regions, **open country** and **woodland**. In the strictest sense, the open country *(campagne)* consists of dry, windswept plains and cultivated fields. The woodland *(bocage)* is typical of the Armorican Massif, although to the east it spills over into the Maine, the Perche and the Auge regions. Typical of the countryside, and sometimes confusing for casual ramblers, a network of dense hedges grows on earthen banks, enclosing fields and meadows and forming a sort of labyrinth.

The people living on the farms and hamlets scattered along the sunken roads have for a long time lived in relative isolation. Lastly, the different parts of the **coast** of Normandy also have distinctive characteristics.

OPEN COUNTRY

The **Pays de Caux** is a vast limestone plateau, stretching from Le Havre to Dieppe, covered with fertile silt, ending along the coast in cliffs famous for their hanging valleys *(valleuses)* and bordered to the south by the Seine Valley. The area produces wheat and industrial crops such as flax, sugar beet and rape. Cattle here are raised for meat.

Bordered by the valleys of the Epte and the Andelle, the **Vexin normand** is covered by a particularly thick layer of alluvial soil which favours the intensive cultivation of wheat and sugar beet.

The **Plaine du Neubourg** and the **Évreux-St-André** district present a flat landscape of open fields, similar to the area known as **Caen-Falaise**. The fertility of the soil in these areas favours large-scale arable farming coupled with cattle-breeding for the production of meat. Vegetables are grown around Caen.

The **Argentan-Sées-Alençon** country, north of the Sarthe Valley and the Alpes Mancelles, is composed of small chalk regions where horses and cattle graze in the open orchards.

TRANSITIONAL REGIONS

The **Roumois** and **Lieuvin** plains, marked by hedges and apple orchards, are separated by the Risle Valley. The **Pays d'Ouche** is more densely forested, whereas the rolling hills of the **Perche normand**, a famous horse-breeding district, form a transition between the Paris basin and the Armorican Massif.

WOODLANDS

The Norman part of the **Pays de Bray** is a vast clay depression, known as the buttonhole, bordered by two limestone heights. It is stock-raising country and has increased its production of meat; it also specialises in fresh dairy produce such as yoghurts and *petits-suisses*.

The **Pays d'Auge**, which contains the river valleys of the Touques and the Dives, differs from the other regions in that the chalk strata have been deeply fissured by streams. High local humidity promotes the growth of grassland and

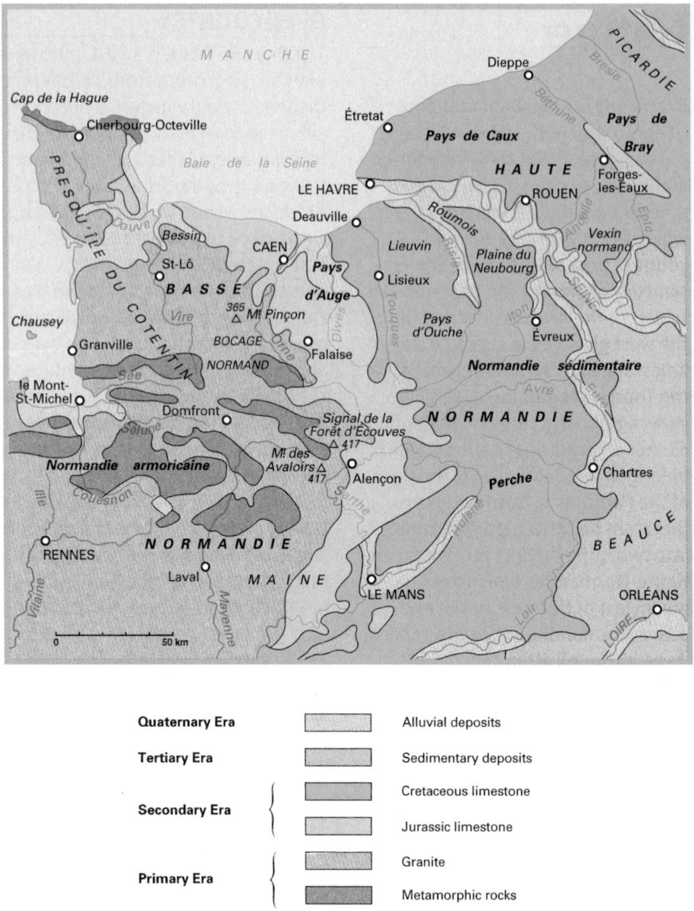

hedges. Apples are turned into cider and Calvados, and milk into Camembert. Horse breeding is also a tradition near the coast and the Perche region.

The **Bessin**, with Bayeux as its capital, lies to the east of the Armorican Massif. Breeding of saddle-horses and trotters is a long tradition, while famed local dairy produce carries the name Isigny.

South of the Bessin is the **Bocage normand**, where meadows, sometimes planted with apple or pear trees, are enclosed by hedges. Dairy farming is still the main activity. In addition to the traditional Normandy cream and butter, farmers produce sterilised milk with a long shelf life and which needs no refrigeration (UHT milk) and a great variety of low-fat dairy produce.

The remote peninsula of **Cotentin**, which lies between the Vire estuary and Mont-St-Michel Bay, is part of the Armorican Massif. The peninsula itself is divided from the Bocage normand by a sedimentary depression, which is flooded at certain times of the year; there are three distinct areas within the peninsula: the Cotentin Pass, the Val de Saire and Cap de la Hague. The region is still largely devoted to stock raising except along the coast where vegetables are grown, as they are in nearby Brittany.

THE COAST

The coast of Normandy from the River Bresle west to the River Couesnon is as varied as its hinterland. Erosion by the sea has transferred material from rocky projections and deposited it in sheltered coves. The sea has brought shingle (stones) to the bays and ports of the Pays de Caux and mud to the Seine estuary; it has silted in more than one port (Lillebonne was a sea port in Gallo-Roman times).

The Pays de Caux meets the sea in what is known as the **Côte d'Albâtre** (Alabaster Coast), a line of high limestone cliffs, like the White Cliffs of Dover, penetrated by shingle-bottomed (stony) inlets. The sea beating at the foot of the cliffs has eroded the cliff face, forming hanging valleys where streams once flowed.

The **Côte Fleurie** offers miles of fine sand beaches where the sea may withdraw more than a mile at low tide; it also enjoys a high level of sunshine. The Calvados coast is composed of the low Bessin cliffs, interspersed with sand dunes and salt marshes (Caen area).

To the west are the sand or sand and shingle (stony) beaches of the bracing **Côte de Nacre** (Mother-of-Pearl Coast). The Cotentin Peninsula resembles Cornwall and Brittany with its rocky inlets, although sand dunes and beaches stretch along the coast where the continental rock base does not reach the shore. Mont-St-Michel Bay is known for its vast sands and mud flats from which the sea seems to withdraw completely at times.

The **lighthouses** along the Normandy coast, which guide navigators in the Channel, also make good vantage points. The Norman engineer **Augustin Fresnel** (1788–1827) replaced the conventional parabolic reflector with compound lenses, which led to great progress in the length of beam projected out to sea. At night, in the more difficult sectors, several lighthouses can be seen at once, each with its own peculiarities: fixed, revolving or intermittent beam.

HORSES: THE PRIDE OF NORMANDY

More than 70% of all French thoroughbreds and trotters are bred in Basse-Normandie as well as the most powerful draught horses (Percherons) and some of the best carriage-horses (cobs).

Thoroughbreds are the fastest and the most refined horses, but their racing career does not exceed three years. The sale of yearlings at the end of August in Deauville attracts international racing stable owners. The sale of brood mares and foals is held in late November.

French trotters were developed from Normandy mares and Norfolk-roadster trotters.

French saddle-horses, a term which first appeared in 1958, encompasses almost all French competition horses, particularly for show jumping.

Whether chestnut or bay, the **Norman cob** is strong, compact, likeable, full of energy and has a pleasant way of trotting. Cobs can work in the fields or be harnessed to a carriage.

Percherons, dappled grey or black, are the most sought-after heavy draught horses in the world; the race was developed from cobs and Arabs, some say as far back as the Crusades.

Finally, one can't ignore the **Cotentin donkey**, recognised by the national stud in 1997, which has a soft grey coat, with a cross of St Andrew on its back. These gentle beasts now carry tourists on treks across the Cotentin.

NATIONAL STUD FARMS

As one of the oldest French institutions – the first was founded by Colbert in 1665 – the system of 23 national stud farms works in close collaboration with the Institut National de la Recherche Agronomique to improve breeding techniques. The system also supervises all equestrian activities, horse racing and betting in France.

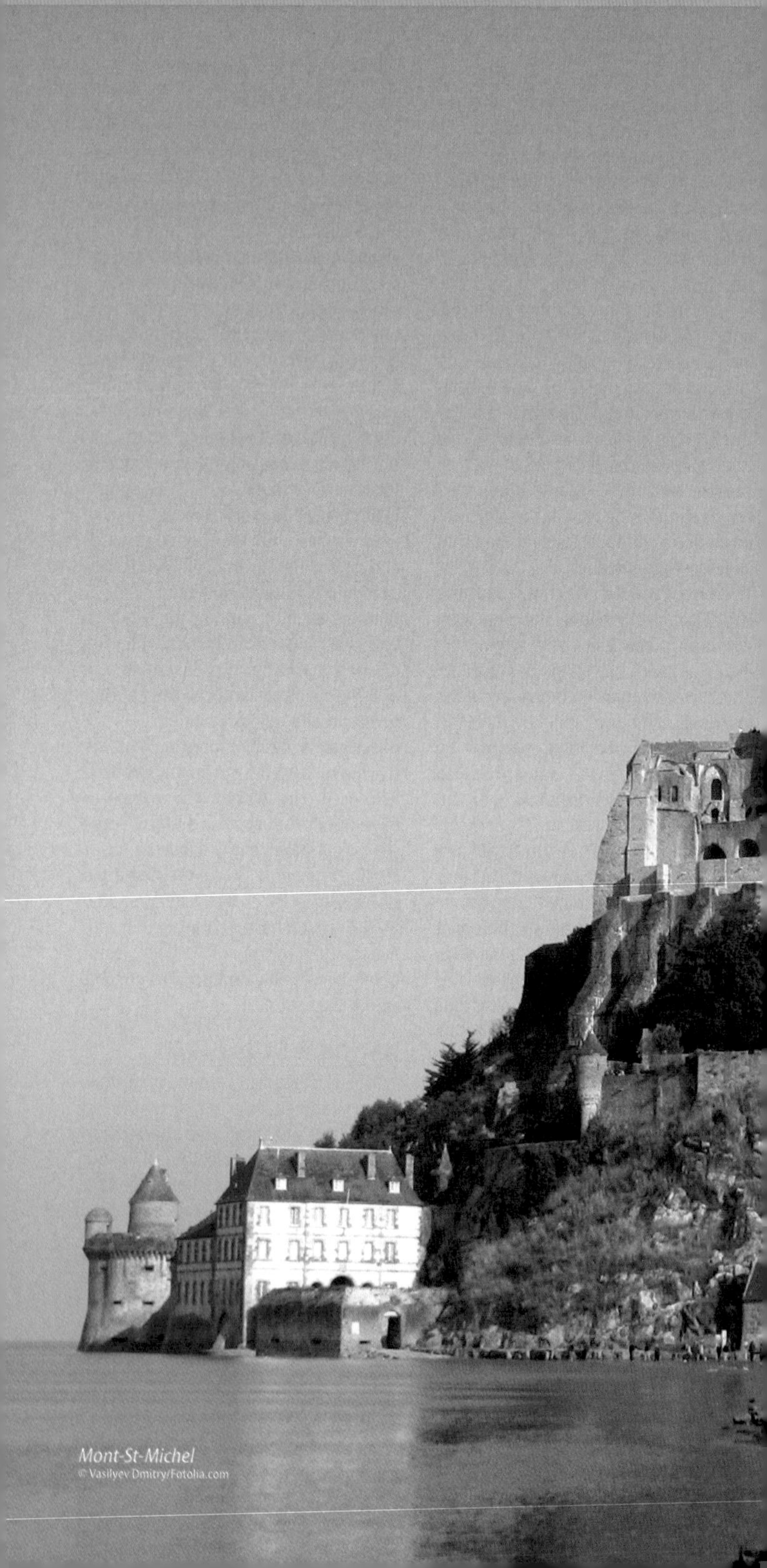

Mont-St-Michel

DISCOVERING NORMANDY

CALVADOS

Part of the region of Lower Normandy (Basse-Normandie), Calvados lies along the English Channel, site both of lovely resort towns celebrated by Impressionist painters and of the D-Day Landing Beaches. Inland, the lush, well-watered countryside is dotted with grazing cows and horses, while orchards furnish apples for cider and the famous local brandy. The bustling capital city, Caen, rose as a triumph of modern architecture from ruins after the last war. Great castles as well as Romanesque churches and abbeys attest to the powerful position of Calvados under William the Conqueror, born in the town of Falaise.

Geography – The name Calvados probably derives from early mariners' charts, where the flat shoreline was described as *calva dorsa*, meaning barren hills in Latin. Today, holidaymakers flock to the wide, sandy beaches along the **Côte Fleurie** (Flowery Coast) and **Côte de Nacre** (Mother-of-Pearl Coast).

Around **Caen**, where rich topsoil lies over a limestone base laid down in the Jurassic era, stretch fields of grain and pastures for beef cattle. To the west, around **Vire**, lies the **bocage country**, where hedgerows provided cover for German soldiers during the fierce battles that followed the D-Day Landings. To the east, the **Pays d'Auge** offers vistas of apple orchards, timber-framed houses and wooded valleys, as well as the cathedral city of **Lisieux**.

Today – Besides cider, calvados and pear cider *(poiré)*, the area is known for Camembert, Livarot and Pont-l'Évêque cheese. The Bessin area around **Bayeux** produces the estimed Isigny butter; the celebrated tapestry recounting the Norman Conquest was made for the town's magnificent 11C cathedral. Easy access to Calvados from Britain via the port of **Ouistreham** near Caen and from Paris by highway draws affluent owners of secondary residences.

Due to the thriving city of Caen, Calvados is less rural and more populous than other parts of Lower Normandy, while the fashionable resorts of **Honfleur**, **Cabourg** and **Deauville** provide a continual seasonal entertainment.

History – On 6 June 1944, astonished German soldiers along the Calvados coast saw coming towards them, through the morning fog, a mighty invasion force. Museums, monuments and cemeteries throughout Normandy recall this event, but nowhere more so than in Calvados.

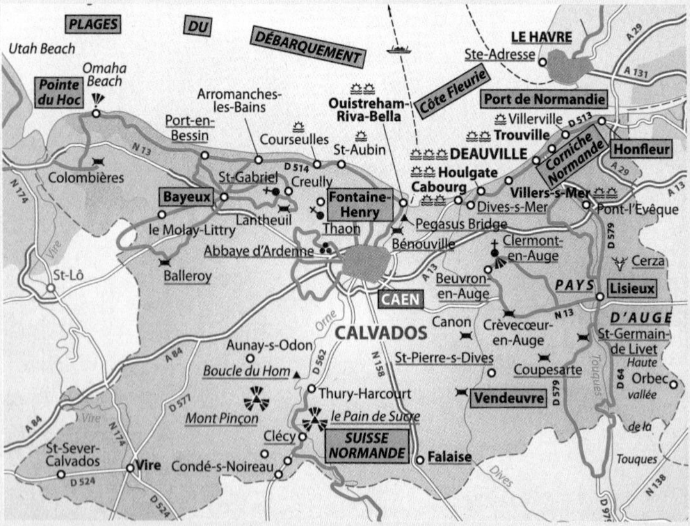

Arromanches-les-Bains

is a modest seaside resort which owes its fame to the gigantic landing operation of June 1944. In the little port are the remains of a Mulberry harbour, the most extraordinary maritime achievement of the war.

- **Population:** 610.
- **Michelin Map:** 303: I-3 – Local map, *see Plages du DÉBARQUEMENT.*
- **Info:** 2 rue Mar.-Joffre. 02 31 22 36 45. www.ot-.fr.
- **Location:** is on the coast, 10km/6.2mi NE of Bayeux via D 516 and 38km/23.6mi NE of Caen via D 516 and N 13.
- **Don't Miss:** The remains of the allied artificial "Mulberry" port.
- **Timing:** In three hours you can see the beach, the museum and the film.

A BIT OF HISTORY

Artificial Port – "If we want to land, we must take our harbours with us."
The Calvados coast offered no natural protection from catastrophic bad weather. A prefabricated port, towed across the Channel, received the code name "Mulberry", perhaps for a restaurant where War Office staff ate.
Mulberries – The Americans' Mulberry A went to Omaha Beach; Mulberry B for British troops at Arromanches enabled 9 000t of material to be landed each day, equivalent to the tonnage handled by the port of Le Havre prior to the war. More than 500 000t had been landed by the end of August.
The best view of the remaining caissons (preferably at low tide) is the belvedere situated on D 514 leading to Asnelles (*see Plages du DÉBARQUEMENT).*

VISIT

Musée du Débarquement

Place du 6 juin. Open May–Aug 9am–7pm; Sept 9am–6pm; Apr 9am–12.30pm, 1.30–6pm; Mar and Oct 9.30am–12.30pm, 1.30–5.30pm; Feb and Nov–Dec 10am–12.30pm, 1.30–5pm. Closed 24–25 Dec, 31 Dec–3rd week in Jan. 6.50€. 02 31 22 34 31. www.musee-arromanches.fr.
The D-Day Landing Museum contains a collection of models, photographs, dioramas, arms and equipment. A large model of the Mulberry port shows how it functioned regardless of the tides. Royal Navy films of the landing are shown.

360

Open Jun–Aug daily 9.40am–6.40pm; Apr–May and Sept–Oct 10.10am–5.40pm; Mar and Nov 10.10am–5.10pm; Feb and Dec 10.10am–4.40pm. 4.20€. 02 31 22 30 30. www.360.com
The Price of Freedom mixes archive footage with scenes re-enacted on the landing sites, on a 360-degree screen.

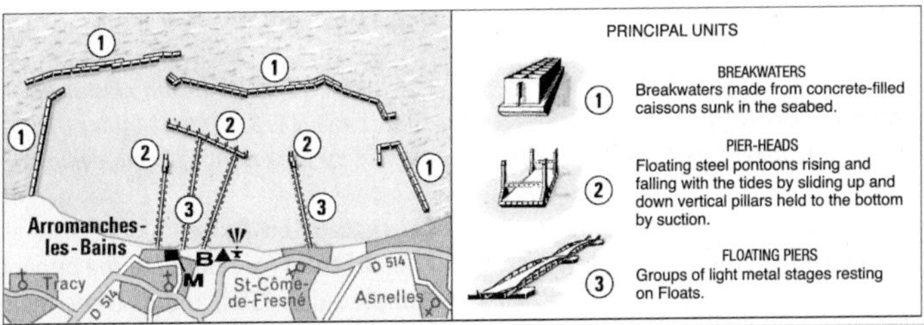

Arromanches-les-Bains
Tracy
St-Côme-de-Fresné
Asnelles
D 514
D 516
B
M
PRINCIPAL UNITS
BREAKWATERS
Breakwaters made from concrete-filled caissons sunk in the seabed.
PIER-HEADS
Floating steel pontoons rising and falling with the tides by sliding up and down vertical pillars held to the bottom by suction.
FLOATING PIERS
Groups of light metal stages resting on Floats.

360 B Musée de Débarquement M

Pays d'Auge★

With its pastures, thatched cottages, manor houses, apple orchards and winding hedgerows, the Pays d'Auge provides a picturesque transition to the beaches of the Côte Fleurie. The heart of traditional rural Normandy, the Auge region is partially covered in original woodland, with a chalk escarpment (30m/98.5ft high), known as the Côte d'Auge, overlooking the Dives Valley and the Caen area.

- **Population:** 149 000.
- **Michelin Map:** 303: M-4–N-6.
- **Info:** 11 rue d'Alençon, Lisieux. ℘02 31 48 18 10. www.pays-auge.fr.
- **Location:** The Pays d'Auge, between the River Dives on the west and the River Touques on the east, surrounds Lisieux, 36km/22.5mi S of Honfleur.
- **Don't Miss:** The beautiful château of Crèvecœur-en-Auge, with its half-timbering typical of the region.
- **Timing:** Give yourself 2hr to visit the Manoir des Évêques de Lisieux, 2hr for the Château de Crèvecœur and some extra time to see the gardens.

DRIVING TOUR

1 CÔTE D'AUGE

66km/41mi – allow 2hr.

Lisieux★★

See LISIEUX, p136.

From Lisieux take N 13 west. In La Boissière turn right onto D 59.

Ancienne Abbaye du Val Richer

Closed to the public.

Following the destruction of the Cistercian abbey during the Revolution, only the 17C hospice remained. François Guizot (1787–1874), a historian and leading politician during the reign of Louis-Philippe (1830–48), retired here after the 1848 revolution until his death in 1874. The Schlumberger brothers, early 20C petroleum engineers, worked here on inventions that would transform the industry (*see CRÈVECŒUR-EN-AUGE, p116*).

At the crossroads turn left onto D 101 and bear right onto D 117. At the next crossroads turn left onto D 16 and right onto D 85.

Clermont-en-Auge★

Chapel. Open Easter–Oct 10am–7pm.

Follow the signs Chapelle de Clermont – Panorama.

Leave the car at the start of the avenue leading to the **chapel** *(15min round-trip)*. From the east end there is an extensive **panorama**★ of the Dives and Vie valleys; in the distance stretches the Caen countryside, bounded by the dark line of the *bocage* hills. The church contains statues of St Marcouf and St Thibeault in polychrome stone in the chancel and on either side of the altar St John the Baptist and St Michael.

Beuvron-en-Auge★

This charming village has kept around 40 lovely old timber-framed houses set around the central square. The former covered market is now a shopping centre. There is a very pretty manor at the south exit from the village, decorated with woodcarvings.

Take D 49 north through Putot-en-Auge; cross N 175 and pass under the motorway. Fork right to Cricqueville.

Crèvecœur-en-Auge

The **château** *(closed to the public)*, completed in 1584, and its three main buildings with vast roofs are typically

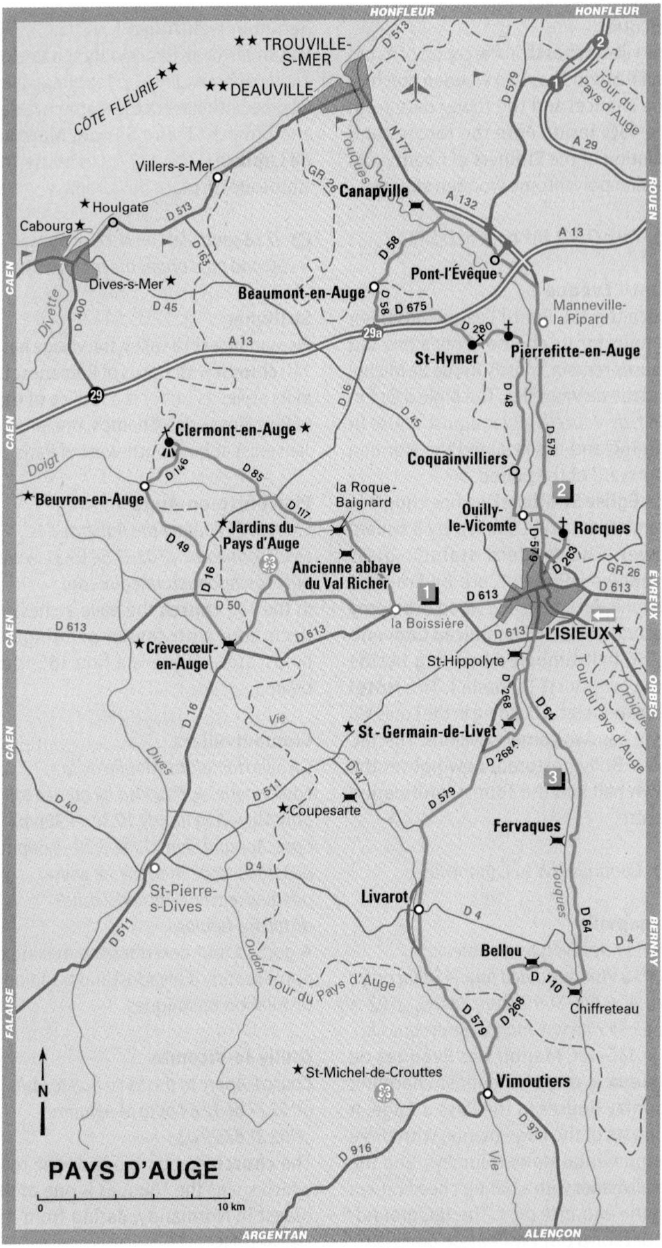

medieval whereas its chequered stone and brick decoration are Norman.

From Sarlabot to Dives there is a beautiful panorama over the Calvados coast.

2 TRADITIONAL NORMANDY: VALLÉE DE LA TOUQUES

60km/37mi – allow 2hr.

Leave Lisieux via boulevard Herbert-Fournet, D 579 north; right onto D 263.

Rocques

The village **church** in the centre of its old burial ground has two wooden porches. The chancel and the tower date from the 13C. Inside note the torches and painting of the Brothers of Charity and several polychrome wooden statues.

Take D 262 NW back to D 579.

Pont-l'Évêque

Since the 13C Pont-l'Évêque has been famous for its cheese. Only a few old houses remain, mostly in rue St-Michel and rue de Vaucelles. The Aigle d'Or Inn *(68 r. de Vaucelles)* was a post house in the 16C and has retained the Norman courtyard of the period.

The **Église St-Michel** is a fine church in Flamboyant style flanked by a square tower. The modern stained-glass windows (1963–64) are by François Chapuis. An interesting wooden balcony decorates the old **Dominican Convent**, a 16C half-timbered building beside the Law Courts (Tribunal). The **Hôtel Montpensier**, a building in the Louis XIII style has two corner pavilions. The 18C Hôtel Brilly (restored) now houses the town hall and the Tourist Information Centre.

Continue NW to Canapville.

Canapville

Manoir des Évêques de Lisieux. Visit by guided tour (45min) only Jul–Aug Tue–Sun 2–7pm. 6€. 02 31 65 24 75.www.manoirdeseveques.fr.

The 13C–15C **Manoir des Évêques de Lisieux** is one of the most charming country houses in the Pays d'Auge. It consists of the large manor, with three monumental stone chimneys, and the small manor with a bishop's head carved on the entrance post. The 18C ground-floor rooms display Chinese porcelain.

Take the N 13 towards Pont-l'Éveque, turn right to rejoin D 58.

Beaumont-en-Auge

This small town, remarkably situated on a spur commanding the Touques Valley, was the birthplace of the mathematician and physicist Pierre **Simon, Marquis de Laplace** (1749–1827). His house and statue are on place de Verdun.

D 58 south; left on N 175; right on D 280 and pass under the motorway.

St-Hymer

Pleasantly set in a valley, the village has a 14C **church** with traces of Romanesque in its style. Its belfry is a replica of that of Port-Royal-des-Champs, the famous Jansenist abbey south-west of Paris.

Pierrefitte-en-Auge

Church. Contact the Auberge des Deux Tonneaux. 02 31 64 09 31. www.aubergedesdeuxtonneaux.com.

In the 13C **church** the nave arches are decorated with cameo paintings of landscapes. There is a fine 16C rood beam.

Coquainvilliers

Distillerie Boulard. Moulin de la Foulonnerie. Visit by guided tour only May–Aug hourly 10.30–4.30pm, 5pm; Apr and Sept 11am, 2.30–4.30pm. 3.30€. 02 31 62 60 54. www.adeauville.com/siteclient/visite-distillerie-boulard.

A guided tour describes the making of apple brandy (Calvados) and traditional distillation techniques.

Ouilly-le-Vicomte

Church. Apply to the town hall to visit. 02 31 61 12 64 or to M Aillaume. 02 31 62 29 02.

The **church** standing beside the road which spans the Touques is one of the oldest in Normandy, dating from the 10C and 11C.

Continue east; at the crossroads turn right onto D 579 to Lisieux.

3 HAUTE VALLÉE DE LA TOUQUES

75km/46.6mi – allow 3hr round-trip from Lisieux – see LISIEUX.

Leave Lisieux via D 579, turn left onto D 64.

Fervaques

Château. Only the exterior can be visited; call for times. 5€ for a brochure. 02 31 32 33 96.

The 16C and 17C **château** overlooking the Touques is a vast building of brick and stone. Fervaques was the retreat of Delphine de Custine, a friend of the author F R de Chateaubriand (1768–1848), who also stayed there.

In Les Moutiers-Hubert turn right onto D 64 towards Gacé. At the crossroads turn left onto D 16 and immediately right. Cross the river in Canapville; turn right onto D 33 and continue south.South of Ticheville station cross the railway line. At the next junction turn right onto D 242; after 1km/0.6mi turn right to Vimoutiers.

Bellou

In the village centre stands Manoir de Bellou, a pleasant 16C timber-framed manor house. The road (D 110) runs southeast through the Moutiers-Hubert Forest and passes the Manoir de Cheffreteau.

Vimoutiers

See VIMOUTIERS, p299.

Take D 579 north and continue along D 579.

Livarot

Home of the cheese of the same name, this village has some beautiful houses.

Continue north on D 579; bear right onto D 268.

St-Germain-de-Livet★

Château. Guided tours (1hr) Feb–Nov and 2nd-half Oct Wed–Mon 11am–6pm (last entry 5pm). Closed 1 May. 6.60€; no charge 1st Sun of month. 02 31 31 00 03.

This delightful **château** consists of a 16C wing, decorated in a highly original stone and brick check pattern, adjoining a 15C half-timbered structure.

The 15C wing contains the guard-room, decorated with 16C **frescoes** (battle scene; Judith bearing the head of Holofernes), and a dining room with Empire-style furniture. On the first floor of the 16C wing are two rooms beautifully tiled in terracotta from the Pays d'Auge, the so-called bedroom of the painter Eugène Delacroix (1798–1863), the gallery with paintings by the Riesener family (19C) and a small round Louis XVI salon.

ADDRESSES

STAY

Chambre d'hôte Le Manoir de Cantepie *– Le Cadran, 14340 Cambremer, 11km/7mi W of Lisieux via N 13, then D 50. 02 31 62 87 27. Closed 15 Nov–1 Mar. 3 rooms. . Reservations required. This splendid 17C manor offers a delightful stay in elegant surroundings at a reasonable price.*

Chambre d'hôte Les Marronniers *– Les Marronniers, 14340 Cambremer. 02 31 63 08 28. www.les-marronniers.com. Closed 15 Nov–15 Feb. 4 rooms.* This charming 17C residence, surrounded by a flower garden, has a superb view over the Dives Valley. The guest rooms are spacious, and breakfast is served on a pleasant terrace.

EAT

Auberge de la Boule d'Or *– pl. Michel-Vermughen, 14430 Beuvron-en-Auge. 02 31 79 78 78. Closed Jan, Tue eve and Wed except Jul–Aug.* A magnificent half-timbered façade and a rustic interior with an open hearth. The Norman menu offers lashings of rich cream, cider and Calvados.

Bayeux★★

Today the Bayeux Tapestry still presents its unique record of the events of 1066 and the Battle of Hastings. Its home, the former capital of the Bessin, was the first French town to be liberated (7 June 1944) in World War II. The town escaped damage during the war, leaving a cathedral and old houses – many tastefully restored – as well as a pedestrian precinct, for explorers in the 21C.

- **Population:** 14 466.
- **Michelin Map:** 303: H-4 – Local map, *see p 90 and Plages du DÉBARQUEMENT.*
- **Info:** Pont St-Jean. 02 31 51 28 28. www.bessin-normandie.fr, www.mairie-bayeux.fr.
- **Location:** A short distance away from the D-Day beaches of Omaha and , Bayeux is midway between Caen (30km/18.6mi SW) and Carentan (47km/29.2mi NW).
- **Don't Miss:** The Bayeux Tapestry; Notre-Dame Cathedral; Battle of Normandy Museum; gardens of the château of Brécy; Priory of St-Gabriel.
- **Timing:** Give yourself at least 1hr to view the Bayeux Tapestry.
- **Kids:** The special children's audioguide will make the tapestry more interesting for them.

A BIT OF HISTORY

Cradle of the Dukes of Normandy – Bayeux, a Gaulish town, became a Roman centre, then was successively captured by the Bretons, the Saxons and the Vikings.

Rollo, the famous Viking, married Popa, the daughter of Count Béranger, Governor of the town. In 905, their son, the future William Longsword, ancestor of William the Conqueror, was born here.

Oath of Bayeux – In the 11C Edward the Confessor ruled over England. He had previously found refuge in Normandy for many years, and Norman accounts claim that he thus chose his cousin, William of Normandy, as his successor. He allegedly sent **Harold**, a powerful favourite of the Saxon nobles, to officially inform the duke.

Harold was shipwrecked on the coast of Picardy and captured by Count Guy of Ponthieu. Freed by **William**, he was received at the Norman court where the duke's daughter, Edwige, was presented as his wife to be.

Harold swore on saintly relics to recognise the Duke's right to the English throne. However, when Edward died on 5 January 1066, Harold accepted the English crown.

The Conquest of England – Harold's accession provoked William to set sail with the Norman fleet on 27 September 1066 from Dives-sur-Mer, to fight for his claim to the throne. On 28 September the Normans set foot on English soil at Pevensey in Sussex and occupied Hastings. Harold dug in on a hill. On 14 October William advanced and emerged victorious by that evening. The Bayeux Tapestry, a propaganda created after the invasion, claims that Harold fell in the fighting with an arrow in his eye.

Only the towers and crypt remain from the original church, which was completed in 1077 by Odo of Conteville, William's turbulent companion-in-arms.

Exterior

The east end is a graceful composition; flying buttresses support the chancel, which is flanked by two bell turrets. The central tower dates from the 15C but was unfortunately recapped in the 19C. The south transept is pure in style; the tympanum over the door shows the

© The Art Archive/Corbis

Detail of Norman Conquest of England from The Bayeux Tapestry

Bayeux Tapestry★★★

The **Bayeux Tapestry** *(Tapisserie dite de la Reine Mathilde)* is displayed in the **Centre Guillaume le Conquérant** in an impressive 18C building which was a seminary until 1970.

Visitors are introduced to this jewel of Romanesque art as they pass through a series of rooms, with films and dioramas explaining the history and content of the tapestry, which is itself displayed under glass round the walls of the specially designed Harold Room.

Wrongly attributed in the 18C to Queen Matilda, the tapestry was probably commissioned in England soon after the conquest from a group of Saxon embroiderers by Odo of Conteville, Count of Kent and Bishop of Bayeux. The embroidery is in coloured wool on a piece of linen, 50cm/19.7in high by 70m/229.7ft long.

The work is the most accurate and lively document to survive from the Middle Ages and provides detailed information on the clothes, ships, arms and general lifestyle of the period.

In 58 detailed scenes, the illustrations give a very realistic account of the events of 1066. The English are distinguished by their moustaches and long hair, the Normans by their short hairstyles, the clergy by their tonsures and the women (three in all) by their flowing garments and veiled heads. Latin captions run above the pictures.

The outstanding sections are Harold's embarkation and crossing (4–6), his audience with William (14), crossing the River Couesnon near Mont-St-Michel (17), Harold's Oath (23), the death and burial of Edward the Confessor (26–28), the appearance of Halley's comet, an ill omen for Harold (32), the building of the fleet (36), the Channel crossing and the march to Hastings (38–40), cooking and eating meals (41–43), the battle and Harold's death (51–58).

Centre Guillaume-le-Conquérant, r. de Nesmond. Open May–Aug 9am–7pm; 15 Mar–Apr and Sept–15 Nov 9am–6.30pm; rest of the year 9.30am–12.30pm, 2–6pm (last entry 45min before closing). Audio-guided tours (14 languages); commentary for children. Closed 1 Jan, 2nd week of Jan, 25 Dec. 7.80€ (children 3.80€, under-10 no charge).

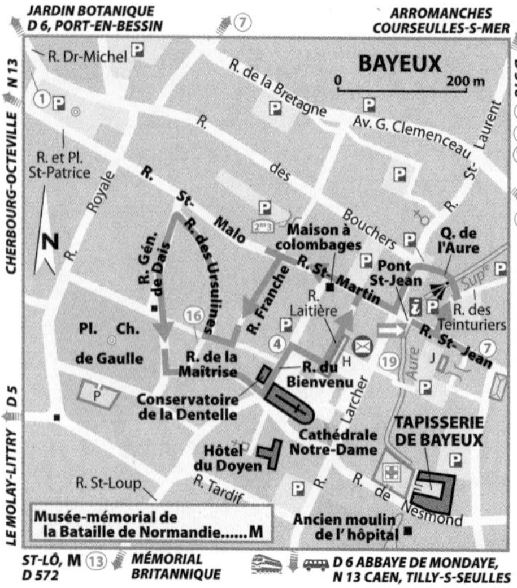

WHERE TO STAY

- Ferme de la Rançonnière (Hôtel)........ ①
- Ferme des Châtaigniers (Chambre d'hôte la)........ ④
- Grand Fumichon (Chambre d'hôte le)........ ⑦
- Manoir de Crépon (Chambre d'hôte le)........ ⑩
- Moulin de Hard (Chambre d'hôte le)........ ⑬
- Petit Matin (Chambre d'hôte le)........ ⑯
- Reine Mathilde (Hôtel)........ ⑲

WHERE TO EAT

- Bristot de Paris (Le)........ ①
- Pommier (Le)........ ④
- Rapière (La)........ ⑦
- Saint-Martin (Hostellerie)........ ⑩

story of Thomas Becket, Archbishop of Canterbury, assassinated in his cathedral on the orders of Henry II.

The small porch further west on the south side is late-12C.

The two Romanesque towers on the west front must have been redesigned in the 13C with massive buttresses to take the weight of the Gothic spires. The only points of interest are on the tympana over the two side doors: the Passion and the Last Judgement.

Interior

The well-lit nave is a harmonious blend of Romanesque and Gothic. The clerestory and the vaulting date from the 13C but the wide arches are in the best 12C style. Their justly famous decoration is typical of Norman Romanesque sculpture. Against an interlaced or knotted ground the spandrels are decorated with low-relief sculptures which show oriental influence transmitted by the illuminators of manuscripts.

The transept crossing is supported by four huge pillars. The south transept contains two interesting pictures low on the right: the Life of St Nicholas and the Crucifixion (15C).

The three-storey chancel, with its ambulatory and radiating chapels, is a magnificent example of Norman Gothic architecture. The great arches are separated by pierced rose windows.

The high altar is a majestic 18C piece; the six candelabras in chased bronze, the tabernacle and the cross are by Caffieri the Elder.

The paintings (restored) on the chancel vault represent the first bishops of Bayeux. The ambulatory, like the transepts, is lower than the chancel and separated from it by handsome wrought-iron screens. The third and fourth chapels on the south side contain 15C frescoes.

Crypt

Beneath the chancel is the crypt (11C). Above the decorative foliage of the capitals are 15C frescoes (restored) of angel musicians. A recess *(left)* contains the recumbent figure of a canon (15C).

Chapter house

This is a beautiful late-12C Gothic construction. The vaulting, which was renewed in the 14C, is supported by consoles decorated with monsters or grotesque figures. A graceful blind arcade adorns the lower walls. The floor of 15C glazed bricks includes a labyrinthine design in the centre. The tiles on the risers at the back of the room depict hunting scenes. The beatification of St Thérèse of Lisieux was signed at the desk.

Old Bayeux

The old stone or timber-framed houses have been splendidly restored.

Rue St-Martin

No 6 is a 17C house known as the Maison du Cadran because of the sundial on the façade. On the corner of rue des Cuisiniers stands a very elegant **half-timbered house**★ with two overhanging upper storeys and a slate roof. Just after the rue Franche, on the right, is the Hôtel d'Argouges, a 15C–16C timber-framed house.

Rue Franche

Several private houses: no 5, Hôtel de Rubercy, is a 15C–16C turreted manor house; no 7, Hôtel de la Crespellière, is set back behind a courtyard and dates from the mid-18C; no 13, Hôtel St-Manvieu, is from the 16C.

Rue du Général-de-Dais

No 10, Hôtel de Castilly (18C), is in the Louis XV style. No 14, Hôtel de la Tour du Pin (18C), has an imposing façade in the Louis XVI style.

Rue du Bienvenu

No 6 is decorated with wooden carvings inspired by religion or legend. It houses the **Conservatoire de la dentelle de Bayeux** (*see Additional Sights*).

Rue St-Jean

East of rue St-Martin, part of this street is within the pedestrian precinct which has been attractively restored. The Tourist Information Centre is housed in the old fish market. No 53 is the Hôtel du Croissant (15C–16C).

Rue des Teinturiers

Two handsome half-timbered houses face a row of stone houses.

Quai de l'Aure

On turning into this street from rue des Teinturiers, one has a fine view of the river, the water mill in what was once the tanning district, the arched bridge, the old fish market and the towers of the cathedral in the background.

ADDITIONAL SIGHTS

Hôtel du Doyen

r. Lambert-Leforestier. Open daily Jul–Aug 10am–12.30pm, 2–7pm; rest of the year 10am–12.30pm, 2–6pm. 3.50€ (no charge with a ticket from the Tapestry Museum). 02 31 92 14 21.

A huge 17C porch leads into the 18C mansion, which houses the collection of the **Baron-Gèrard Museum**, which is closed for repairs (*see below*).

Conservatoire de la Dentelle de Bayeux

6 r. du Bienvenu. Open Mon–Sat 10am–noon, 2–6pm. No charge with a ticket from the Tapestry Museum. 02 31 92 73 80. http://dentellede bayeux.free.fr.

Bayeux lace is characterised by floral motifs. The workshop, where the lacemakers are reviving the Bayeux pattern, has displays of lace specimens.

Musée Baron-Gérard

Closed for renovation until 2012.

Bayeux was once an important manufacturing centre for porcelain. Founded in 1812 by J Langlois, the workshop's famous glazing (red, gold and blue) made the reputation of the town. Production ended in 1951. The museum displays several of these abundantly decorated porcelain pieces, some quite rare.

The upstairs rooms contain furniture and painting, mainly 15C and 16C Italian and Flemish Primitive works and 17C–19C French works including those of Philippe de Champaigne, David, Baron François Gérard, Boudin and Caillebotte.

Musée-Mémorial de la Bataille de Normandie★

Bd Fabian-Ware. Open May–Sept 9.30am–6.30pm; Oct–Apr 10am–12.30pm, 2–6pm (last entry 1hr before closing). Closed 2 weeks in Jan. 6.50€. 02 31 51 46 90.

Situated on the line that separated the British and American sectors in 1944, the Memorial Museum recalls the dramatic events of summer 1944. Two large galleries, named Overlord and Eisenhower, explain the chronology of the Battle of Normandy and give a detailed account of the equipment and uniforms of the various nations involved in the conflict.

The closing of the Falaise Pocket is illustrated by a diorama recreating the village of Chambois where, on 19 August, part of the 90th US Infantry Division joined forces with the 1st Polish Armoured Division.

A great variety of heavy equipment is exhibited. Note in particular the Churchill MK VII tank (GB) – the anti-tank armoured vehicle called Destroyer M 10 (US), the anti-tank Jagdpanzer (Germany) – a quadruple 20mm German Flak gun as well as a Caterpillar D 7 Bulldozer.

Mémorial Charles-de-Gaulle

10 r. Bourbesnour. Open Jun–Aug 9.30am–12.30pm, 2–6.30pm; Sept–Nov and Mar–May 10am–12.30pm, 2–6pm (last entry 30min before closing). 3.50€. 02 31 92 45 55.

The Governor's mansion (15C–17C) houses a museum which retraces the life and career of the General through events associated with Bayeux (liberation of the town and speech of 1946). Personal belongings, newspaper articles and manuscripts are also on display.

Jardin Botanique

55 rte de Port-en-Bessin. Open daily Apr–Sept 9am–8pm; rest of the year 9am–5pm. 02 31 10 10 14. www.bessin-normandie.fr.

The pleasant sloping botanical garden, laid out in 1859, includes 400 trees, among them a huge weeping willow officially recognised as an Important Tree of France, as well as a glasshouse displaying cacti.

EXCURSION

Abbaye de Mondaye

11km/6.8mi – allow 45min. From Bayeux take D 6 S. After 8km/5mi turn right onto D 33; follow the signs. Guided tours (1hr) Jul–Aug Mon–Fri 3pm, Sun 3.30pm; Jun and Sept Sun 3.30pm. 5€. 02 31 92 58 11. www.mondaye.com.

St Martin's Abbey was founded in 1215 but rebuilt in the 18C and 19C. The abbey church, which also serves the parish, is in the Classical style (early 18C). Its uniformity of design is due to its architect and decorator, **Eustache Restout**, a canon in the Premonstratensian Order. The interior contains some fine pieces: high altar, woodwork in the chancel including a beautiful Crucifixion, the Assumption (a terracotta group in the Lady Chapel) and the Parizot organ (restored).

The 18C **conventual buildings** – refectory, sacristy (18C woodwork) and library – are open to the public.

DRIVING TOUR

1 SOUTHWEST OF BAYEUX

Round-trip of 46km/29mi – about 3hr30min.

From Bayeux take D 572.

St-Loup-Hors

The 12C–13C church has retained its Romanesque tower and old tombs.

Noron-la-Poterie

This is a well-known centre producing salt glaze ware; some of the workshops are open to the public.

In La Tuilerie turn left onto D 73, which leads to Balleroy via Castillon.

Château de Balleroy★

See Château de BALLEROY, p94.

On leaving turn left onto D 13. At the Embranchement crossroads take D 13 and D 8 west through Cerisy Forest.

Ancienne Abbaye de Cerisy-la-Forêt

At the exit from the forest of Cerisy near D 572. Allow 2hr in total.

The abbey at Cerisy is a remarkable example of Norman Romanesque architecture. The first monastery dates

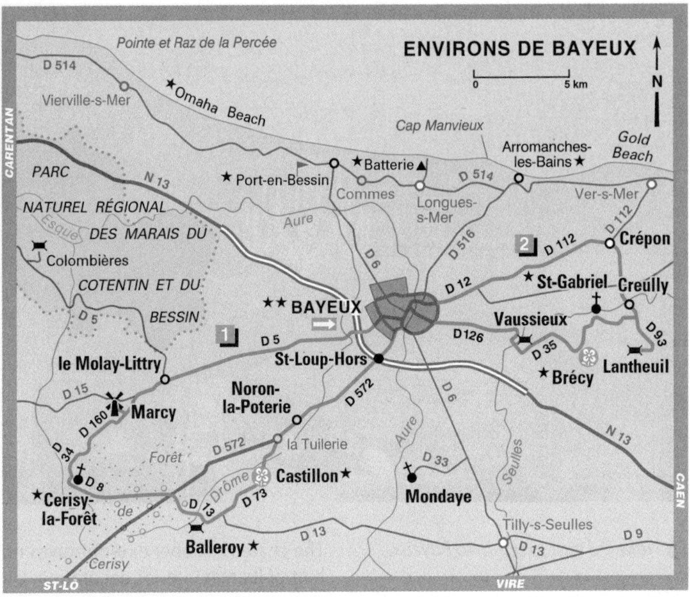

from around 510. In 1032 Robert I of Normandy, the father of William the Conqueror, founded a new monastery here dedicated to Vigor, former bishop of Bayeux.

Église Abbatiale★

Open daily 9am–6pm. Guided tours (45min) of chapel, Salle de Justice, museum Easter–Aug 10.30am–12.30pm, 2.30–6.30pm; Oct Sat–Sun and holidays 10.30am-noon, 2.30–6pm. 4€. 02 33 57 34 63. http://catholique-coutances.cef.fr.

The nave is remarkable for its height. The choir and especially the apse are a striking example of Romanesque architecture characterised by delicacy and abundance of light, when most 11C buildings were massive and sombre. Walk round the church to the east end to admire the **chevet**★ with its tiered effect formed by the apse, the choir and the belfry.

Conventuel Buildings

Same as the église.

Following the Revolution, these 13C buildings were used as a stone quarry.

Musée lapidaire

A low chamber with pointed vaulting houses the Archaeological Museum. At the far end of the chamber, on the left, is a dungeon with 15C and 16C graffiti.

Chapelle de l'Abbé

The Abbot's Chapel, built in the 13C with a gift from St Louis, is a good example of Norman Gothic architecture.

From Cerisy take D 34, D 160 and D 15 northeast to Le Molay-Littry.

Le Molay-Littry

The village was once a busy coal mining centre. The mine was opened in 1743 and flourished until the late 19C. During World War II it was reopened and produced coal until 1950.

The **Musée de la Mine**★ (*open Apr–last Sun in Sept, Tue–Sun and holidays 10am–noon, 2–6pm; 5€ (children 1.50€); 02 31 22 89 10; www.ville-molay-littry.fr*) presents the history of mining and the life of the miners through an audio-visual presentation, a reconstruction of a mining gallery, a scale model of a pithead, and a range of tools.

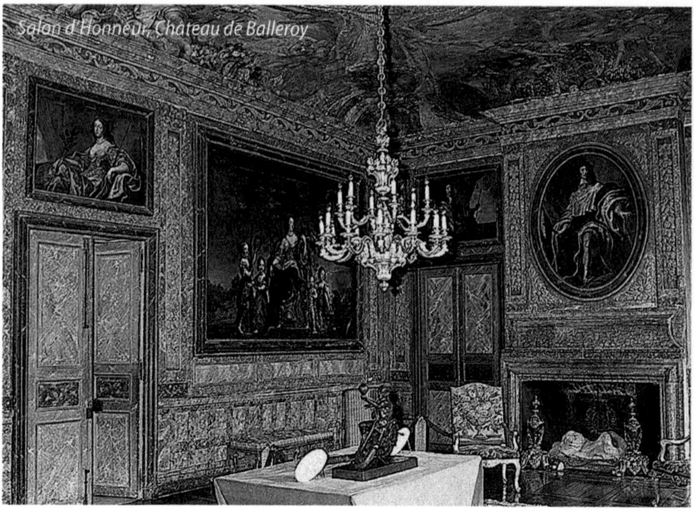

Salon d'Honneur, Château de Balleroy

Take D 5 east to return to Bayeux.

Château de Balleroy★

Also at the exit for the Forest of Cerisy. Allow 2hr to see everything here.

The Château of Balleroy, built between 1626 and 1636, was designed by François Mansart (1598–1666). Owned by successive Marquises de Balleroy for three centuries, it was purchased in 1970 by Malcolm Forbes (1919–90), the American publisher and aeronaut. The plain but majestic brick and stone building dominates the village's main street. Symmetrical outbuildings lie behind formal flower beds designed by Le Nôtre. Don't miss the *salon d'honneur*, reached by one of the earliest cantilevered stairways in France.

Interior

Open Jul–Aug daily 10am–6pm; 15 Mar–Jun and Sept–15 Oct Wed–Sun 10am–noon, 2–6pm. Visit of château by guided tour (45min) only, last tour starts at 5.10pm. Museum and park open out of season Mon and Wed–Fri 10am–noon, 1.30–5pm. Closed holidays off-season. 8€ complete ticket (museum 4.50€, children 3.50€, château 6.50€, park no charge with château and museum ticket). 02 31 21 60 61. www.chateau-balleroy.com.

The château's sober exterior gives no hint of its rich interior decoration. On the ground floor the salons display portraits of past counts. The dining room is painted with scenes from the Fables of La Fontaine.

On the first floor, the bedrooms are decorated lavishly in period styles. The drawing room ceiling portrays the Four Seasons and the signs of the zodiac.

Musée des Ballons

For times and prices see the château.

A museum of hot-air balloons is housed in the stables. Dioramas tell the story of major flights in the history of ballooning.

2 EAST OF BAYEUX

Round-trip of 34km/21mi – allow 2hr.

From Bayeux take D 12 and D 112 towards Ver-sur-Mer.

Crépon

Admire the Romanesque church with its 15C tower and the smart farms.

Turn right onto D 65.

Creully

Guided tours (45min) Jul–Aug Tue–Fri 10am–12.30pm, 2.30–5pm. 3€. 02 31 80 67 08.

The **château** is built on the foundations of an 11C castle. The main 12C building is flanked by a 16C round tower adjoining a square keep. During World War II, the BBC used it to relay news of the Battle of Normandy.
From the terrace there is a view of **Château de Creullet** standing in a loop of the road. On 12 June 1944 King George VI and Sir Winston Churchill met here with General Montgomery.

Grange aux Dîmes

On the Bayeux road, level with no 82.
The Tithe Barn is a powerfully buttressed building where wheat was stored and where the taxes were collected.

Take D 93 south to Lantheuil.

Château de Lantheuil

Guided tours Jun–Oct for groups by appointment only. 7€. 02 31 80 14 00.
This imposing castle built in the reign of Louis XIII has remained in the same family ever since. The rooms have retained their original décor: woodwork, furniture, sculptures and paintings including a remarkable collection of family portraits.

Return to Creully; turn left onto D 35. Enter St-Gabriel-Brécy; turn right.

Ancien Prieuré de St-Gabriel★

Chapel: *Jul–Aug Wed–Mon 2.30–6.30pm; May–Jun and Sept Sat–Sun, call for hours. Unaccompanied visits of gardens during school holidays. No charge except for exhibits. 02 31 80 10 20. www.prieuresaintgabriel.fr.*
The old priory of St-Gabriel was founded in the 11C as a daughter house of Fécamp Abbey. The attractive buildings surround a courtyard with a monumental entrance gate. The church is reduced to the magnificently designed and decorated east end and chancel (11C–12C). Beyond the church is a garden, planted with fruit trees and banks of flowers. The 15C Justice Tower contained a prison on the lower floor and a lookout at the top.

Return to D 35; continue west towards Bayeux; then follow the signs south.

Gardens of the Château de Brécy★

Open Tue, Thu, Sat–Sun and public holidays Jun 2.30–6.30pm; Easter–May and Jul–Oct 2.30–6.30pm. 6€. 02 31 80 11 48.
The castle is approached through a magnificent great **gateway**★ (17C). The terraced **gardens**★ offer a beautiful perspective which terminates in a high wrought-iron grill ornately decorated.

Take D 158; just before the church turn right onto a narrow road; after 2km/1mi turn left onto D 35; after 2km/1mi turn right towards Esquay-sur-Seulles.

Château de Vaussieux

Closed to the public.
In 1778 the American owner of this beautiful 18C mansion gave it to Marshal Broglie to hold manoeuvres designed to intimidate England. The château is an elegant building set in its own park; the outbuildings are half-timbered or of stone.

Continue onto Esquay-sur-Seulles; take D 126 to return to Bayeux.

Ancien Prieuré de St-Gabriel

A. de Valroger/MICHELIN

ADDRESSES

STAY

Chambre d'hôte La Ferme des Châtaigniers – *9 Wall Path, 14400 Vienne-en-Bessin. 7.5km/4.6mi E of Bayeux via D 126. 02 31 92 54 70. 3 rooms.* . Set apart from the farmhouse, this converted stable contains simple yet pleasant, comfortable rooms. Well-equipped kitchen.

Chambre d'hôte Le Grand Fumichon – *14400 Vaux-sur-Aure. 3km/2mi N of Bayeux via D 104. 02 31 21 78 51. www.fermedefumichon.com. 4 rooms.* . This fortified 17C farm is today a dairy and cider-making farm.

Chambre d'hôte Le Manoir de Crépon – *rte d'. 14480 Crépon. 02 31 22 21 27. www. manoirdecrepon.com. Closed Dec–Feb. 5 rooms.* This house, built in the 17C and 18C, is typical of the area. Vast, tastefully furnished rooms. The former kitchen is now a breakfast room.

Chambre d'hôte Le Petit Matin – *2 bis. r. Quincangrogne. 02 31 10 09 27. . 3 rooms. Restaurant* . Intimate hotel in a little street near the cathedral.

Hôtel Reine Mathilde – *23 r. Larcher. 02 31 92 08 13. www.hotel-reinemathilde.com. Closed 15 Nov–15 Feb. 16 rooms. 7€.* This small, family hotel is conveniently situated a stone's throw from the cathedral and the famous Tapestry. Bar, tea room and ice-cream shop.

Chambre d'hôte Le Moulin de Hard – *Area called "Le Moulin de Hard", 14400 Subles, 6km/3.7mi SW of Bayeux. 02 31 21 37 17. 3 rooms.* . Restored 18C watermill near a small river with a beautiful garden. Large, comfortable rooms. Bikes loaned.

Hôtel Ferme de la Rançonnière – *rte d'-les-Bains, 14480 Crépon. 02 31 22 21 73. www.ranconniere.fr. 36 rooms. 12€. Restaurant* . Rustic, well-furnished rooms in a building dating to the 15C and 18C. Breakfast in bed service!

EAT

Le Bistrot de Paris – *pl. St-Patrice. 02 31 92 00 82.* The daily menu of this bistro-style restaurant is based on what the chef finds at the market. Telaxed ambience, reasonable prices.

Hostellerie St-Martin – *pl. Edmond-Paillaud, 14480 Creully. 02 31 80 10 11. www.hostelleriesaintmartin.com.* This 16C building used to house the village market. Curious décor. Classic cuisine. A dozen bedrooms.

Rapière – *53 r. St-Jean. 02 31 21 05 45. Closed 21 Dec–21 Jan, Thu except eve May–Sept, Wed.* A 15C house situated in a picturesque street in old Bayeux. A lovely, rustic interior and tasty food centred on Norman produce.

Le Pommier – *40 r. des Cuisiniers. 02 31 21 52 10. www. restaurantlepommier.com. Closed 7–end Feb, 21 Nov–2 Dec, Tue eve and Wed, except Jul–Aug.* This restaurant near the cathedral has an apple-green façade and offers a celebrated daily menu of Norman specialities, many featuring apple products. The vaulted dining-room with stone walls adds charming authenticity.

SHOPPING

Markets – *r. St-Jean. Open Wed 7.30am –2.30pm and pl. St-Patrice. Sat 6.30am–2.30pm.* Bayeux's two markets are quite unalike, each with its own charm. St-Jean pedestrian street Wednesday market features some 25 stalls including greengrocers, butchers, fishmongers, cheesemakers and honey-sellers. On the Pl. St-Patrice, every Saturday, some 120 merchants offer their wares, about half of them foodstuffs.

Naphtaline – *14–16 parvis de la Cathédrale. 02 31 21 50 03. www. naphtaline-bayeux.com.* Two boutiques housed in a fine 18C building offer antique and modern lace, Bayeux porcelain and reproductions of traditional tapestries woven on Jaquard looms. Next door a third boutique called Autre Temps specialises in medieval objects.

Cabourg☼☼

The large seaside resort of Cabourg, created at the time of the Second Empire (1852–70), centres on the casino and Grand Hôtel on the seafront, from which streets radiate inland, intersecting with two semicircular avenues. Many avenues and streets are lined by attractive houses set in shaded gardens.

- **Population:** 3 965.
- **Michelin Map:** 303: L-4 – Local map, *see Pays d'AUGE, p85.*
- **Info:** Jardins de l'Hôtel de Ville. 02 31 06 20 00. www.cabourg.net.
- **Location:** Take D 513 from Caen (33km/20.6mi to the SW), Deauville (19km/12mi) and Honfleur (51km/31.7mi) to the E; take D 45 from Lisieux (30km/18.6mi to the SE).
- **Don't Miss:** The lovely residences of Cabourg, the magnificent view from promenade Marcel-Proust and the pretty port of Dives-sur-Mer.
- **Timing:** Explore in the morning to avoid crowds.

A BIT OF HISTORY

Cabourg is famous as the place from which William the Conqueror successfully forced Henry I's troops back into the sea.

The holiday towns of Dieppe, Deauville and Trouville were now joined by Cabourg, which, benefiting from a rail link, became a tourist destination of choice. By the 1880s, hotels and villas had sprung up around the **Grand Hôtel** on the seafront; Cabourg was truly established.

EXCURSIONS

Merville-Franceville-Plage

6km/3.7mi W of Cabourg by D 514.

When the Allies landed in June 1944 the strongest point in the defences was the Merville Battery. It was captured by the 6th British Airborne Division. One of the casemates has been converted into a museum, the **Musée de la Batterie** (*open daily Jun–Aug 9.30am–7pm; mid-Mar–May and Sept–mid-Nov 9.30am–6pm; 5€; 02 31 91 47 53. www.batterie-merville.com).*

Grand Hôtel Cabourg

H. Le Gac/MICHELIN

Famous Guest

Marcel Proust went to Cabourg for the first time in 1881, when he was 10. The coastal climate was beneficial to his health (he suffered from asthma), while the town's charm and memories of his childhood drew him to visit frequently as an adult, when he would stay at the Grand Hôtel. *Within a Budding Grove (À l'Ombre des jeunes filles en fleurs)* was a vivid portrayal of the customs of Cabourg and of life in a seaside resort at the turn of the 20C.

Ranville

8km/5mi S of Merville-Franceville-Plage on D 223.

Ranville was captured at 2.30am on 6 June 1944 by the 13th Battalion of the Lancashire Fuseliers of the 6th British Airborne Division; it was the first village to be liberated on French territory. A war cemetery commemorates these events.

ADDRESSES

STAY

Le Moulin du Pré – *Lieu-dit le Moulin du Pré, 14860 Bavent, 7km/4.3mi SW of Cabourg via D 513, rte de Caen. ℘02 31 78 83 68. Closed 1–15 Mar, Oct, Sun eve, Mon, Tue except 15 Jul–15 Aug and public holidays. 10 rooms. Restaurant.* A spacious garden surrounds this charming half-timbered farm from the 19C. Meals are served in an inviting, rustic dining room featuring a fireplace where meat is grilled. Pleasant rooms.

Chambre d'hôte Ferme de l'Oraille – *Chemin de Deraine, 14430 Douville-en-Auge, 7km/4.3mi SE of Dives-sur-Mer via D 45, D 27 between la Maison-Blanche and La Croix d'Heuland. ℘02 31 79 25 49. 2 rooms.* At this 18C Norman farm, which still produces dairy products, you can enjoy simple country comfort and sample farm milk and home-made jam at breakfast.

EAT

Dupont avec un Thé – *6 av. de la Mer. ℘02 31 24 60 32. Closed Tue and Wed out of season, noon on Mon, Thu and Fri out of season except school holidays.* A tea salon offering a range of delicious cakes and sweets, notably chocolate and caramel. Branches are located in Dives, Deauville and Trouville.

Le Champagne – *11 pl. du Marché. ℘02 31 24 23 39. Closed Mon out of season.* Opposite the market, this modest hotel-restaurant is both convenient and well managed. An elegant dining room with a menu specialising in seafood. Upstairs, comfortable guest rooms.

NIGHTLIFE

Bar du Grand Hôtel – *Prom. Marcel-Proust. ℘02 31 91 01 79.* The Grand Hôtel, with its Belle époque style, huge chandeliers and full draperies, is a monument to nostalgia. You needn't be a guest to have tea here, or better yet, enjoy a snifter of 40-year-old Calvados, while gazing out to sea.

Grand Casino – *Prom. Marcel-Proust. ℘02 31 28 19 19.* In addition to its gambling facilities, the casino houses a disco (500 people), a performance hall (500 seats), an Italian-style theatre (up to 500 seats) and a panoramic restaurant facing the ocean. Terrace by the sea.

SPORT AND LEISURE

Les écuries de la Sablonnière – *Av. Guillaume-le-Conquérant, rte de Caen, opposite the Vert Pré campsite. ℘02 31 91 61 70. http://sablonniere.neuf.fr. Open Fri–Wed (open daily during school holidays) 9am–12.30pm, 2-6pm. Lesson 22€/hour. Tours 32€/hour.* This club organises horseback rides on the beach and in the hinterland for all levels of experience.

Caen★★★

Caen is the capital of Calvados and the cultural heart of the Basse-Normandie, a lively city with a distinctive identity. The bombs that fell here in 1944 could have left Caen lifeless for all their violence, but the city proved resilient and drew on the strength of its history to rebuild and re-create. Today Caen is a charming place to visit. It has a modern spirit and a well-regarded university, which was founded in the 15C and now has more than 30 000 students.

- **Population:** 110 399.
- **Michelin Map:** 303: J-4 – Local map, *see Plages du DÉBARQUEMENT.*
- **Info:** 12 place St-Pierre. 02 31 27 14 14. www.caen.fr/tourisme.
- **Location:** At the junction of the rivers Orne and Odon, Caen can be reached by the A 13, some 2.5hr, or 235km/146mi from Paris.
- **Don't Miss:** The Mémorial, the Abbaye-aux-Hommes and the Fine Arts Museum (Musée des Beaux-Arts) housed in the château.
- **Timing:** You need at least 2hr to visit the Mémorial.
- **Kids:** There is an amusement park called Festyland nearby, *see p114.*

A BIT OF HISTORY

William and Matilda

The city achieved importance in the 11C when it became Duke William's favourite place of residence.

After establishing himself as Duke of Normandy, William asked for the hand of Matilda of Flanders, a distant cousin. She replied that she would rather take the veil than be given in marriage to the bastard son of the Beautiful Arlette.

One fine day, mad with love and anger, the duke rode headlong to Lille and burst into the palace of the Count of Flanders. According to the Chronicler of Tours, he seized Matilda by her plaits and dragged her round the room kicking her. Then he left her gasping for breath and galloped off. Proud Matilda was vanquished and consented to the marriage. The Pope, however, objected to the cousins' distant kinship. In 1059, through the efforts of **Lanfranc**, the Pope relented.

As an act of penitence the duke and his wife founded two abbeys – the Abbey for Men and the Abbey for Women. Bayeux remained the episcopal see.

When William departed to conquer England, faithful Matilda became regent of the duchy; in 1068 she was crowned Queen of England. She was buried in the Abbey for Women in 1083.

Abbaye-aux-Hommes

B. Kauffmann/MICHELIN

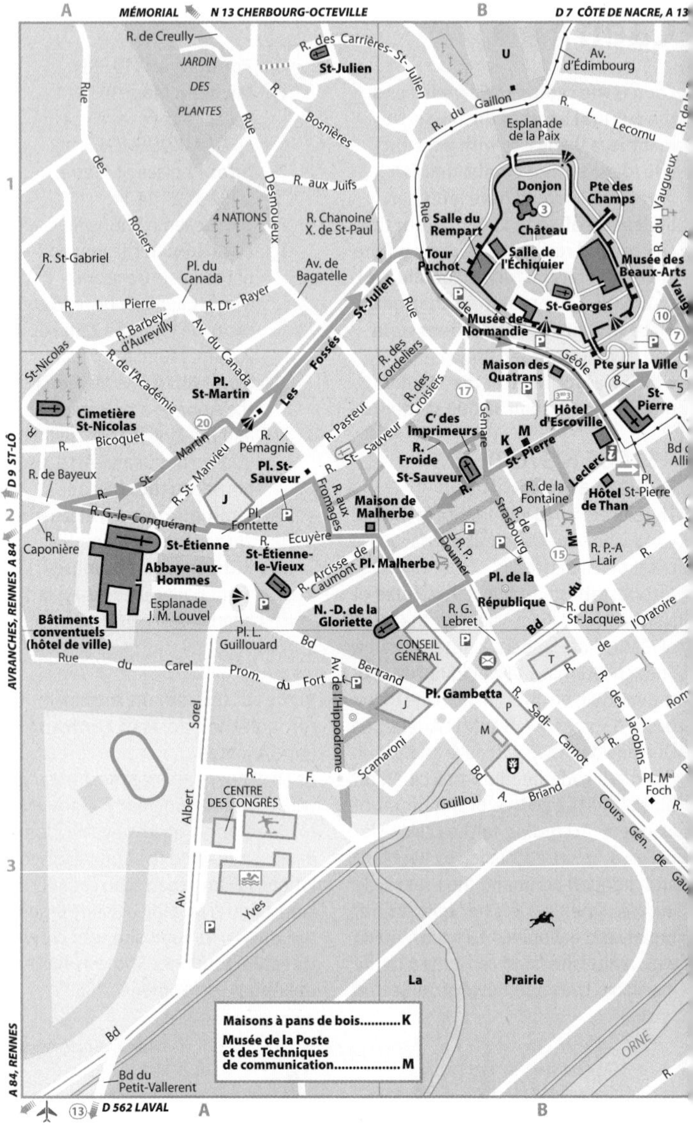

William died in 1087 and was buried in the church of the Abbey for Men.

WALKING TOUR

Hôtel d'Escoville★

pl. Saint-Pierre.

This mansion, which now houses the tourist office and the Artothèque, was built between 1533 and 1538 by Nicolas Le Valois d'Escoville, a wealthy merchant. The bomb damage incurred in 1944 has been repaired. Behind the plain street façade there is a **courtyard** flanked by two wings at right angles; the harmonious proportions, the arrangement of the various elements and the majestic sculptures make an elegant composition.

The main block facing the entrance is surmounted by an unusual ornament, a large two-storey dormer window supported by flying buttresses projecting

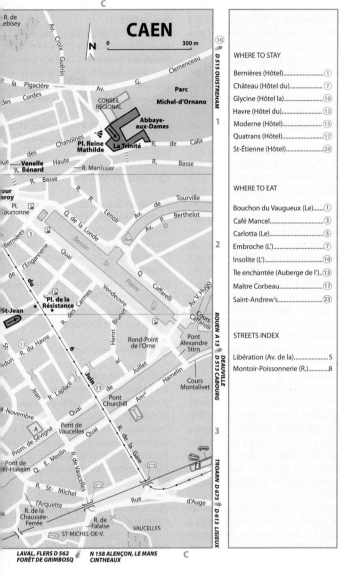

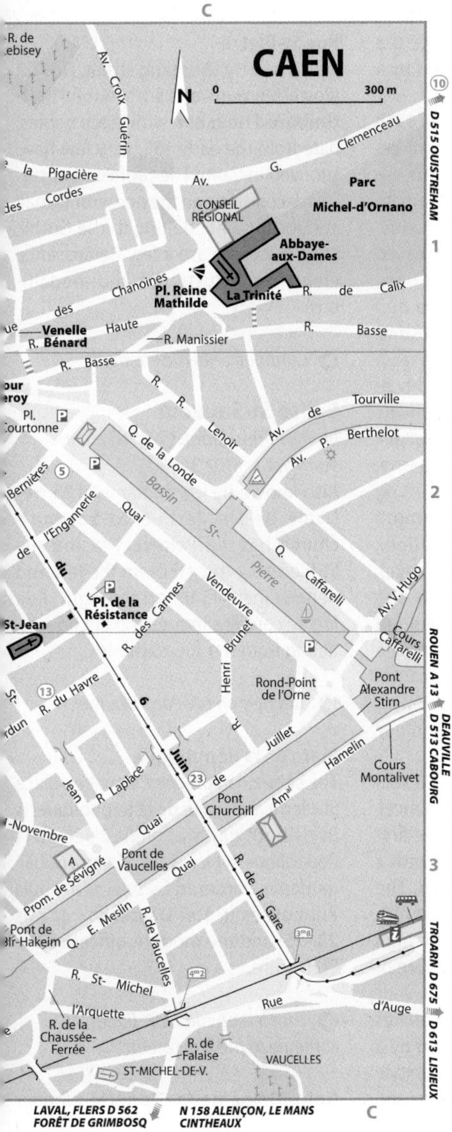

WHERE TO STAY

- Bernières (Hôtel)....(1)
- Château (Hôtel du)....(7)
- Glycine (Hôtel la)....(10)
- Havre (Hôtel du)....(13)
- Moderne (Hôtel)....(15)
- Quatrans (Hôtel)....(17)
- St-Étienne (Hôtel)....(20)

WHERE TO EAT

- Bouchon du Vaugueux (Le)....(1)
- Café Mancel....(3)
- Carlotta (Le)....(5)
- Embroche (L')....(7)
- Insolite (L')....(10)
- Île enchantée (Auberge de l')..(13)
- Maître Corbeau....(17)
- Saint-Andrew's....(23)

STREETS INDEX

- Libération (Av. de la)....5
- Montoir-Poissonnerie (R.)....8

from a steep pavilion roof. Climb up to the loggia for a view of the whole courtyard.

Opposite the Hôtel d'Escoville stands the impressive Église St-Pierre.

Église St-Pierre★

pl. St-Pierre. Open daily except some Sun afternoons. Restoration work is underway.

Although only a parish church, St Peter's is richly decorated. Construction started in the 13C, was continued during the 14C and 15C and completed in the 16C in the Renaissance style. The impressive tower (78m/256ft), which dated from 1308, was destroyed during the Battle of Caen in 1944. "The king of Norman belfries" has, however, been rebuilt as well as the nave into which it fell (all the vaulting has been redone). The west front has been restored to its 14C appearance; the Flamboyant porch is surmounted by a rose window.

The **east end**★★, built between 1518 and 1545, is remarkable for the richness of its Renaissance décor, in which the shapely and graceful furnishings (ornate pinnacles, urns, richly scrolled balustrades, carved pilasters), have replaced the Gothic motifs.

Some of the **capitals**★ *(second and third pillars on the left)* are interesting for their carvings, which are taken from the bestiaries of the period and chivalrous exploits. The third pillar shows *(from left to right)* Aristotle on horseback threatened with a whip by Campaspe, Alexander's mistress; the Phoenix rising from the flames (Resurrection); Samson breaking the lion's jaw (Redemption); the Pelican in her Piety (Divine Love); Lancelot crossing the Sword Bridge to rescue his Queen; Virgil suspended in his basket by the daughter of the Roman emperor; the Unicorn (Incarnation), pursued by hunters; Gawain on his deathbed with an arrow wound *(image is damaged)*.

The Renaissance vaulting in the second part of the nave, near the chancel, contrasts with the vaulting in the first part: each arch is embellished with a hanging keystone, finely carved. The most remarkable keystone, in the fifth arch over the high altar, is 3m/9.8ft high and weighs 3t; it is a life-size figure of St Peter.

The chancel is enclosed by four arches (late 15C–early 16C) surmounted by a **frieze**★★ in the Flamboyant Gothic style with a delicate decoration of flowers and foliage.

The Gothic style prevails up to 2.75m/9ft from the ground but above that level the Renaissance influence increases to predominate in the **vaulting**★★ by Hector Sohier. The vaulting in each chapel is highly ornate; the pendants look like stalactites.

▷ *At the church entrance, turn left onto rue St-Pierre.*

Rue St-Pierre

This is a lively shopping street. Nos **52** (Postal Museum) and **54**, beautiful **half-timbered houses**★ with steep gables, date from the early 16C; very few have survived in Caen. The profusion of carved decoration and the numerous small statues of saints belong to the Gothic style but there are a few Renaissance elements (balustrades and medallions).

▷ *Continue until rue Froide.*

Église St-Sauveur

pl. Pierre-Bouchard. ○*Open daily 9am–5pm.* ☎*02 31 86 13 11.*

Also known by its old name of Notre-Dame-de-Froide-Rue, St Saviour's church has twin chevets facing rue St-Pierre: Gothic (15C) on the left and Renaissance (1546) on the right. Rue Froide contains interesting old houses, dating from the 15C to the 19C.

▷ *Turn left on rue Paul-Doumer.*

Place de la République

The pedestrian precinct, between place St-Pierre and place de la République, is lively both day and night. Place de la République, which is laid out as a public garden is bordered by beautiful Louis XIII houses (Hôtel Daumesnil at nos **23–25**) and the modern offices of the Préfecture.

▷ *Turn left on rue Jean-Eudes, continue to rue St-Laurent.*

Notre-Dame-de-la-Gloriette, a former Jesuit church standing on r. St-Laurent, was built between 1684 and 1689.

▷ *Turn right on rue St-Laurent, which becomes rue Écuyère. Turn right at rue aux Fromages. Cross rue St-Sauveur.*

Place St-Sauveur

A fine collection of 18C houses borders the square, where the pillory stood until the 19C. At the centre is a statue of Louis XIV as a Roman emperor. The northeast side of the square is the site of the old St Saviour's which was destroyed in 1944.

Turn left and continue to a traffic circle. Follow rue Guillaume-le-Conquérant, which takes you to the Abbaye-aux-Hommes and the Église St-Étienne (described below). To continue the walk, turn right on rue Jean-Marot.

On your way, note the row of attractive houses in rue Jean-Marot; they date from the early 20C.

Turn left on rue St-Martin.

Place St-Martin
Note the statue of Constable Bertrand du Guesclin. Interesting view of the two towers of St-Étienne.

Continue NE along the Fossés St-Julien and turn right onto rue de Géôle.

The 15C half-timbered house (no 31) is called **Maison des Quatrans**.

Rue du Vaugueux
Rue Montoir-Poissonnerie leads to this lovely pedestrian street which has kept its quaint charm: cobblestones, stone and timber houses, old-fashioned street lights.

Return to place St-Pierre.

VISIT

The Abbeys★★

Allow 2hr total.

Abbaye-aux-Hommes★★
espl. Jean-Marie-Louvel.
02 31 30 42 81. Guided tours (1hr30min) daily 9.30am, 11am, 2.30pm, 4pm. Closed 1 Jan, 1 May, 25 Dec.
Despite their different styles, St-Étienne Church and the monastery buildings of the Abbey for Men constitute an historical and architectural unit.

Église St-Étienne★★
This is the church of the abbey founded by William the Conqueror; Lanfranc was the first abbot before being appointed Archbishop of Canterbury and it was probably he who drew up the plans. The church was started in 1066 in the Romanesque style, and was completed in the 13C in the Gothic style (east end, chancel, spires). The building was damaged during the Wars of Religion in the 16C and painstakingly restored in the early 17C by Dom Jehan de Baillehache, the Prior.
Following the Maurist reforms of the Benedictine order (1663) the abbey enjoyed a period of prosperity until the French Revolution: the church was richly furnished and the monastery was rebuilt. In the 19C St-Étienne became a parish church and the monastery was converted for use as a school. Fortunately, the buildings survived the Battle of Caen unscathed.
Romanesque art has produced few more striking compositions than this plain **west front**; there are no ornate porches, no rose windows, only a gable end resting on four sturdy buttresses and pierced by two rows of round-headed windows and three Romanesque doors. Lanfranc seems to have exercised the artistic severity of Ravenna and Lombardy in his native country. The austerity of the west front is, however, tempered by the magnificent soaring towers (11C). The first storey is decorated with fluting, the second with single pierced bays and the third with paired bays. The octagonal spires with their turrets and lancets in the Norman Gothic style were added to the two towers in the 13C; the north tower is finer and more delicate in style.
The vast nave is almost bare of ornament except for the great round-headed arches. The construction of the sexpartite vaulting in the 12C altered the arrangement of the clerestory, which is decorated with fretwork typical of the Norman style. At the west end of the church is the organ (1747) flanked by two telamones.

The lantern tower above the transept crossing was constructed in the 11C but rebuilt early in the 17C. The gallery in the north transept houses a large 18C clock in a carved wooden surround. In the 13C the Romanesque chancel was replaced by a Gothic construction, including an ambulatory and radiating chapel; it was the first of the Norman Gothic chancels and subsequently served as a model. With the Gothic style new decorative motifs were introduced: chevrons on the archivolts, rose windows in the spandrels of the lateral arches, trefoils piercing the tympana of the bays in the galleries, capitals ornamented with crochets and foliage. Note the spacious galleries above the ambulatory and the elegant central arches. The handsome stalls and pulpit are 17C.

In front of the altar is a stone inscribed with an epitaph. The sarcophagus containing the body of William the Conqueror was originally placed beneath the lantern but when the church was sacked by the Huguenots in the 16C ,the Conqueror's remains were scattered; all that remains is a femur which is interred beneath the stone. A monumental 18C paschal candlestick stands on the north side of the altar. The chancel is enclosed by a beautiful 19C wrought-iron screen; the cartouches bear the names and arms of the former abbots, priors and other dignitaries of the abbey.

In the sacristy there hangs an unusual portrait of William the Conqueror, painted in 1708, in which he is made to resemble Henry VIII.

Leave the church by the chancel door and skirt the handsome **east end★★** *of St-Étienne (13C–14C) to reach the gardens in Esplanade Louvel, which have been restored according to the 18C plans.*

Monastery Buildings★

Monastery buildings of the Abbaye-aux-Hommes. Guided tours (1hr30min), circuit A (buildings, cloister and chapter-hall) at 9.30am, 2.30pm, 4pm. Circuit B (buildings, cloister, press, guardroom) at 11am. Additional visits (45min) offered Jul–Aug 10.15am, 3.15pm, 5.15pm. Closed 1 Jan, 1 May, 25 Dec. 2.40€ (no charge Sun). 02 31 30 42 81. www.ville-caen.fr/abbayeauxhommes. Entrance through the town hall.

These fine buildings were designed early in the 18C by Brother Guillaume de la Tremblaye, the great master builder of the Congregation of St Maur; the **woodwork★★** is particularly beautiful.

The east wing comprises the monks' **warming room**, now a municipal exhibition hall; the **chapter house**, formerly a collegiate chapel and now a registry office, is panelled in light oak and hung with 17C paintings; the chapel **sacristy**, panelled in oak, contains a painting by Charles Lebrun (1619–90) *(Moses Confronting an Egyptian Shepherd)* and a collection of Norman headdresses.

The hall, which features 18C stairs with a wrought-iron banister, leads to the **cloisters** (18C), where the groined vaulting centres on octagonal coffers. From the southeast corner of the cloisters there is a very fine **view★★** of the towers of St-Étienne and the south side of the church. Fixed to the door into the church is a dark oak timetable of the offices said by the monks (1744).

A doorway leads into the **parlour**, a large oval room with an unusual elliptical vault and beautiful Louis XV wooden doors. The **refectory**, now used for meetings, is sumptuously decorated with late-18C oak panelling and broken barrel vaulting. Some of the paintings above the door and the blind apertures are by Lépicié, Restout and Ruysdael. The wrought-iron banister of the **grand staircase** is decorated with floral motifs. The bold design has no central support. The remarkable Gothic hall in the courtyard, known as the **guard room★**, was built on the remains of a Gallo-Roman structure and is now used for meetings. The panelled ceiling is shaped like an upturned hull. Originally there were two rooms as the two chimneys suggest.

Allied Troops at the Battle of Caen

Battle of Caen

Two Agonising Months – The battle lasted for over two months. On 6 June 1944 there was a heavy bombing raid; fire raged for 11 days and the central area was burnt out. On 9 July the Canadians, who had taken Carpiquet Airfield, entered Caen from the west but the Germans, who had fallen back to the east bank of the Orne in Vaucelles, began to shell the town. The liberation ceremony took place in Vaucelles on 20 July but German shelling lasted another month.

Under the Conqueror's Protection – On 6 June many people sought shelter in St-Étienne Church. During the battle over 1 500 refugees camped out in the abbey church. An operating theatre was contrived in the refectory of the Lycée Malherbe, which was housed in the monastery buildings of the Abbey for Men. The dead were buried in the courtyard. Some 4 000 people found accommodation in the Hospice of the Good Saviour (Bon Sauveur) nearby. The Allies were warned by the Préfet and the Resistance and these buildings were spared.
The quarries at Fleury, 2km/1mi south of Caen, provided the largest refuge. Despite the cold and the damp, whole families lived like troglodytes until the end of July.

View of the Abbey★★

Walk through the gardens in esplanade Louvel to reach the east side of place Louis-Guillouard near Old St-Étienne Church (Vieux St-Étienne), a charming ruin, with the Jesuit church of Notre-Dame-de-la-Gloriette in the background. This is the best view of the 18C monastery buildings flanking the impressive east end of St-Étienne with its bristling bell turrets, flying buttresses, clustering chapels and steep roofs, topped by the lantern tower and the two soaring spires.

Abbaye-aux-Dames★

pl. Reine-Mathilde. 02 31 06 98 98. Guided tours daily 2.30pm, 4pm. No charge. Closed 1 Jan, 1 May, 25 Dec. See following pages for tours of conventual buildings.

Founded in 1062 by **Queen Matilda**, the Abbey for Women is the sister house to the Abbey for Men. It is located on the northeast side of the old city, c. 2km/1mi from the Abbaye-aux-Hommes. From place de la Reine-Mathilde, the towers of St-Étienne Church can just be seen at the end of rue des Chanoines.

Port of Caen

Although the River Orne has always enabled Caen to serve as a port, no major development took place until the middle of the 19C, when Baron Cachin dug a canal parallel to the river. The canal (12km/7.4mi long) was regulated by several locks and served by an outer basin at Ouistreham. Since then the increased output of the Caen steelworks has required the deepening and widening of the canal and the creation of five more docks: St-Pierre for pleasure boats, the New Dock, the Calix Dock, the Hérouville Dock and the Blainville Dock, which came into use in 1974.

Today the transportation of cereals is the chief function of Caen harbour, the largest one in Basse-Normandie, which can receive ships of up to 19 000t fully laden and up to 30 000t partially laden. Because of its broad range of activities, this port is ranked 11th in France.The opening of a cross-Channel car ferry service on 6 June 1986 has established daily links between Caen-Ouistreham and Portsmouth, catering to an estimated one million passengers every year.

Église de la Trinité★★

Open daily 9am–6pm. 02 31 86 13 11.

The old abbey church, which dates from the 11C, is a building in the Romanesque style. Its original plan was inspired by that of Benedictine abbeys, characterised by sturdy tiered apsidioles. The spires were replaced early in the 18C by heavy balustrades.

The vast nave of nine bays is a fine example of Romanesque art. Broken barrel vaulting marks the transition from the nave into the spacious transept. Adjoining the south transept is an attractive chapel, which is now used as the chapter house. It was built in the 13C replacing two Romanesque chapels similar to the two in the north transept. The late-11C groined vaulting in the chancel covers a magnificent span. In the centre of the chancel is Queen Matilda's tomb, a simple monument consisting of a single slab of black marble, which has survived unscathed despite the Wars of Religion and the Revolution.

The crypt *(access by steps in the chapel in the south transept)* is well preserved. The groined vaulting rests on 16 columns, standing close together, which define five bays. An attempt at historiated decoration can be seen on one of the capitals, illustrating the Last Judgement, in which St Michael is portrayed gathering up the dead as they rise from their graves.

Conventual Buildings

Open daily 2–5.30pm (last visit 1hr before closing. Guided tours (1hr15min) daily 2.30pm, 4pm. Closed 1 Jan, 1 May, 25 Dec. No charge. 02 31 06 98 98.

From the French-style garden in the main **courtyard** one can admire the luminous golden façades. The cloisters (only three sides were completed) are a replica of the one in the Abbey for Men. Leading off them is a small oval room, the washroom *(lavabo)*, decorated with stone pilasters and a carved frieze like those in Greek temples; it is furnished with four black-marble basins set in recesses ornamented with a shell. In the **refectory** *(used as a reception room or as a gallery for temporary exhibitions)*, pilasters with Ionic capitals and two columns which flanked the abbess' chair have survived whereas the oak panelling which covered the lower walls has been removed.

The **Great Hall**, which is the focal point of the whole abbey and leads into the church, is graced by **two flights** of stairs decorated at first-floor level with a cartouche bearing a plant motif; the walls are adorned with portraits of the two last abbesses, Anne de Montmorency and Marie-Aimée de Pontécoulant.

CHÂTEAU★

espl. du Château. Allow 3hr including museums. Open daily. Guided tours Jul–Aug (French and English) run by tourist office. No charge. 02 31 27 14 14. www.chateau-caen.eu.

The imposing citadel dominating the mount was begun by William the Conqueror in 1060 and fortified in 1123 by his son, Henry Beauclerk, who added a mighty keep (demolished in 1793). During the 13C, 14C and 15C it was repeatedly enlarged and reinforced. Throughout the 19C it was used as soldiers' barracks and was severely damaged in the bombardment of Caen in 1944. Since then its massive walls have been restored to their early grandeur. The line of the ramparts has changed little since the days of William the Conqueror. In some places the walls date from the 12C, but most of them were built in the 15C. The two main gateways are protected by barbicans.

Enter the castle by the ramp which approaches the south gate opposite Église St-Pierre.

After passing a round tower, a defensive outwork, one enters the citadel by the town gate *(porte sur la ville)*.
From the terrace (east) and the rampart sentry walk there are fine **views**★ of Église St-Pierre and western Caen as far as the Abbey for Men. On the west side of the gate, behind the Normandy Museum, a platform provides an interesting **view**★ over the southwest sector of the town and the belfries of the many churches.
The north rampart, the first to be restored under the current program, can be visited for a remarkable **view**★ of Caen *(guided tour (35min); times posted at the entry to the Musée de Normandie; no charge)*.
The castle precinct encloses the modern **Musée des Beaux-Arts** *(east)* near the **Porte des Champs** (Field Gate), an interesting example of 14C military architecture; the **Chapelle St-Georges**, a 12C chapel which was altered in the 15C; the **Musée de Normandie** *(west)* in a building which was the residence of the bailiff in the 14C and of the Governor of Caen in the 17C and 18C; a rectangular building, incorrectly called the **Salle de l'Échiquier** (Exchequer Hall), which is a rare example of Norman civil architecture in the reign of Henry Beauclerk and was the great hall of the adjoining ducal palace (foundations only visible); adjoining it was the Normandy Exchequer (the Ducal Law Court). Further north lie the foundations of the keep which was built by Henry Beauclerk and altered in the 13C and 14C; it was a huge square structure, a round tower at each corner, surrounded by a moat which was joined to the castle moat. *You can stroll in the castle moat; descend from the porte des Champs.*

Musée des Beaux-Arts★★

Located within the château, east of St-Pierre gate. Open Wed–Mon 9.30am–6pm. Closed 1 Jan, Easter Sunday, 1 May, Ascension, 1 Nov, 25 Dec. Temporary exhibits 5.20€; no charge 1st Sun of month; permanent collection no charge. 02 31 30 47 70. www.ville-caen.fr/mba.

The Café Mancel offers a pleasant break inside the museum, where you can enjoy a meal or a drink (see Addresses).

Situated within the precinct of William the Conqueror's castle, the Fine Arts Museum offers its collections from a chronological, thematic and geographical point of view. Large religious paintings and imposing historical and allegorical scenes hang in vast halls, bathed in light, whereas works of religious fervour and smaller paintings are essentially displayed in the small cabinets. The large galleries display landscapes, battle scenes and portraits.
The first three rooms on the ground floor are devoted to 15C, 16C and 17C Italian painting: the *Marriage of the Virgin* by Perugino, with a remarkable new frame, a triptych representing the *Virgin and Child Between St George and St James* by Cima da Conegliano; in a room entirely devoted to Veronese, two paintings are of particular interest: the *Temptation of St*

Anthony and *Judith and Holofernes*; also worth noting are *Coriolanus Implored by His Mother* by Il Guercino and *Glaucus and Scylla* by Rosa Salvatore.

The next room deals with 17C French painting with outstanding works by Philippe de Champaigne *(Louis XIII's Vow)* and also religious or mythological paintings by Vouet, Vignon, La Hyre and Le Brun.

Three intimate rooms are devoted to Dutch and Flemish 17C painting with works such as *A Seascape* by Solomon van Ruysdael, *Virgin and Child* by Roger van der Weyden and *Abraham and Melchizedek* by Rubens.

In the gallery devoted to the 18C are displayed works by French and Italian portrait and landscape painters: Hyacinthe Rigaud *(Portrait of Marie Cadenne)*, François Boucher *(Young Shepherd in a Landscape)*, Locatelli, Lalemand, Tournières.

On the lower level, the various aspects and the evolution of painting during the 19C and the early 20C are depicted through works by Romantic painters (Géricault, Delacroix, Isabey), Realists (Courbet: *The Lady with the Jewels*, Ribot), landscape painters (Corot, Dupré), Impressionists (Vuillard: *Portrait of Suzanne Desprez*, Bonnard, Dufy, Van Dongen: *Portrait of Madame T Raulet*), and Cubist painters (Gleizes, Villon, Meitzinger). Local artists are also represented: Cals, Fouace, Gernez, Lemaître, Lépine, Lebourg, Rame.

Innovations by contemporary painters such as Tobey *(Appearances)*, Mitchell (*Fields*, 1990), Soulages, Dubuffet *(Migration)*, Vieira da Silva, Szenez, Asse and Deschamps illustrate the different post-war trends: Conceptual art, Abstract landscape, Abstract art, Environmental art. From one end to the other, the museum thus presents an impressive chronology of the history of painting.

Musée de Normandie★

Located within the château, west of the St-Pierre gate. Open Jun–Oct daily 9.30am–6pm; Nov–May Wed–Mon 9.30am–6pm. Closed 1 Jan, Easter, 1 May, Ascension, 1 Nov, 25 Dec. No charge. 02 31 30 47 60. www.musee-de-normandie.eu.

The history and traditions of Normandy are illustrated by the presentation of the many archaeological and ethnographical exhibits.

Abraham and Melchizedek by Rubens, Musée des Beaux-Arts

The first section is devoted to the prehistoric period up to the arrival of the Vikings in 911 and concentrates on the culture and technology of the era: excavated artefacts, miniature replica of the burial mound at Fontenay-le-Marmion, statue of a mother goddess found at St-Aubin-sur-Mer, weapons and jewellery found in medieval cemeteries (tomb of a metalworker buried with his tools).

The second section follows the evolution of agriculture: land use (models comparing different types of cultivation and farms), agricultural techniques (display of ploughs, scythes and millstones).

The third section is devoted to crafts and industrial activities: stock breeding, ceramics (jugs, funerary ornaments and decorative ridge tiles), wood (beautifully carved marriage chests), metallurgy (iron and copper work: craftsman's tools, copperware from Villedieu-les-Poêles), textiles (costumes, headdresses and bridalware in silk lace); the last room concentrates on the work of the candlemaker (interesting collection of candles for Easter, funerals and as votive offerings) as well as ceremonial articles belonging to the different brotherhoods (gold thread embroidery and tintenelles, the tiny hand bells used in processions by the Brothers of Charity).

Musée de la Poste et des Techniques de Communication

52 r. St-Pierre. ○*Open Tue–Sat mid-Jun to mid-Sept 10am–noon, 2–6pm; mid-Sept–mid-Jun 1.30–5.30pm.* ○*Closed public holidays.* ⊕*2.50€.* ℘*02 31 50 12 20. www.ville-caen.fr/museedelaposte.* This Postal and Telecommunications Museum, in a lovely half-timbered 16C house, illustrates the history of the postal service through documents and equipment.

Le Mémorial★★

Allow 3hr. Espl. Général-Eisenhower. ♿○*Open mid-Feb–mid-Nov daily 9am–7pm; rest of the year Tue–Sun 9.30am–6pm (last entry 1hr15min before closing).* ○*Closed 1st 3 weeks of* Jan and 25 Dec. ⊕*17.50€.* ℘*02 31 06 06 45. www.memorial-caen.fr.* ℹ*Directions to the memorial are signposted from the centre-city and from the Péripherique Nord.*

👨‍👧 *A day-care facility welcomes young children while their parents tour the Memorial.*

The memorial erected by the city, which in 1944 was at the centre of the Battle of Normandy, takes the form of a Museum for Peace; it is primarily a place of commemoration and of permanent meditation on the links between human rights and the maintenance of peace.

The façade of the sober building of Caen stone, facing Esplanade Dwight-Eisenhower, is marked by a fissure which evokes the destruction of the city and the breakthrough of the Allies in the Liberation of France and Europe from the Nazi yoke. It stands on the site of the bunker of W Richter, the German general, who on 6 June faced the British-Canadian forces.

The main events of World War II, the causes and the issues at stake, are presented in the light of the latest historical analysis. A particularly imaginative display, centred on a spiral ramp, on such themes as the inter-war years and the advance of Fascism; the use of extensive archive material, including a gripping panoramic projection of D-Day, seen simultaneously from the Allied and the German standpoints, as well as moving testimonies by witnesses of and participants in the drama, confers on this presentation of our recent past the authenticity of living experience.

The film *Hope* uses strong images and original music by Jacques Loussier to trace the alternating outbreaks of war and peace which have followed.

A walk to the Vallée du Mémorial will enable visitors to see the Parc de la Colline aux Oiseaux, in which the Floralies de la Paix has been created. The **Mur de la Liberté** (Wall of Freedom) pays tribute to the hundreds of thousands of American soldiers who fought for freedom in Europe.

▷ *Return to place St-Pierre.*

ADDITIONAL SIGHTS

St-Nicolas Cemetery★

23 r. St-Nicholas. Open daily Mar–Oct 8am–6pm; Nov–Feb 8am–5pm. No charge. Park in the car park to the right of the church.

St Nicholas' Church (deconsecrated) was built late in the 11C by the monks of the Abbey for Men and has not been altered since. The west door is protected by a beautiful triple-arched Romanesque porch, an exceptional feature in Normandy.

The church is surrounded by an old graveyard (entrance left of the west front); one may stroll among the mossy tombstones under the shade of the trees and admire the magnificent apse at the east end beneath its steep stone roof.

Église St-Jean

Place St-Ouen.

The fine Flamboyant Gothic building was begun in the 14C, and repaired in the 15C. The bell tower, of which the base and first storey are 14C, was inspired by the tower of St Peter but, owing to the instability of the marshy ground, the spire and the belfry were never built, nor was the central tower; the lower courses of its second storey were capped with a dome.

The vast nave has a remarkable Flamboyant triforium and a highly ornate cylindrical **lantern tower**★ over the transept crossing. The highly venerated statue of Our Lady of Protection dates from the 17C. In the south transept there is an old retable (17C) from the Carmes Convent depicting the Annunciation and bearing statues of St Joseph and St Teresa of Ávila. In 1964 a statue of Joan of Arc was transferred from Oran to a site near the east end of the church in place de la Résistance.

Église St-Julien

1 r. Malfilâtre. Open Mon–Fri 9.30am–noon, 2–5pm; Sat 9.30am–noon. 02 31 85 44 53.

The old church, which was destroyed in 1944, was replaced in 1958 by this modern building. The sanctuary wall, elliptical in shape, forms a huge piece of latticework like that of a stained-glass window.

EXCURSIONS

Cintheaux

15km/9mi. From Caen take N 158 S – allow 30min.

The village, renowned for its late 12C church, stands on the southern edge of the Caen countryside, in an old mining area marked by solitary slag heaps.

The road from Caen to Falaise passes through country laboriously recaptured during the Battle of Normandy between 8 and 17 August 1944 by the Canadian 1st Army (Gaumesnil cemetery) and its Polish units (Langannerie cemetery).

Troarn

14km/8.5mi – allow 30min.

Leave Caen going E and then take N 175. In Troarn take rue de l'Abbaye (second turn on the right after the church).

This little town, which was founded in 1048 by Roger de Montgomery, contains the remains of a 13C abbey.

DRIVING TOURS

1 NORTH OF CAEN

Round-trip of 31km/19.2mi – allow half a day.

From Caen take D 7 and at the top of the hill, turn right on D 401, then D 60 to the left.

The road bends to the right and there is a panoramic view of Caen.

Biéville-sur-Orne

The blind arcades and oculi which decorate the west front of the church recall the architecture of Tuscany.

Take the road west to Épron.

Épron

This small locality, which was razed in 1944, has been called the Village of the Radio since 1948. The origin of the nickname was a radio programme which sought to determine which of France's

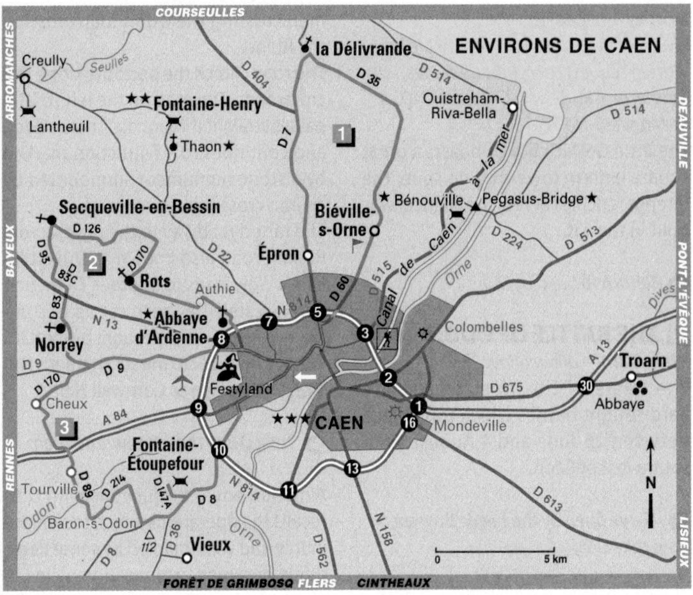

départements had been most severely damaged. Calvados was named, and a lottery draw among ten communes fell to Epron. The village was rebuilt thanks to a collection of small change taken up on its behalf.

2 CHURCHES AND ABBEYS

35km/21mi – allow 2hr

From Caen take D 9 west towards Bayeux on rue de Bayeux and then rue du Général-Moulin. Halfway up a hill on the outskirts of the town turn right onto the road to the abbey.

Abbaye d'Ardenne★

Open Tue–Sun 2–6pm. Guided tour Sat–Sun of convent every 30 min. No charge. Leave the car at the main gate (12C). 02 31 29 37 37. www.imec-archives.com.

The abbey, which was founded in the 12C by the Premonstratensians, fell into ruin during the 19C but has recently benefited from a major restoration project. An exhibit describing its history can be seen at its sister abbey of Mondaye. In the first courtyard stands a huge 13C tithe barn *(back left)* with aisles which is covered by a single asymmetrical wooden roof *(restored – open during temporary exhibitions).* The 13C **abbey church**★ has been damaged on the outside but the nave is a very pure example of the Norman Gothic style.

Since 1998, the abbey has housed a major archive of French publications. The abbey church is now a research library.

Drive west to Rots via Authie.

Rots

The **church** here has an attractive Romanesque west front; the nave dates from the same period; the chancel is 15C.

Take D 170 north; in Rosel turn left onto D 126.

Secqueville-en-Bessin

The 11C **church** has a fine three-storey tower and a 13C spire. The nave and transept are decorated with blind arcading.

Take D 93 and D 83 south.

Norrey-en-Bessin

Church. Guided tour available on written request to M. Roland Audes, Mairie, pl. Charles-de-Gaulle, 14740 St-Manvieu-Norrey.

The little Gothic **church** boasts a great square lantern tower but no spire; the interior is richly carved; the chancel was built in the 13C.

Return to Caen by D 9.

3 THE BATTLE OF ODON

37km/23mi – allow allow 2hr.

The name of this river recalls the hard-fought battles which took place between 26 June and 4 August 1944 southwest of Caen.

Leave Caen by the rue de Bayeux, then take D 9.

The road skirts the airfield which the 12th SS Panzers held for three days, from 4 to 7 July, against the Canadian 3rd Division.

After another 3km/2mi bear left on D 170; in Cheux turn left behind the church onto D 89; after crossing N 175, at the top of a slight rise, follow D 89 round to the right and straight through Tourville.

This is the line of the British advance, which began on 26 June in pouring rain at Tilly-sur-Seulles *(northwest)*; the objective was the River Orne to the southeast. A memorial has been erected *(right)* to pay tribute to the men of the 15th Scottish Division who fell here.

Just when it seems that the road has reached the floor of the Odon Valley it drops into a rocky ravine, hitherto hidden by thickets; the river has created a second valley within the main valley. It is easy to see what a valuable line of defence this natural obstacle would have been and to appreciate the difficulties of the British troops exposed to heavy fire from the Germans on the far side of the valley. In fact the British lost more men crossing the Odon than crossing the Rhine.

The road climbs the opposite slope to a crossroads. The road on the left (D 214) passes straight through Baron-sur-Odon and continues to a T-junction marked by a stone monument surmounted by an iron cross (*right*).

The raised roadway to the right, an old Roman road also known as Duke William's Way, leads to another T-junction where a stele has been set up to commemorate the battles fought by the 43rd Wessex Division. To the south stands **Hill 112** later known as Cornwall Hill.

Take D 8 to the left towards Caen.

A monument at the junction with D 36 recalls the operations which took place in July and were marked by some fierce duels between armoured vehicles. A night attack on 15 June took place by the light of an artificial moon created by the reflection of searchlights on low cloud.

Turn left onto D 147A.

Near a farm on the right the Château de Fontaine-Étoupefour comes into view.

Château de Fontaine-Étoupefour

Access by a track on the right beyond the farm. Guided tours (1hr) Jul–Sept Sun–Tue 2–6.30pm. Closed 26–28 Aug. 5€. 02 31 26 73 20.

Nicolas d'Escoville, who built the Hôtel d'Escoville in Caen, owned this castle. It is surrounded by a moat spanned by a drawbridge which leads to an elegant 15C gatehouse bristling with turrets and pinnacles. The dining room is hung with three interesting paintings of hunting scenes. On the far side of the paved courtyard stand the ruins of one of the two main blocks (late-16C), currently undergoing restoration.

The refectory houses an exhibit about the battle of Hill 112 in 1944, of which the château was the centre.

Return to D 8 to reach Caen.

ADDRESSES

STAY

Hôtel Bernières– *50 r. de Bernières. 02 31 86 01 26. www.hotelbernieres.com.17 rooms. 6€.* The welcome at this hotel is friendly, the breakfast room and lounge are charming and the rooms nicely decorated. All is touched up with bouquets of dried flowers.

Hôtel St-Étienne – *2 r. de l'Académie. 02 31 86 35 82. www.hotel-saint-etienne.com. 11 rooms. 6.50€.* This house, dating to the 1789 Revolution, is located in a quiet district close to the Abbaye-aux-Hommes. Note the fine wooden staircase with its beautiful patined woodwork and the smart bedrooms, some of them with fireplaces. Breakfast served in the dining room.

Hôtel du Château – *5 av. du 6-Juin. 02 31 86 15 37. www.hotel-chateau-caen.com. 24 rooms. 8€.* Well located in the town centre, between the marina and the château. Rooms are small but pleasant, painted in pastel tones.

Hôtel la Glycine – *11 pl. du Commando no.4, 14970 Bénouville. 02 31 44 61 94. www.la-glycine.com. 35 rooms. 8€. Restaurant.* Just a short walk from "Pegasus Bridge", this welcoming hotel offers pleasant lodgings and traditional cuisine.

Hôtel du Havre – *11 r. du Havre. 02 31 86 19 80. www.hotelduhavre.com. 19 rooms. 6€.* Located near La Prairie and its racecourse, this post-war hotel offers modern, colourful and well-soundproofed rooms at very attractive prices.

Hôtel Quatrans – *17 r. Gémare. 02 31 86 25 57. www.hotel-des-quatrans.com. 47 rooms. 8€.* A stone's throw from the town centre, this family hotel offers functional rooms enlivened by bright colours. Rooms at the rear are quieter.

– **Best Western Hôtel Moderne** – *116 bd Mar.-Leclerc. 02 31 86 04 23. www.hotel-caen.com. 40 rooms. 14€.* Discreet post-war building with regularly spruced-up rooms. A view over the rooftops from the 5th floor breakfast room.

EAT

Le Bouchon du Vaugueux – *12 r. Graindorge. 02 31 44 26 26. Closed 3 weeks in Aug, Sun and Mon. Reservations required.* This popular tavern *(bouchon)* is situated near the château and old Caen. Two fixed-price menus are listed on the *carte du jour.*

Maître Corbeau – *8 r. Buquet. 02 31 93 93 00. www.maitre-corbeau.com. Closed 3 weeks in Aug, 1 Jan and 25 Dec.* This place is entirely dedicated to cheese: boxes, adverts, implements, etc. Of course, your task is to choose between this cheese and that cheese, hot cheese, cold cheese and warm cheese! The establishment's generous helpings draw local connoisseurs.

Le Carlotta – *16 quai Vendeuvre. 02 31 86 68 99. www.lecarlotta.fr. Closed Sun.* Art Deco-inspired brasserie serving meats and a wide range of seafood.

L'Embroche – *17 r. Porte-au-Berger. 02 31 93 71 31. Closed Sat lunch, Monday lunch and Sun. Reservations advisable.* This spot in the Vaugueux district has three specialities: a camembert cheese on lettuce dressed with Calvados, steak with a caramelised balsamic sauce, and *tripes Père Michel.* Good selection of cheese and wine.

L'Insolite – *16 r. du Vaugueux at the foot of the château. 02 31 43 83 87. Closed Sun–Mon except Jul–Aug. Reservations advisable.* Take the time to discover this half-timbered 16C house with its unconventional interior, mixing the rustic and the retro: frescoes, mirrors, dried flowers. On your plate, seafood. Heated terrace in winter, and a basement cigar room.

Saint-Andrew's – *9 quai de Juillet. 02 31 86 26 80. http://restaurant.st.andrew.free.fr. Reservations advised.* This is a good place to relax after a stroll along the Orne. In a décor reminiscent of an English pub, you will find a traditional menu, carefully prepared from local products.

– **Auberge de l'Île Enchantée** – *1 r. St-André, 14123 Fleury-sur-Orne, 4km/2.5mi S of Caen. 02 31 52 15 52. www.aubergelileenchantee.com.* Situated by the River Orne, this places offers a warm welcome, serving gourmet French cuisine.

Café Mancel – *Le Château. ℘02 31 86 63 64. www.cafemancel.com.* This café and shop, whose name celebrates the great patron of the museum, offers high-quality local produce, as well as products from Italy, Flanders, Holland and England, partners in the museum.

Stiffler – *72 r. St-Jean. ℘02 31 86 08 94. www.stifflertraiteur.com.* This magnificent pastry shop offers specialties such as the celebrated ***charlotte aux fruits de saison***, the ***bavaroise au chocolat***, or the ***méringue aux amandes***. Pause to enjoy the bounty. The delicatessan counter offers delicious lunch dishes and salads.

NIGHTLIFE

Caen is a highly convivial and lively town. In the evening, tour the small pubs nd restaurants in the Vaugueux district.

Centre dramatique national de Normandie (Comédie de Caen) – *32 r. des Cordes. ℘02 31 46 27 29. www.cdn-normandie.com.* Classical plays alternate with contemporary ones. Two halls, one of 300 seats and one of 700 seats.

Théâtre de Caen – *135 bd du Mar.-Leclerc. ℘02 31 30 48 00. www.theatre.caen.fr.* Operas, ballets and contemporary dance alternate with theatre, classical concerts, jazz sessions and traditional music programmes. Concerts are free on Saturday at 5pm Oct–May, and some evenings in the Café Cour.

SHOPPING

Librairie Guillaume – *98 r. St-Pierre.* The carved-wood façade of this splendid bookshop dates from 1902. There is a choice of books about the region and, on the upper floor, a first-rate selection of antique books.

Poupinet – *8 r. St-Jean.* To taste authentic ***tripes à la mode de Caen***, you must visit Poupinet, where you can buy this speciality put up in jars. You can also find a range of regional specialties including pâtés, terrines, country-style blood puddings, pork ears in jelly, and prepared dishes of highest quality.

MARKETS

Marché St-Pierre (Sun am), rue de Bayeux (Tue am), boulevard Leroy (Wed and Sat am), boulevard de la Guérinière (Thu am), Marché St-Sauveur (Fri), Christmas Market (Dec).

LEISURE

Hippodrome de Caen – *La Prairie. ℘02 33 42 41 07. Open Mar–Jun, Sept–Nov. Closed Jul–Aug.* This racecourse, nearly 2km/1mi long, in located in the heart of Caen. On the second floor, the panoramic restaurant offers a lovely view of the city. Visits are organised on mornings when races are held (30 times a year). Absolutely worth a visit.

Festyland – *rte de Caumont, Boulevard Péripherique N, exit for Carpiquet, 14760 Bretteville-sur-Odon. ℘02 31 75 04 04. www.festyland.com. Check website for opening times.* This leisure park offers typical fairground rides, including big attractions such as *La Vallée aux Dinosaures, Le 1066, Le Carrousel des Arts, Le Valhala, Le Château de Mathilde, Les Cabines, Le Petit-Creux* and more. Great for a day out with the kids.

PARKS AND GARDENS

Caen is a "green city" with parks and gardens open at 8am during the week and 10am on weekends. Tours and exhibits throughout the summer months.

The **Prairie**, a 90ha/36-acre green space in the centre of the city, dates from the Middle Ages. The small lake is frequented by acquatic birds.

Parc floral de la Colline-aux-oiseaux, *av. Amiral-Montbatten.* Opened for the 50th anniversary of the Normandy Landings, this park lies on an old dump, hence the name which means bird hill.

Jardin Botanique – *5 pl. Blot.* This 300-year-old garden is the oldest in Caen and contains remarkable greenhouses with exotic plants.

Le parc Michel-d'Ornano, part of the Abbaye-aux-Dames, is a superb garden *à la française*.

Clécy★

This township, the tourist centre of the Suisse Normande, is close to some of the most picturesque beauty spots in the Orne Valley.

- **Population:** 1 246.
- **Michelin Map:** 303: J-6 – Local map, *see La SUISSE NORMANDE, p380.*
- **Info:** Place du Tripot. 02 31 69 79 95. www.suisse-normande.com.
- **Location:** Clécy is halfway between Caen (40km/24.8mi N) and Flers (23km/14.3mi S) via D 562.
- **Don't Miss:** The many scenic walks, with panoramic views.
- **Timing:** Spend the day enjoying the scenery on foot.
- **Kids:** The Model Railway Museum is a sure bet.

SIGHT

Musée du Chemin de fer miniature

Rue d'Ermington, Clécy. Guided tours (45min), call for times. 5.50€ (children 3.50€) 02 31 69 07 13. www.chemin-fer-miniature-clecy.com. Model locomotives and wagons.

DRIVING TOURS

Croix de la Faverie★

45min round-trip on foot.

Leave from the car park between the post office and the church and head towards La Faverie Cross. At the stop sign turn right; then turn left and continue to climb. Follow the signposts to the cross.

Opposite the cross, a path leads to a grove of pine trees *(picnic site)*, with a very pretty **view**: the Rochers des Parcs overlook the Lande Viaduct.

From Clécy take the route de La Serverie. Cross the bridge over the Orne and the level crossing; after 100m/110yd turn right. A sign (left) shows the start of the path to the Sugar Loaf.

Le Pain de Sucre★

Allow 3hr round-trip on foot. This path *(blazed with red and white markers)* climbs up a valley on the right bank of

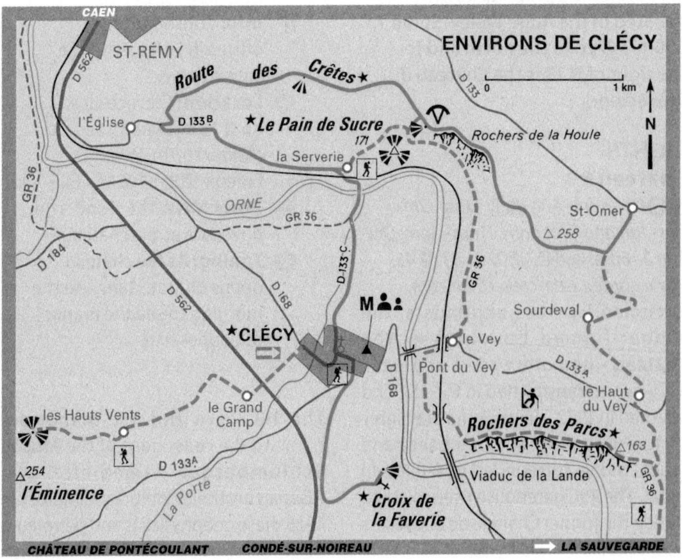

a stream. Cross the stream. Entering the copse, keep to the right of a trail that rises obliquely to the right and leads to the foot of a hillock and a vast **panorama** of the Orne.

Going down, on reaching the foot of the hillock, along the slope opposite the one you came by, follow a winding path (well marked) which, passing below the Rochers de la Houle, comes out at the rustic church of Vey.

From Clécy Church take D 133C towards La Serverie. After the bridge, turn left to St-Rémy; after 1.5km/0.9mi turn sharp right and follow the "Route des Crêtes."

Route des Crêtes★

8km/5mi – allow 45min.

Follow the wooded banks overlooking the valley of the Orne. Bear left on the road *(sharp bend)* which returns to St-Omer. *See Michelin Green Guide France.*

ADDRESSES

EAT

La Guinguette à tartines – *1 Le bord de l'Orne. 02 31 69 89 38. Closed Oct–Mar.* Sandwiches and simple dishes served in a relaxed atmosphere. On the banks of the Orne, enjoy the wide terrace or the dining room with panoramic views. Miniature golf, rental of kayaks.

LEISURE

Vélorail – *02 31 69 39 30. www.rails-suissenormande.fr. Open Jul–Aug daily 10.30am–6pm. Apr–Jun and Sept–Oct Mon–Fri 2–4pm, weekends and public holidays 10.30am–6pm. 13€ for a 4-person railbike (1hr30min trip).* Leave Condé via D 911 towards Pont-d'Ouilly, park at the train station of Pont-Érambourg. You can take a 6km/3.6mi journey by railbike *(vélorail)* until Berjou, 13km/8mi round-trip.

Crèvecœur-en-Auge

Crèvecœur is a pleasant town situated in the Auge Valley. Some 500m/547yd to the north and to the right of N 13 is the Château de Crèvecœur.

- **Population:** 525.
- **Michelin Map:** 303: M-5 – Local map, *see Pays d'AUGE, p85.*
- **Info:** Consult tourist offices in Lisieux and the Pays d'Auge.
- **Location:** Crèvecœur is on N 13 between Caen (43km/26.7mi W) and Lisieux (20km/12.4mi E).
- **Don't Miss:** The wonderful dovecote at the château.
- **Timing:** As the château opens only at 11am, use the morning to see the manor of Coupesarte.

SIGHTS

Château★

Open Jul–Aug daily 11am–7pm; Apr–Jun and Sept daily 11am–6pm; Oct Sun 2–6pm. 6€. 02 31 63 02 45. www.chateau-de-crevecoeur.com.

Encircled by trees and moats, the timber-framed buildings of the **château** – its motte was erected in the 11C – were transformed in the 15C and restored in 1972. They now form a highly picturesque sight: an outer bailey and feudal motte surrounded by a filled-in moat. The 16C gatehouse used to stand beside the former Château de Beuvilliers near Lisieux.

The 16C barn and 15C manor are home to the collections of the **Musée Schlumberger**, named after two Alsatian brothers Conrad and Marcel; in 1928 these geophysicists and petroleum engineers invented the continuous electric logging of boreholes, a technique that was to be extended to countries all over the world.

The museum displays equipment used in oil drilling and prospecting. The **dovecote**, a remarkable construction, is square shaped. Note the projecting eaves formed by the shingled roofing, visible on all four sides of the building. On the side facing winds, is a shelf from which the pigeons are released. The interior woodwork is pierced with 1 500 pigeon-holes *(boulins)*.

The 12C chapel features oak framework in the shape of an upturned hull, as well as fragments of a medieval wall painting. The farm buildings contain the second part of the museum, devoted to **Normandy architecture**, which presents examples of traditional timber-framed architecture from the Pays d'Auge. The History Room (Salle d'Histoire) displays miscellaneous objects retracing the history of Crèvecœur-en-Auge over the centuries.

EXCURSION

Manoir de Coupesarte★

15km/9mi SE. Leave Crèvecœur-en-Auge by D 16 towards St-Pierre-sur-Dives. At Mesnil-Mauger, turn left onto D 47. Cross Authieux-Papion, then just after St-Julien-le-Faucon, turn right onto D 47. Coupesarte is 1.5km/0.9mi further. ***Exterior only:*** *Open daily 9am–7pm. No charge. 02 31 63 82 12.*

This charming half-timbered residence (*interior closed to the public*) surrounded by water on three sides is the main house of a farm building. The construction goes back to the end of the 15C or beginning of the 16C. From the field on the left beyond the small lock there is a good view of the half-timbered façade with its two corner turrets reminiscent of watchtowers.

Deauville★★★

Deauville, a popular resort since the mid-19C, is known for the luxury and refinement of its various establishments and the elegance of its entertainments. Events of the the summer season include racing (including the Grand Prix), the polo world championship, regattas, tennis and golf tournaments, galas, and the international yearling fair. Every year, in early September, the city hosts the prestigious American Film Festival.

- **Population:** 3 973.
- **Michelin Map:** 303: M-3 – Local map, *see Pays d'AUGE, p85.*
- **Info:** Place de la Mairie. 02 31 14 40 00. www.deauville.org.fr.
- **Location:** Located 94km/59mi from Rouen and 43km/27mi from Le Havre, Deauville lies on the Côte Fleurie. The Touques estuary separates Deauville from the older resort, Trouville.
- **Don't Miss:** The pretty villas as well as the view from Mont Canisy and the coastal road from Honfleur to Cabourg.
- **Timing:** Try to see Deauville in the morning; afternoons bring crowds.

VISIT

The Resort

The season in Deauville opens in July and ends with the Deauville Grand Prix on the fourth Sunday in August and the Golden Cup of the international polo championship. Horse racing takes place alternately at La Touques (flat racing) and Clairefontaine (flat racing and steeplechasing) and the international yearling sales are held in Deauville in August. Out of season the resort accommodates numerous conventions as well as seminars.

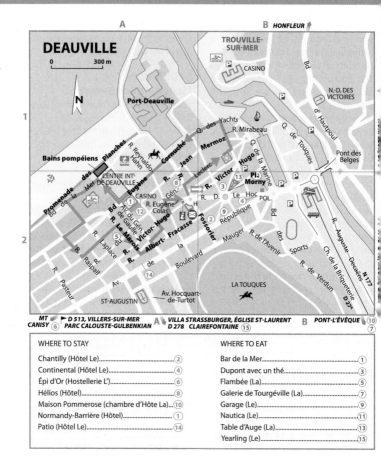

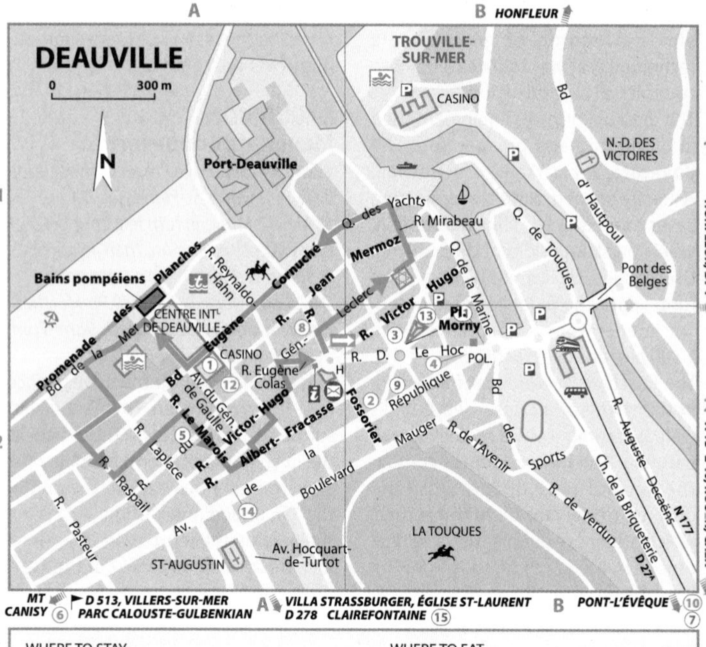

WHERE TO STAY

- Chantilly (Hôtel Le) ... 2
- Continental (Hôtel Le) ... 4
- Épi d'Or (Hostellerie L') ... 6
- Hélios (Hôtel) ... 8
- Maison Pommerose (chambre d'Hôte La) ... 10
- Normandy-Barrière (Hôtel) ... 1
- Patio (Hôtel Le) ... 14

WHERE TO EAT

- Bar de la Mer ... 1
- Dupont avec un thé ... 3
- Flambée (La) ... 5
- Galerie de Tourgéville (La) ... 7
- Garage (Le) ... 9
- Nautica (Le) ... 11
- Table d'Auge (La) ... 13
- Yearling (Le) ... 15

The coming and going on the **Planches** – a wooden plank promenade running the whole length of the beach – is the most distinctive feature of beach life in Deauville. Lined with elegant buildings such as the Pompeian Baths and the Soleil Bar, where stars and celebrities like to be seen, the Planches draws fashionable strollers.

Between the casino and the Planches, the Centre International de Deauville (C.I.D.) is a remarkable ensemble of suspended gardens, fountains and transparent façades which welcomes all kinds of professional, cultural and festive events. A walk along the seafront boulevard Eugène-Cornuché will prove that Deauville is not called the "beach of flowers" *(plage fleurie)* for nothing.

The yacht marina on the Touques and the Yacht Club strike an elegant note.

A little **tourist train** will take you on a guided tour of the city (with commentary), and the tourist office has information about walking tours and bicycle trails.

Deauville Port

The port is enclosed on the west side by a breakwater extending from the beach to the mouth of the Touques and on the east by a jetty marking the port entrance to the channel. The deep access channel means that the port is accessible 80% of the time. It consists of three docks, entered through a double lock, which provide deep water moorings and ample capacity: 800 berths along 4 000m/4 376yd of quays. At the centre are the slate-roofed marinas, the Deauville harbour master's office, an annexe of the Marina Deauville Club (quai des Marchands, near the lock) and space for shops and hotel services.

DRIVING TOURS

The mileage given is calculated from the Pont des Belges, which links Deauville to Trouville.

In summer, the coast between Honfleur and Cabourg is one of the busiest in France, but is lovely despite the crowds.

Le Mont Canisy★

Round-trip of 15km/9mi (about 45min).

Leave Deauville to the SW by the D 513.

Bénerville Church stands overlooking a crossroads.

Turn left up the hill before the church; after about 200m/219yd by the town hall turn left again. At the top bear onto a local road leading to Mont Canisy. Leave the car by a gate.

A path leads to the blockhouses where the view extends from Cap de la Hève to the Orne estuary.

Return to the car and go right.

Once beyond the more recent housing estates of Canisy there are views over the Touques Valley as the road descends to the St-Arnoult crossroads.

Turn left onto D 278 to Deauville.

The Corniche Normande: From Deauville-Trouville to Honfleur★★

21km/13mi – allow allow 1hr.

Leave Deauville-Trouville to the NE by D 513.

This very pleasant tour passes through magnificent scenery and affords views over the Seine estuary between gaps in the hedges and orchards.
Handsome properties are scattered along the road. Just before Villerville there is a fine view of the oil refineries on the estuary. To the left Le Havre can be recognised by its thermal power station and the belfry of St Joseph's Church.

Villerville

This lively seaside resort, with its nearby meadows and woods, has kept its rural character. Notice the Romanesque belfry on the local church. From the terrace overlooking the beach there is a view of Le Havre and Cap de la Hève. The road is thereafter narrow with hidden bends.

Cricqueboeuf

The 12C **church**, with its ivy-covered walls, is a familiar feature on travel posters. The countryside around, with its apple orchards, grazing cows and tranquil ponds, adds to the emblematic beauty.

In Pennedepie, take D 62; after 2.5km/1.5mi turn right onto D 279.

Barneville

The church, tucked away in the greenery, is backed by the magnificent park of the 18C château.

Take D 279 N; after 4km/2.5mi turn left by a château to reach Honfleur via the Côte de Grâce.

12C church in Cricqueboeuf

©World Pictures/Photoshot

Côte de Grâce★★
See HONFLEUR – Additional Sights, p132.

Honfleur★★
See HONFLEUR, p127.

The Côte Fleurie: From Trouville-Deauville to Cabourg

To Cabourg: 19km/12mi.

Leave Deauville to the SW by D 513.

Bénerville-sur-Mer and Blonville-sur-Mer
The hillsides are dotted with villas overlooking a long sandy beach.

Blonville-sur-Mer
Its sweeping sandy beach stretches to the slopes of Mont Canisy. At Blonville, there is an amusement park near the sea as well as extensive sports facilities. The Chapelle Notre-Dame de l'Assomption houses some modern frescoes, the work of the artist **Jean-Denis Maillart**.

Villers-sur-Mer
Musée Paléontologique. Open daily Jul–Aug 9am–7pm; Mar–Jun and Sept–Oct 9.30am–12.30pm, 2–6pm; Nov–Feb 9.30am–12.30pm, 2–5.30pm. Closed Sun afternoon Nov–Jan (except school holidays), 1 Jan, 25 Dec. No charge. 02 31 87 01 18. www.villers-sur-mer.fr.
This elegant seaside resort with its casino and excellent sports facilities is known for its large beach and its wooded hilly countryside crisscrossed with small paths leading down to the town centre. The beachside promenade incorporates a signpost indicating the passage of the Greenwich meridian. The **Musée Paléontologique** *(access through the tourist office on place Mermoz)* has exhibits of fossils and stuffed birds from the area together with a stone armchair and seashells which belonged to Ferdinand Postel, artist and photographer who lived in Villers from 1880 to 1917 and who collected fossils along the area's limestone cliffs.
Just before Houlgate, on a downhill hairpin bend, a viewing table offers a **panorama** from the mouth of the River Dives to the mouth of the River Orne.

Falaise des Vaches Noires★
Between Villers-sur-Mer and Houlgate, the Auberville plateau ends in a crumbling and much-eroded cliff face. It is best to walk along the beach at low tide *(about 2hr on foot round-trip)* to enjoy the panorama, which extends from Trouville to Luc-sur-Mer and over most of the Seine bay.
In places large pieces of limestone have broken away from the cliff top and piled up at the base where they have been colonised by seaweed to form fantastic shapes; these are the Black Cows (Vaches Noires). Fossils found on these cliffs form a large part of the collection at the Villers-sur-Mer museum.

Houlgate
Houlgate is set in the verdant Drochon Valley; the shady avenues and the late-19C houses and gardens, in excellent states of conservation, add to the overall charm of this resort, one of the first to appear on the Côte Fleurie, in 1851.
The promenade Rolland-Garros overlooks the fine sandy beach, which is popular for bathing, and continues to the east towards the cliffs of the **Vaches Noires**. The road runs along the coast and, before Dives-sur-Mer, passes in front of a monument commemorating the departure of **Duke William** for the conquest of England.

Dives-sur-Mer★
See DIVES-SUR-MER, p122.

Cabourg
See CABOURG, p97.

Head to Cabourg via D 45.

ADDRESSES

STAY

⊖ **Hôtel Le Patio** – *180 av. de la République. ☎02 31 88 25 07. www.hotel-lepatio.fr. Closed Feb. 13 rooms.* ☕. The name tells it all: this century-old edifice with an immaculate façade possesses an enticing, flower-filled patio where breakfasts are served as soon as the weather warms up. The rooms, each one different, are regularly spruced up.

⊖⊖ **Chambre d'hôte La Maison Pommerose** – *St-Sylvestre-l'Église, 27260 St-Sylvestre-de-Cormeilles. ☎02 31 57 13 05. www.pommerose.com. 3 rooms.* ☕. *Meals*⊖⊖. Nestled in a thicket of green, this magnificent Norman residence will charm you with its comfort. The stone fireplace warms rooms decorated with tile floors and carved woodwork. Pretty garden with apple trees. Breakfasts are delicious.

⊖⊖ **Hôtel Le Chantilly** – *120 av. de la République. ☎02 31 88 79 75. 17 rooms.* ☕*8.50€.* This townhouse near the hippodrome has well-looked after rooms. Breakfast in a small dining room.

⊖⊖ **Hôtel L'Époi d'Or** – *23 av. Michel-d'Ornano, 14910 Blonville-sur-Mer. ☎02 31 14 46 46. www.hotel-normand.com. Closed 20 Feb–24 Mar and 13–29 Dec. 40 rooms.* ☕*7.50€. Restaurant*⊖⊖. Well-renovated pretty Norman-style building. Bright, functional rooms. Enjoy a traditional menu in the lovely restaurant or quick snack in the brasserie.

⊖⊖ **Hôtel Hélios** – *10 r. Fossorier. ☎02 31 14 46 46. www.hotelhelios deauville.com. 36 rooms.* ☕*8.50€.* A practical address at the centre of the resort. Simple rooms have been freshened up and a small apartment is appreciated by families. Mini-swimming pool.

⊖⊖–⊖⊖⊖ **Hôtel Le Continental** – *1 r. Désiré-Le-Hoc. ☎02 31 88 21 06. www.hotel-continental-deauville.com. Closed 13 Nov–20 Dec. 42 rooms.* ☕*8.50€.* This hotel, built in 1880, is close to the station. Small, nicely furnished rooms. Pleasant breakfast room.

⊖⊖⊖⊖ **Royal-Barrière** – *38 r. Jean-Mermoz. ☎02 31 98 66 22. www.lucien barriere.com. 291 rooms and suites.* ☕. This elegant timber-framed manor house dating from 1912 is situated in the liveliest part of town: facing the sea, near the casino and the shopping district. A sumptuous hotel that will cater to your every desire. The place to be in this town where everything glitters.

EAT

⊖ **Dupont avec un thé** – *20 pl. Morny. ☎02 31 88 20 79. www.patisseriedupont. com. Closed Mon, Thu and Fri out of season, except school holidays 1–2.30pm.* This shop offers wonderful desserts such as lemon-scented sugar biscuita and coffee-flavoured macaroons. Light meals and a hearty breakfast menu.

⊖⊖ **Bar de la Mer** – *Casino Barrière de Deauville. ☎02 31 88 27 51. www. lucienbarriere.com. Closed Nov–15 Feb except public holidays and Fri–Mon during school holidays.* This restaurant, located right on the famous boardwalk, offers a pleasant dining room, an enormous terrace on the beach and a splendid view of the ocean. On the menu: shellfish, grilled meat and salads.

⊖⊖ **Le Garage** – *118 bis av. de la République. ☎02 31 87 25 25. Closed 11 Dec–7 Jan.* This former garage is now a beaming brasserie. Changing menu and a good choice of seafood.

⊖⊖ **Le Nautica** – *2 r. Désir.-Le Hoc. ☎02 31 88 03 27. Closed Wed out of season, except during school holidays.* The atmosphere of an English pub prevails, with a little touch of the sea, in this brasserie near the train station. The menu offers only dishes prepared right in the kitchen, smoked salmon and foie gras included.

⊖⊖**Yearling** – *38 av. Hocquart de Turto. Closed Tue–Wed.* Serving typical French cuisine, its speciality is the grilled Breton lobster served in a *beurre blanc* sauce.

⊖⊖⊖ **La Flambée** – *181 r Gén.-Leclerc. ☎02 31 88 28 46. Closed 2–15 Jan.* In the the vast open hearth are prepared, under your eyes, grilled steaks and chops. There is also more traditional cuisine and, in a tank for your inspection, lobsters.

La Galerie de Tourgéville – *14800 Tourgéville, 6km/3.7mi S of Deauville via D 278 and D 27. ☎02 31 87 31 11. www.galeriedetourgeville.com. Closed Tue–Wed.* A restaurant decorated with sundry bric-a-brac and an art gallery. The menu is simple and trendy; the Deauville Parisians simply *adore* it!

La Table d'Auge – *Pl. du Marché. ☎02 31 88 30 58. www2.allnet.fr/deauville. Reservations advised summer and weekends.* Fresh shellfish, delicious, authentic regional recipes.

ON THE TOWN

Casino – *R. Edmond-Blanc. ☎02 31 14 31 14. www.lucienbarriere.com.* 325 slot machines, punto-banco, and more.

Martine Lambert – *76 bis r. Eugène-Colas. ☎02 31 88 94 04.* Made from Norman cows' milk, Martine Lambert's ice cream is subtle and delicious. Her shops are also found in Paris and Trouville.

Les Planches – *Le Bois Lauret, 14910 Blonville-sur-Mer, 6km/3.7mi SW of Deauville in the countryside. ☎02 31 87 58 09. www.lesplanches.com. Closed Jan.* All of preppy Paris haunts this disco known for its Cuban bar, loft and heated pool.

LEISURE

Le Circuit de Deauville – *rte de Caen, 14800 St-Arnoult, 4km/2.5mi S ofDeauville. ☎02 31 81 31 31 www.dupratconcept.com. From 20€.* Sizeable amusement park specialising in motor sports: go-carting. speed boats and jet skis, safety driving courses and more.

CALENDAR OF EVENTS

Jun – International Sailing Week and Jumping International. Opening of the horseracing season.

Aug – Musical August (Août musical) music festival, polo championship, horse races, sale of yearlings.

Sept – Festival of American Cinema.

Dives-sur-Mer★

If Cabourg is known as a holiday resort, its sister city Dives tends to be associated with history, for it was from here that William the Conqueror, Duc de Normandie, set out to invade England in the 11C.

- **Population:** 5 864.
- **Michelin Map:** 303: L-4 – Local map, *see Pays d'AUGE, p85.*
- **Info:** Rue du Général-de-Gaulle. ☎02 31 28 12 50. www.dives-sur-mer.com.
- **Location:** Dives lies across the estuary of the River Dives from Cabourg.
- **Don't Miss:** The old marketplace (Halles) and the church.
- **Timing:** Give yourself an hour to enjoy the town.

SIGHTS

Halles★

The magnificent oak frame of the covered market (15C–16C) is in very good condition. Wrought-iron signs identify the stalls of the merchants. On the other side of place de la République stands the 16C Bois-Hibou Manor.

Église Notre-Dame de Dives

This massive church, a centre of pilgrimage until the Religious Wars, is 14C and 15C, except for the transept crossing, a remnant of an 11C sanctuary. Inside, the elegant 15C nave contrasts sharply with the massive pillars and plain arches of the Romanesque transept crossing. The transepts themselves, the chancel and the Lady Chapel, were built in 14C Rayonnant Gothic style.

Village Guillaume-le-Conquérant

This pleasant enclave of art and craft shops is located within the precincts of the old inn of the same name, dating from the 16C.

Falaise★

Falaise suffered cruelly during the fighting in the Falaise-Chambois pocket in August 1944. The town's setting in the Ante Valley is dominated by the enormous fortress, one of Normandy's first stone castles, where William the Conqueror was born about 1027. Falaise is a centre for excursions into the Suisse Normande.

- **Population:** 8 475.
- **Michelin Map:** 303: K-6.
- **Info:** Boulevard de la Libération. 02 31 90 17 26. www.falaise-tourisme.com.
- **Location:** Falaise is on N 158 between Caen, 41km/25.5mi to the N and Argentan, 22km/14mi to the SE.
- **Don't Miss:** The château of William the Conqueror.
- **Timing:** Visit the château in the morning, lunch in Falaise and finish the day by touring the valley of the River Laizon.
- **Kids:** Children will enjoy the Automates Avenue exhibit.

THE TOWN

Église de la Trinité★

The west front of the church features a triangular Gothic porch. On the south side note the gargoyles and small carved figures. At the east end the Renaissance flying buttresses are highly ornate.

Fontaine d'Arlette

The fountain of the Val d'Ante (Fontaine d'Arlette) provides an impressive view of the castle towering above.

Église St-Gervais

The church dates from the 11C to the 16C; the lantern tower is 12C. Inside, the contrast between the Romanesque south side and the Gothic north is striking.

Porte des Cordeliers

This lovely stone gateway, part of the town wall, is flanked by a round tower and has a 14C–15C porch.

Château Guillaume-Le-Conquérant★

Open daily Jul–Aug 10am–7pm; rest of the year 10am–6pm (l ast visit 1hr before closing). Closed 1 Jan, 25 Dec. 7€. 02 31 41 61 44. www.chateau-guillaume-leconquerant.fr.

This medieval ensemble (12C–13C), characteristic of defensive Anglo-Norman architecture, has been heavily restored. William the Bastard, Duke of Normandy, was born here in 1027, to a local girl, the Beautiful Arlette.

Château Guillaume-Le-Conquérant

O. Forir/MICHELIN

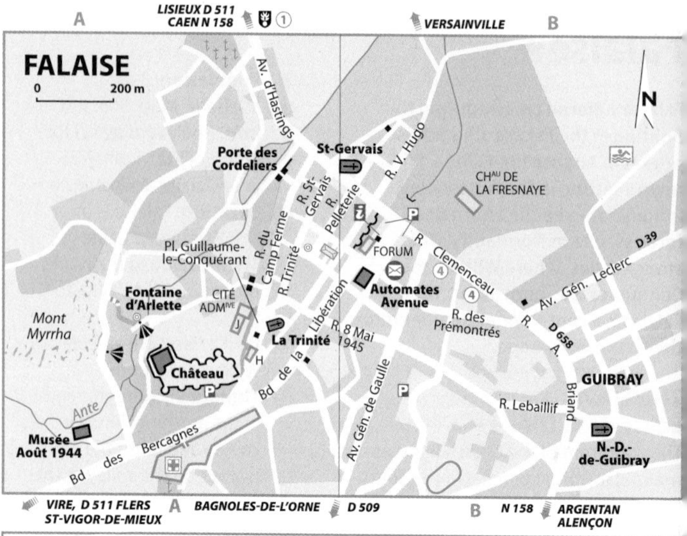

WHERE TO STAY		WHERE TO EAT	
Chêne Sec (Chambre d'hôte le)	①	Attache (L')	①
Poste (Hôtel de la)	④	Fine Fourchette (La)	④

Inner courtyard
Visitors walking through the Porte St-Nicolas enter a large area of about 1ha/2.5 acres, defined by 15 towers.

Main keep
This rectangular 12C structure is surprisingly large; great impregnable-looking flat buttresses mark the line of the walls. Restauration of the huge *aula,* or main reception room, involved sophisticated techniques: the flooring is made of alternating squares of glass and lead, and the ceiling consists of Teflon stretched over an iron frame. Note the Chapelle St-Prix, a small oratory.

Small keep
This luminous, well-balanced construction commissioned by Henri I Plantagenet in the late 12C was designed to guard the main keep from attack from the rock platform.

Tour Talbot
This impressive round tower, 35m/114.8ft tall with walls 4m/13ft thick, recalls John Talbot, governor of the castle in 1449. An incredibly deep well (65m/213ft) provides water to the entire castle. The rock platform commands a lovely **view** of the surrounding countryside.

Guibray Fair
For nine centuries the suburb of Guibray to the southeast of Falaise was famous for its fair. Already in the 11C the horse fair was attended by thousands from all over Europe. The streets, lanes and alleys of Falaise, with their many inns and taverns, were alive with minstrels and dancers. Since the 19C increasing mechanisation has reduced the horse to a minor role.

Musée Août-1944 (Battle of the Falaise Pocket)
Chemin des Roches. Open daily Apr–mid-Nov 10am–noon, 2–6pm. 6€. 02 31 90 37 19. www.normandie-museeaout44.com.

Beautiful Arlette

One evening in 1027, on returning from the hunt, Robert (later known as The Magnificent), younger son of King Richard II, Duke of Normandy, was struck by the beauty of a local girl, her skirts drawn high as she worked with her companions washing clothes. A lad of 17, he watched for her daily and desired her. Arlette's father, a rich tanner, let her decide for herself and she, refusing all secrecy, entered the castle over the drawbridge on horseback, finely apparelled.

Then, as the chroniclers of the time wrote, "When Nature had reached her term, Arlette bore a son who was named William."

his private collection displays heavy English, American and German war equipment. Realistic dioramas depict the ierce fighting of the Falaise Pocket.

Automates Avenue

d de la Libération. Open Jul–Aug daily 10am–6pm; Apr–Jun, Sept and Dec daily 10am–12.30pm, 1.30–6pm; Oct–Nov and Jan–Mar Sat–Sun, holidays and school holidays 10am–12.30pm, 1.30–6pm. 6€ (4–11 years 4.50€). 02 31 90 02 43.

Until the 1950s, the Decamps company decorated the windows of Parisian department stores with animated scenes, of which some 300 are displayed.

Musée André-Lemaître

Same address, ticket booth and hours as Automates Avenue. 6€. 02 31 90 02 43.

Local artist **André Lemaître** (1909–95) s renowned for his paintings of the area around Falaise and Honfleur.

Église Notre-Dame-de-Guibray

The church dates from the days of William the Conqueror. The apse and the apsidal chapels are still pure Romanesque. The organ is by Parizot (1746).

DRIVING TOUR

2.5km/1.5mi north of Falaise by rue Victor-Hugo. After crossing the bridge over the Ante turn right onto the path to Versainville.

Versainville

The 18C château *(closed to the public)* features a central wing with a peristyle, linked by a gallery to a huge pavilion forming the left wing.

4km/2.5mi west of Falaise along D 511. Then turn right onto D 243.

Noron-l'Abbaye

Visit the 13C church with a charming two-storey Romanesque belfry.

26km/16mi round trip – leave Falaise on D 658, N. Allow 1hr.

Vallée du Laizon

Aubigny

At the entrance to the village, on the left, stands a late-16C château. The parish **church** contains statues of six consecutive lords of Aubigny. Notice the 13C belfry of **Soulangy** to the left.

Right onto D 261. In Ouilly-le-Tesson turn right. Right at the next junction.

Assy

A magnificent avenue (left) leads to the **Château d'Assy**, a handsome 18C mansion with an elegant Corinthian portico; the chapel dates from the 15C.

Return to the junction and turn right; turn left onto D 91.

Soumont-St-Quentin

The 12C–14C church belfry is Romanesque below and Gothic above.

Return to Falaise by N 158.

ADDRESSES

STAY

Chambre d'hôte Le Chêne Sec – *14700 Pertheville-Ners, 9km/5.6mi E of Falaise. ℘02 31 90 17 55. Closed in winter. 2 rooms. . Restaurant.* Quiet 15C manor house. The two rooms feature exposed beams, stone walls and country furniture.

Hôtel de la Poste – *38 r. G. Clemenceau. ℘02 31 90 13 14. Closed 23 Jan, Sun and Fri eves, Mon from Oct–Apr. 9€. Restaurant.* Rooms in this postwar bulding are discreet and well kept; those at the rear are quieter. The dining room serves traditional dishes.

EAT

L'Attache – *rte de Caen, 1.5km/0.9mi N. ℘02 31 90 05 38. Closed late Sept–early Oct. Reservations advised.* A former coaching inn with a charming façade and attractive, clasic interior. Focus is on local cuisine with the occasional heirloom variety of herbs and vegetables.

La Fine Fourchette – *52 r. Clemenceau. ℘02 31 90 08 59. Closed 18 Feb–8 Mar, Tue eve off season. Restaurant.* This 195s stone building is home to a restaurant serving modern cuisine in two dining rooms. Attractively presented dshes.

Château de Fontaine-Henry★★

This beautiful building is a fine example of Renaissance architecture. A member of the Harcourt family built it in the 15C and 16C over the dungeons, cellars and foundations of the original 11C–12C fortress.

- **Michelin Map:** 303: J-4.
- **Location:** Fontaine-Henry is in the Mue Valley, near the Côte de Nacre and the D-Day beaches, 18km/11mi N of Caen and 25mi/15.5mi E of Bayeux.
- **Don't Miss:** The stone stalls in the château chapel.
- **Timing:** You need 1hr 30min to see the château.

VISIT

Guided tours (1hr30min) mid-Jun–mid-Sept Wed–Mon 2.30–6.30pm; Easter–mid-Jun and last half Sept Sat–Sun and public holidays 2.30–6.30pm; Oct–2 Nov Sat–Sun and public holidays 2.30–5.30pm. 7€. Evening visits Fri in summer (check schedule). 9€. ℘06 89 84 85 57. www.chateau-de-fontaine-henry.com.

An immense, steeply sloping slate roof, taller than the building itself, covers the 16C pavilion on the left. The main building is a wonder of delicately worked stonework. Inside is similar stonework, including the François I **staircase**. Furnished throughout, the château has some fine paintings. The nave of the 12C chapel was altered in the 16C.

EXCURSION

Allow 15min on foot there and back. The lane branches off D 170 on a corner, about 500m/550yd from Thaon parish church. This downhill path will take you to the bottom of the valley.

Ancienne église de Thaon★

Allow 15min there and back.

Guided tours by volunteers Jul–Aug Sun 3–6.30pm; year-round on request. ℘02 31 80 04 76. http://vieilleeglisedethaon.free.fr . No charge.

This small 12C Romanesque church is enhanced by its attractive setting in an isolated valley. The belfry, one of the most original in Normandy, is capped by a pyramid roof and deeply recessed twin bays.

Honfleur★★

The lovely town of Honfleur is located on the Seine estuary. The impressive Pont de Normandie has made it easier to get to and from the town, and to visit the Pays d'Auge and the Côte de Grâce. You can spend hours wandering around the old dock (Vieux Bassin), Ste-Catherine Church, the narrow winding streets and port where the fishing fleet unloads fresh fish and shellfish every day. Today, Honfleur can rightly claim to be both a river port and a seaport, as evidenced by the many large liners that choose the welcoming city as a stopover: 220m/722ft-long ships, able to accommodate up to 1 200 passengers in optimal conditions, glide along the quays, where the waters are 7.5–9.5m/24.6–31ft deep.

- **Population:** 8 177.
- **Michelin Map:** 303: N-3.
- **Info:** Quai Lepaulmier. ✆02 31 89 23 30. www.ot-honfleur.fr.
- **Location:** The city, 25km/15.5mi from Le Havre and 91km/56.5mi from Rouen, lies on the left bank of the Seine, 3km/2mi from the Pont de Normandie.
- **Parking:** Park on quai de la Tour in the old city.
- **Don't Miss:** Old Honfleur and the wooden Ste-Catherine Church, built by shipwrights.
- **Timing:** Visit Ste-Catherine Quay early in the morning to capture the elongated reflections of the old houses in the still water. In the evening, sunset lights up the *greniers à sel* just opposite.
- **Kids:** The Naturospace offers hundreds of butterflies floating in an immense greenhouse.

A BIT OF HISTORY

Canada, a Norman Colony – Ever since the early 16C, navigators had been anchoring briefly along the coast of a land named Gallia Nova by Verrazano, the discoverer of the site of New York. In 1534, **Jacques Cartier** stepped ashore and claimed the territory for France, naming it Canada. François I was less than impressed with the explorer on his return as he brought back no spices, gold or diamonds. Canada was thus left unexplored until the 17C when the experienced navigator **Samuel de Champlain** received orders to colonise this vast territory. He set sail from Honfleur, and in 1608 founded Quebec.

On Colbert's advice Louis XIV took an interest in Canada and the country rapidly became a Norman and Percheron colony settled by over 4 000 peasants who made their living by agriculture, fishing, hunting and fur trading.

The Iroquois Indians bitterly opposed the French colonists, who by 1665 had to appeal to France for aid against mounting attacks. A thousand soldiers arrived; simultaneously a decree was issued compelling each man to marry, within a fortnight upon her arrival, one of the women, known as the king's daughters *(filles du roy)*, who were sent out from France to help increase the sparse population. The queen took an interest in the selection of the young women, who were to be "not ugly ... not repulsive ... healthy and strong enough for working on the land".

From Canada, **Cavalier de La Salle** journeyed south to explore and colonise Louisiana in 1682. He established the communication route along the Ohio Valley which was to lead to war with the British and finally the loss by the French of Canada in 1760.

Honfleur, an Artist's Paradise – The character and atmosphere of Honfleur has inspired painters, writers and musicians.

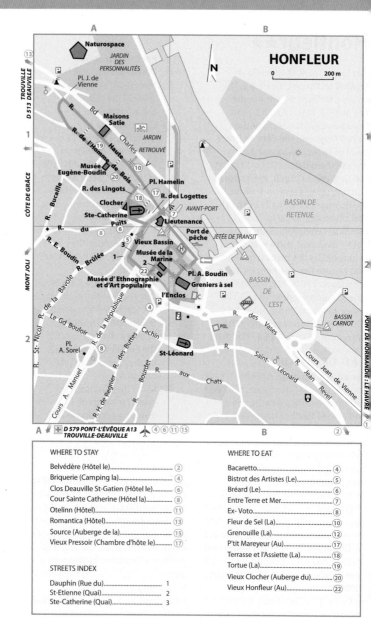

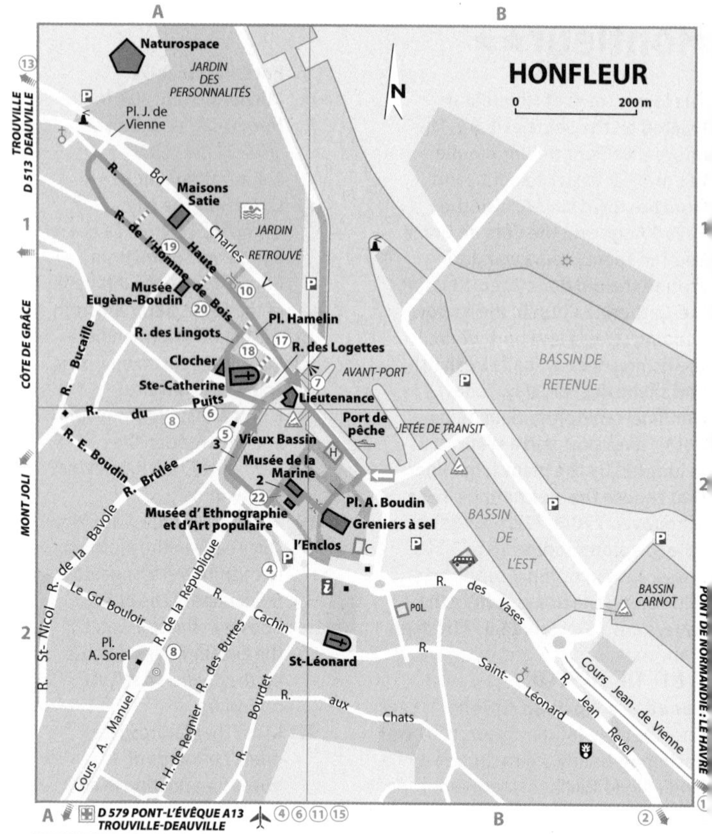

WHERE TO STAY

Belvédère (Hôtel le)........ 2
Briquerie (Camping la)........ 4
Clos Deauville St-Gatien (Hôtel le)........ 6
Cour Sainte Catherine (Hôtel la)........ 8
Otelinn (Hôtel)........ 11
Romantica (Hôtel)........ 13
Source (Auberge de la)........ 15
Vieux Pressoir (Chambre d'hôte le)........ 17

STREETS INDEX

Dauphin (Rue du)........ 1
St-Etienne (Quai)........ 2
Ste-Catherine (Quai)........ 3

WHERE TO EAT

Bacaretto........ 4
Bistrot des Artistes (Le)........ 5
Bréard (Le)........ 6
Entre Terre et Mer........ 7
Ex- Voto........ 8
Fleur de Sel (La)........ 10
Grenouille (La)........ 12
P'tit Mareyeur (Au)........ 17
Terrasse et l'Assiette (La)........ 18
Tortue (La)........ 19
Vieux Clocher (Auberge du)........ 20
Vieux Honfleur (Au)........ 22

Musset came to stay in St-Gatien in the period when the Normandy coast was fashionable with the Romantics. Honfleur began to fill with painters – not only those who were Norman-born such as Boudin, Hamelin and Lebourg, but also Paul Huet, Daubigny, Corot and others from Paris and foreigners such as Bonington and Jongkind.

It was in the small St-Siméon Inn – "chez La Mère Toutain" – that the Impressionists first met. Ever since artists have continued to visit Honfleur. Baudelaire, who stayed in the town with his mother in her old age, declared, "settling in Honfleur has always been the dearest of my dreams" and while there wrote his *Invitation au Voyage*.

Other Honfleur citizens include the composer Erik Satie (1866–1925), the poet and novelist Henri de Régnier (1864–1936), the author Lucie Delarue-Mardrus, the economist Frédéric Le Play and the historian Albert Sorel.

WALKING TOUR

OLD TOWN★★

Allow 1hr30min.

Leave from place Arthur-Boudin to the east of the old dock.

Place Arthur-Boudin

Old slate-shingled houses stand around the square; no 6 is a Louis XIII house with stone and flint chequered decoration. The Saturday-morning flower market brings colour and life to the area.

Greniers à sel

r. de la Ville. Open during temporary exhibits or as part of the city's guided tour. Tourist office 02 31 89 23 30.

These tile-covered stone buildings were constructed in the 17C in order to store the salt required by the cod fishing fleet.

Rue de la Prison

Opposite the Greniers à sel.

Very picturesque with its line of old timber-framed houses. At the end of the street, on the right, is the former church of St-Étienne, its bell-tower rising up above the old port. The building now houses the **Musée de la Marine** (Naval Museum).

Vieux Bassin★★

The quaysides of the old dock – designed by Duquesne on the orders of Colbert – are picturesque, enhanced by the pleasure boats alongside. The contrast is striking between **St-Étienne Quay,** with its splendid two-storey stone dwellings, and **Ste-Catherine Quay**, where the tall – rising up to seven storeys high – slender houses are faced with slate and timber. The Governor's House (La Lieutenance), next to the swivel bridge, completes the scene.

La Lieutenance

Only a relic now remains of the 16C house in which the king's lieutenant, Governor of Honfleur, once lived. The façade facing the square now incorporates, between two bartizans, Caen Gate, one of the two main entrances to the city in the Middle Ages. From the corner of the passenger quay you get a good view of the house, the old dock and, on the other side, the outer harbour.

Rue de Logettes, a reference to the numerous wooden stalls that once lined the street, leads to place **Ste-Catherine**, in the heart of the neighbourhood of the same name. In addition to the pretty street and half-timbered houses, the neighbourhood is famous for its unique church and bell-tower.

Église Ste-Catherine★★

This church is a rare example in western Europe of a building constructed, apart from the foundations, entirely of wood. After the Hundred Years War all masons and architects were employed on the inevitable post-war reconstruction, but the Honfleur axe masters from the local shipyards determined to thank God immediately for the departure of the English and built a church with their own skills.

The interior has twin naves and side aisles, the timber roof over each nave being supported by wooden pillars. The carved panels ornamenting the gallery are 16C, the organ 18C. There are also many wooden statues.

Clocher de Ste-Catherine★

Open same hours as Musée Eugène-Boudin. 2€ (with combined ticket for Eugène-Boudin, no charge). 02 31 89 54 00.

The massive oak belfry, a building covered in chestnut wood, stands apart from the church on a large foundation which contained the bell-ringer's dwelling. Today it is used as an extension of the Musée Eugène-Boudin and contains religious works.

Rue des Lingots, narrow and winding, goes around the tower; the old cobblestones lead to **rue de l'Homme-**

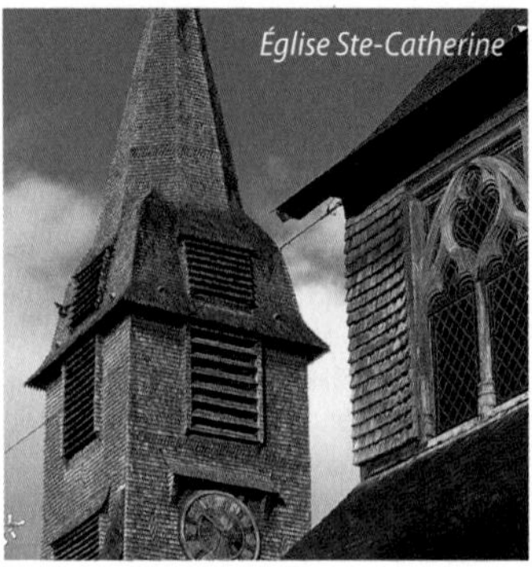

Église Ste-Catherine

G. Targat/MICHELIN

de-Bois, named after a covered wooden head on the house at no **23**.

Turn left onto rue de l'Homme-de-Bois; 400m/437yd further on, across from the Hôtel-Dieu Chapel, take rue du Trou-Miard to the right, then turn right again onto rue Haute.

The hospital's old lighthouse, on place Jean-de-Vienne, is now mostly used by seagulls. **Rue Haute**, formerly a pathway outside the fortifications, was home to many local shipbuilders. The composer Erik Satie was born at no **88**, where the timbers are painted red; inside there is an unusual museum. Continue onto **place Hamelin**, birthplace of Alphonse Allais (no **6**), a French humourist of the late 19C.

End your tour of Honfleur by walking straight on (quai de la Lieutenance and quai de la Quarantaine) to return to place Arthur-Boudin on the right. Or turn and go through the public garden, walking as far as the Seine along the digue de l'Ouest, where a pleasant pedestrian path has been created on the jetty.

SIGHTS

Musée Eugène-Boudin

pl. Érik Satie. Open mid-Mar–Sept Wed–Mon 10am–noon, 2–6pm; mid-Feb–Jun and Oct–Dec Mon and Tue–Fri 2.30–5pm, Sat–Sun and public holidays 10am–noon, 2.30–5pm. Closed 1 May, 14 Jul, 25 Dec. Jul–Aug 5.50€; rest of year 4.80€. 02 31 89 54 00.

An old Augustinian chapel and a more recent building house this museum, which is chiefly devoted to the painters of Honfleur and of the estuary.

On the first floor is a rich collection of household items from 18C and 19C Normandy. The second and third floors display works by 20C artists who, for the most part, worked in the region: Dufy, Marquet, Friesz, Villon, Lagar, Grau-Sala, Saint-Delis, Gernez, Driès, Herbo, Vallotton, Bigot, etc.

Galleries adjoining the chapel feature 19C paintings by Eugène Boudin (the museum possesses 89 of his paintings and drawings) and by Monet, Jongkind, Dubourg, Isabey, Pécrus, Courbet, Cals. A second holds the Hambourg-Rachet bequest of some 300 canvases (19C–20C) by Derain, Foujita, Garbell, Marie Laurencin, Van Dongen and Hambourg. The third is a drawings room in which about 100 works are rotated each year.

Musée du Vieux Honfleur

The museum presents three sections – one on the navy, one on popular art and finally the Manoir du Désert.

Musée de la Marine

quai St-Étienne. Open same hours and conditions as for the Musée d'Ethnographie et d'Art populaire. 3.40€ or 4.60€ for a combined ticket with the Musée d'Ethnographie. 02 31 89 14 12.

The museum, which is housed in Église St-Étienne (deconsecrated), traces the history of the port of Honfleur and contains a large number of scale models and topographical information on the town.

Musée d'Ethnographie et d'Art populaire

r. de la Prison. Open Apr–Sept Tue–Sun 10am–noon, 2–6.30pm; mid-Fev–Mar and Oct–mid–Nov Mon and Tue–Fri 2.30–5.30pm, Sat–Sun 10am–noon, 2.30–5.30pm. Closed 1 May, 14 Jul. 3.40€ or 4.60€ for a

combined ticket with the Musée de la Marine. ✆02 31 89 14 12. www.musees-basse-normandie.fr.
Ten Normandy interiors have been reconstructed in this museum located in 16C residences. Note particularly the timbered manor house, the bourgeois dining room, the weaver's and printer's workshop, the bedroom and a shop on the ground floor.

Maisons Satie★

Entrance at 67 bd Charles-V (running parallel to r. Haute). Audio-guided tour (1hr). Open May–Sept Wed–Mon 10am–7pm; Oct–Dec and mid-Feb–Apr Wed–Mon 11am–6pm. Closed 25 Dec. 5.50€. ✆02 31 89 11 11.
Wearing headphones, you are guided through a series of stage-like settings recalling the career of Erik Satie (1866-1925) – "born young in an old world". The museum offers the opportunity to hear the music and understand more about the life of the man who came out with such conversational pearls as: "Give me a minute to get my skirt on, and I'll be right with you!"; "Although our information is false, we cannot guarantee it."; "What do you prefer, music or cold-cuts?"; "The piano is like money, it's only agreeable when you've got your hands on it."

Église St-Léonard

S of the Vieux-Bassin, take the rue de la République, then left into the rue Cachin, which leads to the place St-Léonard.
The façade of this church is a bizarre combination of an ornate Flamboyant doorway and a 17C belfry tower.
Inside are two immense shells which have been converted into fonts. At the entrance to the chancel stand statues of Our Lady of Victory and St Leonard with two prisoners kneeling; note in the chancel the wooden statues of St Peter, St Paul and the four Evangelists. The narthex is furnished with an 18C copper lectern from Villedieu-les-Poêles.

Naturospace★

Opposite the hospital lighthouse, bd Charles V. Open daily Jul–Aug 10am–7pm; Feb–Mar and Oct–Nov 10am–1pm, 2–5.30pm; Apr–Jun and Sept 10am–1pm, 2–7pm (last entry 1hr before closing). Closed Dec–Jan. 7.80 € (children 6€). ✆02 31 81 77 00. www.naturospace.com.
Inside an enormous greenhouse, 60 species of butterflies from six continents float gracefully in perfect freedom. Surrounded by the whispering of their wings, you stroll among tropical plants and observe cocoons from which, early in the morning, a few caterpillars emerge. Good explanations and special exhibits.

ADDITIONAL SIGHTS

Pont de Normandie

3km/2mi E via the D 580. There is a 5€ toll for cars, but no charge for pedestrians, cyclists and motorcyclists. But watch out – the wind can be very strong!
The bridge was started in 1988 and officially opened in January 1995; it is the third largest bridge to span the Lower Seine after the Pont de Tancarville and the Pont de Brotonne.
Its impact on the economy is three fold: it brings Le Havre and Honfleur closer together by removing the detour via Tancarville Bridge (24km/15mi instead of 60km/37.2mi); it is one of the major motorway links between the Channel Tunnel and the west and south-west of France; it represents one of the many connections in the so-called **Estuaries Route**, which ties up the north and south of Europe without going through Paris.
The Pont de Normandie, a truly remarkable work of art and a technological feat, was seen as a milestone in the history of civil engineering, since it established the record of the longest cable-stayed bridge (more elegant and cheaper to build than a suspension bridge). Although Lisbon's Vasco da Gama Bridge (1998) is now the longest in Europe, the Pont de Normandie is higher. This steel and concrete mass, which seems to defy

the laws of gravity, is surprisingly light and extremely stable. Careful attention was devoted to the subject of safety: the bridge is designed to withstand winds of up to 440kph/274mph; it can resist shocks caused by the largest cargo boats, which could only collide with the north tower, protected by 9m/30ft of concrete; the road surfacing has in-built sensors triggered off by the presence of black ice; tollbooth operators can monitor traffic continually thanks to surveillance cameras.

Besides the standard lighting for road traffic, the Breton architect **Yann Kersalé** conceived a sophisticated lighting system called *Rhapsody in Blue and White* – a bi-coloured display of static lights outline the two towers (blue on the underside, white on the outside), whereas a row of blue twinkling lights run underneath the deck.

Côte de Grâce★★

The peaceful beauty of this famous hillside, appreciated by all Honfleur enthusiasts, is also appealing to passing tourists.

Calvaire★★

Telescope. From the cross there is a good **panorama** of the Seine estuary, the Le Havre roadstead, to the right, the Pont de Normandie and, in the distance, Tancarville Bridge.

Chapelle Notre-Dame-de-Grâce

In the centre of the esplanade beneath tall trees stands the small chapel of Our Lady of Grace and within it the statue after which it is named. This graceful 17C building has replaced a sanctuary said to have been founded by Richard II, 4th Duke of Normandy.

It was here that navigators and explorers came to pray before leaving on journeys of discovery or colonisation to the North American continent; a borough of Montréal bears this name. The north transept chapel is dedicated to all Canadians of Norman origin. There are numerous small, ex-voto vessels.

Mont-Joli viewpoint

The view complements the one from Calvaire: in the foreground are the town, the port and the coast; to the east is the semicircle of hills. Tancarville Bridge can be seen in the distance.

DRIVING TOUR

South Bank of the Seine – Honfleur to Rouen★★

130km/81mi – allow 5hr.

This charming drive takes you through forests and along roads overlooking the river below.

Leave Honfleur via cours Jean-de-Vienne and take D 312 towards Berneville and Pont-Audemer.

The road follows the lower Risle Valley. Beyond Berville, there are many fine views of the estuary. In the spring, the blooming apple orchards turn the landscape into a wonderland.

Pont-Audemer★

See PONT-AUDEMER, p185.

Take D 810.

Ste-Opportune-la-Mare

See QUILLEBEUF-SUR-SEINE, p187.

Take D 95.

After a section on a crest road, between Val-Anger and Vieux-Port, the Seine Valley comes into view again.

Vieux-Port★

The thatched cottages are half hidden by their orchards.

Aizier

The stone bell tower of the 12C church looks very old. Near the church there is a manhole slab – the remains of a covered way dating from around 2000 BC.

From Aizier to Quesney, D 95 and D 65 follow the edge of Brotonne Forest.

Vatteville-la-Rue
The nave of the church dates from the Renaissance; it bears a black mourning band which was painted on the wall for the funeral of the lord of the manor. The Flamboyant chancel is lit by 16C stained-glass windows.

Turn left onto D 65, which leads to La Mailleraye (ferry).

Running alongside the Seine to the right, the road offers views of typical Norman thatched cottages half hidden by trees. After Notre-Dame-de-Bliquetuit, you can see the two ferries which cross at Yainville and Jumièges. Road D 65 then rises in hairpin bends.

Viewpoint★
Picnic area. Viewing table. To the right can be seen the towers of Jumièges Abbey, particularly impressive at sunset, and to the left the Seine Valley.

300m/328yd further on, stop on the right in the La Mailleraye lay-by.

Chêne à la Cuve
100m/110yd from D 913, opposite the 11km post.
Four oak trunks growing from a single bole form a kind of natural vat, 7m/23ft in circumference.

Take D 313 towards Bourg-Achard and turn right on D 101.

Moulin d'Hauville
Open Jul–Aug daily 2.30–6.30pm; May–Jun and Sept Sun 2.30–6.30pm. 2.50€. 02 32 56 57 32.
This 13C windmill is one of the few surviving stone mills in Upper Normandy and once belonged to the monks of Jumièges Abbey. Its cap can be orientated according to the direction of the wind and is supported by oak beams. The stone tower and large sails are most impressive. If weather allows, you can see the mill in operation.

Take D 101 in the other direction and turn left on D 712. Going down the hill, turn onto D 45 (nice views on the forest and the river), then take D 265, which crosses Mauny Forest, then D 64 towards La Bouille.

Between La Ronce and La Bouille, the road goes along the river's edge.

La Bouille
La Bouille, in a lovely site at the foot of the wooded slopes of the Roumois plateau, has always attracted artists, writers, poets and painters.
In the old days, people from Rouen would come here to sample eels stewed in cider, La Bouille cheese and *douillons aux pommes* (apples filled with butter, wrapped in pastry and baked).
Today the village still offers a charming combination of terraces, inns and avenues. Painters set up their easels and draw sketches of the quaint streets and surrounding countryside.
On the quayside, a plaque on one of the houses recalls the critic and novelist **Hector Malot** (1830–1907), born here.

Moulineaux
Church. Make appointment at the mairie to visit. 02 35 18 02 45.
The **church** with its slender spire dates from the 13C. Inside there is an attractive woodwork group formed by the pulpit and rood screen (one side of which is Gothic and the other Renaissance). In the apse is the 13C **stained-glass window**★, a gift of Blanche de Castille.
Note the 16C tableau of the Flemish School depicting the Crucifixion and a monk in prayer.
There is a far-reaching view of the Seine Valley from the cemetery.

Take D 3, a steep hill.

Monument Qui Vive
At the crossroads of D 64 and D 67A.
There is a remarkable view (viewing table) of the Seine as it curves round to encircle Roumare Forest.
Road D 64 goes down to the Seine so that one gets a view of the river bend commanded by Robert the Devil's castle and the Rouen industrial suburbs.

Château de Robert le Diable★
See ELBEUF – Excursions, p332.

Go back to D 64 up a steep climb. Take D 64 right through Londe Forest. At the crossroads known as Le Nouveau Monde, follow D 938 to Orival, to the south.

Orival★
From Oissel to Orival the road is overhung by curious rocks which are part of the chalk escarpment. Orival Church is an unusual semi-troglodytic 15C building.

Return to Le Nouveau Monde.

Roches d'Orival★
Park on D 18 by the sign Sentier des Roches; 1hr on foot there and back by a steep path which is slippery when wet. At the top turn right onto a path which passes in front of some caves hollowed out of the rocks.
The path follows the cliff. By a grassy knoll (300m/328yd) there is a **view** of the Seine and of the rock escarpment, broken by a grassy corniche on which the path continues.

Follow D 18 along the Seine.

Oissel
Pleasant public garden.

To return to Rouen, take D 13, then N 138 to the right.

The pine forest of Rouvray is an oasis of calm, reminiscent of the Landes of southwest France.

ADDRESSES

STAY

Camping La Briquerie – *02 31 89 28 32. www.campinglabriquerie.com. Closed Oct–Easter. 430 sites. Reservations advised. Restaurant on site.* Set on the edge of a forest, this campground has sites separated by hedges of shrubs or flowers. Some small but well-kept self-catered cottages. Large swimming pool, game-room and miniature golf. Restaurant-bar with meals in season.

Chambre d'hôte Le Vieux Pressoir – *Hameau le Clos-Potier, 27210 Conteville, 13.5/8.5mi from Honfleur via D 580, rte de Pont-Audemer then left on D 312. 02 35 57 60 79. www.la-ferme-du-pressoir.com. 7 rooms. Evening meal.* Set in the countryside, this 18C half-timbered farm will delight those who appreciate calm and simplicity. Every room contains 19C and 20C objects and furniture. Flower garden, duck pond and 300-year-old cider press add to the charm.

Kyriad Hôtel– *62 cours A.-Manuel. 02 31 89 41 77. www.kyriad.fr. 50 rooms. . Restaurant.* At a distance from the city centre, this hotel offers rooms at reasonable prices. Small and functional, they make for an agreeable stay. A garden and a terrace let you bask in the gentle Norman sun.

Hôtel Le Belvédère – *36 r. Émile-Renouf. 02 31 89 08 13. www.hotel-belvedere-honfleur.com. Closed Jan. 9 rooms. 7€. Restaurant.* This old town house gets its name from the view from its roof. Peaceful rooms whose cottage setting offers an incomparable view over the Normandy bridge. Pretty garden and good restaurant.

Chambre d'hôte Cour Ste-Catherine – *74 r. du Puits. 02 31 89 42 40. www.giaglis.com. 5 rooms. .* Housed in a 17C convent, this pleasant inn offers five elegant guest rooms, opening onto a flower garden. In the lounge, pretty furniture and a fireplace. Breakfast served in the old cider-press. Charming welcome from the owners.

Le Clos Deauville Saint-Gatien – *4 ch. des Brioleurs, 14130 St-Gatien-des-Bois, 9km/5.6mi S of Honfleur via D 579. 02 31 65 16 08. www.clos-st-Gatien.fr. 58 rooms. 13€.* The charm of the Norman countryside a few short miles from the shore characterises this half-timbered house nestled in a verdant setting. Comfortable, cosy rooms. Three pools, sauna, fitness room.

⊖⊖–⊖⊖⊖⊖ **Hôtel Romantica** – *ch. Petit-Paris, 14600 Pennedepie, 8km/5mi NE of Honfleur. ✆02 31 81 14 00. www.romantica-honfleur.com. 35 rooms. ☕9€. Restaurant⊖⊖.* Perched high in the village, this hotel offers peace and comfort. There is a fine view over the sea from the restaurant. 3 swimming pools.

⊖⊖⊖⊖ **Auberge de la Source** – *14600 Barneville-la-Bertran, 5.5km/3.4mi SW of Honfleur. ✆02 31 89 25 02. www.auberge-de-la-source.fr. Closed 15 Nov–15 Feb. 15 rooms. ☕11€.* Set in the countryside, this beautiful half-timbered farmhouse has a lovely garden with apple orchards.

EAT

⊖ **Bacaretto** – *44 r. de la Chaussée. ✆02 31 14 83 11. Closed Wed and Thu lunch.* This little 2-storey wine bar offers more than 120 bottles to sample, accompanied by a plate of delicious snacks and a piece of "organic" bread.

⊖ **Ex-Voto** – *8 pl. Albert-Sorel. ✆02 31 89 19 69. Closed Wed, 1 Nov, 25 Dec. Reservations advised.* ⊭. One of the few inexpensive yet good-value restaurants in town, this place will make you nostalgic for the neighbourhood bistro. The proprietress concocts special dishes and short orders from fresh market produce. Very few tables, best to reserve.

⊖⊖ **Auberge du Vieux Clocher** – *9 r. de-l'Homme-de-Bois. ✆02 31 89 12 06. Closed 8–28 Jan, 26 Jun–2 Jul, 27 Nov–3 Dec, Tue and Wed.* Small dining rooms are panelled in wood, with touches of pastel colours, and old plates decorate the walls. Traditional cuisine, with an accent on seafood.

⊖⊖ **Le Bistrot des Artistes** – *14 pl. Berthelot. ✆02 31 89 95 90. Closed Jan, Tue from Oct–Apr and Wed from Oct–Jun.* Antiques, paintings of the sea, photos of Honfleur and leather seating make up the décor of this restaurant with a Parisian bistro flair. Tables near the window have a lovely view of the Vieux Bassin. On the menu: salads and slices of bread with various toppings.

⊖⊖–⊖⊖⊖ **Entre Terre et Mer** – *12 pl. Hamelin. ✆02 31 89 70 60. Closed 15 Jan–5 Feb, Wed from 15 Nov–1 Apr.* Two pleasant, modern dining areas. One is rustc wtith wooden beams and rush flooring, the other has tiled floors and is decorated with phorographs of Nomady. Serving modern cuisine including both meat and seafood dishes.

⊖⊖–⊖⊖⊖ **Terasse et l'Assiette** – *8 pl. Ste-Catherine. ✆02 31 89 31 33. Closed 5 Jan–5 Feb, Tue Sept–Jun, Mon.* Half-timbering and brickwork give this restaurant a distinctive atmosphere. Also with an outside dining area overlooking the wooden church. Serves tasty, traditional cuisine.

⊖⊖⊖ **Le Bréard** – *7 r. du Puits. ✆02 31 89 53 40. www.restaurant-lebreard.com.* Near Ste-Catherine Church, this restaurant has a green façade and two dining rooms. Modern cuisine.

⊖⊖⊖ **Au P'tit Mareyeur** – *4 r. Haute. 02 31 98 84 23. www.auptitmareyeur.com. Closed Jan, Mon and Tue. Reservations required.* This tiny restaurant near Honfleur's fishing port is ideal for an intimate meal. Maritime touches add to the cosy feel. Fish and seafood are recommended here.

⊖⊖⊖ **Au Vieux Honfleur** – *13 quai St-Étienne. ✆02 31 89 15 31. www.auvieuxhonfleur.com.* This restaurant by the old harbour extends its terrace along the quay when the weather is fine. Savour Norman dishes and seafood while gazing upon the splendid port.

⊖⊖⊖ **La Fleur de Sel** – *17 r. Haute. ✆02 31 89 01 92. www.lafleurdesel-honfleur.com.* The two small dining-rooms with neo-rustic décor at this gourmet restaurant serve good meat and seafood dishes.

⊖⊖⊖ **La Grenouille Bistro** – *10 quai de la Quarantaine, 14600 Honfleur. ✆02 31 89 04 24. www.absinthe.fr.* Modern décor mixes with traditional French, brasserie-style cuisine, including seafood and, matching the bistro's name, frogs' legs. Heated terrace.

ON THE TOWN
Evenings in Honfleur, the Old Port comes alive. Restaurants, brasseries and bars are clustered on the quais Ste-Catherine, La Quarantaine and St-Etienne. Terraces remain open until 2am in summer.

SHOPPING
Markets – *pl. Ste-Catherine.* Antique market 2nd Sun of each month. Weekly market Sat am featuring local produce and fish. Organic produce market Wed. Evening market Wed in Jul–Aug. Flower market Sat am on place Arthur-Boudin.

Griboulle – *16 r. de l'Homme-de-Bois.* M. Griffoul, nicknamed Gribouille, is an unforgettable local character. He sells Norman shortbread, milk jam, potted rabbit, preserved pork, cider products, etc. Sample the ***pommeau*** or Calvados.

La Cave Normande – *13 r. de la Ville and 12 quai Ste-Catherine.* This is where you'll find top-quality Calvados as well as cider, perry and ***pommeau***.

SPORT
Centre équestre du Ramier – *ch. du Ramier, 14600 Equemauville, 3.6km/2.2mi SW of Honfleur. ✆02 31 89 49 97. Closed 2 weeks in Sept.* This pretty riding centre has 15 training horses available. Rides last for 1hr–1hr30min.

GUIDED TOURS
Honfleur's tourist office offers tours around the town. A tour is the best way to see the famous ***greniers à sel*** (salt stores). Contact the tourist office.

Lisieux★★

Sitting on the east bank of the Touques, Lisieux has become the most important commercial and industrial town in the prosperous Pays d'Auge. The town is renowned for St Theresa of Lisieux and is the second-most important pilgrimage site in France after Lourdes.

- **Population:** 23,343.
- **Michelin Map:** 303: N-5 – Local map, *see Pays d'AUGE, p85.*
- **Info:** 11 rue d'Alençon. ✆02 31 48 18 10. www.lisieux-tourisme.com.
- **Location:** Coming from Évreux (73km/45.4mi E via N13), you immediately see the imposing 20C neo-Byzantine basilica of St Theresa.
- **Parking:** The basilica is equipped for pilgrimages with ample parking nearby.
- **Don't Miss:** The cathedral of St-Pierre and the CERZA zoo.
- **Timing:** Visit Lisieux in the morning, then tour the countryside in the afternoon; enjoy a bite to eat, too (*see Addresses*).
- **Kids:** A short distance outside Lisieux, near Hermival-les-Vaux, is the popular game reserve CERZA.

A BIT OF HISTORY
Thérèse Martin was born on 2 January 1873 to a well-to-do and very religious family in Alençon; she was an eager and sensitive child who soon showed intelligence and will-power. On the death of his wife, M. Martin brought the family to Lisieux where they lived at Les Buissonnets. At 9 years, Thérèse felt the call of the Church.

The authorities considered her too young and it was only in April 1888, after a pilgrimage to Rome and a request to the Holy Father, that she entered the Carmelite Order at the age of 15 years and 3 months. As Sister Theresa of the Child Jesus, she resolved "to save souls and, above all, to pray for the priests". Her gaiety

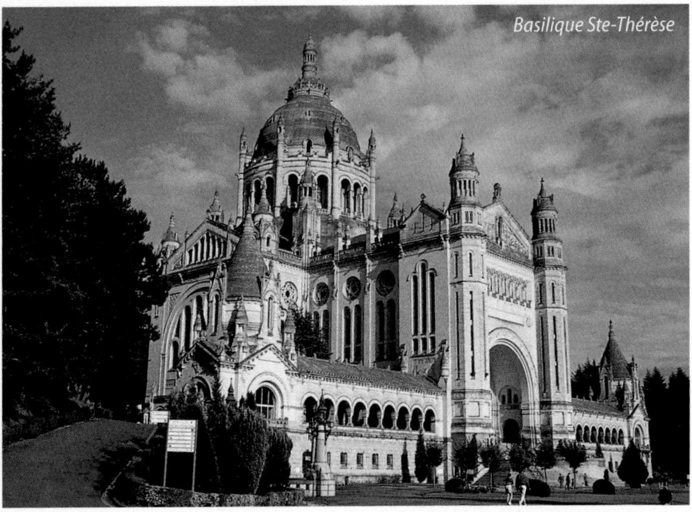

Basilique Ste-Thérèse

S. Sauvignier/MICHELIN

and simplicity cloaked a consuming energy. She wrote the story of her life, *History of a Soul*, finishing the last pages only a few days before entering the Carmelite hospital in which, after an agonising illness, she died in 1897. She was canonised in 1925. On 19 October 1997 Pope Jean-Paul II proclaimed her a Doctor of the Church, an exceptional honour bestowed on saints of great spiritual influence.

THE PILGRIMAGE

Les Buissonnets

Open Easter Mon–Sept daily9am–noon, 2–6pm; Feb–Mar and Oct 10am–noon, 2–5pm; first-half Nov, first-half Dec and Jan 10am–noon, 2–4pm. Closed 1 Jan, 25 Dec. No charge. 02 31 48 55 08. www.therese-de-lisieux.catholique.fr.

This house is where Thérèse Martin lived from the age of 4 to 15. The tour includes the dining room, Thérèse's bedroom, her father's bedroom and a display of mementoes from her childhood days.

Chapelle du Carmel

Open mid-Mar–Oct 7.20am–7pm; rest of the year 7.20am–6.30pm.

The saint's shrine, a recumbent figure in marble and precious wood, is in the chapel on the right and contains her relics.

Basilique Ste-Thérèse

Open Jul–Aug 9am–7.30pm; May–Jun & Sept 9am–7pm; Apr and Oct 9am–6.30pm; Mar and Nov 9am–6pm; rest of the year 9am–5.30pm.

This impressive basilica was consecrated on 11 July 1954 and is one of the biggest 20C churches. The **dome** is open to visitors.

The construction of the bell tower was interrupted in 1975; it ends in a flat roof and contains the great bell, three other bells and a carillon of 44 bells. Notice on the tympanum of the door the carvings by Robert Coin depicting Jesus teaching the Apostles and the Virgin of Mount Carmel. The immense nave is decorated with marble, stained glass and mosaics by Pierre Gaudin, a pupil of Maurice Denis. In the south transept stands a reliquary offered by Pope Pius XI containing the bones of the saint's right arm. The **crypt** (entrance outside, beneath the galleries) is decorated with mosaics (scenes in the life of St Theresa).

Muséé-Diorama: Histoire de Sainte-Thérèse

Beneath the north cloister of the basilica. 25min audio tour. Open Easter–Oct daily 11am–1pm, 2–6pm; Nov–Dec and Feb–Easter weekends, school and public holidays 2–5pm.

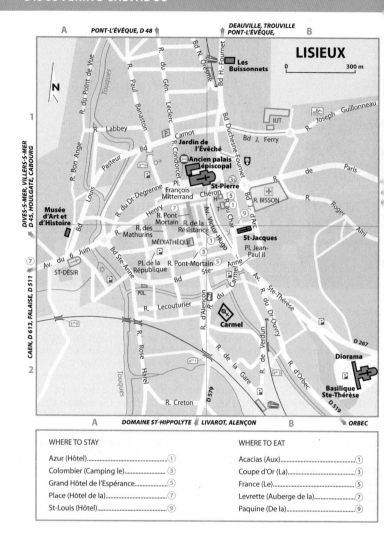

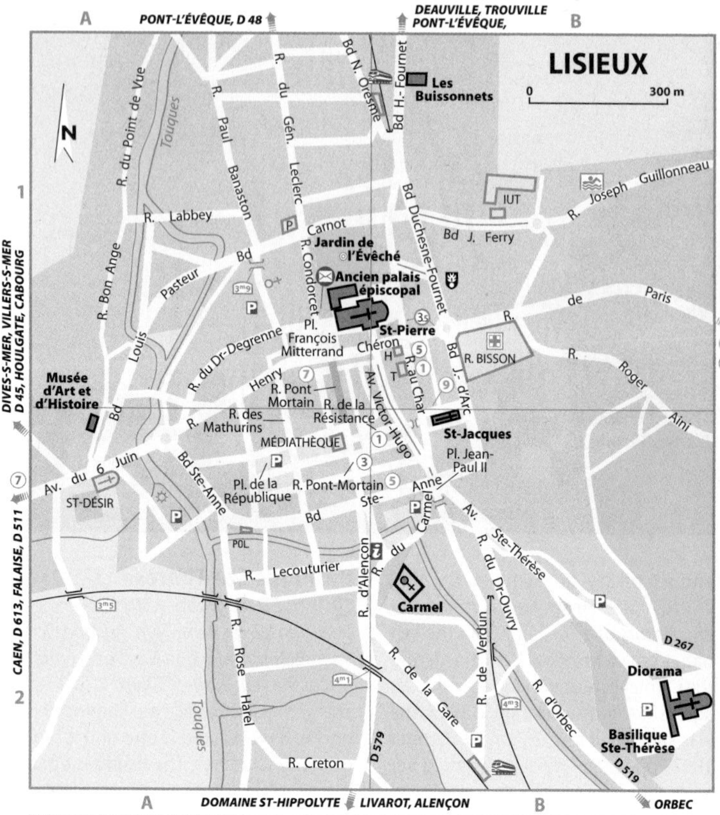

WHERE TO STAY		WHERE TO EAT	
Azur (Hôtel)	1	Acacias (Aux)	1
Colombier (Camping le)	3	Coupe d'Or (La)	3
Grand Hôtel de l'Espérance	5	France (Le)	5
Place (Hôtel de la)	7	Levrette (Auberge de la)	7
St-Louis (Hôtel)	9	Paquine (De la)	9

3€. 02 31 48 55 08. www.therese-de-lisieux.catholique.fr.
This diorama depicts a dozen episodes in the life of St Theresa .

Cathédrale St-Pierre★

Allow 15min.
Open daily 9.30am–6.30pm.
The cathedral was begun in 1170 and completed only in the mid-13C.

Exterior

The façade, raised above the ground on stone steps, is pierced by three doors and flanked by towers.

Walk round the church by the right to the south transept's Paradise Door. The massive buttresses linked by an arch surmounted by a gallery were added in the 15C.

Interior

The transept is extremely simple with the lantern rising in a single sweep at the crossing. Walk round the 13C chancel, to the huge central chapel which was remodelled in the pure Flamboyant style on the orders of Pierre Cauchon, Bishop of Lisieux, after the trial of Joan of Arc. It was in this chapel that Thérèse

Martin attended mass. Note the series of 15C carved low-relief sculptures.

Musée d'Art et d'Histoire

Open Wed–Mon 2–6pm. Closed 1 Jan, 1 May, 25 Dec. 3.50€. 02 31 62 07 70.
Set up in a handsome 16C half-timbered house, a collection of documents and images explains the history, arts and crafts of Lisieux and the Pays d'Auge.

ADDITIONAL SIGHT

Cerza★

12km/7.4mi NE. Leave Lisieux by D 510, E on the plan; 3km/2mi after Hermival-les-Vaux turn right onto D 143. Open daily Jul–Aug 9.30am–7pm; Apr–Jun and Sept 9.30am–5.30pm; Oct–Nov and Feb–Mar 10am–5.30pm (last entry 4pm). 15€ (children 8€). 02 31 62 17 22. www.cerza.com.
The **Centre d'Élevage et de Reproduction Zoologique Augeron (CERZA)** provides a pleasant, natural setting for a great many endangered animal species. The 52ha/129 acres of the domain offer interesting topographical contrasts

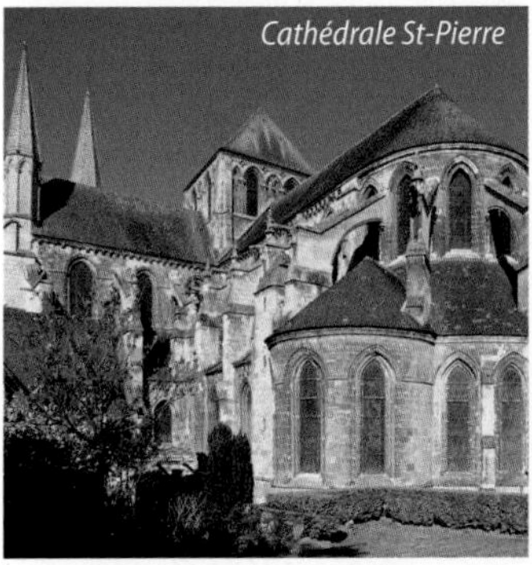
Cathédrale St-Pierre
G. Targat/MICHELIN

– valleys and plains, meadows and forests, barren stretches and lush pockets of vegetation, charmingly dotted with small ponds and burbling streams. Signposted routes will take you through the **African Reserve** (a vast area set aside for rhinoceroses, zebras, watussi, ostriches and giraffes) or on a tour of the valley.
A great many primates (gelada baboons, macaques, capuchins, gibbons) as well as lemurs live in semi-liberty, in a biotope specially designed to meet their needs.

ADDRESSES

STAY

Camping Le Colombier – *14590 Moyaux, 16km/9.6mi NE of Lisieux via D 510 and D 143. 02 31 63 63 08. Closed Oct–Apr. 180 sites. Food service.* This campsite has character, with its manor, timeworn buildings and garden *à la française*. The interior decoration has been conceived with authenticity and warmth in mind. Swimming pool.

Hôtel St-Louis – *4 r. St-Jacques. 02 31 62 06 50. www.hotelsaintlouis-lisieux.com. 17 rooms. 7€.* New, bright wallpaper, new furniture, improved bathrooms: the rooms of this family hotel have benefited from a youth cure. There is a little garden as well.

Best Western Hôtel de la Place – *67 r. Henry-Chéron. 02 31 48 27 27. www.lisieux-hotel-delaplace.com. Closed 16 Dec–7 Jan. 33 rooms. 10€.* The rooms are of varying sizes, but all have been renovated and are bright and modern. Well-stocked breakfast buffet.

Hôtel Azur – *15 r. au Char. 02 31 62 09 14. www.hotel-azur-lisieux.fr. Closed 15 Dec–15 Jan. 15 rooms. 9€.* This hotel occupies a 1960s building. Comfortable rooms. Breakfast served in a winter garden.

Grand Hôtel de l'Espérance – *16 bd Ste-Anne. 02 31 62 17 53. www.lisieux-hotel.com. Closed 22 Oct–Mar. 100 rooms. 9.50€.* Large hotel in pure Norman style dominating the town centre. Traditional beams and calconies. Well-fitted decent-sized rooms. Fine dining guaranteed in the hotel's restaurant.

EAT

Auberge de La Levrette – *48 r. de Lisieux, 14140 Saint-Julien-le-Faucon, 20km/12.4mi SW of Lisieux. 02 31 63 81 20. Closed 26 Jun–2 Jul, 20 Dec–17 Jan, Mon and Tue except public holidays.* Take a break in this 16C coaching inn, set in the heart of the village. Traditional menu and one for the kids, too.

Aux Acacias – *13 r. de la Résistance. ℘02 31 62 10 95. Closed 25–31 Dec, Thu eve Nov–Mar, Sun eve and Mon except public holidays.* An enjoyable restaurant on a small square downtown. The well-prepared regional dishes are interpreted with flair, based on fresh produce. The décor is pastel and the prices are affordable.

La Coupe d'Or – *49 r. Pont-Mortain. ℘02 31 31 16 84. Closed Sun eve.* Although this hotel restaurant is on a busy street, all is calm as soon as you enter the door. Dining room recently renovated. 14 guest rooms also renovated, with a billiards room and internet access. Reasonable prices.

Le France – *5 r. au Char. ℘02 31 62 03 37. Closed Sun eve and Mon Sept–Jun, 6–30 Jan.* Set near the cathedral, this restaurant offers a rustic country theme with exposed beams, copper pots, a wooden apple press and straw-cushioned chairs. The cuisine is traditional, with modern touches, and the wine selection engaging.

De La Paquine – *rte de Moyaux, 14590 Ouilly-du-Houley. ℘02 31 63 63 80. Closed 5 Aug–14 Sept, 14–30 Nov, Sun eve, Tue eve, Wed.* At the village entrance, this place serves traditional cuisine, which varies season by season.

CAFÉS

Pâtisserie Chez Billoudet – *44 r. Henry-Chéron. ℘02 31 62 17 91. Open Tue–Sun 7.30am–7.30pm. Closed 2 weeks during Feb–Mar school holidays, 2 weeks in Jul.* This confectioner/chocolatier offers delicious specialities such as the *caluador* (chocolate with Calvados creme and caramel), *le pom-reine* (chocolate filled with apple ganache) and the traditional apples in Calvados. Tearoom.

SHOPPING

Le Père Jules – *Rte de Dives-sur-Mer, 14100 St-Désir-de-Lisieux. ℘02 31 61 14 57.* Located in a gorgeous 19C Norman house, this family concern established in 1919 is named after the founding grandfather. You'll be invited to visit the Calvados cellars and, naturally, sample a drop or two.

Omaha Beach

The name Omaha Beach, which until 6 June 1944 existed only as an operational code name, has continued to designate the beaches of St-Laurent-sur-Mer, Colleville-sur-Mer and Vierville-sur-Mer, in the memories of the American soldiers of the 1st (5th Corps of the 1st Army) Division, who suffered heavy casualties in the most costly of the D-Day battles.

- **Michelin Map:** 303: G-3 – Local maps, *see below and Plages du DÉBARQUEMENT.*
- **Location:** Omaha Beach is some 20km/12.4mi north-west of Bayeux.
- **Don't Miss:** The American Cemetery at Colleville-sur-Mer holds some 9 400 crosses and Stars of David, perfectly aligned. Note the extreme youth of the fallen soldiers.
- **Timing:** You will need three hours to see the sights.

A BIT OF HISTORY

Normandy Landings – When the American forces landed at Omaha Beach on 6 June 1944, they met an extremely well-organised German defence that was aided by a strong coastal current that swept landing craft off course, and beach shingle that proved at first insurmountable to heavy armour. Companies at first baulked, later rallied and by evening the 116th Regiment had

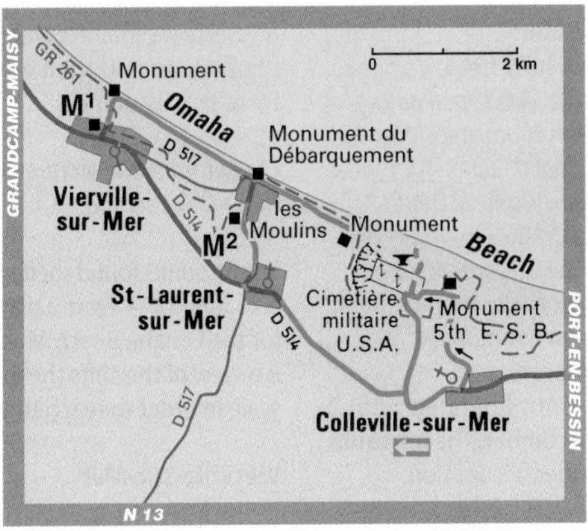

Musée D.-Day-Omaha M1 Musée Omaha-6 juin 1944 M2

taken the Port-en-Bessin-Grandcamp road enabling the motorised units to gain the plateau.

The austere and desolate appearance, especially of the eastern part, a narrow beach backing on barren cliffs, makes the invasion scene easy to imagine.

DRIVING TOUR

COLLEVILLE-SUR-MER TO VIERVILLE

9km/5.6mi – allow 1hr.

Colleville-sur-Mer

The last Germans did not leave the area around the village church until 10am on 7 June. The church has been entirely rebuilt.

Just before the church, turn right towards the coast.

Monument to the 5th Engineer Special Brigade

The monument, built on the remains of a blockhouse, commemorates those who died protecting movements between the landing craft and the beach. This is the best belvedere on Omaha Beach.

American Military Cemetery (St-Laurent-sur-Mer)

The 9 385 Carrara marble crosses and Stars of David stand aligned in an impressive site. A memorial stands in the central alley and is surrounded by trees. The commemorative list includes 1 557 names.

A *bélvèdere* (viewing table showing the landing operation) overlooks the sea. The path down to the beach *(30min there and back)* passes a second viewing table.

A monument to the US 1st Infantry Division stands just outside the cemetery.

Continue west on D 514 to St-Laurent-sur-Mer.

American Military Cemetery, Colleville-sur-le-Mer

St-Laurent-sur-Mer
Musée Omaha 6 juin 1944
Av. de la Libération. Open daily Jul–Aug 9.30am–7.30pm; mid-May–Jun and 1st 2 weeks Sept 9.30am–7pm; mid-Feb–mid-Mar 10am–12.30pm, 2.30pm–6pm; mid-Mar –mid-May and mid-Sept–mid-Nov 9.30am–6.30pm. (Last entry 1hr before closing). 5.80€. 02 31 21 97 44. www.musee-memorial-omaha.com.
This village was not liberated until 7 June after heavy combat. The **museum** describes life under occupation.

Take D 517 down to the beach: the road runs through a valley to another memorial.

Les Moulins
This site is marked by the **Monument to the D-Day Landing.** Turn right onto the road that runs along the beach and follow it to the end; there, at the foot of the American cemetery, you can look out onto the Ruquet Valley and the road opened by the Engineers unit after the blockhouse was destroyed around 11.30am. Heavy equipment, motorised units and the infantry were able to reach the plateau and then advance to the town of St-Laurent.

Return to the Monument to the D-Day Landing.

The first units found shelter here at dawn on 6 June 1944. From a platform erected for the Omaha Beach Monument there is a view of the cliffs the infantry had to scale in order to reach the plateau.

Vierville-sur-Mer

Follow boulevard Maritime west several hundred yards towards Vierville.

Here a stele marks the spot where the first to fall in the Battle of the Beaches were temporarily buried.

The road leaves the coast by another beach exit.

A monument to the American National Guard stands on one of the most redoubtable of the German block-houses.

ADDRESSES

STAY

Chambre d'hôte Ferme du Clos Tassin – *14710 Colleville-sur-Mer, in the village, on D 514. 02 31 22 41 51. www.clostassin.fr.st. Closed Jan. 5 rooms. . Meal.* The owners of this farm make their own cider, calvados and pommeau (a mixture of Calvados and apple juice). Taste the products in the shop, where meals are taken. The bedrooms are simple but very comfortable.

Hôtel du Casino – *r. de la Percée, 14710 Vierville-sur-Mer. 02 31 22 41 02. Closed 15 Nov–15 Mar. 12 rooms. 9.50€. Restaurant.* Sea breezes and fine sand await you when you stay in this seaside hotel dating from the 1950s. Ask for a room with a view, then enjoy seafood in the dining room.

EAT

L'Omaha – *pl. du Monument, 14710 St-Laurent-sur-Mer. 02 31 22 41 46. Closed 15 Nov–15 Feb.*
This restaurant's strongest point is its situation facing the sea, a stone's throw from Omaha Beach. Plain interior and two summer terraces. Cuisine with an accent on seafood. A small souvenir shop.

LEISURE

Eolia Normandie – *Le Cavey Omaha Beach, 14710 Colleville-sur-Mer. 02 31 22 26 21. www.eolia-normandie.com.*
Guided outings on sand-yachts, wake-boards, catamarans and kayaks.

Orbec

Orbec is a small and lively town with a long history, as witnessed by the many old half-timbered houses in the busy shopping street, rue Grande. The town stands quite close to the source of the River Orbiquet in one of the most pleasant valleys in the Auge region. At the entrance to the town stands the famous Pierre Lanquetot factory, which has been producing its delicious Camembert cheeses for the past century.

- **Population:** 2 422.
- **Michelin Map:** 303: O-5.
- **Info:** 6 rue Grande. ℘02 31 32 56 68. www.mairie-orbec.fr.
- **Location:** Orbec is 18km/11mi SW of Bernay via D 131.
- **Don't Miss:** The excursion on foot, following the GR 26 itinerary.

VISIT

Musée municipal

107 r. Grande. Open Jul–Aug Wed and Sat–Sun 10am–noon, 2–6pm, Tue and Thu–Fri 2–6pm; Easter–Jun and Sept–Dec Wed and Sat–Sun 2–6pm. Closed public holidays. No charge. ℘02 31 32 58 89.

The museum is located in a beautiful 16C timber-framed house, the **Vieux Manoir★**, built for a rich tanner. Carved figures and geometric patterns decorate the exterior.

GR 26 WALK

4.5km/2.8mi S of Orbec

A small road *(chemin de la Folletière-Abenon)*, follows along the Orbiquet river. Leave the car by the bridge and take a path on the left. The GR 26 itinerary (signposted in red and white) leads you on a tour of one of the prettiest valleys in the Pays d'Auge.

ADDRESSES

STAY

Le Manoir de l'Engagiste – *15 r. St-Rémi, 14290 Orbec. ℘02 31 32 57 22. www.orbec-hotel-manoirengagiste.com. 4 rooms.* Take the time to fully enjoy this marvellously restored 16C manor. The rooms are veritable cocoons. Wintertime, you'll have a warm breakfast in the exquisite salon by the crackling fireplace.

Detail of the timber-framed Vieux Manoir

Ouistreham-Riva-Bella

Located at the mouth of the Orne and astride the canal from Caen, the combined facilities of the town of Ouistreham and the beach of Riva-Bella make an excellent seaside resort. As the seaport for Caen, the harbour bustles with trawlers, pleasure craft and the cross-Channel ferries plying between Ouistreham and Portsmouth.

- **Population:** 9 396.
- **Michelin Map:** 303: K-4 – Local map, *see Plages du DÉBARQUEMENT.*
- **Info:** Jardins du Casino, 14150 Ouistreham-Riva-Bella. 02 31 97 18 63. www.ot-ouistreham.fr.
- **Location:** Ouistreham is 15km/9mi from Caen.
- **Don't Miss:** Stroll out to admire the yachts anchored in the marina.
- **Timing:** You might consider taking a sea-water cure.

A BIT OF HISTORY

A busy port since medieval times, Ouistreham derives its name from Saxon words meaning "western" (ouistre) and "farm" (ham).

The name "Riva Bella", or "beautiful coast" in Italian, derives from the name of the first of many residences constructed in the 19C, as the splendid 5km/3mi beach attracted fashionable visitors. At dawn on 6 June 1944, the same beach, code-named Sword, became an inferno as a British-French commando force stormed massive German fortifications.

THE TOWN

Église St-Samson★

Place Lemarignier.

This ancient 12C fortress church was built on the site of a 9C wooden church destroyed by Norsemen.

The gabled west front with its three superimposed tiers of blind arcades above the recessed doorway is particularly remarkable. Step back to get a good view of the late-12C belfry supported by buttresses.

In the nave note the round piers with gadrooned capitals and the lovely clerestory windows.

Port de Plaisance

Leave the car in place du Général-de-Gaulle.

A large basin on the opposite bank of the canal (Canal de Caen à la Mer) provides berths for many yachts. In season it is a lively and colourful spot.

Lighthouse

quai Georges-Thierry. Open Jul–Aug Fri,weekends and public holidays 3–6pm; rest of the year depending on the weather and the guardian's availability. 2€.

From the top of the lighthouse (30m/98.4ft high, 171 steps) there is a good view of the harbour and marina.

THE RESORT

Big Bunker (Le Grand Bunker) Musée du Mur de l'Atlantique

av. du 6-Juin near the tourist office. Open Apr–Sept daily 9am–7pm; Oct–Dec and 2nd week Feb–Mar 10am–6pm. 7€. 02 31 97 28 69.

This museum, located in a former German range-finding station, overlooks the mouth of the River Orne from a height of 17m/55.8ft; it sent firing instructions to the artillery units in Ouistreham. Rooms are arranged as they were in 1944. In the range-finding room, you can study the horizon with the range-finder over a 180° angle and a distance of 45km/28mi.

Musée du Débarquement "no 4 Commando"

pl. Alfred-Thomas. Open Mar–Oct daily 10.30am–6pm. 4.50€. 02 31 96 63 10.

The 4th Anglo-French Commando under Commander Philippe Kieffer reduced the enemy strong points on the morning of 6 June. The museum contains original artifacts from the operation.

Casino

pl. Alfred-Thomas. Open daily 10am– dawn. 02 31 36 30 00. www.lucienbarriere.com.
One of a chain, the Casino Barrière d'Ouistreham offers slot machines, table games (blackjack, Texas hold'em poker, roulette, boule), as well as a bar, two restaurants and a disco.

Station nautique

espl. Lofi. Open Apr–Sept daily 10am–1pm, 2–7pm; Oct–mid-Dec and mid-Jan–Mar Fri–Wed 10 am–1pm, 2–6pm. 02 31 96 52 31. www.ouistreham.fr.
The town's nautical centre offers activities such as sailing, cruises, deep-sea fishing, wind-surfing and canoeing, as well as instruction.

ADDRESSES

STAY

Hôtel de la Plage – *39 av. Pasteur, 14150 Riva-Bella. 02 31 9685 16. www. hotel-ouistreham.com. Closed mid Nov–Feb. 16 rooms.* . Early 20C Anglo-Norman villa, on a quiet street near the beach. Renovated guest rooms; some arge ones for families. Pretty garden.

EAT

Le Normandie – *71 av. Michel-Cabieu. 02 31 97 19 57. www. lenormandie.com. Closed 18 Dec–1 Jan, Sun eve and Mon except Apr–Oct.* In an old Norman house on the port, a brightly coloured, well-lit dining room, and an elegant veranda.

Le St-Georges – *51 av. Andry. 02 31 97 18 79. www.hotel-le-saint-georges.com. Closed 8–29 Jan, Sun eve, Mon lunch.* Try the seaside specialities served in both dining rooms: the modern one with its large picture windows offering a panoramic view of the coast, and the traditional one with its wooden ceiling and fireplace. The hotel offers 20 guest rooms.

LEISURE

Thalazur Ouistreham – *av. du Cdt-Kieffer. 02 31 96 40 40. www.thalazur. fr. Closed Dec.* Salt water treatments, massage, beauty care, and fitness programmes. The centre includes the Hotel Riva Bella, with 89 guest rooms.

St-Pierre-sur-Dives★

St-Pierre-sur-Dives, which developed round a rich Benedictine abbey founded in the 11C by Countess Lesceline, aunt of William the Conqueror, still possesses the remarkable old abbey church.

- **Population:** 3 687.
- **Michelin Map:** 303: L-5.
- **Info:** Rue St-Benoît. 02 31 20 97 90. www.mairie-saint-pierre-sur-dives.fr.
- **Location:** St-Pierre-sur-Dives is 43km/21mi SW of Caen.
- **Don't Miss:** The market-place of Saint-Pierre-sur-Dives.
- **Timing:** The Monday morning market is one of the largest in Normandy.

SIGHTS

Église Abbatiale★

Open daily. 02 31 20 97 90.
The original abbey church was burned down in 1106 during the wars between William the Conqueror's sons. The 12C

Romanesque south tower, la **Tour St-Michel**, was originally a dovecote that doubled as a defensive keep; the west front and the north tower were rebuilt in the 14C. A magnificent 13C lantern tower rises at the transept.

A copper strip crosses the floor of the nave. Known as the Meridian, it shows the rays of the noontide sun as they pass through a small bronze plaque in one of the windows.

The **convent buildings** date from the 17C; the **cloister** (*open daily Jun–Aug 9.30am–8pm; Sept–May 9.30am–6pm).* of which only the arcades remain, dates from the 18C.

Salle capitulaire

Entrance at 23 r. St-Benoît.
Open mid-Apr–mid-Oct Mon–Fri 9.30am–12.30pm, 1.30–6pm, Sat–Sun 10am–noon, 2–5pm; rest of the year Mon–Fri 9.30am–12.30pm, 1.30–5.30pm. No charge. 02 31 20 97 90. www.mairie-saint-pierre-sur-dives.fr.
The early-13C Gothic chapter house has a 13C glazed brick pavement, which was previously in the sanctuary.

Halles★

Open daily May–Sept 8am–8pm. No charge. 02 31 20 97 90. Food market Monday mornings. Antiques market 1st Sun of the month.
The 11C–12C market, which was burned down in 1944, has been faithfully rebuilt, even to the use of 290 000 chestnut pegs in its **timber-work**.

EXCURSIONS

Château de Vendeuvre★★

6km/3.7mi SW by D 271.
See Château de VENDEUVRE, p150.

Château de Canon

12km/7.4mi SW of St-Pierre, in Mézidon-Canon, on D 47. Open Jun–Sept daily 2–6pm. Easter–May Sat–Sun and public holidays 2–6pm. 6€. 02 50 67 10 74. www.opatrimoine.com/chateaudecanon.
This Classical château, built between 1720 and 1768, was the birthplace of Léonce Élie de Beaumont (1798–1874), celebrated 19C geologist.

Parks and gardens★
The gardens and grounds are a delightful mix of the formal French style and picturesque English fashion, embellished with statues and follies. The **chartreuses★** are walled gardens where fruits and vegetables are sheltered from the wind.

ADDRESSES

SHOPPING

Market – *Les Halles. 02 31 20 73 28.*
The 16C village marketplace comes alive on Monday morning, when some 150 merchants converge to sell cheese, *charcuterie*, fruit, vegetables and a variety of crafts. On the 1st Sun of the month, from 8am–6pm, it's the turn of antique dealers.

Plaisirs des Mets – *2 r. de Lisieux, St-Pierre-sur-Dives. 02 31 90 33 05. www.plaisirs-des-mets.com. Closed Sun eve, Tue, Wed off-season and Jan.* The pretty façade of this small grocery shop, which has been made to appear old, draws the eye. Inside, the nostalgic theme is pursued: old crates with advertising still evident, elderly furniture and period bric-à-brac support displays of tea, noodles, oils, sweets, sweet liqueurs, preserved flowers and jams.

Thury-Harcourt

The town, rebuilt, stands on the banks of the Orne and is now a tourist centre for the Suisse Normande to the south. Thury adopted the name Harcourt from the Harcourt family which came from the town of Harcourt in the county of Évreux; in 1700 Thury became the Harcourt ancestral seat.

- **Population:** 1 848.
- **Michelin Map:** 303: J-6.
- **Info:** 2 place St-Sauveur, Thury-Harcourt. 02 31 79 70 45. www.suisse-normande.com.
- **Location:** Thury-Harcourt lies 23km/14.4mi south of Caen.
- **Don't Miss:** A drive to the Boucle du Hom, where the River Orne meanders.
- **Timing:** Give yourself a half day to see the château, followed by a walk in the country.

VISIT

Park and Gardens of the Château★

Open May–Sept daily 2.30–6.30pm. Apr Sun and public holidays 2.30–6.30pm. Ask about prices. 02 31 79 72 05.

Near the ruins of the Harcourt family château, burnt by the Germans in 1944, the 70-ha/173-acre park has 4km/2.5mi of walkways bordered with trees, shrubs, flower beds and grassy paths.

DRIVING TOUR

Boucle du Hom★

5km/3mi. Leave Thury-Harcourt on D 6 to the NW. After 1.5km/0.9mi take D 212 to the right.

The road follows the west bank of the Orne and offers good viewpoints overlooking the Orne and its green banks.

Turn right at Le Hom where the road leaves the Orne to enter a deep cutting through the rock at the end of the curve's promontory.

Return towards Thury-Harcourt by D 6.

Mont Pinçon★

14km/8.7mi. Leave Thury-Harcourt on D 6 to the NW. At the Vallée de Hamars, turn left onto D 36, then right on D 108 at the crossroads. At Plessis-Grimault, turn sharp right onto D 54, towards Aunay-sur-Odon.

The **Pré-Bocage** is a picturesque rural countryside which borders the Caen plain, the Bessin and the *bocage*.

At the top of the climb of 365m/1 197ft, near a television transmitter, turn left and continue for another 600m/656yd.

Leave the car to walk over the heathland (*the rough stony path can be difficult in winter, take care*); there is a wide-ranging **panorama** of the *bocage*.

Chapelle St-Joseph

17km/10.5mi. Leave Thury by D 6 towards Bayeux, turn left onto D 166 after a bridge. The route climbs the valley of the Orne. Turn right at Mesnil-Roger to St-Martin-de-Sallen and turn right again here onto a narrow uphill road from which a one-lane road leads off to the right to St Joseph's.

From behind the chapel, there is a beautiful **panorama**★ of the Orne Valley and the heights of the Suisse Normande.

Return to St-Martin-de-Sallen and take the next road on the right to rejoin D 6 to Thury.

Trouville-sur-Mer★★

- Population: 606.
- Michelin Map: 303: M-3.
- Info: 32 quai Fernand-Moureaux, 14360 Trouville-sur-Mer. ℘02 31 14 60 70. www.trouvillesurmer.org.
- Location: Trouville extends along the north side of the estuary, opposite Deauville, 94km/58.4mi E of Rouen.

At Trouville, the cliffs of the Normandy corniche slope away at the mouth of the River Touques, to be replaced by a wonderful beach of fine golden sand. Although up-to-date, the town retains its charm; at the start of the Second Empire (1852), Trouville launched the Côte Fleurie. As in Deauville, the wooden plank promenade *(planches)* runs the full length of the beach. Owing to the comings and goings of the fishermen and the small resident population, Trouville is worth visiting even out of season.

VISIT

Corniche

Make for the corniche road to the north by way of boulevard Aristide-Briand and a left turn. On the way down there is a magnificent **view** of the Trouville and Deauville beaches and the Côte Fleurie. From the Calvaire de Bon-Secours *(viewing table)* the view is breathtaking.

Aquarium

17 rue de Paris. Open Jul–Aug daily 10am–7.30pm; Easter–Jun and Sept–Oct 10am–noon, 2–7pm; rest of the year 2–6.30pm. Closed 25 Dec. 7.50€ (children 3–14 years 5.50€). ℘02 31 88 46 04. www.natur-aquarium.com. Seafront promenade. Fresh and salt water fish together with equatorial forest reptiles provide a colourful spectacle.

Musée de Trouville Villa Montebello

64 r. du Général-Leclerc. Open mid-Mar–Apr and Oct–mid-Nov Mon–Fri 2–5.30pm, Sat–Sun 11am–1pm; May–Sept Mon–Fri 11am–1pm, 2–6pm. 2€. ℘02 31 88 16 26.

This villa is a fine example of seaside architecture during the Second Empire (1852–70). The museum shows work by artists who brought fame to the town.

Trouville-sur-Mer

Galeries d'exposition

In the tourist office. ♿ ⓘOpen Jul–Aug Wed–Mon 10am–1pm, 2–6.30pm; mid-Apr–Jun and Sept 10am–12.30pm, 2–6pm; Oct–Dec during school holidays Wed and Fri–Sat–Sun 10am–12.30pm, 2–5.30pm. 2€. ☎02 31 14 92 06. This gallery hosts temporary art exhibitions.

EXCURSIONS

Corniche Normande from Trouville to Honfleur

21km/13mi. *See DEAUVILLE, p117.*

Côte Fleurie from Trouville to Cabourg

19km/12mi. *See DEAUVILLE, p117.*

Fishmonger in Touville-sur-Mer

G. Targat/MICHELIN

ADDRESSES

STAY

Hôtel Le Fer à Cheval – *11 r. Victor-Hugo. ☎02 31 98 30 20. www.hotel-trouville.com. 34 rooms. 10€.* These two old villas at the centre of the resort, near the beaches, offer functional rooms. The proprietor, a former baker, offers delicious croissants and pastries at breakfast and afternoon tea.

Hôtel les Sablettes – *15 r. Paul-Besson. ☎02 31 88 10 66. www.trouville-hotel.com. Closed Jan. 18 rooms. 7€.* Away from traffic, this hotel offers simple, practical accommodation. Close to the casino and beach.

Hôtel Le Trouville – *r. Thiers. ☎02 31 98 45 48. www.hotelletrouville.com. Closed Jan. 15 rooms. 7 ("breakfast" 14€).* If the façade is a bit tired, the interior is bright and clean. The rooms, 2 of them for family, have complete bathrooms and new beds. Good value for money.

EAT

Le Cap Horn – *20 r. des Bains. ☎02 31 98 45 06. Closed Mon eve, Tue off-season.* Behind the pretty stone façade are two dining rooms. The upper floor has a seaside décor and a terrace. Seafood menu based on the daily catch.

Crêperie Le Vieux Normand – *124 quai Fernand-Moureaux, Trouville. ☎02 31 88 38 79. Closed 10–31 Jan, Thu. Reservations advised.* This first-rate address owes its success to its ideal location facing the wharf, the agreeable rustic setting and the menu of fondues, raclettes, salads and *crêpes*.

Tivoli Bistro – *27 r. Charles-Mozin. ☎02 31 98 43 44. Closed 3 weeks in Jun, mid-Nov–mid-Dec, Wed–Thu. Reservations advised.* The décor of the small pastel dining room is a bit minimalist, but the cuisine is ample and delicious, made with products straight from the market.

La Régence – *132 bd F.-Moureaux. ☎02 31 88 10 71. www.lla-regence.com. Closed 8–18 Mar, 1–27 Dec, Mon, Thu off season. Reservations advised weekends.* Opposite the sea, an elegant dining room decorated with 19C painted wood panels. Very fresh fish and traditional cuisine.

NIGHTLIFE

La Maison – *66 r. des Bains. ☎02 31 81 94 78.* Brunch, lunch, tea or ice cream, wine-tastings, all to beautiful music.

LEISURE

Centre équestre de Trouville-Villerville – *Chemin des Terrois, 14113 Villerville. ☎02 31 14 99 69.* This club offers rides on the beach, in the forest and along the cliffs, offering superb views.

Château du Vendeuvre★★

In 1750 Alexandre le Forestier d'Osseville, Count of Vendeuvre, commissioned the architect Jacques-François Blondel to build him a summer residence on the banks of the Dives. The château and its beautiful gardens, with their delightful surprise fountains, continue to charm.

- **Michelin Map:** 303: L-6
- **Info:** 02 31 40 93 83. www.vendeuvre.com.
- **Location:** The château is 5km/3mi SW of St-Pierre-sur-Dives.
- **Don't Miss:** The Musée du Mobilier miniature is a collection of tiny masterpieces; the park has remarkable waterworks, including surprise spurts.
- **Timing:** You will need 3hr to see the miniature museum and enjoy the garden. You may decide to spend the day here.
- **Kids:** There is an amusing collection of shelters for pets.

VISIT

Open May–Sept 11am–6pm. Apr (during Tulip Festival) and Oct–2 Nov Sun and public holidays 2–6pm. 6.90€–8.90€ (children 5.30€–6.90€). 02 31 40 93 83. www.vendeuvre.com.

The château offers five sights: the **Musée du mobilier miniature** (Miniature Furniture Museum), the château interior, the collection of shelters for pets, the garden and the 18C kitchens. Ticket prices depend on how many venues you want to visit.

Musée du Mobilier miniature★★

The lovely vaulted rooms of the orangery are the setting for an exceptional collection of miniature furniture, models and masterpieces of skilled craftsmen. About 100 pieces dating from the 16C to the present, are exhibited.

Fountain at the water garden, Château du Vendeuvre

© Hemis/Photoshot

Château★

Same hours as museum.

The rooms are attractively furnished. In the dining room, looking out on the evening sunset, the table is laid with a linen cloth woven with the family arms and the rear façade of the château. The reception room has lovely carved panelling.

Two popular 18C games are on display: tric-trac table and loto. Note the special chair for a woman wearing panniers and in the main bedroom the toiletry set, the pastels in the salon, the study (collection of goose feathers), the smoking room (paraphernalia of an 18C smoker) and the kitchens. Behind the château there is a water garden.

Garden of surprises

Among the fanciful delights of the garden, the spray of fountains may catch you by surprise. True to the playful spirit that motivated 18C landscape artists, the many wonders include a not-to-be-missed grotto made of 200 000 seashells. High kitsch!

Vire

Vire stands on a hillock overlooking the rolling Normandy *bocage*. The town grew up around its castle in the 8C. In the 12C Henry Beauclerk, King of England, strengthened the castle's fortifications and built the keep. In the 13C the population increased and trade flourished but the Wars of Religion (1561–98) led to decline and in 1630 Cardinal Richelieu dismantled the castle. The 17C and 18C brought another period of prosperity. Vire is an important road junction and as such it was almost annihilated in 1944.

- **Population:** 12 815.
- **Michelin Map:** 303: G-6.
- **Info:** Square de la Résistance, 14500 Vire. ℘02 31 66 28 50. www.vire-tourisme.com.
- **Location:** On the route between Caen and Fougères.

SIGHTS

Église Notre-Dame

pl. Notre-Dame.

This 13C–15C Gothic church was erected on the site of a 13C Romanesque chapel built by Henry I Beauclerk, son of William the Conqueror. The 13C porch is flanked by a slate-roofed tower. The bell tower is surmounted by a balustrade; its spire succumbed to lightning in the 15C. In the south transept is a gilded Baroque altarpiece and a 19C Pièta by a sculptor from Lisieux. The church suffered heavily during wars and the French Revolution, but has been well restored.

Access via rue du Valhérel. The Vaux de Vire refers to where the steep-sided Vire and Virenne valleys meet, as well as to a collection of 15C drinking songs, origin of the word *vaudeville*.

Tour de l'Horloge

pl. du 6 Juin. Open Jul–mid-Sept Tue–Thu 2–6pm, Fri–Sat 10am–12.30pm, 2–6pm. No charge.

The old main gate (13C) to the fortified town is flanked by twin towers and surmounted by a 15C belfry, built to include both a clock *(horloge)* and a bell. A niche holds a wooden statue of the Virgin dating from the 16C.

EXCURSION

Plan d'Eau de la Dathée

7km/4.3mi S on D 577, then turn right onto D 76.

There are good views and a walk (7km/4.3mi) round the shore, as well as a water sports centre, a bird reserve and picnic area.

S. Sauvignier/MICHELIN

Vire Chitterlings

This well-known local speciality *(andouille)* is prepared to a traditional recipe.

The stomach and the smaller intestines of the pig are cleaned, chopped, salted and marinated and then stuffed into the larger intestine, which is smoked over a beechwood fire for several weeks.

The black colour produced by the process is proof of authenticity. The sausage-like chitterlings are then cooked in water and tied off.

Lighthouse on Cap de la Hague, Soury

The pronounced thrust of the Cotentin Peninsula into the Atlantic corresponds with an equally uncharacteristic landscape: the austere surroundings of La Hague is more like Brittany than Normandy. Geographically speaking, the area can be divided into three parts: the Cotentin Pass is the lower plain, the Val de Saire includes the river valley and the whole northeast part of the peninsula, the Cap de la Hague is the granite spine jutting out into the sea. The wooded hinterland was the cradle of Norman adventurers who once controlled the central Mediterranean area.

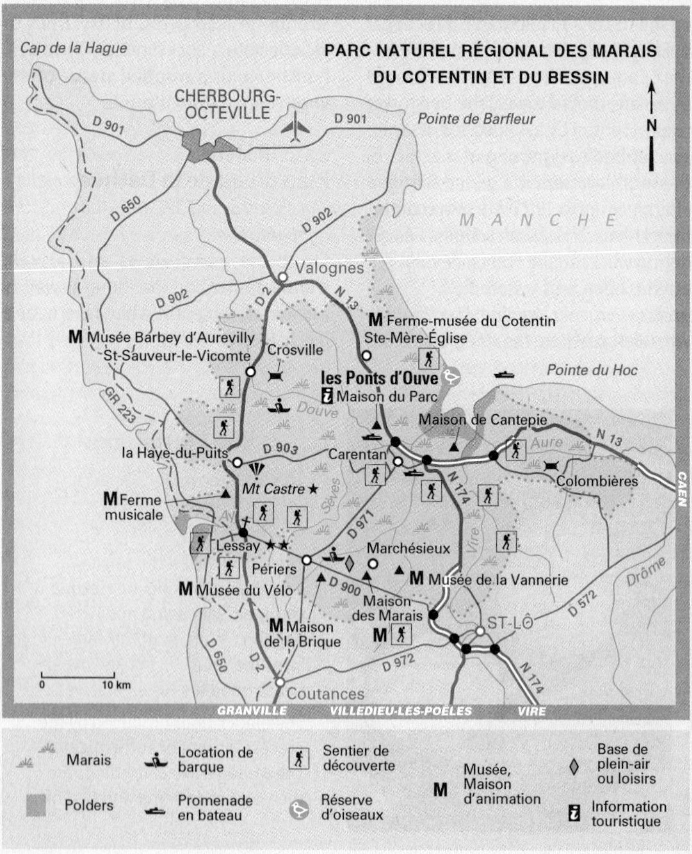

Presqu'île du Cotentin★★

A BIT OF HISTORY

Norman Kings of Sicily (11C–12C) – Early in the 11C, the harsh rule of the Duke of Normandy drove many dissatisfied inhabitants of the Cotentin to set out for the Holy Land. En route they wandered into southern Italy where feudal barons were in a perpetual state of war. A lord in Apulia, in revolt against Byzantium, asked the Normans to return home and raise troops for him; they had no difficulty in finding recruits in the poor and overpopulated Cotentin.

The exploits of three sons of **Tancrède de Hauteville**, a minor baron from the Coutances area, aroused great enthusiasm. The eldest, William, known as Iron Arm, drove out those who had employed him and became William of Apulia in 1102. His two brothers, Robert and Roger, followed his lead. The reign of Roger II from 1101 to 1154 was particularly brilliant. The last Norman king of Sicily was Manfred, who was killed at Benevento in 1265 by Charles of Anjou, brother of St Louis, and whose tragic fate was celebrated by Dante, Byron and Schumann.

MARAIS DU COTENTIN ET DU BESSIN REGIONAL NATURE PARK

Maison d'Acceuil, 50500 St-Côme-du-Mont. ℘02 33 71 65 30. www.parc-cotentin-bessin.fr.

This nature park, formerly known as the Marais de Carentan, was inaugurated in June 1991 and embraces 144 communes, with 65 400 inhabitants. With a total area of 145 000ha/560sq mi these wetlands stretch from the Bay of Veys on the east coast of the Cotentin Peninsula to Lessay haven on the west coast. This area of marshland (30 000ha/116sq mi) and *bocage* with its many canals is rich in plant and animal life. The relatively tall vegetation of these treeless wetlands provides good nesting and wintering grounds for migratory species.

Michelin Map: 303: A-1 to B-2.

Location: Surrounded on three sides by the sea, and separated from the mainland by swamps, the peninsula extends from Portbail to the west (71km/44mi N of Granville) to Carentan on the east (44km/27.3mi W of Bayeux), passing through Cherbourg.

Don't Miss: The splendid view of the Nez de Jobourg and the bay of Écalgrain.

Timing: Spend 2 days; each tour below takes half a day.

Kids: The Ludiver planetarium at La Hague provides a glimpse of the universe.

Les Ponts d'Ouve★ near Carentan is a visitor centre for the Marais du Cotentin et du Bessin Park. In addition to the exhibits indoors on flora and fauna, there is a **discovery trail** through the park with informative panels. There are observation areas set up for birdwatchers.

DRIVING TOURS

East Coast★

1 FROM CARENTAN TO BARFLEUR

75km/46.6mi – allow 2hr45min.

Carentan

Carentan is an important cattle market town and one of the largest centres of the regional dairy industry. The octagonal spire of the belfry of the **Église Notre-Dame** (12C–15C) dominates the whole region. The fine stone house at the corner of rue de l'Église and place Guillaume-de-Cerisay was described by Balzac under the name Hôtel de Dey in his work *Le Réquisitionnaire*.

Routes through the Historical Area of the Battle of Normandy

The following Routes through the Historical Area of the Battle of Normandy, pass through the Parc des Marais: D-Day-Le Choc (The Impact), Objectif-Un Port (Objective-A Harbour) and Cobra-La Percée (The Breakthrough)

www.normandiememoire.com/NM60Neerlandais/1_parcours/parcours.htm

The arcades of the old covered market in **place de la République** date from the late 14C. The **hôtel de ville** (town hall) occupies an 17C–19C convent.

From Carentan take N 13 towards Ste-Mère-Église. Shortly before St-Côme-du-Mont, turn right onto D 913.

Ste-Marie-du-Mont

The impressive **church** is identified by its square 14C tower of which the top storey is a Renaissance addition. The nave is early 12C; the transept and chancel date from the 14C. Inside is a late-16C figured pulpit; in the chancel, on the left, is a funerary statue of Henri Robert aux Espaulles carved in the early 17C.

US Navy memorial at Utah Beach

A roadside monument honours 800 Danish sailors who took part in the **D-Day landings**.

Utah Beach

Despite murderous fire from the German coastal batteries, the troops of the American 4th Division (7th Corps) disembarked on 6 June near La Madeleine and Les Dunes-de-Varreville and managed to make contact with the airborne troops of the 82nd and 101st Divisions, who had landed in the region of Ste-Mère-Église. Three weeks later the whole of the Cotentin Peninsula had been liberated.

Musée du Débarquement

Ste-Marie-du-Mont. Open daily Jun–Sept 9.30am–7pm (last entry 45min before closing); Apr–May and Oct 10am–6pm; Feb–Mar and 1st 2 weeks Nov 10am–5.30pm; mid-Nov–Dec and school and public holidays Sat–Sun 10am–12.30pm, 2–5.30pm. Closed 25 Dec. 6€. 02 33 71 53 35. www.utah-beach.com.

Utah Beach D-Day Museum is undergoing an extensive expansion programme *(current museum is still open during construction)*. Once complete (2011), the museum will display its magnificent collection in an entirely new exhibition space. This will include a hangar to house a full-scale relica of the B-26 *Dinah Might*, whose crew from the 533rd Squadron parahuted safely during the Landings but were later captured.

At **La Madeleine** there is a milestone – the first on the Road to Liberty – erected in 1947 to honour soldiers killed during the landings and a memorial to the 4th Division. A German blockhouse *(left)* is now a monument to the dead of the 1st Engineer Special Brigade; a stele and a crypt commemorate the American 90th Division. On an area of dunes, presented by the commune of Ste-Marie-du-Mont as official American territory, there stands a huge stele erected on the 40th anniversary of the landings by the Americans in homage to those who died at Utah Beach. It provides a fine view of

Port de Barfleur

© Bruno Delacotte/Fotolia

the sea; the wrecks of several blockships are still visible at low tide *(north)*.

Les Dunes-de-Varreville

In an opening in the dunes, 100m/110yd from the route des Alliés, a rose granite monument in the form of a ship's prow and bearing the cross of Lorraine commemorates the landing of the 2nd French Armoured Division under General Leclerc on 1 August 1944.

Quinéville

This is a family seaside resort. Good view of St-Vaast roadstead from the square near the church.

Mémorial de la Liberté retrouvée

18 av. des Plages, Quinéville. Open last week Mar–mid-Nov daily 10am–7pm. 6€. 02 33 95 95 95. www.memorial-quineville.com.
This museum re-creates daily life during the dark days of the Occupation. There is a village street, a blockhouse, and miscellaneous documentary material from the period.

Quettehou

The 13C granite church on a height is flanked by a tall 15C belfry. From the cemetery there is a view of Morsalines Bay, the Hougue Fort and the Pointe de Saire.

Val de Saire★

A detour inland from Quettehou runs through a pleasantly green countryside and affords good views of the east coast of the Cotentin Peninsula.

From Quettehou take D 902 north towards Barfleur; turn left onto D 26, which climbs through apple orchards. In Le Vast turn right.

The countryside offers rolling woodlands and pastures in the valleys.

In Valcanville turn right onto D 125. At D 328 crossroads turn left onto the road to La Pernelle; after 300m/328yd turn right at the sign Église, Panorama.

Beyond the rebuilt church of **La Pernelle** is a former German blockhouse, once an observatory, which commands a **panorama★★** *(viewing table)* extending from the Gatteville lighthouse (north) to the Grandcamp cliffs (south) by way of the Pointe de Saire, Réville Bay, Tatihou Island, Hougue Fort and the St-Marcouf Islands; in clear weather **Percée Point** is visible.

Take D 909 following signs to Pernelle Bourg.

St-Vaast-la-Hougue

See ST-VAAST-LA-HOUGUE, p243.

Continue north on D 1 along the port and the coast.

Beyond Réville the road passes La Crasvillerie, a delightful 16C manor house. As you approach Barfleur, the countryside begins to look a bit like Brittany, with granite houses, rocky bays and gnarled trees bent by the wind. Gatteville lighthouse stands to the north.

Barfleur and Excursions

See BARFLEUR, p206.

North Coast★★

2 FROM BARFLEUR TO CHERBOURG

38km/23.6mi – allow 1hr30min.

Barfleur

See BARFLEUR, p206.

Between Barfleur and St-Pierre-Église, the road crosses the Saire Valley.

Tocqueville

This was the family seat of **Alexis de Tocqueville** (1805–59) the author of *Democracy in the United States* and *The Ancien Régime and the Revolution*.

St-Pierre-Église

The fortified 17C church has a 12C Romanesque doorway. The 18C **château** was the family home of the Abbé de St-Pierre (1658–1743), the author of a plan for peace entitled *Projet de Paix Perpétuelle*.

There are several good **viewpoints**★ from the Fermanville-Bretteville corniche, notably those at the Pointe du Brulay and Brick Bay.

Shortly after Brick Bay turn left at the Auberge Maison Rouge, to climb uphill towards Maupertus-sur-Mer. A track on the right leads to the television relay station.

Belvédère★

There is a magnificent view of the coast and Cherbourg in the distance.

Return to D 116; continue west; in Bretteville take D 320 left towards Le Theil.

Allée Couverte (Gallery Grave)

This collective burial chamber, which dates back 4 000 years, consists of a double row of upright stones supporting flat slabs laid horizontally.

Return to Bretteville; take D 116 west.

On approaching Cherbourg one can see the roadstead and Pelée Island, which serves as an anchor for the mole which, with the great breakwater, divides the harbour from the sea. To the left is Roule Fort.

Cherbourg

See CHERBOURG-OCTEVILLE, p210.

3 FROM CHERBOURG TO BEAUMONT

47km/29.2mi – allow 2hr.

Cherbourg

See CHERBOURG-OCTEVILLE, p210.

Leave Cherbourg by D 901.

Ludiver – Observatoire – Planétarium de La Hague

1700 r. de la Libération. Open Jul–Aug daily 11am–6.30pm, planetarium shows at 11.30am, 3 and 4.30pm (last entry 1hr before closing). The rest of the year Sun–Fri 2-6pm, show at 3pm. Closed Jan, Easter Mon, 1 May, 1 and 11 Nov, 24–25, 31 Dec. 7.50€ (child 5.50€). 02 33 78 13 80. www.ludiver.com.

Set up on the Tonneville and Flottemanville-Hague plateau (180m/591ft), this new centre comprises a museu
m on astronomy and the universe, a planetarium with a seating capacity of 80 and an interior amphitheatre where the images of a 600mm telescope are projected live to the public.

Return to the coast and pass under D 901.

Querqueville

Beside the parish church stands the 10C **Chapelle St-Germain** (*left*), the oldest religious building of the Cotentin area. From behind the church *(path between the chapel and the church)* there is a view over the Cherbourg roadstead stretching from Cap Lévy *(east)* to Pointe Jardeheu *(west)*.

From Querqueville take D 45 west in the direction of Urville-Nacqueville; turn left just before the hamlet of La Rivière.

Château de Nacqueville

Guided tours (1hr) Easter–Sept Tue, Thu, Fri, Sun and public holidays at noon–5pm. Park closes at 6pm. 5€. 02 33 03 21 12. http://naqueville.com.
This beautiful 16C edifice, covered with ivy, makes a romantic sight, standing by a pool in its **park**★ of oak trees and rhododendrons. Only the great hall with its beautiful Renaissance fireplace is open to the public.

Return to D 45; continue west.

At the entrance to Landemer, on the left, are the towers of the old **Manoir de Dur-Écu** restored in the 16C but resting on 9C foundations. Only the courtyards and dovecote can be visited, but the maze in the field opposite is worth seeing *(open Jul–Sept Tue–Thu 11am–1pm, 3–7pm; 4€; 06 10 58 68 41; http://durecuf.wordpress.com)*.

After Landemer the road rises in the Habilland Ravine, soon a perspective (right) opens up from the Cap Lévy lighthouse to Pointe Jardeheu.

Gréville-Hague

The small church was a model for the painter **Jean-François Millet** (1814–75) in his works of Norman landscapes. The artist's bust sits on a rock at the crossroads and the **house** where he was born in **Gruchy** is open to the public *(guided tours (45min) daily Jul–Aug 11am–7pm; Jun and Sept 11am–6pm; Apr–May and school holidays except Christmas 2–6pm (last entry 1hr before closing); 4.20€; 02 33 01 81 91)*.

From Gréville-Hague, take the D237 to the right for Gruchy.

Rocher du Castel-Vendon★

Allow 1hr round-trip on foot. Leave the car at the entrance to the village and continue on foot to the public wash-house by a sunken road which then becomes a footpath: parts of this itinerary are difficult.
The path follows the right-hand side of the valley. From a rocky promontory, there is a **view** of the coast from Cap Lévy to Pointe Jardeheu. In the foreground stands the granite rock spine called the Rocher du Castel-Vendon.
In **Omonville-la-Petite** is a graveyard where the poet **Jacques Prévert** (1900–77) is buried *(left of the entrance)*.
To visit the **Maison Prévert** park on the church square *(open daily Jul–Aug 11am–7pm; Jun and Sept 11am–6pm; Apr–May and school holidays except Christmas 2–6pm (last entry 1hr before closing); 4.20€; 02 33 52 72 38)*.
The road towards St-Germain-des-Vaux affords views of the tiny hamlet of **Port-Racine**, one of France's smallest ports. At the entrance to **Auderville** a road down to Goury leads to the north end of the Cap de la Hague. Beyond the shore is the lighthouse of La Hague and, in the distance, the steep cliffs of Alderney.

Goury★

The small harbour is an important coastguard and lifeboat station. In its octagonal station, the lifeboat swivels around a turntable so it can be launched from two slipways: towards the port at high tide or towards the open sea at low tide.

Baie d'Écalgrain★★

This desolate beach backed by heathland is one of the area's wild beauty spots. To the left of Alderney are Guernsey and Sark and on the horizon the west coast of the Cotentin Peninsula.

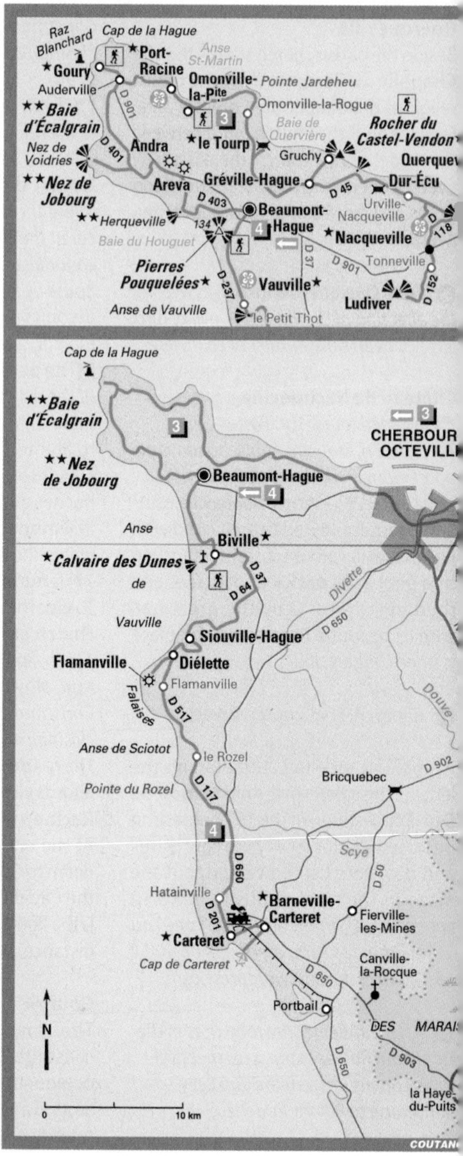

From Dannery take D 202 to the headland, Nez de Jobourg.

Nez de Jobourg★★

Off D901 in Beaumont-Hague. The information centre at the Avra Centre for storage of nuclear waste is open Mon–Fri 8.30am–noon, 1.30–5pm. Guided tour (2hr) Mon–Fri by reservation. No charge; identification required. Parking inside site. 03 33 01 69 00. www.andra.fr.

The long, rocky and barren promontory is now a bird sanctuary (seagulls). Walk along the **Nez de Voidries**. From the Auberge des Grottes there is a view north of Écalgrain Bay, the lighthouse off Cap de la Hague and the Channel

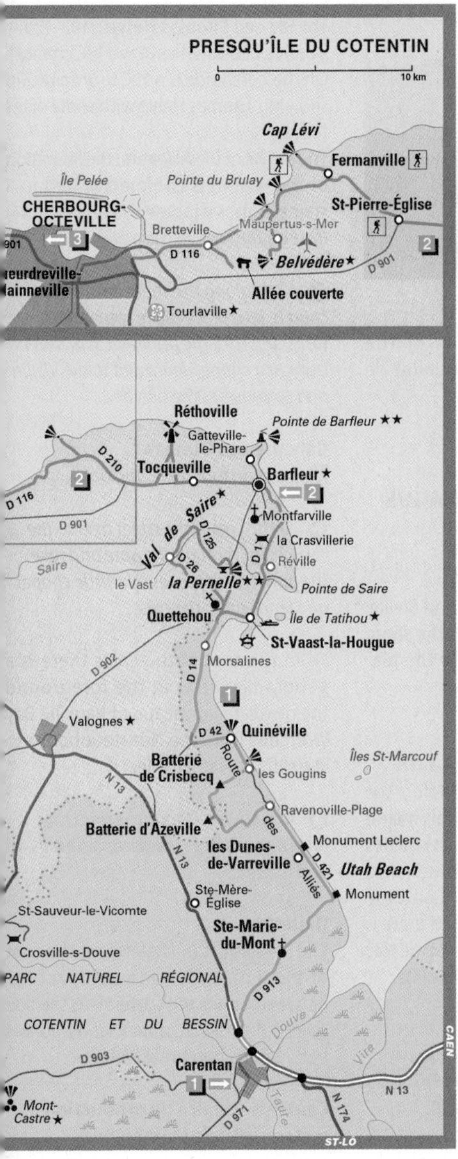

Islands: Alderney, the nearest, Sark, Guernsey and Jersey. Farther south the Nez de Jobourg itself comes into view, separated from the Nez de Voidries by Senneval Bay. In the distance Vauville Bay curves south to the cliffs at the Cap de Flamanville.

Take D 403, a steep downhill road, opposite the **Usine Areva**.

Leave the car in a lay-by in a bend beyond Herqueville to look at the **vista**★★ across Vauville Bay and over the Flamanville cliffs. The descent continues with Houguet Bay on the right.

Baie d'Écalgrain

G. Targat/MICHELIN

Beaumont-Hague

This was the home town of the 17C smuggling family, the Jallot de Beaumont.

West Coast★★

4 FROM BEAUMONT-HAGUE TO CARTERET

45km/28mi – allow 1hr30min.

Between Beaumont-Hague and Biville, the road goes down towards the shore and then climbs up again to the plateau.

Pierres Pouquelées★

45min round-trip on foot from D 318.

Leave the car 200m/219yd before the first houses of Vauville and walk inland up a path on the right. When it reaches the plateau turn left to reach the Pierres Pouquelées gallery grave. Continue right to a small rise from which there is a **panorama**★ of the coast from the Nez de Jobourg to the Flamanville cliffs.

Vauville

Botanical Garden: *Open Apr–Sept daily 2–6pm; Oct Tue and Fri–Sun 2–6pm. 6€. 02 33 10 00 00. http://jardin-vauville.fr.*

The 12C church and the 17C manor make an attractive picture. The **botanical garden**★ on the grounds of the manor specialises in evergreen plants.

Beyond the village of Petit Thot the road affords a good **view**★ of the moorland around the bay of Vauville.

Biville★

The village is set on a plateau overlooking the desolate shoreline of Vauville Bay. The Blessed **Thomas Hélye** (1187–1257), a native of Biville, lies in the 13C chancel. On the north side is a 19C bronze group showing Thomas Hélye with some of his followers.

The arrival of the Allies and the liberation of the region is commemorated in a stained-glass window by Barillet (1944) *(first on the right in the nave).*

Walk along the street beside the church; by a fence make some sharp turns and take the path which passes in front of a chapel dedicated to the Virgin and continue to the Calvary.

Calvaire des Dunes★

45min on foot there and back.

At the end of the street next to the church, go through the gate and take the path which passes by a little chapel and leads up to the cross.

From the foot of the cross there is a panoramic view: in the foreground the desolate landscape of Vauville Bay stretches from the Nez de Jobourg to the cliffs at Flamanville.

At Siouville-Hague the road runs once again beside the dunes, the hills and the sea.

Diélette

The small port of Diélette, at the foot of the dark cliffs, is the only refuge between Goury and Carteret. As the tide goes out, a beach of fine sand appears between its two breakwaters.

Centre nucléaire de production d'électricité de Flamanville

For security reasons, the nuclear power station no longer receives visitors. 02 33 78 70 17.

This nuclear power station, occupying 120ha/296 acres, stands in part on the granite bedrock, and in part on an artificial platform that juts into the ocean. Two production units have an installed capacity of 1 300 million kW each. Each unit produces 9 000 million kWh.

Between Flamanville and Le Rozel the road overlooks a small bay, the **Anse de Sciotot**; Cap de Flamanville and, to the south, the Pointe du Rozel are visible. The cliffs become lower, giving way to dunes.

Between Hatainville and Carteret the road runs along the dunes, the highest on the Norman coast. The grass covered hollows between the dunes are known locally as *mielles*.

Carteret★

See BARNEVILLE-CARTERET, p207.

ADDRESSES

STAY

Chambre d'hôte La Dannevillerie – *50630 Le Vast, 5km/3mi NW of Quettehou via D 902 and D 26, then 2km/1mi further on, take the road on the right before Le Vast. 02 33 44 50 45. www.ladannevillerie.com. 3 rooms.* Nestling in the Val de Saire, this farm offers peace and repose. Delicious breakfasts.

Hôtel-Restaurant L'Escapade – *28 r. du Dr-Caillard, opposite the train station, 50500 Carentan. 02 33 42 02 00. Closed Dec–Feb. 15 rooms. Restaurant.* Under Napoleon III, this stately edifice covered with Virginia creeper was a coaching inn. Today it offers rooms of varying sizes and a handsome rustic dining room with an impeccably waxed parquet.

Château de Quinéville – *50310 Quinéville. 02 33 21 42 67. www.chateau-de-quineville.com. Closed Jan–Mar. 30 rooms. Restaurant.* Rooms in the former stables are more modern than those in the 18C château. The garden has Roman ruins, a 14C tower and a pond. Atractive dining room, traditional fare.

EAT

L'Estaminet – *pl. de l'Église, 50480 Ste-Marie-du-Mont-Village. 02 33 71 57 01. Closed Jan, Tue eve and Wed Oct–May.* Stop on the tiny, charming square next to the church, which on 6 June 1944 was stormed by thousands of Allied vehicles on their way from Utah Beach. This lovely Norman inn is the right place to recover from your emotions. Seafood on the menu. A few rooms.

Ferme-auberge La Huberdière – *Le Pommier, 50480 Liesville-sur-Douve, 8km/5mi NW of Carentan via D 913 to St-Côme-du-Mont then D 270. 02 33 71 01 60. www.chevrerie-ferme-auberge.com. Closed Sun evening and Mon. Reservations required.* You can tour this farm which breeds dairy cows and nanny goats. You may also sit down directly for a meal and enjoy the specialities of the house without delay.

Le Moulin à Vent – *50440 St-Germain-des-Vaux, 9km/5.6mi N of Nez de Jobourg via D 202, D 901 then D 45. 02 33 52 75 20. www.le-moulin-a-vent.fr. Closed Dec–Jan, Sun evening and Mon, except Jul–Oct.* This spruce, flower-decked granite house stands on a cliff at the end of the Cotentin Peninsula. In the dining room with its exposed beams, you will enjoy fresh seafood and sea views.

SHOPPING

Dupont d'isigny – *99 rte Américaine, 50500 Carentan. 02 33 71 66 66. Open Mon–Fri 9am–noon, 1.30–5pm.* This deluxe sweetshop, founded in 1894, offers 8 sorts of caramel and a wide range of candies. The factory can be visited by appointment.

LEISURE

École de Surf du Cotentin – *14 bis bd Deveaud, 50340 Siouville-Hague. 06 81 33 57 07. http://cotentin.surfclub.free.fr. Closed Dec–mid-Mar.* Lessons and rentals for surfers.

Club de kayak de mer du Nord-Cotentin – *Rte de Becquet, 50110 Tourlaville. 02 33 22 59 59. http://cotentinkayak.free.fr. Closed Feb and Christmas holidays.* This club offers lessons and kayak trips both on sea and in rivers, as well as rentals.

As the River Eure flows from its source in the hills of Perche northeast to join the Seine below Louviers, it passes through the *département* that carries its name. Wooded plateaux and rich, well-drained farmland lie on soil laid down over chalk formed in the Cretaceous Era, ending 70 million years ago. The landscape is characterised by half-timbered houses, châteaux and abbeys, medieval fountains and doorways, crooked streets, small hotels and restaurants. Great castles and dramatic ruins remind the visitor that the Eure, on the frontier between Normandy and France, has a long history of warfare, most recently in 1940 and 1944, when Évreux and Louviers suffered intense aerial bombardment. Yet pristine villages such as Lyons-la-Forêt and Vernon abound. Today, agriculture predominates, with orchards, fields of wheat, flax and sugarbeet, and pastures where dairy cows and Norman horses graze.

The small town of **Les Andelys** is dominated by the massive 12C **Château-Gaillard**, built by Richard the Lionheart in only one year, a remarkable engineering feat that introduced to Europe the round tower, a major defensive improvement over the square Norman tower. Nearby lie the gardens and water lily ponds of **Giverny**, created by Claude Monet around his home,and a magnet for tourists. **Le Bec-Hellouin** abbey, founded in 1034, abandoned at the Revolution and re-occupied by Cistercian monks in 1949, is magnificent. Besides the great castles of **Champ-de-Bataille**, **Harcourt**, and **Gisors**, a profusion of châteaux, grand and more modest, punctuate the countryside. Champs-de-Bataille and Harcourt also have notable gardens, as do **Acquigny** near Louvier and the **Abbaye de Mortemer** near Lyons-la-Forêt; keep an eye open for the many lovely parks and gardens around abbeys and châteaux and along village streets. The **Forêt de Lyons**, stretching 10 700ha/41sq mi, is the glory of French beech forests, with trunks reaching 20m/60ft tall. The small cities of **Évreux** and **Louviers**, reconstructed after World War II, as well as small towns such as **Conches-en-Ouche**, **Bernay**, **Pont Audemer** and **Verneuil** have retained half-timbered residences and narrow medieval streets. Because of the Eure's proximity to Rouen and Paris, many residents work in the city and villages are quiet on weekdays. *See also Fôret de Brotonne (p313).*

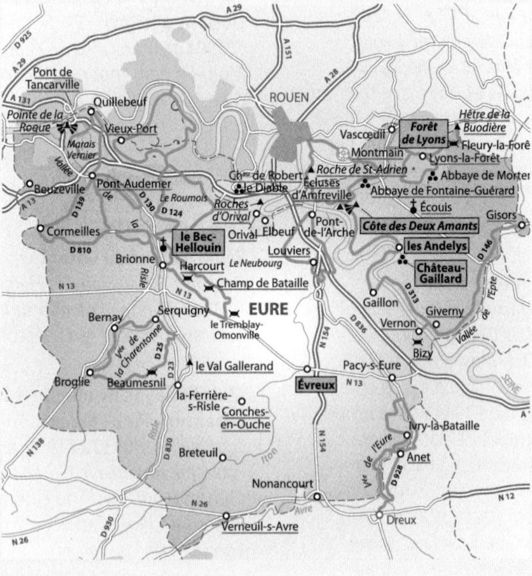

Les Andelys★★

Les Andelys, dominated by the impressive ruins of Château-Gaillard, lies in a lovely setting along the Seine. It once consisted of two distinct areas, Le Petit Andely to the west and Le Grand Andely to the east. The latter was the site of a 6C monastery founded by Clotilde, who converted her husband, King Clovis, to Christianity. At a fountain at 29 rue Ste-Clotilde, she is said to have turned water into wine for workmen building the monastery chapel.

- **Population:** 9 047.
- **Michelin Map:** 304: I-6 – Local map, *see Guide Vert VALLÉE DE LA SEINE.*
- **Info:** 24 rue Philippe-Auguste. ℘02 32 54 41 93. www.ville-andelys.fr.
- **Location:** The two Andelys are linked by avenue de la République and rue du Maréchal-Leclerc. Paris is 100km/62mi away, and Rouen 40km/25mi.
- **Don't Miss:** The view of the Seine Valley from the heights of the château.
- **Timing:** Visit the château in the morning, then enjoy Les Andelys and its surroundings.
- **Kids:** Children will be thrilled by the massive fortress.

A BIT OF HISTORY

In 1196 **Richard the Lionheart**, King of England and Duke of Normandy, decided to bar the King of France's way to Rouen along the Seine Valley by building a massive fortress on the cliff commanding the river at Andely. Within the year Château-Gaillard was erected and Richard cried "See my fine yearling!" **Philippe Auguste**, King of France, did not at first dare attack so formidable a redoubt. But when the vacillating King John succeeded Richard in 1199, the French beseigned the castle, filled in the moat, mined the walls and took the castle by storm on 6 March 1203.

Château-Gaillard★★

Allow 1hr. To reach the château by car: from Grand Andely, follow the signs from rue Louis-Pasteur. On foot (allow 30min ascent): from Petit Andely, follow rue Richard-Cœur-de-Lion, near the Office de Tourisme. Open mid-Mar–mid-Nov Wed–Mon 10am–1pm, 2–6pm (last entry 1hr before closing). Closed 1 May. 3€. ℘02 32 54 41 93 .http://les-andelys.com/chateau-gaillard.

From the car park there is a **view**★★ of the castle, the Seine and Les Andelys.

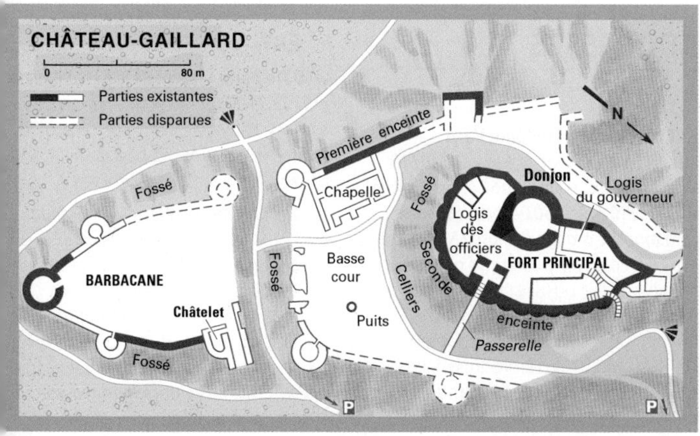

Barbican

The redoubt, separated from the main castle by a deep moat, possessed five towers of which only one, the barbican, remains, encircled by a narrow path.

Castle

The outer ward, the esplanade, is situated between the redoubt and the castle. Around the wall to the left are the foundations of the keep, which rises from the natural rock. At the far end of the wall there is a fine **viewpoint**.

Returning along the bottom of the moat, one passes casemates (*right*) hollowed out of the rock to store the garrison's food. The keep is round (8m/26ft in internal diameter) with thick walls (5m/16.4ft). Adjoining *(right)* are the ruins of the Governor's residence.

Outside the perimeter wall a path leads to the edge of the rocky escarpment, which provides an extended view of the Seine Valley.

Take the one-way descent to rue Richard-Cœur-de-Lion to return to the town.

ADDITIONAL SIGHTS

Église Notre-Dame★

Grand Andely. Open daily Jun–Sept 9am–noon, 2–6pm; Oct–May 9am–noon, 2– 5pm. 02 32 54 41 93.

A well-balanced façade of twin towers flanked by a square staircase tower fronts the church. The 16C south side is in the Flamboyant style and the 16C and 17C north side is Renaissance in style with round arches, Ionic pilasters, balustraded roofs, caryatids and antique-style statues.

Inside, the nave is 13C; the delicately ornamented triforium was remodelled in the 16C and the windows enlarged; the **organ**★ and loft are Renaissance. In the north transept and a nearby chapel are two lovely paintings by Quentin Varin, teacher of Les Andelys native Nicholas Poussin (1594–1665). The Entombment in the south aisle beneath the tower is 16C, the Christ in the Tomb is 14C.

Église St-Sauveur

pl. St-Sauveur, Petit Andely. Open daily 9am–6pm. 02 32 54 41 93.

St Saviour's is Greek cross in ground plan and Gothic in style; the chancel is late-12C, the nave early 13C. The wooden porch stands on an early 15C stone foundation. Inside there is an organ dating from 1674.

Musée Normandie-Niémen

r. Raymond-Phelip. Open Jun–mid-Sept Wed–Mon 10am–noon, 2–6pm; rest of the year Wed–Mon 2–6pm. Closed 1 Jan, 1 May, 24, 25, 31 Dec. 3.50€. 02 32 54 49 76.

The Normandie-Niémen squadron of the Free French Air Force fought with the Soviet Union on the Eastern Front from 1943–45.

ADDRESSES

STAY

Chambre d'hôte Mme Vard – *29 r. de l'Huis, village of Surcy, 27510 Mézières-en-Vexin, 13km/8mi SE of Les Andelys via D 1. 02 32 52 30 04. http://simone.vard.monsite.orange.fr. Closed Nov–Mar. 4 rooms.* Fresh air, peace and quiet, plus the charm of a bustling farm. Although the house's façade is rather glum, the old furniture, fine half-timbered stairway and rustic bedrooms make for an authentic sojourn. Farm products for sale.

EAT

De Paris – *10 av. de la République. 02 32 54 00 33.* Attractive residence from the early 20C, with a restaurant in a style part bourgeois, part rustic. A few simple rooms are also available.

La Chaîne d'Or – *27 r. Grande. 02 32 54 00 31. http://giverny.org/hotels/chainedor. Closed 1 Jan–4 Feb, Sun eve, Tue lunch, Mon–Tue in Nov–Mar.* This pleasant house on the banks of the Seine offers lovely views of the river. Try for a window seat, but wherever your table, you will enjoy the renowned cuisine. Rooms are available.

Le Bec-Hellouin★★

Le Bec-Hellouin Abbey, a medieval religious and cultural centre, produced two great Archbishops of Canterbury for England.

- **Population:** 415.
- **Michelin Map:** 304: E-6.
- **Info:** Place du Mal-Leclerc, 27110 Le Neubourg. ℘02 32 35 40 47. www.le-neubourg.fr/tourisme.
- **Location:** The abbey is 35km/22mi SW of Rouen and within 40km/25mi of Honfleur (NW), Lisieux (W) and Évreux (SE). Rouen is 52km/32mi NE, Harcourt 10km/6mi SE.
- **Don't Miss:** The abbey of Le Bec-Hellouin, the château and gardens at Champ-de-Bataille, and the Harcourt fortress with its arboretum.
- **Timing:** Spend your morning at the abbey, then go to Champ-de-Bataille or Harcourt in the afternoon.

A BIT OF HISTORY

In 1034 the knight **Herluin** found God and founded the Bec Abbey; its pious reputation attracted an Italian scholar, **Lanfranc**, who later became young Duke William's trusted adviser.

Pope Alexander II, a former student of Lanfranc at Bec, appointed him Archbishop of Canterbury, which made him virtual Regent of England whenever William returned to Normandy. On Lanfranc's death in 1093, **Anselm**, the theologian who was now Abbot of Bec, was transferred to Canterbury.

In the 17C Bec rose to new eminence under **Guillaume de la Tremblaye** (1644–1715), one of the greatest sculptors and architects of his period.

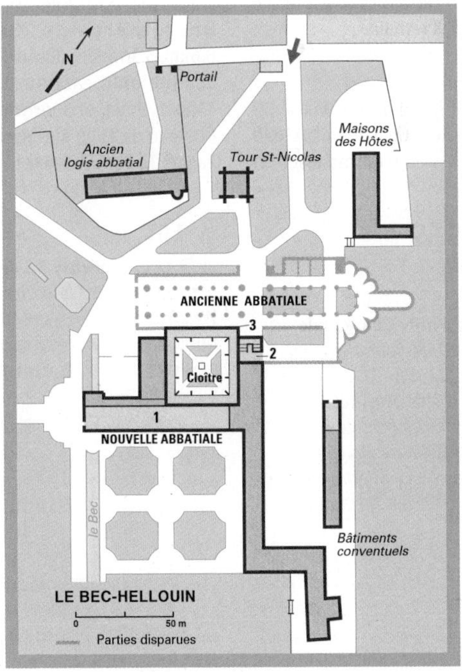

The monks were driven out during the Revolution and the church, one of the largest in Christendom, was demolished under the empire. In 1948 the site was restored to the Benedictine Order.

VISIT

Abbaye de Bec-Hellouin★★

Open for unaccompanied visit daily 8am–9pm. Guided tours (45min) Wed–Sat and Mon 10.30am, 3pm and 4pm, Sun noon, 3pm and 4pm. 5€ (tour). 02 32 43 72 60. www.abbayedubec.com.

New Abbey Church

The new abbey stands in the former Maurist refectory. At the entrance is a 14C statue of the Virgin; the Fathers of the Church are 15C. The altar was presented in 1959 by Aosta, birthplace of Bishop Anselm. Before the high altar lies the 11C sarcophagus of Herluin, founder of Bec **(1)**. Turn left on leaving to reach the other sights.

Old Abbey Church

Only the column, foundations and fragments of the south transept of the old abbey church remain.

Cloisters

A monumental 18C grand staircase **(2)** leads to the cloisters. Built between 1640 and 1660, the cloisters were modelled on those of Monte Cassino (Italy). Northeast of the cloisters is a beautiful, 14C gothic doorway **(3)**.

Tour St-Nicolas

Closed for security reasons.

The 15C tower is the most important remainder of the old abbey church. A plaque recalls the abbey's ties with England in the 11 and 12C.

EXCURSIONS

Château de Tilly (1500)

7km/4.3mi NE of Bec-Hellouin. Guided tours of interior (30min) mid-Jul–mid-Aug 2–6pm. 4€. Tours of exterior 10am–6pm. 2.50€.

Lozenge-patterned stone and glazed-brick front, perimeter wall quartered by pointed turrets. The winding **staircase**★ in brickwork in the courtyard recalls that of the Rihour Palace in Lille.

Tour of Village churches

Churches worth a visit include those at **Bouquetot** (11C–12C, 11km/7mi N of Château de Tilly), **Bourg-Achard** (15C–16C, 3km/2mi E of Bouquetot), **Bourgtheroulde** (Renaissance, 8.6km/5.3mi SE of Bourg-Achard) and **Écaquelon** (beautiful 16C panelling, 14.8km/9mi E of Bourgtheroulde, past Château de Tilly) and **Routot** (Romanesque, 12.5km/7.7mi N of Écaquelon).

ADDRESSES

STAY

Chambre d'hôte Château de Boscherville – *27520 Bourgtheroulde, 10km/6mi NE. 02 35 87 62 12. 5 rooms.* The rooms of this small 18C family château are comfortable and bright. A must, if only to enjoy following in the footsteps of Jean de La Fontaine while strolling among the centuries-old oaks in the park.

EAT

Le Canterbury – *r. de Canterbury. 02 32 44 14 59. Closed Sun, Tue eve, Wed.* The aim here is not to impress, but to satisfy. The result: scrupulously well-prepared cuisine served in a fine half-timbered 18C house. Over 60 kinds of Calvados to sample. Small terrace open in fine weather.

Bernay

Bernay developed rapidly around an abbey founded early in the 11C by Judith of Brittany, wife of Duke Richard II. The town, which nestles in the Charentonne Valley, has a number of interesting, renovated, half-timbered houses.

- **Population:** 10 635.
- **Michelin Map:** 304: D-7.
- **Info:** 29 rue Thiers. 02 32 43 32 08. www.ville-bernay27.fr.
- **Location:** Bernay lies at the junction of the Charentonne and the Cosnier rivers. Take N 138 from Rouen (65km/40.5mi NE) or Alençon (92km/57mi SW), or the N 13 from Lisieux (34km/21mi NW) or Évreux (52km/32mi SE).
- **Don't Miss:** The view from boulevard des Monts, the municipal museum, and the lovely château de Beaumesnil.
- **Timing:** Spend a morning in town, then drive along the Risle river.
- **Kids:** The museum has activities for children.

SIGHTS

The principal streets are rue Thiers and du Générale-de-Gaulle, along which the abbey, the museum and the Ste-Croix Church are clustered. The information office is also here.

Boulevard des Monts★

This lovely hillside road north of the centre commands good views of the town and the Charentonne Valley.

Hôtel de ville★

The 17C town hall buildings, which were formerly Bernay Abbey, are in the style of the Maurists, a Benedictine order.

Ancienne église abbatiale

Same as for the municipal museum, below.

The abbey church was begun in 1013 by **Guglielmo da Volpiano**, summoned from Fécamp by Judith of Brittany. In the 15C the semicircular apse was replaced by a polygonal one. Note the carved capitals above the nave and the twin bays in the galleries. The north aisle, rebuilt in the 15C, has diagonal vaulting.

Musée municipal

pl. Guillaume-de-Volpiano Open Tue–Sun mid-Jun–mid-Sept 10am–noon, 2–7pm; rest of the year 2–5.30pm. Closed 1 Jan, 1 May, 25 Dec. 3.60€ ticket combined with the abbey church (no charge for under-16s, Wed and 1st Sun of month). 02 32 46 63 23.

The museum is housed in the 16C abbot's lodge. Exhibits include a fine collection of Rouen, Nevers and Moustiers faïence and old Norman furniture.

Église Ste-Croix

r. Thiers.

Started in the 14C, the church is heavily restored and contains fine works of art from Le Bec-Hellouin. The remarkable **tombstone** of Guillaume d'Auvillars, Abbot of Bec (1418), stands at the entrance to the sacristy. Sixteen great statues of Apostles and Evangelists from the end of the 14C are in the nave.

Basilique Notre-Dame-de-la-Couture

Access by rue Kléber-Mercier, about 1km/0.6mi S of town centre. Ask for information at the presbytery, 12 rue Alexandre. Open for unaccompanied visits Sat 2–6pm. 02 32 43 06 82.

The interior of this 15C church, established as a basilica in 1950, has wooden vaulting; the statue Notre-Dame de laCouture (16C), highly venerated by pilgrims is placed on a modern altar in the north transept.

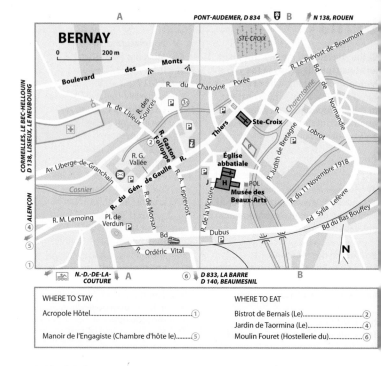

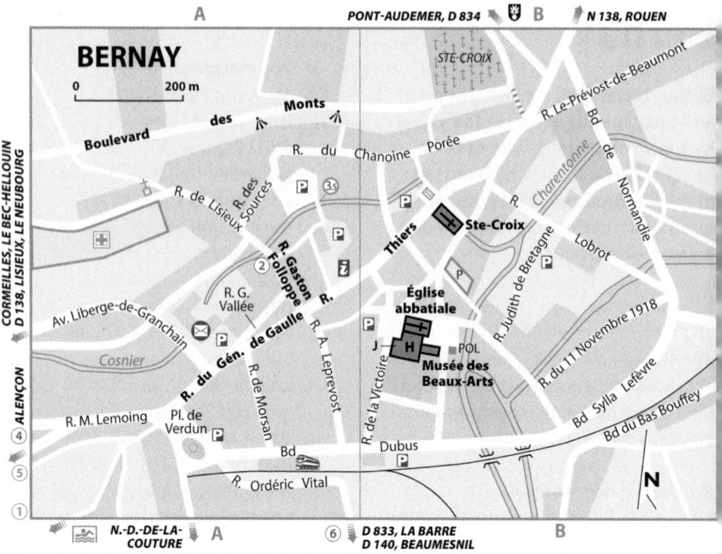

WHERE TO STAY		WHERE TO EAT	
Acropole Hôtel	①	Bistrot de Bernais (Le)	②
		Jardin de Taormina (Le)	④
Manoir de l'Engagiste (Chambre d'hôte le)	⑤	Moulin Fouret (Hostellerie du)	⑥

EXCURSION

Château de Beaumesnil★

13km/8mi SE by D 140. Open Jul–Aug daily 11am–6pm; Easter–Jun Fri–Mon and public holidays 2-6pm; Sept Mon–Wed 2–6pm. 7€. 02 32 44 40 09. www.chateaubeaumesnil.com.

The château, a masterpiece of the Louis XIII style, is built of brick and stone. The formal gardens and the 60ha/149-acre **park** echo the sumptuous lines of the château.

ADDRESSES

STAY

Acropole Hôtel – *10 r. Grande-Malouve, 3km/2mi SW by rte de Broglie. 02 32 46 06 06. www.hotel-acropole.com. 51 rooms. 9€.* Set in the countryside, this hotel has comfortable, spacious rooms.

Chambre d'hôte Manoir de l'Engagiste, *see ORBEC (p143)*

EAT

Le Bistrot de Bernais – *21–23 r. Gaston-Follope. 02 32 46 23 60. Closed 2 weeks in Aug, Sun and Mon.* A narrow passage leads to a delightful courtyard, where there is a terrace in fine weather. Behind a creaking door is a medieval room (the house dates from the 15C) with an enormous fireplace. Traditional cuisine and cheese specialities.

Le Jardin de Taormina – *2–4 pl. du Parvis, 14290 Orbec, 18km/11mi SW. 02 31 32 01 15. www.le-jardin-de-taormina.com. Closed Sun eve, Mon.* Near the church Notre-Dame-d'Orbec, three dining rooms offer excellent Italian cuisine in a southern décor. In summer, sit on the terrace from which you can admire, in the evening, the illuminated church tower.

Hostellerie du Moulin Fouret – *27300 St-Aubin-le-Vertueux, 3.5km/2mi S. 02 32 43 19 95. www.moulin-fouret.com. 8 rooms. 10€. Restaurant.* In the middle of a large park,traversed by a river, rooms are comfortable. Peaceful surroundings.

Brionne

In medieval times Brionne was a stronghold commanding the Risle Valley. While William of Normandy was besieging Brionne from 1047 to 1050, he encountered the monks of Bec-Hellouin Abbey, an event which had a profound impact on religious life in England.

- **Population:** 364.
- **Michelin Map:** 304: E-6.
- **Info:** 1 rue du Générale-de-Gaulle. 02 32 45 70 51.
- **Location:** Brionne is 40km/25mi NW of Évreux via N 13 and D 130, and nearly the same distance E of Lisieux.
- **Don't Miss:** The square Norman keep and the banks of the Risle.
- **Timing:** After 1–2hr n the village, visit Le Bec-Hellouin and the châteaux of Harcourt and Champ de Bataille nearby.

SIGHTS

Donjon

Park in place du Chevalier-Herluin or by the church.

Take rue des Canadiens and 45m/50yd farther on turn right onto sente du Vieux-Château. 15min on foot there and back.

The steep path leads to the ruins of one of the best examples of a square Norman keep (11C), once supported by solid buttresses. From the base of the keep *(viewing table)* there is a pleasant view over the town and the Risle Valley.

Église St-Martin

The nave is 15C and the Gothic wood vaulting in the chancel 14C. The marble altar and altarpiece (17C) come from Bec-Hellouin Abbey. The modern windows are by Gabriel Loire.

DRIVING TOUR

28km/17.4mi – allow about 1hr.

The Lieuven is a region of pastures and cereal crops. Together with the Roumois, from which it is separated by the Risle Valley, it forms the transition between the Caux and the Auge regions.

From Brionne take D 46 north. In Authou turn left onto D 38.

Livet-sur-Authou

A picturesque village with half-timbered houses, a castle and a church.

St-Benoît-des-Ombres

Beyond the miniature town hall, the chapel *(right)* is hidden in greenery. Its 15C wooden porch is crowned by a wooden statue of St Benedict. Inside, a fine vault and 16C font.

Bear right towards St-Georges-du-Vièvre.

Château de Launay

Guided tours (45min) mid-Aug–Sept. 5€. www.chateaudelaunay.com.

From the main gate, approached on foot, there is a good view of this attractive early 18C building. Noteremarkable **dovecote**★ with beams carved to depict monsters and grotesque characters, and attractive formal gardens.

Return to Brionne by D 137 and D 130.

Château du Champ de Bataille★

The name, which means "Castle of the Battlefield", may recall a battle in 935 between forces of the Count of Cotentin and of William Longsword, ancestor of the Conqueror. Or it may be that a peasant named Bataille owned the field ("champ"). The 17C château was built by Alexandre de Créqui and occupied by the Harcourt family before it was looted in 1795. In the 20C it was used as a hospice, a camp for war prisoners and a jail for women. The Duke of Harcourt bought it in 1947 and began restoration, continued by the present owner, Jacques Garcia.

- **Michelin Map:** 307: F-7 – 4km/2.5mi NW of Le Neubourg.
- **Info:** www.chateauduchampdebataille.com.
- **Location:** The château is just outside Le Neubourg, 23km/14mi SW of Rouen, by N 138, then D 83 S.
- **Don't Miss:** The park.
- **Timing:** Allow 1hr for the château and surrounding gardens.

VISIT

Gardens: *Open Jul–Aug 10am–6pm; Jun–May and Sept daily 2–6pm; Easter–Apr and Oct Sat–Sun and holidays 2–6pm. 12€.* ***Principal rooms:*** *Audio-guided tour Jul–Aug daily 3.30–5.30pm. Easter–Jun, Sept–Oct Sat–Sun 3.30–5.30pm. 24€ (including garden). 02 32 34 84 34. www.chateauduchampdebataille.com.*

Park

A French-style garden of vast proportions has been re-created, offering spectacular perspectives and subtle plantings reflecting 18C philosophical notions of the orders of nature: animal, vegetable, mineral, etc.

Main Courtyard

This quadrangle is entered through a gate pierced in a wall adorned with pilasters; it is closed off by a monumental gate.

Interior

Entrance through the main courtyard on the left.

The entrance (inspired by the 16C Italian architect Andrea Palladio) gives access to the grand staircase embellished with wrought-iron banisters. On the first floor, north wing, is a Louis XVI dining hall and a billiards room decorated with 16C **tapestries** from Brussels.

The south wing has an outstanding collection of antiques and sumptuous neo-Egyptian furniture. A small gallery features Chinese and Japanese porcelain (17C–18C). The visit ends with the chapel (17C–18C), which has recently been restored.

EXCURSIONS

Harcourt★

7km/4.3mi SE of Brionne by D 26 and D 137.

This small town near Le Neubourg is at the intersection of roads leading to the banks of the River Risle and River Charentonne and Beaumont Forest.

Not far from the 13C **church** *(open Mon–Tue and Thu–Fri 9am–noon, 1.30–4.30pm, Sat 9am–11.30am; get key at town hall; 02 32 45 02 40)* the old wooden market place stands intact.

Château d'Harcourt★

Open mid-Jun–mid-Sept daily 10.30am–6.30pm; Mar–mid-Jun and mid-Sept–mid-Nov Wed–Mon 2–6pm. 4€ 02 32 46 29 70.

Since 1827 the château (*see Illustration in Introduction: Military architecture, p65*) and its park have belonged to the French Agricultural College.

The castle was built in the late 12C by Robert II of Harcourt, companion to Richard Lionheart. It was modernised

Château du Champ de Bataille

B. Kaufmann/MICHELIN

in the 14C by John IV of Harcourt and, in the 17C, was converted into a comfortable residence. At the end of the drive stands the imposing mass of the castle, sheltered by its curtain wall, 20m/65.6ft-wide moat, and ramparts flanked by dilapidated towers. The medieval entrance and its bridge have been restored.

Arboretum★

Same as for the château.

Adjoining the main courtyard, a 10ha/25-acre arboretum presents over 400 tree species coming from the five continents.

Conches-en-Ouche★

The town of Conches, on the edge of the woodlands that mark the northern limits of the Pays d'Ouche, is remarkably situated on a spur encircled by the River Rouloir. There is a particularly good view of the town if it is approached along the Rouloir Valley (from Évreux). The keep of the ruined castle is illuminated from April to September.

- **Population:** 5 072.
- **Michelin Map:** 304: F-28.
- **Info:** Place Aristide-Briand. 02 32 30 76 42. www.conches-en-ouche.fr.
- **Location:** From Aigle (30km/18.5mi SW) or Évreux (14km/8.5mi NE) take D 830. From Bernay (30km/18.5mi NW) take D 140, and from Rouen (50km/31mi N).
- **Don't Miss:** The beautiful windows of the Ste-Foy Church.
- **Timing:** Visit Conches in the morning, then stroll along the many paths in the area.

A BIT OF HISTORY

From Rouergue to the Pays d'Ouche – On his return from the *Reconquista de Iberia* (1034), **Roger de Tosny** made a pilgrimage to Conques, in Rouergue (southwest France) and brought back relics of St Foy. This may be the origin of the town's name. Roger dedicated a church to **St Foy**; at the end of the 15C it was replaced by the present building.

Walking Tours

Pick up a walking guide to the area from the tourist office called *Les Circuits Touristique*; also shows bike and horse riding trails.

SIGHTS

Jardin de l'Hôtel de Ville

The Gothic doorway of the town hall – entrance to the former castle – leads to a garden in which stands the ruined keep of the lords of Tosny, surrounded by 12C towers.

From the terrace there is a fine view of the Rouloir Valley and the elegant Flamboyant apse of St Foy Church. Below another terrace offers a similar view.

Rue du Val

There are two interesting buildings here. One is the 16C half-timbered **maison Corneille**, home to the family of the famous dramatist (1606–84). At the end of the street, the **hospital** stands on the site of the abbey; the vaulted cellars are open to visitors.

Église Ste-Foy★

r. Ste-Foy. Open daily 9am–7pm.

The south tower is crowned by a tall spire of wood and lead, a copy of the one blown down in a storm in 1842. The fine carved panels of the façade doors are early 16C. Notice the many gargoyles. Inside there are some beautiful statues including that of St Roch (17C) in the south aisle and near the great organ.

Stained-Glass Windows★ – The Renaissance windows, dating from the first half of the 16C, have retained their unity in spite of restoration. Those in the north aisle depict the life of the Virgin. The seven windows (10.5m/34.4ft) in the chancel are divided into two, the upper part illustrating the Life of Christ, the lower to that of St Foy and portraits of the donors.

The windows in the south aisle were made in either Île-de-France or at Fontainebleau. The Mystical Wine Press (fifth window) is the best known.

The houses facing the church are 15C and 16C. The vaulted cellars (11C–12C) are open to visitors.

Musée du Terroir Normand

r. Paul-Guilbaud. Open Jun–Sept Wed–Sat 10am–noon, 2–5.30pm, Sun 3–6pm. Closed public holidays. 3€ (ticket combined with Musée du Verre). 02 32 37 92 16.

The Museum presents an exhibition of old tools and farming implements as well as re-creations of various workshops.

Musée du Verre

rte de Ste-Marguerite. See Musée du Terroir Normand. 02 32 30 90 41.

This museum has a collection of objects made of molten glass by the man known as the sorcerer of Conche, François Décorchement (1880–1971).

EXCURSION

Breteuil-sur-Iton

14km/8.5mi S by D 840.

The town stands on the eastern edge of Breteuil Forest in a loop of the River Iton which forms a small lake in the public gardens laid out on the site of the old castle. In the 11C **church**, of local reddish stone *(grison)*, William the Conqueror's daughter Adèle the Beautiful married Stephen, Count of Blois, in 1081. The belfry is a large square tower above the transept crossing. The interior is dominated by the great nave arches supported on 12 massive stone pillars. The balustrade of the organ loft is decorated with Italian Renaissance motifs and 12 angelic musicians.

ADDRESSES

LEISURE

Village équestre de Conches – Horse riding. *02 32 30 22 56.*

Lac de la Noë – *1 rte d'Évreux, 27190 La Bonneville-sur-Iton. Closed Oct–May. 02 32 37 61 87. www.conches-en-ouche.fr.* Miniature golf, tennis, swimming, fishing, boating. Equipment rentals.

Markets – Thursdays and Sundays.

Écouis★

The village of Écouis centres on the twin towers of its old collegiate church, built between 1310 and 1313 by Enguerrand de Marigny, Superintendant of Finances to Philip the Fair. Opponents accused him of sorcery, and he died on the gibbet in 1315. His artistic patronage may be seen from the remarkable works of art in the church.

- **Population:** 745.
- **Michelin Map:** 304: I-6.
- **Info:** 6 place du Cloître. ☏02 32 69 43 08. www.collegiale-ecouis.asso.fr.
- **Location:** Écouis is 12km/7.4mi S of Lyons-la-Forêt via D 2.
- **Don't Miss:** Collégiale Notre-Dame; Abbaye de Fontaine Guérard.

Collégiale Notre-Dame★

Open daily 7am–7pm. For a guided tour, make an appointment at the presbytery. ☏02 32 69 43 08.

The roof timbers were replaced by the present brick and stone vaulting at the end of the 18C. The immense chancel, which contains some beautiful furnishings and remarkable **statues**★ dating from the 14C to the 17C, terminates in a three-sided apse.

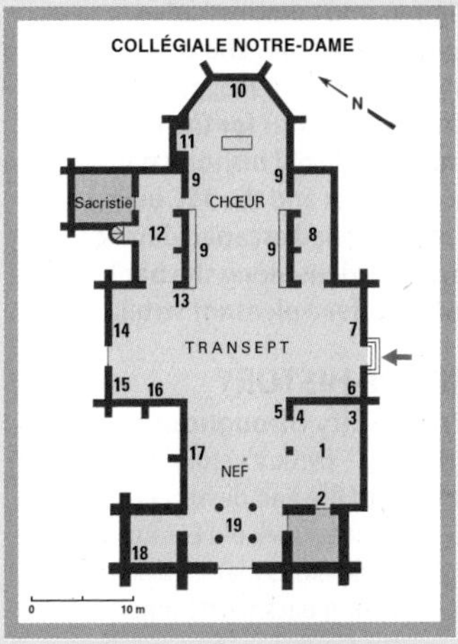

1) Chapel of the Immaculate Conception (16C).
2) Christ on the Cross (13C).
3) St Nicaise.
4) St Ann and the Virgin (14C).
5) Our Lady of Écouis (14C).
6) Statue of St Margaret (14C).
7) Statue of Jean de Marigny, brother of Enguerrand, who was Archbishop of Rouen when he died in 1351.
8) St John Chapel – The wooden vault enables us to imagine the former vault of the nave. Statue of Alips de Mons, wife of Enguerrand de Marigny. Stained glass (14C) depicting the Crucifixion with St John and Mary at the foot of the Cross.
9) 14C choir stalls; 16C doors and woodwork.
10) Door of former rood screen.
11) Christ and his Shroud (16C).
12) North side chapel: St Martin, St Francis, St Laurent (14C), St Cecilia.
13) Madonna of the King (14C).
14) St Agnes (14C).
15) St Veronica (14C).
16) Ecce Homo in wood (15C).
17) Annunciation (15C) – The statue of the Virgin is supported by a charming group of small angels reading prophecies relating to the mystery of the Incarnation. The hands and face of the Virgin, together with the face of Archangel Gabriel, are in marble encrusted in stone.
18) St John the Baptist (14C).
19) Organ case (17C).

In a **room** on the first floor beautiful works of art are displayed including a cope chest and the chalice of Jean de Marigny (14C).

EXCURSION

Abbaye de Fontaine-Guérard★

12km/7.4mi NW via N14. Just before Fleury-sur-Andelle, take D 321 left, then the second road on the right. Allow 30min to visit.

The ruins of the 12C abbey, on the north bank of the Andelle, are both evocative and moving, owing to their isolation and the threat of flooding.

Beside the path stands the 15C St Michael's Chapel (left). The abbey church dates from 1218; the square chevet and some apsidal vaulting have survived. The **chapter-house** (right) is a fine example of early 13C Norman architecture.

Évreux★★

Évreux, on the River Iton, is the religious and administrative capital of the Eure. The city centre was rebuilt after 1945, providing attractive settings for the town ramparts, the old bishop's palace, the cathedral and the 15C belfry, all of which had escaped damage. Flower gardens along the banks of the Iton offer a pleasant stroll.

- **Population:** 53 254.
- **Michelin Map:** 304: G-7.
- **Info:** 3 place du Général de Gaulle. ✆02 32 24 04 43. www.ot-pays-evreux.fr.
- **Location:** Évreux is 96km/60mi W of Paris, 58km/36mi S of Rouen and 48km/30mi NE of Dreux.
- **Parking:** There is parking (fee) behind the cathedral, near the tourist office and near the Cloître des Capucins public garden.
- **Don't Miss:** The Flamboyant beauty of Notre-Dame Cathedral and the rich collections of the museum.
- **Timing:** Allow yourself 2hr to see the museum.
- **Kids:** The Roman ruins at Gisacum will interest them as will the train through the valley of the Dure.

A BIT OF HISTORY

A French City throughout the Wars of History – Évreux's story is a lengthy chronicle of fire and destruction:

5C – Vandals sack old Évreux, a prosperous market town dating back to the time of the Gauls.

9C – Vikings destroy the fortified town established by the Romans on the present site beside the Iton.

1119 – Henry I, King of England, sets fire to the town when fighting the Count of Évreux.

1193 – King Philippe Auguste burns the city in reprisal.

1356 – Jean the Good, King of France, lays siege to Évreux in his struggle against the House of Navarre, and sets fire to the town.

1379 – Charles V besieges the town, which suffers cruelly.

June 1940 – Following German air raids the centre of the city burns for nearly a week.

June 1944 – Allied air raids raze the district round the station.

SIGHTS

Cathédrale Notre-Dame★★

r. Charles-Corbeau. Open Mon–Fri 8.30am–7pm, Sat–Sun 9am–7pm.

The great arches of the nave are the only extant part of the original church, rebuilt between 1119 and 1193. The chancel was built in 1260. The chapels are 14C. Following the fire of 1356 the lantern tower and the Lady Chapel were added. The magnificent north transept façade and doorway are early 16C.

The upper parts of the cathedral suffered in the 1940 conflagration: the

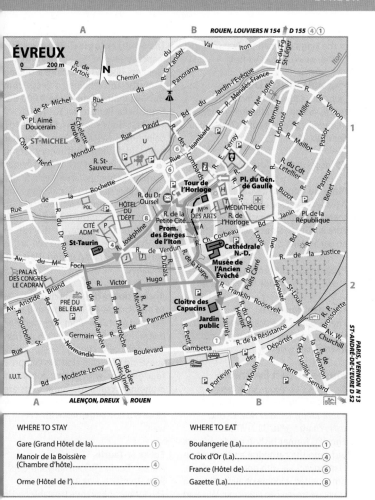

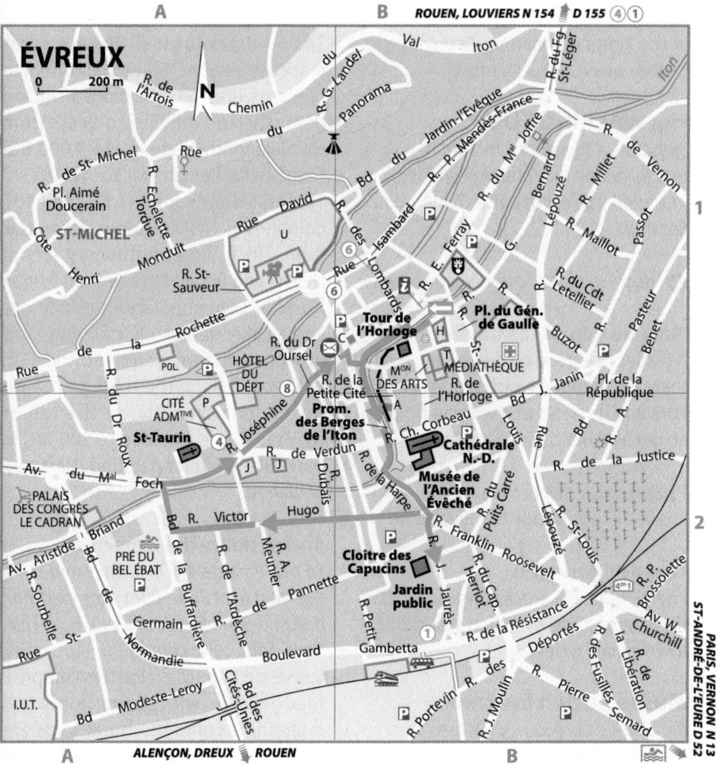

WHERE TO STAY		WHERE TO EAT	
Gare (Grand Hôtel de la)	①	Boulangerie (La)	①
Manoir de la Boissière (Chambre d'hôte)	④	Croix d'Or (La)	④
Orme (Hôtel de l')	⑥	France (Hôtel de)	⑥
		Gazette (La)	⑧

silver belfry melted and the west façade towers lost their crowns.

Exterior

Walk along the north side.

The aisle windows were redesigned in the 16C in the Flamboyant style. The north door is a perfect example of the Flamboyant style, then at its height.

Interior

To view the **stained glass★** (*see Illustration in the Introduction: Religious architecture, p64*) and the **carved wood screens★** of the ambulatory chapels stand in the transept, between the pillars supporting the graceful lantern tower.

The chancel is closed by a 18C wrought-iron grill and is very beautiful. The apse windows are perhaps the most beautiful of the 14C. Fine Renaissance wood screens mark the ambulatory entrance.

The 15C Treasury Chapel is quite unique: closed off by wrought-iron bars to which an iron frame has been attached. The **screen★** to the fourth chapel is a masterpiece of imagination and craftsmanship, particularly the lower figures; the chapel glass is early 14C. The central or Lady Chapel, given by Louis XI, has 15C windows of considerable documentary interest. The upper parts depict the peers of France at the king's coronation. Two windows further on is Louis XI himself.

WALKING TOUR

3km/2mi. Allow about 1hr30min (not including the cathedral and the museum). Park at place Clemenceau. See map.

Begin at place du Général de Gaulle.

Place du Général de Gaulle

A castle once stood on this square. Today, there is a fountain which represents the Eure and its rivers as a woman holding an oar and the city's coat of arms.

Promenade des remparts

The walk runs beside the River Iton.

Tour de l'Horloge

The elegant 15C clock tower stands on the site of a tower which flanked the town's main gateway.

Musée Ancien Évêché★★

6 r. Charles-Corbeau. Open Tue–Sun 10am–noon, 2–6pm. Closed 1 Jan, 1 May, 1 and 11 Nov, 25 Dec. No charge. 02 32 31 81 90.

The 15C former bishop's palace looks out onto the cathedral and has a fine Flamboyant air with dormer windows, ornamented window pediments and a staircase tower. The Municipal Museum is inside.

The first two rooms on the ground floor are devoted to the history and geography of the Eure region and of the town itself. The former chapter house (Room 3) has a monumental fireplace and contains medieval and Renaissance collections. Notice the series of 17C Aubusson tapestries on the theme of the Prodigal Son. Room 4 contains medieval exhibits: tomb inscriptions in engraved stone, capitals.

The **Archaeological Room**★, dramatically sited in ruined Gallo-Roman ramparts, displays collections including domestic and religious objects from the Palaeolithic Age (up to 9 000 BC) to the Gallo-Roman era (1C–4C AD).

The first floor contains 17C and 18C paintings as well as various decorative items, including apothecary jars in Nevers and Rouen faïence from Évreux Hospital. Contemporary art exhibitions and a collection of 19C paintings and objects (Lebourg, Jongkind) take up the second floor; the third floor, with its diagonal vaulting at the top of the stairway, is devoted to 20C art, in particular abstract painting (Hartung, Soulages).

Ancien cloître des Capucins

96 r. de Panette. Open daily mid-Apr–mid-Sept 8am–8pm; Mar–mid-Apr and mid-Sept–Oct 8am–7pm; Nov–Feb 8am–5pm. No charge.

These old Capuchin cloisters comprise four galleries with timber roofs and monolithic columns; moral texts are inscribed on the walls. In the cloister close is a flower garden with a central well.

Église St-Taurin

Place St-Taurin. Open daily Jun–Sept 9am–7pm; Oct–May 9am–8pm.

This former abbey church established in 660 and dedicated to the first Bishop of Évreux dates back to the 14C and 15C. The well-proportioned 14C chancel is lit by superb 15C windows. Three windows in the apse trace the life of St Taurinus.

Châsse de St-Taurin★★

This masterpiece of 13C French craftsmanship in the north transept was given to the abbey by St Louis to contain St Taurinus' relics and was probably made in the abbey workshops. The silver gilt reliquary enriched with enamel is in the form of a miniature chapel and even shows St Taurinus with his crosier.

ADDRESSES

🛏 STAY

🍽🍽 **Chambre d'hôte Manoir de la Boissière** – *Hamlet "La Boissaye", 27490 La Croix-St-Leufroy, 16km/10mi NE.* 📞*02 32 67 70 85. www.chambres-la-boissiere. com. 5 rooms.* ☐. This 15C manor is a working farm. The rooms are each different, with family furniture. Pretty duck pond and veranda. Meals by reservation.

🍽🍽 **Grand Hôtel de la Gare** – *61 bd Gambetta.* 📞*02 3238 67 45. Restaurant*🍽🍽*. 29 rooms.* ☐*6.50€.* Just 2min from the town centre, rooms here offer a reasonable degree of comfort. The restaurant serves traditional food.

🍽🍽 **Hôtel de l'Orme** – *13 r. des Lombards.* 📞*02 32 39 34 12. www.hotel-de-lorme.fr. Closed Sat–Sun from Oct–Mar. 39 rooms.* ☐*9€.* This In the town centre, this hotel has functional rooms.

🍴 EAT

🍽 **La Boulangeraie** – *130 av. Aristide-Briand, 27930 Gravigny, 2km/1mi N.* 📞*02 32 62 22 35. Closed Sun.* A café-cum-bakery where you can sit and enjoy a sandwich, a pizza, an omelette or a *salade.* All food is very fresh.

🍽🍽 **La Croix d'Or** – *3 r. Joséphine.* 📞*02 32 33 06 07. www.la-croix-dor.fr.* Seafood served in a long, sober dining room or on the veranda is the star of this establishment. A local favourite.

🍽🍽 **Hôtel de France** – *29 r. St-Thomas.* 📞*02 32 39 09 25. Closed Sat lunch, Sun eve and Mon. Reservations advised.* This eatery offers seasonal menus. 16 guest rooms.

🍽🍽–🍽🍽🍽 **La Gazette** – *7 r. St-Sauveur.* 📞*02 32 33 43 40. www.restaurant-lagazette.fr. Closed Aug, Sat lunch, Sun.* Well looked-after establishment with modern furnishings and copies of old newspapers lining the walls. Intimate, contemporary place.

🎭 ON THE TOWN

Le Grand Café – *11 r. de la Harpe.* 📞*02 32 33 14 01.* Located in a pedestrian street on the banks of the canal, this traditional café has two terraces that offer a view of the cathedral. Brasserie-style meals at lunch and Thu–Sun.

🛒 SHOPPING

Chocolatier Auzou – *34 r. Chartraine.* 📞*02 32 33 28 05. Closed 1 Jan, 1 May, Sun in Jul–Aug.* This confectioner's produces several house specialities, all with evocative names such as the Zouzous d'Auzou and the macaroons of Grand'Mère Auzou.

Gisors★

Gisors is the capital of the Norman Vexin: it was once a frontier town belonging to the dukes of Normandy. The town owes its origins to the castle, which formed part of a line of defence running from Forges-les-Eaux to Vernon and included the castles of Neaufles-St-Martin and Château-sur-Epte.

VISIT

Château Fort★★
r. de Ponthièvre. 👣*Guided tours (1hr) Apr–Sept Wed–Mon 10am, 11am, 2.30pm, 3.45pm and 5pm; Oct–Nov and*

▶ **Population:** 11 809.
🎯 **Michelin Map:** 304: K-6.
ℹ **Info:** 4 rue du Général de Gaulle. 📞*02 32 27 60 63.* www.tourisme-gisors.fr.
🅿 **Location:** Gisors is 76km/47mi NW of Paris and 64km/40mi NE of Rouen.
🏞 **Don't Miss:** The château and the Tree of Jesse in St-Gervais-et-St-Protais.
🕐 **Timing:** See Gisors in the morning, then tour the Epte Valley.

The History of the Dukedom of Normandy

It was at St-Clair-sur-Epte in 911 that Charles the Simple – a nickname, meaning honest and straightforward – met with Rollo, the ruler of the Vikings. Dudon de St-Quentin, Normandy's first historian, recounts that, to ratify the agreement creating the Dukedom of Normandy, the Viking placed his hands between those of the French king. This informal deal, concluded in the manner of tradesmen, carried the same legal weight as a formal exchange of seals and signatures, for a written treaty was never signed. The dukedom is bordered by the River Epte north of the River Seine and by the River Avre to the south. Normandy's boundaries were often fought over throughout history by the kings of France and the dukes of Normandy, who became the kings of England in the late 11C.

Feb–Mar weekends and public holidays 10.30am, 2.30pm and 4pm. Closed 1 May. 5€. The park is open daily Apr–Sept 8am–7.30pm; Oct–Mar 8.30am–5pm. No charge. 02 32 55 59 36. www.ville-gisors.fr.

The castle was built as early as 1097 by William II of England, son of the Conqueror. In 1193 it was taken by Philippe Auguste of France. During the Hundred Years War the castle changed hands several times before returning to the French crown in 1449.

The 11C **keep**, on its 20m/65.6ft artificial mound in the centre of the fortified perimeter and surrounded now by a public garden, is flanked by a watchtower. A staircase leads to the top from where there is a fine **view** over the surrounding woodland.

Église St-Gervais-et-St-Protais★

r. de Vienne.

The oldest parts of the church date back to the 12C, but construction continued to the end of the 16C, as is evident both outside and inside. The Gothic chancel was completed in 1249; the side chapels adjoining the ambulatory were added in 1498 and 1507. The transept doors are 16C and Gothic, as is the very tall nave. The monumental west front is Renaissance: the doorway is flanked by two towers, that on the north being built in 1536, that on the south left unfinished in 1591.

In spite of the mixture of architectural styles the church as a whole appears perfectly harmonious.

The large monochrome window in the chapel on the right of the choir dates from the 16C. The chapel below the South Tower contains a charming spiral staircase by Jean Grappin and a huge late-16C Tree of Jesse.

DRIVING TOUR

Epte Valley

41km/25.5mi – allow 2hr.

The road from Gisors to Vernon follows the shady west bank of the Epte, which contrast with the bare slopes hewn out of the chalk bed of the Vexin plateaux.

From Gisors take D 10 W.

Neaufles-St-Martin

The village is dominated by a keep standing upon a perfectly preserved artificial mound.

At the junction turn left onto D 181.

Dangu

Church. Can be visited on request at the town hall. 02 32 55 22 15.

The main features of the Gothic **church** are the 18C woodwork and painted panelling in the chancel, the 16C Montmorency Chapel in which a *grisaille* window above the altar shows St Denis, St Lawrence and, on his knees, William, fifth son of Anne of Montmorency.

Take D 146 south into the valley.

Château-sur-Epte
quai Fossé aux Tanneurs, Gisors. *Closed to the public.* *02 32 27 60 63.*
Standing on an artificial mound surrounded by a moat are the remains of a massive keep built by William Rufus,King of England from 1087 to 1100, to protect the Norman frontier.

ADDRESSES

STAY

Chambre d'hôte Le Four à Pain – *8 r. des Gruchets, 27140 St-Denis-le-Ferment, 7km/4.3mi NW. 2 rooms.* *02 32 55 14 45 . http://lefour-apain.monsite.orange.fr.* One room is built in an old bread oven amid a charming garden. Another, in the farm renovated *à l'ancienne*, is larger and has a handsome wood frame ceiling.

Giverny★

Claude Monet lived in this village from 1883 until his death in 1926, and attracted many other artists to the area. It was here that he painted the huge canvases of the water lilies which can be seen in Paris at the Orangerie Museum and the Marmottan Museum.

- **Population:** 530.
- **Michelin Map:** 304: J-7 – 2km/1mi SE of Vernon.
- **Info:** An information point is open Apr–Oct daily 10am–7pm, in the car park opposite the Musée des Impressionismes. www.giverny-village.fr. 02 32 51 39 60.
- **Location:** Giverny is 2km/1mi SW of Vernon, which is (69km/43mi) from Rouen via D 313/D 5.
- **Parking:** Car parks (free) are found on both sides of D 5.
- **Don't Miss:** The home of Claude Monet and the Impressionist Museum.
- **Timing:** Give yourself 2hr for each of the museums.

VISIT

Maison de Claude Monet★

Open Apr–Oct daily 9.30am–6pm. 6€ (to avoid long queues, purchase tickets via the website and take them to the "Groupe" entry). 02 32 51 28 21. www.fondation-monet.com.
Claude Monet's garden *(only part of site accessible)* slopes gently to the banks of the River Epte. The house now displays reproductions of his greatest paintings; the originals hang in musems in Paris and around the world. The tour includes the blue salon, the bedroom with the roll-top desk, the old studio, the yellow dining room with its painted wooden furniture and the tiled kitchen.
The walled garden *(clos normand)*, is planted according to Monet's own design, and *(via a tunnel to the other side of the road)* the Japanese-inspired water garden is fed by the River Epte.

Musée des Impressionismes Giverny★

99 r. Claude-Monet. Open May–14 Jul daily 10am–6pm; 15 Jul–Oct Tue–Sun 10am–6pm (last entry 30min before closing). 5.50€ (free first Sun of month). 02 32 51 94 65. www.museedesimpressionismesgiverny.com.
This museum, opened in May 2009 in the former premises of the Musée d'Art Américain *(www.maag.org)*, holds temporary exhibits on the subject of Impressionist art. The museum gardens, composed of sections separated by hedges, burst with bright colour.

ADDRESSES

STAY

Chambre d'hôte Au Bon Maréchal – *1 r. du Colombier. ℘02 32 51 39 70. www.giverny.fr. 3 rooms.* This house used to be a small café where Monet and his artist friends would meet. Ideally situated near the gardens, it now offers cosy, comfortable rooms with reasonable prices to match.

EAT

Restaurant, Musée des Impressionismes – *99 r. Claude-Monet. ℘02 32 51 94 61. Closed Nov–Apr.* Overlooking renowned gardens, with a shaded terrace, the former Terra Café has delighted a generation of museum-goers.

Le Moulin de Fourges– *38 r. du Moulin, 27630 Fourges, 11km/7mi NE. ℘02 32 52 12 12. www.moulindefourges.com. Closed Nov–Mar, Sun eve, Mon except Jul–Aug.* A former watermill on the banks of the Epte, a place Monet would have appreciated. No water lilies, but a country setting. Traditional cuisine.

Restaurant-Musée Baudy – *81 r. Claude-Monet. ℘02 32 21 10 03. www.giverny.fr. Closed Nov–Mar, Sun eve, Mon except public holidays.* The former Hôtel Baudy used to lodge Impressionist painters. Savour the dish of the day and salads. Delectable old rose garden concealing the studio just beyond ... A must!

Louviers★

Badly damaged in 1940, Louviers has been carefully reconstructed, sparing the remaining old houses and delightful avenues along the River Eure. The old town north of Notre-Dame Church has pretty half-timbered houses, such as in rue Tatin, rue du Quai and rue Pierre Mendès-France. Louviers remains an industrial centre, especially in the north of the town.

- **Population:** 18 785.
- **Michelin Map:** 304: H-6.
- **Info:** 10 rue du Maréchal-Foch. ℘02 32 40 04 41. www.tourisme-seine-eure.com.
- **Location:** Louviers is 32km/20mi S of Rouen and 103km/64mi NW of Paris via A 13.
- **Don't Miss:** The Flamboyant Notre-Dame Church and Acquigny park.
- **Timing:** You will need 1hr30min to see the town.

WALKING TOUR

From the Notre-Dame Church in the town centre, take rue de la Poste, which crosses both branches of the Eure river.

Ancien couvent des Pénitents

Allow 30min.

All that remains of this Franciscan convent, built in 1646 on a tributary of the Eure, is the inhabited main building together with three small arcaded galleries belonging to the cloister. The western gallery is in a ruinous state and overlooks a square with lawn and trees.

Rue de la Trinité *(on the left)* leads into the former manufacturing district and to **rue Terneaux**, where the buildings have large attics once used for drying out dyed fabrics.

Take the short rue Polhomet to the right, then turn right again on rue du Quai. Pretty half-timbered houses line the street. Rue au Coq, on the left, leads to the museum; rue Pierre-Mendès-France takes you back to the east end of Notre Dame Church.

Normandy's Literary Ghosts

Many of Normandy's towns, villages, manor houses, coastal and rural scenes were described often under a fictional name by one of the region's celebrated writers.

Cabourg – the Balbec in Marcel Proust's *À la recherche du temps perdu.*
Ry – the Yonville-l'Abbaye of Gustave Flaubert's *Madame Bovary* (1857).
Le Havre – Guy de Maupassant's *Pierre et Jean* (1888).
Inland from Yport – Maupassant's *Une Vie* (1883).
The Cotentin – Barbey d'Aurevilly's (the Walter Scott of the region) *Le Chevalier des Touches, Une vieille maîtresse* and *L'Ensorcelée.*

Musée municipal

pl. Ernest Thorel. Open Wed–Mon 2–6pm. Closed 1 Jan, 1 May, 25 Dec. No charge. 02 32 09 58 55. www.ville-louviers.fr/ville/musee.

The museum hosts temporary exhibitions of faïence, furniture and painting. One room is devoted to the clothing industry.

Maison du Fou du Roy

10 r. du Maréchal-Foch.

This half-timbered house in the main street is also the tourist office. It once belonged to Guillaume Marchand, an apothecary, who became Henri IV's jester (Fou du Roy) after the previous incumbant was killed in battle.

Église Notre-Dame

pl. du Parvis. *See p182.*

EXCURSIONS

Acquigny French Gardens

6km/3.7mi S of Louviers via D 71. 1 r. Aristide Briand. Open daily Jul–Aug 2–7pm; mid-Apr–Jun and Sept–mid-Oct weekends and public holidays 2–6pm. 7€. 02 32 50 23 31. www.parc-et-jardins-acquigny-27.com.

The formal **French gardens**, lying at the confluence of the River Eure and River Iton, have retained their long avenues and orangery. Waterfalls, artificial streams and a series of fords are reminiscent of the Romantic period.

Vironvay

5km/3mi E by N 155, then the minor road on the left which crosses A 13 and N 15.

The isolated church overlooks the Seine Valley. The **view**★ on approaching extends over the river spanned by the bridge at St-Pierre-du-Vauvray and, further east, the ruins of Château-Gaillard.

Église Notre-Dame

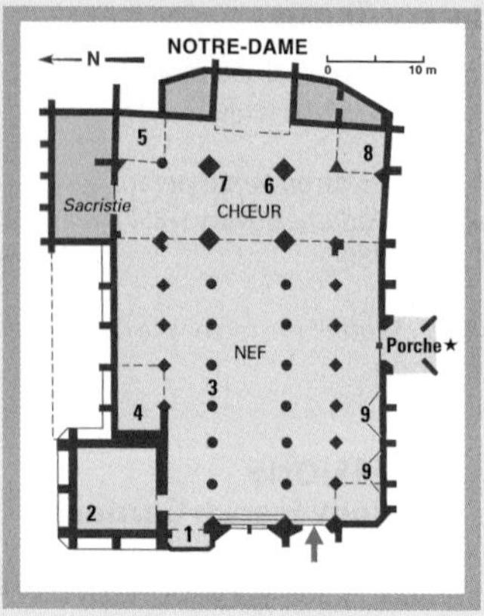

Église Notre-Dame★

The plain 13C church was redecorated in the late 15C in the Flamboyant style and it is for this that it has become famous.

The **south front**★ is outstanding for its profusion of Flamboyant features. Pointed gables rival with openwork balustrades, pinnacles, festoons and gargoyles. The **south porch**★, with all its delicately carved detail, looks more like silverwork than masonry. Note the Renaissance door panels and the hanging keystones of the Gothic arcades.

Interior

The 13C nave with double side aisles is an elegant interior which shelters several fine **works of art**★.

1) Entombment (late-15C).
2) Salome and her sons, James and John (16C).
3) Throne.
4) Above the altar are three statues: Christ, the Virgin and St John (15C). On each side are carved panels depicting the Virgin Mary and the Centurion at Calvary (14C).
5) Altar decorated with carved panels depicting the life of the Virgin (16C).
6) & 7) Early-17C tableaux by local artist Jean Nicolle: the Nativity and Adoration of the Magi.
8) Mausoleum by Robert d'Acquigny (late-15C).
9) Restored Renaissance stained glass.

Pont-de-l'Arche

11km/7mi E by D 321 along the south bank of the Seine.

The small town, named after the first bridge to be built over the lower Seine, is pleasantly set in a valley. On the south side is Bord Forest.

The **Église Notre-Dame-des-Arts** exhibits the Flamboyant Gothic style in the doorway and the ornate south side. The interior is lit by 16C and 17C windows. The Louis XIII altarpiece shows the Resurrection by CLF Le Tourneur (1751–1817).

ADDRESSES

STAY

Manoir de La Haye le Comte – *4 rte de La-Haye-le-Comte, 700m/0.5mi S. 02 32 40 00 40. www.manoir-louviers.com. Closed 23 Dec –15 Jan. 14 rooms. Restaurant*. A stunning 16C family residence. Luxurious, comfortable rooms. Cosy lounge and dining rooms.
The park offers romantic strolls, tennis, pétanque, croquet, a golfing range and mountain biking.

EAT

Le Jardin de Bigard – *39/41 r. du Quai. 02 32 40 02 45. Closed Feb holidays, 2 weeks in Aug, Sun. Reservations advised.* A traditional restaurant behind a brick façade, located in a neighbourhood that survived World War II unscathed. View of Notre-Dame Church, a park and a manor; terrace in the summer.

Lyons-la-Forêt★

The half-timbered houses, old brick buildings and sylvan setting in the heart of the Forêt de Lyons create a picture-book vision of Normandy. Unusually in the French language, the final "s" of Lyons is pronounced, indicating the town's Scandinavian origins.

- **Population:** 774.
- **Michelin Map:** 304: I-5.
- **Info:** 20 rue de l'Hôtel de Ville. ✆02 32 49 31 65. http://paysdelyons.com.
- **Location:** Lyons-la-Forêt is 43km/27mi E of Rouen via N 31 and D 921, and 20km/12.5mi N of Andelys via D 2, on the River Lieurre.
- **Don't Miss:** The château of Vascœuil and the beautiful Forêt de Lyons.

THE VILLAGE

Halles

pl. Benserade.

The old covered market in the centre of place Benserade was used for scenes in Jean Renoir's film *Madame Bovary*. The fountain appeared in Claude Chabrol's 1990 version of the same novel.

Pretty half-timbered houses surround the square. In the steep street west of the square, **Maurice Ravel** composed *Le Tombeau de Couperin* and completed the orchestration for Moussorgsky's *Pictures at an Exhibition*.

Église St-Denis

r. Bout-de-Bas leads to St-Denis Church, at the edge of the village, on the riverside. Open only to groups.

The 12C church was completely renovated in the 15C. The stonework and the timber belfry are admirable, and in the chancel the statue of St Christopher carrying the infant Jesus dates from the 16C.

DRIVING TOUR

FORÊT DE LYONS★★

70km/43.5mi – allow one day.

The forest covers 10 700ha/26 440 acres and is known for its glorious beech trees. You can also admire an old abbey and two interesting châteaux.

1 LYONS TO LES BORDINS

Leave Lyons to the W via D 6.

Notre-Dame-de-la-Paix

From this statue there is a fine view of the town of Lyons.

Take D 169 left.

Chapelle St-Jean

Behind the 17C chapel a path leads to the Chêne St-Jean (St John's Oak) which has a circumference of 5m/16ft at a height of 1.30m/4ft from the ground.

Take the second road on the left (D 11) towards Rosay.

Rosay-sur-Lieure

The **church** and churchyard are in a pleasant setting.

D 11 goes on to Ménesqueville.

Ménesqueville

The small 12C country **church,** skilfully restored, contains some very old statues. The stained-glass windows by contemporary artist F E Décorchemont portray the Song of Songs.

From here, D 12 goes along the pretty Fouillebroc Valley as far as Lisors.

Lisors

The church contains a 14C crowned Virgin which was found buried in 1936.

Take D 175; on the right, you will see the ruins of the abbey.

Abbaye de Mortemer

Guided tours (45min) available. Unaccompanied access to park year-round 1.30–6pm. Park and museum

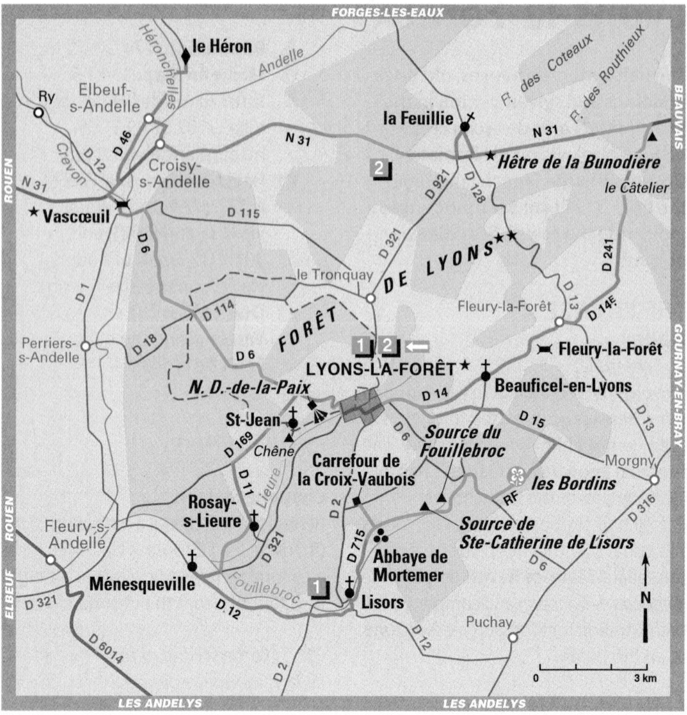

8€. Park alone 6€ ℘02 32 49 54 34. www.mortemer.fr.

In the forest stand the ruins of the 12C–13C Cistercian abbey. A **museum** below the conventual building, reconstructed in the 17C, explains monastic life and evokes legends connected with the abbey.

Across from the abbey, on the left-hand side of D 175, a short path leads to the Croix-Vaubois crossroads.

Carrefour de la Croix-Vaubois

The monument erected here recalls the foresters who died in the Resistance.

As you continue along D 175, look for two springs (sources) off to the left.

Source de Ste-Catherine-de-Lisors

A footbridge spanning the Fouillebroc leads to an oratory, traditionally visited by young girls in search of a husband.

Source du Fouillebroc

This spring is set in pleasant forest surroundings.

Les Bordins Arboretum

Free to visit year round; guided tours by request. ℘02 32 49 04 09.

Opened in 1994, this 11 000-acre/4 451.5ha area abounds with trees from across the world, grouped by continent.

2 NORTH OF THE FOREST

60km/37mi – allow about 2hr30min.

Leave Lyons to the E via D 14.

Beauficel-en-Lyons

Church. Guided tours by appointment with Mme Dufour, 1 rte de Fleury, 27480 Beauficel-en-Lyons. ℘02 32 49 62 51.

The **church** is preceded by a 17C porch and contains beautiful statues, including a 14C virgin in polychrome stone.

D 14 runs alongside Fleury-la-Forêt Castle (to the right).

Château de Fleury-la-Forêt

Guided tours available. 7€ 02 32 49 63 91. www.chateau-fleury-la-foret.com.
Beyond a wrought-iron gate, an avenue of lime trees leads to the 17C château built of red brick, flint and sandstone. The interior contains interesting displays of dolls, toys and furniture. There is also a huge kitchen abundantly decorated.

Turn left after Bosquentin and follow D 241.

Hêtre de la Bunodière★

Indicated by a signpost on the right as you leave N 31 to enter the forest, this magnificent beech, at 40m/131ft tall, stands near the Câtelier Reserve. Its circumference measures 3.3m/11ft.

N 31-E 46 leads back to La Feuillie.

La Feuillie

At 54m/177ft, the slender church **spire**★ is a bold piece of carpentry.

Le Héron

This pleasant tree-shaded area was designed by La Nôtre.

Rejoin the D 46 to Vascœuil.

Vascœuil

This little village (pronounced Va-coy) on the edge of the forest is famous for its 14C–16C **château**★ (*open Jul–Aug daily 11am–6.30pm; Apr–Jun and Sept–Oct Wed–Sun 2.30–6pm; 8€; 02 35 23 62 35; www.chateauvascoeuil.com*). On the grounds is the **Musée Michelet**, dedicated to the historian Jules Michelet (1798–1874), who stayed here.
The church, Église St-Martial (*guided tours by appointment, rue des Canadiens; 02 35 02 11 69*). Inside this church is the tomb of Hugues de Saint-Jovinien, a holy man who died in the 12C.

Pont-Audemer★

This quaint town of 16C houses is sometimes called the Venice of Normandy in reference to its canals, which once served a prosperous tanning trade.

- **Population:** 9 058.
- **Michelin Map:** 304: D-5.
- **Info:** Place Maubert. 02 32 41 08 21. www.ville-pont-audemer.fr.
- **Location:** 24km/15mi E of Honfleur and 58km/36mi W of Rouen.
- **Parking:** Car park on place Général de Gaulle.
- **Don't Miss:** Compass cards painted on the ground, let you explore the town at your own pace.

WALKING TOUR

OLD TOWN

Allow 45min. Start from place du Général de Gaulle. Take rue des Carmes and turn left on rue de la République; 100m/109yd further on, turn left again onto impasse de l'Épée. Further down the street, also on the left, is impasse St-Ouen.

Walk down these lanes to view the half-timbered houses the church.

Take rue Thiers to the left.

From the **bridge over the Risle**, there is a nice view of slate-roofed river houses.

From place Victor-Hugo, continue to place Louis-Gillain, to the right, and enter rue des Cordeliers.

At the corner of rue des Cordeliers and rue Notre-Dame-du-Pré stands a building with a small tower, the timber beams resting on a ground floor of stone.

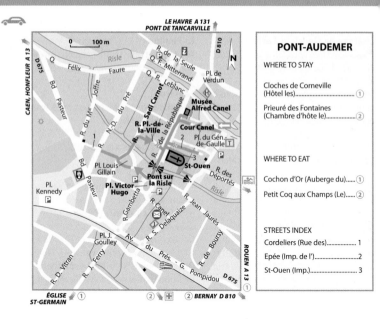

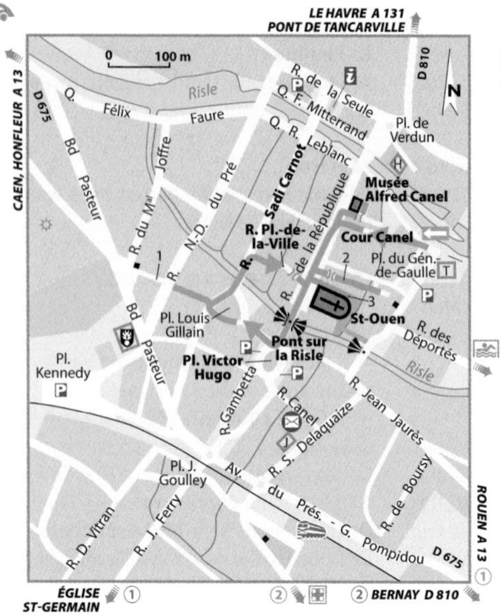

PONT-AUDEMER

WHERE TO STAY

Cloches de Corneville (Hôtel les)....... ①

Prieuré des Fontaines (Chambre d'hôte le)....... ②

WHERE TO EAT

Cochon d'Or (Auberge du)....... ①

Petit Coq aux Champs (Le)....... ②

STREETS INDEX

Cordeliers (Rue des)....... 1

Epée (Imp. de l')....... 2

St-Ouen (Imp.)....... 3

Return to place Louis-Gillain, cross the the Risle and take rue Sadi-Carnot.

Note the sculpted doorways. **Rue Place-de-la-Ville**, crosses a bridge into rue de la République, at St-Ouen Church.

Go up rue de la République and take the first passage right, after rue des Carmes.

Cour Canel also has some lovely half-timbered buildings to admire.

CHURCHES

Église St-Ouen

r. de la République.

The church was begun in the 11C and enlarged in the 16C. The nave received a 15C Flamboyant veneer. There are magnificent Renaissance **stained-glass windows**★.

Église St-Germain

Open Mon 2–6.30pm, Wed and Fri 4.30–6pm, Thu 10am–noon.

Parts of this church date back to the 11C, 14C and 19C.

ADDRESSES

STAY

Chambre d'hôte Le Prieuré des Fontaines – *rte de Lisieux, 27500 Les Préaux, 5km/3mi SE by D 139. 02 32 56 07 78. www.prieure-des-fontaines.fr.* This restored 17C building has spacious, comfortable rooms.

Les Cloches de Corneville – *rte de Rouen, 27500 Corneville-sur-Risle, 6km/3.7mi E via D 675. 02 32 56 7 21. www.cloches-de-corneville.fr. 11 rooms, 1 suite.* The Corneville bells peal from the top floor of this hotel, a historic monument.

EAT

Auberge du Cochon d'Or – *27210 Beuzeville, 14km/8.7mi W via D 675. 02 32 57 70 46. www.le-cochon-dor.fr.* Locals appreciate the changing menus.

Le Petit Coq aux Champs – *La Pommeraie Sud, 27500 Campigny, 6km/3.7mi S via D 810 and D 29. 02 32 41 04 19. www.lepetitcoqauxchamps.fr. Closed 2–29 Jan. Reservations required.* This beautiful thatched cottage houses a restaurant of solid renown, and 12 guest rooms.

Quillebeuf-sur-Seine

Population: 1 020.
Michelin Map: 304: D-5.
Info: 6 Grande Rue, 27500 Bourneville. 02 32 57 32 23. www.tourisme-quillebeuf.com.
Location: Quillebeuf-sur-Seine lies 11km/7mi E of the Tancarville Bridge via A 131, opposite Port-Jérôme. From the west, take N 178.

Until the 19C captains waited here for high tide, to pass through the dangerous channel known as the cemetery of ships. Today, the old port is overwhelmed by oil refineries and petrochemical installations in Port Jérôme on the north bank. Nonetheless, the town has managed to retain its traditional character. The town has an excellent view of Port Jérôme from the lighthouse. Église Notre-Dame-de-Bon-Port has a fine but incomplete Romanesque tower.

DRIVING TOUR

Quillebeuf to Roque Point

23km/14.3mi – allow 1hr.

The Vernier Marsh cuts a vast bay of 5 000ha/20sq mi out of the Roumois plateau between Quillebeuf and the Pointe de la Roque. It forms part of the **Parc naturel régional des Boucles de la Seine**.

Ste-Opportune-la-Mare

Follow the signs *Panorama de la Grande Mare* to a viewpoint over the Great Marsh and beyond to the reclaimed Marshland.

Réserve naturelle des Mannevilles

Guided tours (3hr) leaving from Ste-Opportune-la-Mare. Jul–Aug Sun 2–5pm. 3€. Information and reservations. 02 32 37 23 16. Wear boots.

The visitor can observe the flora and fauna of the Marais (marshland) area and approach Camargue horses and Scottish highland cattle.

W of Bouquelon, take D 39 north to St-Samson-de-la-Roque. A narrow winding road leads to the headland.

Pointe de la Roque★

Picnic area.

From the lighthouse on the cliff the **panorama** extends over the Seine estuary to Cap de la Hève and the Côte de Grâce. Tancarville cliffs and bridge can be seen to the right.

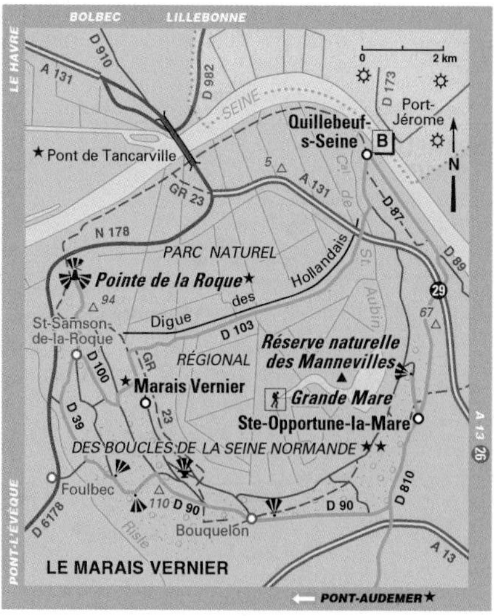

Verneuil-sur-Avre★

- **Population:** 6 699.
- **Michelin Map:** 304: F-9.
- **Info:** 129 place de la Madeleine. ✆02 32 32 17 17. www.verneuil-sur-avre.fr.
- **Location:** 36km/22.4mi W of Dreux on N 12.

Verneuil comprises three districts, the main streets of which are rue de la Madeleine, rue Gambetta and rue Notre-Dame. In the past each district was like a mini-town protected by a fortified wall and a moat, just as the whole town was surrounded by an outer wall and moat. Some fine half-timbered houses and old mansions have been preserved in the town.

A BIT OF HISTORY

Verneuil was formerly a fortified city created in the 12C by Henry Beauclerk, Duke of Normandy, third son of William the Conqueror. Together with Tillières and Nonancourt it formed the Avre defence line on the Franco-Norman frontier. In 1204, the town became French under Philippe Auguste, who built the Grise Tower and its defence system.
After many battles with the English, the French victory of 1449 was achieved through the guile of miller Jean Bertin.

SIGHTS

Tour Grise

The sentry walk at the top of this 13C tower is built of red agglomerate *(grison)*, from which it takes its name.
To the south, cross the small bridge over the Iton river to view the tower together with a charming little house at its base. The pleasant and relaxing **Fougère Park** lies near the bridge.
The partly ruined **Église St-Jean** has retained its 15C tower and its Gothic doorway.
The term Promenades refers to boulevard Casati and its prolongation. Remains of several of the old outer fortifications are visible. From avenue du Maréchal-Joffre and avenue du Maréchal-Foch are interesting views of the town.

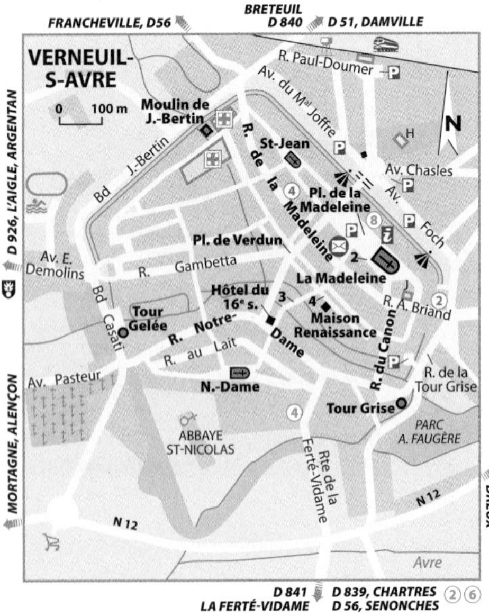

WHERE TO STAY

- Château de la Puisaye (Chambre d'hôte)....②
- Hostellerie Le Clos....④
- Moulin des Planches (Hôtel le)....⑥
- Saumon (Hôtel du)....⑧

WHERE TO EAT

- Brocante Gourmande (La)....②
- Madeleine (Le)....④

STREETS INDEX

- Poissonnerie (R. de la)....2
- Pont-aux-Chèvres (R. du)....3
- Tanneries (R. des)....4

Tour gris

G.Targat/MICHELIN

The many old houses are extremely well restored and add to Verneuil's charm. Note for instance the 15C residence at the corner of rue de la Madeleine and rue du Canon, with its chequered walls and turret, which now houses the public library. Between rue Canon and rue Thiers, on rue de la Madeleine, stand a number of attractive stone or timbered houses. The 18C Hôtel Bournonville has wrought-iron balconies. Note also the houses at nos 532 (behind a courtyard), 466 and 401.

A Renaissance house stands at no 136 rue des Tanneries, with a carved wooden door surmounted by wooden statues. At the corner of rue Notre-Dame and rue du Pont-aux-Chèvres stands a 16C town house with decorated turret. On place de Verdun, place de la Madeleine, rue de la Poissonerie are more picturesque old wooden houses.

Église de la Madeleine★

pl. de la Madeleine. Ask at tourist office about ascending the tower. ⊜1.20€.

The **tower**★ abutting the church dates from the late 15C–early 16C. The third of the four tiers is surmounted by a richly decorated belfry.

The Renaissance-style porch is flanked by mutilated but beautiful 16C statues of the Virgin and of St Anne. The interior is lit by 15C and 16C stained-glass windows and has several 15C and 16C artworks. The nave ceiling is vaulted in wood.

Église Notre-Dame

pl. Notre-Dame.

The church, built of the red stone known as *grison* in the 12C, has been remodelled and possesses a number of 16C **statues**★ carved by local sculptors. The illustration shows: **1)** St Denis (14C). **2)** St James the Great. **3)** St Christopher. **4)** St Christine. **5)** St Fiacre. **6)** St Susanna. **7)** St Barbara. **8)** St Francis of Assisi. **9)** St Benedict. **10)** Joan of Arc, as a Lorraine country girl. **11)** Renaissance Pietà. **12)** St Lawrence. **13)** St Augustine. **14)** St Denis with open skull. **15)** St Louis

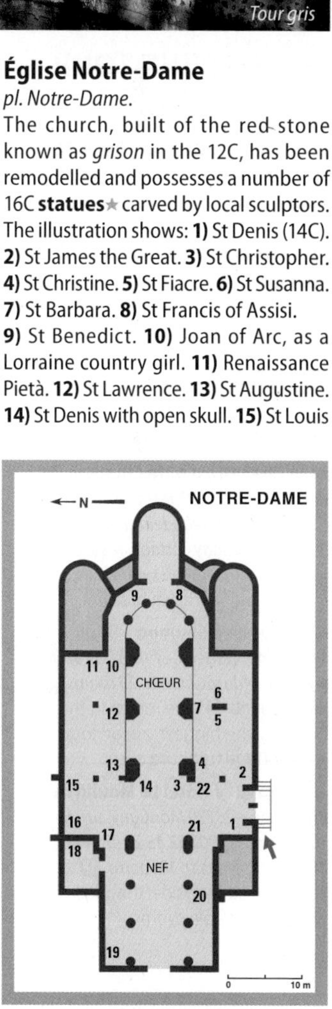

(17C). **16)** Two Prophets (Renaissance woodwork). **17)** St Sebastian (17C woodwork). **18)** 15C chest and altar base. **19)** 11C font. **20)** 14C Trinity (early Norman Renaissance). **21)**Virgin at Calvary (13C). **22)** St John.

EXCURSION

Francheville

9km/5.6mi NW on D 56.

The village, set attractively beside the River Iton, has a pretty church, restored. On the square *(place Modeste Leroy)* stands a small **Musée de la Ferronnerie** (Ironwork Museum: *02 32 60 18 89. www.francheville-eure.fr*).

DRIVING TOUR

VALLÉE DE L'AVRE: From Verneuil-sur-Avre to Nonancourt

20km/12.5mi – Allow 45min.

From Verneuil, take N 12 E for 13km/8mi.

Tillières-sur-Avre

Tillières was the first Norman fortified town built (1013) to guard the Avre defence line. The church, with its Romanesque nave and panelled vault, was rebuilt in the 16C. From the garden called the Grand Parterre there is a fine view of the Avre Valley.

Continue along N 12 for 12km/7.5mi.

The Flamboyant **Église St-Lubin** *(south of the river in St-Lubin-des-Joncherets)* was rebuilt in the 16C; the façade is Renaissance in style.

Head N over the river (0.7km/0.4mi.

Nonancourt

Église St-Martin. Guided tours by request. 02 32 58 28 74.

Nonancourt was built in 1112 by Henry Beauclerk. The Flamboyant-style **Église St-Martin** dates from 1511, the belfry from 1204, the organ from the Renaissance.

Take N 12 W to Verneuil-sur-Avre.

ADDRESSES

STAY

Chambre d'hôte Chiateau de la Puisaye – *27130 Verneuil. 02 32 58 65 35. www.chateaudelapuisaye.com. 5 suites, 1 holiday cottage.* A stunning Napoleon III château with characterful rooms. Hearty English breakfasts.

Hôtel du Saumon – *89 pl. de la Madeleine, Verneuil. 02 32 32 02 36. www.hoteldusaumon.fr. 29 rooms. . Restaurant*. The rooms in the main building, the biggest, are decorated with antique furniture.

Hôtel Le Moulin des Planches – *28270 Montigny-sur-Avre, 10km/6mi E. 02 37 48 25 97. www.moulin-des-planches.fr. 18 rooms. 9€.* Set in the countryside, this place has very comfortable rooms.

Hostellerie Le Clos – *98 r. Ferté-Vidame. 02 32 32 21 81. www.hostellerieduclos.fr. Closed 11 Dec–20 Jan, Mon and Tue lunch. 4 rooms. . Restaurant*. Elegant mansion with superb façade, refined rooms and spacious suites. Bikes loaned.

EAT

La Brocante Gourmande – *ruelle de l'Abreuvoir. 02 32 60 11 11. Closed Sun eve, Mon–Wed.*

Le Madeleine – *206 r. de la Madeleine. 02 32 37 78 26. Closed Wed.* Small, unpretentious restaurant with traditional menu. Jazz cocerts 1st and 3rd Thu of the month.

Vernon★

Vernon, which is close to the forest of the same name, was created by Rollo, first Duke of Normandy, in the 9C. It became French early in the 13C and is now an extremely pleasant residential town.

- **Population:** 622.
- **Michelin Map:** 304: I-7.
- **Info:** 36 rue Sadi-Carnot. ℘02 32 51 39 60. www.cape-tourisme.fr.
- **Location:** Vernon is 65km/ 40.4mi SE of Rouen on A 13.
- **Parking:** Two car parks are located at each end of the Clemenceau bridge.
- **Don't Miss:** The Église Notre-Dame and the park of the château of Bizy.
- **Timing:** Guided tours of the château of Bizy take some 45min. The park can be seen in 30min.

WALKING TOUR

Park near the Clemenceau Bridge (access from boulevard du Maréchal-Leclerc or rue de la Ravine).

Bridge Viewpoint

From the bridge there is a view of Vernon, the wooded islands in the Seine and the ruined piles on which the 12C bridge stood. On the right bank are the towers of Tourelles Castle, which formed part of the defences of the old bridge.

Turn left and walk along the Seine.

The walk takes you by the 18C Bourbon-Penthièvre house, named for the last Duke of Vernon. The street of the same name leads into the **old town**. Notre-Dame Church stands at the end of the pretty street with some half-timbered houses. Notice the 16C façade embellished with Gothic sculptures at no 15.

Église Notre-Dame★

1 r. du Chapitre.

This 12C collegiate church was remodelled several times before the Renaissance. The 15C west front has a beautiful rose window flanked by galleries. In rue du Chapitre, on the right side of the church, is a 17C house (nos 3-5). There are other interesting old houses in rue Carnot and rue Potard, in particular.

Côte St-Michel★

Allow 1hr round-trip on foot.

Old bridge over the Seine at Vernon

G.Targat/MICHELIN

From Vernonnet (north); rue J.-Soret to the church, turn right; follow signs.

From the top of the hill there is a good view of Vernon and the Seine Valley.

SIGHT

Musée A.-G.-Poulain

Entrance on rue Dupont. Open Apr–Sept Tue–Fri 10.30am–12.30pm, 2–6pm, Sat–Sun 2–6pm; Oct–Mar Tue–Sun 2–5.30pm. Closed public holidays. 2.80€. 02 32 21 28 09. www.vernon27.fr/musee.

The museum occupies several buildings dating from the 15C to the 19C. The collection includes works by Monet, Rosa Bonheur, Maurice Denis, Pierre Bonnard, Vuillard and Steinlen (1859–1923).

EXCURSIONS

Giverny★

See GIVERNY, p179.

Château de Bizy★

2km/1mi W of Vernon by D 181. Avenue des Capucins. Guided tours of the interior (45min) Apr–Oct daily except Mon 10am–noon, 2–6pm; Mar Sat–Sun 2–5pm. Closed Nov–Feb. 7.50€. 02 32 51 00 82. http://giverny.org/castles

The château was begun in 1740 for the Maréchal de Belle-Isle, and was remodelled by subsequent occupants. The Classical front faces the park. The rooms are decorated with beautiful Regency woodwork, 18C tapestries and Empire style furniture. The **park** was laid out in the 18C and redesigned in the English style by King Louis-Philippe. Thanks to recent renovation work, the *chemin d'eau* (waterway) has been restored to its former glory.

Signal des Coutumes

8km/5mi from Vernon. Take N 15 out of town and after 5km/3mi, just before Port-Villez, turn right on D 89.

Notre-Dame-de-la-Mer

The **look-out point**★ gives a view of the river between Bonnières and Villez.

Carry on along D 89; left at the town hall of Jeufosse and leave the paved road on the right. Outside the hamlet of Les Coutumes, take a paved road to the right, which leads to the edge of the woods.

Signal des Coutumes

There is a lovely, broad **view**★ over the Bonnières meander.

DRIVING TOUR

The Vexin Normand★★

From Vernon to Rouen

100km/62mi – allow 5hr (includes visits).

The road runs parallel to the right bank of the Seine through farmlands and between the river bank and the escarpment found at each hollow bend.

From Vernon take D 313 north.

Near the D 10 junction at the entrance to Port-Mort village, in a field, stands a dolmen, known as the **Gravier de Gargantua** (Gargantua's Pebble).

Courcelles-sur-Seine; cross to south bank along D 316.

Château de Gaillon

Closed for renovation. www.chateaugaillon.com.

The vast **château** *(the access roads branch N off N 15 going W to Rouen)* was made famous in the late 15C by **Georges d'Amboise**, the first of France's great Cardinal-Ministers. After an expedition to Italy, the prelate rebuilt the château, launching the Renaissance style in Normandy.

From Gaillon take D 65 north. In Villers-sur-le-Roule turn right onto D 176.

There is a fine **view**★ south of Tosny. A suspension bridge carries the road over the Seine to Les Andelys.

Les Andelys★★

See Les ANDELYS, p163.

From Les Andelys to Muids, the road (D 313) runs at the foot of chalk escarpments bordering the river. Beyond Muids (D 65) the escarpment is visible across the river.

In Amfreville-sous-les-Monts turn right onto D 20 which climbs rapidly to the top of the hill; park 50m/55yd beyond the TCF viewing table.

Côte des Deux-Amants★★

From a bend in the road there is a magnificent view of the Seine Valley: Amfreville locks and dam and the bend in the Seine.

In the 12C, Marie de France, the first French woman writer, told the story of the a king who he decreed that his daughter's bridegroom would have to be strong enough to run non-stop to the top of a nearby hill with her in his arms. Raoul died at the summit; Caliste, the daughter, fell dead beside him,and so the hill acquired their names.

Écluses d'Amfreville★

The locks and the Poses Dam control water flow in the Lower Seine. Follow the towpath over a distance of 1.7km/1mi to reach the river boat Musée de la Batellerie sur la Seine (River Transport Museum). Take the footbridge overlooking the locks to see the water pouring over the Poses Dam.

Le Manoir

The new church is a plain, modern building. A vast composition in glass gives a warm light to the interior.

In Igoville turn right onto N 15, which cuts across a promontory that points towards Elbeuf on the south bank.

Les Authieux-sur-le-Port-St-Ouen

The church has a fine series of Renaissance stained-glass.

North of St-Adrien turn right onto D 7; continue to the plateau at Belbeuf.

Chapelle St-Adrien

Situated 20m/65.6ft below the road, the 13C chapel is partly built inside the cliff and partly thatched.

South of Belbeuf turn sharp right onto rue de Verdun; bear left, then right, cross a forest crossroads and take the first right; park near the housing development; take the path (45min on foot there and back) to the rocks.

Roches St-Adrien★

A very attractive view of the river and of the city of Rouen to the north.

Belbeuf

The small church is guarded by its old yew tree.

Turn left onto N 14. As the road descends below the basilica in Bonsecours, there is a grand **panorama★★**.

ADDRESSES

STAY

Hôtel d'Évreux – *11 pl. d'Évreux. 02 32 21 16 12. www.hoteldevreux.fr. 12 rooms. 7€. Restaurant.*

The Count of Évreux lived in this 17C residence, later a coaching inn. The drawing room is chic and the remodelled rooms retain their elegance.

EAT

Les Fleurs – *71 r. Carnot. 02 32 51 16 80. Closed 4–13 Mar, 1–27 Aug, Sun eve, Mon. Reservations required.*

This 15C house in the heart of town opens its doors onto an intimate, rather bourgeois décor featuring Louis XV furniture. Enjoy the pleasant setting while choosing one of the set menus that have contributed to its fine reputation. Also has 2 guest rooms.

EURE-ET-LOIR

The part of Normandy known as the Perche lies in the southwest corner of the département of Eure-et-Loir, and spreads into the département of Orne. With its humid valleys and forests, the Perche offers a sharp contrast to the flat, dry plains of the French Beauce to the east. The countryside is typified by picturesque villages, marshy bocage country and wooded hills crisscrossed by narrow roads and hiking trails. In the pastures graze dairy cows and sturdy Percheron draught horses. The principal cities, Dreux and Nogent-le-Rotrou, grew up around fortified hills.

At the place where the River Blaise flows into the Eure, **Dreux** has been a crossroads since ancient Gallo-Roman times and has both prospered and suffered as a result. Fortified by the Normans and their successors, it was sacked by Henri IV in 1593. After an 18C tussle within the royal family, the city found itself the family seat of the Orléanist faction, and site of the elaborate family crypt, containing a remarkable collection of 19C funerary monuments, in the **Collégiale St-Étienne**.

Long a bustling manufacturing centre, Dreux now counts light industry and pharmaceuticals as major employers. Outside the city lie the **Dreux and Ivry forests**, along the River Eure, which offer lovely drives. Not far away lies the spectacular Renaissance **Château d'Anet**, built between 1547 and 1552 by Diane de Poitiers, mistress to Henri II; she retired here after the king's death, to avoid the formidable royal widow, Catherine de' Medici. Nearly demolished after the French Revolution, the château has been lovingly restored by a succession of owners.

To the southwest, within the **Parc naturel régional du Perche**, lies **Nogent-le-Rotrou**, dominated by the massive 12C–13C castle of the counts of Perche, under whom this was a powerful feudal state. The city centre retains remarkable late Gothic Flamboyant and Renaissance buildings, including the tomb of the Duc de Sully (1560–1641), renowned financier of of Henri IV.

The surrounding nature park is a delight of country roads, manor houses, small châteaux and pretty villages, constructed of the white, grey and beige local stone and brick, with red-tiled roofs. This rural charm, so accessible from Paris, has created a lively maket for secondary residences.

The celebrated **Percheron horses**, dappled grey or black, conduct visitors on circuits within the park and can be admired during exhibitions.

See also Fôret de Brotonne, p313.

Dreux★

Dreux is set on the boundary between Normandy and Île-de-France; it is a lively regional market town earning its living from diverse industrial activities. The town is the final resting place of members of the Orléans family, one of France's royal lines; they can be viewed in the crypt of the Royal Chapel of St-Louis where their tombs comprise an impressive collection of 19C sculpture. Nearby, the Eure Valley contains lovely surprises, notably the château of Anet.

- **Population:** 32 565.
- **Michelin Map:**311: E-3.
- **Info:** 6 r. des Embûches. 02 37 46 01 73. www.ot-dreux.fr.
- **Location:** Dreux is 85 km/52.8mi W of Paris via N 12, and 48km/29.8mi E of l'Aigle. The historic centre is on the left bank, and the Grande-Rue (rue Maurice-Violette) is the liveliest street.
- **Don't Miss:** The Royal Chapel and the Renaissance château of Anet.
- **Timing:** You'll need 2hr to see the town, and another 2hr for the château of Anet. Make time for a picnic on the site of the château d'Ivry.
- **Kids:** The musée Marcel-Dessal has a children's itinerary.

A BIT OF HISTORY

Dreux rose to importance when the Normans settled west of the River Avre and Dreux Castle had to defend the French frontier against a very belligerent neighbour. The castle, which stood on the hill now occupied by St Louis' Chapel, was besieged many times. It was dismantled on the orders of Henri IV, who razed the town in 1593 after a three-year siege.

In 1556 the Paris Parliament decided that the County of Dreux should in the future be the exclusive property of the French royal family. In 1775 Louis XVI ceded Dreux to his cousin, the Duc de Penthièvre, son of the Comte de Toulouse. Eight years later, when at the king's insistence the duc was forced to give up his magnificent property at Rambouillet, he arranged for the family tombs in the parish church of Rambouillet (subsequently destroyed) to be transferred to the collegiate church adjoining Dreux Castle. When the duc's daughter married Louis Philippe d'Orléans, known as Philippe Égalité, her dowry included the County of Dreux. It was thus that Dreux, which until the Revolution had been a simple family burial place, became the mausoleum of the Orléans family.

SIGHTS

Belfry★

Closed for renovation.

At the end of the old Grande-Rue (Maurice-Violette) rises the ornate façade of the Hôtel de ville (town hall), which was built from 1512 to 1537. The ground and first floors are decorated in the Flamboyant style; the Renaissance second floor shows the skill of a young architect from Dreux, **Clément Métézeau** (1479–1555).

Église St-Pierre

pl. Métézeau, opposite Belfry.

Open daily 9am–noon, 2–7pm.

Built in the early 13C and partly damaged during the Hundred Years' War, St Peter's Church was heavily remodelled from the 15C to the 17C. The façade dates from the 16C. Of the two towers designed to flank it, only the left one was actually completed. The gate, chancel and left arm of the transept are 13C. The right arm of the transept dates from the 16C to the 17C.

The church interior is notable for its fine 15C and 16C **stained-glass windows**, to be found especially in the side chapels *(1st, 2nd and 3rd on the right; 2nd, 3rd and 4th on the left)* and apsidal chapel. The outstanding organ case (1614) is the work of the local cabinetmaker Toussaint Fortier.

Grande-Rue

The former Grande-Rue, now rue Maurice-Violette, hums with activity most days of the week, particulary during summer festivals. Note at the corner of rue Illiers two 15C half-timbered houses whose upper storeys extend over the street.

Chapelle royale St-Louis

2 sq. d'Aumale. Guided tours (1hr) Wed–Mon Jul–Aug 9.30am–12.30pm, 1.30–6.30pm; Apr–Jun and Sept 9.30am–noon, 2–6pm. 7€. Access to park 1€. 02 37 46 07 06.

Before the Revolution this site was occupied by the Collegiate Church of St Stephen (St-Étienne). In 1783 it received the remains of members of the Toulouse-Penthièvre families.

In 1816 the dowager Duchess of Orléans, widow of Philippe Égalité, erected a chapel in the Neoclassical style. It was enlarged by her son Louis-Philippe (1773–1850) when he became king, and the exterior was embellished with bell turrets and Gothic pinnacles. The building as a whole is a monument to the 19C for both the quality of its architecture and the work of talented artists.

The side windows make it possible to admire the stained-glass representations of the patron saints of France and the royal family: *(left)* St Philip, St Amelia, St Ferdinand (the heads are portraits). The stained glass in the apse illustrates the life of St Louis.

The main crypt contains the tombs of the Princes of Orléans; the recumbent figures form a little museum of 19C statuary by Mercié, Pradier, Dubois, Chapu, Millet, Lenoir, etc.

On the lower level, five extremely rare **glass panes painted with enamels**★★ catch the visitor's attention. They were made in the Sèvres workshops, as was the other glasswork.

The park contains several remains of old fortifications. A fine **view** can be had of the town.

Musée d'Art et d'Histoire Marcel-Dessal

Place du Musée. Open Wed–Sat 2–6pm. Closed public holidays (except 14 Jul) and 2nd-half Dec. 2.17€ (under 10 years no charge). 02 37 50 18 61. www.musees.regioncentre.fr

Set up in a neo-Romanesque chapel, the museum displays furnishings taken from the Collégiale St-Étienne, a 12C church which stood on the site of the Royal Chapel. Shown alongside local archaeological exhibits, dating from Prehistoric, Gallo-Roman and Merovingian times, are exhibits evoking the history of the Dreux region. A set of 18C furniture taken from the Château de Crécy-Couve, formerly owned by the Marquise de Pompadour, is also on show.

The painting gallery displays both ancient and contemporary works. Impressionist and post-Impressionist movements are well represented with canvases by Vlaminck, Montezin and Le Sidaner, arranged around a painting by Claude Monet *(Wisteria)*.

DRIVING TOURS

FROM DREUX TO PACY-SUR-EURE

49km/30.5mi – allow 3hr (including château visit).

Leave Dreux via D 928 north and take D 161 to the left.

Outside Dreux, the aqueduct crosses the valley, carrying water from the Avre to Paris. Off to the right, you can see the church in the little town of Montreuil as you drive by, and Dreux Forest off to the left. In Ézy-sur-Eure, an old humpback bridge (Pont St-Jean) crosses the river to Saussay.

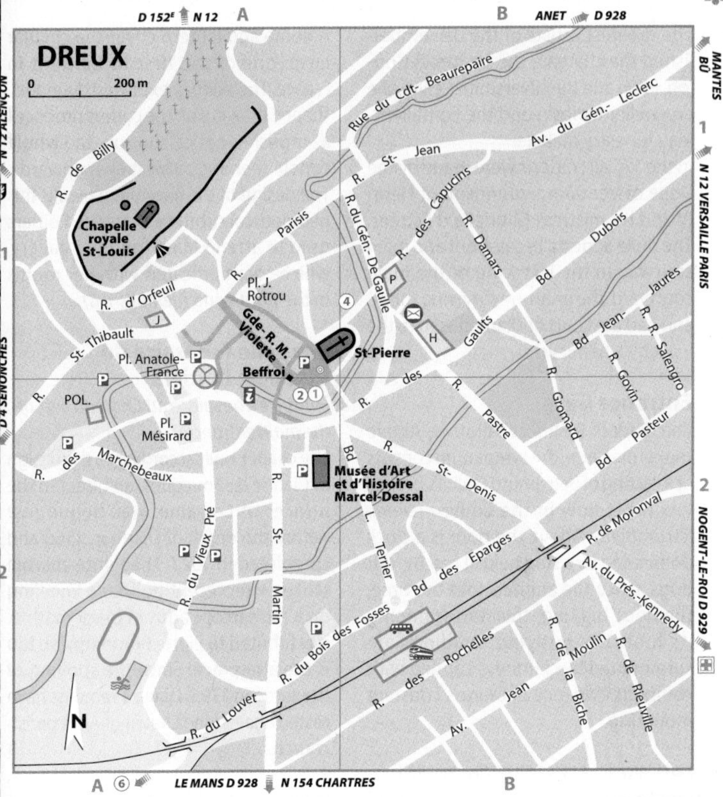

WHERE TO STAY		WHERE TO EAT	
Beffroi (Hôtel le)	①	Quatre Vents (Aux)	②
		Saint Pierre (Le)	④
		Vallée Verte (Auberge de la)	⑥

CHÂTEAU D'ANET★

Guided tours (45min) Apr–Oct Wed–Mon 2–6pm; Feb–Mar and Nov Sat–Sun 2–5pm. 7.30€. 02 37 41 90 07. www.chateaudanet.com

Of all the French Renaissance châteaux, Anet was reputedly the most ornate. Successive owners since 1840 have endeavoured to maintain the original appearance of the buildings.

A Queen without a Crown

Shortly after her arrival at court, **Diane de Poitiers** (1490–1566), widow of Louis de Brézé, Seneschal of Normandy and Lord of Anet, caught the attention of Henri, second son of François I and 20 years her junior. Beautiful, intelligent and a patron of the arts, Diane was 32 when the dauphin met her and he was still fascinated by her when he became King Henri II. When in 1559, Henri was killed by Montgomery during a tournament, Diane had reigned for 12 years over sovereign, court, artists and royal finances. Anet, which she had rebuilt, was the symbol of her power and taste. In 1559 Henri's widow Catherine de' Medici took Chenonceau but left Anet to Diane, who died there in 1566. Work began c. 1548 under the architect **Philibert Delorme**.

The centrepiece of the main building overlooking the courtyard was well ahead of its time; it now stands in the courtyard of the Fine Arts School (École des Beaux-Arts) in Paris.

The greatest artists of the day embellished the château: the sculptors Goujon, Pilon and the silversmith Cellini, the enameller Limosin and the Fontainebleau tapestry makers.

In the 17C alterations were made by the Duke of Vendôme, grandson of Henri IV and his mistress Gabrielle d'Estrées. The duke added a break-front and main stairway to the left wing of the main courtyard, the only one surviving today, and had the court of Diane closed to the west by a hemicycle.

Entrance Gate

The work of Philibert Delorme. Above the central arch, the tympanum consists of a casting of Benvenuto Cellini's bronze low relief now in the Louvre *(Diane Recumbent)*. Above the door is a clock dominated by a stag held at bay by four dogs. Once the animals told the time, the dogs barking, the stag stamping its foot. The outlying buildings are surmounted by chimneys capped with coffins as evidence of Diane's constant mourning.

Left Wing of the Main Courtyard

The visit begins on the first floor with Diane's bedroom. The main attraction is the Renaissance bed, decorated with the three crescents of Diane. The stained-glass windows include fragments of the original greyish monochrome designs (*grisailles*), a discreet decoration in keeping with Diane's mourning.

The **main stairway**, added by the Duke of Vendôme in the 17C, affords views of the lake and park. The vestibule, dating back to the same period, leads to the Salon Rouge containing furniture from the French and Italian Renaissance.

The Faïence Room, which has kept part of its original tiling, leads into the dining room where the huge fireplace is supported by two atlantes by Puget. In the centre note the Jean Goujon medallion depicting Diane snaring the royal stag.

Chapel

It was built in 1548 by Philibert Delorme and is in the form of a Greek cross. A dome and lantern cover the circular nave, one of the first to be built in France. The skilfully executed diamond-shaped drawing on the coffers produces a surprising optical illusion, the whole cupola seeming to be drawn upwards. The design of the floor tiling recalls this geometrical subtlety. Diane de Poitiers used to attend Mass from the gallery, which communicated with her rooms in the right wing *(demolished)*.

Chapelle funéraire de Diane de Poitiers

Entrance from place du Château, left of the main entrance.

The chapel, built according to the design of Claude de Foucques, architect to the princes of Lorraine, was begun just before the death of Diane in 1566 and completed in 1577. The white-marble **statue**★ representing Diane kneeling on a tall sarcophagus in black marble, is attributed to Pierre Bontemps; so too is the altarpiece. Since the spoiling of the tomb in 1795, Diane's remains have rested against the chevet of Anet parish church.

Ivry-la-Bataille

The battle referred to in the town name took place on 14 March 1590, when Henri IV defeated the Duc de Mayenne and the Catholic League during the Wars of Religion (1561–98). There are a few picturesque timber-framed houses in the village: a typical local house *(no 5 rue de Garennes)* may have been the lodging of Henri IV in 1590; the 11C doorway *(at the end of rue de l'Abbaye)*, decorated with three sculpted key stones (renovated), may have been part of Ivry Abbey, which ceased to exist at the Revolution. Diane de Poitiers was the founder of the **Église St-Martin**, a late-15C to early 16C church, attributed in part to the famous architect, Philibert Delorme.

Take D 833 northwest.

In the little village of **Couture-Boussey**, a centre of woodwind manufacture since the 16C, is a **Musée des Instruments à**

Vent (🕐 *open Tue–Sun 2–6pm;* 🕐 *closed 20 Dec–10 Jan, 1 May.* ◉4€; 📞*02 32 36 28 80; www.lacoutureboussey.com*).

▶ *Return to Ivry via D 833, continue north on D 836.*

Between Neuilly and the mills of Merey, the 16C **Château de la Folletière** (🗝 *closed to the public*) can be seen through the foliage in a park.

▶ *From Chambine to Pacy, D 836 rises above the Eure and there are pleasant views upstream.*

ADDRESSES

🛏 STAY

🍽🍽 **Hôtel Le Beffroi** – *12 pl. Métézeau.* 📞*02 37 50 02 03. Closed 23 Jul–16 Aug. 15 rooms.* ▭. In the heart of the old city, this hotel is not particularly luxurious but the rooms are functional and adequate to the task.

🍴 EAT

🍽 **Le Saint Pierre** – *19 r. de Sénarmont.* 📞*02 37 46 47 00. www.lesaint.pierre. com. Closed 7–15 Mar, 12–28 Jul, Sun eve, Thu eve, Mon.* Delectable menus and reasonable prices have brought renown to this small restaurant in the town centre. Bistro-style décor.

🍽🍽 **Aux Quatre Vents** – *18 pl. Métézeau.* 📞*02 37 50 03 24. www.aux-quatrte-vents.eu. Closed eves except Fri.* Located in the heart of Dreux, this family eatery offers an array of traditional dishes served in a brasserie-style dining room. Terrace by the river the summer.

🍽🍽 **Auberge de la Vallée Verte** – *6 r. Lucien-Dupuis. 28500 Vernouillet, 2km/1mi S.* 📞*02 37 46 04 04. www.auberge-vallee.com. Closed 1–25 Aug, 25 Dec–9 Jan, Sun–Mon.* Tradition rules in this family-owned inn. Here, you will sample traditional dishes based on what appears in the market. Rustic dining room, with mezzanine. 16 guest rooms.

Nogent-le-Rotrou

The capital of the Perche region lies on the banks of the River Huisne, dominated by its castle. The old town borders the main road (N 23) at the foot of St John's Hill; the new town covers the flat land beside the River Huisne.

A BIT OF HISTORY

Between 925 and 1226 the Gallo-Roman town became a powerful fief of the Rotrou family, counts of Perche, who gave the town its name (Nogent derives from the Gallic term *noviomago* meaning new market). Nogent was burned down in 1449 at Charles VII's command to prevent the English from capturing it. The town was rebuilt soon afterwards, in the Flamboyant or Renaissance style.

▶ **Population:** 12 484.
🔢 **Michelin Map:** 311-A-6.
ℹ **Info:** 44 rue Villette-Gate. 📞*02 37 29 68 86. www. ville-nogent-le-rotrou.fr.*
📍 **Location:** Nogent-le-Rotrou is 91km/56.5mi SW of Dreux and 77km/47.8mi S of L'Aigle.
🅿 **Parking:** Park in place de la République.
👁 **Don't Miss:** Château St-Jean; the tomb of Sully.
🕐 **Timing:** Take time to tour the surrounding Parc naturel régional du Perche.

SIGHTS
Église Notre-Dame
Corner of rue Gouverneur and rue de Sully 🕐*Open daily 8am–7pm.*

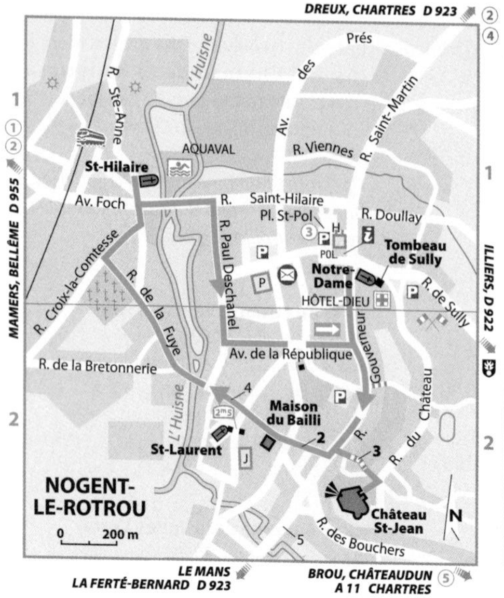

WHERE TO STAY

Brit Hôtel du Perche 1
Jardin François (Chambre d'hôte le) 2
Lion d'Or (Hôtel Au) 3
Vallées du Perche (Hôtel les) 5

WHERE TO EAT

Alambic (L') 2
Hostellerie le Chêne Doré 4

STREETS INDEX

Bourg-le-Comte (R.) 2
Marches St-Jean (R. des) 3
St-Laurent (R.) 4
St-Lazare (R.) 5

The building was formerly the chapel of the Hôtel-Dieu (workhouse) and dates from the 13C and 14C. At the end of the north aisle there is a 16C–17C crib; the figures are of painted terracotta.

Tombeau de Sully

Access is through rue de Sully: a courtyard contains the oratory and tomb. Open daily 9am–4.30pm.
The doorway to the Hôtel-Dieu (17C) displays Sully's coat of arms and emblems on the pediment. As Sully was a Protestant, his tomb is next to the church but not part of it. His empty tomb was sculpted by Barthélemy Boudin from Chartres.

Château St-Jean

Access on foot by rue des Marches-St-Jean, or by car along rue de Sully, then rue du Château-St-Jean. Open Wed–Mon 10am–noon, 2–6pm (last entry 5.30pm). Closed 1 Jan, 1 May, 1 Nov, 25 Dec. 2.60€. 02 37 52 18 02.
This impressive castle stands on a rocky spur. The Rotrous, counts of Perche, lived in the huge rectangular keep (35m/115ft high), which is supported by unusual buttresses. The enclosing wall with its semicircular towers was built from the 12C to the 13C. The remarkable gatehouse is flanked by round towers with arrow slits and machicolations. The courtyard provides a view of the town.

A path runs round outside the walls.

Rue Bourg-le-Comte

Several of the houses are of interest: a 13C turreted house (no **2**), which is better seen from rue des Poupardières; a 16C house (no **4**); a Renaissance house with mullioned windows (no **3**).

Famous Names

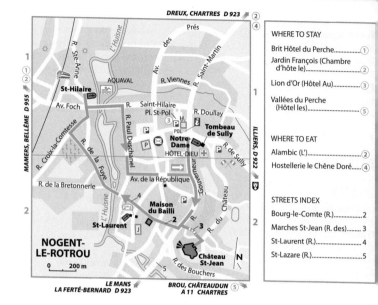

Poet **Rémi Belleau** (1528–77), born in Nogent-le-Rotrou and one of the founders of the Pléiad group, glorified the art of living; he also described rural landscapes and the beauty of natural shapes.
Nogent-le-Rotrou is closely associated with **Maximilien de Béthune**, Duc de Sully (1560–1641), renowned financier of Henri IV. The duke owned Rosny, Sully, La Chapelle-d'Angillon, Henrichemont and Villebon. In 1624 he purchased the château and manor of Nogent from Henri II de Condé.

Maison du Bailli

47 r. St-Laurent. Exterior only.
Two turrets flank the entrance to the 16C mansion built by Pierre Durant, Bailiff of St Denis' Abbey, and his wife Blanche Dévrier. The dormer windows are particularly fine.

Église St-Hilaire

The church (13C–16C) stands beside the River Huisne. Its square tower dates from the 16C. The unusual polygonal chancel (13C) was modelled on the Holy Sepulchre in Jerusalem.

Église St-Laurent

By appointment: ask at town hall.
The building is in the Flamboyant style, surmounted by a tower with a Renaissance top.

ADDRESSES

STAY

Brit Hôtel du Perche – *r. de la Bruyère. 02 37 53 43 60. www.brit hotel.fr. 40 rooms.* . Set in the heart of the Perche countryside, this modern hotel is still just 900m/0.5mi from the train station. Garden terrace. Rooms are pleasant and functional.

Chambre d'hôte L'Aulnaye – *rte d'Alençon, 1km/0.6mi W of Nogent-le-Retrou. 02 37 52 01 11. 3 rooms.* . 19C bourgeois property in superb surroundings. A beautiful stairway leads to the rooms, which have parquet flooring.

Chambre d'hôte Le Jardin François – *Le Clos, 61340 Préaux-du-Perche, 10km/6mi W of Nogent-le-Retrou. 02 37 49 64 19. www.jardin-francois.com. 5 rooms.* . Pretty rooms with kitchenettes in an old house located near a magnificent garden created by the owner, a keen gardener. Concerts and exhibitions are held in the orangerie or the outdoor theatre.

Hôtel Auberge des Vallées du Perche – *Lieu-dit l'Ambition, 28480 Vichères, 9km/5.6mi SE. 02 37 29 47 58. 14 rooms. Restaurant . 7€.* Rooms are in the annex of this small country inn. Some newer than others. Good soundproofing.

Hôtel au Lion d'Or– *28 pl. St-Pol. 02 37 52 01 60. Closed 3–28 Aug, 31 Oct–5 Nov, 26 Dec–4 Jan. 18 rooms. 7€.* A small, practical town-centre hotel with fully renovated rooms and clean bathrooms.

EAT

L'Alambic – *20 av. de Paris, Maragon, 2km/1mi NE. 02 37 52 19 03. 18 rooms.* Traditional cuisine served in a choice of three dining rooms. Terrace in summer.

Hostellerie de la Papotière – *31 r. Bourg-le-Comte. 02 37 52 18 41. Closed Sun eve and Mon.* The modest, intimate restaurant in this timber-framed house offers a unique menu.

Hostellerie le Chêne Doré – *12 pl. de l'Hôtel de Ville, 28240 La Loupe, 25km/15/5mi N of Nogent-le-Retrou. 02 37 81 06 71. Closed Fri eve, Sat eve, Sun eve.* Situated in the centre of the small town of La Loupe, the dining room offers traditional cuisine using regional, seasonal ingredients. 12 guest rooms.

SHOPPING

Virginie Berthier – *41 r. du Paty. 02 37 52 12 81. www.patymetiersdart.com. Visits by appointment, 10 people maximum. 30€ per hour.* Creation and restoration of stained-glass windows, painting on glass. Lessons.

Long, windswept beaches, rocky cliffs, coves, dunes, the piercing calls of seabirds, and happy vacationers strolling and bathing along the shore, these are the images inspired by the Manche, whose name is the French word for the English Channel. The Cotentin Peninsula, shaped like a snail's head, reaches north into the Channel, with the great port of Cherbourg-Octeville at the tip, while inland stretches the *bocage* country of hedgerows and narrow roads, with many churches, castles and houses made of local granite. The numerous abbeys include Mont St-Michel, a miracle of art and engineering.

Most of the Manche, like Brittany, lies on the Armorican Massif, a landscape of marshes, granite escarpments and low hills, remains of an ancient mountain range that rose some 286 to 350 million years ago.

The word "Amor" comes from the ancient Gaulish language and means "land of the sea." While the coastline to the east of the penninsula presents long stretches of beach from **St-Vaast-la Hogue** southwards to **Utah Beach**, the coast on the west, descending south to the Bay of Mont St-Michel, is cut by coves and rocky headlands surmounted by lighthouses. Warmed by the Gulf Stream, pleasant bathing beaches and marinas attract summer holidaymakers. Despite 350km/217mi of coastline, the Manche has no large natural harbours. The port at **Cherbourg**,strategically located opposite Bournemouth in England, grew from an artifical breakwater laid to create a naval base in the 18C. During World War II, the Germans mined the port; the city emerged devastated, but today is a lively commercial and military port, with much to see on both walking and nautical tours.

At **Coutances**, also pummelled in the war, the Gothic cathedral, the greatest in Normandy, miraculously survived. For history buffs, the town of **Avranches** offers dramatic relics of seraphic visions, war, rebellion and the murder of an Archbishop of Canterbury.

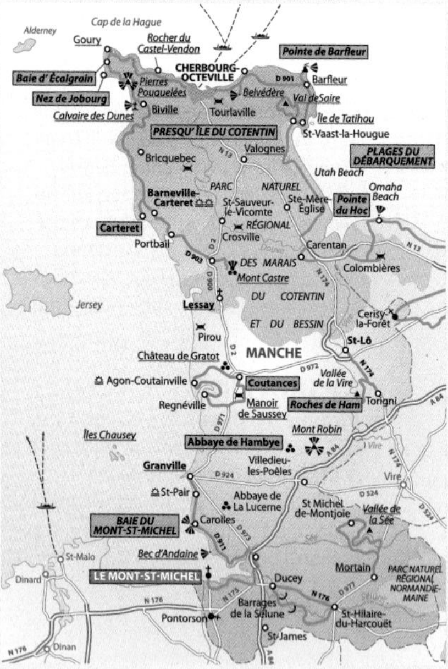

For summer vacationers, the splendid beaches at **Barneville-Carteret**, **Granville**, **St-Vaast-la-Houge** and around **Coutances** beckon; seaside stations rent watercraft and offer cruises.

East of Cherbourg lies **Barfleur**, one of the prettiest villages in France. The capital of the Manche, **St-Lô**, left almost entirely in ruins in 1944, has rebuilt its homes and monuments around the high ramparts of the old town.

Rural rambles, such as the **Vallée de la Vire**, and enchanting ruins, like **Hambaye**, invite exploration.City gardens in **Avranches** and Cherbourg are celebrated.

Avranches★

The pretty and lively city of Avranches is one of the oldest towns in Normandy; its origins date back to early antiquity. St Aubert, Bishop of Avranches in the 8C, instigated the foundation of Mont-St-Michel and the two centres are therefore closely linked not only geographically but also historically. The surrounding area is known for the Avranchin breed of sheep.

- **Population:** 8 239.
- **Michelin Map:** 303: D-7 – Local map, see *MONT-ST-MICHEL, p224.*
- **Info:** 2 rue Général de Gaule. 02 33 58 00 22. www.ot-avranches.com.
- **Location:** The town, on a granite spur, has a commanding view of Mont-St-Michel, 25km/15.5mi to the W. It can be reached by A 84, linking Villedieu-les-Poêles (23km/14.3mi) to the NE and Rennes, 87km/54mi to the SW.
- **Parking:** At the town centre, near the museum, Plate-forme and gardens.
- **Don't Miss:** The superb view of Mont-St-Michel from the Jardin des Plantes.
- **Timing:** One can easily spend a half-day at Avranches, between the museums and the Jardin des Plantes.
- **Kids:** At the Scriptorial, children are welcomed with a special tour led by the elf Titivillus.

A BIT OF HISTORY

The Vision of Bishop Aubert (8C) – Legend has it that St Michael appeared twice before **Aubert** and commanded him to raise a chapel in his honour on the rock then called Mount Tombe, but the sceptical Bishop of Avranches vacillated. St Michael reappeared and dug an imperious finger into the doubting man's skull. Aubert could delay no longer. A skull with a hole in it displayed in the Treasury of the St Gervase Basilica recalls this legend.

Henry II Repents (12C) – Relations between the King of England, **Henry Plantagenet**, who was also Duke of Normandy, and his Archbishop of Canterbury, **Thomas Becket**, became very bitter. One day the King cried out, "Will no one rid me of this insolent priest?" Four knights took the words as a command and, on 29 December 1170, Thomas Becket was murdered in Canterbury Cathedral.

The Pope excommunicated Henry II, who begged absolution. Robert of Torigni, Abbot of Mont-St-Michel, held a council attended by the king at Avranches, and so it was that at the door of the cathedral (collapsed in 1794) Henry II, barefoot and dressed only in a shirt, made public penance on his knees on 22 May 1172.

Barefoot Peasants' War – Imposition of a salt tax in 1639 brought a revolt of the Avranches saltworkers (les Nu-Pieds), led by Jean Quétil.

The Avranches Breakthrough – It was from Avranches on 31 July 1944 that General Patton began the swift advance which smashed the German Panzer counter-offensive launched from Mortain, beginning the attack which was to take the American 3rd Army through to Bastogne in Belgium.

SIGHTS

The museum, the Plate-forme and the town hall (Mont St-Michel manuscripts) are located around the site of the former episcopal palace while the botanical gardens are slightly down the hill. The Basilica of SS Gervais and Protais is a short walk from the town hall.

Entry to the Basilica Treasury is included in the museum and manuscript ticket. The Patton Monument is a 20-minute walk down rue de la Constitution.

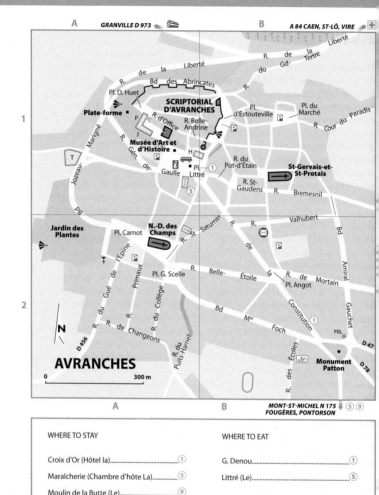

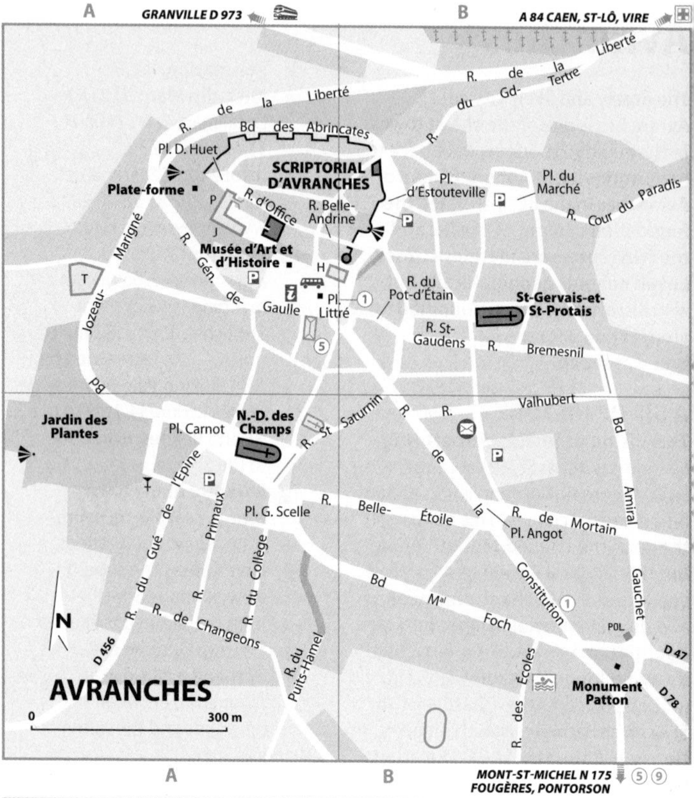

WHERE TO STAY

- Croix d'Or (Hôtel la)........ ①
- Maraîcherie (Chambre d'hôte La)........ ⑤
- Moulin de la Butte (Le)........ ⑨

WHERE TO EAT

- G. Denou........ ①
- Littré (Le)........ ⑤

Jardin des plantes

pl. Carnot. Open 8.30am–dusk.

The botanical gardens were once the property of a Capuchin monastery that was destroyed during the Revolution. From the terrace at the far end of the garden is a **panorama**★ of the bay.

La Plate-forme

From place Daniel-Huet, walk along the garden of the Sous-Préfecture to reach the site of the old cathedral. This little square contains the paving stone on which Henry II made public penance in 1172. From the terrace there is a wide **view**★ embracing Mont-St-Michel.

Monument Patton

This memorial commemorates the deployment of General Patton's troops towards Brittany and the Basse-Normandie (in July 1944 with the American 3rd Army). The square on which it stands is now American territory.

Musée d'Art et d'Histoire

pl. Jean de St-Avit. Open Jun–Sept daily 10am–noon, 2–6pm. 1.50€. 02 33 58 00 22. www.ville-avranches.fr.

Housed in the outbuildings of the former episcopal palace restored in the late 15C the museum contains rich and varied collections illustrating the history of the town.

Manuscrits du Mont-St-Michel

pl. d'Éstouteville. Open Jul–Aug daily 10am–7pm; May–Jun and Sept, Tue–Sun 10am–6pm; Oct–Dec and Feb–Apr Tue–Fri 10am–12.30pm, 2–5pm, Sat–Sun 10am–12.30pm, 2–6pm (last ticket 1hr before closing). Closed 1 May, 1 Nov, 25 Dec. 7€ (children 3€). 02 33 79 57 00. www.scriptorial.fr.

The Scriptorial d'Avranches, a centre incorporating up-to-date technology, houses a collection of precious 8C–15C **manuscripts**★★, largely from Mont-St-Michel Abbey, including very old copies of famous texts from ancient Greece and Rome as well as medieval works.

Basilique St-Gervais-et-St-Protais Treasury

pl. St-Gervais. Open Jul–Sept daily 10am–noon, 2–6pm; Jun Mon–Sat 10am–noon, 2–6pm, Sun 2–6pm. No charge. 02 33 58 00 22. www.ville-avranches.fr.

This vast late-19C basilica contains several gold objects, including a gold and silver **reliquary** containing the skull of St Aubert, the 8C bishop, which legend says was pierced by St Michael's finger.

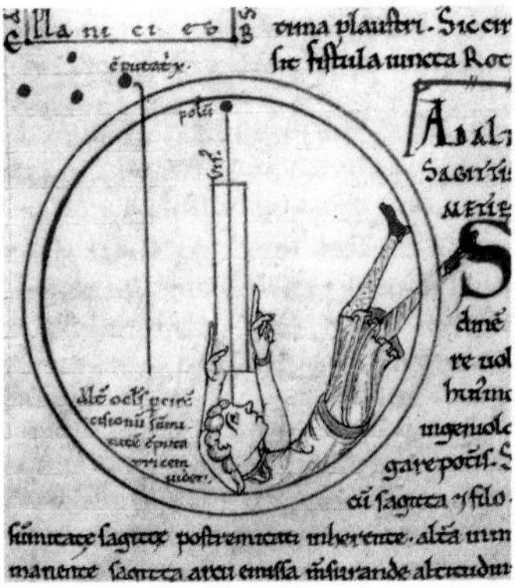

Manuscrit Mont-St-Michel

Manuscrit Mont-St-Michel [Scriptorial d'Avranches] © Ville d'Avranches

Musée de la Seconde Guerre mondiale

At Le Moulinet, Le Val St-Père, 5km/3mi S on N 175. Open daily Jul–Aug 9am–7pm; Apr–Jun and Sept–mid-Nov 9.15am–12.15pm, 2–6.30pm; mid-Nov–Mar 10am–noon, 2–5pm. Closed 1 Jan, 25 Dec. 7€. 02 33 68 35 83.

The German exhibits are on the ground floor (note the bell that sounded the alarm on the morning of 6 June 1944 on Pointe du Hoc); the Allied exhibits are upstairs.

ADDRESSES

STAY

Chambre d'hôte La Maraîcherie – *1 La Maraîcherie, 50300 Le Val-St-Père, 5km/3mi SE. 02 33 58 10 87. www.chambre-hotes-maraicherie.c.la. 3 rooms.* The former stables of this pretty 18C farm, just 200m/656ft from the bay of Mont-St-Michel, have been transformed into guest rooms furnished in Norman style.

Le Moulin de la Butte – *11 r. du Moulin-de-la Butte, 50170 Huisnes-sur-Mer, 18km/11mi SW. 02 33 58 52 62. 5 rooms.* At the entrance tothe village, opposite Mont-St-Michel, this large, modern house has light, modern, spacious rooms. Bicycles on loan.

Hôtel La Croix d'Or – *83 r. de la Constitution. 02 33 58 04 88. www.hoteldelacroixdor.fr. Closed Jan, Sun eve from 15 Oct–25 Mar. 27 rooms.* P. This low, half-timbered house extends into an attractive garden full of flowers in season. The guest rooms are pretty; some overlook the garden.

EAT

G Denou – *9 pl. Littré. 02 33 58 05 74. Closed Mon, end Jan–start Feb, 2 weeks in Jun, 2 weeks in Oct.* This pleasant tearoom is great for a quick lunch: sandwiches, *crêpes* and more.

Le Littré– *8 r. du Dr-Gilbert. 02 33 58 01 66. Closed last 2 weeks Jun, Sun and Mon.* The regulars occupy low chairs in the bar, but you can sit comfortably at a table in one of the two dining rooms.

Barfleur★

This charming fishing port, with its granite houses and its quays, is one of the most beautiful villages of France. Tradition has it that the boat that carried William, Duke of Normandy, to England was built here. A bronze plaque placed in 1966 at the foot of the jetty marks his departure (1066). In 1194 Richard Lionheart also embarked from Barfleur on his way to be crowned King of England.

- **Population:** 652.
- **Michelin Map:** 303: E-1 – Local map, *see Presqu'île du COTENTIN, p152.*
- **Info:** 2 rond-point Guillaume-le-Conquerant. 02 33 54 02 48. www.ville-barfleur.fr.
- **Location:** Barfleur is reached from Cherbourg (29km/18mi to the W) via D 116, which follows the coast, or by D 901, which is more direct.
- **Don't Miss:** The view from the top of the Gatteville lighthouse, and the arrival of the day's catch from fishing boats in the port.
- **Timing:** The area requires at least a half day of your time.

SIGHTS

Église St-Nicholas

Set in a cemetery on a rocky promontory, this squat 17C church has the appearance of a fort. In the south transept is a remarkable 16C Pietà while in the north transept above the font is a stained-glass window of Ste Marie-Madeleine Postel (1756–1846).

Maison de Julie Postel

Open 9am–7pm. No charge. 02 33 54 02 17. La Bretonne hamlet.
Julie Postel was born in Barfleur in 1756. As Sister Marie-Madeleine she founded the Sisters of the Christian Schools of Mercy (La Congrégation des Sœurs de la Miséricorde), now called Sisters of Saint Marie-Madeleine Postel. She lived in this house, which was also a school of domestic science, for 30 years. Scenes from her life are depicted in the stained-glass windows of the adjoining chapel.

POINTE DE BARFLEUR★★

4km/2.5mi N by D 116 and D 10.

Gatteville-le-Phare

The church, rebuilt in the 18C, still has its original 12C belfry. The Mariners' Chapel (Chapelle des Marins), in the square, is built over a Merovingian necropolis. Beyond Gatteville the scenery is wilder and rough seas pound the rocky coast.

Phare★★

Open May–Aug 10am–noon, 2–7pm; Apr and Sept 10am–noon, 2–6pm; Mar and Oct 10am–noon, 2–5pm; Feb and Nov–Dec 10am–noon, 2–4pm. Closed Jan, 1 May, 25 Dec, and if winds are too high. 2€. 02 33 23 17 97.
The lighthouse, on the north-eastern extremity of the Cotentin peninsula, is one of the tallest in France (71m/233ft). The light, with a range of 56km/35mi, and the radio beacon, installed in a small 18C tower, guide ships into Le Havre. From the top (365 steps) there is a **panorama**★★ stretching over the east coast of the Cotentin peninsula, St-Marcouf Islands, Veys Bay and, in clear weather, the cliffs at Grandcamp.
The shallow waters and swift currents have caused many shipwreks, including the *White Ship* in 1120, with Henry's heir, William Atheling, and 300 members of the Anglo-Norman nobility on board.

Montfarville

2km/1mi S by D 155.
This 18C granite church has a chapel and belfry dating from the 13C and a highly colourful **interior**★. The paintings on the vaulting are by a local artist, Guillaume Fouace. Note the 18C rood beam and a 14C polychrome Virgin.

Barneville-Carteret

This popular seaside resort, the closest port to the Channel Islands, is lively, the dunes windswept, and the long beach is of fine sand.

- **Population:** 2 398.
- **Michelin Map:** 303: B-3 – Local map, *see Presqu'île du COTENTIN, p152.*
- **Info:** 10 rue des Écoles. 02 33 04 90 58. www.barneville-carteret.fr.
- **Location:** Valovnes is 28km/17.5mi NE, Cherbourg 37km/23mi NE via D 650 and Caen 120km/74.5mi to the E.
- **Don't Miss:** You may want to tour Carteret on the tourist train, before trying some of the hikes and walks giving views over the sea.
- **Timing:** The Saturday morning market is worth your time.
- **Kids:** The tourist train.

CARTERET★

Tourist train operates 10km/6mi between Carteret and Portbail. Contact for times, which vary by season. 8€. Le Clos St-Jean. 02 33 04 94 54 (Barneville) or 02 33 04 03 07 (Portbail). http://ttcotentin.monsite.wanadoo.fr.

A magnificent rocky headland to the north protects the Gerfleur estuary and the delightful small beach (*beware coastal currents*), making this one of the most pleasant seaside resorts on the Cotentin Penninsula.

WALKING TOUR

Cap de Carteret★★

Allow a total of 2hr for these two walks.

Follow the signs La Corniche, le Phare; park near the roundabout by Carteret beach. Take sentier des Douaniers *(left)* ,which is very narrow and requires care. The view changes constantly on the way to Carteret's second beach, the extensive Plage de la Vieille-Église.

Take the road leading down to this beach to return inland. At the crossroads either turn right up to the **lighthouse** *(phare)* for an overall view or turn left *(avenue de la Roche-Biard)* to a viewing table: **views**★ of the coast, the Channel Islands and inland.

Alternatively, continue straight ahead at the crossroads to return to the car.

BARNEVILLE

Église

The 11C church of St Germain of Auxerre, standing high on the town's central hill, was given a fortified tower in the 15C. A late-19C restoration disfigured the chancel, which lost its ceiling, but the arches and capitals of the Romanesque nave have delightful **decoration**★. On one of these capitals, note the figure portraying the Prophet Daniel confronting a fierce lion. The monument on the way out of Barneville commemorates the cutting-off of the Cotentin Peninsula on 18 June 1944 during the Battle of Normandy.

Barneville-Plage – The seafront boulevard bordered by villas leads to the very popular beach.

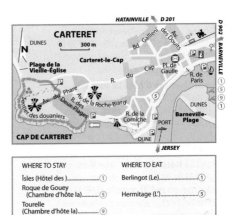

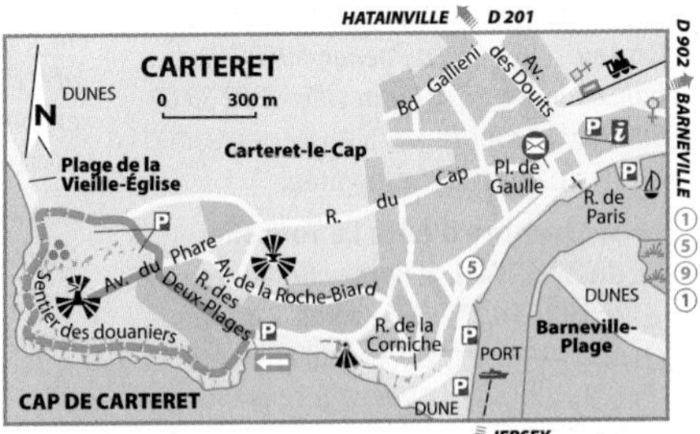

WHERE TO STAY		WHERE TO EAT	
Îsles (Hôtel des)	1	Berlingot (Le)	1
Roque de Gouey (Chambre d'hôte la)	5	Hermitage (L')	5
Tourelle (Chambre d'hôte la)	9		

EXCURSION

Fierville-les-Mines

9km/5.6mi E. Leave Barneville S on D 903 until La Picauderie, then turn left onto D 50 to Fierville-les-Mines and follow signs to Le Moulin à vent du Cotentin.

Moulin à vent du Cotentin

Guided tours (30min) Jul–Aug 10am–noon, 2–7pm; May–Jun and Sept Tue–Sun 2–7pm (Sept until 6pm); Mar–Apr and Oct–Nov Wed, Sat–Sun 2–6pm. School holidays except Christmas Tue–Sat 2-6pm. Closed Dec–Jan. 3.50€ (children 1€). 02 33 53 38 04. www.moulin-du-cotentin.com.
This 18C mill was restored in 1997 and continues to produce flour. The tour explains the mechanism and aspects of this traditional profession.

DRIVING TOUR

29km/18mi – allow 2hr15min.

Mont Castre

From Barneville-Carteret take the Coutances road. At La Picauderie, bear right onto D 50.

Portbail

This popular resort has two beaches of fine sand, a sailing school and a marina. A 13-arch bridge links the town to the harbour and the beaches. The 11C early Romanesque **Église Notre-Dame** was built on the site of a 6C abbey founded in the reign of Childebert. The tower was added in the 15C.

Église Notre-Dame

Open Apr–Sept 10.30am-noon, 3–7pm; guided tours available in Jul–Aug hourly Tue–Sat 10.30am–12.30pm, 3.30–6.30pm, Sun 3.30-6.30pm; Sept and Jun visits by appointment at tourist office. 2€. 02 33 04 03 07.

Take D 15 and D 903 inland via La Haye-du-Puits towards Carentan. 1.5km/0.9mi from the first level crossing east of La Haye-du-Puits turn right onto a narrow uphill road.

Mont Castre★

Beyond the houses, take the path to the church ruins, then go round a field to the ruins of a Roman watch post – still a strategic point in July 1944 during the Battle of Normandy. The **view** extends from Carteret to St-Côme-du-Mont. Committed hikers can climb up to the ruins of the Roman watch post by following the signposted route. There are one or two rocky areas to climb over.

ADDRESSES

STAY

Chambre d'hôte La Roque de Gouey – *16 r. Gilles-Poërier, 50580 Portbail, 8km/5mi SE of Barneville. 02 33 04 80 27. 4 rooms.* Simply decorated rooms, pleasant garden area.

Chambre d'hôte La Tourelle – *5 r. du Pic-Maillet, in Barneville-Bourg. 02 33 04 90 22. 5 rooms.* This 16C house faces the village church: an old-fashioned place offering a good breakfast.

Hôtel des Îles – *9 bd Maritime. 02 33 04 96 76. www.hoteldes isles.com/gb.swf. 31 ooms. 12€.* Maritime décor characterises this hotel with spacious rooms.

EAT

Le Berlingot – *rte de Bricquebec (D 902), 50270 Sortosville-en-Beaumont, 7km/4.3mi NE of Barneville. 02 33 53 87 16. Closed mid-Nov–Mar, Tue and Wed out of season.* This restaurant, specialising in crêpes is popular with locals. The meat dishes are also good.

L'Hermitage – *4 prom. A.-Leboutellier, Carteret. 02 33 04 96 29. Closed 3 weeks in Nov–Dec, Jan, Mar and Wed out of season.* Great for seafood. Terrace facing the port.

Îles Chausey★

According to legend, the Chausey Islands were part of the ancient Scissy Forest submerged by the sea in 709. The islands are a popular day excursion *(1hr by boat)* and are uninhabited except for Grande Île, which has a population of up to 400 in summer, and only a dozen in winter.

- **Michelin Map:** 303: B-6.
- **Location:** The islands are 17km/10.5mi from Granville.
- **Don't Miss:** The remarkable spectacle of the high tide.
- **Timing:** The excursion takes a day; you can spend the night.

VISIT

La Grande Île★

The Island (2km/1mi long by 700m/2 297ft at its widest point) is the largest and the only one accessible to visitors. Spring flowers are especially lovely. The **lighthouse** stands 37m/121.4ft above the sea. The beam carries 45km/28mi.

Fort

The fort was built between 1860 and 1866 against a British attack that never came. It now serves as a shelter for local fishermen.

Go round the fort. The path goes past an old cemetery with four tombs.

Vieux fort

The Old Fort was rebuilt in 1923 on the remains of one built in 1558. It dominates all the coastline. Below it, on the beach at Plage de Port Homard, the enormous tidal range is 14m/46ft.

The Moines and the Éléphant

These granite rocks, which can be reached at low tide, are thought to resemble monks and an elephant. More than 200 rocks, known locally as *grunes*, are revealed when the tide is out.

Sailors should get some advice and double-check charts before setting out on an adventure.

Sailing around the islands

G.Targat/MICHELIN

ADDRESSES

STAY & EAT

Hôtel Fort et des Îles – *50400 Îles Chausey. 02 33 50 25 02. Closed 27 Sept–mid-Apr. 8 rooms: half-board only. Reservations essential. Restaurant.* The only hotel on the island, the sounds of wind and waves lull you in this white house set in a flower garden. A few simple rooms. Seafood gathered or bred on the island can be enjoyed in the dining room.

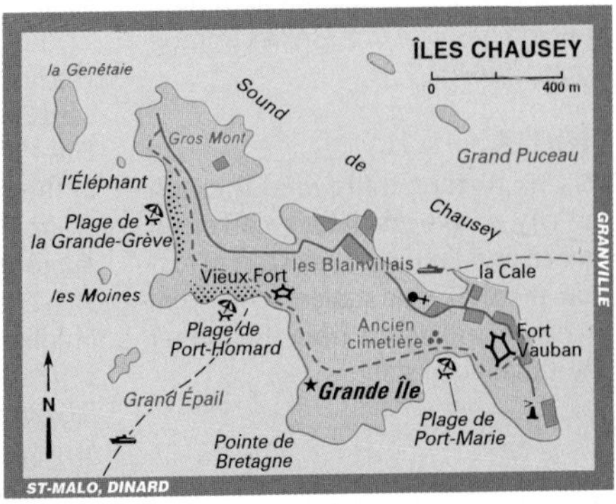

Cherbourg-Octeville

Cherbourg is a seafaring town with the largest artificial harbour in the world. Here, on the northern shore of the Cotentin Peninsula, this city boasts beautiful monuments, and is known for its remarkable breakwater.

- **Population:** 42 328.
- **Michelin Map:** 303: C-2 – Local map, see *Presqu'île du COTENTIN, p152.*
- **Info:** 2 quai Alexandre III, 50100 Cherbourg-Octeville. 02 33 93 52 02. www.cotentin-tourisme.com; www.ville-cherbourg.fr.
- **Location:** The N 13 ends in Cherbourg, after passing through Caen (123km/77mi SE) and Bayeux (96km/60mi).
- **Don't Miss:** The Cité de la Mer and a boat tour of the port area.
- **Timing:** Count on 3hr to see the Cité de la Mer.
- **Kids:** See the aquarium and the submarine at Cité de la Mer.

A BIT OF HISTORY

Titanic Undertakings – The great military architect **Vauban** (1633–1707) saw the possibilities of Cherbourg as an Atlantic port. An attempt in 1776 to create an offshore barrier by submerging 90 huge timber cones filled with rubble failed when the sea washed it all away. However, over time all of the material that had accumulated on the seabed began to form an artificial island. A fortified breakwater was eventually completed in 1853.

Today the breakwater remains essential for maintaining a safe haven against often violent storms.

Frogmen at Work – The capture of Cherbourg on 26 and 27 June 1944 marked a decisive stage in the Battle of Normandy, allowing for the landing of heavy equipment on a large scale. When the American 7th Corps took Cherbourg they found the harbour completely devastated and mined. Mines were cleared by Royal Navy frogmen, so that Cherbourg could supply the Allied armies. The undersea pipeline **PLUTO** (**P**ipe **L**ine **U**nder **T**he **O**cean) from the Isle of Wight emerged at Cherbourg, bringing gasoline to the Allies from 12 August 1944.

SIGHTS

Six historic trails wind through the city, with explanatory markers in French and English. They start across from the SNCF train station, across from St-Trinité and across from the former Transatlantique station.

Parc Emmanuel-Liais

The park, created by the naturalist and astronomer **Emmanuel Liais** (1826–1900), is famous for its tropical plants.

Place Napoléon

A bronze statue of the emperor dominates the square. Nearby is the **Église de la Trinité**, a Flamboyant Gothic church.

Musée Thomas-Henry

4 r. Vastel. Open May–Sept Tue–Sat 10am–noon, 2–6pm, Sun–Mon 2–6pm; Oct–Apr Wed–Sun 2–6pm. Closed public holidays. No charge. 02 33 23 39 30.

The first gallery is devoted to paintings with Cherbourg and the sea as themes. The 15C–19C paintings are on display in the other galleries: Fra Angelico's altarpiece panel, *The Conversion of St Augustine*, Filippo Lippi's *Entombment*. The 17C–19C collection has works by Murillo, Vernet and Chardin as well as canvases by Poussin, Largillère and Rigaud and a Nude by David. The local artist **Jean-François Millet** (1814–75) is well represented.

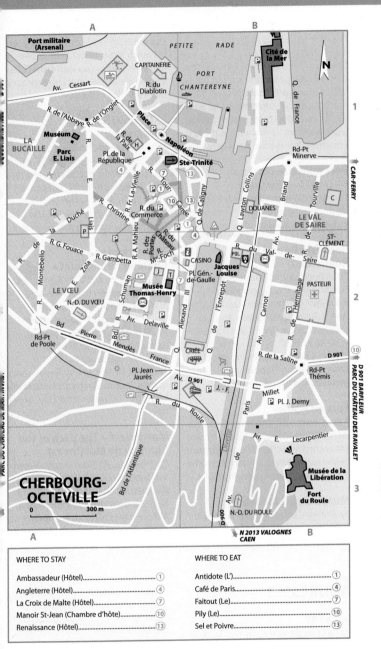

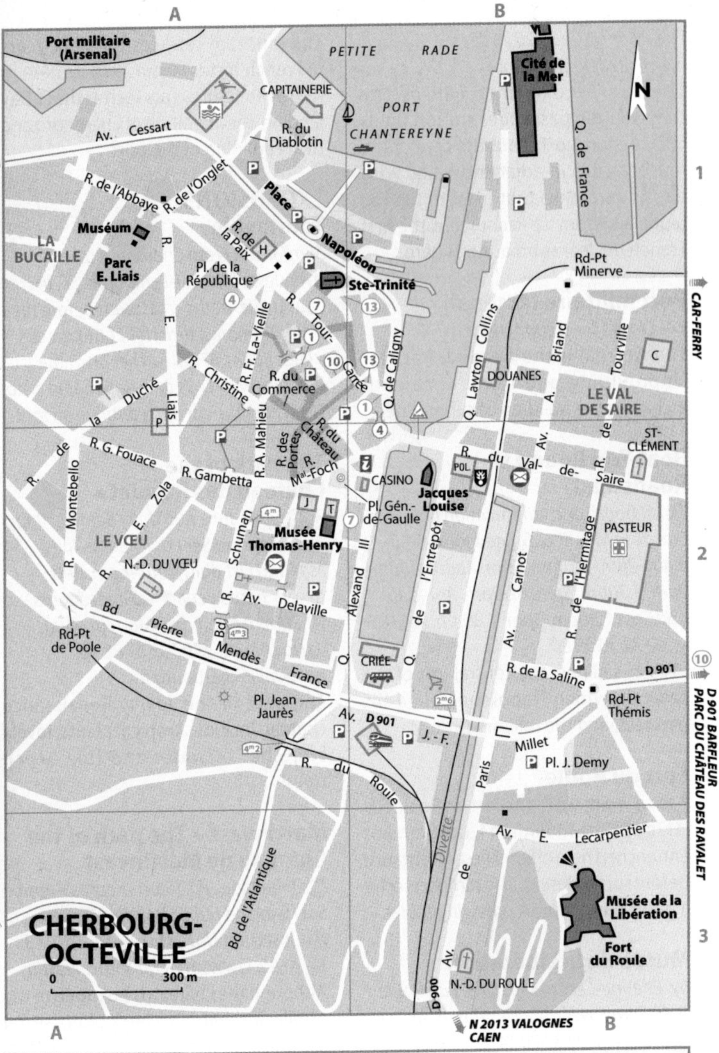

WHERE TO STAY

- Ambassadeur (Hôtel)........ ①
- Angleterre (Hôtel)........ ④
- La Croix de Malte (Hôtel)........ ⑦
- Manoir St-Jean (Chambre d'hôte)........ ⑩
- Renaissance (Hôtel)........ ⑬

WHERE TO EAT

- Antidote (L')........ ①
- Café de Paris........ ④
- Faitout (Le)........ ⑦
- Pily (Le)........ ⑩
- Sel et Poivre........ ⑬

Muséum d'histoire naturelle d'archéologie et d'ethnographie

Rond point Leclerc, Parc Emmanuel Liais. Same as Musée Thomas-Henry. No charge. 02 33 53 51 61.

On the ground floor are exhibits of shells, mammals and birds. Upstairs Egypt, Asia, Africa, Oceania and the Americas are represented.

Cité de la Mer★★

Gare Maritime Transatlantique, facing the marina. Contact for hours. 18€ Apr–Sept; 15.50€ Oct–Dec and

Feb–Mar. ℘02 33 20 26 69. www.citedelamer.com.
The Art Deco former hall of the transatlantic passenger station holds information kiosks, but the core of the museum lies in adjacent wings with basins and tanks that present marine fauna and flora. *Le Redoutable*, the first French nuclear submarine, is here.

Port militaire (Arsenal)

Closed for security reasons.
The Arsenal is the headquarters for shipbuilding and naval armament including the building of submarines.

Boat Trip Round the Roadstead

Ticket booth and embarcation point at Cité de la Mer. Guided tours 6 Jul–3 Aug 2pm, 3.30pm, 5pm; Aug 11.30am, 2pm, 3.30pm, 5pm, 6.30pm; Apr–5 Jul and Sept 1.30pm, 3pm, 4.30pm. 13€. ℘02 33 20 09 00.
Visitors sail past the central fort of the seawall, which Napoleon called his pyramid, and the military port.

Fort du Roule

A road winds up to the fort on Roule Hill (112m/367ft). In Jun 1944, the Germans entrenched here offered fierce resistance before surrendering. The ramparts offer a good **panorama★** *(viewing table).*

Musée de la Libération

av. Étienne-Lecarpentier, Fort du Roule. Same as Musée Thomas-Henry. 3.40€. ℘02 33 20 14 12.
The museum retraces the dark years of French history from 1940 to 1944 as well as hopeful events such as the D-Day landing, the liberation of Cherbourg and the rebuilding of the port.

EXCURSIONS

Tourlaville

5km/3mi E. From Cherbourg take avenue de l'Amiral-Lemonnier SE. In Tourlaville, at the crossroads before the Hôtel Terminus, turn right onto rue des Alliés. 800m/875yd farther on at the junction with D 63 turn right again onto D 32. Park the car and continue on foot.

The Park of the Château des Ravalet★

Open Jun–Aug daily 8am–7.30pm; Apr–May and Sept daily 8am–7pm; Mar and Oct daily 8am–6pm. Rest of year hours vary. Guided tours (1h30min) offered on Mon Jul–Aug. No charge. ℘02 33 87 88 98. www.ville-cherbourg.fr.
The park of this lovely Renaissance château includes tropical plants, lovely stretches of water and fine beech trees.

Martinvast – The park of the Château de Martinvast

Open Mon–Fri 10am–noon, 2–6pm, Sat–Sun and public holidays 2–6pm. Closed Sat Nov–Mar. 6€. ℘02 33 87 20 80. www.chateau-martinvast.fr.
Although the château is not open to the public, its charming **park** offers seven signposted trails.

ADDRESSES

STAY

La Croix de Malte – *5 r. des Halles. ℘02 33 43 19 16. Closed 15 days at Christmas. 24 rooms.* . A stone's throw from the theatre and the casino. The rooms, furnished in pine, are well soundproofed. Ask for one of the larger rooms when you reserve.

Hôtel Angleterre – *8 r. P.-Talluau. ℘02 33 53 70 06. www.hotelangleterre-fr.com. 23 rooms.* . Situated in a quiet part of the town centre, a simple hotel with a white façade. Rooms are a bit small, but renovated and perked up with pastel colours. Reasonable prices.

Hôtel Ambassadeur – *22 quai de Caligny. ℘02 33 43 10 00. www.ambassadeurhotel.com. 40 rooms.* This hotel overlooks the port, providing a view of constant activity.

But have no doubts, the rooms are well soundproofed. Reasonable prices.

⊖⊖⊖ **Hôtel Renaissance** – *4 r. de l'Église. ☎02 33 43 23 90. www.hotel-renaissance-cherbourg.com. 12 rooms.* ☕. This name is accuate: the hotel has bright, soundproofed rooms, modern bathrooms.

⊖⊖ **Chambre d'hôte Manoir St-Jean** – *Le hameau St-Jean, 50110 Tourlaville, 1km/0.6mi beyond the château des Ravalet via D 322 and the road marked centre aéré, Rte de Brix. ☎02 33 22 00 86. 3 rooms.* ⊭☕. Located on the edge of the châtau des Ravalet park, this converted 18C farmhouse overlooks the green Trotebec Valley. You will be well taken care of by the owner, who has a great knowledge of the natural and cultural wealth of her region. Two self-catering cottages.

EAT

⊖ **L'Antidote** – *41 r. au Blé. ☎02 33 78 01 28. Closed Sun–Mon. Reservations advised.* A pleasant terrace and a wood-panelled dining room. The specialities include *rillets de saumon de Cherbourg* (a salmon patty), black pudding with pineapple, ginger and apples, and foie gras. Warm welcome.

⊖⊖ **Café de Paris** – *40 quai Caligny. ☎02 33 43 12 36. Closed 16 Jan–7 Feb, 7–22 Nov, Mon lunch and Sun from 29 Sept–13 Apr.* This bistro-style restaurant is bright and warm. Enjoy a selection of seafood while admiring the view of the harbour in one of the two dining rooms.

⊖⊖ **L'Au Tire-Bouchon** – *17 r. Notre-Dane. ☎02 33 53 54 69. Closed Sun. Reservations advised.* The owner also has a wine shop and a grocery, and the bistro specialities are meant to accompany a good bottle. Dishes include confit de canard and the andouillette sausage as well as fresh seafood.

⊖⊖ **Le Faitout** – *25 r. Tour-Carrée. ☎02 33 04 25 04. www.restaurant-le-faitout.com. Closed 2 last weeks Dec. Reservations required.* An attractive retro façade outside, a handsome wood-panelled décor like that of a ship inside. Traditional cuisine and Norman specialities.

⊖⊖ **Sel et Poivre** – *17 r. du Port. ☎02 33 01 24 09.* A pinch of salt, a dusting of pepper and a good dollop of know-how bring out the best in typical local fare served in a charming dining room.

⊖⊖ **Le Pily** – *39 Grande Rue. ☎02 33 10 19 29. Closed Sat lunch and Wed.* Warm welcome in a fashionable prune and cream dining room, with a cosy lounge area. Delicious contemporary cuisine.

ON THE TOWN

Cherbourg is a sailors' town and under its peaceful daytime atmosphere runs a fun-loving, wild streak which surfaces after midnight.

Café du Théâtre– *8 pl. du Gén.-de-Gaulle. ☎02 33 43 01 49. Closed Sun.* A great place to meet after a movie or show, or just to hang out. A glass-enclosed terrace let you enjoy the view over the public square in all weather. A lounge with red plush seats recalls days when this was a theatre.Reasonably, priced, traditional cuisine.

Casino de Cherbourg– *18 quai Alexandre III. ☎02 33 43 00 56.* Built in 1827, this casino is the oldest in France. Gamblers can try their luck, but others might prefer the leather armchairs of the elegant bar, or the 1950s style pub "Fifty's Diner". The disco plays golden oldies.

SHOPPING

La Cave au Roy – *47 r. Tour-Carrée. ☎02 33 53 05 21.* This well-stocked wine store in the town centre carries a variety of regional specialities.

Les 3 Marches – *13 r. Grande-Rue. ☎02 33 53 24 94.* One of the oldest shops in Cherbourg, a grocery featuring products from all the regions of France, with an accent on Normandy.

LEISURE

Station Voile Nautisme et Tourisme de Cherbourg Hague – *r. du Diablotin, quartier Chantereyne. ☎ 02 33 78 19 29.* This club offers many activities: canoeing, kayaking, sailing, diving, beach sports, mountain biking, paragliding, hang-gliding, etc. Lessons and rentals are available.

Coutances★★

Coutances is perched on a hillock crowned by a magnificent cathedral, miraculously saved from the bombardments that destroyed two-thirds of the town in June 1944. The name of this religious and judicial centre of the Cotentin Peninsula recalls the Roman Emperor Constantins-Chlorus (293–306). In the 14C Coutances acquired an aqueduct *(ancien aqueduc)* of which only three arches remain standing to the northwest of the town on the Coutainville road.

- **Population:** 10 904.
- **Michelin Map:** 303: D-5.
- **Info:** Place Georges-Leclerc. ℘02 33 19 08 10. www.coutances.fr.
- **Location:** Coutances is at a crossroads: D 972 links it to St-Lô (29km/18mi E), D 900 heads towards Cherbourg (77km/48mi N) and D 971 leads to Granville (29km/18km S). The sea-coast is 10min to the W.
- **Don't Miss:** The cathedral, a miracle of Gothic architecture, and the display of old Nativity crèches at the manor of Saussey.
- **Timing:** Take 2hrs to see the town and cathedral, before embarking on one of the excursions in the area.
- **Kids:** The cathedral offers guided tours for children in July–August

Cathédrale★★★

Guided tours for children (6–12 years); call or enquire within. Tour of the cathedral, art project, stone-carving, visit to cathedral tower. 6.50€. ℘02 33 19 08 10.

One of the best views of the cathedral is when arriving at Coutances from the south; the elegance of the proportions and the purity of the lines are starkly outlined against the sky.

Geoffroy de Montbray, one of those great prelate knights Duke William gathered round him, completed the first nave in 1056. Then, thanks to the generosity of the sons of Tancrède de Hauteville whose amazing Mediterranean adventure had just begun, he built the chancel, transept, central tower and the façade with its twin octagonal towers reminiscent of those at Jumièges.

In 1218, after the town had been burned down, a new Gothic cathedral was literally mounted on the remains of the 11C church, involving prodigious adaptations of style as can be seen from the way the Romanesque towers of the old façade were incorporated into a new rectangular front and surmounted by spires.

Exterior

Above the great window a beautiful gallery crowns the façade whereas on either side rise the towers, quartered at their highest, octagonal level, by graceful elongated pierced turrets. The profusion of ascending lines, so remarkable in their detail, culminates in the flight of the spires, which rise to 78m/256ft. The bold turreted lantern tower at the transept crossing is noteworthy for its slender ribbing and fine, narrow windows.

Interior

Pause at the beginning of the nave for a remarkable general view of this singular building with its upswept lines: to right and left wide arcades are lined above by galleries where the lower windows, surmounted by blind rose windows, have been blocked up; above again, along the bottom of the clerestory windows, a second balustrade of a different design lines the walls.

Dominating the transept crossing is the octagonal **lantern tower**★★★. It is 41m/134.5ft high at its apex and the best example of its type in Normandy. At the

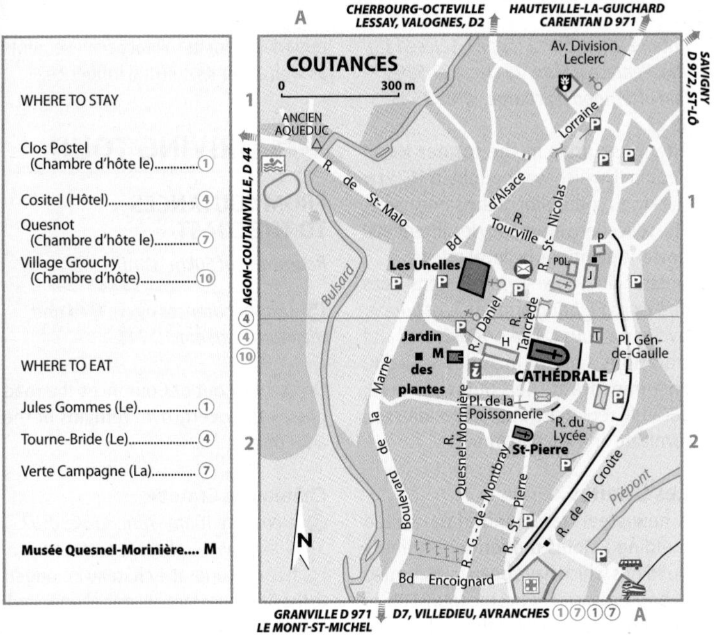

base of the south transept pillar stands the beautiful and deeply venerated 14C statue of Our Lady of Coutances, which miraculously survived the 1944 bombing of St Nicholas' Church. The north transept contains the oldest, 13C stained-glass windows; the south, a 14C window, in sombre tones, of the Last Judgement. The chancel, with the same architectural simplicity as the nave, is later in date and wider. As you walk round the two ambulatories, note the false triforium formed from two arches each covering twin bays. The radiating chapels are shallow and the ribs of their vaulting combine with the corresponding ambulatory bay rib to form a single arch. The central apsidal chapel, known as the Circata, was enlarged during a late-14C rebuilding by Sylvestre de la Cervelle. Above the slender painted columns small figures and animals peer out from the foliage of the capitals.

Upper Storeys★★

Guided tour (1hr30min), reserve beforehand. Jul–Aug Sun–Fri 11am, 3pm, Sun3pm; Jun and 1st 3 weeks Sept Tue and Sun 3pm. ✆02 33 19 08 10. 6.50 € (under 10 years not permitted).

The walk, which explores the the Romanesque parts of the original building, starts at a west front tower, continues through the attic of the aisle then on to the third-floor galleries to finish at the top of the lantern tower. The **panorama** extends from Granville, over the Chausey Islands to Jersey and on a clear day even Mount Pinçon is visible.

SIGHTS

Jardin des Plantes★

r. Quesnel-Morinière. Open daily Jul–Aug 9am–11pm; Apr–Jun and Sept 9am–8pm; Oct–Mar 9am–5pm. Sound and light show in Jul–Aug. No charge. ✆02 33 19 08 10.

The garden's entrance is flanked by an old cider press on one side and the Quesnel-Morinière Museum on the other. The terraced promenade traverses the sloping gardens with its many flower beds and pine trees.

Musée Quesnel-Morinière

2 quai Quesnel-Morinière. Open Jul–Aug daily 10am–noon, 2–6pm; Sept–Jun Wed–Sat and Mon 10am–

noon, 2–5pm, Sun 2–5pm. Closed 1 Jan, Pentecost Mon, 25 Dec. 2.50€; Sun afternoon no charge. 02 33 45 19 22.

The museum is in the former Hôtel Poupinel, which was bought in 1675 by the king's counsellor of the same name. The collections are mainly local: regional pottery, paintings by local artists. Outstanding, however, are Rubens' *Lions and Dogs Fighting* and the *Last Supper* by Simon Vouet. The popular arts and traditions section includes 18C–20C costumes from the Coutances area, 18C–19C regional pottery, headdresses, furniture and kitchen utensils.

Les Unelles

A new steel frame and glass-walled building adjoins the former seminary buildings which have been transformed to house an arts centre, the tourist office and the local authority offices. The name is derived from the Unelli whose capital was Cosedia, present day Coutances.

Église St-Pierre

This fine 15C–16C church built by Bishop Geoffroy Herbert was given a lantern tower over the transept crossing. In accordance with Renaissance custom, it was decorated ever more richly as the height increased.

EXCURSION

Hauteville-la-Guichard

15km/9mi NE. Leave Coutances to the N on D 971 heading for St-Sauveur-Landelin, then turn right onto D 53. Just after Moncuit, turn left towards Hauteville (D 435).

The **Musée Tancrède de Hauteville** (*open Jul–Aug Tue–Sun 2–6.30pm, last 2 weeks Jun and 1st 2 weeks Sept Sun 2–6pm, closed public holidays; 4€; 02 33 19 19 19*) plunges you into the heart of the Norman conquest of Sicily and southern Italy at the beginning of the 11C. Tancrède and his 12 children (the most famous were Robert Guiscard and Roger I of Sicily) were the true founders of Norman power in the Mediterranean. Incredibly well organised and extremely cunning, they created a powerful state remarkable for its military achievements as well as for its cultural influence.

DRIVING TOUR

FROM COUTANCES TO THE COAST

Round-trip of 50km/31mi.

Leave Coutances by ④, D 44 and then turn right onto D 244.

On the way out of Coutances the road passes the overgrown remains of the aqueduct.

Château de Gratot★

Open daily 10am–7pm. 3€. 02 31 45 18 49. www.chateaugratot.com.

For five centuries the château belonged to the Argouges family. Long abandoned, the château has been restored and converted into an arts centre.

A small three-arched bridge over the moat leads to the entrance gatehouse and then the inner courtyard. Within the courtyard from left to right are the 18C pavilion and the 17C main building, flanked by the Round Tower, and the Fairy's Tower with the North Tower to the rear.

Maison seigneuriale

Two flights of steps lead to the entrance of the now roofless former living quarters. The ground floor was lit by tall windows, the upper floor by dormers.

Tour ronde

This early 15C round tower is quite medieval in appearance. The narrowing of the staircase as it moved upwards was devised to hinder an attack as only one person could pass at a time.

The entrance to the basement is at the foot of this tower.

Caves

The groined vaulting of these fine cellars is supported by stout piers. The masonry is composed of stones placed edgewise.

The late-15C tower, now called the Fairy's Tower, is reinforced by a powerful buttress. It is octagonal at the base but becomes square at the top and is crowned by a saddleback roof.

Tour d'angle

This corner tower, the only part of the medieval castle which remains, probably dates from the late 13C or the early 14C; the door has been walled up.

Communs

One of the rooms in these 16C outbuildings hosts an exhibition on the château, its construction and restoration.

In St-Malo-de-la-Lande take D 68 towards Tourville-sur-Sienne then turn right onto D 272 to Agon-Coutainville.

Agon-Coutainville

Coutainville is one of the more popular resorts on the west coast of the Cotentin Peninsula,bounded by the Channel to the west and the Sienne estuary to the east. At low tide these great wet sandy stretches are popular for those looking for shrimps, cockles and clams.

Take the road leading to the Pointe d'Agon.

Pointe d'Agon

The line of stones on the right-hand side of the road is a memorial to the author **Fernand Lechanteur** (1910–71), who wrote in the Norman dialect. From the headland there is a good view of this part of the Channel coast and especially of the port of Regnéville on the other side of the estuary.

Return to Agon-Coutainville, then follow the road to the hamlet, rue d'Agon.

The D 72 road soon overlooks the silted up port of Regnéville.

Tourville-sur-Sienne

The roadside statue is of Admiral de Tourville, who lost the Battle of La Hougue (1692). From the terraced cemetery *(road from the statue)* there is a good view of Regnéville harbour closed off by the sandy headland, Montmarin belfry, the Rocher de Granville, and in clear weather, the Chausey Islands.

Drive to Pont-de-la-Roque along D 650, then to Regnéville-sur-Mer along D 49.

Regnéville-sur-Mer

From the 13C **church**, follow signposts to the **Musée du Littoral et de la Chaux** *(14 rte des Fours-à-Chaux; open year round, call for precise hours; 4.20€; 02 33 46 82 18)* set up in the former Rey lime kilns. This splendidly restored example of mid-19C industrial architecture presents traditional activities connected with the Channel coast.

Leave Regnéville on D 49 towards Montmartin-sur-Mer, then Hyenville (D 73). Continue on D 73 until you cross D 7 and drive towards Coutances via Saussey.

Manoir de Saussey★

Open Easter–Sept daily 2–6.30pm (last entry 30min before closing). 6€. 02 33 45 19 65.

The 17C buildings are enhanced by a pretty rose garden, an orchard, a vegetable patch and a series of delightful flower beds. Note the collection of **Nativity scenes** and a lovely exhibition of **glassware**.

Go back to D 7 and follow signs to the Manoir d'Argences.

Jardins d'Argences

Open mid-May–mid-Oct daily 2–6pm. 5.50€. 02 33 07 92 04.

The grounds surrounding this manor house (15C–18C) are enchanting and laid out along a series of pretty itineraries.

Drive back to Coutances.

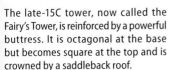

ADDRESSES

STAY

Chambre d'hôte Village Grouchy – *11 r. du Vieux-Lavoir, 50560 Blainville-sur-Mer, 2km/1mi N of Agon-Coutainville via D 72. 02 33 47 20 31. Closed Jan–Mar. 5 rooms.* This little village used to comprise exclusively fishermen's homes. In this house, large bedrooms with wood panelling make for a fine halt right near the sea. A summer kitchen is at guests' disposal in the garden.

Chambre d'hôte Le Quesnot – *3 r. du Mont-César, 50660 Montchaton, 6.5km/4mi SW of Coutances via D 20 then D 72. 02 33 45 05 88. Closed 15 Nov–Easter. 3 rooms. 9€.* Guests have the use of a small 18C stone-built house with its own terrace and tiny garden and a view of a little church perched on a promontory. Modern bedrooms above the large country-style dining room.

Chambre d'hôte Le Clos Postel – *5 rte d'Urville, Village d'Urville, 50590 Regneville-sur-Mer, 10km/6mi SW of Coutances via D 20, rte de Montmartin-sur-Mer and D 49. 02 33 07 12 38. Closed Dec–Jan. 4 rooms.* This fomer presbytery has been totally restored and benefits from a great view of the Baie de la Seine. A calming atmosphere prevails in the garden. The four, well-kept rooms (two of them in the old pigeon house) offer plenty of comfort.

Hôtel Cositel – *rte Coutainville-Delasse. 02 33 19 15 00. http://en.hotelcositel.com. Closed Dec–Jan. 55 rooms. 9€.* Modern construction in the town. Rooms are functional; the bistro offers light fare.

EAT

Le Jules Gommes – *34 r. du Vaudredoux, 50590 Regneville-sur-Mer, 10km/6mi SW of Coutances via D 20, rte de Montmartin-sur-Mer and then D 49. 02 33 45 32 04. www.le-jules-gommes.com. Closed Mon–Tue except school holidays. Reservations required weekends.* This address, which shares its name with a late-19C three-masted schooner, positively exudes charm. Handsome rustic interior featuring exposed stone, a fireplace and watercolours. Both seafood and inland cuisine, crêpes and a pub featuring a healthy choice of ales and whiskies.

Le Tourne-Bride – *85 r. d'Argouges, 50200 Gratot. 02 33 45 11 00. Closed 1–15 Jul, Feb holidays, Sun eve and Mon.* The proprietors of this former post-coach relay, Martine and Denis Poisson, offer a warm and attentive welcome. In the two rustic-style dining rooms, the menu accents traditional Norman cuisine, with produce straight from the sea and local fields.

La Verte Campagne – *Le Hameau Chevalier, 50660 Trelly, 13km/8mi S of Coutances via D 7, D 49, then D 539 and a minor road. 02 33 47 65 33. www.lavertecampagne.com. Closed 17–24 Mar and 22 Nov–15 Dec.* This 18C farm, covered with Virginia creeper in summer, has retained its authentic charm: wide ceiling beams, stone walls and old fireplaces. This renowned restaurant serves dishes prepared with care. A few rooms available upstairs.

SHOPPING

Market – *pl. du Gén. de Gaulle, 50560 Blainville-sur-Mer.* A very animated and colourful market. Country produce of every kind can be found here, including, ***naturellement***, the local cheese: le Coutances.

LEISURE

Several beaches are found on this part of the west coast, within 12–15km/7.5–9mi of Coutances. From north to south: **Anneville-sur-Mer**, a little beach with fine sand set in the dunes; **Gouville-sur-Mer**, a beach 6km/4mi long with several acres of oyster beds (*for a guided tour of the oyster beds, 02 33 47 84 33)*; **Blainville-sur-Mer**, another beach with a reputation for oysters, also offers fishing and a wide sand beach much appreciated by families; **Agon-Coutainville** is the furthest south, and you will find here a golf course, a casino and all sorts of sports and nautical activities.

Granville★

This lively seaside resort, set on a rocky promontory, is also a busy port with an active fishing fleet and a marina. Granville is also the departure point for ferries to the Chausey and Channel islands.

- **Population:** 13 782.
- **Michelin Map:** 303: C-6.
- **Info:** 4 cours Jonville. ✆02 33 91 30 03. www.ville-granville.fr.
- **Location:** As the crow flies, Granville is 150km/93mi from Paris; 106km/65.8mi from Cherbourg; 109km/67.7mi from Caen; 50km/31mi from Mont St-Michel.
- **Don't Miss:** A look at haute couture in the Villa Dior.
- **Timing:** Try to fit in a day trip to the Îles Chausey.
- **Kids:** There is an aquarium they will enjoy.

A BIT OF HISTORY

In the 15C, the English fortified the rocky promontory as a base from which to attack Mont-St-Michel, then occupied by the Normans. The town was recaptured permanently by the knights of Mont-St-Michel in 1442. Prosperity came with deep-sea fishing in the 18C, and Granville flourished with the rising popularity of sea bathing in the 19C.

UPPER TOWN

Allow 2hr.

The Main Gate (Grand Porte) with its drawbridge remains the principal entrance to the fortified, upper part of town which concentrates all Granville's military and religious past within its ramparts.

Église Notre-Dame

pl. du Parvis, Upper Town.

The oldest parts of this austere granite church with a fine tower go back to the 15C. The nave itself and the west front were erected in the 17C and 18C. The 14C statue, in the north chapel, of Our Lady of Cape Lihou is greatly venerated locally.

Pointe du Roc

This is an exceptional **site**★. The point which marks the northern limit of Mont-St-Michel Bay is linked to the mainland only by a narrow rocky isthmus. In the 15C the English dug a trench, known as Tranchée aux Anglais, as part of their fortifications.

The walk (the path starts from the harbour) to the lighthouse offers a fine view of the sea and the rocks.

RAMPART WALK★

Park on the parvis of Notre-Dame Church.

Go through the Grand'Porte and over the drawbridge. Turn right onto rue Lecarpentier to follow the south rampart to place de l'Isthme.

The **view**★ from the square extends, on a clear day, to the coast of Brittany *(viewing table).*

Continue along the inside of the ramparts by rue du Nord.

At this point the view is spectacular in stormy weather. The Chausey Islands lie to the northwest.

Turn left onto rue des Plâtriers to reach rue St-Jean, then turn right.

Note, at no 7 rue St-Jean, an old house with a ground-floor shop and then, at no 3, a house dating from 1612.

The street opposite, montée du Parvis, leads back to the starting point.

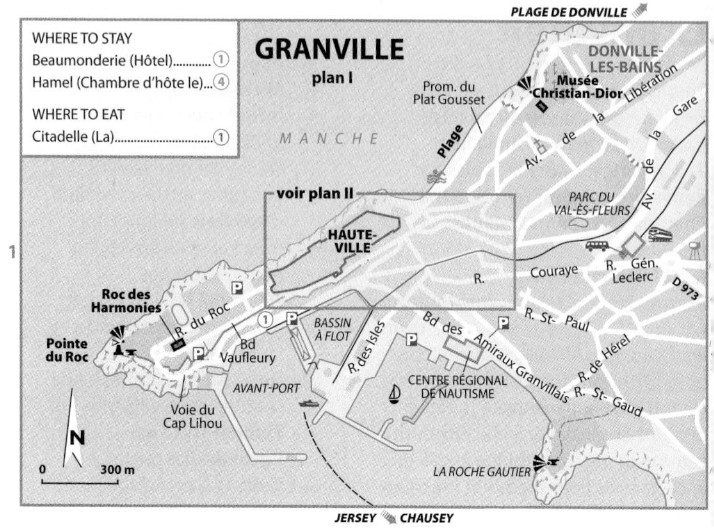

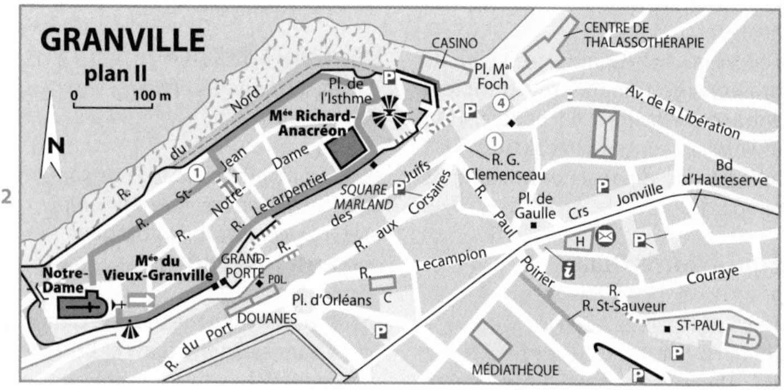

WHERE TO STAY	WHERE TO EAT
Hôtel des Bains......①	Échauguette (Créperie Grill l')......①
	Horizon (L')......④

LOWER TOWN

La Plage

The narrow beach at the foot of shale cliffs is overlooked by the Plat-Gousset Breakwater promenade.

Jardin public Christian-Dior et Villa des Rhumbs

Garden open daily 9am–8pm. No charge. Museum open mid-May–mid-Sept daily 10am–6.30pm. 5€. 02 33 61 48 21.

This public garden and museum are located in the childhood home of the famous couturier. From the upper terrace you look down on the Granville promontory, north towards Regnéville and out to the Chausey Islands.

The cliff path passes the cemetery to reach the great expanse of Donville Beach. Low tide reveals numerous stakes used for growing mussels.

Aquarium du Roc

Enter from 1 bd Vaufleury. Open Feb holidays–11 Nov daily 10am–12.30pm, 2–7pm (last entry 1hr before closing). Closed Mon in Mar. 7€. 02 33 50 19 83. www.aquarium-du-roc.com.
The **tanks** contain fish from local waters – note the sea perch with its powerful jaw and conical – as well as exotic and freshwater species.

Musée du Vieux Granville

In the fortified gatehouse, Grand'Porte. *Open Jul–Sept Wed–Mon 10am–noon, 2–6.30pm; Apr–Jun Wed–Mon 10am–noon, 2–6pm; Oct–mid-Dec and Feb holidays–Mar Wed and Sat–Sun 2–6pm (last entry 30min before closing). Closed 1 May, 1 Nov. 1.70€. 02 33 50 44 10. www.ville-granville.fr*
On the first floor is a collection of Norman costumes and headdresses as well as household furnishings, notably the **toiles de Hambaye**, which is pieces of canvas or even gunny sacks painted in stylised decoration, and used as bed curtains. On the second floor are exhibitions about the sea.

Musée Richard-Anacréon

pl. de l'Isthme. Open Jun–Sept Tue–Sun 11am–6pm; Oct–May Wed–Sun 2–6pm. Closed 1 and 8 May and when exhibits are being changed. 2.60€. 02 33 51 02 94.
This museum of modern art presents a permanent collection of works by major 20C artists including Derain, Utrillo, Signac and Van Dongen, as well as temporary exhibits. A yearly exhibit of rare books draws bibliophiles.

The Carnival at Granville

This long-standing tradition was originated by local fishermen. Before leaving for long fishing expeditions out in Newfoundland, cod fishermen would go out to spend their money in the streets of the city, dressing up in various costumes for the occasion. Today the Carnival takes place during Shrove Tuesday celebrations (the day before the beginning of Lent); it lasts for four days and includes a funfair with a procession of floats, an orchestra and majorettes.
On the last day the residents, dressed up and masked, pay a visit to their friends; a Carnival effigy is burned on the beach, marking the end of festivities.

EXCURSION

Îles Chausey
See Îles CHAUSEY, p209.

St-Pair-sur-Mer

St-Pair has a breakwater promenade protecting a beach of golden sand which is perfect for children. The **church** is said to have been founded in the 6C by two local Evangelists, St Pair and St Scubilien. The building consists of the Romanesque belfry and the bay beneath, the 14C chancel and a 19C neo-Gothic nave and transepts. Inside are several religious artworks from the 15C to the 18C, as well as 6C sarcophagi.

ADDRESSES

STAY

Chambre d'hôte Le Hamel – *"Le Hamel", 50380 St-Aubin-des-Préaux, 8km/5mi from Granville. 02 33 51 42 65. 4 rooms. Closed last 2 weeks Sept.* An old stone farm building in a peaceful, verdant setting with spacious, comfortable rooms. Lounge and breakfast room with a fireplace that is welcome on cold days. Pretty garden.

Hôtel des Bains – *19 r. Clemenceau. 02 33 50 17 31. www.hoteldesbains-granville.com. 54 rooms.* Right on the coast in the bay of Mont-St-Michel; ask for a room with a view over the sea, or one equipped with a relaxing jacuzzi.

Villa Beaumonderie – *20 route de Coutances, 50290 Bréville-sur-Mer, 4.5km/2.8mi NE of Granville. 02 33 50 36 36. 13 rooms, 3 suites. 10€. Restaurant.* Charming early 20C villa with a cosy atmosphere and some spacious rooms. Ask for a room with a sea view.

EAT

Crêperie l'Échauguette – *22–24 r. St-Jean. ℘02 33 50 51 87.* Nestling in one of the narrow streets of old Granville, you can enjoy excellent buckwheat galettes and pancakes.

L'Horizon – *pl. Maréchal Foch. ℘02 33 50 00 79. www.casino-granville.com. Closed Mon–Tue from Oct–Mar.* This restaurant belongs to the stylish Casino. You'll have a first-rate view of the sea from the dining room. Seafood and contemporary cuisine.

La Citadelle – *34 r. du Port. ℘02 33 50 34 10. www.restaurant-la-citadelle.com. Closed Feb and Christmas school holidays, Tue from Oct–Mar and Wed.* Before setting off for the islands, stop and have a meal in the dining room with its blue-wood panelling or sit on the small raised terrace. Specialities: seafood, including lobster.

LEISURE

Institute de Thalassothérapie Préwithal – *3 r. Jules-Michelet. ℘02 33 90 31 10. www.prewithal.com.* Granville's invigorating climate has favoured the creation of a physical therapy and re-education centre lies directly on the sea coast. Spa treatments are offered in the afternoon, while the morning is spent on revivifying hikes studying flora and fauna.

Old ships – Granville is famous for its traditional fishing vessels, such as la bisquine, a sailing ship that challenged those of Cancale during fierce regattas as early as the 1850s. Today, cruises are offered aboard some of these, superbly restored by ardent craftsmen:
La Granvillaise (℘02 33 90 07 51),
Le Charles-Marie (℘02 33 46 69 54)
Le Lys Noir (℘02 33 90 48 63),
Le Courrier des Îles (℘02 33 50 49 80)
Le Strang Hugg (℘02 33 90 69 06).

Lessay★

Lessay grew up round a Benedictine abbey founded in 1056 by a Norman lord. The first monks came from Le Bec-Hellouin. The town is particularly lively in September during the Holy Cross Fair, which originated in the 13C.

- **Population:** 2 046.
- **Michelin Map:** 303: C-4.
- **Info:** 11 place Saint-Cloud. ℘02 33 45 14 34. www.canton-lessay.com.
- **Location:** Lessay lies between Coutances, 21km/13mi to the S on D2, and Valognes, 36km/22.4mi N on D 900.
- **Don't Miss:** The impressive view of the abbey nave.
- **Timing:** In July and August, concerts are held at the abbey.
- **Kids:** There are several nature trails; ask at the tourist office.

Abbey Church★★

Allow 30min. Av. Paul Jeanson. Open daily 9am–6pm, except during services. No charge. Guided tours (1hr) Jul–Aug Wed 3pm (check dates at tourist office). 4P.

The magnificent Romanesque abbey church, damaged during the war, was reconstructed between 1945 and 1957, using original building materials wherever possible; the result is one of the most perfect examples of Romanesque architecture in Normandy.

Building of the original church started in 1098 with construction of the apse, chancel transept and two bays of the nave with their vaulting; the remaining bays of the nave were completed several years later.

La Foire de Sainte-Croix

Lessay is extraordinarily lively during the days of the Holy Cross Fair (second weekend in September). The origins of the fair are lost in the 11C – it is supposed that the Benedictines were the first sponsors.

Friday is fair day for horses, donkeys, dogs, ferrets and fowl; Saturday welcomes cattle, sheep and goats. More than 1 500 exhibitors attend and dozens of carnival rides are set up alongside. To feed the 400 000 visitors, about 2 800 local lambs are grilled up along an alleyway reserved for this purpose.

Exterior

The full beauty of the lines of the apse, abutting on a flat gable, can best be seen from the War Memorial Square. The rather squat square belfry with its Hague schist slates is also worth noting.

Interior

The seven broad bays of the nave and the transepts are roofed with pointed vaulting; there is rib-vaulting in the aisles. The gallery in front of the clerestory windows passes round the entire building in the thickness of the walls. The chancel terminates in an oven-vaulted apse lit by two rose windows. A 15C chapel with a cobbled floor *(right of the chancel)* contains the baptistery and the font. The new glass windows are inspired by Irish manuscripts.

Abbaye de La Lucerne

The sizeable ruins of Lucerne Abbey stand in a fine parkland setting in the Thar Valley. The abbey was founded in 1143, but it was not before 1164 that construction started. Largely demolished at the Revolution, it has been restored.

- **Michelin Map:** 303: D-7.
- **Location:** The abbey is 12km/7.5 mi SE of Granville via D 973, then D 580 until just before St-Pierre-Langers. It is on the road between Sartilly and St-Léger-en-Avranchin.
- **Don't Miss:** The remarkable 12C bell tower.

VISIT

Abbey Church

Open mid-Mar–Sept Mon–Sat 10am–noon, 2–6.30pm, Sun 2–6.30pm; mid-Oct–mid-Nov and Christmas school holidays Mon–Sat 10am–noon, 2–5pm, Sun 2–5pm. Closed during religious holidays. Guided tours available afternoons Jul–Aug daily; Sept Sat–Sun. 5€. 02 33 48 83 56. www.abbaye-lucerne.fr.

The doorway in the 12C façade is Romanesque. The nave is Cistercian-style. The transept crossing (restored) supports a late-12C Gothic square **bell tower**★, pierced with narrow lancets.

The south transept houses a fine 18C **organ**★ with 33 stops. Concerts are given throughout the year.

Cloisters and Conventual Buildings

The arcades of the northwest corner and the entrance to the chapter house still stand. In the southwest corner, near the door to the old refectory, is a 12C *lavatorium* with four beautiful little Romanesque arcades.

Note the old tithe barn and the dovecot, a huge round tower with 1 500 pigeon-holes.

Mont-St-Michel★★★

Why is the world fascinated by Mont-St-Michel? No doubt it is not just the beauty of the architecture and the length of the mount's history. Perhaps it is the sense of mystery in the movement of the tides that separate this rocky outcrop from the mainland, or the play of twilight on the water and walls, or the cry of gulls gliding above the salty grass marsh. It is impossible to take the measure of Mont-St-Michel without including its unique natural setting: the rock and the bay of this UNESCO World Heritage Site are truly one.

- **Population:** 41
- **Michelin Map:** 303: C-8.
- **Info:** Corps de garde des Bourgeois. ℘02 33 60 14 30. www.ot-montsaintmichel.com, www.abbaye-saintmichel.com.
- **Location:** Mont St-Michel is at the northern limit of D 976, which connects with D 175 at Pontorson, 10km/6mi S, which in turn leads to Avranches (21km/13mi NE) via N 175 and major national arteries.
- **Parking:** Car parks (4€ per day per vehicle) stretch over 2km/1mi of dykes. Arrive early in the morning to get a space closer to the Mount, or park as near as you can along the acces road if just there to admire the Mount or take photos. During very high tides, car parks are inundated and you must park along the access road. Attendants are there to help.
- **Don't Miss:** Try to catch the miraculous spectacle of sunset over the bay from the steps of the church.
- **Timing:** In the summer, night visits are organised, to musical accompaniment *(Mon–Sat 7–11.30pm; last entry at 10.30pm).* ℘02 33 89 80 00.
- **Kids:** The Maison de la Baie offers guided tours of the bay covering a large distance (check beforehand). The nature centre at Relais de Vains-St-Léonard explains the fauna and flora of the Bay *(see Relais des Genêts p231).* Aligator Bay (*see p232*) displays alligators, crocodiles, turtles, etc.

A BIT OF HISTORY

An amazing achievement – The abbey dates back to the early 8C when the Archangel Michael appeared to Aubert, Bishop of Avranches. He founded an oratory on the island, then known as Mount Tombe. In the Carolingian era (8C–10C) the oratory was replaced by an abbey. From then until the 16C a series of increasingly splendid buildings, in the Romanesque and then the Gothic style, succeeded one another, on this mount dedicated to the Archangel Michael. The abbey was remarkably well fortified and never fell to the enemy. The construction is an amazing achievement. The blocks of granite were transported from the Chausey Islands and Brittany, then hoisted up to the foot of the building. The crest of the hill was very narrow, so the foundations had to be built up from the lower slopes.

Pilgrimages – Pilgrims flocked to the mount, even during periods of attrition like the Hundred Years' War. The English, who had possession of the area, granted safe conduct to the faithful in return for payment. People of all sorts made the journey: nobles, rich citizens and beggars who lived on alms and were granted free accommodation by the monks.

Mont-St-Michel
A. Coupe/MICHELIN

Hotels and souvenir shops flourished. The pilgrims bought medals bearing the effigy of St Michael and lead amulets which they filled with sand from the beach.

In periods of widespread disaster the pilgrimage incited such excess of fervour that the church authorities were obliged to intervene.

Of the many thousands of people crossing the bay, some drowned, others perished in the quicksands. The deaths led to the lengthening of the prayer to St Michael in Peril from the Sea.

Decline – The abbey came to be held *in commendam* (by lay abbots who received the revenue without exercising the duties) and discipline among the monks grew lax. In the 17C the Maurists, monks from St Maur, were made responsible for reforming the monastery, but they only made some disappointing architectural changes and tinkered with the stonework. Further dilapidation ensued when the abbey became a prison. In 1811, after the Revolution, it was converted into a national prison for political prisoners. In 1874 the abbey and the ramparts passed into the care of the Historic Monuments Department (Service des Monuments Historiques). Since 1966 a few monks have again been in residence conducting the services in the abbey church.

Stages in the Abbey's Construction
The buildings date from the 11C to the 16C.

Romanesque Abbey

11C–12C: Between 1017 and 1144 a church was built on the top of the mount. The previous Carolingian building was incorporated as a crypt – Notre-Dame-sous-Terre (Our Lady Underground) – to support the platform on which the last three bays of the Romanesque nave were built. Other crypts were constructed to support the transepts and the chancel, which projected beyond the natural rock. The convent buildings were constructed on the west face and on either side of the nave. The entrance to the abbey faced west.

Gothic Abbey

13C–16C: This period saw the construction of:

- The magnificent Merveille buildings (1211–28) on the north side of the church, used by the monks and pilgrims and for the reception of important guests.
- The abbatial buildings (13C–15C) on the south side comprising the administrative offices, the

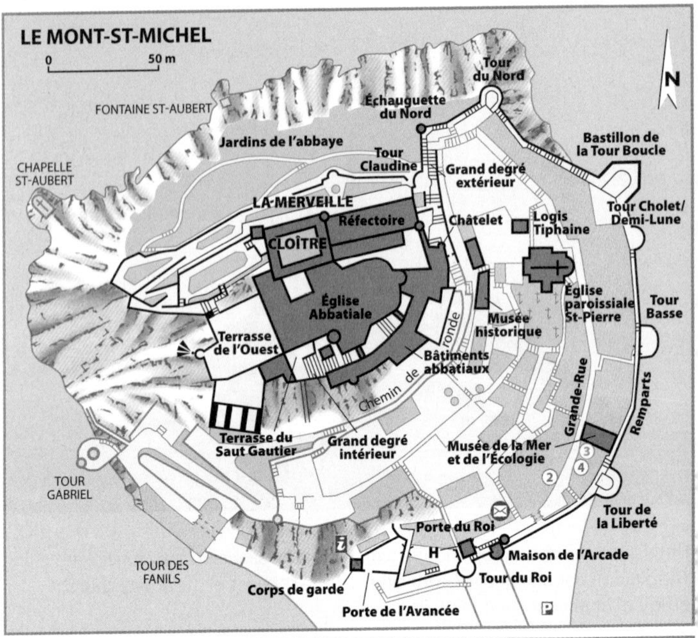

WHERE TO STAY	WHERE TO EAT	
St-Pierre (Auberge)..............③	Mère Poulard (La)................②	Sirène (La)...............................④

abbot's lodging and the garrison's quarters.

- The main gatehouse and the outer defences (14C) on the east side, protecting the entrance, which was moved to this side of the mount.
- The chancel of the Romanesque church had collapsed and was rebuilt more magnificently in the Flamboyant Gothic style (1446–1521) above a new crypt.

Alterations

18C–19C. In 1780 the last three bays of the nave and the Romanesque façade were demolished.

The present bell tower (1897) is surmounted by a beautiful spire that rises to 157m/515ft and terminates in a statue of St Michael (1879) by Emmanuel Frémiet. The 4.5m/15ft-tall archangel, in position for over 100 years, was recently restored after lightening has struck off St Michael's sword.

THE VILLAGE

The cobbled streets are uneven and steep here, and the abbey is a labyrinth of corridors and cloisters. Wear the most comfortable shoes you own.

Outer Defences

The outer gate opens into the first fortified courtyard. On the left stands the Citizens' Guard room (16C) occupied by the tourist office; on the right are the Michelettes, English mortars captured in a sortie during the Hundred Years' War.

A second gate leads into a second courtyard. The third gate (15C), complete with machicolations and portcullis, is called the King's Gate because it was the lodging of the token contingent maintained by the king to assert his rights; this gate opens onto the Grande-Rue where the abbot's soldiers lodged in the fine arcaded house *(right)*.

Grande-Rue★

This picturesque narrow street climbs steeply between old (15C–16C) houses and ends in a flight of steps. In summer it is crowded with stalls of souvenir merchants just as in the Middle Ages.

Ramparts★★

These are 13C–15C. The sentry walk offers fine views of the bay; from the North Tower the Tombelaine Rock, which Philippe Auguste had fortified, is clearly visible.

Musée de la Mer et de l'Écologie

Open Jul–Aug 9am–7pm; Feb–Jun, Sept–mid-Nov and Christmas school holidays 9.30am–6.30pm. 8€ (children 4.50€). 02 33 60 85 12.

Films and an audioguided tour explain the environment of the Mount, including the tides, the dangers in the bay and the silting-up process. There are also 150 models of old boats.

Musée historique

Same hours and conditions as for the Musée de la Mer. 02 33 60 07 01.

This historical museum retraces the history of the Mount back 1 000 years, using a sound and light show and glass cases of old objects and weapons. The tour ends in the dungeons.

Église paroissiale St-Pierre

The 11C parish church has been much altered. The apse spans a narrow street. The church contains a Crucifix and other furnishings from the abbey; the chapel in the south aisle houses a statue of St Michael covered in silver; in the chapel to the right of the altar there is a 15C statue of the Virgin and Child and another of St Anne and the Virgin as a child.

Logis Tiphaine

Same hours and conditions as for the Musée de la Mer. 02 33 60 23 34.

When the 14C warrior Bertrand du Guesclin was captain of the Mount, he had this house built (1365) for his wife Tiphaine Raguenel, an attractive and educated woman from Dinan, while he went off to the wars in Spain. The house was heavily restored in the 19C.

THE ABBEY★★★

Open daily May–Aug 9am–7pm (last admission 1hr before closing); Sept–Apr 9.30am–6pm. Guided tours (1hr). Closed 1 Jan, 1 May, 25 Dec. 8.50€ (under 18 years no charge); no charge to attend Mass, during which visits are not allowed: Tue–Sun noon–12.15pm. 02 33 89 80 00. www.monum.fr.

The tour passes through a maze of corridors and stairs floor by floor, not from building to building or period by period.

Restoring the Bay

A project to dredge the Bay of St-Michel is in full swing. The entire project is extremely complex project, but its ultimate aim it to reverse the silting-up that has gone on for years, particularly since construction of the 1877 causeway. In the first stage, begun in 2006, a dam is being constructed on the River Couesnon to restrain the influx of sand. Finally, the causeway will be partially replaced by a bridge planned for 2012, which will allow tidal water to swirl freely around the bay. Tourist access to the Mount will not be interrupted during these major works and a temporary visitor centre has been set up.

For more information, you can consult the website www.projetmontsaint-michel.fr or visit the red **project information booth** located near the causeway (*open Jul–Aug daily 10am–7pm, Apr–Jun and Sept daily 10am–12.30pm, 2–6pm, Oct–mid-Nov and 2nd week Feb–Mar Wed–Sun 2–8pm).*

From 2010, car parks will be located further inland and shuttles will ferry tourists to and from the Mount while construction continues.

Outer Defences of the Abbey

A flight of steps, the Grand Degré, once cut off by a swing door, leads up to the abbey. At the top on the right is the entrance to the gardens; more steps lead up to the ramparts.

Through the arch of an old door is a fortified courtyard overlooked by the fort, which consists of two tall towers linked by machicolations. Even this military structure shows the builder's artistic sense: the wall is attractively constructed of alternate courses of pink and grey granite. Beneath a flattened barrel vault a steep and ill-lit staircase, the Escalier du Gouffre (Abyss Steps), leads down to the beautiful door which opens into the guard room, also called the Porterie.

Salle des Gardes or Porterie

This gatehouse was the focal point of the abbey. Poor pilgrims passed through on their way from the Merveille Court to the Almonry.

Abbey Steps

An impressive flight of 90 steps rises between the abbatial buildings *(left)* and the abbey church *(right)*; it is spanned by a fortified bridge (15C).

The stairs stop outside the south door of the church on a terrace called the Saut Gautier **(Gautier Leap)**, after a prisoner who is supposed to have hurled himself over the edge. The tour starts here.

Cloisters, Mont-St-Michel

©Jameson Weston/iStockphoto.com

West Platform

This spacious terrace, which was created by the demolition of the last three bays of the church, provides an extensive **view**★ of the Bay of Mont-St-Michel.

Church★★

The exterior of the church, particularly the east end with its buttresses, flying buttresses, bell turrets and balustrades, is a masterpiece of light and graceful architecture. The interior reveals the marked contrast between the severe, sombre Romanesque nave and the elegant, luminous Gothic chancel.

La Merveille★★★

The name, which means the Marvel, applies to the superb Gothic buildings on the north face of the Mount. The eastern block, the first to be built between 1211 and 1218, comprises, from top to bottom, the refectory, the Guests' Hall and the Almonry; the western block, built between 1218 and 1228, consists of the cloisters, the Knights' Hall and the cellar.

From the outside the buildings look like a fortress although their religious connections are indicated by the simple nobility of the design. The interior is a perfect example of the evolution of the Gothic style, from an almost Romanesque simplicity in the lower halls, through the elegance of the Guests' Hall, the majesty of the Knights' Hall and the mysterious luminosity of the Refectory, to the cloisters, which are a masterpiece of delicacy and line.

Cloisters★★★

The cloisters seem to be suspended between the sea and the sky. The gallery arcades display heavily undercut sculpture of foliage ornamented with the occasional animal or human figure (particularly human heads); there are also a few religious symbols. The double row of arches rests on delightfully slim single columns arranged in quincunx to enhance the impression of lightness.

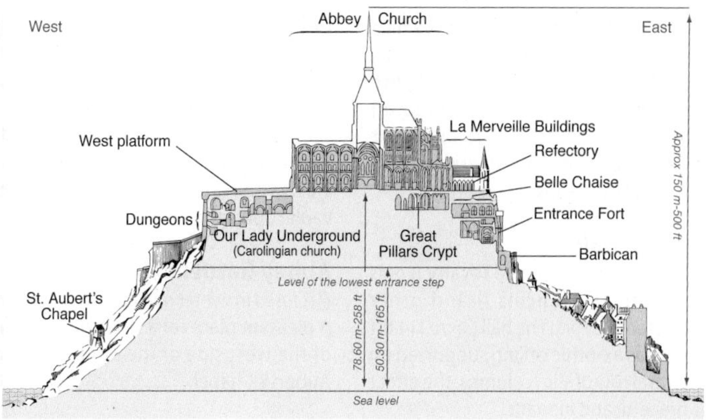

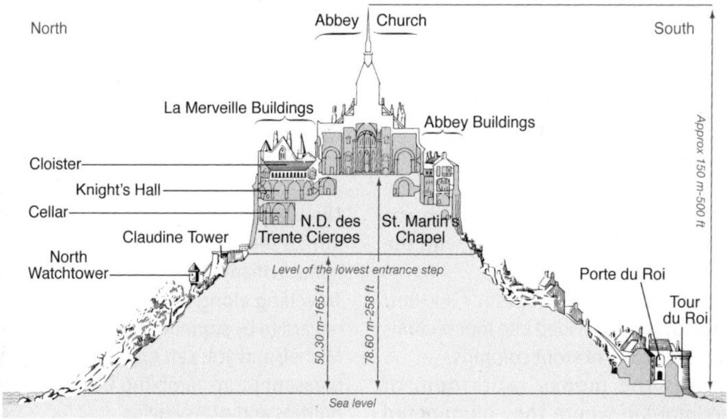

The different colours of the various materials add to the overall charm. The *lavatorium* (lavabo) on the right of the entrance recalls the ceremonial washing of the feet every Thursday.

Refectory★★

The effect is mysterious; the chamber is full of light although it appears to have only two windows in the end wall.

To admit so much light without weakening the solid side walls which support the wooden roof and are lined with a row of slim niches, the architect introduced a very narrow aperture high up in each recess. The vaulted ceiling is panelled with wood and the acoustics are excellent.

Old Romanesque Abbey

The rib vaulting marks the transition from Romanesque to Gothic. The tour includes the Monks' Walk and part of the dormitory.

Great Wheel

The wheel belongs to the period when the abbey was used as a prison. It was used to haul provisions and was operated by five or six men turning the wheel from within as if on a treadmill.

Crypts

The transepts and chancel of the church are supported by three undercrofts or crypts; the most moving is **Notre-Dame-sous-Terre** *(accessible only during guided tours)*: the Carolingian structure which stands where St Aubert officiated, is a simple rectangle (8x9m/26.9x29.5ft), divided into two small naves by a couple of arches resting on a central pillar. The place is awe-inspiring because of the complete silence which prevails and because of the memory of events which took place here more than 1 000 years ago! The most impressive is the **Crypte des Gros Piliers**★ (Great Pillared Crypt), which has ten pillars (5m/16.4ft in circumference) made of granite from the Chausey Islands.

Guests' Hall★

Here the abbot received royalty (Louis IX, Louis XI, François I) and other important visitors. The hall (35m/114.8ft long) has a Gothic ceiling supported on a central row of slim columns; the effect is graceful and elegant.

At one time it was divided down the middle by a huge curtain of tapestries; on one side was the kitchen quarters (two chimneys) and on the other the great dining hall (one chimney).

Knights' Hall★

The name of this hall may refer to the military order of St Michael, which was founded in 1469 by Louis XI with the abbey as its seat.

The hall is vast and majestic (26x18m/85.3x59ft) and divided into four sections by three rows of stout columns.

It was the monks' workroom or *scriptorium* where they illuminated manuscripts, read and studied religious or secular texts and, for this reason, it was heated by two great fireplaces. The almonry and cellar occupy the rooms on the lower floor.

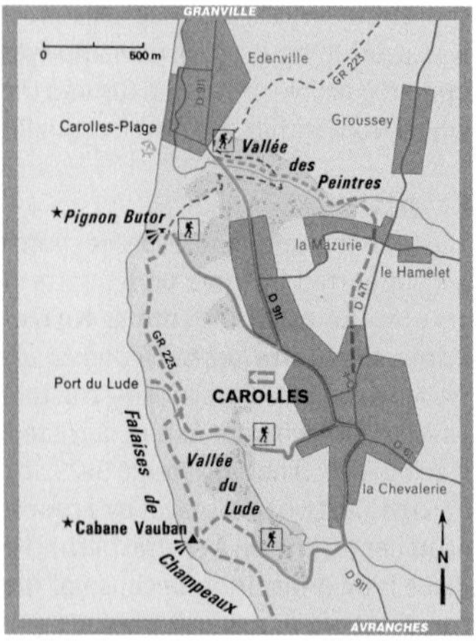

Cellar

This was the storeroom; it was divided into three by two rows of square pillars supporting the groined vaulting.

Almonry

This is a Gothic room with a Romanesque vault supported on a row of columns.

Abbey Gardens★

Closed in winter and in bad weather.

A pleasant place for a stroll with a view of the west side of the Mount and St Aubert's Chapel.

DRIVING TOURS

Mont-St-Michel Bay★★

About 100km/62mi of coastline border the bay.

The islands, cliffs, beaches and dunes form a series of ecosystems which are home to many species of flora and fauna. Travelling along the coast, you will be rewarded by stunning views of Mont-St-Michel, and you can enjoy walks along pleasant paths rambling between the polders and grassy fields.

Tall Tales and Natural Phenomena

Pilgrims liked to tell frightening tales of the perils of Mont-St-Michel, but the natural phenomena of the site are now well understood. What used to be called quicksand is really the effect of swathes of firm sand sitting on top of pockets of more liquid sand. The fearsome fog which occasionally envelops the whole bay with such speed can now be predicted by weather forecasters, and there is no longer a need to ring the church bell to warn of its imminence. And the tide racing in faster than a galloping horse? Although there are specific points where the action of the spring tide combines with geological features to create a movement of water at a speed of up to 25–30kph/15.5–18.6mph, the average rate of speed of the incoming tide is 3.7kph/2.3mph – about the speed of a person walking.

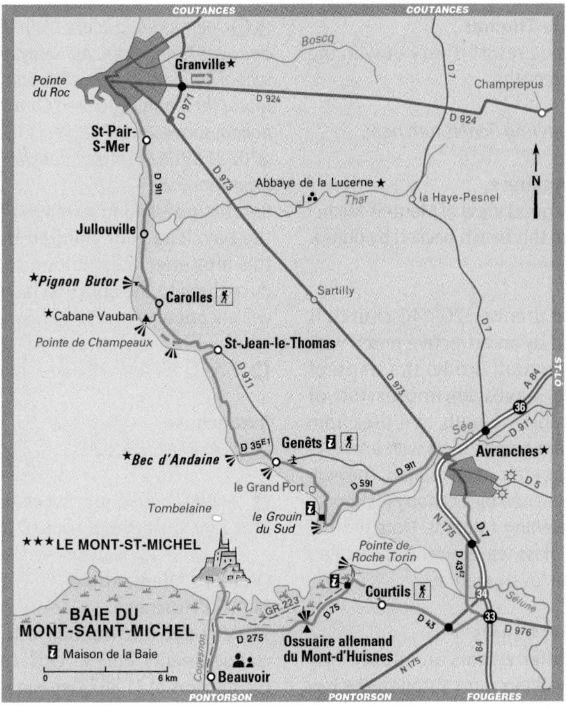

From Granville to Mont-St-Michel

40km/25mi – allow 2hr30min.

Between Granville and Carolles, there is a wide open view of the bay.

St-Pair-sur-Mer

See GRANVILLE – Excursion, p221.

Jullouville

The town is renowned for its fine sand beach. A pleasant walk leads along the seafront, passing 19C houses scattered among pine trees. The view extends from Pignon Butor to the Point du Roc.

Carolles

The village is set on the last headland before the sandy expanse of Mont-St-Michel Bay. As you drive between Carolles and St-Jean-le-Thomas, there is a splendid **view** ★★ of the bay. Don't hesitate to stop the car!

In the vicinity there are also several attractive walks with fine views.

The **Vallée des Peintres** (Artists' Valley) is an attractive spot, green and rock-strewn (*P car park at Carolles-Plage, N of Carolles*).

The **view** ★ from **Le Pignon Butor** *(viewing table)* on the clifftop extends north to Granville Rock and west to the Pointe du Grouin and Cancale in Brittany *(1km/0.6mi – 1hr on foot there and back, NW of the village).*

The path through the **Vallée du Lude** crosses an area of gorse and broom to reach the lonely cove, Port du Lude, on the coast. *P Follow the signs to the car park, 1hr on foot there and back.*

South of Carolles on D 911 beyond the small bridge turn right; park at the end of the road; take the downhill path (left) which then climbs (right) towards the cliff.

The **view** ★ from the Vauban Hut, a stone building standing on a rocky mound, includes Mont-St-Michel in the middle of the bay.

St-Jean-le-Thomas
This seaside resort is very busy in the summer months.

On entering Genêts turn right.

Bec d'Andaine★
There is a good **view** of Mont-St-Michel here from this beach backed by dunes.

Genêts
The solid granite 12C–14C **church** is preceded by an attractive porch with a wooden roof. Inside, the transept crossing leaves an impression of considerable strength, as it rises from four square granite piers with animalC- and foliage-decorated capitals. The high altar is crowned by a canopy resting on gently swelling columns. Note the 13C stained-glass window at the east end and some lovely statues.

Relais des Genêts
Guides offer visitors an opportunity to join walking tours through the bay area, some with special themes, and all centred around enjoying the natural beauty, learning about the flora and the fauna *(4 pl. des Halles, 50530 Genêts; open Apr–Sept daily 9am–6pm; Oct–Mar Mon–Fri 9am–1pm, 2–5.30pm; 02 33 89 64 00)*. Reservations are required, and you are asked to wear boots and warm clothing in winter, and carry a wind-breaker, a snack and water at all times.

On leaving Genêts turn right before the calvary.

The coastal road goes through Le Grand Port and offers good views, at very close quarters, of Mont-St-Michel, especially from the **Pointe du Grouin du Sud** (Grouin du Sud Point). The famous salt-marshes can also be seen.

Maison de la Baie-Relais de Vains-St-Léonard (Bay Centre)
Relais de Vains Saint-Léonard, rte du Grouin du Sud, 50300 Vains.
Open Jul–Aug 10am–7pm. Jun and Sept 10am–6pm. Apr–May and school holidays 2–6pm. Guided tours (1hr30min). Closed Christmas holidays. 4.20€ (7–15 years 1.75€). 02 33 89 06 06. http://manche.fr/patrimoine.
Before undertaking a walking tour of the bay, lead your children through this multimedia exhibition to introduce them to the flora and fauna they will encounter.

Take D 591 and D 911 to Avranches.

Avranches★
See AVRANCHES, p203.

At Bas-Courtils, turn left onto D 75; after 2km/1mi turn right onto D 107.

Ossuaire Allemand du Mont-d'Huisnes
This circular construction with its 68 compartments, built in 1963, contains the remains of 11 887 German soldiers fallen in France. From the belvedere there is a good view of Mont-St-Michel.

Continue along D 275.

The coastal road skirts the salt-marshes where flocks of sheep are put out to graze on the special grass there. The lambs are prized for their succulent tender meat. Again there are fine views of Mont-St-Michel.

Alligator Bay
Located at the entrance to Beauvoir, on the edge of D 976. 62 rte Mont-St-Michel. Open Apr–Sept daily 10am–7pm; Feb–Mar and Oct–Nov daily 2–6pm; Dec–Jan Sat–Sun and school holidays 2–6pm. 11€ (children 4–12 years 7€, 13–18 years 9€). 02 33 68 11 18. www.alligator-bay.com.
Thrills are guaranteed at this reptile breeding centre where you can see a wide variety of tortoises, snakes and crocodiles.

ADDRESSES

STAY

Chambre d'hôte Amaryllis – *Le Bas-Pays, 50170 Beauvoir, 2.5km/1.5mi S of Mont-St-Michel dir. Pontorson. 02 33 60 09 42. 5 rooms.* This stone house was renovated specifically as a B&B. The impeccably clean rooms feature well-equipped bathrooms and a furnished terrace. An extra treat: you can visit the farm next door.

Hôtel Bretagne – *r. Couesnon, 50170 Pontorson, 8km/5mi S of Mont-St-Michel via D 976. 02 33 60 10 55. www.lebretagnepontorson.com. Closed 15–30 Jan. 13 rooms. Restaurant.* This regional-style house has lovely 18C wood panels, a grey-marble fireplace and a plate-warming radiator (very unusual!) in a little dining room. Cosy, typically British bar and spacious, pleasantly furnished rooms.

Hôtel La Tour Brette – *8 r. Couesnon, 50170 Pontorson, 9km/5.6mi S of Mont-St-Michel. 02 33 60 10 69. http://fraysse.phpnet.org. Closed 14–22 Mar, 1–20 Dec, Wed except Jul–Aug. 10 rooms. Restaurant.* This well-situated little hotel owes its name to an old tower that protected Normandy from the dukes of Brittany. Rooms are small but recently renovated. At the restaurant, extensive traditional menu.

Chambre d'hôte Mme Gillet Hélène – *3 Le Val-St-Revert, 35610 Roz-sur-Couesnon, 15km/9mi SW of Mont-St-Michel via D 797, the coast road to St-Malo. 02 99 80 27 85. 4 rooms.* This 17C family house overlooks the bay and offers a beautiful view of Mont-St-Michel and the surrounding countryside. Four rooms where an old-world charm lingers on: three on the sea side and a more recent and brighter one with a terrace facing the garden.

Âuberge St-Pierre – *Grande-Rue. 02 33 60 14 03. www.auberge-saint-pierre.fr. 21 rooms. 14€. Restaurant.* This half-timbered inn is home to a restaurant and small well-kept bedrooms. The bigger rooms are in an adjacent wing and offer sea views. Choose between a brasserie on the road side, a dining room upstairs or the terrace bult against the ramparts.

EAT

La Gourmandise – *21 rte du Mont-St-Michel, 50170 Beauvoir, 4km/2.5mi S of Mont-St-Michel. 02 33 58 42 83. Closed Nov–Mar and Tue except Jul–Aug* This Breton house transformed into a crêperie enlivens the tiny village. Simple décor, lit up by large bay windows. The extensive menu offers a choice of crêpes and galettes. A few guest rooms.

Auberge de la Baie – *44 rte de la Rive, 50170 Ardevon, 3km/2mi SE of Mont-St-Michel dir. Avranches via D 275. 02 33 68 26 70. www.aubergedelabaie.fr. Closed Nov and Tue–Wed except Jul–Aug.* This restaurant on a departmental road is a welcome break from the bustling tourism of Mont-St-Michel, at least for an hour or two. On the menu: traditional and regional dishes, plus a short list of galettes. 13 guest rooms.

La Mère Poulard – *Grande-Rue. 02 333 89 68 68. www.merepoulard.com.* This hotel-restaurant is famous for Mother Poulard's omelette, which rubs shoulders with appetising regional recipes. Inviting rooms, some of which command a panoramic view.

La Promenade – *pl. du Casino, 50610 Jullouville. 02 33 90 80 20. www.la-promenade.fr. Closed Mon–Tue. Reservations advised.* It would be difficult to find a better view of Mont-St-Michel Bay than at this elegant restaurant-tearoom on the ground floor of the former casino hotel (1881). Handsome antique furniture and tableware. Menu with an accent on seafood.

La Sirène – *16 Grande-Rue. 02 33 60 08 60. Closed 10 Jan–2 Feb, 15 Nov–20 Dec.* Take the spiral staircase to enter the crêperie in this 14C house that was an inn for many years. The frosted-glass windows, their panes separated by metal mullions, confirm the genuine flavour of the place.

Mortain★

This small, pleasantly well-kept town is built halfway up a hillside in an attractive setting★ where the River Cance, cutting through the last of Basse-Normandie's southern hills, emerges on to the vast wooded Sélune basin, leaving in its wake a rock-strewn countryside. The name of the town is derived from the word Maurus and could refer to the Moors who served in the Roman army. During the Middle Ages Mortain was the capital of the county held by Robert, the stepbrother of William the Conqueror. The town has been rebuilt over the ruins left after the Battle of Normandy.

- **Population:** 2 191.
- **Michelin Map:** 303: G-8.
- **Info:** Rue du Bourglopin. ℘02 33 59 19 74. www.ville-mortain.fr.
- **Location:** Mortain is 25km/15.5mi S of Vire via D 577 and D 977. Avranches is 42km/26mi W via D 5.
- **Don't Miss:** The picturesque Grande and Petite Cascades and the "Chrismal" treasury at St-Évroult Church.
- **Timing:** You will need a half day to tour the Cascades, which involve considerable walking and the Abbaye Blanche.

SIGHTS

Grande Cascade★

Either park in avenue de l'Abbaye-Blanche in the car park at a bend in the road and take the path downhill or park in rue du Bassin (signposted) and take the path that follows the river bank.

The waterfall (25m/82ft) is created by the River Cance flowing through a wooded gorge; the foaming waters recall the mountain streams of the Pyrenees or the Alps.

Petite Cascade★

45min on foot there and back. From place du Château take the downhill path S (left) along the wall of the Caisse d'Épargne (signpost).

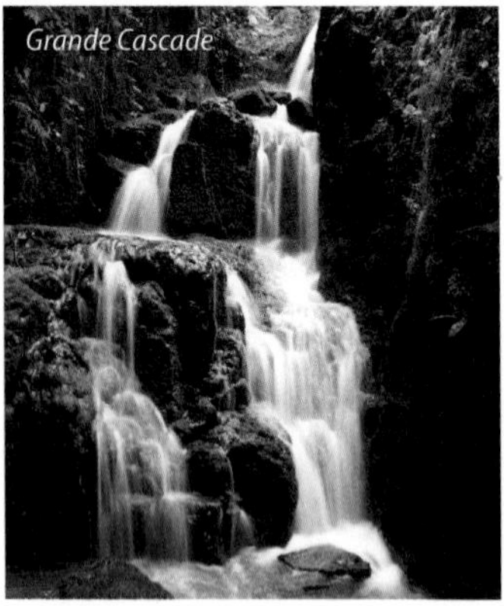
Grande Cascade

© Laurent Renault/Fotolia

The path crosses the River Cance and follows the bank upstream past the Aiguille Rock. It then crosses the Cançon stream on stepping stones before reaching the waterfall (35m/114.8ft) in a rock amphitheatre.

Petite Chapelle★

From Mortain take the road S towards Rancoudray; in front of the Gendarmerie turn left. Park in the car park at the top of the hill; walk up the avenue of fir trees.

To the left and beyond the chapel there is a belvedere *(viewing table)* providing a **view**★ of the wooded heights of Mortain and Lande-Pourrie. On a clear day Mont-St-Michel and the Breton coast are visible on the horizon *(right)*.

Abbaye Blanche

At edge of town, going towards Villedieu-Sourdeval. Open Apr–Dec Wed–Mon 10am–noon, 2.30–7pm. No charge. ℘02 33 79 47 47.

This 12C former monastery in a landscape of rocky outcrops was founded in the 12C by Adeline and her brother Vital, chaplain to Count Robert, stepbrother of William the Conqueror.

The chapter house is composed of two bays with pointed vaulting. The sisters usually sit by order of seniority on the white-stone benches which run round the walls.

The cloister gallery, contrary to other Romanesque cloisters in the region, which have twinned columns or clusters as at Mont-St-Michel, consists of a simple row of single columns. The vaulting is of timberwork.

The church displays the usual features of the Cistercian plan: flat east end with its oculus and transept chapels. The diagonal ribs are a precursor of the Gothic style. The groined vaulting of the Lay Sisters Refectory is supported by two central columns.

The storerooms have two barrel vaults of four bays each; the capitals are carved with foliage and scrolls.

Collégiale St-Évroult

Town centre. Open daily 9am–7pm. To see the treasury, ask at the tourist office Jul–Aug. No charge. 02 33 59 19 74.

This old collegiate church reconstructed in the 13C is built of sandstone in a somewhat severe Gothic style. The 13C belfry is attractively plain and simple. The fine door in the second bay shows all the decorative elements known to Norman Romanesque. The single arch relies neither on columns nor capitals. The chancel stalls have carved miseericords representing satyr-like figures. The **treasury** contains the Chrismal, an exceptional 7C casket of Anglo-Irish origin. The casket or portable reliquary is made of beechwood, lined with copper and engraved with runic inscriptions and images of sacred personages.

EXCURSIONS

Ger

On the road to Flers. 15km/9mi from Mortain on D 157. Then take D 60 on the left, heading towards Le Placître.

Musée régional de la Poterie★

3 r. du Musée-Le Placître. Open Jul–Aug 11am–7pm; Apr–Jun and Sept 2–6pm, Easter and All Souls school holidays 2–6pm (last ticket 1hr before closing). 4.20€ (children 1.75€). 02 33 79 35 36. www.sitesetmusees.cg50.fr.

The museum comprises 12 buildings: a potter's house, three long tunnel-kilns from the 17C and 18C, a drying device for pots, various workshops, a bakery, etc. There is an interesting **demonstration**★ of manufacturing techniques. Pottery is still made on the premises and is available for sale.

DRIVING TOUR

Vallée de la Sée

Round-trip of 58km/36mi – allow 3hr. From Mortain take D 977 N towards Vire.

North of La Tournerie, where the road winds downhill, there is a view of the vast Sourdeval basin, through which runs the River Sée.

In Sourdeval turn left onto D 911.

From Pewterers to Guy Degrenne

In the early 19C men would leave their native village and take to the roads to try their luck throughout France. They would buy used cutlery made of pewter from farms and would melt it to make new kitchen utensils. These men, who were born in Sourdeval, Gathemo or Fresne-Porêt, were known as *grillous*: they were the ancestors of the industrialists who gradually converted their old paper mills into small metalworking factories. Over the years the manufacture of cutlery was to become a speciality of the canton. It was originally made in pewter, then in steel-coated metal and eventually in stainless steel, as is the custom today. The firm Guy Degrenne, named after its original founder, is one of France's most prestigious manufacturers of cutlery today.

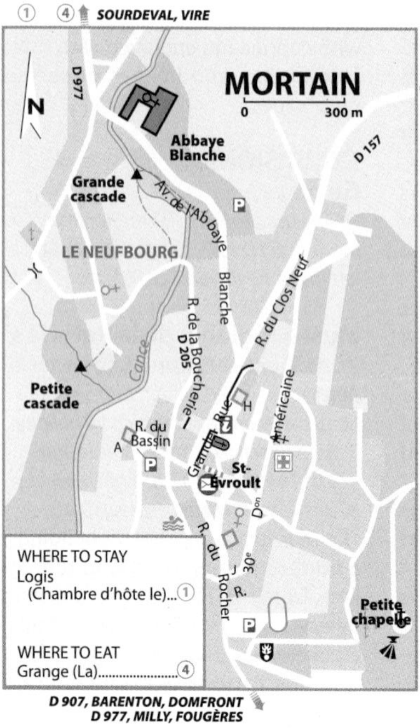

The road follows the curves of the narrow **Sée Valley**★, offering a new view at each bend.

Moulin de la Sée

Brouains. Open Jul–Aug Mon–Fri 9am–7pm, Sat–Sun and public holidays 11am–7pm; Mar–Jun and Sept–Oct Mon–Fri 9am–12.30pm, 2–6pm, Sat–Sun and public holidays 2–6pm (last entry 30min before closing). 5€. 02 33 59 20 50.

This mill is also known as the Écomusée de la Vallée de Brouains, a museum devoted to rivers and related activities, including fish breeding (the river Sée is one of France's finest Salmon runs), the development of hydraulic energy, and the development of water-powered industries, from pewterware to stainless steel cutlery.

After passing the church in Chérencé-le-Roussel, turn right onto D 33.

St-Pois

Fine views south of the Sée Valley.

In St-Pois turn right and right again onto D 39 which climbs uphill.

St-Michel-de-Montjoie

Musée du Granit. Open Jun–mid-Sept daily 2–6pm; May Sun 2–6pm (last entry 1hr before closing). 4€. 02 33 59 02 22.

At the southwest entrance to the village, a terrace affords a fine view which, on a clear day, extends to Mont St-Michel. The village is known for its granite quarry (*NW off D 282 towards Gast*) and for its mineral water, Eau de Montjoie.

The **Musée du Granit** describes quarrying and displays granite objects – capitals, pediments, sarcophagi, balusters, millstones – in a wooded park.

Return to Chérencé-le-Roussel. Turn left onto D 33 towards Mortain.

ADDRESSES

STAY

Chambre d'hôte Le Logis – *50520 Juvigny-le-Tertre, 12km/7.5mi W. 02 33 59 38 20. http://gitefillatre.free.fr. Closed 15 Nov–15-Mar. 5 rooms. . Meal.* Housed in 17C buidings, the rooms have a rustic feel.

EAT

Auberge La Grange – *In the Village enchanté de Bellefontaine, 50520 Bellefontaine, 7km/4.3mi N. 02 33 59 01 93. www.village-enchante.fr. Closed 15 Jan–15 Mar.* Situated at the entrance to the village, this old barn converted into a restaurant is truly bewitching with its old beams. Guest rooms and self-catering cottages for groups.

Château de Pirou★

The 12C fortress, which once stood on the coast beside an anchorage, since silted up, served as an outpost for the defence of Coutances under the lords of Pirou. The castle passed to other noble families until the late 18C, when it was used as a hideout for smugglers dealing in tobacco from Jersey.

- **Michelin Map:** 303: C-4.
- **Info:** 02 33 46 34 71. www.chateau-pirou.org.
- **Location:** 10km/6mi SW of Lessay, 17.8km/11mi NW of Coutances.
- **Don't Miss:** The tapestry describing the conquest of Sicily by the Normans.
- **Timing:** For a relaxed visit, take 1hr30min.

Château de Pirou

S. Sauvignier/MICHELIN

VISIT

Allow 30min. Open daily Apr–Sept 10am–noon, 2–6.30pm; mid-Oct–Nov and Feb–Mar 10am–noon, 2–5pm. 5€.

Three fortified gatehouses – there were originally five – lead to the old sheepfold, the outer bailey and then to the castle itself, a massive structure encircled by a moat.

The room where justice was dispensed displays a **tapestry** similar in style to the Bayeux Tapestry, recounting the conquest of southern Italy and Sicily by the Cotentin Normans. The original tapestry can be seen only in July and August; otherwise a copy is on display.

ADDRESSES

EAT

La Mer – *2 r. Fernand-Desplanques, 50770 Pirou-Plage, 2.5km/1.5mi W of Château de Pirou via D 94. 02 33 46 43 36. Closed Jan, 10 days in Oct, Sun, Mon and Tue eves and Wed off-season.* From your table you see the coastline and the Channel Islands appear offshore in good weather. The cuisine has a definite sea flavour.

The Legendary Geese of Pirou

When the Norse invaders failed to take the fortress they decided to lay siege to it. After several days of waiting they realised that there was no longer any sign of activity within the castle but, being suspicious, they decided to delay a little longer before making the final assault. Imagine their surprise when they found that the only remaining occupant was a bedridden old man, who informed them that the lord, his wife and other occupants of the castle had transformed themselves into geese, to escape from the hands of their attackers. Indeed the Norsemen recollected having seen a skein of wild geese flying over the castle walls the previous evening. According to Norse traditions, the human form could only be reassumed once certain magic words had been recited backwards. The geese came back to look for their book of magic spells but alas, the Norsemen had set fire to the castle. Legend has it that the geese come back every year in the hope of finding their book of spells, which explains why there are so many skeins of geese in the vicinity of the castle.

Pontorson

Pontorson is a favourite stopping place for visitors on their way to Mont-St-Michel. The town is named after a local baron, Orson, who in 1031 built a bridge (*pont* in French) over the Couesnon.

- **Population:** 4 203.
- **Michelin Map:** 303: C-8.
- **Info:** Place de l'Hôtel-de-Ville. ℘02 33 60 20 65. www.mont-saint-michel-baie.com.
- **Location:** Pontorson is 9km/5.6mi S of Mont-St-Michel on D 976.
- **Don't Miss:** The chapel of the St-James American Military Cemetery.

VISIT

Église Notre-Dame

Open daily.

The 11C church is said to have been founded by **William the Conqueror** to thank the Virgin for saving his army from the Couesnon quicksands. The episode is portrayed in a stained-glass window and also in scene 17 in the Bayeux Tapestry. The church was given pointed vaulting at a later date and has been remodelled several times. The massive rough granite west front has kept its Romanesque appearance, with a great arch, only slightly pointed. Note the tympanum on the south doorway, carved with a man and a bird. A Gothic arch opens into the chapel of St Saviour, where there is a fine 15C altarpiece: the Broken Saints. Despite being mutilated during the Wars of Religion and the Revolution, it is a work of great richness.

EXCURSION

St-James

15km/9mi E by D 30.

This is one of western Normandy's oldest cities, founded by William the Conqueror in 1067. Several old streets and 15C ramparts recall the historic past. The **Cimetière américain et Mémorial de Bretagne** is on the outskirts of St-James (*take D 230 in the direction of Louvigné*). This cemetery holds the graves of over 4 400 Americans. In the chapel are regimental colours, stained-glass windows, coats of arms and maps commemorate the events of 1944.

St-Lô

In 1944 St-Lô acquired the sad title of Capital of Ruins. On 19 July, the day the town was liberated, only the battered towers of the collegiate church and a few houses in the suburbs remained standing. Since then St-Lô has been rebuilt and it is now the site of one of the largest stud farms in France.

- **Population:** 19 643.
- **Michelin Map:** 303: L-5.
- **Info:** Place Général de Gaulle. ℘02 33 77 60 35. www.st-lo.fr.
- **Location:** St-Lô lies between Coutances (29km/18mi W) and Bayeux (37km/23mi NE).
- **Don't Miss:** The outdoor pulpit at the Église Notre-Dame.
- **Timing:** In late summer, attend the Thursday exhibition at the stud farm.
- **Kids:** Haras National stud farm.

A BIT OF HISTORY

Key Town – St-Lô, a vital communications centre, was destined to play a strategic role in the Battle of Normandy. Owing to its position at a crossroads, the town underwent heavy bombing from 6 June aimed at dispersing enemy forces.

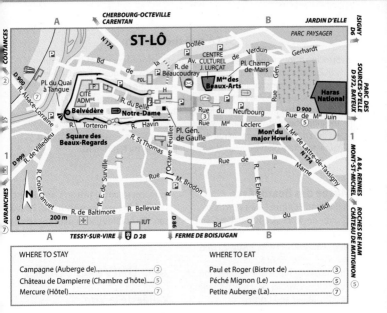

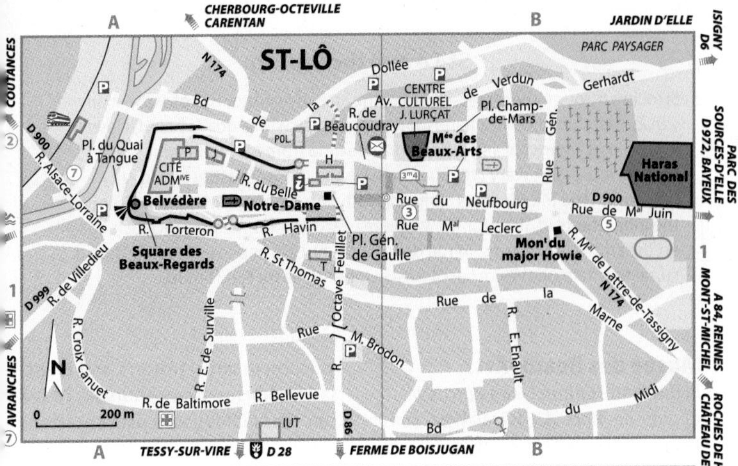

WHERE TO STAY

Campagne (Auberge de) ②
Château de Dampierre (Chambre d'hôte) ⑤
Mercure (Hôtel) ⑦

WHERE TO EAT

Paul et Roger (Bistrot de) ③
Péché Mignon (Le) ⑤
Petite Auberge (La) ⑦

The battle for St-Lô began early in July in the middle of the War of the Hedgerows to capture the Lessay-St-Lô road, the base for Operation Cobra.

The town, which was the centre of German resistance, fell on 19 July. A monument, erected in memory of Major Howie of the American army, recalls a moving episode in the town's liberation. Howie had wanted to be one of the first to enter St-Lô, but he was killed on 18 July. To fulfil his wish, the first Allied troops to enter St-Lô carried his coffin in with them, setting it down in the ruins of the belfry of Holy Cross Church.

A week later, after an unprecedented aerial bombardment – when 5 000 tonnes of bombs fell on an area of 11sq km/4sq mi – the German front broke in the west and the Avranches breakthrough was launched.

Reconstruction – A new town has arisen from the ruins, planned so that one can now clearly see the outline of the rocky spur, ringed by ramparts and towers, which have become the landmark. The oldest district, the Enclos, in the upper part of the town includes the Préfecture and administrative buildings, which make an interesting post-war architectural group.

The extremely modern tower in place Général de Gaulle is an amazing contrast to the former prison porch nearby, now a memorial to Resistance fighters and the victims of Nazism.

SIGHTS

Église Notre-Dame

r. de la Chancellerie (facing the Préfecture) Open daily 8.30am–7pm.

The west front of the church (13C–17C) and the two towers have been shored up but otherwise left as they were in 1944 as a witness to the ferocity of the bombardment.

In St. Thomas à Becket's chapel, note the large window by Max Ingrand. There is an outside pulpit against the north wall, level with the chancel.

Belvédère

From the tower overlooking the spur on which the town stands there is a view of the Vire Valley and the *bocage.*

Hôpital-Mémorial France-États-Unis

By rue de Villedieu to the SW.

The hospital was built jointly by the two nations and has a Fernand Léger mosaic on one of its façades.

St-Lô and the Unicorn

Strolling through the streets of St-Lô, the attentive visitor will glimpse many versions of the unicorn, a handsome white horse with a goat's beard, cloven hooves and a narwhal's spiralled horn growing from his forehead. Considered as shy, wary creatures embodying purity, chastity and loyalty, unicorns in the Middle Ages came to symbolise the Virgin Mary. The devotion of the inhabitants of St-Lô for the Virgin may account for the presence of a unicorn on the city's coat of arms, in rue de la Porte-au-Lait, and even leaping from a stone fountain on the corner of rue Leturc and rue du Neufbourg.

Musée des Beaux-Arts

In the Centre Culturel Jean-Lurçat, pl. Champ-de-Mars. Open Wed–Sun 2–6pm. Closed 1 Jan, Easter Sun and Mon, 1 May, Ascension, 1 Nov, 25 Dec. 2.55€. 02 33 72 52 55.

The museum has a good collection of tapestries as well as 19C French painting: Boudin, Miller and Corot.

Haras national★

437 r. du Maréchal-Juin, dir. Bayeux. Guided tours hourly (1hr) Jul–Aug Mon–Sat 11am, 2.30pm–4.30pm, Sun 2.30pm–4.30pm; Jun and Sept Sat–Tue 2.30pm–4.30pm; May Fri–Sun 2.30pm–4.30pm. 6€ (12–16 years 2.50€). Presentation of stallions at 3pm every Thu from the last Thu of Jul to 1st Thu of Sept. 6€ (children 6–16 3€). 02 33 55 29 09.

The St-Lô stud, the biggest of the 23 national studs, specialises in breeds such as Norman cobs, trotters and French saddle-horses. Every Thursday in season, the stables hold a **presentation**★ of the stallions.

DRIVING TOURS

Vallée de la Vire

20km/12.5mi SE of St-Lô by N 174.

Torigni-sur-Vire

Château des Matignon. Guided tours (1hr30min) Jul–Aug daily 2.30–6pm (last entry 5pm); last 2 weeks of Jun and 1st 2 weeks of Sept Sun and public holidays 2.30–6pm. 3.50€. 02 33 56 71 44.

Since the 19C the **Château des Matignon** has consisted of only the west wing (restored). The main staircase (17C) leads to the reception rooms, which contain a very fine collection

Vire River Valley

G. Targat/MICHELIN

of tapestries, Louis XIII, Louis XV and Louis XVI furniture and works by the wildlife artist Arthur Le Duc. The park includes three ponds encircled by shaded paths.

From Torini take N 174 north; after 5km/3mi turn left onto D 286.

Roches de Ham★★

Alt 80m/262.5ft.

From the magnificent escarpment (above the river) there is a **view** of a beautiful bend in the River Vire.

Return downhill; turn right onto D 551 and right again; pass through Troisgots and descend towards La Chapelle-sur-Vire.

La Chapelle-sur-Vire

This small village has been a centre of pilgrimage since the 12C. In the church stand a statue of Our Lady of Vire (15C) and a low relief of St Anne, the Virgin and Child.

Continue along D 159.

The shaded road crosses the River Vire, then follows its course.

At the crossroads with D 511, turn right.

There is a view of the **Château de l'Angotière** *(closed to the public).*

ADDRESSES

STAY

Hôtel Armoric – *15 r. de la Marne 02 33 05 61 32. www.hotel-armoric.com. 20 rooms.* This 1950s building is out of the town centre yet close to the ramparts and the old town. Simple rooms are well kept, with veneer or wicker furniture.

Auberge de Campagne – *Château de la Roque, 50180 Hébécrevon, 7.5km/4.7mi W of St-Lô towards Coutances, then towards Périers via D 900. 02 33 57 33 20. www.chateau-de-la-roque.fr. 15 rooms. 9€.* This beautiful 16C–17C residence appears at the end of a poplar-lined approach. Tastefully decorated rooms, lovely park for strolls, spa, sauna and plenty of activities on offer. The *restaurant* offers fine local cuisine in its dining room, which displays exposed beams. Friendly welcome.

Chambre d'hôte Château de Dampierre – *14350 Dampierre, 9km/5.6mi from Torigny-sur-Vire via D 13, then right on D 53. 02 31 67 31 81. 5 rooms.* A magnificent tree-lined approach leads to this 16C manor. Well-kept rooms overlooking the moat, the gatehouse and a superb dovecot, in the midst of the *bocage* countryside.

EAT

Bistrot de Paul et Roger – *40 r. du Neufbourg. 02 33 57 19 00. Closed 1st week Aug.* In the middle of this crazy bric-à-brac of glazed tiles, Louis XVI chairs, old posters and black-and-white photographs, don't miss the priceless collection of old radio sets. Copious cuisine.

La Petite Auberge – *1216 rte de Candol, exit towards Canisy. 02 33 05 34 11. www.aubergedecandol.fr. Closed Mon.* After long years of travel, the chef has settled here to create delicious seafood dishes served on the terrace or near the fireplace.

Le Péché Mignon – *84 r. du Maréchal-Juin. 02 33 72 23 77. Closed Sun eve and Mon, except for group bookings.* Near the Haras national, the owner/chef prepares regional dishes adapted to today's tastes. Two dining rooms, including a more modern one with brightly coloured tablecloths.

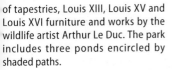

St-Sauveur-le-Vicomte

St-Sauveur-le-Vicomte, standing on the banks of the Douve in the heart of Cotentin, is closely associated with the 19C writer Jules Barbey d'Aurevilly and St Mary Magdalen Postel, who founded the Sisters of the Christian Schools of Mercy in the 19C.

- **Population:** 2 118.
- **Michelin Map:** 303: C-3.
- **Info:** Le Vieux Château. 02 33 21 50 44. www.ville-saint-sauveur-le-vicomte.fr
- **Location:** St-Sauveur-le-Vicomte is 15km/9.6mi S of Valognes on D 2 and 19km E of Barneville-Carteret via D 650 and D 15.
- **Don't Miss:** The keep of the Vieux Château.
- **Timing:** You will need 3hr to see the château and the abbey.

SIGHTS

Château

Guided tour (1hr) Jul–Aug Tue–Sun 3pm, 4.30pm. Gardens open all year. 2€. 02 33 21 50 44.

The bust at the entrance is that of Barbey d'Aurevilly, by Rodin. This 12C castle was the ancestral home of two Norman families, the Néels and the Harcourts. The castle has suffered many a siege, notably by the English in 1356 and the French in 1375. Louis XIV had the castle converted into a hospice in 1691.

Église

Only the transept dates from the 13C,;the rest of the church was rebuilt in the 15C. At the entrance to the chancel are a 16C *Ecce Homo (left)* and a 15C statue of St James of Compostela *(right)*.

Musée Barbey-d'Aurevilly

64 r. Bottin-Desylles. Enter the castle precinct (which now contains an old people's home), climb the stairs (left) beyond the vault. Open Wed–Mon Jul–Aug 11am–6pm; mid-Apr–Jun and Sept–Oct 1–6pm. Guided tours available. 4€. 02 33 41 65 18.

The museum contains mementoes of Jules Barbey d'Aurevilly (1809–89), a critic and writer of popular fantastical novels who was born in the town and is buried in the castle cemetery *(round the castle, along the curtain walls in the moat, and across the large courtyard)*.

Abbaye

Open daily 10am–noon, 2–6pm. No charge. Guided tours available on request. 02 33 21 63 29.

The abbey was founded in the 10C by Néel de Néhon, Vicomte de St-Sauveur. The Hundred Years' War brought ruin on the abbey and forced the monks into exile.

At the Revolution the building was further dismantled. In 1832 it was bought by Mother Marie-Madeleine Postel to serve as the mother house for the order, which she had founded in Cherbourg in 1807. Although damaged in World War II, the abbey was repaired in 1945–50.

Abbatiale

The plain round-headed windows in the south aisle of the abbey church date from the Romanesque period.

The lovely 15C carved-wood altar portrays scenes from the childhood of Christ. The tomb of St Marie-Madeleine Postel lies in the north transept.

Parc

The well-tended park with its fine trees and colourful flower beds is a pleasant place for a stroll. The well-restored convent buildings add an elegant note.

EXCURSION

Château de Crosville-sur-Douve

Proceed towards Valognes for 5km/3mi and in Rauville-la-Place take D 15 towards Pont-l'Abbé, then follow the signposts. Open Easter–Oct and 1–24 Dec daily 2–6pm. 5€ (fee includes the garden). 02 33 41 67 25.

The oldest part of this imposing 17C château is the round, machicolated tower with its staircase turret. Note the granite staircase and remnants of painted decoration in the great hall.

St-Vaast-la-Hougue

Among the good reasons to visit this popular seaside resort with a marina and a mild climate are the delicious *huîtres* (oysters). The fortifications protecting the harbour date back to Vauban (17C). Offshore lies the "warrior island", Tatihou, which is definitely worth visiting.

- **Population:** 2 128.
- **Michelin Map:** 303: E-2.
- **Info:** 1 place du Général-de-Gaulle. 02 33 23 19 32. www.saint-vaast-reville.com.
- **Location:** St-Vaast is 12km/7.5mi S of Barfleur; 18km/11mi NE of Valognes.
- **Don't Miss:** Vauban's Tower.

SIGHTS

Île de Tatihou★

Crossing (10min) every 30min (high tide) and every hour (low tide). Crossing from Apr–Sept 10am–6pm; rest of the year Sat 2–5.30pm. Max 500 visitors per day; book in advance. 7.80€ return fare (ticket includes visit of the museum and the Tour Vauban). Reduction offered with recent ticket from Cité de la Mer, Ludiver or the Cotentin train. 02 33 23 19 92. http://manche.fr/tatihou. Visitors can reach the island by foot at low tide through a road in the oyster beds known as "Le Run".

Vauban's Tower, Île de Tatihou

© Jakezc/Dreamstime.com

An amphibious vehicle takes visitors over to Tatihou, which means mound surrounded by water; "hou" is Norse for water. The **Musée maritime départemental** (Maritime Museum) has sections on naval architecture and history as well as objects recovered underwater at the site of the Battle of La Hougue (1692): guns, shoes, bowls, china, pipes, cutlery, part of the upper works and deadeyes which give a good idea of life on His Majesty's ships. **A nature reserve** (20ha/50 acres), covering moorland, sand dunes and shingle (stony) beach offers opportunities for birdwatching. In the old fort built by Vauban, there is a bookshop, a caféteria and a restaurant.

DRIVING TOUR

Take D 1 north towards Réville; after crossing the bridge over the Saire turn right to the Pointe de Saire.

Pointe de Saire

Beyond the hamlet of Jonville, by the sea, is an old blockhouse that offers a good **view**★ of the attractive rock-strewn beaches of Pointe de Saire and of Tatihou Island with St-Vaast in the background.

Continue north on D 1.

Beyond Réville the road passes La Crasvillerie, a delightful 16C manor house. This is market gardening country where they specialise in cabbages. As you approach Barfleur, the countryside becomes more Amorican in character, in fact resembling the neighbouring region of Brittany, with housesmade of granite hewn from local rocks, rocky bays and gnarled trees bent by the wind. Gatteville lighthouse stands to the north.

ADDRESSES

STAY

Chambre d'hôte La Ferme de Cabourg – *10 rte du Martinet, 50760 Réville, 3.5km/2.2mi N of St-Vaast via D 1, then D 328 dir. Jonville. 02 33 54 48 42. 3 rooms.* A poplar-lined alley leads to this fortified 15C farm. The guest rooms are nice and bright.

Hôtel de France et Fuchsias –*20 r. du Mar.-Foch. 02 33 54 40 41. www.france-fuchsias.com. Closed 3 Jan–1 Mar, Mon, Tue in Mar, Nov, Dec and Tue lunch from Apr–Oct. 34 rooms. Restaurant.* When the fuchsias are in bloom, they cover the walls of this 100-year-old hotel set back from the harbour. Some rooms overlook the garden. Meals in the dining room, on the veranda or the terrace.

EAT

Crêperie Léoncie – *27 quai Vauban. 02 33 44 42 50.* You'd better book ahead for this little place with a good reputation. Try the delicious crêpes with scallops or with three kinds of apples.

Le Chasse Marée – *8 pl. du Gén. de Gaulle. 02 33 23 14 08. Closed 5–27 Jan, 15–30 Nov, Mon lunch in Jul–Aug, Sun eve and Mon from Sept–Jun.* The dishes are mostly seafood. On the walls, the flags of prestigious yacht clubs (mainly British) and old marine photos form an appropriate setting for the refined cuisine.

SHOPPING

Market – *r. de Verrüe, pl Belle-île and pl. de la République. Sat 7am–2pm.* Some 80 merchants sell fruit, vegetables, charcuterie, cheese, seafood and more.

Ste-Mère-Église

This town entered modern history brutally on the night of 5–6 June 1944 when troops from the American 82nd Airborne Division landed to assist the 101st Division in clearing the exits from Utah Beach. Ste-Mère-Église was liberated on 6 June but fighting continued until tanks advanced into the town from Utah Beach the following day.

- **Population:** 1 585.
- **Michelin Map:** 303:E-3.
- **Info:** 6 rue Eisenhower. 02 33 21 53 91.
- **Location:** The N 13 between Bayeux (59km/37mi E) and Valognes (16km/10mi NW) passes by Ste-Mère-Église. Well signposted.
- **Don't Miss:** Look up to the church steeple at the paratrooper dangling there.
- **Timing:** Take 2hr to see the village and the Airborne Museum.
- **Kids:** The Cotentin Farm Museum.

SIGHTS

Church

The solid 11C–13C church was damaged particularly during the dislodging of German snipers from the belfry. A dummy at the end of a parachute hangs from the steeple as a reminder of Private

Église Ste-Mère with paratrooper

A. Coupe/MICHELIN

John Steele's ordeal: dropped over the area during the night of 6 June 1944, he was caught dangling from the steeple by his parachute. He played dead for 2hr, a few feet from a bell which never stopped ringing. The Germans eventually unhooked him.

Borne O de la Voie de la Liberté

In front of the town hall.

This is the first of the 12 000 symbolic milestones (*bornes*) along the Road of Liberty followed by General Patton's 20th Corps of the American Third Army to Metz and Bastogne.

Musée Airborne★

14 r. Eisenhower. ♿ *Open daily Apr–Sept 9am–6.45pm; Oct–Nov, Feb–Mar abd Christmas school holidays daily 9.30am–noon, 2–6pm. 7€. 02 33 41 41 35. www.musee-airborne.com.*

A parachute-shaped building in a large park at the entrance to the town houses the Airborne Museum, which contains mementoes of the fighting on D-Day. The museum has plans for extension.

Ferme-Musée du Cotentin

chemin de Beauvais. ♿ *Open Jul–Aug 11am–7pm (last entry 1hr before closing); Jun and Sept 11am–6pm; Apr–May and school holidays (except at Christmas) 2–6pm. 4.20€. 02 33 95 40 20.*

Housed in the Beauvais farm (16C), this Cotentin Farm Museum re-creates rural life of the early years of the 20C.

ADDRESSES

STAY

Chambre d'hôte Saint-Méen – *15 pl. du 6-Juin-1944. 02 33 21 52 17. www.chambres-de-saint-meen.com. 5 rooms.* ♿ P. Set in the town centre, a few yards from the church, this 18C stone house stands right on the street, but with a small garden in back. One family room, one is handicapped accessible.

EAT

Le John Steele – *4 r. du Cap-de-Laine, 50480 Ste-Mère-Église. 02 33 41 41 16. http://auberge-hotel-restaurant.aubergejohnsteele.com. Closed Sun eve and Mon Oct–Jun.* Situated near the famous church, this inn (1730) pays homage to the soldier John Steele. Typically Norman dining room with exposed beams and stone walls. Regional cuisine. A few simple rooms.

Valognes★

Valognes is an important road junction at the heart of the Cotentin Peninsula and is the market town for the surrounding agricultural area. The aristocratic town described by Barbey d'Aurevilly was partially destroyed in June 1944; it has been rebuilt in the modern style and expanded. Several traces of the past have survived including Gallo-Roman ruins, 11C–18C churches, and private mansions built in the 18C when local high society made Valognes the Versailles of Normandy.

- **Population:** 7 274.
- **Michelin Map:** 303: D-2 – Local map, *see Presqu'île du COTENTIN, p152.*
- **Info:** Place du Château. ℘02 33 40 11 55. www.ot-cotentin-bocage-valognais.fr.
- **Location:** Valonges is at a major crossroads: Cherbourg is 20km/12.5mi N, Barnville-Carteret 29km/18mi SW, St-Sauveur-le-Vicomte is 16km/10mi SW.
- **Don't Miss:** Hôtel de Beaumont.

SIGHTS

Hôtel de Beaumont★

11 r. Barbey-d'Aurevilly. Guided tours (1hr) Jul–mid-Sept daily 10.30am–noon, 2.30–6.30pm; weekends of Easter, Pentecost, 1 May and the Ascension 2.30–6.30pm (last entry 1hr before closing); rest of the year open for groups (20+) only. 5€. ℘02 33 40 12 30. www.hoteldebeaumont.fr.

This noble 18C residence, miraculously spared by the bombings, has a splendid front in dressed stone. Inside, the sweeping flight of steps with its double winding stairwell gives access to the upper floor by a stone arch ending in mid-air. The terraces are laid out as formal gardens.

Hôtel de Grandval-Caligny

32 r. des Religieuses. Guided tours (45min) on request 1 day before to Mme Fauvel. Jun–Aug Mon–Sat 11am–noon, 2.30–6pm. 4€. ℘06 98 89 31 64.

The 19C novelist **Jules Barbey d'Aurevilly** once lived in this handsome 17C–18C mansion.

Hôtel de Beaumont

Note the staircase with its wrought-iron bannistor, the Empire-style ceramic stove in the dining room, and alcoved bedrooms.

Musée Régional du Cidre

r. du petit-Versailles and r. Pelouze. Open Apr–Jun and Sept Mon–Tue and Thu–Sat 10am–noon, 2–6pm, Sun 2–6pm; Jul–Aug Mon–Sat 10am–noon, 2–6pm, Sun 2–6pm; Oct–Mar open for group bookings only (02 33 95 82 00). 4€. 02 33 40 22 73. www.mairie-valognes.fr.

The Cider Museum is set up in the **Maison du Grand Quartier**, one of a group which housed a 15C–18C linen factory.

Musée de l'Eau-de-Vie et des Vieux Métiers

Open same hourse as Cider museum.

Housed in the **Hôtel de Thieuville** (16C–19C), this museum displays equipment for distillation, stonemasonry, iron and copper work from the 11C to the 20C.

EXCURSIONS

Bricquebec

From Valognes, go west on the D 902, about 13km/8mi. Guided tours (1hr30min) of the castle Jul–Aug Wed–Mon 2–6.30pm. 1.80€ 02 33 87 22 50 (town hall).

The town is known for its old **castle** and its Trappist monastery. The inner courtyard of the castle is still enclosed by its fortified wall. The 14C **keep** is a handsome polygonal tower (23m/75.5ft high). The sentry walk between the keep and the clock tower offers a view of the town. The **Tour de l'Horloge** (clock tower) houses a small regional museum.

From Bricquebec take D 50 and D 121 north; just before the Calvary turn left onto a path.

Abbaye Notre-Dame-de-Grâce

From Bricquebec, 2km/1mi via D50, then D 121 and the road to the left, just before a stone cross. The abbey is not open for tours but it is possible to attend services, watch an audio-visual presentation at 3pm and purchase items. 02 33 87 56 10.

The Trappist monastery, which is occupied by a community of Cistercian monks, was founded in 1824 by Abbot Dom Augustin Onfroy, a priest from the village of Disgoville near Cherbourg.

ADDRESSES

STAY

Chambre d'hôte Le Haut Pitois – *50700 Lieusaint, 2km/1mi S of Valognes via D 2, small road to left on leaving the village. 02 33 40 19 92. 5 rooms.* A superb woodland road leads to this former farm in a calm setting. The rooms, located upstairs in an outbuilding (2 can sleep 4 or 5 people) are sparse but functional with complete bathrooms. Ideal for a tight budget and for families.

Grand Hôtel du Louvre – *28 r. des Réligieuses. 02 33 40 00 07. www.grandhoteldulouvre.com. Closed 15 Dec–15 Jan. 18 rooms. Restaurant.* Near the centre of town, this hotel has character: Barbey d'Aurevilly, a 19C Gothic novelist, stayed in Room no 4. Rooms, reached by a spiral staircase, have been renovated but retain their 19C character, as does the dining room.

EAT

L'Agriculture – *18 r. Léopold-Delisle. 02 33 95 02 02. www.hotel-agriculture.com.* In the centre of Valognes, this vine-covered building sits on a quiet little square. The interior is charming and grustic. Delicious house specialities. Guest rooms are modern and comfortable.

GUIDED TOURS

In Jul–Aug, Valognes offers several tours led by expert guides trained by the Ministry of Culture. *Contact Le Clos de Cotentin. 02 33 95 01 26 or the tourist office.*

Villedieu-les-Poêles

- **Population:** 3 950.
- **Michelin Map:** 303: E-6.
- **Info:** Place des Costils. ✆02 33 61 05 69. www.ot-villedieu.fr.
- **Location:** From Granville, Villedieu is 26km/16mi E.
- **Kids:** The zoo in Champrepus.

The town occupies a bend in the River Sienne and is an important road junction. It takes part of its name (*poêle* means pot or frying pan) from the making of pots and pans – a local activity here since the 12C. By 1740, there were 139 workshops in the town.
From making the great round-bellied copper milk churns *(cannes)* the local factories now make copper and aluminium boilers for domestic and industrial use. The town has retained its medieval appearance with many attractive inner courtyards, stepped streets and alleys and old houses.

SIGHTS

Église Notre-Dame

This 15C church in the Flamboyant Gothic style was built on the site of a 12C church. The square transept tower over the crossing is emblazoned with various heraldic emblems. The chancel contains an 18C gilt wooden tabernacle.

Atelier du Cuivre

54 r. Général Huard. Guided tours (45min) Sept–Jun Mon–Fri 9am–noon, 1.30–5.30pm, Sat and Jul–Aug until 6pm. Closed public holidays. 5.20€ (combined ticket with the Maison de l'Étain 9€). ✆02 33 51 31 85. www.atelierducuivre.com.

The story of copper working in Villedieu is explained: the copper deposits, techniques of copper working and a tour.

Musée de la Poeserie and Maison de la Dentellière (Boiler's Museum and Lacemaker's House)

25 r. Général Huard, cour du Foyer. Open May–Sept Mon and Wed–Sat 10am–12.30pm, 2–6.30pm, Tue and Sun 2–6.30pm; Oct–Dec and Apr until 6pm. Closed Easter Sun and Mon, Pentecost

VILLEDIEU-LES-PÔELES

WHERE TO STAY

Gaieté (Chambre d'hôte la)............ ①

WHERE TO EAT

Acherie (Manoir de l')........................ ①

Ferme de Malte (La)............... ④

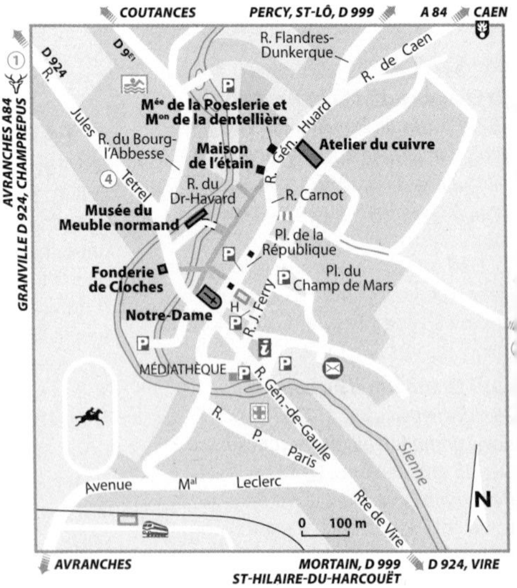

Mon, 14 Jul, 25 Dec. 4€ (combined ticket with the Musée du Meuble normand 5€). 02 33 61 11 78.
A reconstruction of an old workshop shows the copperware-making process. The lacemaker's house displays Villedieu lace, popular in the 18C.

Fonderie de Cloches★

r. du Pont-Chicnon. Guided tour (1hr) mid-Jul–Aug daily 9am–6pm; Sept–mid-Nov and mid-Feb–mid-Jul Tue–Sat 10am–12.30pm, 2–5.30pm. 4.90€. 02 33 61 00 56. www.cornille-havard.com.
The foundry still produces bells for belfries, ships and other public buildings, exported worldwide.

Maison de l'Étain

15 r. Général Huard. Open May–Sept Mon–Sat 9am–noon, 1.30–5.30pm; Mar–Apr and Oct Tue–Sat 1.30–5.30pm. 3.50€ (combined ticket with the Atelier du Cuivre 9€). Closed public holidays. 02 33 51 05 08.
In a house dating to the middle ages, an exhibit illustrates the art of pewter-working in the past.

Musée du Meuble normand

9 r. du Reculé. See Musée de la Poeslerie. 02 33 61 11 78.
The collection of Norman furniture dates from 1680 to 1930.

EXCURSIONS

Abbaye de Hambye★★

12km/7.5mi N of Villedieu by D 9 and D 51. Guided tour (45min, last tour 30min before closing) Apr–Oct Wed–Mon 10am–noon, 2–6pm. 4.20€. 02 33 61 76 92.
Beside the River Sienne are the majestic ruins of Hambye Abbey, which was founded around 1145. The **church**★ is imposing, although it lacks a roof, a west front and the first bay of the nave. The narrow 13C nave was extended in the 14C by three bays. The exceptionally large Gothic chancel has pointed arches, an ambulatory and radiating chapels. The tombstones are those of Jeanne Paynel, last descendent of the founders of Hambaye, and her husband, Louis d'Estouteville. The lay brothers' refectory (now used as a conference room) is furnished with 17C Rouen tapestries and a collection of old furniture.

Mont Robin

13km/8mi N by D 999. About 2km/1mi beyond Percy turn right towards Tessy-sur-Vire and right again almost immediately to Mount Robin.
From this point (276m/906ft) there is an expansive **view** east in the direction of the Suisse Normande.

Parc zoologique de Champrepus

8km/5mi W by D 924 toward Granville. Picnic area and adventure playground. Open Apr–Sept daily 10am–7pm; Feb–Mar and Oct Sat–Sun 11am–6pm. 12.80€ (3–12 years 7€, 13–19 10.80€). 02 33 61 30 74. www.zoo-champrepus.com.
Over 80 species are presented in a pleasantly shaded setting of parkland covering 6ha/15 acres. There is also an amusement park and snack shops.

ADDRESSES

STAY

Chambre d'hôte La Gaieté – *2 r. St-Georges, 50320 Beauchamps, 10km/6mi W. 02 33 61 30 42 . 5 rooms.* This impressive stone house with adjacent garden has nicely decorated rooms.

EAT

Manoir de l'Acherie – *37 r. Michel de l'Epinay, 50800 Ste-Cécile, 4km/2.5mi E. 02 33 51 13 87. www.manoir-acherie.fr. Closed Mon (except mid-Jul–Aug) and Sun eve mid-Oct–Apr.* Enjoy a meal (or a night) in this beautiful 17C manor house. The fare at this hotel-restaurant is plentiful, with grills sizzling on a wood fire.

Restaurant La Ferme de Malte – *11 r. Jules Tétrel. 02 33 91 35 91.* A touch of luxury at this comfortable, highly rated restaurant in town.

The portion of the Mayenne *département* that extends into Normandy is also known as the lower Maine or the black Maine, remnants of a former province. Through it flows the River Mayenne, on which sit the ancient fortress cities of Laval and Mayenne. The navigable river system once formed a vital transport artery, defended by picturesque forts and castles; today, recreational marinas line the river banks. The landscape, part of the Amoricain Massif, is rocky and forested, crisscrossed with hedgerows planted to contain the marshy soil, and dotted with gardens, orchards and pastures where horses graze.

Laval, a thriving modern city, nevertheless possesses a captivating old town composed of medieval and Renaissance buildings clustered under the castle on the left bank of the Mayenne river. Its terraced **Perrine gardens**, noted for magnificent trees and water features, offer views of the town and river. Folded into the surrounding countryside are abbeys, castles and Roman ruins to be seen on driving tours. **Mayenne**, a city surrounded by picturesque villages and a pretty forest, holds ruins of a Carolingian); often reinforced, it was once taken by William the Conqueror. In the countryside around the ancient market town of **Lassay-les Châteaux**, with its great castle, pleasant walking paths have been traced among the hedgerows. At the little village of **Pontmain**, site of an apparition of the Virgin at the end of the Franco-Prussian War, the beautiful **La Pellerine gardens** bloom all summer. The well-preserved town of **Évron**, set among forests and lakes, has a magnificent basilica, while the 11C keep at **Ste-Suzanne**, set on a commanding promontory above the river Erve, offers splendid views. A walk along the ramparts encircling the town provides both views and historical perspective, taking in a 16C castle built by Henri IV and a quarry. But perhaps the most affecting sight in the Mayenne is the ancient Roman garrison town at **Jublains**, with its massive fortress, temple, amphitheatre and public baths, as well as small shops and pottery works. Built on a strategic crossroads in the Roman road network linking the English Channel to the city of Tours, the town was abandoned in the late 3C, as Gaul descended into the Dark Ages.

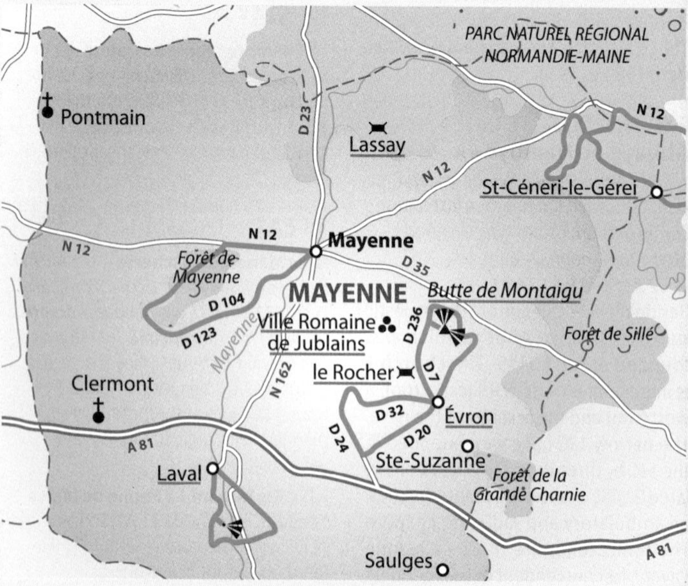

Évron★

This small town at the foot of the Coëvrons possesses one of the finest churches in the Mayenne, visible from 10km/6mi away. In the 19C the town's linen mills prospered; today it is classified as a "station verte de vacances" – recognised for the beauty and preservation of the natural surroundings.

- **Population:** 7 152.
- **Michelin Map:** 310: G-6.
- **Info:** 4 Place de la Basilique. 02 43 01 63 75. www.evron.fr.
- **Location:** Évron, surrounded by forests and lakes, is 26km/16mi SE of Mayenne via D 7, and 33km/20.5mi NW of Laval via D 20, then N 157.
- **Don't Miss:** The St-Crespin chapel in the Notre-Dame Basilica.
- **Timing:** After 1hr seeing the town, make an excursion to the surrounding countryside.

Basilique Notre-Dame★

pl. de la Basilique. Open daily. Guided tours (1hr) of the basilique, crypt and St-Crespin Chapel Jul–Aug Tue–Sat 2, 3, 4pm. Leave from Basilique information point. 4€.

A massive square 11C tower, embellished with corner buttresses and turrets, links the Romanesque part of the nave to the 18C abbey buildings.

The nave's four original bays are Romanesque, while the remainder of the basilica was rebuilt in the 14C in the Flamboyant Gothic style. Note the very fine 16C organ case and in the trefoil the fragments of a fresco depicting the Nursing Virgin.

The bare Romanesque nave enhances the sense of space, soaring height, luminosity and contrasts with the Gothic decoration elsewhere (restored 1979).

Chancel

Slender columns, pure lines and subtle decoration give the chancel considerable elegance. The overall effect is embellished by five windows with 14C stained glass, restored in 1901. During repair work to the chancel paving, a crypt and several sarcophagi were discovered, one dating to the 10C.

Chapelle St-Créspin★★

The 12C St Crespin's Chapel opens off the north side of the ambulatory. Christ is shown in a mandorla surrounded by the symbols of the Evangelists. Four lovely Aubusson tapestries represent Abraham's Sacrifice of Isaac, Hagar and Ishmael in the desert, Lot and his daughters leaving Sodom and Jacob's Dream.

At the altar is a large 13C statue of Our Lady of the Thorn (the full name of the basilique is Notre-Dame-de-l'Épine) in wood plated with silver. Beneath a remarkable 13C Crucifix, a cabinet contains two outstanding pieces of metalwork: a delightful 15C silver Virgin and a 16C reliquary.

DRIVING TOURS

Le Bois de Mirebeau

Allow 1hr45min.

35km/22mi. From Évron take D 20 north.

As the road climbs there are views to the west over woods and lakes.

Beyond Ste-Gemmes-le-Robert turn right onto the Mont Rochard road, which is sometimes in poor repair.

Le Gros Roc

From this rocky escarpment surrounded by vegetation there is an extensive view over the *bocage* countryside.

Turn left onto D 241 just before a bridge.

Frescoes in Chapelle St-Créspin

The itinerary passes the **Château de Montesson**, encircled by a moat; the entrance pavilion is crowned by an unusual roof. The adjoining round tower has a highly original onion-domed roof.

In Hambers, opposite the church, turn left onto D 236. After 2.5km/1.5mi turn left again onto the narrow road leading to the Butte de Montaigu.

Butte de Montaigu★
Allow 15min on foot there and back from the car park.
The mound, crowned by an old chapel, is only 290m/952ft high but, because of its isolation, makes an excellent viewpoint from which to see the Coëvrons rising to the southeast, Évron, Ste-Suzanne on its rock spike, to the south, Mayenne and its forest, to the northwest and the forests of Andaines and Pail to the north and northeast.

Return to D 236 and continue south through Chellé. At the T-junction turn left onto D 7 at the entrance to Mézangers village; turn right to the Château du Rocher.

Château du Rocher★
Allow 30min on foot there and back. Exterior of château: mid-Jun–Sept daily 10am–noon, 2–6pm. No charge.

A gallery of five low rounded arches runs the length of the Renaissance façade. Delicate sculptures adorn the buildings. The more austere 15C façade faces the lake in the park.

Return to D 7 and continue south to return to Évron.

Les Bois des Vallons
36km/22.5mi – allow about 1hr.

From Évron take D 32 west. On the west side of Brée turn right onto D 557. On approaching St-Ouen-des-Vallons turn right to the Château de la Roche-Pichemer.

Château de la Roche-Pichemer
Open Jul–mid-Aug 2–6pm. No charge. Park near the moat, outside the gate.
The château consists of two main Renaissance wings built at right angles and covered with tall slate roofs. Massive square pavilions project from each corner, adding considerable dignity to the building, fronted by formal gardens.

From St-Ouen-des-Vallons take D 129 and D 24 south via Montsûrs to La Chapelle-Rainsouin.

La Chapelle-Rainsouin
A room off the church chancel contains a beautiful 16C polychrome stone **Entombment★**.

Take D 20 NE. In Châtres-la-Forêt turn right onto D 562. Further, turn right again to the Château de Monteclerc.

Château de Monteclerc
Closed to the public. Leave the car at the beginning of the avenue.
The château, built at the very beginning of the 17C, stands in sober dignity at the far end of a vast courtyard. The drawbridge lodge has a rounded roof crowned by a lantern turret.

Return to Châtres-la-Forêt; turn right onto D 20 to return to Évron.

Ville Romaine de Jublains★

This archaeological site offers a valuable insight into urban life under the Romans. The baths, the ruins of a Roman fort, the temple and the theatre are the best Gallo-Roman period remains in the region.

- **Population:** 689.
- **Michelin Map:** 310: G-5
- **Info:** 02 43 04 3033. www.jublains.fr.
- **Location:** The remains of the Roman city are 10km/6mi SE of Mayenne; 14km/8.5mi NW of Évron.
- **Don't Miss:** The remarkably preserved theatre.
- **Timing:** If you are near Jublains in late July or early August, try to attend a musical performance organised by Les Nuits de la Mayenne (www.nuitsdelamayenne.com).

A BIT OF HISTORY

Following the conquest of Gaul by Julius Caesar (50 BC), the Romans divided the country into districts and built towns; the town of Noviodunum (Jublains) was built at an ancient crossroads as an important link in the road network of the Roman Empire. Its main role as a sanctuary is shown by the alignment of the public buildings along the axis of the temple.

SIGHTS

Musée départemental d'Archéologie

Situated at the entry to the fortress, 13 r. de la Libération. Open May–Sept daily 9am–6pm; Oct–Apr Tue–Sun 9.30am–12.30pm, 1.30–5.30pm (open Mon on holidays). Closed 1 Jan, 25 Dec. 4.50€. 02 43 04 30 16.

This museum uses modern techniques to present archaeological themes of the Mayenne region, in particular the palaeolithic site at Saulges with its decorated cave, the Gaulish and Gallo-Roman sanctuaries and the development of the Roman town, then called Noviodunum. A large model gives a good idea of what the town looked like in ancient times.

Forteresse gallo-romaine

The fortress consists of three concentric parts. The central building, the oldest part of the fortress dating from the early 3C, is a massive rectangular storehouse with four angle towers. During the crisis which shook the Roman Empire at the end of the 3C (invasions, military anarchy, peasant rebellions, etc.), the storehouse was surrounded by a rampart of raised earth and a moat. This moat was later filled in and fortified walls were erected around AD 290, just before the whole site was abandoned.

Public baths

Below the church; entrance through the Syndicat d'Initiative. See museum opening times.

The building, which dates from the late 1C, was altered in the 3C and transformed into a Christian church at the end of the Gallo-Roman period. The layout of the baths is shown on a plan; one can see the main rooms: the cold bath *(frigidarium)* paved in blue schist, the warm room *(tepidarium)*, the sweating room *(laconicum)*. The hot bath *(cella soliaris)* is situated beyond the excavated part.

Theatre

The theatre was offered to the town by a rich Gaul, Orgetorix (c. 81–83).

Temple

The temple can be visited freely; brochures are distributed at the museum or at the Syndicat d'Initiative.

The temple is situated at the other end of the Roman town, 800m/0.5mi from the theatre. Its proportions were vast (each side 80m/262.5ft long) and limestone was brought from the Loire region.

Lassay-les-Châteaux★

On the edge of this ancient market town stands an imposing fortress. A few buildings have been restored, revealing some splendid red-granite façades such as the Maison du Bailly.

- **Population:** 2 450.
- **Michelin Map:** 310: G-4.
- **Info:** 8 rue du Château. ℘02 43 04 74 33.
- **Location:** Lassay lies on D 34 between Bagnoles-de-l'Orne (17km/10.6mi NE) and Mayenne (19km/12mi SW).
- **Don't Miss:** For a good overall view of the castle take the path under the stone bridge at the foot of the towers.
- **Timing:** Walks are traced in the surrounding countryside among the hedgerows *(bocage)*.

The Château★

Guided tours (1hr) Jun–Sept daily 2.30–6.30pm. Easter–May Sat–Sun and public holidays 2.30–6.30pm. 5.50€. ℘02 43 04 71 22.

The castle, which dominates the village with its eight pepper-pot towers linked by a strong curtain wall, was built in 1458 in place of an older building dismantled in 1417 during the Hundred Years' War. A prime example of military architecture under the reign of Charles VII, the castle evokes three famous people: King Henri IV, the writer and poet Victor Hugo and the chemist A L de Lavoisier, who was a prisoner in the castle during the Revolution. The bridge spanning the moat leads to the barbican, a fortified structure defending the entrance. The two towers guarding the drawbridge are linked by living quarters, in which 16C and 17C weapons and furniture are displayed. The casemates can be seen at the foot of the barbican. The tour ends with a stroll in the park.

ADDRESSES

STAY

La Ferme de la Prémoudière – *61330 St-Denis-de-Villenette, 11.5km/7mi N via D 117 dir. Domfront, then D 52 at Sept-Forges. ℘02 33 37 23 27. www.lapremoudiere.com. 5 rooms. Restaurant.* Former cellars have been converted into very pleasant guest rooms. Peace and quiet are guaranteed and you can enjoy farm produce and home-made redberry jam as part of your breakfast.

Laval★

The first thing that strikes any visitor to Laval is the River Mayenne, which flows gently through the centre of town, as it has since the city was founded in the year 1000. The town has a picturesque château and old half-timbered houses, and has produced many distinguished citizens *(see sidebar, p256)*.

You can tour the old city by yourself: it should take about 1hr, not counting visits to the château, museums and churches.

- **Population:** 148 964.
- **Michelin Map:** 310: E-6.
- **Info:** 1 allée du Vieux-St-Louis. ℘02 43 49 46 46. www.laval-tourisme.com.
- **Location:** Laval is 32km/20mi S of Mayenne by D 162. Le Mans is 86km/53.4mi to the E on N 157.
- **Don't Miss:** A walk along the docks to see the old *bateau-lavoir* St-Julien.

WHERE TO STAY

Grand Hôtel de Paris.......... ①
Le Bas du Gast (Chambre d'hôte)............. ④
Marin'Hôtel.......................... ⑦
Village Vacances Pêche (Camping)............. ⑩

WHERE TO EAT

Antiquaire (L').......................... ①
Bonne Auberge (À la)......... ④
Edelweiss (L')......................... ⑦
Gerbe de Blé (La).................. ⑩
Table Ronde (La).................. ⑬

STREETS INDEX

Allègre (Promenade Anne d')........1
Grande-Rue..............................2
Orfèvres (R. des)...................3
Trinité (R. de la)......................4

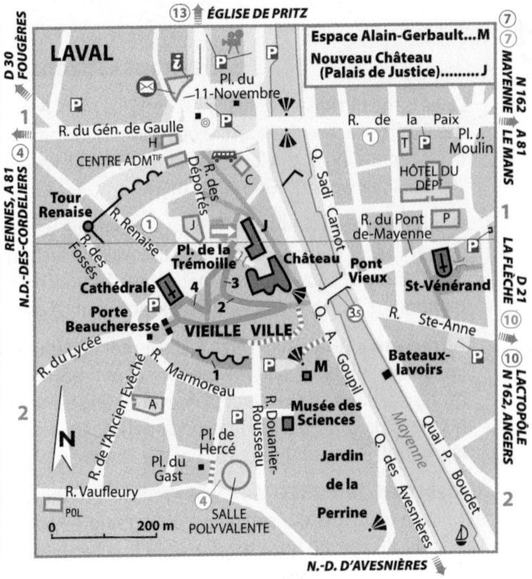

WALKING TOUR

OLD TOWN★

Allow 1hr.

Place de la Trémoille

The square is named after the last of the local lords, guillotined during the Revolution. On the east side stands the Renaissance façade of the 16C **Nouveau Château** built for the Count of Laval; it was enlarged in the 19C and now houses the law courts.

Rue des Orfèvres

The narrow street which runs south into Grande-Rue is lined with beautiful 16C overhanging houses and 18C mansions. At the T-junction stands the Renaissance house (1550) of the Master of the Royal Hunt (Grand Veneur).

Grande-Rue

This was the main street of the medieval city; it descends to the River Mayenne between rows of old houses, some half-timbered with projecting upper storeys, others in stone with Renaissance decoration.

Turn right onto rue de Chapelle.

The street climbs between medieval and Renaissance houses to a charming statue of St René in a niche *(right)* at the top.

Go straight ahead onto rue des Serruriers.

South of the Beucheresse Gate are two slightly askew half-timbered houses.

Porte Beucheresse

In former days this 14C gate, then called Porte des Bûcherons, opened directly into the forest; its two round towers, topped with machicolations, were once part of the town walls. Henri Rousseau was born in the south tower, where his father worked as a tinsmith.

Cathédrale

The building has been altered many times but the nave and the transept crossing are covered with Angevin vaulting, characterised by curved rib vaulting in which the keystones are at different heights.

The walls are hung with Aubusson tapestries (early 17C) depicting the story of Judith and Holofernes in six panels. On the left pillar near the chancel is a very beautiful triptych painted by the Antwerp Mannerist School in the 16C; it presents the Martyrdom of St John the Apostle when closed and three scenes

Famous Citizens

Laval is the birthplace of many exceptional men. **Ambroise Paré** (1517–90) was the first to practise the ligature of arteries during amputations and is deserving of his reputation as the father of surgery: yet he was modest about his success, "I dress their wounds, God cures them."

Henri Rousseau (1844–1910), whose nickname was Le Douanier (the Customs Officer), was a tax collector in Paris. He was the archetype of the modern naïve artist, and was known for the meticulous approach which he brought to his paintings of lush jungles, wild beasts and exotic figures.

Alfred Jarry (1873–1907) was the inventor of pataphysics, the science of imaginary solutions, and the forerunner of the Surrealists. He created the grotesque satirical character of *Père Ubu, King of Poland*, when he was still in his teens. Jarry died destitute and largely unappreciated. Today, however, he is honoured as one of the creators of the Theatre of the Absurd.

Alain Gerbault (1893–1941) was a renowned tennis player, as well as sailor. In 1923 he made the transatlantic crossing single-handed; he died in the Polynesian islands. His second boat, the *Fire-Crest II*, is exhibited in the Jardin de la Perrine.

Jean Cottereau, called Jean Chouan, led Royalist troops during the French Revolution. In 1793 the Royalists *(Les Blancs)* occupied Laval and beneath its walls defeated the Republican army of General Lechelle. The name **Chouan** was adopted from their rallying cry, the hoot of the tawny owl *(chat-huant)*.

from the life of John the Baptist when open. In the north transept there is an imposing revolving door, which was carved in the 18C.

On leaving the cathedral, walk round the east end to admire the northeast door (facing the law courts), which is decorated with 17C terracotta statues.

Rue de la Trinité

One of the old houses dates from the 16C and is adorned with statues of the Virgin and the Saints.

Turn left onto rue du Pin-Doré which ends in place de la Trémoille.

Quays★

The bateau-lavoir St-Julien, quai Paul-Boudet: Jul–Aug Tue–Sun 2–6pm. No charge.

The quays on the east bank provide the best overall **views**★ of Laval across the River Mayenne. From the **Pont Vieux**, a 13C humpback bridge, there is a more detailed view of the old town.

The **bateaux-lavoirs**, the last public wash houses in Laval, are moored along quai Paul Boudet. One of these, the **St-Julien**, has been restored.

Jardin de la Perrine★

The terraces of these public gardens command attractive views. As well as a rose garden there are many tall trees, ponds, waterfalls, lawns and flower beds.

The Château★

Allow 1hr.

Pl. de La Trémoille. Open Tue–Sun May–mid-Sept 10am–6pm (14 Jul and 15 Aug 2–6pm); rest of the year 2–5pm. Unaccompanied visit 1€. Guided tours Tue–Sat 2–5pm, Sun 2–6pm (last departure 1hr before closing). 2€. 02 43 53 39 89. www.laval-tourisme.com.

To the right of the railings in front of the law courts stands a noble 17C porch, next to an early 16C half-timbered house. Through the porch is the courtyard of the old castle enclosed by ramparts (from the top of the walls there is a picturesque **view**★ of the old town). In its present state the bulk of the castle dates from the 13C and 15C; the windows and dormers in white tufa, carved with scrolls in the Italian style, were added in the 16C. The crypt and the keep are the oldest parts (12C–13C).

Donjon
Originally separated from the courtyard by a moat, the keep was later incorporated between the two wings of the castle. Within the keep, the most interesting feature is the extraordinary **timber roof**★★, which was built c. 1100 to an ingenious circular design. Great beams, radiating from the centre like the spokes of a wheel, project beyond the walls (which are over 2m/6.6ft thick) to support the wooden defensive gallery that projects out to permit defence of the gate and the base of the walls.

SIGHTS
Musée d'Art naïf★
Within castle. ○*Same hours as for the old château.* ◉*1€.*
The Museum of Naïve Painting, which can be visited separately from the castle and the keep, displays a number of canvases by painters from France, Croatia, Germany, Brazil, etc. A reconstruction of Rousseau's (Le Douanier) studio contains mementoes of the artist.

Musée des Sciences
21 r. Douanier-Rousseau. ○*Open daily except public holidays 10am–noon, 2–6pm.* ○*Closed between exhibits.* ◉*2€ (1st Sun of month no charge).* ℘*02 43 49 47 81.*
The Science Museum is housed in an imposing building. The archaeological exhibits are the result of excavations carried out in the Laval region. The 19C astronomical clock in its carved wooden case is a fine exhibit.

Notre-Dame-d'Avesnières Basilica
1.5km/1mi S, via the quai d'Avesnières.
This ancient sanctuary dedicated to the Virgin Mary was made into a basilica in 1898. The Romanesque **east end**★ is best seen from Avesnières Bridge: the

chancel, the ambulatory and the five radiating chapels. The attractive Gothic-Renaissance spire is an identical copy, made in 1871, of the original which was erected in 1538.
The fine Romanesque chancel consists of three storeys of arches and bays. The modern stained glass is by Max Ingrand.

Église St-Vénérand
The nave of the church is flanked by double aisles. The north front, facing the street, has a Flamboyant **door**★ decorated with an attractive 17C terracotta figure of the Virgin.
Tour Renaise – This 15C round machicolated tower belongs to the old walls.

Église Notre-Dame-des-Cordeliers★
Built between 1397 and 1407, this former chapel of a Franciscan monastery contains a remarkable set of seven **altarpieces**★★ from the 17C. Six of them can be seen in the north aisle *(lighting is essential; token available from the tourist office)*; they were carved out of tufa and marble by the local architect **Pierre Corbineau** (1600–78).

Ancienne Église de Pritz
2km/1mi N. Leave Laval by allée de la Résistance, rue du Vieux-St-Louis and D 104. ○━*Closed to the public.*
This simple church stands on the right of the road in the hamlet called Pritz and is surrounded by a garden. It dates from about the year 1 000 and was altered and enlarged in the Romanesque period.

🚗 DRIVING TOUR

▷ *15km/9mi west by rue du Général-de-Gaulle and N 157.*

Abbaye de Clermont
♿○*Open daily Mar–mid Sept 9am–6.30pm; rest of the year 9.30am–4.30pm.* ◉*4€.* ℘*02 43 02 11 96.*
The ruins stand in open country watered by many streams. The abbey was

founded in 1152, as a daughter house of Clairvaux, by St Bernard with the support of Guy V, Count of Laval; it was a thriving monastic community until the Revolution.
The square east end of the **church** comes into view before the dilapidated west front and the austere Romanesque porch with its three round-headed openings. South of the church is the **cloister garth**. The wooden cloister galleries have not survived, but the **lay brothers' range** (west) contains the cellar and the refectory.

Return to Laval and then take quai d'Avesnières and D 1 south out of town.

The road goes down to the banks of the Mayenne, providing a nice view over the former Porte de l'Huisserie.

Bear left onto D 112 towards Entrammes; after 1km/0.6mi fork left onto a narrow road to L'Enclos et Bonne (Lock).

The road descends to the bank of the River Mayenne, offering a very attractive **view★** of the river, the lock, a mill and a castle.

Return to D 112 and continue south; bear left onto D 103.

Trappe du Port-du-Salut

No charge.
Until 1959 the famous Port-Salut cheese was made here by the Trappist monks. They still make cheese today but under a different name.
The **large and small chapels** are open to the public.

Continue east on D 103.

Entrammes

Ancient baths. Guided tour (1hr15min) daily mid-Jul–mid-Aug 10.30am–12.30pm, 3–7pm; last weekend Jun–mid-Jul and mid-Aug–1st weekend Sept 3–7pm; rest of the year (except last weekend Oct–1st weekend Apr) Sat–Sun and public holidays 3–6pm. 2.80€ 02 43 49 46 46.
During recent restoration work inside the church, remains of the town's **ancient baths** were discovered (*see Ville Romaine de JUBLAINS*). An audiovisual presentation explains the site.

Parné-sur-Roc

The church belonging to the village on the rock was built in the 11C and contains some interesting **mural paintings** (late-15C to early 16C). On the left one sees the silhouette of the resurrected Christ against a background of red stars and a Madonna Dolorosa; on the right, Cosmas and Damian, two brothers who practised medicine and were popular in the Middle Ages.

Take D 21 to return to Laval.

ADDRESSES

STAY

Camping Village Vacances Pêche – *53170 Villiers-Charlemagne, 20km/12.5mi S of Laval via N 162. 02 43 07 71 68. www.sudmayenne.com. Closed Nov–Mar. 20 sites. Reservations advised.* Keen anglers will be able to indulge in their hobby at leisure. The lake abounds in pike, pike-perch and carp. Campers have their own bathroom installations and room to store fishing tackle. You can rent small chalets with individual terraces raised on piles.

Marin'Hotel – *102 av. Robert-Buron. 02 43 53 09 63. www.marin-hotel.fr. 25 rooms. 7€.* On a street corner near the train station, the building is decorated with grotesque masks that testify to its age. The rooms, however, are up to date, functional and well soundproofed from the street noise. The breakfast room has a nautical theme.

Best Western Hôtel de Paris – *22 r. de la Paix. ☎02 43 53 76 20. Closed 24–26, 31 Dec–2 Jan. 50 rooms. ☕8€.* Hotel situated right in the town centre, close to the shopping area. The simple rooms with their white roughcast walls and coloured wood furniture are well soundproofed.

Chambre d'hôte Le Bas du Gast – *6 r. de la Halle-aux-Toiles, across from the Salle Polyvalente. ☎02 43 49 22 79. www.chateaulebasdugast.fr. Closed Dec–15 Mar. 4 rooms. ☕.* Built in the centre of Laval's old quarter, this 17C–18C castle is surrounded by a beautiful garden featuring trimmed box trees. As you go in, note the lovely smell of wax on the oak parquet flooring and period furniture. The spacious guest rooms have been thoughtfully decorated.

EAT

L'Édelweiss – *99 av. R-Buron. ☎02 43 53 1100. Closed 16–24 Feb, 15 Jul–12 Aug, Sun eve, Mon and holidays.* Next to the train station, a contemporary dining room in pastel tones, where you can enjoy traditional cuisine without fuss and in a friendly setting.

À La Bonne Auberge – *170 r. de Bretagne. ☎02 43 69 07 81. www.alabonneauberge.com. Closed 19–26 Feb, 1–22 Aug, 24 Dec–8 Jan, Fri eve, Sun eve and Sat.* The pastel-coloured decoration of the dining room gives this inn an intimate, muted atmosphere. The veranda adds light and an impression of spaciousness. Well-prepared cuisine at reasonable prices. Selection of comfortable rooms.

L'Antiquaire – *5 r. Béliers. ☎02 43 53 66 76. Closed 16–24 Feb, 13 Jul–5 Aug,Sat lunch, Sun evening and Wed.* This restaurant occupies the ground floor of an old Laval house. In the well-furnished dining room, turn of the 20th century British décor in tones of red. Generous portions of traditional cuisine, with a few modern touches.

Gerbe de Blé – *83 r. Victor-Boissel. ☎02 43 53 14 10. www.gerbedeble.com. Closed 1st 2 weeks Aug and Sat.* This renowned family-run establishment is worth a detour. The warm décor of wood panelling in shades of golden wheat is conducive to relaxation. The traditional cuisine is well prepared and appetising. A few guest rooms as well.

La Table Ronde – *Pl. de la Mairie, 53810 Changé, 4km/2.5mi N of Laval via D 104. ☎02 43 53 43 33. Closed 1 week in Feb, 3 weeks in Aug, Sun eve, Wed eve and Mon.* Opposite the château. Upstairs, the gastronomical restaurant: Louis XVI-style chairs and handsome tables laid with care; downstairs, the bistro.

NIGHTLIFE

Le Johannesburg –*5 r. de la Trinité, Old Laval, near the Cathedral. ☎02 43 53 21 21 . Open Sun–Tue, Thu 9pm–2am; tavern noon–2.30pm and after 7pm. Closed last week Jul, 1st 2 weeks Aug.* Behind a 17C façade, an old Cistercian abbey now serves as a tavern and a pub, tucked away in a very deep cellar. An amiable way to while away evening hours, one of the most pleasant spots in Laval.

SHOPPING

Abbaye de la Coudre – *r. St-Benoît. ☎02 43 02 85 85. www.abbaye-coudre.com. Closed Easter, 25 Dec.* Under beautiful rafters and lit by lightwells in the roof, this boutique offers products made by monastic communities: fruit pastes, jams, preserves of beer and wine, Chimay beer, coffee from Cameroon, spirits, biscuits, Bonneval chocolate, honey, nougat, caramels ... and the speciality of the house, Trappist cheese aged two months in the abbey cellars.

LEISURE

Golf de Laval-Changé – *La Chabossière, 53810 Changé. ☎02 43 53 16 03. www.laval53-golf.com. Closed 25 Dec–5 Jan.* Laid out on ondulating ground covering 82ha/203 acres, this splendid golf course offers two rounds of 9 and 18 holes by the River Mayenne. From the bar/restaurant, there is a superb view of the course. Beginners' courses and equipment rental.

TOURS

Guided tours – Laval, which is classified as a City of Art and History, offers tours conducted by highly qualified guides trained by the Ministry of Culture. Contact the tourist office.

CALENDAR

The Nights of the Mayenne – *Mid-Jul–mid-Aug.* Shows and performances at three major sites: Ste-Suzanne, Jublains and Laval. Creativity is unleashed as the Mayenne region celebrates its rich heritage with musical and theatrical programmes. *℘02 43 53 63 90. www.nuitsdelamayenne.com.*

Night-time musical tours – *Mid-Jul–mid-Aug, every Tue.* A pleasant way to visit the sights of Laval, guided by actors in period costmes. Contact the tourist office.

Les Uburlesques – *1st weekend of Sept.* A street festival in the spirit of *Ubu roi*, the play – or rather, theatrical gesture, by Alfred Jarry.

Mayenne

Mayenne is a bridgehead town whose strategic importance in the past was compounded by the existence of a powerful fortress.

- **Population:** 299 000.
- **Michelin Map:** 310: E-5.
- **Info:** Quai de Waiblingen. ℘02 43 04 19 37. www.mairie-mayenne.net.
- **Location:** Mayenne is on the route from Le Mans (104km/64.5mi SE) to Mont-St-Michel. It is also between Caen (120km/74mi N) and Laval (32km/20mi S).
- **Don't Miss:** The pretty villages in the forest of Mayenne.
- **Timing:** Take a day to see the town, and to enjoy the many nautical activities on the Mayenne river.

A BIT OF HISTORY

Cardinal Mazarin originally undertook to make the River Mayenne navigable from Lavalle to Mayenne in the 17C. The town's key role was proved during World War II. By 8 June 1944, Mayenne had been nearly levelled, but the bridge remained intact. Thanks to the heroism of an American sergeant, Mack Racken, the only bridge still spanning the River Mayenne was saved to serve the Allies.

SIGHTS

Château Carolingien

pl. Juhel. ♿ Open Jul–Aug daily 10am–7pm; Apr–Jun and Sept Tue–Sun 9am–6pm; rest of the year Tue–Sun 9am–12.30pm, 2–7pm; open Mon public holidays. Closed 1 Jan, 1 May, 25 Dec. 4€. ℘02 43 00 17 17. www.museeduchateaudemayenne.fr.

During construction work on a new cultural centre in 1993, workers discovered an old fortress dating from the time of the Carolingian kings, (751–987) who included Charlemagne. Archaeologists were called in; the new museum presents artefacts from 15 years of digs, in lively displays.

The present castle, reinforced several times in the 11C–15C, stands on the hill on the west bank of the river. It suffered frequent siege, and William the Conqueror took it by cunning.

The perimeter wall remains, giving the castle a truly feudal appearance. The promenade between the curtain walls and the town gardens commands an attractive **view**★ of the town.

Basilique Notre-Dame

This church has been remodelled several times. The west front along with the pillars and arches in the nave are 12C; the transept walls and windows are 16C. The church was rebuilt at the end of the 19C in the Gothic style.

Église St-Martin

Located opposite the château, on the hillside on the other side of the river. Open Easter–Oct daily 9.30am–5pm. In the 11C the church belonged to Marmoutiers Abbey in Tours, and both the apse and transept date from this period.The modern stained glass, like that in the Basilique Notre-Dame, is by the master glazier Maurice Rocher.

EXCURSIONS

Forêt de Mayenne (oak, elm and coppice): **Fontaine-Daniel** (a pool overlooked by an attractive chapel and an **exhibition centre**), flower-decked houses and an old Cistercian abbey; **Chailland** (statue of a Virgin on top of a rocky escarpment). *Exhibition centre displaying fabrics including Mayenne cloth (toile de Mayenne). No charge. 02 43 00 34 80. www.toilesdemayenne.com. Open Mon–Sat 9am–noon, 1.30–6pm. Closed public holidays.*

ADDRESSES

EAT

Beau Rivage – *Rte de St-Baudelle, 53100 Moulay, 4km/2.5mi S. 02 43 00 49 13. www.restaurantbeaurivage.com. Closed Sun eve and Mon.* The River Mayenne flows just below the shaded terrace. In cool weather, relax in the vast dining room with exposed timber-work and watch meat and fish being grilled in the brick-built fireplace.

La Marjolaine – *Le Bas-Mont, 53100 Moulay, 6.5km/4mi S. 02 43 00 48 42. www.lamarjolaine.fr. Closed 3–9 Jan, Feb school holidays, Mon lunch and Sun eve.* This stone house stands in a peaceful park. In the cosy dining room modern cuisine and a good selection of wine. At lunchtime, a bistro for fast meals. 23 comfortable, spacious rooms.

LEISURE

Base de bateaux électriques et location de vélos – *Halte Fluviale. 02 43 32 10 32. www.paysdemayenne-tourisme.fr. Closed Tue in May–Jun and Sept, and Oct–Apr.* Hire of boats and bicycles.

Canoe-Kayak – *17 r. Pasteur. 02 43 04 18 33. www.kayak-mayenne.fr.st. Open Wed and Sat 2–4pm.* This friendly club, open all year, offers lessons, rentals and storage.

Sailboards and dinghies – *Base Départementale de Voile, La Haie-Traversière. 02 43 04 00 68. Closed Dec–Feb.* Offers lessons, rentals, a snack-bar and overnight accommodations, even for visiting sailors.

Pontmain

In this village on the border of Brittany on 17 January 1871, during the Franco-Prussian War, the Virgin appeared to several of the village children, including Eugène and Joseph Barbedette, with a message of prayer and hope; 11 days later an Armistice was declared.

- **Population:** 879.
- **Michelin Map:** 310: C–4.
- **Info:** 5 rue de la Grange. 02 43 05 07 74.
- **Location:** Pontmain is 16km/10mi NE of Fougères, 45km/28mi NW of Mayenne, 6km/4mi SW of Landivy and 35km/22mi SW of Mortain.
- **Don't Miss:** The lovely garden of la Pellerine, with its water-lilies, just 21km/13mi S of Pontmain.

SIGHTS

Grange Barbedette

It was from this thatched barn that the children, and then the other villagers, saw the Virgin in the sky above the house of Augustin Guidecoq on the far side of the square.

Basilique

The vast neo-Gothic basilica with its twin granite spires was built at the end of the 19C. The ten stained-glass windows in the chancel depict the Virgin's Apparition in Pontmain in Lourdes and La Salette, as well as scenes from the life of Christ.

Chapelle des Missionaires Oblats

Musée des Missions. Open Sun and public holidays 2.30–6pm. Other days on request to M. Elie. No charge. 02 43 30 27 51.

Behind the basilica are the park and Mission of the Oblate Fathers of Mary Immaculate. The 1953 chapel has a heavy appearance from outside – but is surprisingly pleasing within, illuminated by a golden light diffused by stained-glass windows.

Jardin de la Pellerine★

21km/13mi S of Pontmain, on N 12 between Fougères to the W and Ernée to the E. La Larderie, 53220 La Pellerine. Open May–Oct Thu–Fri 10am–6.30pm, Sat–Sun and public holidays 2–6.30pm. 6€. 02 43 05 93 31.

Lovely gardens surround a 17C house: roses, shrubs, arbours and ponds with acquatic plants, including water lilies, on a 2ha/5-acre site.

Ste-Suzanne★

This peaceful village occupies a picturesque setting★ on a rocky promontory commanding the north bank of the Erve. In the 11C, the viscounts of Beaumont built on the site one of the most important Maine strong points, the only one to successfully resist William the Conqueror.

- **Population:** 960.
- **Michelin Map:** 310: G-6.
- **Info:** 1 rue du Chenil. 02 43 01 43 60.
- **Location:** Ste-Suzanne is 50km/31mi E of Le Mans, 32km/20mi W of Laval.
- **Don't Miss:** The view from the castle keep.
- **Timing:** Half a day.
- **Kids:** Look into the Théatrales Pitchoun, a summer programme for children.

SIGHTS

Viewing Table

Via rue du Grenier à Sel.

From the tower you see the town nestled around its 11C keep, the new town beyond the ramparts and the surrounding countryside.

Promenade de la Poterne

The walk along the ramparts starts at the Tour du Guet (watchtower), and passes the castle and the Porte de Fer (Iron Gate). The second half of the walk, ending at the Porte du Guichet (Wicket Gate), provides distant views *(northeast)* of the Coëvrons Hills and *(north)* of Mont Rochard and the Butte de Montaigu topped by St Michael's Chapel.

Church

Interesting statues include a gracious St Suzanne, a 16C polychrome wood statue and a 14C stone Virgin and Child.

Dolmen des Erves

3km/2mi by D 143 or the Assé-le-Béranger road.

This megalithic monument was built during the 4th millennium BC.

Musée de l'Auditoire

7 Grande-Rue. Open Jul–Aug daily 2–6pm. 4€ (children 2.50€). 02 43 01 42 65. www.museeauditoire.com

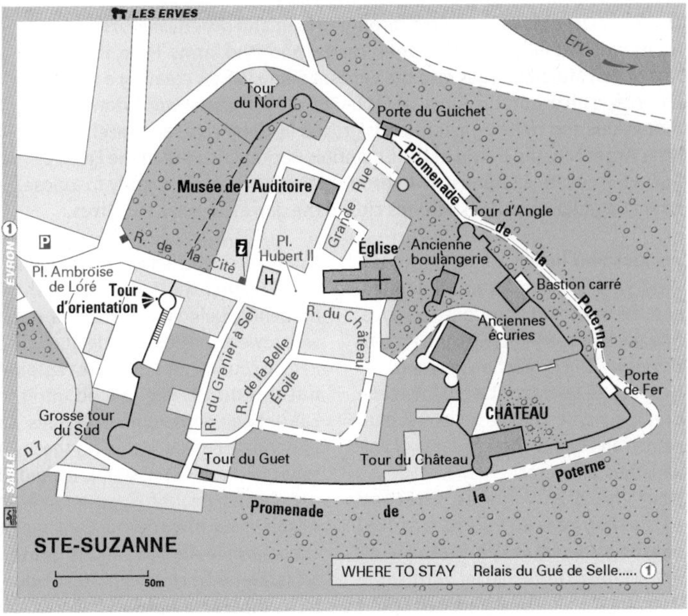

The building, a courthouse in the 17C and 18C, now houses an exhibition on the medieval town of Ste-Suzanne.

Château

Open May–Sept daily 9am–6pm; rest of the year Tue–Sun 9.30am–12.30pm, 1.30–5.30pm (open Mon when public holiday). Closed 1 Jan, 25 Dec. No charge. 02 43 01 40 77.

The second floor of this early 17C château has an astonishing **timberwork roof** in the form of an upturned keel.

DRIVING TOUR

Saulges

19km/12mi S by D 125 and D 235.

The road follows the Erve Valley. In Saulges, in the square opposite the parish church stands **Église St-Pierre**. Steps in the 16C **Chapelle St-Sérénède** lead down into a rare Merovingian building, the 7C **Chapelle St-Pierre**.

Grottes de Saulges

Guided tours (45min) Jul–Aug daily 10am–11.30am, 2–6pm; Sept–mid-Nov and mid-Mar–Jun Mon–Sat 2–4.30pm, Sun 10am–11.30am, 2–5.30pm. 8.70€ (2 caves); 5.70€ (1 cave). 02 43 90 51 30. www.grottes-de-saulges.com.

The caves **Grotte à Margot** and **Grotte de Rochefort** present some interesting geological formations and traces of human habitation.

Take D 554 NW towards Vaiges; after 1km/0.6mi turn left onto a downhill road to a car park; walk over footbridge.

Oratoire St-Cénéré

The hermitage is secluded at the foot of a rocky slope, near where the Erve forms a small lake known for its fishing.

ADDRESSES

STAY & EAT

€€€–€€€€ **Relais du Gué de Selle** – *rte de Mayenne, 53600 Évron – Mézangers, 5km/3mi N. 02 43 91 20 00. www.relais-du-gue-de-selle.com. Closed Mon lunch Jun–Sept, Fri and Sun eves Oct–May. 24 rooms. 11€.* Old restored farm with well fitted-out rooms and a lovely garden.

ORNE

The River Orne flows to the sea through this inland *département*, renowned for its wooded hills, pretty villages, castles and stud farms. Here, the stony Armorican Massif merges into the verdant Seine Valley, creating a varied landscape incorporating ancient (360–286 million years) worn-down mountains and rolling pasturelands grazed by dairy cows and racehorses. Near Argentan, the Battle of the Chambois Pocket (also called the Falaise Pocket) from 18–22 August 1944 brought the Battle of Normandy to a close, when Canadian and Polish troops closed the gap at Tournai-sur-Dives.

Walkers and hikers are drawn to the rugged hills of the **Alpes Mancelles**, and the forests of Perseigne, Écouves, Andaines and Bellême, with their splendid views. Once, great abbeys and castles such as **Domfront** were the scene of epic dynastic struggles involving both French and English descendants of William the Conqueror.

Near the great moated **Château of Carrouges**, the **Parc naturel régional Normandie-Maine** covers 2 350sq km/907sq m, with some 2 500km/1 553mi of signposted paths. **Bagnoles-de-l'Orme**, in a superb setting on a lake next to the forest of Andaines, sprung as a thermal spa town from a 19C developer's plans; its centre is still a Belle Époque jewel. The nearby horse farm at the picturesque village of **Juvigny-sous-Andaine** offers a horse-show and rides to please children. To the southeast, the **Perche** area around the town of **Bellême**, is home to the sturdy Percheron horses; the old houses here vary from the typical Norman half-timbering, being made of stone, often with towers and defensive features. The Perche country and the **Parc régional naturel du Perche** extend into the Eure-et-Loir département. At **Sées**, an episcopal seat since the 4C, the twin spires of the 13C–14C Gothic cathedral rise above a beautifully restored little village. **Vimoutiers** gave us Camembert cheese, while **Alençon** and **Argentan** are renowned for lacework. Near Argentan is the **Haras National du Pin**, the celebrated stud farm, set up by Colbert in 1665 and occupying an 18C château on grounds designed by André le Nôtre (1613–1700), gardener to Louis XIV. To the west, the *bocage* country surrounds the town of **Flers**, whose 16C château holds an art museum. From the nearby **Mont de Cerisy** are views over the hedgerows and a spring rhododendron display.

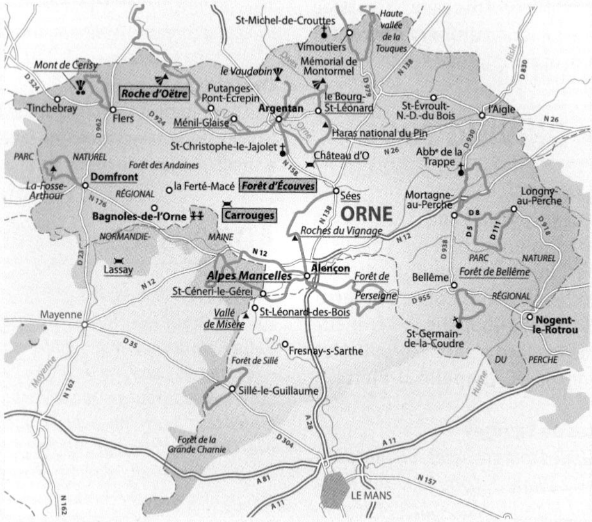

L'Aigle

L'Aigle is at its best on Tuesday, when it holds the third-largest market in France. One of the main towns in the Upper Risle Valley, L'Aigle is a centre for traditional metalwork industries: steel drawing mills produce pins, needles, staples and more. The historic centre is place St-Martin, with its attractive church.

- **Population:** 8 489.
- **Michelin Map:** 310: M-2.
- **Info:** Place Fulbert-de-Beina. 02 33 84 16 10. www.paysdelaigle.com.
- **Location:** L'Aigle lies between the Pays d'Ouche and the Perche, on the road linking Dreux, 59km/37mi to the E, to Argentan. Lisieux is only 56km/35mi NW on D 519.
- **Parking:** You will find parking on the public squares: de la Halle, de l'Europe, de Verdun and de Bois-Landry.
- **Don't Miss:** The Tuesday market; the museum of La Grosse Forge at Aube.
- **Timing:** Give yourself half a day at L'Aigle before visiting the museums at Aube.
- **Kids:** The museum of the Comtesse de Ségur (1799–1874), France's most famous children's author, and the machinery at the Grosse Forge museum at Aube.

CHÂTEAU

Musée de la Vigne et du Vin and Musée de l'Étiquette: *Open Apr–Jun and Sept–Oct Tue–Sun 11am–6pm; Jul–Aug daily 11am–6pm. 9€. 02 44 66 21 30. www.chateauaigle.ch.*

The château, which houses the town hall and **two museums**, was built in 1690 on the site of an 11C fortress, by Fulbert de Beina, Lord of L'Aigle and vassal of the dukes of Normandy. He is said to have discovered an eagle's nest on the site, hence the name of the town.

The plans were the work of Mansart (Jules Hardouin 1646–1708), who designed the Château of Versailles for Louis XIV.

Musée Municipal d'Aigle

Located in the buildings surrounding the château. Open Apr–Oct Tue–Wed and Sat–Sun 2–6pm. 3.60€.

The museum houses le Musée Juin 44, the Météorite de l'Aigle exhibition and an archaeology exhibition:

Musée Juin 44

Located beside the castle, the Battle of Normandy Museum contains wax figures of De Gaulle, Churchill, Leclerc, Roosevelt, Stalin, etc. and their recorded voices. The Battle of Normandy is represented on a 36sq m/387.5sq ft relief map and events are traced on dioramas. A small archaeological museum houses some interesting objects.

SIGHTS

Église St-Martin

Centre of town, presbytery, r. des Emangeards. 02 33 24 08 30.

An elaborate late-15C square tower contrasts with a small 12C one built of red iron agglomerate *(grison)* and surmounted by a more recent spire. Beautiful modern statues stand in niches between the windows of the south nave, added in the 16C.

Above the high altar (1656) is a beautiful carved wooden altarpiece, consisting of four twisted columns capped by Corinthian capitals and decorated with vine leaves, bunches of grapes and cherubs. The central composition, attributed to Charles Lebrun (1619–90), a celebrated artist under Louis XIV, shows the Descent from the Cross.

Musée des Instruments de Musique

Located in the town hall. Call for opening times. No charge. 02 33 84 16 10.

A double spiral staircase leads to the first floor of the museum. A collection of musical instruments, the gift of a former bandmaster, includes an archaic bass wind instrument known as a serpent used in military music.

EXCURSION

St-Sulpice-sur-Risle

3km/2mi NE by D 930. Open Mon–Fri 3–5pm, telephone beforehand. 02 33 24 15 76.

The **church** adjoins the 13C priory, which was partially rebuilt in the 16C. Among its artworks are a 16C tapestry, a 17C painting of St Cecilia, a statue of St Anne and two stained-glass windows from the 13C and 14C.

AUBE

Musée de la Comtesse de Ségur

7km/4.3mi SW of L'Aigle by N 26. 3 r. de l'Abbé-Derry. Open mid-Jun–mid-Sept Thu–Mon 2–6pm, Wed 4–6pm (last entry 5pm). Closed public holidays. 4€ (6–12 years old 1.50€). Ticket combined with Grosse Forge 6€(children 2€). 02 33 24 60 09. www.musee-comtessedesegur.com.

The Russian-born countess (1799–1864), languishing in the country while the count enjoyed other society, produced very late in life a series of tales for her grandchildren. The books met great success and are still cited, especially *Les Malheurs de Sophie*, but mostly as examples of tedious moralising. The museum's considerable charm lies in its lovely rural setting and frequently changing exhibits evoking 19C children's pastimes as well as aristocratic life and attitudes.

Musée de la Grosse Forge d'Aube

r. de la Vielle-Forge. Open mid-Jun–mid-Sept Wed–Mon 2–6pm (last entry 5.15pm). Guided tours (45min) 15min past every hour. 4€ (6–12 years old 1.50€). Ticket combined with Musée de la Comtesse de Ségur 6€ (children 2€). 02 33 24 60 09.

The **Château des Nouettes**, now a medico-pedagogical institute, was once the residence of Countess Eugène de Ségur.

In the former presbytery at the foot of the church stands the **Musée de la Comtesse de Ségur**, which contains exhibits evoking the life and literary career of the countess. Characters from the writer's novels are represented by a collection of dolls and exhibits (toys, games, books, furniture, etc.).

On the River Risle, as you leave Aube towards L'Aigle, stands the **Musée de la Grosse Forge d'Aube**, which retraces five centuries of metallurgy. This museum has changed very little since the 17C. Note the furnace for refining metals, the massive camshaft hammer and the wooden bellows (a 1995 replica) operated by a paddle wheel.

ADDRESSES

STAY

Hôtel du Dauphin – *pl. de la Halle. 02 33 84 18 00. 30 rooms. 10€. Restaurant.* The older of these two buildings was already a hotel in 1618. The rooms are comfortable, with a mixture of old and modern furniture. A shop sells local products, while the restaurant offers a daily menu in the pleasant dining room. A nice, old-fashioned Renaissance sort of place.

EAT

Le Manoir de Villers – *61550 Villers-en-Ouche, 9km/5.6mi N of St-Évroult via D 230 dir. Bocquencé. 02 33 34 98 00. http://perso.wanadoo.fr/le.manoir.Closed Jan, Tue–Thu, except for hotel guests. Reservations suggested.* This 17C farm includes an equestrian centre and small hotel, as well as the restaurant. The proprietors offer their native Italian cuisine, with delicious home-made pasta, served in friendly, rustic surroundings.

Alençon★

A royal lace manufactory under Louis XIV, Alençon has a rich architectural heritage, a Fine Arts Museum with a collection of lacework and paintings from the 15C–19C, and pleasant waterways and gardens surrounding the pedestrian town centre. Alençon was liberated on 12 August 1944 due to the decisive role of the French 2nd Armoured Division in the Battle of the Falaise-Mortain Pocket.

- **Population:** 28 935.
- **Michelin Map:** 310: J-4.
- **Info:** Maison d'Ozé, place de la Madeleine. 02 33 80 66 33. www.paysdalencon tourisme.com.
- **Location:** From Alençon, roads lead to Paris (195km/122mi E via N 12), and to Brittany, Belgium and Spain. The A 28 leads to Le Mans (58km/36mi to the S) and to Rouen (160km/100mi to the N).
- **Don't Miss:** The little villages of the Alpes Mancelles, especially St-Léonard-des-Bois and St-Céneri-le-Gérei.
- **Timing:** Take a half-day in the town, then enjoy the lovely countryside in the forest of Perseigne or in the Alpes Mancelles.
- **Kids:** At St-Léonard-des-Bois, the domaine of Gasseau offers nature hikes under the trees.

SIGHTS

Musée des Beaux-Arts et de la Dentelle★

Cour carré de la Dentelle. Open Jul–mid-Sept daily 10am–noon, 2–6pm; rest of the year Tue–Sun 10am–noon, 2–6pm. Closed 1 Jan, 1 May, 25 Dec. 3.10€ (no charge 1st Sun of the month). 02 33 32 40 07.

Located in the former Jesuit college (17C), the Museum of Fine Arts and Lace houses paintings from the 15C to the 19C as well as collections of lace. The French and Nordic Schools of the 17C are well represented with canvases by Philippe de Champaigne, Jean Jouvenet, Allegrain, Voet, Ryckaert, Wyck. There is also a fine selection of 19C French painting with works by Boudin, Courbet, Fantin-Latour, Lacombe, Laurens, Legros, Veyrassat, etc.

The presentation of the **lace collection**★ offers a broad review of the principal lacemaking centres in Italy and France. Its display of Alençon lace, which uses a needlepoint technique unique in France, includes the elegant creations of the Alençon lacemakers from the 17C to the present day.

There is also a collection of Cambodian objects brought back by **Adhémar Leclère** (1853–1917), a native of Alençon and 19C governor of Cambodia.

Descent from the Cross, Église Notre-Dame

E. Lambère/MICHELIN

Église Notre-Dame★

Grand-Rue. Allow at least 15min. Open daily 9am–noon, 2–5.30pm. Guided tours available Jun–Aug; ask at the tourist office.

The beautiful 14C–15C Flamboyant Gothic Church of Our Lady was begun

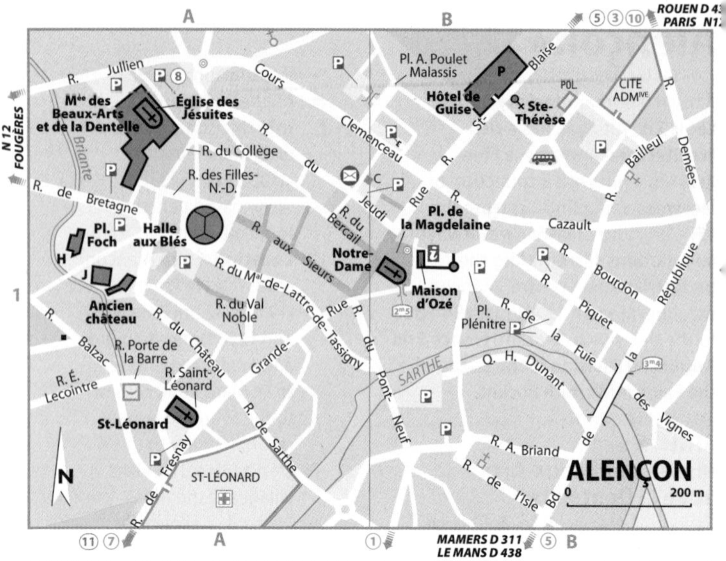

WHERE TO STAY	
Garencière (Chambre d'hôte la)	1
Marmotte (Hôtel)	3
Mercure (Hôtel)	5
Moulin de Linthe (Chambre d'hôte le)	7
Sarceaux (Chambre d'hôte Château de)	10

WHERE TO EAT	
Normande (Auberge)	5
Petit Vatel (Au)	8
Saint-Léo (Le)	11

during the Hundred Years' War. The tower, transept and chancel were rebuilt in the 18C. The elegant three-sided **porch**★, built by Jean Lemoine from 1490 to 1506, is an example of the purest Flamboyant style. All the decoration is concentrated on the upper parts of the church. The Transfiguration in the central gable shows Christ with the Prophets Moses and Elijah; below are the Apostles Peter, James and John, with their backs to the street.

Inside, the sweeping lines of the nave rise to the lierne and tierceron **vaulting** which is highly decorated. The lines of the triforium merge with those of the clerestory to form a unified whole. Note the admirable **stained glass**★ by the master-glaziers of Alençon and the

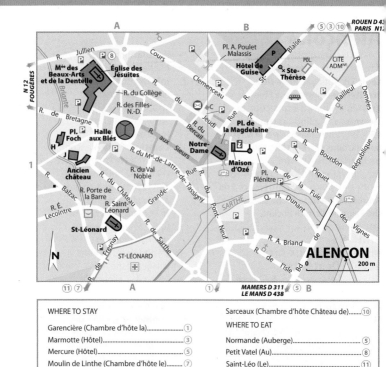

From the Venice Point to the Alençon Point

Around 1650, Madame de la Perrière perfected the Venice Point, very fashionable at the time in all the European courts, and taught her skill to the young women of Alençon. As a result, lacemaking developed and soon 8 000 people were involved in the manufacture of point lace. In order to keep up with fashion, men and women were tempted to spend large sums of money and to buy lace abroad, which prompted Colbert in 1665 to ban imported lace and to establish a royal factory in Alençon to produce French point lace. The needlewomen of Alençon subsequently developed their own style based on a specific technique and a new pattern consisting of delicate motifs arranged in close symmetry on a plain background. This was the origin of Alençon lace, which, by the end of the 17C, was the only one in fashion. The Atelier National du Point d'Alençon (National Workshop of Alençon Lace, *closed to the public*) has preserved this ancient tradition of needlepoint lace, acknowledged in the 19C as the best lace.

Maine region. The glass in the clerestory windows dates from 1530.
The first chapel off the north aisle is where Marie-Françoise-Thérèse Martin (1873–97) was baptised. She is better known as St Theresa of Lisieux.
In place de la Madeleine, to the left of the church, is the attractive 15C **Maison d'Ozé** (Ozé House), now the Tourist Information Centre, where the future King Henri IV is said to have stayed in 1576.

ADDITIONAL SIGHTS

Ancien Château

49 r. du Château.
From place Foch, you can see the 14C and 15C towers of the old castle, built by Jean II le Beau, first Duke of Alençon and ally of Joan of Arc.
The central tower, known as the crowned tower, has an unexpected outline: the main tower with machicolations is itself crowned by a slimmer, round tower. The other two towers, which defend the main gate, can be seen from rue du Château.

Halle au Blé

r. des Filles Notre-Dame. Open daily 9am–noon, 2–6pm.
This circular grain market was covered towards the end of the 19C with a glass dome which the ladies of the town nicknamed the hoopskirt of Alençon. It is today a cultural centre.

Église St-Léonard

pl. Marguerite-de-Lorraine. Apply to the presbytery to visit. 02 33 26 20 89.
The rebuilding of the present church was begun in 1489 by René, second Duke of Alençon, and was completed in 1505 by his widow, Marguerite de Lorraine.
Nearby (*no 10 rue Porte-de-la-Barre*) is a 15C house (Maison à l'Étal) with a slate-hung façade.

Chapelle Ste-Thérèse

r. St-Blaise. Open Jun–Sept daily 9am–noon, 2–6pm; Oct–Dec and Feb–May Tue–Sun 9.30am–noon, 2–5pm. Visit by guided tour (30–45min). No charge. 02 33 26 09 87. www.famillemartin-therese-alencon.com.
Opposite the Préfecture (a fine 17C building and former military headquarters) a double staircase leads to the chapel, which adjoins the house (*50 rue St-Blaise*) where St Theresa of Lisieux was born on 2 January 1873.

DRIVING TOUR

FORÊT DE PERSEIGNE★

Round-trip 53km/33mi – allow about about 3hr.

From Alençon take D 311 southeast in the direction of Chartres. Beyond Le Buisson turn left onto D 236. After 4km/2.5mi turn sharp right onto a forest road towards Aillières-Beauvoir and right again towards Ancinnes; at the Rond de Croix-Pergeline turn left by a milestone to Gros Houx.

La Belle Échappée

8 r. de la Forêt de Perseigne, La Fresnaye-sur-Chédouet. Open April–Sept Wed–Sun 10am–noon, 2–7pm; Oct–Mar Sat–Sun 10am–12.30pm, 2–6.30pm (last entrance 1hr before closing). Closed 25 Dec–2 Jan. 5€. 02 43 34 39 11. http://vttsi.free.fr.
Exhibitions retrace the history of cycling and of its great champions.

At the Carrefour des Trois-Ponts turn left uphill.

The road enters the picturesque **Vallée d'Enfer** (Hell Valley). The tower-belvedere (30m/90ft high) is the highest point (349m/1 145ft) in the Sarthe district.

There are 8km/5mi of waymarked paths round the belvedere and in Hell Valley.

Take D 234 southeast to the twin villages Aillières-Beauvoir and take D 116 south via Villaines-la-Carelle. At the crossroads with D 311 continue southwest on D 310.

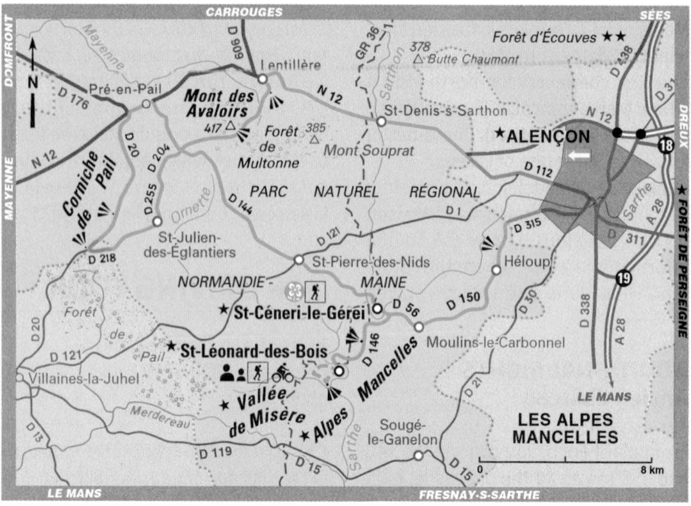

Chapelle Notre-Dame-de-Toutes-Aides

The doorway of this graceful pilgrimage chapel is surmounted by a Virgin and Child. Above the 17C altarpiece is an Assumption; below is a painting of the Annunciation.

In St-Rémy-du-Val turn right in front of the church onto the road to Neufchâtel-en-Saosnois (D 117). Turn left onto D 165. From Ancinnes take D 19 to Alençon.

EXCURSIONS

Fresnay-sur-Sarthe

Allow 1hr30min. Michelin map 310: J-5. Fresnay is 21km/13mi S of Alençon.

Fresnay occupies a picturesque site perched high above the River Sarthe. The town is a centre for excursions into the Alpes Mancelles or Sillé Forest, but also has plenty to offer on-site in the form of a preserved network of narrow streets bordered by beautiful medieval houses. In 1063 the town was occupied by the troops of William, Duke of Normandy; he put down revolts in 1068 and 1078 himself. In 1100, following incessant local fighting, Henry I of England abandoned the region of Maine, which allied itself with Anjou. Peace lasted until the end of the 14C, when the Hundred Years' War reignited strife.

Église Notre-Dame

Open Jul–Aug 3.30–6pm, by appointment. 02 43 97 24 98.

The Church of Our Lady, built of local rust-coloured stone in the transitional Romanesque style, is dominated by a remarkable octagonal belfry. The round-headed doorway frames the oak door (1528); its carved panels depict *(left)* the Tree of Jesse and *(right)* Christ

L'Encerclement

The itinerary known as L'Encerclement (The Encircling Movement), one of several in the Historical Area of the Battle of Normandy, runs from Alençon to L'Aigle, tracing the progress of the 2nd Armoured Division under General Leclerc.

Find out about this and other routes at http://www.normandie-tourisme.fr/normandy-tourism/main-menu/things-to-do/sites-and-attractions/d-day-and-the-battle-of-normandy-172-2.html.

Terrace de l'Hôtel de Ville
A public garden has been laid out in the castle's former precincts. From the terrace there is a **view★** down over the Sarthon with its attractive bridge and old houses.

Cave du Lion
Open Jul–Aug Tue–Sun 4–7pm, by appointment with M. Jean-Gilles 4 days in advance. No charge. 02 43 33 64 42.
This underground cellar opens off ruelle du Lion, on the far side of the covered market. The chamber has an octagonal central pillar and ribbed vaulting.

Sillé-le-Guillaume

Michelin map 310: I-5. Sillé-le-Guillaume is on D 304, 35km/22mi NW of Le Mans, 41km/25.5mi SE of Mayenne and 17km/10.5mi SW of Fresnay-sur-Sarthe..
The small town of Sillé-le-Guillaume had a rich and eventful past as one of the strong points, like Ste-Suzanne and Mayenne, which protected northern Maine from Norman invasion.

Château
Guided tours available. 2.50€. 02 43 20 10 32 (tourist office). www.tourisme.sille-le-guillaume.fr.
At the end of the Hundred Years' War (1337–1453), the English sacked the 11C fortress. The 15C castle was built on the ruins.

Église Notre-Dame
The church stands upon the site of a former Romanesque church of which the **crypt** and the south transept gable remain. A beautiful 13C door restored in the 15C is decorated with a statue of the Virgin and Child.

EXCURSION IN FORÊT DE SILLÉ

Allow 1hr. From Sillé-le-Guillaume head north on rue du Château. Maps available at tourist offices.
The classic excursion in the Forest of Sillé takes in the Étang du Defais, also known as the Lac de Sillé; the 16C Château de Foulletorte, and view from La Croix de la Mare.
The road rises before entering Sillé Forest, which covers the eastern crest of the Coëvrons chain of hills and is well organised for walkers, with shelters, signposted footpaths and special riding lanes.
The forest was over-exploited at the turn of the 20C and today it is composed trees under tall stands or plantations of conifers on the poorer soils.

After 4km/2.5mi turn left onto the forest road; after 800m/875yd turn left again onto a forest road which skirts the north end of Defais Pool.

Étang du Defais
This stretch of water, also known as the Lac de Sillé, with its attractive surroundings, is a favourite spot with the local townspeople. There is a good bathing area with facilities for yachting, canoeing, swimming, camping, etc.

From the west side of the pool take the road west; right at crossroads to D 16.

There is a good view of the Norman *bocage* from the north of the forest

Left in La Boissière; St-Pierre-sur-Orthe, take D 143 southwest via Vimarcé.

Château de Foulletorte
Park beside D 143; walk up the avenue, which leads to the (closed) castle.
The attractive moated château (the water is supplied by the River Erve) was built by Antoine de Vassé at the end of the 16C.
The staircase loggia on the entrance front, the projecting cornice on the two wings at right angles, the round-headed or mullioned windows and the tall chimneys are the only decorative notes on this sobre granite building.

Return to St-Pierre-sur-Orthe; turn right onto D 35. After traversing the wooded Coëvrons ridge, the road descends towards Sillé: attractive view

of La Croix de la Mare (La Mare Cross) – 290m/952ft.

DRIVING TOUR

THE ALPES MANCELLES★

See map p270. 82km/51mi – about 3hr round-trip from Alençon (excluding the Misère Valley).

The Alpes Mancelles is part of the Normandie-Maine Regional Park.

On leaving Alençon take N 12 west via St-Denis-sur-Sarthon; in Lentillère turn left towards Champfrémont; then bear right to Mont des Avaloirs.

Mont des Avaloirs

A belvedere marks the summit (417m/1 368ft), one of the highest points in western France.

At the second crossroads turn left onto D 204 and then fork right onto D 255. In St-Julien-des-Églantiers turn right onto D 245, then right onto D 218 and right again onto D 20.

Corniche de Pail

The road, which climbs slowly, provides a view over the Mayenne basin.

In Pré-en-Pail take N 12 east and D 144 south via St-Pierre-des-Nids.

St-Céneri-le-Gérei★

This village has a charming setting: hilltop Romanesque church, bridge spanning the Sarthon and stone houses.

From St-Céneri-le-Gérei take D 56 south; turn right onto D 146.

St-Léonard-des-Bois★

This village is an ideal excursion centre for the Alpes Mancelles.

Vallée de Misère★

Round-trip 1hr30min on foot.

On the church square take the path from the corner by the Hôtel Bon Laboureur. At the crossroads marked by a stone cross take a path uphill. Beyond Le Champ-des-Pasfore turn left. At the next crossroads turn left onto a path marked in red and white. From a bench there is an attractive **view**★ of the wild Misère Valley, St-Léonard and the Manoir de Linthe further downstream.

From St-Léonard-des-Bois take D 146 N. Turn right onto D 56; in Moulins-le-Carbonnel turn left onto D 150, which becomes D 315, which will take you back to Alençon.

ADDRESSES

STAY

Hôtel Marmotte – *Les Grouas, 61250 Valframbert, 1km/0.6mi N of Alençon centre, dir. Dreux. ☎02 33 27 42 64. 46 rooms.* *Restaurant*. Since the town centre offers limited accomodation, head towards the outskirts where you will find this traditional family hotel. Its rooms offer contemporary furnishings and modern plumbing. A good base from which to explore the area.

Chambre d'hôte La Garencière – *72610 Champfleur, 6.5km/4mi SE of Alençon dir. Mamers and Champfleur via D 19, then towards Bourg-le-Roi. ☎02 33 31 75 84. Closed Jan. 5 rooms. Restaurant.* At the time of the Crusades, this hamlet was the fief of the knights of Garencière and a stop on the pilgrimage route to Compostelle in Spain. Today, you will enjoy the prettily decorated rooms and the covered swimming pool facing the countryside. Billiards room and second-hand crockery on sale to guests.

Chambre d'hôte Le Moulin de Linthe – *rte de Sougé-le-Ganelon, 72130 St-Léonard-des-Bois. ☎02 43 33 79 22. www.moulindelinthe.fr. Closed Jan–Feb. 5 rooms.* The bedrooms have character in this old mill which looks quite picturesque even if its paddle wheel no longer turns. Anglers can fish for trout or pike in the River Sarthon.

Mercure – *187 av. Gén-Leclerc, 2.6km/1.6mi SW. 02 33 28 64 64. Closed 24 Dec–1 Jan. 53 rooms. 10€.* Fairly recent building in a small commercial park. Rooms are practical and well soundproofed, those on the first floor are modern and renovated.

Château de Sarceaux – *61250 Valframbert. 02 33 28 85 11. www.chateau-de-sarceaux.com. Closed Jan. 5 rooms.* A large park with a pond surrounds this château built in the 17C and 19C. The south-facing rooms are elegantly decorated with antique furniture and family portraits. Candlelight dinners in the guest dining room, with classic cuisine.

EAT

Auberge Normande – *Le Pont-du-Londeau, 61250 Valframbert. 02 33 29 43 29. Closed 1 May, 24-25 Dec, Sun eve and Mon. Reservations advised.* This restaurant is often fully booked for lunch; the locals appreciate the updated regional cuisine and reasonable prices.

Le Saint-Léo – *pl. de l'Église, 72130 St-Léonard-des-Bois. 02 43 33 81 34. Closed Wed off-season and Tue.* A simple, convivial stop in this picturesque village in the Alpes Mancelles. The dining room faces the Sarthe and offers local fare with an accent on fresh ingredients, galettes and crepes.

Au Petit Vatel – *72 pl. Cdt-Desmeules. 02 33 26 23 78. Closed 27 Jul–10 Aug, Sun eve, Wed.* There is nothing "petit" about the cuisine of this restaurant with its pleasantly rustic décor, where the chef offers traditional fare enlivened by regional touches. One menu is devoted entirely to Norman specialities.

ENTERTAINMENT

La Luciole – *171 rte de Bretagne. 02 33 32 83 33. www.laluciole.org. Opening times follow the calendar of performances. Closed Aug, Sun and Mon.* This music hall is no doubt the locals' favourite haunt, with more than 70 concerts each year. Pop-rock is the main genre, but both established and aspiring young groups of all horizons perform here.

SHOPPING

Les Caves de la Rotonde – *5 r. des Filles-Notre-Dame. 02 33 26 20 76. www.cavesdelarotonde.com. Closed Sun, Mon and public holidays except 1 Jan and 25 Dec.* This unpretentious shop holds treasures of vintage Calvados, cider, ***pommeaux***, ***poiré*** (pear cider) and apéritifs as well as wine from France and elsewhere. Tastings are held from time to time.

Argentan

From its hillside site, the small town of Argentan overlooks the confluence of the River Orne and the River Ure. The marked itinerary known as L'Encerclement (The Encircling Movement), one of several in the Historical Area of the Battle of Normandy, goes through this town. France's most renowned stud farm, the Haras du Pin, lies nearby.

- **Population:** 15 465.
- **Michelin Map:** 310: I-2.
- **Info:** Chapelle St-Nicholas, 6 place du Marché, 61200 Argentan. 02 33 67 12 48. www.argentan.fr.
- **Location:** Argentan lies on the River Orne, surrounded by forests, between Flers and Alençon, each 45km/28mi away.
- **Don't Miss:** Examples of local lacemaking at the Maison des Dentelles; Château of Bourg-St-Léonard.
- **Timing:** Allow 1 day.

A BIT OF HISTORY

From Kingly Disputes to Lacemaking – It was in Argentan in the 12C that the papal legates assembled to settle the disagreement between the English king, Henry II Plantagenet, and his chancellor,

ARGENTAN

WHERE TO STAY

- Ariès (Hôtel)............ ①
- Ferme de la Gravelle (Chambre d'hôte)............ ⑦
- Pavillon de Gouffern............ ⑩
- Refuge du P'tit Fischer (Le)............ ⑬

WHERE TO EAT

- Fleuré (Restaurant de)............ ①
- Renaissance (La)............ ⑤

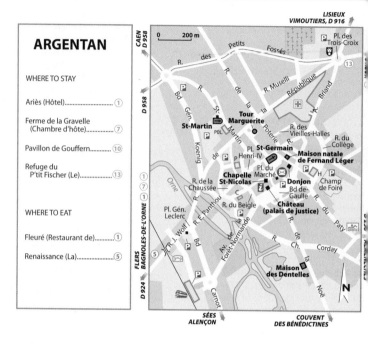

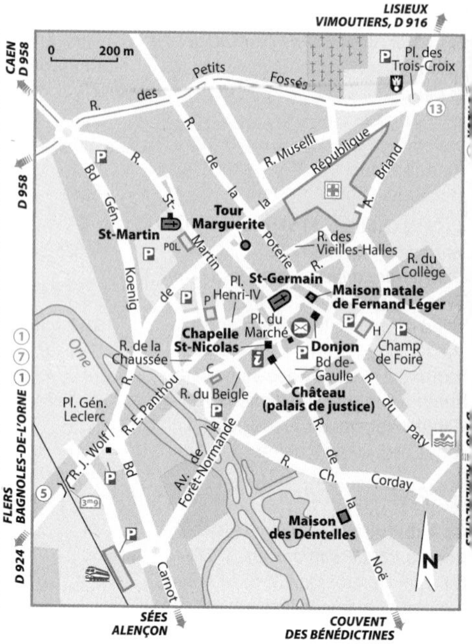

Thomas Becket, Archbishop of Canterbury. The assassins of the sainted archbishop set out from here to accomplish their dire deed.

Although Colbert set up a lace factory in Alençon, he did not neglect the lacemakers of Argentan. The rediscovery of 18C lace patterns for the Point d'Argentan in 1874 enabled the characteristic Argentan pattern to regain its popularity.

VISIT

Église St-Germain★

pl. du Marché. Open Jun–mid-Sept Mon, Wed, Thu, and Fri 9am–noon, 2–6pm, Tue 2–6pm, Sun 3–6pm. Closed public holidays. 02 33 67 12 48 (tourist office).

The church, badly damaged by shelling in 1944, was built in the Flamboyant style from the 15C to the 17C.

Walk round the church clockwise to view the unusual pentagonal east end (16C) and the unusual circular chapels terminating the transepts. At the base of the belfry a fine Flamboyant **porch** opens on to rue St-Germain.

ADDITIONAL SIGHTS

Château

Closed to visitors.

The castle now serves as the Law Courts. This imposing rectangular castle, flanked by two square towers, was built in 1370 by Pierre II, Count of Alençon.

Ancienne chapelle St-Nicolas

pl. du Marché.

The chapel, which was built in 1773, belonged to the castle. Marguerite de Lorraine, founder of the monastery of Ste-Claire, took her vows here.

The Tourist Information Centre occupies the ground floor, and the first floor houses a lovely carved 17C altarpiece *(displayed on request).*

Église St-Martin

r. St-Martin. Guided tours Jun–Sept by appointment with the tourist office. 02 33 67 12 48.

The church, which was damaged in 1944, is dominated by an octagonal tower surmounted by a decapitated spire. The overall style is Flamboyant Gothic but presents several Renaissance innovations.

The Point d'Argentan (Argentan Lace Stitch)

Take boulevard du Général-de-Gaulle and rue de la Noë SE, following signs to Abbaye des Bénédictines.

Benedictine Abbey

2 r. de l'Abbé. Open Mon–Sat 10.30am–noon. Guided tours 2.30–4pm. 2€. Closed one week late Dec–Jan. 02 33 67 12 01.
The enclosed order of nuns has exclusive rights to the Argentan stitch, a needlepoint lace comprising a variety of motifs on a honeycomb-like background.
There are no workshops, but one can ask to see specimens illustrating steps in the working of Argentan lace and samples of old and modern needlepoint lace.

Maison des Dentelles

34 r. de la Noë. Open Apr–mid-Oct Tue–Sat 9am–11.30am, 2–5.30pm, Sun 3–5.30pm. 3€. Guided tours available. 02 33 67 50 78.
This museum presents a charming incursion into the history of lacemaking right up to the present day. A number of dresses and other outfits are on show, many the work of famous designers.

DRIVING TOURS

Pays d'Argentan

The region around Argentan is a plain circled by woods: Écouves to the south, Gouffern to the north. The Orne Valley, separating this region from the Pays d'Auge, entered into military history in August 1944.

1 MEANDERS OF THE RIVER ORNE

32km/20mi – 1hr from Argentan and back.

Leave Argentan travelling southwest on D 924.

Écouché

Church. Open Jul–Aug daily 2.30–5pm. If it is closed, apply to the Syndicat d'Initiative. 02 33 36 88 82.
The 15C-16C **church** was never completed and the ruined 13C nave never rebuilt. The Renaissance triforium in the transepts and the chancel are worthy of note.

Take D 29 north towards Falaise; turn left.

Ménil-Glaise★

The **view**★ from the bridge takes in the rock escarpment crowned by a castle on the south bank of the Orne; there is another good view from a terrace.

Turn round; continue straight ahead passing (left) the path from the bridge and (right) the Batilly road; turn left onto D 924 to Argentan. 9km/5.6mi south.

Take N 158 from Argentan.

2 ST-CHRISTOPHE-LE-JAJOLET

The village church is a place of pilgrimage to St Christopher, the patron saint of travellers. On the day of pilgrimage *(last Sun in Jul and first Sun of Oct)* a procession of cars files past.

Château de Sassy

Open Easter–Sept. Guided tours (45min) daily mid-Jun–mid-Sept 10.30am–12.30pm, 2–6pm; Easter–mid-Jun and last half Sept, Sat–Sun and public holidays 3–6pm. 6€. 02 33 35 32 66.
Building began in 1760, was interrupted by the Revolution and continued in 1817 by the Marquis d'Ommy. In 1850 the château became the property of Étienne-Denis Pasquier (1767–1862), an important political figure.
The main salon presents several 17C tapestries and mementoes of Pasquier. The **chapel**, partly hidden by trees, contains a 15C Flemish oak altarpiece carved with scenes from the Passion, formerly in St Bavon Abbey in Ghent. Don't miss the **terraces** and **gardens** of the château.

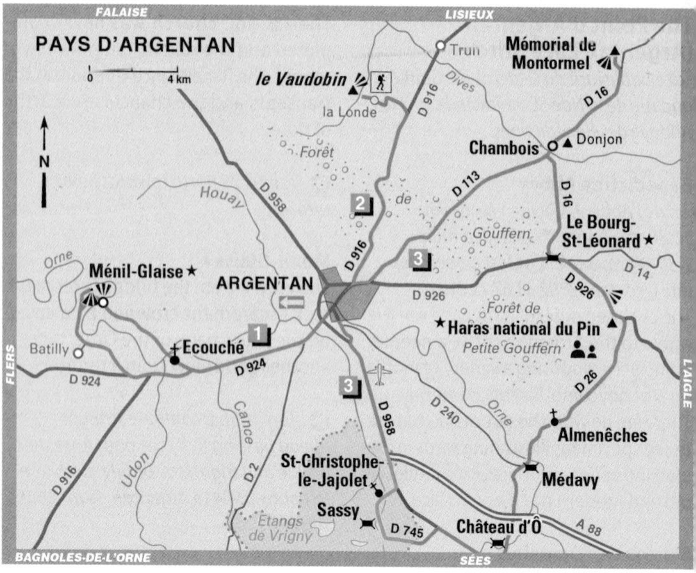

3 LE VAUDOBIN

12km/7.4mi – plus 15min walk round trip on slippery paths.

From Argentan take D 916 northeast; after 7km/4.3mi (beyond Gouffern Forest) turn left and cross La Londe. Park near the quarry; take the path left of the quarry entrance.

The path crosses the Meillon stream, bears left round a large rock and climbs uphill past a rock bearing fossil imprints. From the top of the grassy mound there is a view of the Meillon Gorge and the Dives Valley.

4 GOUFFERN FOREST

About 3hr30min.

Leave Argentan to the northeast via N 26, then take D 113 to the left.

As you leave Argentan, the road crosses Gouffern Forest, then winds back down into the Dives Valley.

Chambois

A stele near a central crossroads recalls the joining up of Polish (1st Canadian Army) and American 3rd Army troops on 19 August 1944 to cut off the retreat of the German 7th Army.

Battle of Normandy

In 1944 the closing stages of the Battle of Normandy were fought around Argentan. Following the success of the American breakthrough at Avranches and the failure of the German counter-attack of 7 August, the enemy rear guard was vulnerable. On 13 August the French 2nd Armoured Division at Écouché together with the American 5th Armoured Division in the Argentan sector formed the southern arm of the pincer action. When the Canadians took Falaise on 17 August, the German 7th Army retreated via Dives Valley.

A chaotic rush ensued. On 19 August the allied troops met at Chambois and by nightfall (6.30pm) on 21 August the fall of Tournai-sur-Dive marked the final stage in the Battle of Normandy.

The huge rectangular **keep** *(donjon)* buttressed by four towers is a good example of 12C military architecture. The church has an 11C stone spire and a fine Descent from the Cross.

Take D 16 uphill to Montormel.

Mémorial de Montormel

Visit by guided tour (1hr) only daily May–Sept 9.30am–6pm; Apr 10am–5pm; Oct–mid-Dec and mid-Jan–Mar Wed and Sat–Sun 10am–5pm. 5€. 02 33 67 38 61. www.monument-montormel.org.

The **Battle of the Chambois Pocket**, raged from 18 to 22 August 1944, causing 10 000 to 12 000 deaths. Marshall Montgomery declared that it marked the "beginning of the end of the war". A monument commemorates the fierce fighting. From the American tank there is a wide **view**★ over the plain.

Two galleries have particular interest: in one, a large relief map describes the battle; the other is devoted to the soldiers of the Polish 1st Armoured Division.

Le Bourg-St-Léonard★

11km/7mi E by N 26. Château.

Guided visit (45min) Jul–Aug daily 2.30–5.30pm; May–Jun and 1st 3 weekends Sept and holidays. 2.30–4.30pm. 3€. 02 33 36 68 68.

The 18C **château** was built by Jules David Cromot while chief of the Treasury under Louis XV.

The elegance of its lines and the harmony of its design make it a most attractive building. The interior is embellished with panelling, tapestries and 18C furniture. The sweeping views from paths in the 400ha/988-acre English-style park are well worth exploring.

Haras national du Pin★

See Haras national du Pin, p294.

From the stud farm, to the south, you can see the outline of the Écouves Forest.

Almenêches

The Renaissance church used to belong to a Benedictine **abbey**. The altars are decorated with sculptures representing, on the left, the canonisation of St Opportune, a well-known local abbess.

Médavy

Château: *Visit by guided tour (45min) only Jul–Aug daily 3–7pm. (call to confirm times and hours, possibly affected by restoration work). 6€. 02 33 35 05 09.*

A 11C fortified house built to defend the Orne crossing was replaced by a 16C stronghold. A sombre 18C **château**, now undergoing restoration, occupies the site, with gardens *à la française*. In the chapel are remains of the fortress.

Château de Bourg-St-Léonard

S. Targat/MICHELIN

ADDRESSES

STAY

Le Refuge du P'tit Fischer – *1 pl. des Trois-Croix. 02 33 67 05 43. 17 rooms. . Restaurant. Closed Sun eve.* Just at the entrance to Argentan, on a busy street, this hotel offers modern, fuctional rooms on three storeys, well soundproofed. The restaurant is brasserie style.

Arlès – *Z.A. Beurrerie, 1km/0.6mi via 4 on map. 02 33 39 13 13. 43 rooms. 8€. Restaurant (closed Fri eve).* A very well insulated hotel situated by quite a busy road. Simple and functional accommodation, bistro-style furniture and simple table settings in a restaurant proposing classic cuisine, buffet menus and dishes of the day.

Chambre d'hôte Ferme de la Gravelle – *41 r. de la Gravelle, Sarceaux, 2.5km/1.5mi W. 02 33 67 04 47. Closed Sun eve. 3 rooms. . Restaurant.* There is a calm atmosphere in this country house in a small rural village. Rooms are pretty and a gîte is also available.

Pavillon de Gouffern – *61310 Silly-en-Gouffern, 11km/7mi E. 02 33 36 64 26. www.pavillondegouffern.com. 20 rooms. . Restaurant.* At this former 19C hunting lodge, the hotel exterior is rustic, with typical Norman half-timbering, the renovated interior is chic and contemporary.

EAT

Restaurant de Fleuré – *61200 Fleuré, 6.5km/4mi SW. 02 33 36 10 85. Closed Sun eve, Thu eve, Mon.* Just outside Argentan, this family restaurant is a local favourite with carefully prepared cuisine and a cordial ambience.

Hostellerie La Renaissance – *20 av. de la 2e Division-Blindée. 02 33 36 14 20. www.hotel-larenaissance.com. Closed Sun eve, Mon.* This hotel *(12 guest rooms; 10€; closed Sun eve)* has a restaurant with a quiet, friendly atmosphere.

LEISURE

Hippodrome d'Argentan – *rte de Crennes (D 113), 61200 Urou-et-Crennes. 02 33 67 08 02. www.hippodrome-argentan.com.* Vast racecourse. The timetable is available at the tourist office.

Bagnoles-de-l'Orne

In addition to its healing waters, Bagnoles-de-l'Orne has a lovely lakeside setting★ that invites calm. The lake is formed by the Vée, a tributary of the Mayenne, before it enters a deep gorge cut through the massif of the Andaines Forest. The site can be seen best by walking from Tessé-la-Madeleine to the Roc au Chien.

- **Population:** 2 561.
- **Michelin Map:** 310: G-3.
- **Info:** Place du Marché. 02 33 37 85 66. www.bagnolesdelorne.com.
- **Location:** Bagnoles is 2km/1mi N of the N 176, which links Alençon (47km/29mi SW) to Mont-St-Michel (90km/56mi W). The town comprises two distinct parts: to the W Bagnoles-Château and E, Bagnoles-Lac.
- **Parking:** Near the château, the museum, the casino and the place du Marché.
- **Don't Miss:** Roc au Chien.
- **Timing:** Half a day for the spa waters.
- **Kids:** Forêt des Andaines.

A BIT OF HISTORY

The spot known as Capuchin's Leap received its name when a Capuchin monk, cured of his ills by a magical spring, fulfilled a vow by making a gigantic leap (4m/13ft) between the rock spikes high above the water.

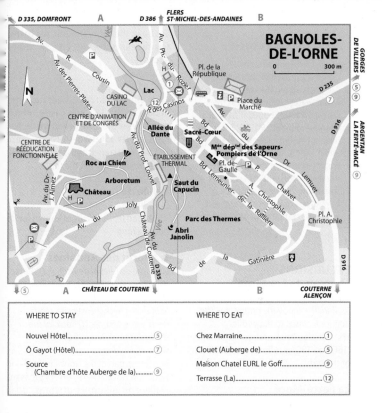

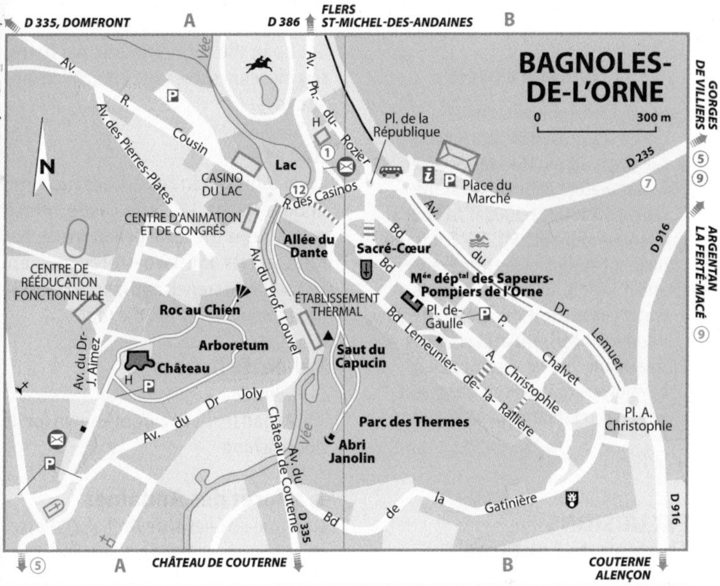

WHERE TO STAY		WHERE TO EAT	
Nouvel Hôtel	5	Chez Marraine	1
Ô Gayot (Hôtel)	7	Clouet (Auberge de)	5
Source (Chambre d'hôte Auberge de la)	9	Maison Chatel EURL le Goff	9
		Terrasse (La)	12

SIGHTS

Parc de l'établissement thermal★

The park surrounding the spa building is planted with pines, oaks and chestnut trees. The Allée du Dante on the east bank of the Vée, which is often crowded with bathers, leads from the lake to the spa building. Other alleys in the park wind towards Capuchin's Leap and to the site known as the Abri Janolin. Shops line the lake front rue des Casions.

Le Roc au Chien★

Tours by tourist train (30min) Jun–Sept Mon–Fri 3.15 and 4.30pm; Apr–May and Oct Sat–Sun and public holidays 3.15 and 4.30pm. 5€. 02 33 30 72 70. www.bagnolesdelorne.com.

45min round-trip on foot. Start from the church and walk up the avenue du Château; the main gateway opens on to the avenue and the public park of Tessé *(arboretum containing 150 different tree species, bird-watching trail, children's playground and other amusements).*

The château, built in the 19C in the neo-medieval style. now houses the town hall. Take the avenue on the right which overlooks the Bagnoles Gorge and leads to the rocky promontory, the Roc au Chien, where there is a lovely **view**★ of Bagnoles beside the lake *(left)* and the spa building and its park *(right).*

Musée départemental des Sapeurs-Pompiers de l'Orne

16 av. Albert-Christophle.

Open daily Apr–Oct 2–6pm (last entry 30min before closing). 3.80€. 02 33 38 10 34.

A deconsecrated church houses the Fire Brigade Museum with its collection of horse-drawn hand pumps, the oldest pre-dating1790, badges, medals, helmets, uniforms, equipment, breathing apparatus and radios.

Healing Waters

The establishment in the Vée Gorge is supplied exclusively by the Great Spring (Grande Source) where water gushes forth at the rate of 50 000l/11 000gal an hour at a temperature of 25°C/77°F. It is the only hot spring in western France and its acidic, mildly radioactive waters have a low mineral content. Bathing, the essential part of any treatment, can be accompanied by showers or localised treatment with water jets, and pulverisations.

EXCURSIONS

Château de Couterne

1.5km/0.9mi S of Bagnoles by D 335.
Park the car by the bridge. ⊶The interior is closed to the public.
The massive brick and granite château (16C and 18C) is reflected in the waters of the Vée.

La Ferté-Macé

6km/4mi N via D 916.
This small town has retained a number of 18C and 19C buildings and houses that recall its past role in the textile industry. Its gastronomic renown is due to *tripes en brochettes*, skewered onto hazelwood sticks.

A large tourist complex includes a leisure park (pedalos, windsurfing, fishing, climbing, swimming, golf, etc.) and a dozen holiday houses. A lively market is held on Thursday mornings. An 11C Romanesque tower is all that remains of the old church demolished in 1861.

The **hôtel de ville** (town hall) houses works by the local artist **Charles Léandre**, as well as fascinating 19C paintings celebrating the postal service and local manufacturing.

♟♟ Musée du Jouet

32 r. de la Victoire. ○Open Jul–Aug daily 3–6pm. Apr–Jun and Sept Sat–Sun and public holidays 3–6pm. ⊚3.30€ (under 6 years no charge). ℘02 33 37 47 00 or 02 33 37 04 08.

Set up in the former municipal baths, this museum shows 19C and 20C games and toys.

Rânes

13km/8mi from La Ferté-Macé via D 916.
Rebuilt in the 18C, the castle, which now houses the local *gendarmerie*, has retained its 15C two-storeyed keep, fortified with crenels and machicolations. (*panoramic view from the top*).

Vallée de la Cour

5km/3mi SE.
A road leads to a pool known for its good fishing.

♟♟ Forêt des Andaines

La Ferme du Cheval de Trait. ♿○Horse shows Jul–Aug Wed, Thu, Sat–Sun, 14 Jul and 15 Aug at 3.30pm; Apr–Jun and Sept–Oct, check the website. ⊚9€ (5–12 years 4€). ⌂ P Book for lunch on the farm. ℘02 33 38 27 78. www.chevaldetrait.com.

This forest, part of the Normandie-Maine Regional Nature Park, offers pleasant walks and glimpses of stags, does and the smaller roedeer. Of particular interest are: **Tour de Bonvouloir**, a slender observation tower; **Chapelle Ste-Geneviève**, a picnic site; and **Juvigny-sous-Andaine**, where the **Ferme du Cheval de Trait**, offers a 1hr horse show sure to please youngsters.

ADDRESSES

⬠ STAY

⊖ **Auberge de la Source**– *La Peras, 61600 La Ferté-Macé, 5km/3mi NW via D 908, towards Mont-St-Michel. ℘02 33 37 28 23. 5 rooms. ⊡. Restaurant⊖.* This new building follows the old Norman style with bricks and half-timbering. Upstairs, the rooms, one for families, have excellent beds and parquet floors. The restaurant has an open hearth and regional fare.

Ô Gayot – *2 av. de la Ferté-Macé. ℘02 33 38 44 01. Closed 21 Dec–7 Feb, Apr–9 Nov, Mon–Wed 9 Nov–Mar. 16 rooms. 8.50€. Restaurant*. Completey renovated town centre hotel offering a "total concept": minimalist rooms, bar, tea room and gourmet boutique. Contemporary cuisine at reasonable prices in the modern bistro. Terrace.

Nouvel Hôtel – *ave du Dr-Pierre-Noal, 61140 Tessé-la-Madeleine, 0.5km/0.3mi S. ℘02 33 30 75 00. www.nouvel-hotel-bagnoles.fr. Closed Nov–Mar. 30 rooms.* This lovely, thoroughly renovated villa dating from 1900 lies close to the thermal spa. Modern rooms are decorated in warm colours. Covered terrace.

EAT

Maison Chatel – Le Goff – *31 r. St-Denis, 61600 La Ferté-Macé. ℘02 33 37 11 85. Closed Sun afternoon, Mon.* If you like rural treats such as calf's head or tripe cooked in beer or with vegetables, you can purchase them in the renowned shop, or enjoy them in the small restaurant.

Auberge de Clouet – *Le Clouet, 61600 La Ferté-Macé, 7km/4.3mi NE of Bagnoles via D 916. ℘02 33 37 18 22. Closed 1–15 Nov, Sun eve, Mon Nov–Easter.* In spring, the terrace of this peaceful inn overlooks a small vale covered in flowers. Regional cuisine from local produce, chickens from the farm and vegetables from the garden in season. Six rooms decorated in 1970s style are available.

Chez Marraine – *6 r. du Square. ℘02 33 37 82 91. Closed 15 Feb–15 Mar.* "To be happy, be discreet!" This motto surely applies to this restaurant hidden in a narrow street between town and lake. Meals are served on the pleasant covered terrace, a good opportunity for you to try calf's head, a speciality of the house, or langoustine in a cider cream sauce.

La Terrasse – *r. des Casinos. ℘02 33 37 81 44. Closed 26 Nov–4 Jan, Sun eve, Mon.* With an unexceptional exterior, this restaurant may escape your notice. But you'll be glad you walked in when you taste the good regional cuisine and the fish specialities. Inviting rustic interior and sheltered terrace.

Bellême

Bellême, a very typical village of the region, overlooks the forest and the beautiful Perche countryside. The town had a particularly turbulent history in the Middle Ages, when Blanche of Castile and the future St Louis (Louis IX, 1214–70) took the fortress by storm in 1229.

- **Population:** 652.
- **Michelin Map:** 310: M-4 – Local map, *see MORTAGNE-AU-PERCHE, p290.*
- **Info:** Bd Bansart-des-Bois. ℘02 33 73 09 69. www.lepaysbellemois.com.
- **Location:** Bellême is 22km/13.5mi NW of Nogent-le-Rotrou and 17km/10.5mi S of Mortagne-au-Perche, its long-time rival.
- **Don't Miss:** The old houses of the Ville-Close, and the forest walks.
- **Timing:** Give yourself 1hr to see the town, and 3hr to visit the Écomusée at Ste-Gauburge.

SIGHTS

Ville-Close

The **gate**, flanked by two reconstructed towers, together with towers now incorporated into domestic buildings, are the only remains of the 15C ramparts, which once enclosed the town and were built upon 11C fortress foundations. Rue Ville-Close, on the site of the former citadel, is lined with fine 17C and 18C houses. Outstanding are no **24**, the

Governor's house, and especially no **26**, the **Hôtel Bansard des Bois**.

Église St-Sauveur

pl. de la République. Open Sat–Sun 9am–6pm.

The late-17C St Saviour's Church has a richly decorated interior. Note in particular the imposing high altar and canopy (1712) made of stone and marble, the chancel woodwork from the old abbey of Valdieu, and the windows, each composed of six scenes from the life of Christ. The font, decorated with garlands, stands against a three-panelled altarpiece.

DRIVING TOUR

Forêt de Bellême★

27km/17mi – about 1hr30min.

This forest (2 400ha/5 930 acres) is one of the most beautiful in the Perche region with its majestic oaks and its beautiful and varied site.

From Bellême take D 938 northwest.

From the road there is a very pretty **view** of the town. It then crosses woodland before reaching the Herse Pool.

Étang et Fontaine de la Herse

A path circles the pool – 15min on foot.

The calm waters of the pool reflect the surrounding greenery and offer freshness much appreciated by tourists. Opposite the forester's lodge is a Roman fountain and two blocks of stone bearing Latin inscriptions.

Turn round and continue straight ahead; turn right at the Colbert crossroads.

The forest road (surfaced) affords lovely **views**.

At the Creux Valley crossroads, turn left. Follow the road along to the edge of the forest. Turn first right and enter the forest once again. Before reaching the Montimer crossroads the road crosses a thicket. Descend on the left for 400m/0.2mi.

Chêne de l'École

This oak tree stands 40m/131ft tal and has a circumference of 22m/72ft Even after 300 years it is still perfectl straight.

Return to the Montimer crossroads and continue to La Perrière.

La Perrière

The name comes from the Latin *petraria* meaning stone quarry. Many of the houses have been built with dark-rec ferruginous sandstone *(grison)*.

The village offers one of the bes **panoramas**★ of the Perche countryside including Perseigne Forest *(W)* anc Écouves Forest *(NW)*, which can be seen from the cemetery path near the church.

To admire the old dwellings (15C–17C) and streets of the town, follow the discovery path *(sentier de la découverte plan available locally)*. To organise cycle tours and country walks, contact Les Marcheurs du Perche Ornais *(La Grange Rouge, 61130, St-Germain-de-la-Coudre; 02 33 83 22 90.*

Return to the forest road that crosses Bellême Forest from west to east and passes through the delightful Creux Valley. At the Rendez-vous crossroads turn right onto D 310.

St-Martin-du-Vieux-Bellême

The houses of this picturesque village are clustered round the 14C–15C church.

Continue on the road which joins D 955 and turn left to Bellême.

PERCHE TOURS

Owing to its rich meadows the Perche is devoted to stock raising, particularly to the breeding of the draught horses known as **Percherons**. The region is subdivided into two areas, the Normar

Perche, and the southern sector, the Perche-Gouet or Lower Perche.

Whereas manors in the Pays d'Auge appear as country houses, those in the Norman Perche resemble small castles, built of stone and fortified. Although most of these late-15C or early 16C lordly houses are now farmhouses, they have retained features such as towers, elegant turrets and the delicately carved ornaments decorating many façades.

1 FROM BELLÊME TO LONGNY-AU-PERCHE

68km/42mi – allow about 2hr.

From Bellême take D 7 south.

Château des Feugerets

Closed to the public.

A cluster of buildings – two square pavilions with a fine balustrade and moat and an elegant 16C central block – form a harmonious, well-balanced ensemble.

In La Chapelle-Souëf turn left onto D 277.

St-Cyr-la-Rosière

The church has a beautiful Romanesque doorway, a remarkable 17C polychrome terracotta **Entombment**★ and a 17C painting of St Sebastian.

Take the road south towards Theil.

Manoir de l'Angenardière

Closed to the public.

This manor house, built in the 15C and 16C, is circled by well-preserved ramparts. Note the massive towers with machicolations.

Continue to the south.

La Pierre Procureuse

According to legend, this stone serving as a roof to a late Neolithic (2 500 BC) dolmen brings luck if you touch it.

At the T-junction turn right; go through Gémages.

H. Dewynter/MICHELIN

Percheron

St-Germain-de-la-Coudre

The church has an 11C crypt containing a beautiful Virgin and Child in stone.

Return to Gémages and take the road to Ste-Gauburge.

Priory of Ste-Gauburge

At St-Cyr-la-Rosière. Open Apr–Sept daily 10.30am–6.30pm; rest of the year daily 10.30am–6pm (closed Sat–Sun morings in Dec–Jan) Closed 1 Jan, 24–25, 31 Dec. Guided tour of the priory during school holidays, public holidays and Sat–Sun 2–6pm. 5.20€. 02 33 73 48 06. http://museeatp.free.fr.

The church has been transformed to house the Écomusée du Perche. Crafts of the past – blacksmith, saddler, cartwright, woodcutter, cooper – are brought to life again.

Adjoining the church is an imposing monastic ensemble (13C–18C) laid out around the courtyard.

Continue along D 277. Turn left at the crossroads onto D 9. In Colonard-Corubert turn right onto D 920.

East of Rémalard the country is greener and hillier; the road is picturesque.

In Moutiers turn left onto D 918 to Longny-au-Perche.

2 FROM MORTAGNE-AU-PERCHE TO LONGNY

25km/15.5mi –allow about 30min.

See MORTAGNE-AU-PERCHE, p290.

3 FROM MORTAGNE-AU-PERCHE TO BELLÊME

35km/22mi – allow about 1hr.

See MORTAGNE-AU-PERCHE, p290.

D 95 from Mortagne-au-Perche.

Château de Carrouges★★

For almost five centuries this immense château and park (10ha/25 acres), belonged to a famous Norman family, Le Veneur de Tillières; in 1936 it was bought by the nation. The town of Carrouges is part of the Parc naturel régional Normandie-Maine.

- **Population:** 735.
- **Michelin Map:** 310: I-3.
- **Info:** Rue du Crochet. 02 33 26 78 43.
- **Location:** Set on a high point NW of the Écouves forest, Carrouges is 26km/16mi E of Bagnoles-de-l'Orne and 30km/18.5mi NE of Alençon.
- **Don't Miss:** The majestic grand staircase at the château.
- **Timing:** Count on at least 90min to see the château.

The Château

Guided tours (45min, last tour 45 min before closing); mid-Jun–Aug 9.30am–noon, 2–6.30pm; Apr–mid-Jun and Sept 10am–noon, 2–6pm; rest of the year 10am–noon, 2–5pm. Closed 1 Jan, 1 May, 1 and 11 Nov, 25 Dec. 7€. 02 33 27 20 32.

Park

From the park with its fine trees and elegant flower beds there are good

Château de Carrouges

views of the château.
The Conservatoire botanique des pommiers de Bretagne et de Normandie, at the entrance to the property, includes 152 varieties of apple trees.

Exterior

The 16C **gatehouse★** is an elegant brick building with decorative geometric patterns.
It was almost certainly built by Jean Le Veneur, Bishop of Lisieux and Abbot of Bec, who helped fund Jacques Cartier's 1534 expedition to Canada.
The château itself is austere but imposing. Surrounded by a moat, the buildings are arranged around an inner courtyard. The stables and domestic quarters occupy the ground floor; the apartments and state rooms are on the first floor.

Interior

The **kitchen** presents an imposing array of copper pans. The **Louis XI Bedroom** was named after the king's visit on 11 August 1473.
The panelling is adorned with delicate panels of foliage highlighted in a different colour.
In the principal **antechamber** the chimney breast is decorated with a hunting scene. The remarkable fireplace in the **dining room** is flanked by two polished granite piers with Corinthian capitals. The sideboards are Louis XIV; note the Restoration chairs.
The **portrait gallery** with its Louis XIII chairs assembles past lords and owners.
The **drawing room** occupies part of one of the corner towers. The straw-coloured panelling dates from the late 17C or early 18C.
The visit ends with the monumental great **staircase★** and its brickwork vaulting and round headed arches as they wind up and round the square stair well.

The Village

La Maison du Parc, BP 05, 61320 Carrouges. Open Jun–Sept Wed–Mon 10.30am–6.30pm; rest of the year

Gatehouse of Château de Carrouges

S. Sauvignier/MICHELIN

Tue–Fri 10.30–noon, 2–5pm. No charge. 02 33 81 75 75. www.parc-naturel-normandie-maine.fr.
Carrouges stands within the boundary of the **Parc naturel régional Normandie-Maine**. The **Maison du Parc** (park's visitor centre) occupies the restored buildings of a 15C chapter of canons, an outbuilding of the château.

Normandie-Maine Regional Nature Park

Created in 1975 and spread over two regions (Basse-Normandie and the Pays de Loire), the **Parc naturel régional Normandie-Maine** covers 2 350sq km/907sq mi and includes 150 communes from the Orne, Manche, Mayenne and Sarthe *départements*.
Lying on the boundaries of both Normandy and Maine, the park can be divided into an upper stretch *(haut pays)*, featuring crests and wooded escarpments in the Alpes Mancelles, and a lower stretch *(bas pays)*, characterised by a *bocage* landscape, the rolling hills of Saosnois and open fields around Sées and Alençon.
The park can be explored by car or on a bicycle via four itineraries: the **Route des Trois Forêts** (three forests); the **Route Historique des Haras et Châteaux de l'Orne** (historic châteaux and stud farms); the **Circuit au Pays de**

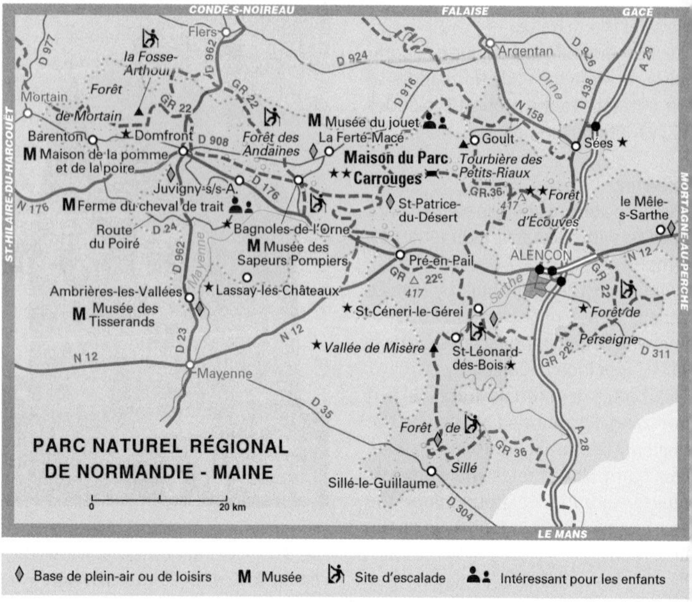

Lancelot du Lac; the **Route du Poiré,** (techniques of making cider, Calvados and perry).

There are 2 500km/1 553mi of signposted paths, including 250km/155.3mi associated with different themes.

Goult

13km/8mi E of Carrouges via D908, then left on D204.

A road lying between two farms leads to the **Chapelle St-Michel**, all that remains of the La-Lande-de-Goult Priory, once a stop on the medieval pilgrimage route to Mont-St-Michel.

The 12C Romanesque porch has remarkable capitals carved with complex designs of birds and mythical beasts, as well as hunting scenes. From the cross, there is a fine view of the Écouves forest. Nearby earthworks indicate remains of a Roman military camp.

ADDRESSES

EAT

Le Jean-Anne – *2 r. de la Fée-d'Argouges, 61150 Rânes, 11km/7mi NW of Carrouges via D 908 and D 909. 02 33 39 75 16. Closed last 2 weeks of Feb, Tue eve, Wed except public holidays.* Enjoy the view of the small Romanesque church and the château while dining in this simple, spick-and-span restaurant. The wife presides over the stoves while the husband takes your order. Traditional bourgeois cuisine.

SHOPPING

La Maison des métiers – *Maison du Parc, 61320 Carrouges. 02 33 81 75 75. www.parc-naturel-normandie-maine.fr. Closed Sept–Nov and Jan–Jun.* Located in the restored buildings of the 15C chapter house at the château, the House of Crafts of the Parc naturel régional Normandie-Maine offers arts and crafts exhibitions and has objects for sale.

Domfront★

Domfront lies spread along a rocky ridge over a gorge carved by the River Varenne, affording a panorama of the Passais *bocage* country. In addition to its strategic site★ on the old route between Mont-St-Michel and Paris, the town features historic ruins and a well-restored town centre.

- **Population:** 953.
- **Michelin Map:** 310: F-3.
- **Info:** 12 place de la Roirie. ✆02 33 38 53 97. www.domfront.com.
- **Location:** Domfront is on between Mayenne (36km/22.4mi S) and Flers (22km/13.5mi N).
- **Don't Miss:** Notre-Dame-sur-l'Eau.
- **Timing:** Several bike tours have been mapped by the tourist office.
- **Kids:** The tourist office has a guidebook for children.

A BIT OF HISTORY

Under English Rule

In 1092 the townspeople of Domfront rose up against their overlord Roger de Montgomery and rallied to **Henry Beaucler**, the son of William the Conqueror.

In 1100 Henry became King of England and Domfront an English possession.

In the 12C Henry II Plantagenet and his queen, Eleanor of Aquitaine, often visited with their brilliant court.

In August 1170 papal legates met here to attempt to reconcile Henry and his estranged Archbishop of Canterbury, Thomas Becket. Domfront passed from English to French hands and back again during the Hundred Years' War. it became French for good in 1450.

Matignon's Siege – In 1574 Gabriel, Comte de Montgomery (1530–74), who had mortally wounded the French King Henri II in a tournament, defended Domfront against the royal forces under the Comte de Matignon. Montgomery surrendered believing that his life would

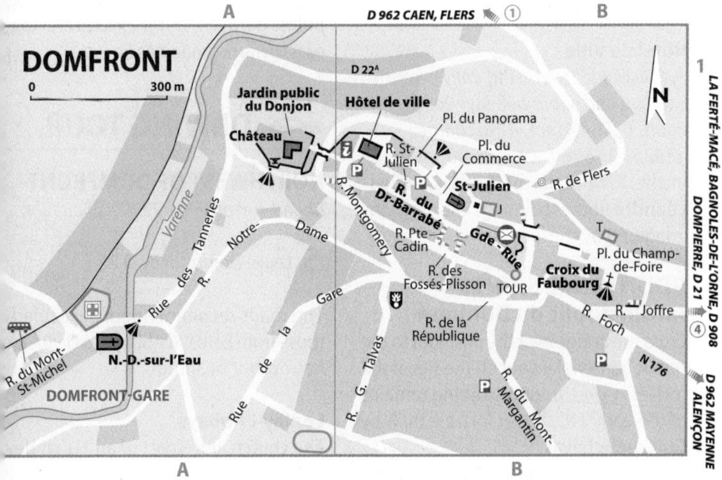

WHERE TO STAY	WHERE TO EAT
M. et Mme Roussel (Chambre d'hôte)........ ①	Relais de la Forêt (Le)........ ④

be saved but was executed on the orders of Henri's widow, Catherine de' Medici.

OLD TOWN CENTRE★

Allow 30min.

The old town is enclosed by a wall and 13 of the original 24 towers. The best preserved are those on the south side; one is still crowned with machicolations. For a good view walk along rue des Fossés-Plisson. Several 16C stone houses, formerly inhabited by noble or well-to-do families, have been restored.

Grande-Rue

This sloping street, now a pedestrian zone, has kept its original paving.

Rue du Docteur-Barrabé

There are some lovely timber-framed houses, notably at no 40 and at the corner of ruelle Porte-Cadin.

Église St-Julien

This modern church (1924) in neo-Byzantine style is dominated by a tall cement belfry. Inside, an immense mosaic depicts Christ in Majesty. The area around the church, in particular rue St-Julien and place du Commerce, is a pleasant area for a stroll.

Hôtel de Ville

Guided tours (1hr) daily except Sat–Sun and public holidays 9am–noon, 1.30–4.45pm. No charge. 02 33 30 60 60. www.domfront.com.

In the town hall, the **Salle Charles-Léandre** houses paintings and drawings imagined by the local artist.

ADDITIONAL SIGHTS

Jardin public du Donjon★

Cross the bridge over the old moat to the public gardens laid out on the site of the fortress razed in 1608. Nothing remains of the early 11C timber fortress built by Guillaume Talvas.

Of Henry Beauclerk's 1092 fortress there remain two imposing sections of the keep's walls and two towers from the flattened curtain wall. Inside the curtain walls stand the ruins of the late-11C Chapelle St-Symphorien. Eleanor of Aquitaine's daughter was born in Domfront and christened in this very chapel. Skirt the ruins of the keep to reach the terrace *(viewing table)* which affords a **panorama**★ of the Passais countryside and its three rivers, the Mayenne, Varenne and Égrenne.

Église Notre-Dame-sur-l'Eau★

Under the château, on the Varenne river.

This charming Romanesque Church of Our Lady on the Water (late-11C) was badly mutilated in the 19C when five of the seven nave bays were destroyed to make way for a road. Following damage in 1944 the church was restored.

According to legend, at Christmas in 1166 Thomas Becket, Archbishop of Canterbury, celebrated Mass in this church while in exile in France.

Several 12C frescoes have been uncovered in the south transept representing the Doctors of the Church (theologians who expounded the Christian doctrine). A Gothic canopy covers a recumbent figure with a lion at its feet.

Croix du Faubourg

From the foot of the Calvary, there is a **panorama**★ similar to the one from the public gardens, but it extends further east towards Andaines Forest.

DRIVING TOUR

NORTHWEST OF DOMFRONT

Round-trip of 35km/22mi – about 2hr.

Leave Domfront by D 22.

The roads recommended, particularly those from Lonlay-l'Abbaye to D 907, are narrow but beautiful.

Lonlay-l'Abbaye

The church, once part of an 11C abbey, enjoys a pleasant country setting. It was damaged in 1944. The 15C porch opens directly into the transept; the south arm is typical of Romanesque construction and decoration. The Gothic chancel and its granite pillars have been restored.

5km/3mi west of the village turn left onto D 134.

La Fosse-Arthour

The most interesting part of the drive is between two bridges. From a rock height on the left there is a view of La Fosse-Arthour with the River Sonce running swiftly between two steep sandstone banks and opening out into a pool before continuing on its way in a series of small cascades. Fishing and canoeing enthusiasts are able to ply the 3ha/7-acre stretch of water.

Take D 134 south towards St-Georges-de-Rouelley; at the first junction turn left onto the Rouellé road. In Rouellé turn left onto D 907 to Domfront. After 1.5km/0.9mi turn right onto a narrow road, unsurfaced towards the end, which leads to the Saucerie Manor.

Manoir de la Saucerie

The entrance pavilion flanked by two round towers with loopholes is all that remains of this 16C manor house. The combination of different building materials (stone, brick and timber) provides a certain charm.

Return to D 907 for Domfront.

ADDRESSES

STAY

Chambre d'hôte M et Mme Roussel – *"La Roculière", 61700 St-Bômer-les-Forges, 10km/6mi N. 02 33 37 60 60. 4 rooms.* A pretty farm with rooms to match.

EAT

Le Relais de la Forêt – *Le Bourg, 61700 Dompierre, 9km/5.6mi NE. 02 33 30 44 21. Closed Mon–Thu eves.* Slightly old-fashioned décor, local, seasonal produce is used, accompanied by local cider.

Flers

Situated in the heart of a *bocage* – a region of traditional hedgerows – Flers has managed to modernise itself: textiles, originally based on local linen and hemp, have given way to new industries, notably mechanical engineering and electrical appliances.

- **Population:** 16 947.
- **Michelin Map:** 310: F-2.
- **Info:** 2 pl. du Dr-Vayssières. 02 33 65 06 75. www.flerstourisme.com.
- **Location:** Flers is at the crossroads of the Paris-Granville and Caen-Laval routes: 92km/57.5mi S of Caen via D 562; 58km/36mi N of Mayenne via D 962 and D 23; 30km/18.6mi SE of Vire; 44km/27mi W of Argentan via D 924.
- **Don't Miss:** The view from the château at Mont de Cerisy.
- **Timing:** You need half a day to see Flers and its surroundings.

THE CASTLE

Musée du Château

av. du Château. Open Apr–Oct Mon–Fri 10am–noon, 2–6pm, Sat–Sun 2–6pm. Closed 1 May, 13 Jul. 2.10€. 02 33 64 66 49. www.agglo-paysdeflers.com.

The present castle, with a moat on three sides, has a 16C main building by the alchemist **Nicolas Grosparmy**, lord of Flers from 1527 to 1541, with an 18C Classical main front. The first-floor rooms contain the painting and decorative art sections. In the gallery devoted to the regional schools of the 19C there are works from the Barbizon School by Corot and Daubigny, pre-Impressionists such as Boudin and Lépine and Impressionists (Caillebotte).

AROUND MONT DE CERISY

Round-trip of 24km/15mi – allow 3hr.

Take D 924 W.

La Lande-Patry

Two giant yews grow in the old cemetery.

Continue west on D 924.

Tinchebray

Prison royale, 34 Grande-Rue, corner r. de la Prison. Guided tours Jul–Aug Wed–Sun 2–5pm. May be closed for renovation; check at tourist office. 4€. 02 33 64 23 55.

On 28 September 1106 a battle took place near this market town between two of William the Conqueror's sons. As a result the elder son, Robert Curthose, was forced to cede the Duchy of Normandy to Henry I of England, known as Henry Beauclerk.

The **Prison royale** houses an Ethnographic Museum. The revolutionary tribunal was set up on the first floor. Two cells have fireplaces, as some prisoners could pay for coal. The thick walls and wooden doors with impressive locks bear graffiti – some dates from 1793.

From Tinchebray take D 911 northeast. In St-Pierre-d'Entremont turn right onto D 18. Before crossing the River Noireau turn right onto a narrow road along the river bank.

Les Vaux

After passing between Mont de Cerisy *(left)* and St-Pierre Rocks *(right)*, the road ends in the old hamlet of St-Pierre where a small Roman bridge spans the river.

Continue southeast on D 18 to Cerisy-Belle-Étoile.

Mont de Cerisy★

Open daily 9am–6pm.

A road *(fee)*, bordered by rhododendrons, climbs up the slope to the ruined castle, which commands extensive **views**★ over the countryside even to the foothills of the Suisse Normande. The plateau is the venue for the **Rhododendron Festival**.

Continue on D 18 to return to Flers.

Mortagne-au-Perche

This pretty village retains a medieval design with the houses clustered together, presenting a jumble of brown-tile roofs contrasting with the lighter-coloured façades. The village was once a stronghold of the Perche region.

- **Population:** 4 210.
- **Michelin Map:** 310: M-3.
- **Info:** Halle-aux-Grains. 02 33 85 11 18. www.ot-mortagne auperche.fr.
- **Location:** Mortagne is 35km/21.7mi S of L'Aigle; 74km/46mi SW of Dreux
- **Don't Miss:** Approaching from the N, on D 930, you will enjoy an excellent view of the town.
- **Timing:** After 1–2hr in town, take one of the described driving tours.

VISIT

Jardin Public

These gardens *à la française* offer good views of the Perche countryside. An outstanding equestrian statue by E Frémiet (1824–1910) depicts Neptune as a horse, setting out to conquer Ceres.

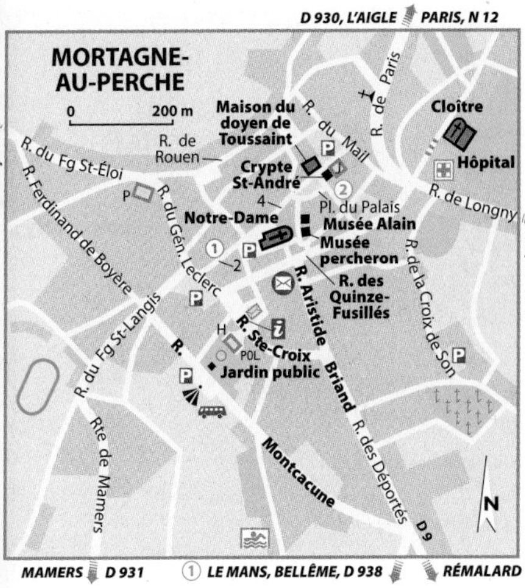

WHERE TO STAY

Miottière (Chambre d'hôte la)........①

Tribunal (Hôtel le)........②

WHERE TO EAT

Hostellerie Genty-Home........①

STREETS INDEX

Notre-Dame (R.)........2

Hôpital

Delightful 16C cloisters with panelled vaulting and an 18C chapel are all that remain of the former convent of St Clare.

Porte St-Denis

Musée Percheron , rue du Portail-St-Denis. Open mid-Jun–mid-Sept Tue–Sun 3–6pm. Closed 14 Jul. No charge. 02 33 25 25 87.

The St-Denis Gate is the sole remnant of the town's fortifications. In the 16C two storeys were added to the original 13C Gothic arch and they now house the **Musée Percheron**.

Maison des Comtes du Perche

This 17C house stands on the site of a former manor house. The ground floor houses the public library, and the first floor contains the Musée Alain.

Église Notre-Dame

The church was built between 1495 and 1535 and combines both Flamboyant Gothic and Early Renaissance styles on the exterior decoration.

There is a magnificent 18C **altarpiece**★ in the apse. The stained-glass window in the third chapel, off the north aisle, recalls the role of local people in the colonisation of Canada in the 17C.

Musée Alain

8 r. du Portail St-Denis. Open Tue, Thu–Fri 2–6pm, Wed 9.30am–noon, 1.30–6pm, Sat 10am–noon, 2–5pm. Closed public holidays, 25 Dec–5 Jan and public holidays. No charge. 02 33 25 25 87.

The French philosopher **Alain** (1868–1951), whose real name was **Émile Chartier**, was born in Mortagne. The museum displays personal belongings.

DRIVING TOURS

THE PERCHE AND TRAPPE FORESTS

Round-trip of 51km/31.5mi – allow about 1hr30min.

From Mortagne take N 12 north and after 12km/7.5mi turn right onto D 290.

Parc naturel régional du Perche, created in 1998, covers 1 820sq km/702.7sq mi of gentle hills, deep forests, hidden ponds, hedgerows, green valleys and interesting architecture.

Autheuil

The Romanesque church (restored) has a fine chancel arch at the transept, handsome capitals on the square piers and a 16C statue of St Leonard.

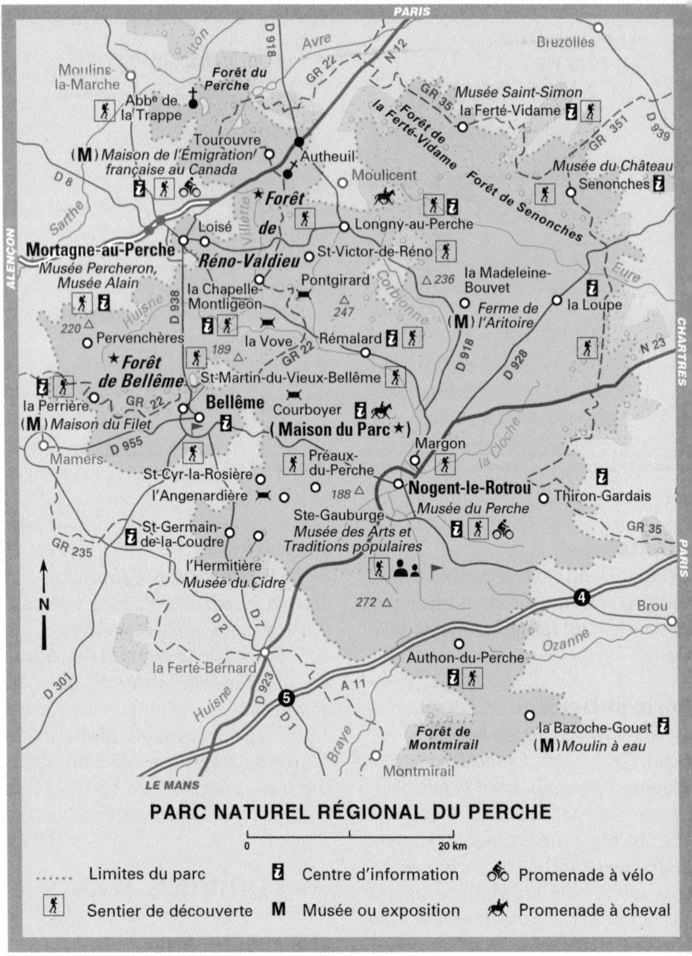

Make a U-turn and take D 290 west in the direction of Tourouvre.

Tourouvre

Two stained-glass windows in the church tell about local families associated with the founding of Quebec.

Beyond the church turn right onto a road which climbs steeply towards Perche Forest.

After a steep climb the road enters Perche Forest and, after 2km/1mi, reaches the beautiful Étoile du Perche crossroads. Continue straight ahead and on reaching the Avre Valley turn left to admire the various pools. West of Bresolettes the road enters Trappe Forest.

At the road junction turn right onto D 930 and then left onto the minor road.

Abbaye de la Trappe

Soligny-La-Trappe. Monastery store open Jul–Aug Mon–Sat 10.30am–noon, 3–6.30pm, Sun 11.45am–1pm, 3–6.30pm; Sept–Jun Mon–Sat 10.30am–noon, 2.45–5.45pm, Sun 11.45am–1pm, 2.45–6.30pm. All services open to public. Check schedule. No charge. 02 33 84 17 00. www.latrappe.fr.

The 12C abbey was named after an area where hunters caught game using a *trappe*. The name was adopted by monasteries which, like La Trappe, form the Order of Reformed Cistercians of the Strict Observance.

Make a U-turn and take D 930 south to Mortagne.

FROM MORTAGNE-AU-PERCHE TO LONGNY

25km/15.5mi – allow about 30min.

Loisé

The 16C church is flanked by a monumental square tower.

Forêt de Réno-Valdieu

This 1 600ha/4 000-acre forest has beautiful stands of very old trees. A farm has replaced the former Abbaye de Valdieu. West of the forest the road (D 8) traverses a remarkable landscape of hills, passing Château de la Goyère.

On leaving the forest, take D 291 right.

Monceaux-au-Perche

Manoir du Pontgirard. Open May–Sept Thu–Tue 10am–6pm. No charge. 02 33 73 61 49.http://pontgirard.free.fr.

This village standing at the confluence of two small valleys is one of the prettiest in the area. Nestling along the banks of the River **Jambée**, the **Manoir du Pontgirard** (16C) features some fine terraced **gardens** tucked away behind its walls.

Longny is reached by taking D 11, which runs through the shady Jambée Valley.

Longny-au-Perche

A pleasant location beside the River Jambée. There is a good view of Longny from the charming 16C **Chapelle de Notre-Dame-de-Pitié** *(access by rue Gaston-Gibory on the right of the town hall)*. The carved wooden doors are by a local 19C-20C artist, Abbé Vingtier.

The **Église St-Martin** dates from the late-15C and the early 16C. The square belfry is supported by carved buttresses and the stair tower.

ADDRESSES

STAY

Chambre d'hôte La Miottière – *61400 Le Pin-La-Garenne, 12km/7.5mi S. 02 33 83 84 01. 3 rooms.* Set in the countryside in an area of 53ha/130 acres. Rooms are spacious and the breakfasts quite adequate.

Hôtel Le Tribunal – *4 pl. du Palais. 02 33 25 04 77. 18 rooms. 9€.* Welcoming, family-run house built between 13C an 18C. Nearby arethe church and museum. Rooms are characterful and the terrace is pleasant on warm days.

EAT

Hostellerie Genty-Home – *4 r. Notre-Dame. 02 33 25 11 53. Closed Sun eve except public holidays. 8 rooms.* This traditional hostelry gives onto a nice little square in the city centre. The hotel rooms have a modern flair, whereas the elegant dining room is Louis XV. Regional specialities.

Haras National du Pin★

Le Pin Stud Farm, one of the most famous horse-breeding establishments in France, is attractively set amid woods and meadows. Its activities include racing and training for the staff of other national and private stud farms (smithery, artificial insemination, etc.).

- **Michelin Map:** 310: J-2.
- **Info:** Association Haras du Pin Tourisme. 02 33 36 68 68. www.haras-national-du-pin.com.
- **Location:** The Haras is some 15km/9mi E of Argentan via D 926.
- **Don't Miss:** The Cour d'Honneur on Thursdays with stallions and carriage teams.

A BIT OF HISTORY

The stud farm dates from 1665, when Jean-Baptiste Colbert, chief minister of Louis XIV, founded the national stables. The buildings, designed by Pierre Le Mousseux, a disciple of the great architect François Mansart, date from 1715 to 1730; the grounds were designed under the king's landscape architect, André Le Nôtre.

VISIT

Guided tours (1hr) Apr–Sept 10am–6pm; school holidays (other than Jul–Aug long holiday) 10.30am–noon, 2–7pm; rest of the year 2–5pm. Closed 1 Jan, 25 Dec. 9€. Display of horsemanship Jun–Sept Thu 3pm in the Cour Colbert. 5€.

Three magnificent woodland rides converge on the horseshoe-shaped courtyard known as the Cour Colbert.

The château *(not part of tour)* holds offices and reception rooms.

The brick and stone stable wings can accommodate the 40 or more stallions grouped according to their breed, colour and size, although most of the year only 20 horses are in residence; the others are stabled at regional stud farms. Other outbuildings house the collection of 19C carriages used for official events in France and abroad.

EXCURSION

St-Germain-de-Clairefeuille

10km/6mi SE (via Nonant-le-Pin).

The church is distinguished by its magnificent woodwork including 13 **painted panels**★ of the Life of Our Lord by the early 16C Flemish School.

Haras National du Pin

St-Évroult-Notre-Dame-du-Bois

The ruins of this abbey, a great centre of intellectual life in the 11C and 12C, are set in a lovely valley, through which the River Charentonne flows.

- **Michelin Map:** 310: L-2.
- **Info:** Place Fulbert-de-Beina, L'Aigle. 02 33 24 12 40. www.paysdelaigle.com.
- **Location:** The abbey is 27km/17mi NW of L'Aigle on D 13.
- **Don't Miss:** Enjoy the driving tour through the lovely countryside.
- **Timing:** Take time for a stroll in the woods near the abbey.
- **Kids:** Nearby, at Saints-Pères pond, there is a recreation area.

VISIT

Abbey Ruins

Destroyed in the 10C by wars, the Romanesque abbey of Ouche revived in the 11C. It was rebuilt in the 13C in the Gothic style, but little remains.

In front of the main entrance stands a monument to Orderic Vital (1075–1142), an English historian whose work described the abbey in its heyday.

DRIVING TOUR

THE CHARENTONNE VALLEY

From St-Évroult to Serquigny, 65km/40.4mi – about 2hr30min.

Leave St-Évroult by D 31 travelling northeast. After 5km/3mi, take D 14 left. At La Ferté-Frênel, take D 252 and D 33 north.

This tour takes you between Anceins and Notre-Dame-du-Hamel.

In Mélicourt, take D 819 left.

St-Denis-d'Augerons

From the war memorial there is an attractive view of the two churches of St-Denis-d'Augerons and St-Aquilin.

Return to Mélicourt; take D 33 north.

Broglie

This small town was the fief of the famous Broglie (pronounced Broy) family. The 18C **château** *(private)* is built around a medieval fortress. The pillars and the chancel of the church are Romanesque; the rest is 15C and 16C.

Jardin aquatique

Open daily. No charge. *02 32 44 60 58.*

This charming little water garden is irrigated by the River Charentonne.

Étang Saints-Pères

Open daily. No charge. *02 32 44 60 58.*

The banks of this little pond offer picnic tables, peddle-boats, walks and recreation facilities.

Ferrières-St-Hilaire

This remains of the forge and the forge master's manor still stand.

St-Évroult-Notre-Dame-du-Bois

© Jmalo/Wikimedia Commons

St-Quentin-de-Isles
Below the 19C château, there is a textile plant. A dovecote stands on an island.

Bernay
See BERNAY, p167.

Take D 144 east along the opposite side of the river.

Menneval
The country church with its renovated façade is delightful. The local Brotherhood of Charity dates from 1060.

5km/3mi further along, cross the bridge over the Charentonne.

Fontaine-l'Abbé
A pretty Norman village with a Louis XIII château and a **church** (*closed to the public)*. Inside are displayed the banners of the local Brotherhood of Charity.

Return to D 133 and continue onto Serquigny.

Serquigny
The church façade, chequered in blank flint and white stone, is pierced by a Romanesque doorway. Inside are a Renaissance chapel *(left)* with stained-glass windows of the same period. Note the carved wooden panels on the pulpit and the old wooden statues in the nave.

ADDRESSES

STAY

Le Manoir de Villers – *61550 Villers-en-Ouche, 9km/5.6mi N by D 230, direction Bocquencé. 02 33 34 98 00. Closed Jan, Tue–Thu except hotel. 6 rooms.* .
On this 17C farm is a riding school, an Italian restaurant and six small bedrooms. Rustic dining room.

Sées★

Sées has been the seat of an episcopal see since St Latuin converted the district to Christianity in the year 400. The quiet old cathedral town, with its several religious communities, has been sensitively restored.

- **Population:** 4 967.
- **Michelin Map:** 310: K-3.
- **Info:** place du Général de Gaulle. 02 33 28 74 79.
- **Location:** 22km/13.5mi SE of Argentan, or 19km/11.8mi N of Alençon, near the Forêt d'Écouves.
- **Don't Miss:** The chancel of the cathedral; Forêt d'Écouves.
- **Timing:** Take a day to see the town and enjoy the forest.

CATHÉDRALE★★

Allow 15min.
Open daily 9am–6.30pm.
Despite its difficult history, the cathedral is one of the finest examples of 13C and 14C Norman Gothic.
Exterior – The porch on the west front is disfigured by heavy buttresses added in the 16C when it began to lean alarmingly.
Interior – In the **chancel**★★ and the **transepts**★★ the triforium is an interesting example of Gothic art, lit by magnificent 13C **stained glass**★★ and rose windows in the transept.

SIGHTS

Église Notre-Dame-de-la-Place

Guided tour available from the tourist office. 02 33 27 81 76.
The organ loft is Renaissance and the 12 low-relief sculptures illustrating scenes from the New Testament are 16C.

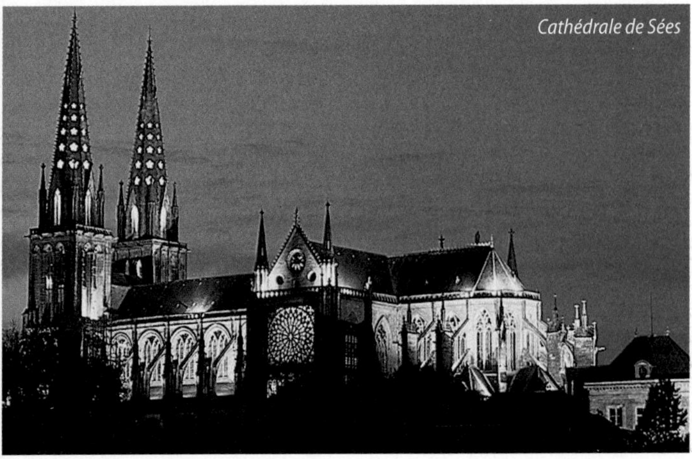
Cathédrale de Sées

B. Kaufmann/MICHELIN

Musée départemental d'Art religieux

pl. du Gén. de Gaulle. Open Jul–Sept Wed–Mon 10am–6pm. 2€ (under 12 years no charge). 02 33 81 23 00.

The museum, in the former canons' residence, presents a varied collection (12C–19C) of religious art and objects.

Ancienne abbaye St-Martin

Closed to the public.

The old abbey is now a children's home. Through the great main door one can see the gracious 18C abbot's lodging.

Ancien évêché

This palace was built for Bishop Argentré in 1778.

The beautiful wrought-iron gate has an escutcheon and foliated scrolls.

Anciennes halles

This unusual covered market, a rotunda with a peristyle, dates from the 19C.

EXCURSIONS

Château d'O★

8km/5mi NW by N 158 and a right turn. Guided tour of gardens and part of château (30min) mid-Jul–Aug Mon–Sat 10am–noon, 2–5pm. No charge. 02 33 39 55 79 (M. Gascoin).

This late-15C château combines the Flamboyant Gothic and Renaissance styles. For many generations the château belonged to the O family, who were royal courtiers. The name "O", pronounced the same as *eau* ("water" in French), is appropriate, for the many sloping roofs, slim turrets, delicate ornamentation and façade of brick and stone are beautifully reflected in the moat.

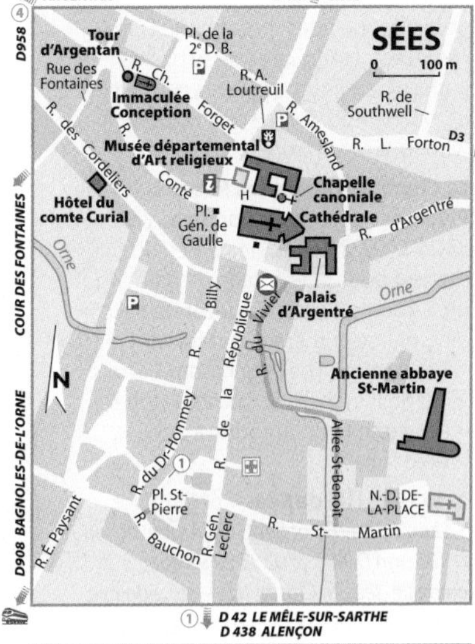

WHERE TO STAY		WHERE TO EAT	
Ferme Équestre des Tertres (Chambre d'hôte)	1	Cheval Blanc (Le)	1
Île de Sées (Hôtel)	4		

From Sées to Alençon

29km18mi – 2hr15min.

Écouves Forest

Guided tours on foot or on horseback through the forest massifs (Écouves, Andaines, Bellême and Perche-Trappe, Réno-Valdieu, Moulins-Bonsmoulins) are available on request one month in advance from the Office National des Forêts (National Forestry Commission), 36 r. St-Blaise, 61000 Alençon. 02 33 82 55 00. www.onf.fr.

This **forest** (14 000ha/34 600 acres) covers the eastern promontory of the hills of Basse-Normandie.

The **Signal d'Écouves** is with the Mont des Avaloirs the highest point (417m/1 368.6ft) in western France.

Take D 204 south. At the Rochers du Vignage crossroads bear right onto D 26 and again right onto a forest road; park the car.

Rochers du Vignage★

1hr45min round-trip on foot.

The path *(marked with yellow blazes)* leaves the forest road to a low rock crest from which there are outstanding views over the forest. The path reaches the Chêne-au-Verdier, then parallels the Aubert forest road for 300m/328yd, forks right, then returns downhill to the forest road and the car.

Take D 26 south to Alençon.

ADDRESSES

STAY

Chambre d'hôte Ferme Équestre des Tertres – *61500 La Chapelle-près-Sées, 4km/2.5mi S of Sées dir. La Ferté-Macé via D 908 then Bouillon via C 14. 02 33 27 74 67. www.fedestertres.com. 5 rooms.* This farm is the starting point for fine rides through the Écouves Forest. Hikers can follow blazed paths whereas other guests could try a barouche ride. Three stylish bedrooms with robust furniture.

Chambre d'hôte Les Roses et les Pivoines – *26 r. du Dr Hommey. 02 33 26 17 02. 2 rooms.* Behind this modest bourgeois façade, 2 charming guestrooms pleasantly decorated according to flower themes and furnished with antiques. The larger room, in a wing built in the 18C, boasts a stone fireplace. In the bathroom, a claw-footed tub.

Hôtel Île de Sées – *61500 Macé, 5.5km/3.5mi NW of Sées, dir. Argentat, via D 303 and D 747. 02 33 27 98 65. www.ile-sees.fr. Closed Nov–Feb, Sun eve, Mon. 16 rooms.* Enjoy the peace and quiet of the countryside at this former dairy, set in a park. Dark woodwork adds warmth to the interior decoration. Nice rooms in pastel shades with sedate stained furniture.

EAT

Le Cheval Blanc – *1 pl. St-Pierre. 02 33 27 80 48. Closed Feb, Nov and Fri.* A charming "Old France" atmosphere prevails in this century-old half-timbered inn. Traditional dishes in a rustic setting. Guest rooms are clean and simple.

Le Gourmand Candide – *14 pl. du Gén.-de-Gaulle. 02 33 27 91 28. Closed Feb school holidays, Sun eve, Tue eve, Mon.* The pretty green façade of the restaurant draws the eye. Inside, a contemporary dining room, and a more elegant room with a veranda. Traditional dishes such as the ***tête de veau du gourmand Candide***.

SOUND AND LIGHT

Les Musilumières – *Jul–mid-Sept, Fri–Sat eve. 45min. Reserve at tourist office.* Sound and light show in the cathedral, retracing its history.

Vimoutiers

The small town of Vimoutiers is tucked away in the valley of the River Vie between hills covered with apple trees which supply the local cider factories. Vimoutiers has close ties with Marie Harel, who gave us the famous Camembert cheese. A statue to her memory, offered by an American cheesemaker, stands on the town hall square.

- **Population:** 4 029.
- **Michelin Map:** 310: K-1.
- **Info:** 21 place Mackau. *02 33 67 49 42.*
- **Location:** Vimoutiers is 28km/17.5mi S of Lisieux via D 579, and 45km/28mi SW of Bernay.

VISIT

Musée du Camembert

10 av. du Gén. de Gaulle. Audio-guided tours (30min) Mar–Oct Tue–Sat 9am–noon, 2–6pm, Mon 2–6pm, Sun and public holidays 10am–noon, 2.30–6pm. 3€. 02 33 39 30 29.
The exhibition describes the history and manufacturing process of Camembert. Note the collection of Camembert labels. The legend has it that, during the French Revolution, Marie Harel protected a fugitive priest who, in compensation, revealed to her his secret cheese recipe.

EXCURSIONS

Camembert

5km/3mi S by D 246.

Maison du Camembert

Open May–Aug daily 10am–6pm. Feb–Apr and Sept Wed–Sun 10am–6pm. No charge. 02 33 12 10 37. www.maisonducamembert.com.
This modern museum (1992), shaped like an open Camembert cheese box, lies at the heart of this tiny village, facing the 13C church. Here is information on this famous cheese and where it is made. Next to the church, opposite the museum, stands the **Ferme Président**, producer of a popular brand of Camembert. (*open Jun–Aug daily 10am–noon, 2–6pm; tour and tasting 5€ (half-price with a label from a Ferme Président product). 02 33 36 06 60. www.fermpresident.com,* A few farms where cheese is still made in the traditional way can also be visited.

Prieuré St-Michel de Crouttes★

5km/3mi W via the D 916, then take the third road to the right. Open May–Sept Wed–Sun 2–6pm (last admission 30min before closing). 6€. 02 33 39 15 15. www.prieure-saint-michel.com
The origin of this monastic house dates from the 10C. The noble rustic architecture of the buildings is admirably set off by an orchard, gardens and water. Beyond the 18C dairy is the 13C **tithe barn**. One can also see the 18C prior's lodging, the chapel (13C) and the bakery, an 18C timber-framed building. Part of the priory is operated as a bed-and-breakfast, with reception rooms and tea room.

Camembert labels

S. Sauvignier/MICHELIN

The choice of Normandy as the landing point for the invasion of Europe was not evident. Defended by the Atlantic Wall, the coast had choppy water and tricky tides. Italy seemed a more likely option, but the invasion begun in July 1943 proved slow and costly; on the east, the Germans still besieged Leningrad. At the Teheran Conference in late 1943, Churchill, Roosevelt and Stalin agreed on a French front. Men and arms were massed in Britain and intense bombing raids over Germany and France were intended to soften defences. The tour described in this section includes that part of the Calvados coast between the mouths of the Orne and the Vire, also known as the Côte de Nacre, where the D-Day landings took place on 6 June 1944. The marked itineraries, known as Overlord-L'Assaut (Overlord-The Onslaught) and D-Day-Le Choc (D-Day-The Impact), are two of several such itineraries in the Historical Area of the Battle of Normandy.

- **Michelin Map:** F3-K4
- **Info:** Pont St-Jean, Bayeux. 02 31 51 28 28. www.bessin-normandie.fr.
- **Location:** This section covers the Calvados coast between the mouths of the Orne and the Vire, also known as the Côte de Nacre (Mother-of-Pearl coast) where the Normandy landings took place on D-Day, 6 June 1944.
- **Timing:** Each of the circuits described below takes half a day.

Operation Overlord

The Normandy Landings, or D-Day, for which the code name during preparations for this massive Allied invasion was Operation Overlord, were commanded by US General Dwight D Eisenhower, with British General (later Field Marshal) Bernard Montgomery in charge of land forces. Transport involved an armada of 7 000 ships and landing craft, and 12 500 aircraft. Some 156 000 troops landed, supported by 195 000 sailors. Preparations were epic: finally, all depended on the tides, to bring landing craft to shore.

See The D-Day Landings on p303 for a more detailed history of events.

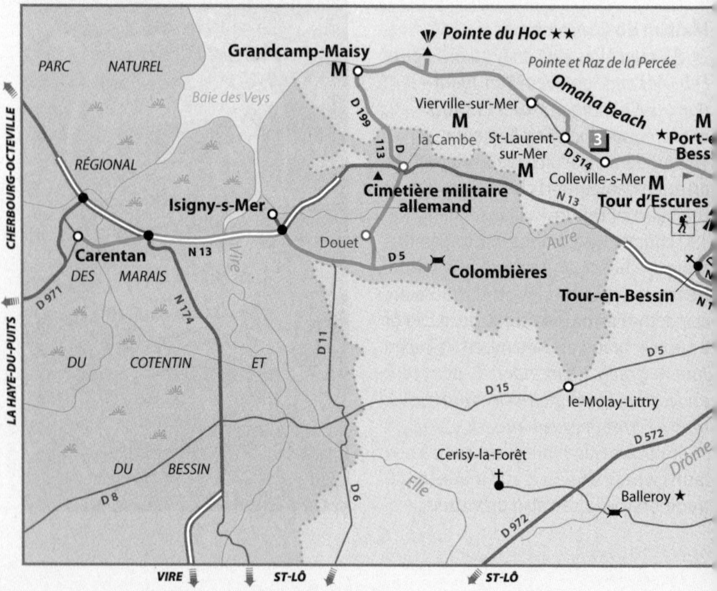

D-Day Landings: A Turning Point

Field Marshal Erwin Rommel, inspecting the Atlantic Wall, pointed out that if the Allies succeeded in breaching it, the Third Reich would fall. Germany fell on 8 May, 1945, after a long stuggle, but the end had begun 11 months earlier.

65th Anniversary: 2009

Leaders of France, Great Britain, the USA and Canada met on the beaches of Normandy to mark the June 1944 landings, probably the last commemoration where significant numbers of veterans will be able to take part.

DRIVING TOURS

1 SWORD BEACH–JUNO BEACH–GOLD BEACH

71km/44mi – allow 1hr15min. From Caen take D 515 northeast.

The road to Riva-Bella runs down the lower Orne Valley west of the ship canal.

Bénouville

Château. Open during temporary exhibitions, usually late Jun–Sept Wed–Mon 2–6pm. 1.50€. 02 31 95 53 23. www.cg14.fr/chateau_benouville.

The town hall, which stands alone in a fork in the road near Pegasus Bridge, was occupied by the British 5th Parachute Brigade at 11.45pm on 5 June.

The **château**★, one of the major works by the Parisian architect **Claude-Nicolas Ledoux** (1736–1806), is a fine example of French Neoclassical architecture at the end of the 18C.

The interior contains a suite of five rooms and a magnificent **staircase**★★ rising through three landings to the first floor. The château was virtually undamaged in the war.

Pegasus Bridge★

The two Ranville-Bénouville bridges were captured soon after midnight during the night of 5–6 June 1944 by the British 5th Parachute Brigade: **Pegasus** was their emblem. Major Howard had won the Battle of Pegasus – a field where the Horsa and Hamilcar gliders could land, a mobile bridge made of steel, a house at the water's edge ... and the Gondrée family, who waited until **Lord**

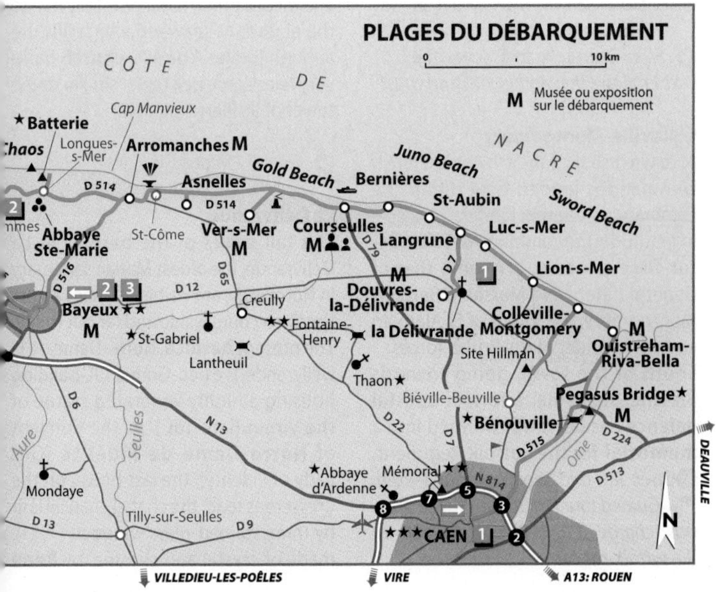

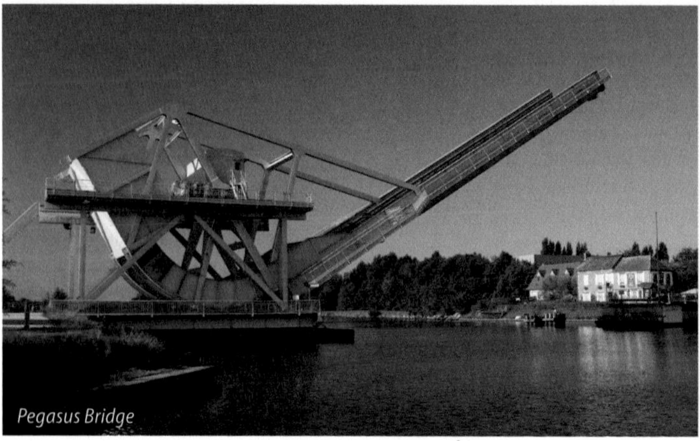
Pegasus Bridge

© Stephen Meese/Dreamstime.com

Lovat (1911–95) and his Green Berets arrived, to the strains of Bill Millin's bagpipes *(see sidebar, p304)*.

Mémorial Pegasus★

Av. du Major-Howard, Ranville.
Open daily Apr–Sept 9.30am–6.30pm; Feb–Mar and Oct–Nov 10am–1pm, 2–5pm. 6€. 02 31 78 19 44. www.normandy1944.com.
Near the commemorative stelae stands a museum devoted to life during the Occupation and the Normandy landings.

Ouistreham-Riva-Bella

See OUISTREHAM-RIVA-BELLA, p144.

From Riva-Bella to Asnelles, the D 514 follows the Mother-of-Pearl coast.

Colleville-Montgomery

At dawn on 6 June the 4th Anglo-French commandos landed here under the command of Captain Kieffer.
In gratitude, the commune of Colleville-sur-Orne added to its name that of General (later Field Marshall) Bernard Montgomery, the Victor of El Alamein and commander of the British forces.
South of the town, going towards Biéville-Beauville, a former coastal defence has been transformed into a **memorial** for the Suffolk Regiment. *Open Jul–mid-Sept Mon–Sat 3–7pm. Guided tour (1hr30min) Tue at 3pm. No charge. 02 31 97 12 61. www.amis-du-suffolk-rgt.com.*

Lion-sur-Mer

This seaside resort has a 16C–17C **château**. The **church** has a 11C Romanesque tower and handsome capitals.

Luc-sur-Mer

Luc is a seaside resort known for its bracing air. The spa *(see Addresses, p309)* offers hydro-sodium-iodate cures. The beautiful **municipal park**★ *(35 r. de la Mer)*, is an oasis of greenery.

Langrune-sur-Mer

The name of this resort on the Mother-of-Pearl coast is Scandinavian in origin and means green land, probably due to the abundant seaweed which fills the air with iodine. The 13C **church** has a very handsome bell tower similar to the tower of St-Pierre in Caen.

Take D 7 inland.

La Délivrande

The tall spires of the basilica in La Délivrande, the oldest Marian sanctuary in Normandy, are visible for miles across the Caen countryside and far out to sea. The present **basilica**, Notre-Dame de la Délivrande, is a neo-Gothic 19C building housing a highly venerated statue of the Virgin (late-16C). At the Convent of **Notre-Dame-de-Fidélité** (Our Lady of Fidelity), the last house on the Cresserons road, the chapel chancel is lit by three stained-glass windows (1931), made of crystal and chrome, by **René**

The D-Day Landings

D-Day Invasion, Omaha Beach

© Bettmann/CORBIS

Dawn of D-Day – The formidable armada, which consisted of 4 266 barges and landing craft together with hundreds of warships and naval escorts, set sail from the south coast of England on the night of 5 June 1944 (*for further details, see The Battle of Normandy in the Introduction*); it was preceded by flotillas of minesweepers to clear a passage through the mine fields in the English Channel.

As the crossing proceeded, airborne troops were flown out and landed in two detachments at either end of the invasion front. The British 6th Division quickly took possession of the Bénouville-Ranville bridge, since named Pegasus Bridge after the airborne insignia, and harried the enemy positions between the River Orne and the River Dives to prevent reinforcements arriving. West of the River Vire the American 101st and 82nd Divisions mounted an attack on key positions such as Ste-Mère-Église or opened up the exits from Utah Beach.

British Sector – Although preliminary bombing and shelling had not destroyed Hitler's Atlantic Wall, they succeeded in disorganising German defences. Land forces were able to reach their objectives, divided into three beachheads.

A German counter-attack was crushed under naval bombardment.

Sword Beach – The Franco-British commandos landed at Colleville-Plage, Lion-sur-Mer and St-Aubin. They captured Riva-Bella and the strongpoints at Lion and Langrune and then linked up with the airborne troops at Pegasus Bridge. The main strength of the British 3rd Division then landed. This area, exposed to the Germans' long-range guns in Le Havre, became the crucial point in the battle.

Juno Beach – The Canadian 3rd Division landed at Bernières and Courseulles, reaching Creully by 5pm. They were the first troops to enter Caen on 9 July 1944.

Gold Beach – The British 50th Division landed at Ver-sur-Mer and Asnelles; by the afternoon they held and the artificial Mulberry harbour could be brought into position. The 47th Commandos advanced and captured Port-en-Bessin during the night of 7 June. On 9 June the British sector joined up with the Americans from Omaha Beach. On 12 June, after the capture of Carentan had enabled the troops from Omaha and Utah beaches to join forces, a single beachhead was established.

American Sector – The events involved in the landing of American troops at **Omaha Beach** and **Utah Beach** are described under *OMAHA BEACH* and *Presqu'île du COTENTIN*.

Bill Millin and his Bagpipes

"Down the road came Lord Lovat's commandos, cocky in their green berets. Bill Millin marched at the head of the column, his pipes blaring out *Blue Bonnets over the Border.* On both sides the firing suddenly ceased, as soldiers gazed at the spectacle. But the shock didn't last long. As the commandos headed across the bridges the Germans began firing again. Bill Millin remembers "just trusting to luck that I did not get hit, as I could not hear very much for the drone of the pipes".

The most famous literary work about the Battle of Normandy is undoubtedly *The Longest Day*, written by the late Irish author **Cornelius Ryan** (published by Simon & Schuster in New York).

Lalique, who was also responsible for the door of the tabernacle.

Continue on D 7 for 3km/2mi until you reach D 404 leading to Courseulles-sur-Mer. Follow signs for the Musée-Radar up to D 83 on the right.

Douvres-la-Délivrande

Musée-Radar, Rte de Basly. Open daily mid-Jun–mid-Sept Tue–Sun 10am–6pm; May–mid-Jun holiday weekends 10am–6pm (last entry 30min before closing). 5.50€. 02 31 37 74 43.

The **Musée-Radar** retraces the history of radar equipment. Blockhouses, situated on the site of the German radar station at Douvres, have been renovated and provide insight into the daily life of German soldiers stationed along the Atlantic Wall. The role of aerial or maritime search equipment in the last war and their evolution since 1945 is explained with the help of realistic scenery.

St-Aubin-sur-Mere

Bracing seaside resort with an offshore reef for shrimping and crab catching.

Bernières-sur-Mer

The French–Canadian Chaudière Regiment landed on this beach. Press and radio reporters came ashore here and sent the first reports of the landings.

The church has a justly famous 13C **bell tower**★; the three storeys and the stone spire together measure 67m/220ft.

Courseulles-sur-Mer

Centre Juno Beach

Voie des Français-Libres. Open daily Apr–Sept 9.30am–7pm; Mar and Oct 10am–6pm; Feb and Nov–Dec 10am–1pm, 2–5pm. Closed 25 Dec. 6.50€. 02 31 37 32 17. www.junobeach.org.

At Centre Juno Beach, a short film introduces you to the role of Canadian soldiers and sailors, as well as the heroic performance of Canadian industry in the war effort. Multimedia guideposts and interactive exhibits enliven the displays.

In 1944 several important people landed on the west beach at Courseulles, then part of Juno Beach: on 12 June Winston Churchill, on 14 June General de Gaulle on his way to Bayeux and on 16 June George VI on a visit to the British troops. Courseulles is also a seaside resort well known for its large marina.

The **Maison de la Mer**, at the entrance to the harbour, displays an astonishing collection of sea shells and is equipped with an aquarium (100 000l/22 000gal of sea water) containing local marine fauna.

Closed for renovation. Scheduled to open 2010 or 2011. 02 31 37 92 58.

Ver-sur-Mer

On 6 June 1944 this tiny resort was the main British bridgehead in the Gold Beach sector. A monument commemorating the landing stands where D 514 meets avenue du Colonel-Harper. The **tower**★ of St Martin's Church

is the original robust 11C Romanesque structure of four storeys.
The **lighthouse** works in conjunction with the lights of Portland and St Catherine's Point in England and at Antifer, Le Havre and Gatteville in France to guide the shipping in the Channel. There is an extensive view from the lantern.

America-Gold Beach Museum

2 pl. Amiral-Byrd. Open Jul–Aug daily 10.30am–5.30pm; Apr–Jun and Sept Wed–Mon 10.30am–5.30pm. 4€. 02 31 22 58 58. www.goldbeachmusee.fr.
The first exhibit describes pioneering transatlantic flights, notably that of the triple-engine Fokker *America* which landed at Ver in 1927. Homage is also paid to the British troops who landed at Gold Beach on 6 June 1944 to liberate Bayeux. West of Ver-sur-Mer, the cliffs of come into view.

Asnelles

This little resort with its sandy beach lies at the eastern end of the artificial harbour established at Arromanches. From the sea wall there is a good view of the cliffs and the roads of (traces of the Mulberry harbour still exist). On the beach stands a monument raised to the memory of the British 231st Infantry Brigade.
West of Asnelles the road climbs to the eastern edge of the Bessin plateau; the Romanesque church in St-Côme comes into view. West of St-Côme, on the right-hand side of the road, a belvedere *(viewing table and parking area)* offers a beautiful **view★** down over the harbour of and the last remaining elements of the Mulberry harbour.

Arromanches-les-Bains

See ARROMANCHES-LES-BAINS, p83.
After , the road goes through the fields of Bessin. Further on you can see the bell towers of Bayeux.

2 OMAHA BEACH★

From Bayeux to Carentan 75km/46.6mi – allow 2hr45min.

Leave Bayeux by the north 13 going west.

Tour-en-Bessin

The church has a 12C doorway. The spire above the transept crossing dates from the early 13C. The Romanesque nave with its pure lines has been renovated. Admire the beauty of the Gothic chancel (early 15C). On the columns of the arcade to the right, notice 12 sculpted scenes representing the months of the year.

Tour d'Escures

Park beside D 100; take the private path (left) uphill (15min on foot there and back).
Steps on the outside of the wall lead to the top of the round tower, which provides an extensive view of the rolling Bessin countryside and of Bayeux.

Port-en-Bessin★

See p308. From Port-en-Bessin, as far as Grandcamp-Maisy, the road continues through the Bessin region, which is crisscrossed by hedgerows.

Omaha Beach

See OMAHA BEACH, p140.

Pointe du Hoc★★

From D 514 coming from Bayeux, just after a manor house, turn right to the P car park. 1hr on foot.
The Pointe du Hoc was heavily defended by the Germans; their observation post

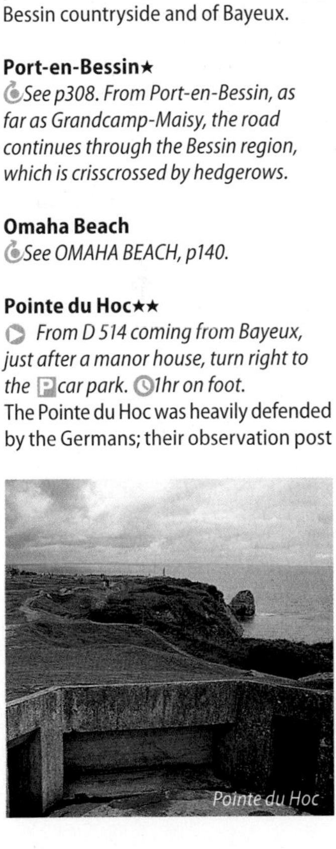
Pointe du Hoc
S. Sauvignier/MICHELIN

Crabs and AVREs and DD Tanks

Ingenious Fighting Machines to Breach the Atlantic Wall

These bizarre fighting machines, known as Hobart's Funnies, formed the 79th Armoured Division, commanded by their foremost inventor Major-General Sir Percy Hobart. The tanks were designed to swim ashore (Duplex Drive: Sherman amphibious tank); to clear a path through the minefields (Crab: Sherman flail tank); to double as flame-throwers (Crocodile: Churchill VII tank); to lay matting on soft sand (Bobbin); and to double as bridges to carry other tanks over obstacles (Ark: Churchill tank). The tanks were a complete surprise to the enemy and after the Normandy landings the 79th Armoured Division pursued its advance, crossing the Rhine and entering Germany.

Eisenhower paid a vibrant tribute to Hobart's Funnies, pointing out that many lives had been saved thanks to the "successful utilisation of our mechanical inventions". A Duplex Drive can still be seen on Canada Beach (Plage du Canada) at Courseulles-sur-Mer.

covered all the area where the American invasion fleet appeared on the morning of 6 June 1944. As the troops landing on **Omaha Beach** would have been particularly vulnerable to attack from this battery, the **Texas** fired 600 salvoes of 35.5cm/14in shells.

The 2nd Battalion of Rangers captured the position by assault at dawn on 6 June, scaling the cliffs with ropes and extendible ladders but with heavy losses – 135 Rangers out of 225. Commandos of the 116th Regiment of the US infantry, assisted by tanks, subdued the German defence. The gaping craters and battered blockhouses give some idea of the intensity of the fighting. Fine **views**★ of the sea and the coast westwards to the Cotentin Peninsula.

Continue west on D 514.

Grandcamp-Maisy

Quai Crampon. Open May–Sept Tue–Sun 9.30am–1.30pm, 2.30–6.30pm, Mon 2.30–6.30pm; Feb–Apr and Oct Tue–Sun 1–6pm. 4€. 02 31 92 33 51.

Little fishing port and marina. A small **museum** describes the exploits of the American Rangers.

Take D 199 and D 113 inland.

Cimetière militaire allemand de la Cambe

This impressive German cemetery with its rectangular lawn (2ha/5 acres) is the last resting place of 21 500 German soldiers who fell in the fighting in 1944.

Château de Colombières

Guided tours (45min) Jul–Aug Mon–Fri 2.30–6.30pm; Sept Sat–Sun 2.30–6.30pm (last entry 30min before closing). Closed public holidays. 5€. 02 31 22 51 65. www.chateaudecolombieres.com.

The **château** was one of the most important strongholds in the Bayeux region and today it makes a most attractive picture with its massive 14C machicolated round towers reflected in the waters of the moat. The rest of the château was heavily restored in the 17C and 18C. It served as HQ for the American press after the Normandy landings.

Isigny-sur-Mer

The town has been famous for production of milk and butter since the 17C.

Carentan

See Presqu'île du COTENTIN – East Coast, p153.

3 LA CÔTE DU BESSIN

From Bayeux to Port-en-Bessin – 34km/21mi – allow 1hr45min. Leave Bayeux on D 516.

Arromanhes-les-Bains
See ARROMANCHES-LES-BAINS, p83.

After visiting, return to the road you came in on and, about 1km/0.6mi outside of town, turn right on the road to Port-en-Bessin. At Longues-sur-Mer, turn right on D 104 towards the sea.

Batterie allemande de Longues-sur-Mer★
Half a mile down this road, a surfaced road *(left)* leads to the site of the powerful German battery. In spite of the release by 124 RAF planes of 600t of bombs during the night preceding 6 June, the four German guns began firing at 5.37am on June 6. The French cruiser *Georges-Leygues* returned fire, followed by the *Montcalm* and the American battleship *Arkansas*.
The Germans were silent for a while but resumed firing in the afternoon; the battery was finally silenced at 7pm by two direct hits from the *Georges-Leygues*. Built on a picturesque cliff, it was composed of four 150mm/5.6in guns with a range of 20km/12.5mi which enabled it to control Omaha and Gold beaches. The observation post and control room, on the cliff-edge, appeared in a famous scene from the film *The Longest Day* (1962).

Le Chaos
The track descends steeply and is liable to rockfalls; there is a view of the coast from Cap Manvieux in the east to the Pointe de la Percée in the west.
This part of the Bessin coast has eroded into a chaotic jumble: entire sections have collapsed into heaps of fallen rocks, perched in the most extraordinary positions.

Take D 104 south towards Bayeux.

Abbaye Ste-Marie
Open 1–20 Jul and 1–10 Sept Mon–Fri 2–6pm; rest of the year Thu 2–6pm. For other days, apply to guardian. 4€. 02 31 21 78 41.
All that remains of the 12C abbey church is the main door and a few footings of the chancel and transept. The tombstones of the lords of Argouges can be admired in the refectory.

Return north to D 514; continue west to Port-en-Bessin.

The Norman Ancestors of Walt Disney?

As is well known, in 1066, Duke William of Normandy sailed across the Channel and conquered England. After these historic events, two Norman soldiers who had accompanied his troops, **Hugues d'Isigny** and his son **Robert**, chose to settle on British soil. They were born in Isigny-sur-Mer, a small village near the mouth of the River Vire.

Over the years, their surname d'Isigny underwent a series of changes, becoming Disgny, then Disney, which sounded decidedly more Anglo-Saxon. In the 17C, a branch of the Disney family emigrated to Ireland. In 1834, Arundel Elias Disney and his brother Robert, along with their families, embarked on a voyage to North America. Leaving from Liverpool, they arrived on Ellis Island off New York on 3 October, after travelling for one month. That was the start of their American adventures. On 5 December 1901, Elias Disney's fourth child was born in Chicago: he was to become the famous illustrator **Walt Disney**, whose legendary animated cartoon characters like Mickey Mouse and Donald Duck have delighted many a generation of children. He died on 15 December 1966.

Port-en-Bessin★

The town, which is known locally as Port, is made more picturesque by its narrow confines.

From the jetties, a favourite haunt of rod fishermen, there is a view of the cliffs of the Bessin coast, from Cap Manvieux to the Pointe de la Percée. A tower erected by Vauban in the 17C dominates the eastern outer harbour. There is a good **view** of the whole harbour from the blockhouse on the clifftop.

Just outside Bayeux on D6, there is a good **view** of the **Château de Maisons** (15C–18C), surrounded by a moat fed by the river.

ADDRESSES

STAY

Chambre d'hôte La Ferme d'Escures – *Escures village, 14520 Commes, 2.5km/1.5mi S of Port-en-Bessin via D 6. ℘02 31 69 62 95. 4 rooms and a campsite.* Located a few miles from the beaches and Bayeux, this 17C farm, built with local Caen stone, is the ideal starting point for a tour of the area. The decoration of the rooms is simple but pleasant and the self-catering cottage, located in the former bakery, has its own garden.

Chambre d'hôte Le Logis – *Escures village, 14520 Commes, 2.5km/1.5mi SE of Port-en-Bessin via D 6. ℘02 31 21 79 56. http://monsite.wanadoo.fr/le.logis. 4 rooms.* You will be won over by the charm of these old houses inhabited by a family with a great sense of hospitality. Breakfast is served in the former stable, which still has a stone drinking trough. The rooms and the self-catering cottage are comfortable.

Chambre d'hôte La Faisanderie – *14450 Grandchamp-Maisy. ℘02 31 22 70 06. 3 rooms.* Attractive house covered in Virginia creeper in the midst of a horse farm. Pretty rooms, each different. Breakfast is served in pleasant dining room with fireplace.

Chambre d'hôte Ferme du Mouchel – *At "Le Mouchel", 14710 Formigny. ℘02 31 22 53 79. www.ohotes.com/fermedumouchel. 4 rooms.* On a little country road, a pleasant dairy farm probably from the 16C. Three pretty rooms, with another in an annex where breakfast is served.

Chambre d'hôte Le Petit Val – *24 r. du Camp-Romain, 14480 Banville, 3km/2mi SW of Courseulles-sur-Mer via D 12. ℘02 31 37 92 18. www.ferme-le-petitval.com. 5 rooms.* Dating most likely from the 17C, this typical Bessin farm is the ideal spot for a nature break. Discreet décor in the cosy bedrooms, attractive breakfast room and a garden filled with flowers.

Domaine de L'Hostréière – *r. du Cimetière américain, 14170 Colleville-sur-Mer. ℘02 31 51 64 64. www.domainedelhostreiere.com. Closed mid-Nov–Easter. 20 rooms.* Modern, well-equipped rooms, each with a terrace, now occupy the outbuildings of this old farm, next to the American cemetery of St-Laurent-sur-Mer. Gym and swimming pool.

Chambre d'hôte Château de Vouilly – *14230 Vouilly-Église, 8km/5mi SE of Isigny via D 5. ℘02 31 22 08 59. www.chateau-vouilly.com. Closed 11 Nov–20 Mar. 5 rooms.* A moat abounding with fish, handsome gardens, an orangery, imposing drawing rooms and dual-coloured paving in an 18C residence.

Chambre d'hôte Manoir de l'Hermerel – *14230 Géfosse-Fontenay, 7km/4.3mi N of Isigny via D 514 then D 199. ℘02 31 22 64 12. www.manoir-hermerel.com. Closed 15 Nov–15 Feb. 4 rooms.* This fortified 17C farm once belonged to the local squire, as the dovecote facing the entrance porch testifies. Visit the small 15C Gothic chapel before retiring to one of the attractive bedrooms. Simple, convivial welcome.

EAT

⊖ **Les Alizés** – *4 quai Ouest, 14470 Courselles-sur-Mer. ✆02 31 36 14 14. www.les-alizes.net.* This kitchen has won a loyal clientèle. In a comfortable dining room with a nautical theme, you can sample oysters and mussels at any hour, against a background of classical music. Some guest rooms.

⊖ **Café Gondrée** – **Pegasus Bridge** – *12 av. du Cdt-Kieffer, 14970 Bénouville, 9km/5.6mi N of Caen via D 514. ✆02 31 44 62 25. Closed 15 Nov–8 Mar.* This small, authentic pre-war café, the first house on French soil to be liberated in 1944, has strong historic and emotional connotations. Arlette Gondrée, who was four at the time, still prepares the traditional family omelette with salad.

⊖ **La Flambée** – *2 r. Émile-Demagny, 14230 Isigny-sur-Mer. ✆02 31 51 70 96. Closed 2 weeks Feb–Mar, 2 weeks Jun–Jul, Tue in winter and Wed.* Fish and meat are grilled in over a vast fireplace in the dining room of this typical Norman restaurant with its exposed beams.

⊖⊖ **Le Bistrot d'à Côté** – *12 r. Michel-Lefournier, 14520 Port-en-Bessin. ✆02 31 51 79 12. www.barque-bleue.fr. Closed Jan, Tue–Wed from 15 Sept–15 Jun.* This dining room, a study in contrasting blues and yellows, features old photographs of the harbour. The day's fish and shellfish dishes are listed on the large blackboard menu.

⊖⊖ **La Pêcherie** – *pl. du 6-Juin, 14470 Courseulles-sur-Mer. ✆02 31 37 45 84. www.la-pecherie.fr.* Storm lanterns, oars and port-holes announce a nautical theme. The cuisine follows suit, with oceanic specialities. A few guestrooms decorated like ships' cabins.

⊖⊖ **Hotel Mercure Omaha Beach** – *On the golf course, 14520 Port-en-Bessin. ✆02 31 22 44 44. /www.omaha-beach-hotel.com/GB_restaurants.htm. Closed 22 Dec–12 Jan.* This hotel-restaurant, open to the public, has a superb view over the Omaha Beach Golf Club, whose facilities it shares. The Sunday brunch is particularly generous. A brasserie-type restaurant at the club house.

⊖⊖ **La Trinquette** – *7 rte du Joncal, 14450 Grandcamp-Maisy. ✆02 31 22 64 90. www.restaurant-la-trinquette.com. Closed Oct–Easter Tue–Wed.* Fresh fish, leeks slowly melted in butter, simmered in an earthenware dish or served as a soup. Try the local fishermen's dish, *la marmite grandcopaise*.

⊖⊖ **Le Vauban** – *6 r. du Nord, 14520 Port-en-Bessin. ✆02 31 21 74 83. www.restaurant-levauban.com. Closed mid-Dec–mid-Jan, Tue eve and Wed.* One of the locals' favourite eating places. The owner-chef uses fresh produce.

⊖⊖⊖ **L'As de Trèfle** – *420 r. Léopold-Hettier, 14990 Bernières-sur-Mer. ✆02 31 97 22 60. Closed 2 Jan–10 Feb and Mon–Tue except Jul–Aug.* This building, constructed after the war, is unattractive, but the quality of the kitchen is well worth the trip. Delicious seafood. Terrace for fine weather.

⊖⊖⊖ **Le Manoir d'Hastings et la Pommeraie** – *18 av. de la Côte-de-Nacre (near the church), 14970 Bénouville, 10km/6mi NE of Caen via D 515. ✆02 31 44 62 43. www.manoirhastings.com. Closed Feb school holidays, 10 Nov–14 Dec, Sun eve and Mon except school holidays.* This former 17C priory, enclosed within its garden, has retained its old-world aspect with weathered stone walls and exposed beams. Several dining rooms including an attic one. A few bedrooms.

LEISURE

Spa **Le Hammam de la Mer** – *2 r. Guynemer, 14530 Luc-sur-Mer. ✆02 31 97 32 22. www.thalasso-normandie.com. Closed 3–23 Jan.* An authentic steam bath, with perfumes, olive-oil soap, clay scrubbing compounds, loofah sponges. Tea is served along with delicate pastries.

SEINE-MARITIME

The populous, fertile plateau of the Pays de Caux, cut by the valley of the Seine as it flows through Rouen to the sea at Le Havre, lies on a bed of limestone, covered by rich soil that supports intense agriculture. High chalk cliffs overlook the English Channel along the Alabaster Coast. Inland, along the meanders of the Seine lie lovely, forested rural landscapes and small villages. in the Bray Buttonhole, to the northeast, the landscape changes abruptly to the *bocage* country of picturesque hedgerows, forests, streams and marshes.

Rich land, seaports and easy access inland via the Seine have given the area that now forms the département of Seine-Maritime a lively history. Roman settlers left an amphitheatre at **Lillebonne**. Norse settlers are recalled in many place names derived from Scandinavian; the Viking longship often appears in local imagery. Kings, lords and saints left castles, manor houses, churches and abbeys in profusion. The great river port of **Rouen**, to many, evokes Joan of Arc and her fiery end during the Hundred Years' War between French and English. Its cathedral has survived as one of the most perfect French Gothic monuments. **Le Havre**, a deep-water port at the mouth of the Seine, suffered grievously during World War II, but emerged from the ruins as a model of city planning. **Dieppe**, an old fishing port, hideout of privateers and a redoubt against the English, has both a sturdy castle and lovely beaches, as France's oldest seaside resort. The city suffered in the Dieppe Raid of 19 August 1942, but has maintained its charming old quarter. The ancient abbey at **Jumièges**, founded in the 7C, was destroyed by Vikings, magnificently rebuilt in the 10C, then destroyed in 1793 during the Revolution, creating the most beautiful ruins in France. Charming seaside resorts include **Le Tréport**, **St-Valéry-en-Caux**, **Fécamp**, **Varengeville-sur-Mer**, and **Veules-les Roses**. Walks along the cliffs, such as at **Veulette-sur-Mer**, give breathtaking views over the beaches and headlands. For the sheer drama of its chalk cliffs overlooking sweeps of beach, **Étretat** requires a visit. **Fécamp**, from which intrepid fishermen sailed to Newfoundland for cod, has a magnificant ducal church and a 19C Benedictine palace, where the liqueur is made. Forests of **Arques**, **Ewy**, **Eu**, **Roumare** and, on the south bank of the Seine, **Brotonne**, invite hikers and nature lovers.

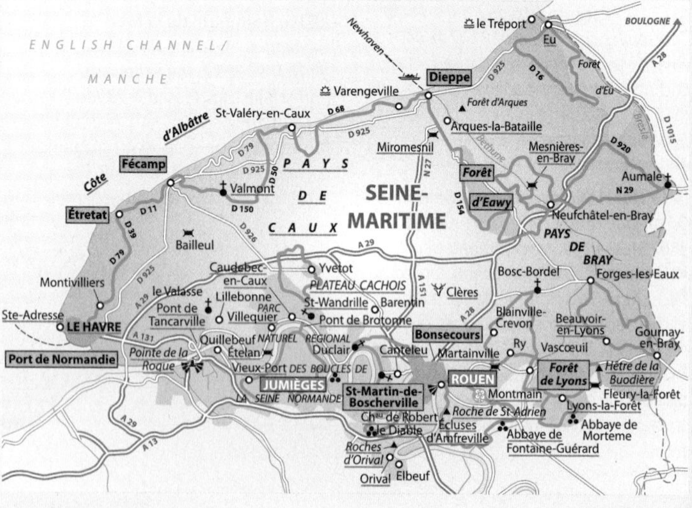

Arques-la-Bataille★

Arques lies under a massive medieval fortress where the future Henri IV won a celebrated battle. A nearby château, Miromesnil, was the birthplace of writer Guy de Maupassant.

- **Population:** 2 468.
- **Michelin Map:** 304: G-2.
- **Location:** Arques is 8km/5mi SE of Dieppe, near the confluence of the rivers Varenne and Béthune. The Forest of Arques lies to the NE.
- **Don't Miss:** The medieval fortress offers a magnificent view of the countryside; the gardens of Miromesnil are splendid.
- **Timing:** You can visit only the exterior of the fortress, which takes 30min. Plan at least 1hr30min for the Miromesnil château.
- **Kids:** Cool off the kids at the waterpark.

A BIT OF HISTORY

When **Henri IV** (1553–1610) was still a king without a kingdom, he possessed the fortress of Arques, said to be "capable of withstanding cannon". He gathered within the ramparts every piece of artillery he could find and dug in, with 7 000 men, to await 30 000 soldiers under the Duke of Mayenne. The battle took place on 21 September 1589. A fog delayed the artillery action but finally Henri's cannon thundered into the besiegers. Mayenne, who had promised to bring back his enemy "tied and bound", beat a hasty retreat. Near Arques, on the edge of a lake, the recreational centre **Varenne Plein Air** offers facilities for water sports and other nautical activities.
Varenne Plein Air: *Base de Loisir, 76510 St-Aubin-le-Cauf. Open daily 9am–noon, 1.30–5.30pm. 02 35 85 69 05. www.varennepleinair.fr.*

SIGHTS

Château★

Allow 30min. From place Desceliers, where the town hall (Mairie) is located, take the second road to the right, uphill to the castle entrance, about 45min; the road is very narrow, steep and winding. Closed for safety reasons. Château grounds, no charge.

The 12C keep occupies the highest point. The earliest part was built between 1038 and 1043. In 1053 it was attacked by William the Conqueror, then reconstructed by Henri I in 1123. Two new towers were added in the 14C. It played a vital role in the wars of religion that raged in the late 16C, as Protestant forces under the future Henri IV repelled the Catholic League in 1589. A triple door leads into the castle. On the back of the last one a carved low relief depicts Henri IV at the Battle of Arques. Follow the old sentry path along the moat to enjoy a view of the Arques Valley.

Église Notre-Dame-de-l'Assomption

Rue des Bourguignons.

Rebuilt around 1515, the church was given a belfry in the 17C. The nave was roofed in the 16C with wood cradle vaulting. The apse windows are 16C (restored). A chapel to the right of the chancel contains a small bust of Henri IV and an inscription commemorating the battle. Note a 15C Pietà in the south chapel.

EXCURSIONS

Château de Miromesnil★

4km/2.5mi SW of Arques. Visit of château by guided tour (1hr) only, Apr–Oct daily 2–6pm. 6.50€; garden and park Jul–Aug 10am–1pm, 2–6pm. 4€. 02 35 85 02 80. www.chateaumiromesnil.com

The château was built after the Battle of Arques (1589). Facing the main courtyard is the monumental Louis XIII central façade, capped by a great slate roof.

In the hall there is a display of documents connected with the birth of the great writer Guy de Maupassant in the château on 5 August in 1850.

The **south front**, in the Henri IV style, is flanked by two cylindrical pepper-pot towers; brick predominates with stone trim round the windows and corners. Beyond a magnificent stand of beech trees is a 16C **chapel**, part of an earlier château. The sober flint and limestone walls contrast with the rich interior decoration dating from 1780.

Jardins et potager fleuri★

Flowers border the tidy vegetable plots. Brick walls enclose the garden and support espaliered fruit trees.

Forêt d'Arques

From Arques-la-Bataille take D 56.

The forest roads are sometimes narrow; drive carefully.

This beech forest lies between the rivers Eaulne and Béthune, which flow into the Arques. D 56 crosses the river, then the southern part of the forest, alongside traces of an ancient Roman road. Pretty villages in the area include St-Nicholas-D'Allermont, a "street-village" which grew up in medieval fashion along either side of the road. Envermeu has an unfinished Gothic church with Renaissance touches; its remarkable **chancel**★ has hanging keystones. On D 1 between Enverneu and Arques an obelisk commemorates the battle of Arques. From the site *(15min walk from the car park)* is a view of the château of Arques-la-Bataille across the river.

Blainville-Crevon

This small village located in the Crevon Valley is the birthplace of the artist Marcel Duchamp (1887–1968), forerunner of the New York School of painting (*see The Green Guide New York City*). Many artists from the School of Rouen stayed in the town, including Gustave Flaubert (1821–80) and Eugène Tirvert (1881–1948). Blainville-Crevon hosts the annual Archéo-Jazz Festival (June), which comprises dance, cinema, theatre and music

- **Population:** 1 125.
- **Michelin Map:** 304: H-4.
- **Info:** Maison de l'Abreuvoir, 76116 Ry. 02 35 23 19 90. www.blainville-crevon.fr.
- **Location:** Blainville-Crevon is 20km/12.4mi NE of Rouen via N 31, then D 7.
- **Don't Miss:** The church, with its statue of St Michael killing the dragon, and the tour of Emma Bovary country. A map is available in tourist offices in the area.
- **Timing:** You can tour the village in an hour; a 60km/37.2mi marked itinerary around Ry lets you pass time with Emma Bovary.

SIGHTS

Église St-Michel

Guided tours Jun–Sept Sat–Sun 2–6.30pm; Oct–May, contact the town hall. 02 35 34 01 60.

The Collégiale de Blainville, which was founded in 1488, has a chequered sandstone and silex facing. The interior is in the Flamboyant style. In the left transept there is a monumental late-15C statue in painted wood of St Michael slaying the dragon.

Château

Visits by appointment only. 01 42 88 95 29.

Excavations begun in 1968 on the ruins of a medieval castle have exposed a staircase buried by an 11C motte, a stretch of curtain wall, ditches and two towers.

DRIVING TOUR

South of Blainville

Tour of 10km/6mi by D 12.

Ry

The village of half-timbered and brick houses is said to be the model for Yonville-l'Abbaye, where **Gustave Flaubert** (1821–80) set his novel *Madame Bovary* (1857).

The 12C **church** is surmounted by a lantern tower entered through a Renaissance wooden **porch**★.

Take D 13 southwest.

Château de Martainville★

Open Apr–Sept Wed–Sat and Mon 10am–12.30pm, 2–6pm, Sun 2–6.30pm; Oct–Mar Wed–Sat and Mon 10am–12.30pm, 2–5pm, Sun 2–5.30pm. Closed 1 Jan, 1 May, 1 and 11 Nov, 25 Dec. 3€. 02 35 23 44 70.

The elegant brick and stone château, little changed since its construction in 1485–1510, has a massive dovecote (16C) and a half-timbered cart shed (18C). The château houses the **Musée Départemental des Traditions et Arts Normands**★, with displays of furniture from Rouen and the Pays de Caux, chests, 17C buffets, 18C cupboards, earthenware and pottery, glass, pewter and copper, regional ceramics and costumes.

Forêt de Brotonne

(Parc naturel régional des Boucles de la Seine)

The creation of the Parc naturel régional des Boucles de la Seine in 1974 and the construction of the Brotonne Bridge in 1977 have made the Brotonne Forest readily accessible. La Haye-de-Routot is part of the Écomusée de la Basse-Seine (regional open-air museum), which preserves ancient crafts.

- **Michelin Map:** 304: D-5 to E-5.
- **Info:** Maison du Parc, 76940 Notre-Dame-de-Bliquetuit. 02 35 37 23 16. www.pnr-seine-normande.com.
- **Location:** The park extends on either side of the Seine below Rouen. Bridges at Tancarville and Brotonne as well as ferries pass from one bank to the other.
- **Don't Miss:** The many marked paths in the forest, as well as Vieux-Port and its surroundings.
- **Timing:** Find lodging outside the park, near Pont-Audemer, and pack a lunch.

DRIVING TOUR

FROM ROUTOT TO CAUDEBEC-EN-CAUX

39km/24.2mi – allow 1hr30min.

Take D 686 N, then E on D90.

Moulin de Hauville

Open Jul–Aug daily 2.30–6.30pm; May–Jun and Sept Sun 2.30–6.30pm. 02 32 56 57 32. 2.50€.

This 13C grain mill belonged to the Abbey of Jumièges (*see Abbaye de JUMIÈGES, p352*). The oak roof beams are covered in reed thatch, the tower is made of stone, and you can observe the works inside. The miller's house holds a small museum.

Return to D 686, continue north to La Haye-de-Routot.

La Haye-de-Routot

Church

Open Sun 2–6pm.

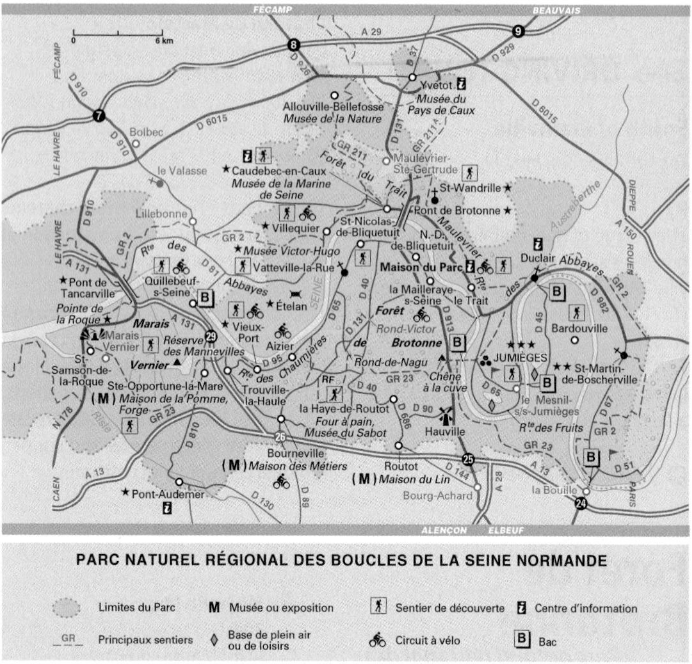

PARC NATUREL RÉGIONAL DES BOUCLES DE LA SEINE NORMANDE

The cemetery surrounding the little **church** is shaded by two **yew trees**★ more than 1 000 years old.

Bread Oven

Open 14 Jul–Aug 2–6.30pm; Mar–13 Jul and Sept–Nov Sun and public holidays 2–6.30pm. Closed 1 Jan, 8 May, Pentecost Mon, 11 Nov, 25 Dec. 1.80€. 02 32 57 07 99.

In an 18C thatched brick building, the **bread oven** dating from 1845 revives ancient baking methods.

Musée du Sabot

Same hours as Bread Oven. 2€ 02 32 57 59 67.

The **Musée du Sabot** set up in a 17C house presents tools and techniques used by makers of wooden shoes.

Take D 40 for 4.5km/3mi; turn left onto the narrow forest road which crosses D 131.

This pleasant road passes through beautiful woods as descends into the Seine Valley. Near the river *(3km/2mi from D 131)* is a spectacular **view** (*left*) of the Seine Valley west as far as Tancarville Bridge.

Turn right onto D 65; at Le Quesney bear right onto the road to La Mailleraye and right again onto the forest road to St-Maur Chapel.

The road passes through one of the thickest parts of the forest.

Turn left onto D 131; continue north via Rond-Victor to St-Nicolas-de-Bliquetuit. Turn left onto D 65.

Maison du Parc

Notre-Dame-de-Bliquetuit.

Open Jul–Aug Mon–Fri 9am–6.30, Sat–Sun 10am–6.30; Apr–Jun and Sept Mon–Fri 9am–6pm, Sat–Sun noon–6pm; rest of the year Mon–Fri 9am–6pm. 02 35 37 23 16. www.pnr-seine-normande.com.

The visitors' centre, just outside the village, occupies a group of old farm buildings.

A 2km/1.25mi walk from the centre leads through a garden, hedgerows, and a marsh.
From St-Nicolas-de-Bliquetuit pretty gardens and half-timbered houses are strung along the River Seine.

Pont de Brotonne★
Toll bridge. The bridge, which spans the Seine above Caudebec-en-Caux, was opened in 1977.

Return to Caudebec via D 982.

Caudebec-en-Caux★

Caudebec settles around the Seine where the Ste-Gertrude Valley runs into the river. The Brotonne Bridge leads directly to the forest of the same name. A fire in 1940 destroyed most of the old buildings, but the fine Church of Our Lady was virtually undamaged and three old houses to the left of the church give some idea of what Caudebec must once have looked like.

- **Population:** 2 336.
- **Michelin Map:** 304: E-4.
- **Info:** Place du Général-de-Gaulle. 02 32 70 46 32. www.caudebe-cen-caux.com.
- **Location:** Midway between Rouen (48km/30mi E) and Le Havre (52km/32.5mi W), Caudebec is on the banks of the Seine.
- **Parking:** Public lots are located on Place du Marché (except Saturday mornings), Place Henri-IV and Place d'Armes.
- **Don't Miss:** The Flamboyant architecture of Notre-Dame church, and the pretty town of Villequier.
- **Timing:** You need a day at Caudebec.

A BIT OF HISTORY

A Short-Lived Prestigious Past – The name Caudebec first appears in the 11C on a charter granted to the monks of St-Wandrille Abbey. In the 12C the town was fortified to resist the English who were nevertheless victorious in 1419. After submitting to Henri IV in 1592, during the Wars of Religion, it became a flourishing glove- and hat-making centre. The Revocation of the Edict of Nantes in 1685, which revived the persecution of Protestants, put an end to this period of prosperity.

Église Notre-Dame★

30min. Place du Parvis.
This fine Flamboyant edifice (*see illustration in Introduction: Religious architecture, p62*) which Henri IV described as "the most beautiful chapel in the kingdom" was built between 1425 and 1539.

Exterior

The belfry (53m/174ft high) adjoining the south wall has a delicately worked upper part surmounted by a stone crown spire.

The west face is pierced by three beautiful Flamboyant **doorways** – the larger of the two is said to portray 333 different characters – and by a

West portal of Église Notre-Dame

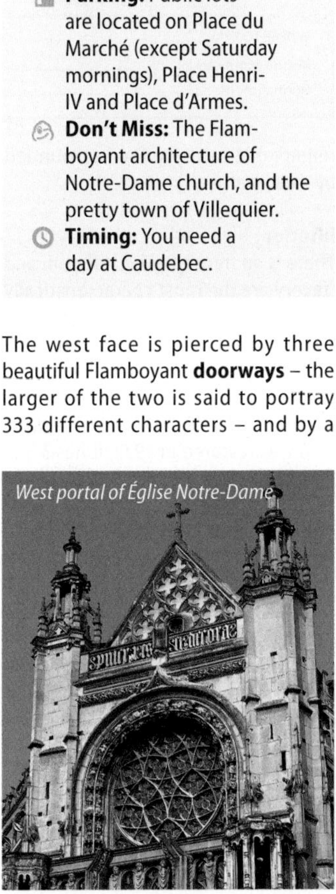

G. Targat/MICHELIN

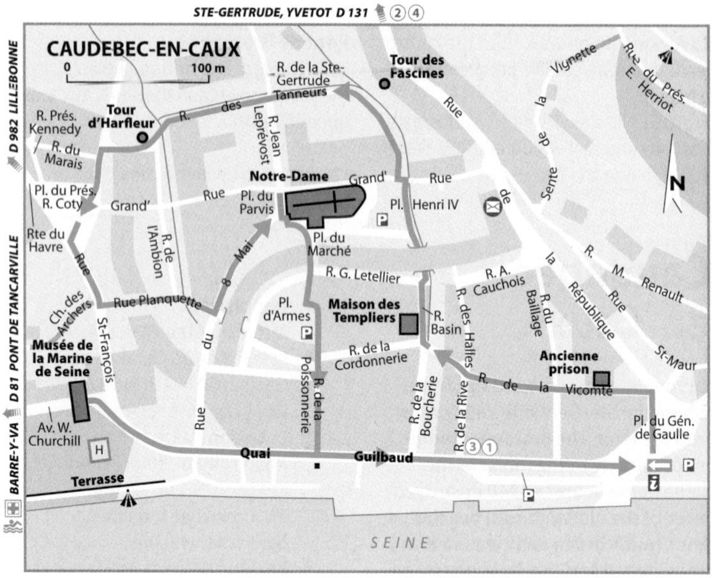

WHERE TO STAY		WHERE TO EAT	
Marine (Normotel la)	①	Rendez-Vous des Chasseurs (Au)	②
Normandie (Hôtel le)	③	Val de Cesne (Auberge du)	④

remarkable rose window surrounded by small statues.

Interior

There is no transept. The triforium and tracery are the most characteristically Flamboyant features.

The 17C **font** *(left)* is decorated with intricately carved panels. The **great organ**★ (early 16C – *see illustration in Introduction: Religious architecture, p63)* was restored in 1972; it has 3 345 pipes of repoussé pewter.

Chapelle du St-Sépulcre

The chapel inspired Fragonard to sketch it. Beneath the 16C baldaquin a recumbent Christ, carved in incredible detail, faces some very large stone statues – all from Jumièges Abbey. The Pietà between the windows is 15C.

Chapelle de la Vierge

The Lady Chapel is famous for its **keystone**★, a 7t monolith supported only by the dependent arching and forming a 4.3m/13ft pendentive. The architect of this feat, Guillaume Le Tellier, lies buried in the chapel and is commemorated in a plaque beneath the right window.

WALKING TOUR

2km/1mi. About 1hr starting from the tourist office. From place du Général de Gaulle, take rue de la Vicomté.

The Sentier de la Gribane (signposted and dotted with explanatory panels) provides an interesting itinerary for visiting the city. The promenades of La Vignette and Mont-Calidu offer lovely vistas of the town. On the right , the old prison is set in the 14C ramparts.

Continue along rue Thomas-Basin.

Maison des Templiers

1 r. Thomas-Basin. Open Apr–Oct Wed–Fri and Sun 2.30–6.30pm, Sat 10am–noon, 2.30–6.30pm; Jan–Mar Tue and Thu 4–6pm. Closed 25 Dec. 5€. 02 35 96 95 91.

The Templars' House is a precious specimen of 13C civil architecture which has retained its two original gable walls.

Follow cours de la Ste-Gertrude.

You walk by two towers: **Tour des Fascines** and **Tour d'Harfleur**.

Take rue du Havre, on the left, and then left again on rue Planquette.

Église Notre-Dame
See entry, p315.

Musée de la Marine de Seine

av. Winston-Churchill. Open daily Apr–Sept 2–6.30pm; Oct–Mar 2–5.30pm. Closed 1 Jan, 25 Dec. 3.30€. 02 35 95 90 13.
The museum is devoted to the history of navigation along the River Seine: ports, commercial exchanges, shipbuilding, crossings. Visitors can learn about a bygone phenomenon, the **tidal bore, which used to rip down the Seine**.

Return to Place du Général de Gaulle along the quai Guilbaud.

DRIVING TOURS

AROUND ST-WANDRILLE

Round-trip of 8km/5mi. Leave Caudebec by rue St-Clair and follow chemin de Rétival keeping to the right.

The road runs along the top of a small escarpment with tantalising glimpses of the bend in the river.

At the bottom of a steep descent take D 37 on the left.

The road goes up a delightful little **valley**★ with thatched farmhouses scattered here and there.

Before Rançon, turn right on D 33 to St-Wandrille.

Abbaye de St-Wandrille★
See Abbaye de ST-WANDRILLE, p377.

Take D 22 and D 982 back to Caudebec.

Latham-47 Monument
This commemorates the polar explorer **Roald Amundsen** and his companions, who disappeared in the Arctic in 1928.

Take D 22, than D 982 to return to Caudebec.

AROUND BARRE-Y-VA

Round-trip of 21km/13mi. Leave Caudebec to the north on the Yvetot road and turn left onto D 40.

Ste-Gertrude
The small **church** stands in attractive surroundings. It was consecrated in 1519 and is Flamboyant in style.

Head west on D 40, then D 30. Turn south on D 440 towards Anquetierville. At the junction with D 982 turn left, then at St-Arnoult right onto D 440. Turn right onto D 281 and almost immediately left down a steep hill to Villequier.

Villequier★
Musée Victor-Hugo. Access through the rue Ernst-Binet. Open Apr–Sept Wed–Sat 10am–12.30pm, 2–6pm, Sun 2–6pm; Oct–Mar Wed–Sat 10am–12.30pm, 2–5.30pm, Sun 2–5.30pm. Closed 1 Jan, 1 May, 1 and 11 Nov, 25 Dec. 3€. 02 35 56 78 31.
Villequier occupies a beautiful **site**★ on the banks of the Seine at the foot of a wooded height crowned by a castle. In 1843, six months after their marriage, Charles Vacquerie and his wife, Léopoldine Hugo, the daughter of the novelist and poet Victor Hugo, were drowned in the Seine at Villequier.
A house once owned by the Vacquerie family, rich boat builders from Le Havre, has been converted into the **Musée Victor-Hugo**★.

Take D 81 back to Caudebec.

Barre-y-Va
This tiny hamlet is named after the tidal wave or bore *(barre)* which used to swell upstream along the Seine.

Return to Caudebec via D 81.

AROUND YVETOT

22km/14mi – 1hr30min. Leave Caudebec and go north on D 131. After 4km/2.5mi, turn right on D 33 then left on D 37 towards Yvetot.

Yvetot

The town, made famous in a song as the capital of an imaginary kingdom, is in fact a large market town on the Caux plateau. The **Église St-Pierre** *(open Mon–Sat 9am–noon, 2–6pm, Sun and holidays 8.30am–noon; audio guides available at tourist office)*, built in 1956, contains remarkably large **stained-glass windows**★★ by Max Ingrand, which produce a dazzling effect; other windows show founders of religious orders, saints of the Rouen diocese and the saints of France. The Lady Chapel *(behind the altar)* windows depict episodes in the life of the Virgin.

Take D 131 south; turn right on the by-pass; turn left on D 34.

Allouville-Bellefosse

The village is known for the **oak tree** *(chêne)* which grows in front of the church; it is believed to be more than 1 300 years old, one of the oldest in France and the most famous tree in Normandy.

Follow the signs to the Musée de la Nature (1.5km/1mi).

Musée de la Nature

12 r. du Musée, Allouville-Bellefosse. Open Jul–Aug daily 10am–noon, 2–6pm; Apr–Jun and Sept daily 2–6pm; Oct–Mar Wed, Sat–Sun and school holidays 2–6pm. Closed 1 Jan, 25 Dec. 3.50€. 02 35 96 06 54. www.chene.asso.fr.

The Nature Museum is located in an old Caux farmhouse. Two diorama displays show local bird families and a reconstitution of the Normandy countryside (coastline, marsh, plain, forest and farmyard). The coastline is shown before and after the effects of pollution.

Return to Allouville, take D 34 then turn left on D 40; take D 131 back to Caudebec.

ADDRESSES

STAY

Hôtel Le Normandie – *Quai Guilbaud. 02 35 96 25 11. www.le-normandie.fr. 15 rooms. 7.50€. Restaurant.* Located along the road skirting the Seine, this small, unpretentious hotel offers simple, very tidy rooms; some with balconies. Traditional Norman cuisine in the restaurant.

Normotel La Marine – *18 quai Guilbaud. 02 35 96 20 11. www.normotel-lamarine.fr. 31 rooms. Restaurant.* On the quai along the Seine, this large hotel's best rooms have balconies overlooking the river. Traditional cuisine in the restaurant. In summer, enjoy the terrace on the water.

EAT

Au Rendez-Vous des Chasseurs – *Hameau de Sainte-Gertrude, 76490 Maulévrier Ste-Gertrude, 3.4km/2mi. 02 35 96 20 30. Closed Sun eve and Mon.* Beautiful half-timbered building with pretty garden terrace, smart décor and traditional, regional cuisine.

Auberge du Val au Cesne – *Le Val au Cesne, 76190 Yvetot. 02 35 56 63 06. www.valaucesne.fr. Closed 10 Jan–1 Feb, 23 Aug–7 Sept, Mon–Tue.* Lying in a remote vale, this Norman inn, with an exuberant garden and an aviary, is delightful. The cuisine is in harmony with the décor: it tastes of the authentic. A few comfortable guest rooms.

Pays de Caux★

The Caux is mainly known for its impressive coastline. Visitors delight in the natural beauty of the area, returning each year to the vast beaches below the splendid chalk cliffs. The surrounding countryside offers a swathe of remarkable churches, castles and manor houses.

- **Michelin Map:** 512 folds 7-10, 19-22.
- **Info:** Several villages have their own tourist offices. Those of Dieppe, Étretat, Le Havre and Caudebec-en-Caux also serve the Caux region.
- **Location:** The Pays de Caux is bounded on the S by the Seine Valley, on the W and N by the Alabaster Coast and on the E along a line extending between Dieppe and Rouen.
- **Don't Miss:** The resorts and little villages of the Alabaster Coast, as well as the charming villages of the interior and the Parc des Boucles de la Seine.
- **Timing:** You will need several days to tour this region.
- **Kids:** The outdoor centre on Lac de Caniel offers sports and games.

See Addresses, p323.

GEOLOGY

Côte d'Albâtre – Along the Alabaster Coast the chalk cliffs, with alternate strata of flint and yellow marl, are worn away ceaselessly by the action of the tides and the weather.

The Étretat needle rocks and underwater shelves 1.6km/1mi from the shore indicate the former coastline. At the particularly exposed point of **Cap de la Hève** erosion is 2m/6.5ft a year; the water is milky with chalk, and flints are pounded endlessly upon the beaches. The hollows *(valleuses)* cut into every clifftop as far as the eye can see are dry former river valleys, truncated by the retreating coastline. Some rivers were powerful enough to carve valleys right down to the coastline, and that is where ports and resorts have appeared.

Caux Farmsteads – The farms appear as green oases surrounded by 2m/6.5ft-high windbreaks topped by a double row of oaks, beeches or elms.

The **farmstead** comprises a meadow planted with apple trees in which stand the half-timbered farm buildings. The entrance is often through a monumental gateway. In spring cattle and horses pasture tethered to a post *(tière)* and each animal marks out its territory in the form of a perfect circle. Milk is the chief source of income.

DRIVING TOURS

1 CÔTE D'ALBÂTRE★

From Dieppe to Étretat, 104km/64.5mi – about 5hr.

Glimpses of the sea and cliffs and pleasant views of resorts are the main features of the drive, which is at its best in the morning.

Dieppe★★

See DIEPPE, p325.

Leave Dieppe by D 75.

Pourville-sur-Mer

This seaside resort, pleasantly situated near jagged cliffs, has risen from the ruins of the Dieppe commando raid of 19 August 1942; the Cameron Highlanders and a Canadian Regiment, the South Saskatchewan, landed to the sound of bagpipes, inflicted severe damage on the enemy and, under cover of the Navy and by sacrificing their rearguard, re-embarked early in the afternoon.

A commemorative stele of pink marble stands on the seafront.

Continue west on D 75.

Varengeville-sur-Mer

See VARENGEVILLE-SUR-MER, p379.

Ste-Marguerite-sur-Mer

The 12C church, which has no transept, was considerably remodelled in the 16C. Inside, four of the original **arches**★ remain on the north side; those on the south date from 1528. The high altar dates from 1160 and is one of the very few of this date extant.

At St-Aubin bear left onto D 237.

Le Bourg-Dun

Notre-Dame-du-Salut is a vast composite church, remarkable for its **tower**★ built on a massive square 13C base.

The hatchet-shaped roof is 17C. A Renaissance door opens into the south aisle. Beneath Flamboyant vaulting in the south transept are a Renaissance bay and piscina;three arches in the chancel open into the beautiful south aisle, added in the 14C. The font in the north aisle is Renaissance.

Return to St-Aubin.

Veules-les-Roses★

The seaside resort, sheltered in a small valley, has pretty surroundings, notably windmills and picturesque villas dating from the 19C, when the town attracted fashionable Parisians. **St-Martin**, in the town itself, is a 16C–17C church with a 13C lantern. A timber-framed roof covers the nave and aisles. Inside are five 16C twisted, limestone columns and ancient statues.

The local tourist office has traced five walks in the village area that take in the prettiest spots *(27 r. Victor-Hugo; 02 35 97 63 05; www.veules-les-roses.fr).*

Turn left onto D 37.

Église de Blosseville

The church, surmounted by a 12C belfry, possesses beautiful Renaissance stained-glass windows and some old statues.

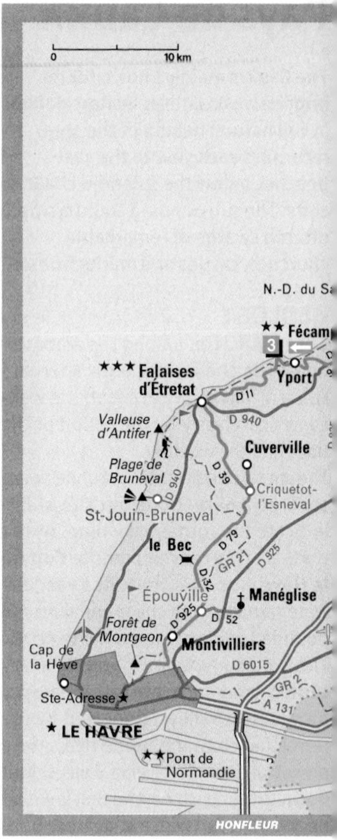

Continue towards Ermenouville on D 37.

Château du Mesnil-Geoffroy

Ermenouville. Guided tours (45min) May–Sept Wed–Sun 2.30–6pm. Closed 1 May. 6€. 02 35 57 12 77. www.chateau-mesnil-geoffroy.com. Guest rooms available ( ).

Surrounded by a 9ha/22.2-acre formal French park with a famous rose garden (2 500 species), this 17C and 18C château is an interesting testimony to the gentle art of living under Louis XV.

After leaving the château, turn onto D 70.

Le Mesnil-Durdent

Make sure you visit this charming village and its wild garden, the Jardin communal d'Amouhoques, an irregular

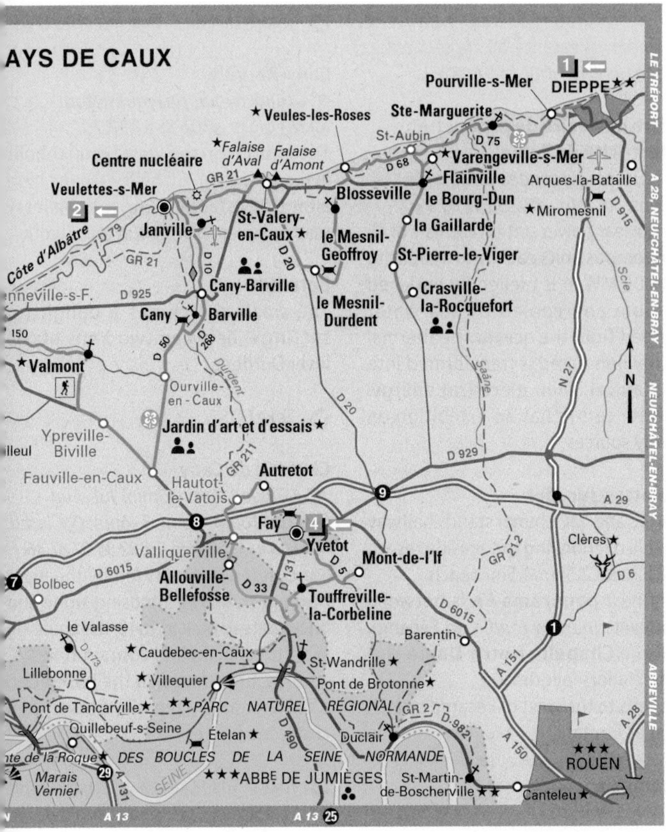

plot of land with many paths and embankments, planted with all manner of herbs carrying quaint, old-fashioned names.

St-Valery-en-Caux★

St-Valery is both a popular seaside resort, with a promenade overlooking the long shingle beach, and a fishing and coastal trading port.

The **Falaise d'Aval**★ (West Headland) *(access on foot via sentier des Douaniers and steps)* is crowned by a monument commemorating the battles of June 1940 (51st Highland Division and the French 2nd Cavalry Division). The view embraces the Ailly lighthouse and, on a clear day, Dieppe. The **Maison d'Henri IV** *(quai du Havre)* is a beautiful Renaissance house with carved beams. On the **Falaise d'Amont** (East Headland) *(access by steps)* stands the 51st Highland Division Monument overlooking the town, harbour and beach. The more modern monument nearby was erected in memory of Coste and Bellonte, who in 1930 made the first flight from Paris to New York.

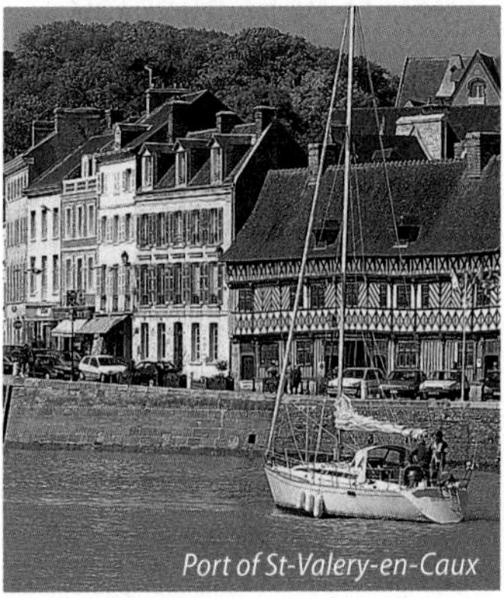

Port of St-Valery-en-Caux

G. Targat/MICHELIN

The area around St-Valery-en-Caux offers many pleasant walks *(tourist office, Maison Henri IV; ℘02 35 97 00 63).*

Centre nucléaire de production d'électricité de Paluel

Tours are suspended for security reasons. For Info: ℘02 35 57 69 99.

The nuclear power station consists of 45 autonomous units each with a capacity of 1 300 MW. It is fuelled by enriched uranium and cooled by sea water pumped from the ocean. The thermal energy generated is transformed into mechanical, then electrical energy. A visitor centre has an exhibition on energy sources.

Veulettes-sur-Mer

The 11C and 13C church stands halfway up a hill overlooking the seaside resort, which has a 2.5km/1.5mi beach.

The finest **panorama**★★ is between Senneville *(narrow road)* and Fécamp, near the **Chapelle Notre-Dame-du-Salut** (sailors' pilgrimage).

The cliffs to the west of Fécamp stretch as far as Étretat.

Fécamp★★

See FÉCAMP, p337.

Yport

Yport,a seaside resort tucked away in a valley, had a fishing fleet until 1970.

Étretat★★

See ÉTRETAT, p332.

2 VALLÉE DE LA DURDENT

From Veulettes-sur-Mer to Fécamp, 36km/22.4mi – about 3hr

Veulettes-sur-Mer

See above.

From Veulettes take D 10 south. In Paluel turn left onto D 68. After a sharp right hand bend, turn left at the top of a rise to the chapel.

Chapelle de Janville

This pilgrimage church has an attractive wrought-iron grille in the chancel.

Return to Paluel. Turn left onto D 10.

Cany-Barville

Guided tours on request from tourist office. ℘02 35 57 17 70.

The **church** on the west bank, rebuilt in the 16C, has a 13C belfry. On the high altar (18C) stands a Christ in Majesty made of over 80 angels in relief work.

Barville

The small church has a delightful **setting**★ between two arms of the River Durdent.

Take D 131.

Château de Cany

Guided tours (45min) Jul–Aug Sat–Thu 10am–noon, 3–6pm. Closed 4th Sun in Jul. 6€. ℘02 35 97 87 36.

Surrounded by moats fed by the River Durdent stands an imposing stone and brick château built in 1640, the Louis XIII era. The apartments contain fine 17C and 18C furnishings. In the basement, a kitchen contains utensils, crockery and costumed figures.

Take D 50 to Ourville, then turn right onto D 150, which descends into the Valmont Valley.

Valmont

See FÉCAMP – Excursions, p340.

Return to D 150 towards Fécamp.

Fécamp★★

See FÉCAMP, p337.

3 VALLÉE DE LA LÉZARDE

Étretat to Le Havre, 33km/21mi – allow 1hr.

Étretat★★

See ÉTRETAT, p332.

Leave Étretat by D 39. At Criquetot-l'Esneval turn left onto D 239.

The road descends into the pleasant Lézarde Valley.

Château du Bec

Closed for visits.

The 12C–16C castle has an enchanting setting of trees and still waters.

In Épouville turn left onto D 925 and then right onto D 52.

Manéglise

The small church is agraceful example of Romanesque architecture.

Return to Épouville; continue south.

Montivilliers

See Le HAVRE – Excursions, p350.

The road leaves the Vallée de la Lézarde via Rouelles, just outside Le Havre.

The road skirts the edge of Montgeon Forest, and leads to the Jenner tunnel, which leads to the town centre.

Le Havre★★

See Le HAVRE, p344.

4 PLATEAU DE CAUX★

Round-trip starting from Yvetot – *See CAUDEBEC-EN-CAUX, p318.*

ADDRESSES

STAY

Chambre d'hôte Le Château de Grosfy – *61 r. du Calvaire, 76570 Hugleville-en-Caux. 02 35 92 63 60. www.chateaudegrosfy.com. 4 rooms.* A lovely alley of lime trees leads to this 18C–19C family home, formerly a hunting lodge. Both rustic and reproduction antique furniture in the large, peaceful guest rooms. Billiards, library, board games and kitchen available. Large park with a little wood.

Chambre d'hôte Mme Genty – *5 rte de Quiberville, Hameau de Ramouville, 76740 St-Aubin-sur-Mer, 4km/2.5mi N of Bourg-Dun, then dir. Quiberville. 02 35 83 47 05. www.fermettederamouville.com. 5 rooms.* Skilful restoration work has revived the ancient appeal of this typical late-18C farm. Bedrooms are decorated in the country spirit. Mornings, the scent of warm bread will draw you towards the breakfast room.

Chambre d'hôte Château de Mesnil Geoffroy – *76740 Ermenouville, 12 km/7.5mi S of St-Valery-en-Caux via D 20 and D 108. 02 35 57 12 77. www.chateau-mesnil-geoffroy.com. 5 rooms.* A 17C–18C château, ranked as an historic monument, surrounded by a park with a superb rose garden. Guestrooms are refined and furnished with antique family furniture and art objects. Pleasant welcome by true princes, fortunate proprietors of this remarkable site.

EAT

La Boussole– *1 r. Max-Lerclec, 76460 St-Valery-en-Caux. 02 35 57 16 28. Closed Nov–Feb, Mon–Tue in Jan.* Prettily set in a navy blue half-timbered house, this restaurant opposite the port is entirely devoted to seafood. Two cosy rooms with bistro chairs and wooden tables. Shellfish platters in summer and many fish specialities. Piano music in the evening.

Le Belvédère – *76280 St-Jouin-Bruneval, 10km/6mi S of Étretat via D 940 then D 111. 02 35 20 13 76. www.restaurant-lebelvedere.com. Closed 10 Jan–9 Feb, Wed eve, Sun eve, Thu.* A curious blue building perched upon the cliffs of the Pays de Caux. The comfortable dining room, nicely renovated, offers an exceptional view of the sea. Enjoy fish, mussels and other shellfish while gazing over the deep blue sea.

LEISURE

Parc de Loisirs "Eu et Natur" – *Societé du Lac de Caniel, 76450 Cany-Barville, between St-Valery-en-Caux and Fécamp. 02 35 97 40 45. www.lacdecaniel.com. Open year round daily.*

25 outdoor activities on offer including wake-boarding, bowling, skate-park. There's a brasserie and bar for the adults, too!

Clères★

One of Normandy's greatest attractions is the animal park at the château of Clères. The original castle, now in ruins, was built in the 11C. The present château consists of a 19C western wing in the neo-Gothic style, and an eastern wing dating from the 15C, which was remodelled towards 1505. In the market square stands the wooden structure and slate roof of an 18C covered market.

- **Population:** 1 303.
- **Michelin Map:** 304: G-4.
- **Info:** 59 av. du Parc. 02 35 33 38 64. www.ot-cleres.fr.
- **Location:** Clères is 30km/18.5mi N of Rouen, following A 150, A 151 and D 6, or about 50km/31mi S of Dieppe by N 27 and D 6.
- **Don't Miss:** The rare birds in the aviary at Clères.
- **Timing:** Give yourself a good 2hr to tour the zoo.
- **Kids:** After the Clères zoo, visit the amusement park at Bocasse.

SIGHT

Parc Zoologique de Clères-Jean-Delacour★

Open daily Apr–Sept 10am–7pm; Mar and Oct 10am–6.30pm; last 3 weeks Feb and Nov 1.30–5.30pm. 5.50€ (children 4€). 02 35 33 23 08. www.ot-cleres.fr. The best time to visit is before end Jun.

In an exceptional natural setting, the park of Clères provides a wonderful opportunity to see the birds and mammals collected by the botanist and ornithologist **Jean Delacour** (1890–1985). In the garden are pink flamingos, ducks and exotic geese. Antelope, kangaroos, gibbons, cranes, peacocks and deer roam in partial liberty. Indoor and outdoor aviaries are reserved for lesser-known birds, some endangered species: around 2 000 birds. In the former main room of the château, a gallery houses rare exotic birds.

EXCURSIONS

Parc du Bocasse

2km/1mi W by D 6. Park includes a **children's amusement park** *and picnic area. Call or see website for details. 12€ high season; 11€ low season. 02 35 33 22 25. www.parcdubocasse.fr.*

With 30 attractions including mini golf and plenty of head-spinning fairgound rides, this place will keep children (and adults accompanying them) amused for hours. You can bring a picnic.

Montville

6km/4mi S on the D 155.

Musée des Sapeurs-Pompiers de France

Rue Baron Bigot, Montville. Open Apr–Oct Mon–Fri 10am–noon, 2–6, Sat–Sun 2–6pm; Nov–Mar Mon–Fri 10am–noon, 2–5pm, Sat–Sun 2–5pm. Closed public holidays. 4€ (children 1.50€). 02 35 33 13 51. http://museesp.free.fr.

A fine collection of red fire engines, banners and uniforms, tall ladders and gleaming helmets retrace the glorious history of the French fire brigades.

ADDRESSES

EAT

Au Souper Fin – *76690 Frichemesnil, 4km/2.5mi NE of Clères via D 6 and D 100. 02 35 33 33 88. www.souperfin,com. Closed 24 Mar–1 Apr, 11 Aug–2 Sept, 22 Dec–6 Jan, Sun eve Oct– Apr, Wed–Thu.* This restaurant is situated in a brick house that was once Frichemesnil's grocery shop-café. The owner-chef puts his heart into preparing imaginative cuisine. Attractive dining room, garden terrace. Three charming bedrooms.

Dieppe★★

Dieppe, the beach closest to Paris, is France's oldest seaside resort. The harbour is modern but many old corners and alleys remain, along with churches, a castle and a museum. In the square du Canada stands a monument commemorating the men of Dieppe who explored Canada in the 16C, 17C and 18C, a reminder of more than 350 years of common history. A plaque recalls the Commando Raid in 1942.

- **Population:** 33 618.
- **Michelin Map:** 304: G-2 – Local map, *see Pays de CAUX, p321.*
- **Info:** Pont Jehan-Ango. ✆02 32 14 40 60. www.dieppetourisme.fr.
- **Location:** Dieppe is 65km/40.5mi N of Rouen and 108km/67.5mi from Le Havre. The city is cut in two by the River Béthune, with the picturesque old districts on the right bank and the commercial and government buildings on the left bank around the Grande-Rue and the rue de la Barre.
- **Parking:** Look for free parking along the seafront (bd de Verdun), along the quai de Bérigny (cultural centre) and behind the train station. The car park opposite the town hall (Mairie) on Maréchal-Joffre is paying.
- **Don't Miss:** The 18C buildings along rue de la Barre and the wonderful view of the city from the château museum, as well as the Forest of Eawy.
- **Timing:** You need a day to see Dieppe, and half a day to tour the Forest of Eawy.

A BIT OF HISTORY

Jean Ango and the Privateers' War (16C) – When the Portuguese decided to treat any vessel found off the African coast as a pirate ship, François I riposted by issuing letters of marque.
The seamen of Dieppe took the lead. **Jean Ango**, shipbuilder and naval adviser to François I, produced a fleet of privateers, "which would make a king tremble". Among his captains was **Verrazano** from Florence who discovered the site of New York (1524). Within a few years Ango's ships had captured over 300 Portuguese vessels. Fearing ruin, the King of Portugal forced Ango to give up his letter of marque. The captain built himself a splendid mansion in Dieppe and a country residence in Varengeville. In 1535 he was appointed Governor of Dieppe. In 1551 he was buried in a chapel of St James' Church.

Dieppe Spa – According to the chronicler Pierre de l'Estoile, in 1578 Henri III, who was suffering from scabies (a skin disease), was advised by his doctors to bathe in the sea at Dieppe.
Later Madame de Sévigné mentioned in her letters that some of the court ladies, who had been bitten by a dog, went to Dieppe. She wrote of one of them, "The sea received her bare naked and thus was made proud; I mean to say the sea was proud, for lady was greatly embarrassed."
Throughout the 19C the baths and casinos of Dieppe attracted extravagant people showing off their fine clothes and celebrities such as King Louis-Philippe, Napoleon III, Eugène Delacroix, Camille Saint-Saëns, Alexandre Dumas and Oscar Wilde.

Canadian Commando Raid in 1942 – On 19 August 1942, Operation Jubilee, the first Allied reconnaissance in force on the coast of Europe, was launched, with Dieppe as the primary objective. Seven thousand men, mostly Canadians, were landed at eight points between Berneval and Ste-Marguerite, but the Churchill tanks floundered hopelessly

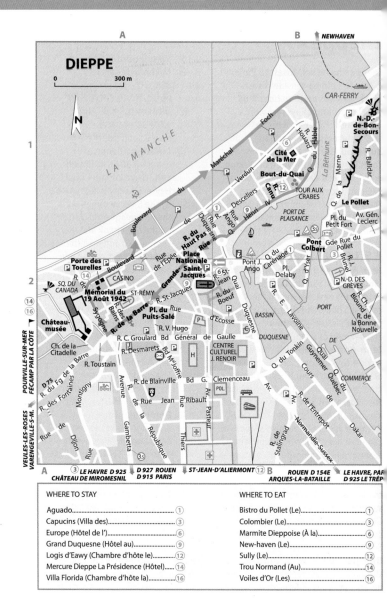

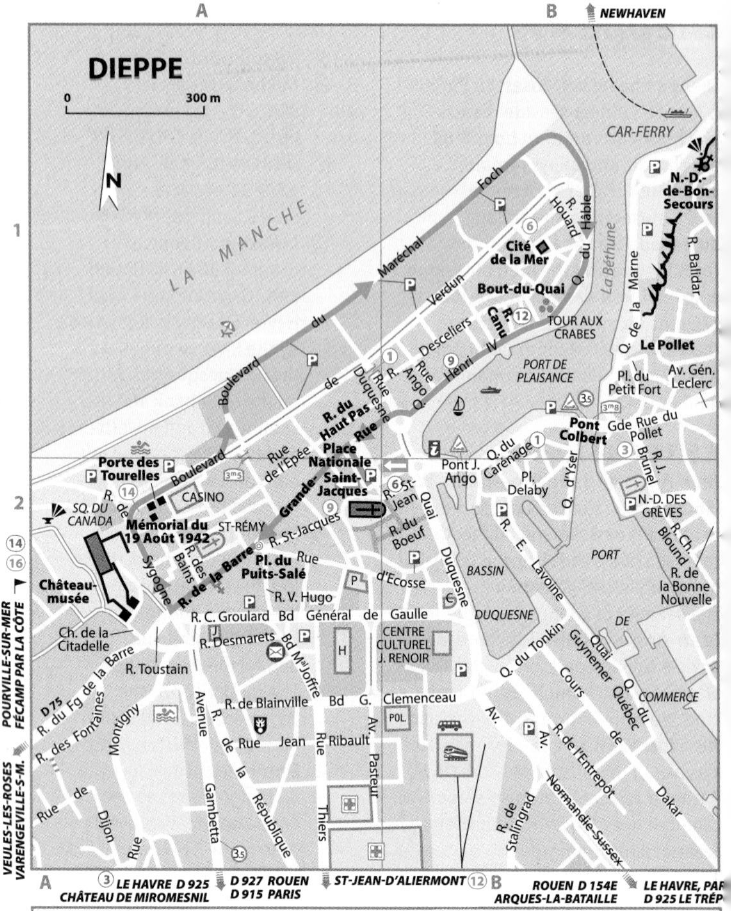

WHERE TO STAY

- Aguado 1
- Capucins (Villa des) 3
- Europe (Hôtel de l') 6
- Grand Duquesne (Hôtel au) 9
- Logis d'Eawy (Chambre d'hôte le) 12
- Mercure Dieppe La Présidence (Hôtel) 14
- Villa Florida (Chambre d'hôte la) 16

WHERE TO EAT

- Bistro du Pollet (Le) 1
- Colombier (Le) 3
- Marmite Dieppoise (À la) 6
- New-haven (Le) 9
- Sully (Le) 12
- Trou Normand (Au) 14
- Voiles d'Or (Les) 16

on the beach under intense fire. Five thousand men were killed or taken prisoner; the Allies learned from this raid that German defences were concentrated round the ports and, as naval losses were small, that amphibious operations on a larger scale might be successful; the Germans, however, concluded that future Allied attacks would be directed particularly at the ports. They were wrong; the Allies developed artificial ports, the famous Mulberries, which they towed across the Channel for the Normandy Landings, avoiding highly defended ports like Dieppe.

WALKING TOURS

DOWNTOWN AND THE BEACH

About 1hr30min from the parking at place Nationale, near St-Jacques.

Place Nationale

In the centre of the circle stands a statue of Abraham Duquesne (1610–88), famous for defeating the Dutch navy and for hunting down and disarming pirate ships in the Mediterranean. Two of the buildings on place Nationale (nos **18** and **24**) date from the early 18C.

Église St-Jacques★

pl. St-Jacques.

Begin by going round the outside of the church, which has been considerably rebuilt over the centuries. Over the 14C central doorway is a fine rose window; the façade tower is 15C, the east end and radiating chapels are 16C; the unrenovated south transept, on the other hand, is a good example of early Gothic.

Interior

The well-proportioned nave, which is 13C, was ornamented in the 14C with a triforium and given tall windows a century later.

The first chapel in the south aisle, the Chapel of the Holy Sepulchre, is 15C. The transept, the oldest part of the church, supports the dome, which was rebuilt in the 18C. A fine 17C wooden statue of St James stands above the high altar. The Sacred Heart Chapel on the right facing the high altar has original Flamboyant vaulting; the centre chapel is known for carved organ consoles (1635). Left, above the sacristy door, is a frieze of Brazilian Indians that recalls the voyages of Dieppe explorers.

Grand-Rue

Many of the houses in white brick date from the reconstruction of Dieppe after the British naval bombardment of 1694. No **21** (now the Globe Café) was once the home of the dreaded pirate Balidar, terror of the English Channel. In the courtyard of no **77**, there is a fountain dating from 1631. At no **186**, an apothecary's old sign on the first floor illustrates three elements of nature: an obelisk (mineral), a palm (vegetable) and a sun (fire).

Place du Puits-Salé

At the junction of six roads, this is the liveliest quarter of Dieppe. The name recalls an old salt-water well (the current well is purely decorative). The large white façade of the early 18C Café des Tribunaux has a clock from 1709.

Rue de la Barre

The pharmacy at no 4 was founded in 1683. Voltaire lodged here when he returned from exile in England, at the home of his friend the apothecary **Jacques Féret**. The houses here are once again early 18C, with period balconies (nos 40, 42, 44). The Protestant church at no 69 was once the chapel of a Carmelite convent (1645).

Take rue de Sygogne, which overlooks the château, to the right.

A monument in the **square du Canada** recalls the 350 years of history uniting Dieppe and Canada, starting with the 17C colonists who left for Québec and continuing through the raid of 19 August 1942. In the summer, you can enter the château-museum from the square.

Boulevard de Verdun leads to the beach through the monumental gate **Les Tourelles**, the only survivor of five gates (15C) in the old fortifications.

Continue along quai du Hâble in the neighbourhood known as **le Bout du Quai**. The little streets off place du Moulin-à-Vent have traditionally been home to local fishermen. The **Maritime Museum** *(Estran-Cité de la Mer Museum, see below)* is on the north side. Just before the corner of rue de la Rade and quai du Hâble, are the vestiges of a 14C tower (Tour aux Crabes). Follow quai Henri IV along the marina.

Return to place Nationale on the left, via Grand-Rue.

THE PORT, LE POLLET AND THE CLIFF

About 2hr, starting from the tourist office.

Go up the cliff from the fishermen's neighbourhood known as Le Pollet for a great view.

Avant-Port

Tall, dark stone buildings surround the basin where the Newhaven–Dieppe ships used to moor.

A yachting marina designed to accommodate up to 400 boats was recently built following the 1994 transfer of the car ferry terminal onto the new outer port. To reach the terminal on foot, cross two bridges, Pont d'Ango and Pont Colbert, built in 1889 from designs by Gustave Eiffel. They lead to the Pollet district. Follow along the base of the cliffs, where you can see *gobes*, former cliff dwellings, now walled up.

Go back to the Colbert Bridge and take ruelle des Grèves (next to a butcher's shop). From rue Guerrier, take rue du Petit-Fort, which ends in a stairway to the top of the cliffs.

Le Pollet and Cliff

There is a very old street leading off rue Guerrier, rue Quiquengrogne; the strange name was a rallying cry of pirates on the Channel in the 15C. Next to no 3 rue du Petit-Fort, a tiny fisherman's cottage, its roof caved in, predates the 1694 bombardment of Dieppe by the English. On top of the cliff stands the **Chapelle Notre-Dame de Bon-Secours**, built in 1876. The military light signal is operational 24hr. Step away from the mast for an extensive **view★** of the city and harbour.

Port de pêche (bassin Duquesne)

Dieppe has a large fishing fleet which goes out to sea on shortish expeditions (one to five days), bringing back fish and seafood for auction. The early-morning fish market is a colourful sight. Dieppe is France's leading source of scallops *(coquilles St-Jacques)*, as well as of sole and other fine fish.

CHÂTEAU AND MARITIME MUSEUM

Château

From the east end of **boulevard de la Mer**, there is a magnificent **view★** of the city and the beach. Dieppe Castle was built round a massive circular tower which formed part of the earlier, 14C, town fortifications. Note the 17C curtain walls linking the castle to the square St-Rémy Tower. Formerly belonging to the governors of the town, it now houses the Municipal Museum.

Museum★

Within château. Open Jun–Sept daily 10am–noon, 2–6pm; Oct–May Wed–Mon 10am–noon, 2–5pm (Sun 6pm (last entry 30mn before closing). Closed 1 Jan, 1 May, 1 Nov, 25 Dec. 3€. 02 35 06 61 99.

The collections centre on two themes: the navy and ivory. At the entrance is a display of ship models, maps and navigational tools. On the first floor, several rooms are devoted to Dutch painting and furniture – many seascapes and still-life pictures of fish (Pieter Boel, 17C) – as well as to 19C and 20C French and international painting: Isabey, Noël, Boudin, Renoir, Pissarro, Mebourg, Sisley, Jacques-Émile Blanche and Walter Sickert. There is an important collection of Pre-Colombian (Peruvian) pottery.

On the first floor is an incomparable collection of **Dieppe ivories★**.

The craftsmanship is meticulous: model ships and navigational instruments, as well as religious items and secular pieces (toilet articles, sewing requisites, fans, snuff boxes, etc.).

A small workshop has been reconstituted to show the tools of local craftsmen who carved ivory imported from Africa and the Orient. In the 17C there were 350 ivory carvers in the town.

One **gallery** is dedicated to the musician **Camille Saint-Saëns**.

Estran-Cité de la Mer★

37 r. de l'Asile-Thomas. Open daily 10am–noon, 2–6pm. Closed 1 Jan, 25 Dec. 5.80€. 02 35 06 93 20. http//:.estrancitedelamer.free.fr.
Situated at the heart of an old fishermen's district, this museum is devoted to local maritime professions and to the ecosystem of the eastern Channel.

EXCURSIONS

Varengeville-sur-Mer★

See VARENGEVILLE-SUR-MER, p379.
8km/5mi SW via D 75.

Offranville

12km/7.4mi SW via D 54B/D54.
Standing next to a 16C church is a thousand-year-old tree more than 7m/23ft around. The William-Farcy gardens are planted with lovely flowers and trees.

Arques-la-Bataille

See ARQUES-LA-BATAILLE, p311.
5km/3mi S via D 154 or D 154E.

Château de Miromesnil★

12km/7.5mi S via D 915 or D 54B. *See ARQUES-LA-BATAILLE – Excursions, p311.*

Forêt d'Eawy

67km/41.6mi from Dieppe to Neufchâtel-en-Bray.
This beautiful beach wood covers a jagged ridge (6 600ha/16 300 acres) flanked by the Varenne and Béthune valleys. A straight ride, allée des Limousins, bisects it. Leaving from Dieppe (D 915) the road crosses the plateau between the River Varenne and the River Scie. Going downhill (D 107) from Le Bois-Robert there are pretty views of the wooded crest separating the Varenne from one of its tributaries. Brick manor houses are dotted all along the Varenne Valley *(D 149, D 154)*. A pretty detour is offered by the Road of the Long Valleys *(D 97)* between Rosay and the carrefour de l'Épinette junction. The village of **St-Saëns** lies on the road back through the woods *(D 12)*.

ADDRESSES

STAY

Aguado – *3 bd Verdun. 02 35 84 27 00. 56 rooms. 10€.* The building is on a street leading to the seafront. The rooms on the promenade side or overlooking the town and harbour have efficient soundproofing.

Chambre d'hôte Le Logis d'Eawy – *1 r. du 31-Août-1944, 76680 St-Saëns, 57km/36mi S. 06 19 15 52 04. www.logisdeawy.com. 2 rooms and 2 suites.* This former post-coach relay in a charming village has, behind a half-timbered façade, a pretty paved courtyard. The interior, much of it original, is splendid. Delicious breakfasts. Good value for money.

Chambre d'hôte La Villa Florida – *24 ch. du Golf. 02 35 84 40 37. www.lavillaflorida.com. 4 rooms.* This hotel's rooms are modern and stylish; each with a terrace. Generous breakfasts.

Hôtel au Grand Duquesne – *15 pl. St-Jacques. 02 32 14 61 10. http://augrandduquesne.free.fr. 12 rooms. Restaurant.* While the guest rooms are somewhat spartan, the restaurant is remarkable. Vegetarian menu, along with traditional dishes.

Mercure Dieppe La Présidence – *1 bd de Verdun. 02 35 84 31 31. www.hotel-la-presidence.com. 81 rooms and 4 suites. 14€. Restaurant.* This luxury hotel's rooms were entirely renovated in 2008. Ideally located near the beach, breakfast in bed is available from 6.30am–noon. Pleasant bar and lounge area.

Villa des Capucins – *11 r. des Capucins. 02 35 82 16 52. www.villa-des-capucins.fr. 2 rooms and 2 suites.* In the old Pollet quarter, this villa is set in splendid surroundings. Pretty rooms.

Hôtel de l'Europe – *63 bd de Verdun. 02 32 90 19 19. www.hoteldieppe.com. 60 rooms. 9€.* A bland façade belies an interior with touch of class. Rooms are tidy and of a good size.

EAT

Le Bistrot du Pollet – *23 r. de Tête-de-Bœuf. ☎02 35 84 68 57. Closed Sun and Mon, 20–29 Apr, 17 Aug–1 Sept and 8 Jan.* A pretty façade of marine tiles. Flavoursome cuisine blending the best of surf and turf.

Le New Haven – *53 quai Henri IV. ☎02 35 84 89 72. Closed Tue and Wed except in Jul–Aug.* A straight-forward and pleasant restaurant. Charming view of the marina. The chef produces traditional cuisine, generously served.

Le Trou Normand – *76550 Pourville-sur-Mer, 5km/3mi W. ☎02 35 84 59 84. www.letrounormand.fr. Closed Sun eve and Wed.* This inn overlooks Juno Beach. On the menu: produce of both sea and land.

Le Colombier – *r. Loucheur, 76550 Offranville. ☎02 35 85 48 50. Closed Sun eve, Tue eve and Wed.* This typical Norman building (1509) has attractive traditional furnishings to match its cuisine. Well worth a try!

La Marmite Dieppoise – *8 r. St-Jean. ☎02 35 84 24 26. Closed Sun eve and Mon, Thu eve from Sept–Jun, 20 Jun–3 Jul, 21 Nov–8 Dec and 15–end Feb. Reservations recommended.* The yellow-brick façade in the centre of town conceals a small restaurant. Cuisine with a spotlight on seafood.

Les Voiles d'Or – *1 ch. de la Falaise. ☎02 35 84 16 84. Closed 13 Nov–1 Dec, Sun eve, Mon and Tue. Reservations recommended.* Modern place in the Pollet quarter with colourfulr furtniure. Contemporary cuisine.

LEISURE

Armement Legros – *54 r. du Dauphin-Louis-XI. Closed Sept–Jun except public holidays.* Fishing trips and 40min sea cruises. Equipment may be hired.

M. Dubois – *10 r. de la Charpenterie. ☎02 35 84 93 51.* Sea-fishing excursions. By reservation.

Elbeuf

Elbeuf was once an important centre for French cloth-making, an industry that began here in the 15C. The decline of this industry, described by the famous novelist André Maurois, has since been offset by modern manufacturing, including chemicals, electrical goods, machinery, metallurgy and automobiles.

- **Population:** 17 277.
- **Michelin Map:** 304: G-6.
- **Info:** 28 rue Henry. ☎02 35 77 03 78. www.tourisme-elbeuf.org.
- **Location:** Elbeuf is reached by N 15 and D 7 from Rouen (20km/12.4mi N) or by the D 313 from Louviers (14km/8.5mi S).
- **Don't Miss:** The old cloth-making neighbourhoods; a River Oison excursion.
- **Timing:** Attractions are more likely to be open on afternoons.

WALKING TOUR

Old Town *Allow 45min.*

Leave your car in the car park. P Across from the town hall. Take rue Henry and when you reach St-Jean Church, turn left on rue Guyemer.

Place St-Jean and the Puchot district are at the heart of the old town.

Straight along rue R.-Poulain and take the first right to place de la République.

On the square the old cloth manufactory (18C, attic and chimneys 19C) is being restored. More than 350 people worked here in 1889; it closed in 1961.

Rue aux Bœufs; cross rue Boucher-de-Perthes. Go through the gardens to

CAEN A 13 · D 938 ROUEN · A · D 7 · ST-AUBIN-LES-ELBEUF · D 144 · A 13-E 05 ROUEN · B

LA SEINE

Pont Jean Jaurès

Musée municipal

St-Jean-Baptiste

St-Étienne
JARDIN DE LA SOURCE

CHAMP DE FOIRE

IMMACULÉE CONCEPTION

ELBEUF
0 200 m N

D 840 · LE NEUBOURG

WHERE TO EAT
Pomme (La)..............②

D 840 · LE NEUBOURG · A · B

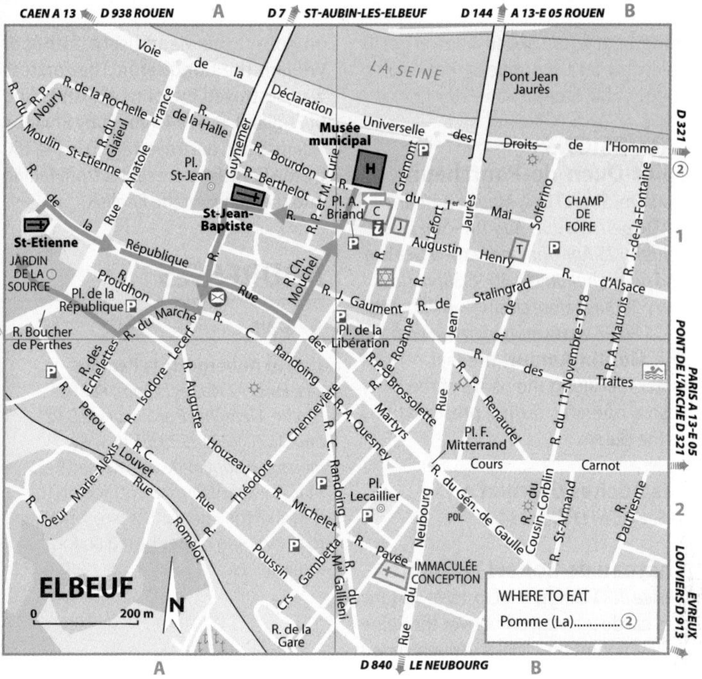

St-Étienne Church, then continue up rue de la République on the right.

The **Jardins de la Source**, opened 1994, enlivened this old manufacturing area.

○ *Continue straight on rue des Martyrs and take the first left to the town hall.*

SIGHTS

Église St-Jean-Baptiste
pl. St-Jean. ○*Open Mon–Fri 9am–1.30pm.* ⊶*Choir closed for repairs.*
Gothic church with Classical ornamentation and furnishings. Notice the 16C stained-glass windows on the 1st, 3rd, 4th and 5th windows in the north aisle and the first in the south aisle. They are the oldest (1500) and best conserved.

Église St-Étienne
r. de la République. ○*Open May–Oct Sat 10.30am–1pm.*
This Flamboyant church has retained its 16C stained-glass windows. Note the Crucifixion on the top window to the right in the apse and other windows retracing scenes from the life of the Virgin

in the north aisle. Near the Lady Chapel in the north aisle there is a fine stained-glass representation of the Tree of Jesse. St Roch is depicted in the stained glass of a chapel in the south aisle. One of the panels shows the drapers in working clothes. Woodcarving is represented by a Louis XV-style rood beam, a 13C

18C house in the Old Town

G. Targat/MICHELIN

recumbent figure of Christ (lower north aisle) and, on either side of the chancel, statues of St Stephen and St John.

EXCURSIONS

Saint-Ouen-de-Pontcheuil

8km/5mi S via D 840. Moulin Amour – Open mid-Jul–Aug Tue–Sun 2.30–6.30pm; 25 Apr–Jun and Sept–4 Oct Sun and public holidays 2.30–6.30pm (last entry 30min before closing). 4€. 02 32 35 80 27. www.moulinamour.com.

The **Moulin Amour**, the last official water mill along the banks of the River Oison, operates during presentations to the public.

Les Roches d'Orival ★

See HONFLEUR, p134.

Château de Robert le Diable★

Musée des Vikings. Closed to visitors.

The castle is a viewpoint over the Seine Valley. Robert the Devil is vaguely based on Robert the Magnificent, father of William the Conqueror. The fortress was destroyed by John Lackland, King of England, in 1204, rebuilt by Philippe Auguste and destroyed again in the 15C by the French to prevent it from falling into the hands of the English.

ADDRESSES

EAT

Auberge de la Pomme – *44 r. Eure, 72340 Les Damps, Pont de l'Arche, 11km/7mi E of Elbeuf via D 921 and D 321. 02 35 23 00 46. www.laubergedelapomme.com. Closed 9–25 Aug.* A pretty Norman cottage on the banks of the Eure with a pleasant dining room serving dishes based on local ingredients.

Étretat★★

The elegant resort of Étretat is renowned for its magnificent setting. The grandeur of the high cliffs and crashing waves has inspired many writers, artists and film directors. Maurice Leblanc described the Aiguille Creuse through his famous character, Arsène Lupin.
Maupassant spent his childhood here, "leading the life of a wild foal". Other famous habitués include Alexandre Dumas, André Gide, Victor Hugo, Gustave Courbet, Jacques Offenbach and Claude Monet.

- **Population:** 1 531.
- **Michelin Map:** 304: B-3.
- **Info:** Place Maurice-Guillard. 02 35 27 05 21. www.etretat.net.
- **Location:** This seaside resort is located 47km/29.2mi N of Honfleur, 90km/56mi NW of Rouen and 219km/136mi from Paris.
- **Parking:** Place du Général-de-Gaulle (fee). Free car parks: the Grand Val (rue Guy de Maupasssant, 300m/275yd from the centre), the route du Havre to the S and near the former train station to the N.
- **Don't Miss:** Panoramic view from the cliffs of Aval and Amont.
- **Kids:** The Tourist Train between Étretat and Les Loges.

CLIFF WALKS

Falaise d'Aval★★

Allow 1hr on foot there and back. From the west end of the promenade climb the steps (180 steps, handrail) to the path which scales the cliff face. Walk along the edge of the cliff as far as the ridge of Porte d'Aval.

Falaise d'Aval

G. Targat/MICHELIN

The view is magnificent: the massive Manneporte arch (left), the Aiguille opposite and the Amont Cliff on the far side of the bay. The variations of colour according t time of day and natural lighting are truly enchanting.

Falaise d'Amont★★

Allow 1hr on foot there and back. From the east end of the promenade take the steps cut into the chalk cliffs and the path to the clifftop.
Access by car: take D 11 Fécamp par la Côte; just before the sign indicating the end of the built-up area, turn sharp left onto a steep and narrow uphill road. Park near the monument.

From **Notre-Dame-de-la-Garde** there is a magnificent **view**★ of Étretat and its surroundings. Below is the long shingle beach between the Aval arch and the Aiguille. Behind the chapel an immense spire points towards the sky. The memorial was erected to Nungesser and Coli, French aviators who made the first, unsuccessful attempt to fly the Atlantic on 8 May 1927. It was here that their aircraft, the *Oiseau Blanc*, was seen for the last time.

SIGHTS

Halles

This wooden covered market in place du Maréchal-Foch is a reconstruction.

Église Notre-Dame

Rue Notre-Dame at corner of rue Nungesser et Coli.

This church has a Romanesque doorway with a 19C tympanum. The rest of the building is 12C. Go forward to the transept crossing to admire the 13C lantern turret.

Le Clos Lupin★

15 r. Guy-de-Maupassant. Open Apr–Sept daily 10am–5.45pm; Oct–mid-Nov and mid-Dec–Mar Fri–Sun and school holidays 11am–4.45pm. Audioguided tours (45min). Closed 1 Jan, 25 Dec. 6.75€. 02 35 10 59 53. www.arsene-lupin.com.

Arsène Lupin is a gentleman burglar created by Maurice Leblanc. The museum, in a vast Norman family home, mingles mementoes of the two.

EXCURSION

To Le Havre-Antifer Port and Terminal

15km/9mi S.

Leave Étretat by D 940; turn right onto D 111, direction La Poterie, cap d'Antifer.

The cliffs can collapse without warning. Do not walk directly beneath them; beware tides.

> *"On a sun-drenched beach when the galloping waves toss the fine shingle, a charming sound rings out, dramatic as the tear of a canvas sail and merry as an elfin peal of laughter, a soft rumbling that echoes all along the coastline, racing against the foamy peaks, resting a while, then resuming its lively, intoxicating dance with the ebbing of the ocean waters. The very name Étretat – spirited and lively yet deep and melodious – seems to have sprung from the sound of pebbles being rolled by the receding waves. And its beach, whose beauty has been immortalised by so many painters, is the embodiment of magic, with its two formidable tears in the cliff face known as the doors."*
> Guy de Maupassant – *Étretat*

Bruneval

A German radar installation near the beach was the objective of an Allied raid on the night of 27–28 February 1942. Three detachments of British parachutists destroyed the position and re-embarked almost without loss.

Between Bruneval and St-Jouin, the road passes through picturesque countryside and leads to the oil terminal.

Le Havre-Antifer Terminal

The Le Havre-Antifer port was created in 1976 to receive oil tankers too big for the facilities at Le Havre. On the way back to St-Jouin, a narrow road on the right (signalled Port du Havre/Antifer/Belvédère), leads to a belvedere with a fine **view**.

ADDRESSES

STAY

Chambre d'hôte M. et Mme Delahais – *54 r. du Prés.-René-Coty, 76790 Le Tilleul, 3km/2mi S of Étretat via D 940. ℘02 35 27 16 39. Closed 2 weeks in Oct. 4rooms.* Basic comfort, a very considerate reception, ambient quietude and, above all, highly attractive prices for a room just 3min from Étretat by car!

Hôtel La Résidence – *4 bd René-Coty, BP 24. ℘02 35 27 02 87. 15 rooms.* This downtown mansion was built in the 14C. Pleasant rooms with amusing, eclectic furniture. Cycle hire.

EAT

Lann Bihoué – *45 r. Notre-Dame. ℘02 35 27 04 65. www.lannbihoue.com. Closed Dec, Tue except during school holidays and Wed.* To make a change from Norman cuisine, try this crêperie near the town centre. Besides the classic Breton crêpes, there's a speciality with Guémémé sausages and caramelised apples. Friendly service.

Le Clos Lupin – *37 r. Alphonse-Karr. ℘02 35 29 67 53. www.le-clos-lupin.fr. Closed Mon–Tue except school holidays. Reservations required weekends.* Behind the stylish painted façade and lace trimmings, you'll find a long dining room in the heart of town. The menu features classic fare at decidedly reasonable prices.

Le Galion – *Bd René-Coty. ℘02 35 29 48 74. Closed 15 Dec–26 Jan, Tue–Wed.* Situated in the town centre, this house, built with materials taken from an old Lisieux residence, has a noteworthy 14C ceiling of carved beams. Good cuisine and competitive prices.

LEISURE

Étretat Tourist Train – Vélorail – *At the train station. 6km/3.7mi from Étretat via D 940, 76790 Les Loges. ℘02 35 29 49 61. www.trains-fr.org. Reservations required. Closed Nov–Mar.* Across the green countryside between Étretat and Les Loges. You can pedal the vélorail (a sort of bicycle on train tracks) from Loges.

Eu★

Eu is a small town on the River Bresle set between the sea and the forest from which it gets its name. The town centres around its beautiful 11C collegiate church. It was in Eu that the two Anguier brothers, François (1604–69) and Michel (1612–86), were born: these Baroque sculptors contributed to the building of the Louvre and the Val de Grâce in Paris.

- **Population:** 7 571.
- **Michelin Map:** 304: i-1.
- **Info:** Place Guillaume-le-Conquérant. 02 35 86 04 68. www.ville-eu.fr.
- **Location:** Eu is 4km/2.5mi E of Le Tréport by D 1915 and 34kim/21mi NE of Dieppe by D 925.
- **Parking:** There is parking on the square between the château and the church.
- **Don't Miss:** The château and its museum; the historic centre of town for its lively pedestrian streets.
- **Timing:** Spend the morning seeing the city, then head towards the pretty forest of Eu.
- **Kids:** Take them to the archaeological site at Bois-Abbé and the Glass-Making Museum.

SIGHTS

Collégiale Notre-Dame et St-Laurent★

pl. Guillaume-le-Conquérant. Open daily Apr–Oct 9am–noon, 2–6pm (except Sun during mass); Nov–Mar 9am–noon, 2–5pm (except Sun during mass). Closed 1 Jan. No charge. 02 35 86 19 34.

The collegiate church, dedicated to Our Lady and St Lawrence O'Toole, Primate of Ireland who died in Eu in 1180, was erected in the 12C and 13C in the Gothic style. In the 15C the apse was remodelled and in the 19C Viollet-le-Duc, the architect and restoration specialist, undertook a general restoration of the building.

The **interior** is striking for its size and harmonious proportions. The second ambulatory chapel on the right, the Chapel of the Holy Sepulchre, has, beneath a Flamboyant canopy, a 15C **Entombment**★; opposite is a magnificent head of Christ in Sorrow, also 15C.

Crypt

The crypt, which is beneath the chancel, was restored in 1828 by the Duke of Orléans, who reigned as King Louis-Philippe from 1830 to 1848. The 12C–

Château d'Eu

G. Targat/MICHELIN

13C recumbent statue of St Lawrence O'Toole is believed to be one of the oldest in France.

Château

Nothing remains of the original castle where William the Conqueror married Matilda of Flanders in 1050. It was destroyed in 1475 on the orders of Louis XI. The present château, a huge brick and stone building begun by Henri of Guise and Catherine de Clèves in 1578, has been restored several times since. It passed to the Orléans family and became one of the favourite residences of Louis-Philippe, who received Queen Victoria there twice. Viollet-le-Duc was commissioned to redecorate it between 1874 and 1879 for the Count of Paris, grandson of the king. The château, which now belongs to the town of Eu, is occupied by the town hall and the communal archives, and houses the **Louis-Philippe Museum**.

Musée Louis-Philippe

Open mid-Mar–early Nov Wed–Thu and Sat–Mon 10am–noon, 2–6pm, Fri 2–6pm (last entry 1hr before closing). 4€. 02 35 86 44 00.

On the ground floor visitors are shown the grand staircase and the Duchesse d'Orléans' suite, redecorated by Viollet-le-Duc in 1875, as well as the two salons and the bedroom where Queen Victoria and Prince Albert slept in 1843 and 1845, embellished with a superb inlaid parquet floor made under Louis-Philippe.

In the restored portico overlooking the garden, note the dazzling **wall of light** conceived by Viollet-le-Duc and master-glazier Oudinot.

On the first floor you can visit the 19C bathroom, the gold bedroom with its pretty green and gilt wainscoting bearing the monogram of the Grande Demoiselle (Princesse Anne Marie Louise d'Orléans, 1627-1693, who once lived here), the Louis-Philippe **dining hall** with its lovely 17C coffered ceiling, the Black Salon, with its strange pink and black colour scheme, and the vast **Galerie des Guise**, currently being renovated to house 145 family paintings purchased in 2000. The gallery contains 10 000 volumes, including books from Eu's Jesuit College and those belonging to the last Comte d'Eu.

The south wing of the first floor, which once housed the private suites of Louis-Philippe and Marie-Amélie, is being restored to its former glory.

The Park

Most of the trees are beeches, one of which, known as the Guisarda, was planted in 1585.

Chapelle du Collège★

The Jesuit college now bears the name of the 17C Anguier brothers, who studied here. The chapel was commissioned in 1624 by Catherine de Clèves, widow of Henri de Guise, to whom she brought the County of Eu as a dowry in 1570.

The Louis XIII **façade**★ is quite remarkable. The beautifully restored brick and stone masonry lends both warmth and harmony to the whole ensemble.

Musée des Traditions Verrières

r. Semichon, follow the signs from the Salle Audiard. Open Jul–mid-Sept Tue, Wed, Sat–Sun and public holidays 2.30–6pm; Apr–Jun and mid-Sept–Oct Tue, Sat–Sun and public holidays 2.30–6pm. 3€ (under 12 years no charge) 02 35 86 04 68.

The former stables of the Bresle cavalry house this museum devoted to glass-making techniques.

The Forêt d'Eu

This beech wood covers three isolated massifs with beautiful beech glades: St Martin's Priory Chapel (pretty doorway); **St Catherine's Viewpoint** (a 45min walk leads up to a view of the Yères Valley); **La Bonne Entente** (an oak and a beech growing intertwined); **St-Martin-le-Gaillard** (13C **church**).

The interior has cornices carved with humorous human figures; 18C Virgin and Child. Note that that Baby Jesus is receiving a fig.

ADDRESSES

STAY

Hôtel restaurant Maine – *20 pl. de la Gare. 02 35 86 16 64 www.hotel-maine.com. 19 rooms. . Restaurant.* Built in 1897, this bourgeois house has an old-fashioned, discreet appeal. Rooms, generally plainly fitted out, may be embellished with small touches from the past. Belle Epoque dining room brightened up by knick-knacks, paintings and bouquets.

Chambre d'hôte Manoir de Beaumont – *rte de Beaumont, 2km/1mi E via D 49, dir. Forêt d'Eu. 02 35 50 91 91. www.demarquet.com. 4 rooms. .* This former hunting lodge of the Château d'Eu overlooks the valley. From your comfortable rooms, you'll savour the tranquillity of the park, the charm of the house and, above all, the first-class welcome.

EAT

La Gare aux Gourmets – *2 r. de la Gare, 80520 Woincourt, 8.5km/5.3mi E via D 925. 03 22 30 92 42. http://gare-aux-gourmets.picardieresto.com. Closed Aug and Sat lunch.* A stone's throw from the Channel, near the village train station, this friendly inn offers traditional fare in a family atmosphere.

LEISURE

Cycles Joostens – *1 r. Charles Morin. 02 35 86 22 24. Closed 2 weeks in Feb and Aug. Bike rentals. Tourist offices have maps for some marked trails.*
If you dislike dirt paths, head for the Bois de Cise (before Ault and N of Mers), where the trails are paved and lead you to a little-frequented beach. The Hyères valley circuit (50km/31mi), starting from the beach at Mesnil-Val, passes through lovely countryside but you need to be in shape. There's an alternate, more relaxed circuit of only 25km/15.5mi.

Fécamp★★

Fécamp is a fishing port as well as a centre for pleasure boats. The town is also the home of Benedictine liqueur – a link with its monastic past. Guy de Maupassant was one frequent visitor to the town, which features in several of his works.

- **Population:** 19 424.
- **Michelin Map:** 304: C-3. Local map, *see Pays de CAUX, p320.*
- **Info:** Quai Sadi-Carnot. 02 35 28 51 01. www.fecamp-tourisme.com.
- **Location:** Fécamp is 43km/26.7mi NE of Le Havre and 72km/44.7mi NW of Rouen.
- **Don't Miss:** The rich collections of the Bénédictine palace, the abbey of La Trinité and the superb view from Cap Fagnet and Valmont Abbey.
- **Timing:** Fécamp and its surroundings will take up a day.
- **Kids:** The museum of Terre-Neuvas et de la Pêche.

A BIT OF HISTORY

As early as the 7C there was a monastery in Fécamp with a relic of the Precious Blood. Richard II, Duke of Normandy from 996–1027, established a Benedictine community here. Before the rise of Mont-St-Michel, this was the foremost place of pilgrimage in Normandy.

SIGHTS

Abbatiale de la Trinité★

pl. des Ducs Richards.

The abbey church built by Richard II was struck by lightning and burned down. The subsequent building (12C–13C) was modified several times between the 15C and 18C.

Exterior

The cathedral is one of the longest (127m/417ft) in France. The Classical façade does not accord with the rest of the building and the nave walls are austere. Skirt the south porch: the tympanum above the door is a good example of Norman Gothic decoration.

Above the transept crossing rises the square lantern tower (65m/213.3ft high), designed in the typical Norman style.

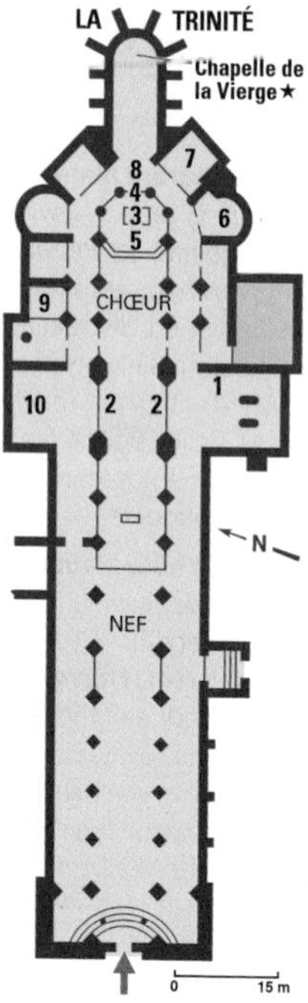

Interior

The south transept contains a beautiful late-15C **Dormition of the Virgin**★. On the right of the altar is the Angel's Footprint. In 943, when the reconstructed church was being consecrated, an angel appeared and left his footprint on the stone.

The chancel's dimensions make it magnificent. The stalls, baldaquin and high altar are all good 18C works by the Rouen artist De France. A Renaissance altar stands behind the high altar. In the centre of the sanctuary is an ancient shrine adorned with low-relief sculptures dating from the 12C. The chapels off the chancel aisles and radiating chapels were embellished with wonderful **carved screens**★ in the 16C. In the fourth chapel, on the right, is the **tomb**★ of Abbot Thomas of St-Benoît, who died in 1307; the tomb is decorated with scenes from the abbey's history on its base.

The 15C **Lady Chapel**★forms a separate group in the Flamboyant style. The wood medallions are 18C; the windows are 13C, 14C and 16C. Facing the chapel is the white-marble **tabernacle**★ of the Precious Blood. The 17C tomb in the chapel of the Sacred Heart belongs to **Guglielmo da Volpiano**, first abbot of Fécamp, who died in 1031.

Palais Bénédictine★★

110 r. Alexandre-le-Grand. Open daily mid-Jul–Aug 10am–6pm; Apr–mid-Jul and Sept–mid-Oct 10am–1pm, 2–6.30pm; 7 Feb–Mar and mid-Oct–Dec 10.30am–12.45pm, 2–6pm (last

Palais Bénédictine

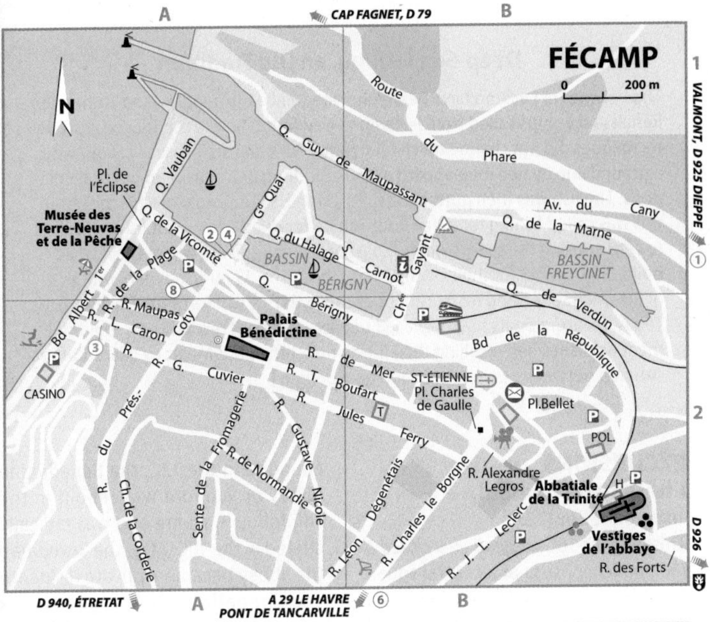

WHERE TO STAY

Le Thuillier (Chambre d'hôte Mireille)........ (1)

Plage (Hôtel de la)........ (3)

WHERE TO EAT

Nounoute (Chez)........ (2)

Maritime (Le)........ (4)

Rouge (Auberge de la)........ (6)

Vicomte (Le)........ (8)

entry 1hr before closing). Closed 5 Jan –6 Feb, 25 Dec, 1 May. 6.50€. 02 35 10 26 10. www.benedictine.fr/anglais/lepalais_frame.html.

The building, designed by Camille Albert in the late 19C, is a mixture of neo-Gothic and neo-Renaissance styles.

The **museum** displays a large collection of objets d'art: silver and gold work, ivories, Nottingham alabasters (late-15C), wrought-iron work, statues and many manuscripts.

The Gothic Room is covered by a fine pitched roof made of oak and chestnut, shaped as the upturned hull of a ship; it houses the library: 15C Books of the Hours with fine **illuminations**, numerous **ivories**, a collection of **oil lamps** dating from the early days of Christianity and a Dormition of the Virgin, a painted low-relief wooden carving of the German School.

The Alexander Le Grand Room, named after the Fécamp merchant who first marketed the Bénédictine liqueur in 1863, displays objects and documents relating to its history.

Musée des Terre-Neuvas et de la Pêche★

27 bd Albert I. Open Jul–Aug daily 10am–6.30pm; Sept–Jun Wed–Mon 10am–noon, 2–5.30pm. Closed 1 Jan, 1 May, 25 Dec. 3€. 02 35 28 31 99.

The Newfoundland and Fishing Museum evokes memories of the Fécamp fishing industry. The lower gallery explores the great adventure of the cod fishermen on the Newfoundland banks in the days of the sailing ship and the dory, a flat-bottomed craft rising at bow and stern.

One room is devoted to shipbuilding, featuring a model of the Belle Poule, the naval training ship built in Fécamp in 1931.

Exhibits trace the development of fishing methods and types of craft.

The outdoor terrace provides a magnificent **view**★ of the sea.

Deep-Sea Fishing, an Old Tradition

The herrings of Fécamp have been renowned since the Middle Ages. During the Renaissance ships sailed from Fécamp to Newfoundland to fish for cod. Fishing techniques did not change much for nearly 400 years: the fish was caught with a ground line by two men aboard a 5m/5.5yd-long flat-bottomed boat called a doris. The fish was then gutted, cleaned, boned, salted and stored in the hold; this was called fishing for green cod. Fishing for dried cod meant fishermen had to settle during the season on the coast of Newfoundland, where they would build drying racks for their catch. During the 1970s, 15 huge trawlers with a crew of 900 men salted and froze 21 000t of cod in the icy waters of the North Atlantic. Today, pleasure boats have replaced trawlers, but until recently one could still meet old fishermen recalling their memories at the Bout Menteux (Liars' Corner, situated between quai Vicomté and quai Bérigny).

EXCURSIONS

Château de Bailleul

10km/6mi SE by D 73.

This elegant 16C château *(closed to the public)* consists of a central square building flanked by four pavilions. The medieval side façades are almost blind. A chapel stands in the wooded park.

Valmont

11km/7mi E via D 150.

Located in the very heart of the Pays de Caux and dominated by a castle built on a rocky spur, the village of Valmont possesses the ruins of a Benedictine abbey.

Abbey★

Church open Feb–Dec daily 9am–6pm; Chapelle de la Vierge and mausoleum open Jul–Sept Wed–Mon 2.30–5pm. Closed Easter Sun, Pentecost Sun, 15 Aug, 25 Dec. 2€. 02 35 27 34 92. http://abbayevalmont.free.fr.

Founded in the 12C, the Benedictine abbey of Valmont was rebuilt in the 14C following a fire and was radically altered in the 16C. After the Revolution the abbey became a private residence The **Chapelle de la Vierge**★, or Six o'Clock Chapel (the monks celebrated Mass at this time every day), which has remained intact among the ruins, has an overall effect of great grace. Above the altar is a tiny room which has exquisite decorations and also a picture of the Annunciation attributed to Germain Pilon.

Château

Closed to the public.

Property of the Estoutevilles, lords of Valmont, this former military fortress preserves a Romanesque keep flanked by a Louis XI wing, crowned by a covered watch-path, and a Renaissance wing.

ADDRESSES

STAY

Chambre d'hôte Mireille Le Thuillier – *37 Le Val de la Mer – 76400 Senneville-sur-Fécamp, 5km/3mi E of Fécamp, dir. Dieppe, then secondary road. 02 35 28 41 93. www.val-de-la-mer.com. Closed mid-Aug–mid-Sept. 3 rooms.* This charming Norman house, which appears quite old, is named for the little road that runs by it, leading to the sea. Guest rooms are decorated with exquisite taste. The biggest, sun-filled room is on the ground floor.

Hôtel de la Plage – *87 r. de la Plage. 02 35 29 76 51. www.hotel-delaplage-fecamp.com. 22 rooms.* Situated close to the waterfront, this very simple family hotel is a modest stopover. Rooms are spic-and-span and the breakfast room is picturesque with its marine décor and counter shaped like a ship's hull.

EAT

Chez Nounoute – *3 pl. Nicholas-Selle. ℘02 35 29 38 08. Closed Wed from Sept–Feb. Reservations advised.* Occasionally one likes to find an unusual place, managed by a rather special but friendly owner. Here you find seafood *choucroute* and fresh fish wonderfully cooked.

Le Maritime – *2 pl. Nicolas-Selle. ℘02 35 28 21 71. Reservations advised.* This restaurant situated in the marina displays navigational instruments and wood panelling for a maritime décor. The menu offers seafood, as well as meat for famished buccaneers.

Le Vicomté – *4 r. du Prés.-René-Coty. ℘02 35 28 47 63. Closed mid-Aug–1 Sept, 20 Dec–3 Jan, Wed eve, Thu, holidays.* Near the great Benedictine palace, where a celebrated liqueur is produced, this small bistro is decorated with old engravings. The chef uses ingredients sourced from local markets to make delicious dishes.

Auberge de la Rouge – *rte du Havre, St-Léonard. ℘02 35 28 07 59. www.auberge-rouge.com.* The restaurant in this hotel is just 5min from Fécamp. There is a most charming garden and the traditional menu is highly praised.

LEISURE

Tourisme et loisirs maritimes – *15 r. Vicomte. ℘02 35 28 99 53.* A variety of excursions on boats along the Norman coast are proposed, including fishing expeditions, both from Fécamp and from Le Havre.

The tourist office has suggestions for bicycle excursions and hikes in the area.

Forges-les-Eaux

Located in the green heart of the Pays de Bray, Forges-les-Eaux is a spa resort and source of iron-rich waters reputed to be both refreshing and stimulating.

- **Population:** 3 542.
- **Michelin Map:** 304: J-4.
- **Info:** Rue Albert-Bochet. ℘02 35 90 52 10. www.ville-forges-les-eaux.fr.
- **Location:** Forges-les-Eaux is 60km/37mi NE of Rouen.
- **Don't Miss:** Excursions into the Pays de Bray to see the pretty villages.
- **Timing:** After a morning in town, see the Pays de Bray.

SIGHTS

Collection Faïence de Forges

In the tourist office. Open Tue–Fri. Closed public holidays. 2.50€. ℘02 35 90 52 10.

A hundred or so examples of Forges faïence, manufactured until the 19C, are displayed at the town hall.

Musée de la Résistance et de la Déportation

r. du Général-Leclerc. Open daily 2–6pm (last entry 5.30pm). Closed 1 Jan, 14 Jul, 15 Aug, 25 Dec. 5€. ℘02 35 90 64 07

Insignia, arms and uniforms as well as documents recount the dark days of the Occupation in Haute Normandie.

The Spa

Rue de la République boasts some half-timbered façades (17C–18C), and leads onto avenue des Sources, where it passes under the old railway line (now a footpath).

The resort grounds and casino are to the left, just after the bridge. The **park** and spa are managed by the Club Méditerranée in an elegant setting.

Parc Montalent and Épinay Forest

On the other side of avenue des Sources, four pleasant and well-marked **nature trails** wind among the ponds and into the woods.

EXCURSION

La Ferme de Bray

Leave Forges via D 915 NW; after 8km/5mi, turn left before Sommery and follow the signs. 281 Chemin de Bray. ♿ ⏲Open Jul–Aug daily 2–7pm. Easter–Jun; Sept–Oct Sat–Sun and public holidays 2–7pm. ⚭6€. ☏02 35 90 57 27. http://ferme.de.bray.free.fr.

On the banks of the Sorson, this restored site shows what a prosperous 17C–18C farm was like. The bread oven, the cider press and the mill are in use. There are regular exhibits in the main house, a spacious 16C building whose façade was redone in the 17C.

DRIVING TOURS

Southern Pays de Bray

52km/32.3mi. Leave via D 921 south.

The Pays de Bray is a lush strip at the centre of the vast bare stretches of the Caux plateau. It owes its chief characteristic, known as the Bray "Buttonhole", to a geological accident, which created a hollow in the surrounding chalk. Running parallel to the valley of the River Seine, the region is a sparsely inhabited patchwork of vales, limestone bluffs, hills, meadows and forests.

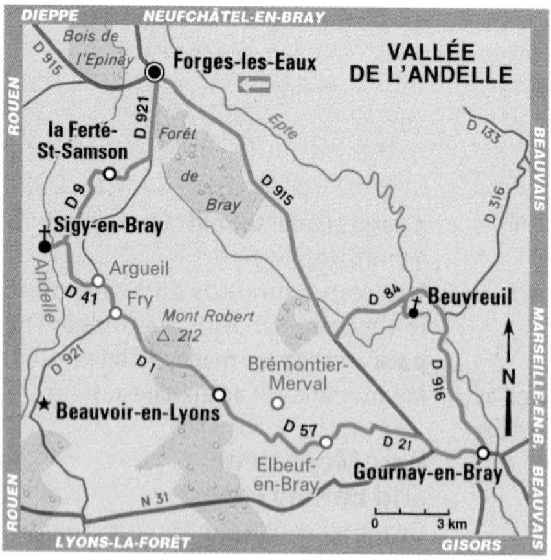

La Ferté-St-Samson

The village is perched just before the main edge of the Bray Buttonhole and from the approach to the church there is an extended view of the depression with its clearly defined rim. In the main square is the 16C house of Henri IV.

In Fry, before church, turn left onto D 1.

The road runs along the southwest Bray escarpment of massive bare mounds crowned with beech trees (Mont Robert).

Beauvoir-en-Lyons

Park beyond the town hall; walk up the street on the left to the church.

From the east end there is a **view**★ of the green Bray Valley cutting away in a straight line southeast. In clear weather Beauvais Cathedral is visible.

Return to the car and continue southeast on D 1. At a crossroads, turn left downhill onto D 57. Then follow D 21.

Gournay-en-Bray

Gournay and Ferrières are the busiest towns in the Pays de Bray. The local dairy industry supplies most of the fresh cheese consumed in France.

Collégiale St-Hildevert

The church, which is largely 12C, has withstood several wars but the late 12C doors have suffered from excessive restoration. Inside, the massive columns are surmounted by carved capitals. The oldest and most worn, at the end of the south aisle, are among the earliest examples of attempts at human portrayal during the Romanesque period.

Take D 916 north.

Beuvreuil

Church. *Closed for repairs.*
The wooden porch of the small 11C country **church** is decorated with enamelled bricks. Inside the church are an 11C font stoup, a 15C holy-water stoup, Gothic statues, a 15C altarpiece and a 16C lectern.

Take D 84 west; turn right onto D 915 to Forges.

Vallée de l'Andelle

56km/35mi – from Forges take D 919 and D 13 southwest. Allow 2hr30min.

Sigy-en-Bray

The **abbey church** is all that remains of Sigy Abbey, founded in the 11C by Hugh I. It has kept its 12C chancel and seven-sided apse, a 13C portal and the nave vaulting, restored in the 18C. The 15C bell tower overlooks a cemetery with a late 15C sandstone calvary.

Take D 41 E towards Argueil, then D 921 south.

Le Héron

This small village enjoys a pleasant site alongside the park – designed by Le Nôtre – of the château where, it is said, Gustave Flaubert, then 16 years old, discovered the worldly life, an inspiration used in *Madame Bovary*.

Continue to Vascœuil by the D 46.

Vascœuil

At the **château** (*open Jul–Aug 11am–6.30pm; mid-Mar–Jun and Sept–mid-Nov Tue–Sun 2.40–6pm; closed public holidays; 7.50€*) the historian Jules Michelet (1798–1874) wrote his famous *Histoire de France*.
The road continues past a surprising sight, the ruins of a spinning mill built at the turn of the 20C in imitation of the medieval and Gothic styles.

Nature trail, Épinay Forest

© CDT CALVADOS

Pont-St-Pierre

The town, which stretches across the Andelle Valley, owes much to its 12C–18C château and surrounding park, glimpsed through a gap in the main street.
The 11C–12C church is decorated with **woodwork★**, complemented by Henri II stalls and a 17C altarpiece from Fontaine-Guérard. A 14C Virgin in the chancel wears a dress inlaid with cabochon stones.

After Romilly station turn right; follow D 19 which crosses D 20. After the Sabla factory, turn left along the Seine.

Écluses d'Amfreville★

The locks, together with the Poses Dam, control the water flow in the Lower Seine and divide the stretch below Paris from the tidal section flowing into the Channel. Take the footbridge overlooking the locks to see water pouring over the Poses Dam; go over to the left bank where the 8 000kW power station stands. A spillway specially designed for fish with an observation room shows how different species make their way upstream.

To return to the coast, continue on D 19 as far as Amfreville-sous-les-Monts and take D 20 up a steep hillside.

Le Havre★

In 1945 Le Havre was Europe's most badly damaged port; today the town, including the residential area of Ste-Adresse and the old port of Harfleur, is a remarkable example of large-scale reconstruction and successful town planning. Le Havre's university is new, it opened here in 1986.

- **Population:** 182 580.
- **Michelin Map:** 304: A-5.
- **Info:** 186 boulevard Clemenceau. ℘02 32 74 04 04. www.lehavre tourisme.com.
- **Location:** 197km/122.4mi from Paris and 90km/56mi from Rouen.
- **Don't Miss:** Car ferries operate to England and the Republic of Ireland.
- **Timing:** The best time to visit is Wednesday or weekends, when all sites are open.
- **Kids:** The Malraux museum has a tour map for children.

A BIT OF HISTORY

A Judicious Choice – In 1517 **François I** ordered the construction of a new port, called Havre-de-Grâce, to replace Harfleur, which had silted up. The marshy site chosen by Bonnivet, Grand Admiral of France, had the crucial advantage of a high tide that lasted for over two hours.

An Ocean Port – The career of Le Havre as a trading and transatlantic port began during the American War of Independence when supplies for the rebels were shipped from Le Havre.

Le Havre bustled in the 19C when great transatlantic passenger liners reduced the journey time in New York.

Le Havre during the War – Le Havre suffered 146 raids, in which more than 4 000 were killed. The siege of the town began on 2 September 1944 – the Battle of Normandy was over and Paris liberated, but Le Havre was still occupied.

Allied air raids went on ceaselessly for eight days from 5 September; the Germans were determined to blow up any port installations still in existence. On 13 September 1944 Le Havre was liberated. It took two years to clear the destruction and reconstruction began only in 1946.

THE PORT★★

Traffic

Le Havre is a deep-water port situated in the Seine estuary; it ranks first among French ports for exports and container traffic, and fourth in Europe for total traffic. Le Havre also has frequent car-ferry links with Great Britain (Le Havre–Portsmouth) and Ireland (Le Havre–Rosslare, Le Havre–Cork).

Each year 7 000 merchant ships dock in Le Havre, including 2 250 container ships.

Port Tour

Allow 1hr15min. Information from the tourist office.

For information about the port and shipping movements, see the receptionist at the Centre Administratif, Port Autonome, Terre-plein de la Barre. Audio-guides can be hired for unaccompanied visits of the port.

Boat trips from quai de la Marine take their passengers round the port facilities.

WALKING TOURS

THE MODERN TOWN★

The old town was virtually wiped out in 1944. A new town was planned by **Auguste Perret** (1875–1954), the pioneer of reinforced concrete construction, who achieved remarkable architectural unity. *See map, p346.*

Le Volcan by Oscar Niemeyer, Basin du Commerce

A. de Valroger/MCIEHLIN

Bassin du Commerce and Espace Oscar-Niemeyer

The commercial dock is the focal point of the new district accessible by an elegant footbridge, designed by the architects Gillet and Du Pasquier.

At the west end, facing the war memorial, is the **Espace Oscar-Niemeyer** complex on place Gambetta. The main pavilion (Grand Volcan) has a large theatre, a cinema and exhibition rooms.

Head N along Place de l'Hôtel de Ville for 0.5km/0.3mi.

Place de l'Hôtel-de-Ville★

The square, which was designed by Auguste Perret, is bordered by three-storey buildings, punctuated by taller ten-storey blocks. The open space is laid out with fountains, lawns, arbours and yew hedges. The **hôtel de ville**, an austere building, is distinguished by a great tower (72m/236ft high) in concrete.

Leave the square E and walk along Avenue Foch.

Avenue Foch★

The central roadway is bordered by lawns shaded by trees; the Porte Océane marks the west end of the street on the seafront.

North dyke and the beach

The north breakwater, supplemented by a jetty, encloses the marina. The Le Havre and Ste-Adresse Beach stretches from the North Breakwater to the Hève Cape.

When you reach the "Porte océane", head S along bd Clemenceau, which runs alongside anse des Régates and anse de Joinville. Turn left down rue Frédérick Lemaître.

Église St-Joseph★

Bd François 1er.

This sober **church** typical of Auguste Perret's style was built of concrete between 1951 and 1957. It is surmounted by an octagonal lantern-belfry (109m/357.6ft high). The **interior**★★ is monumental and impressive.

Return to bd Clemenceau. Follow it to avant-port past the Musée des Beaux-Arts André-Malraux (see entry, p348).

Sémaphore

The view from the end of the pier embraces the harbour entrance and the long southern breakwater protecting the outer harbour.

Continue along the seafront and take quai South Hampton up to Maison de l'Armateur. Take the first left (rue du Général Faidherbe) then the Notre-Dame bridge. Take a right (quai Videcoq) then rejoin rue Drapiers on the left. Once you hit rue de Paris, head north.

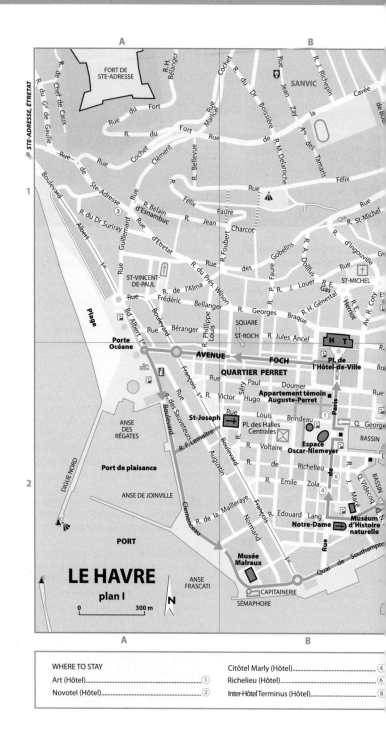

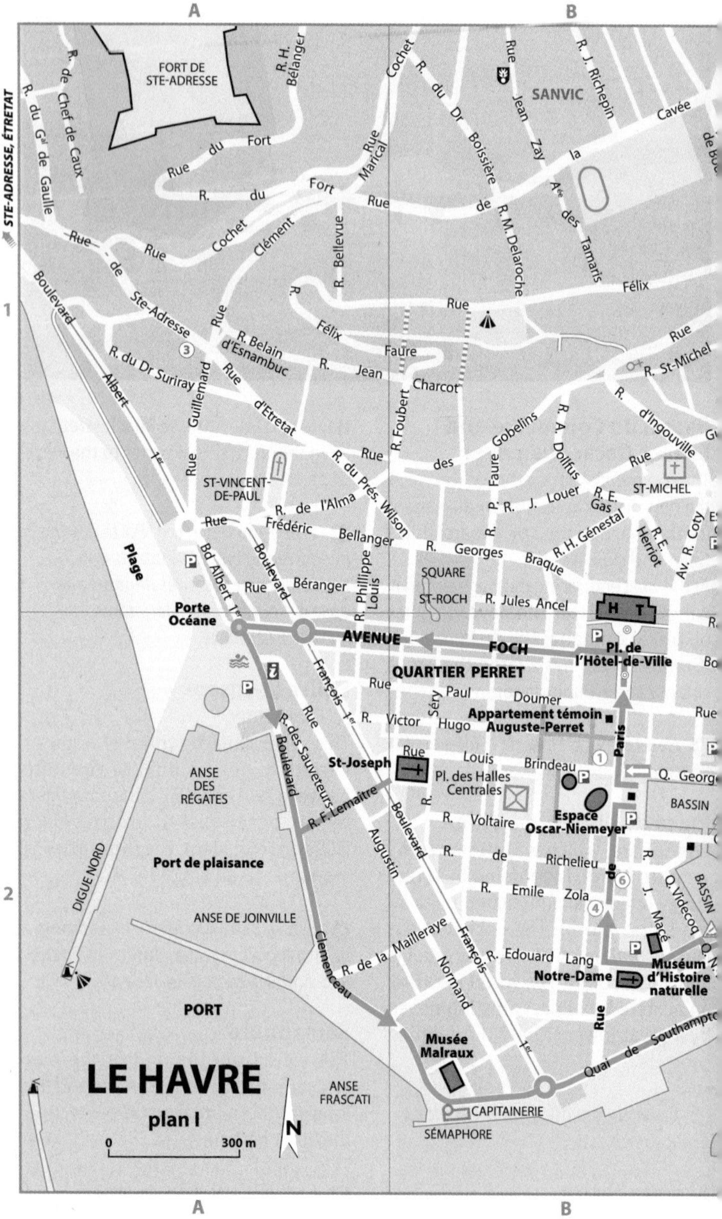

WHERE TO STAY

Art (Hôtel) ①

Novotel (Hôtel) ②

Citôtel Marly (Hôtel) ④

Richelieu (Hôtel) ⑥

Inter-Hôtel Terminus (Hôtel) ⑧

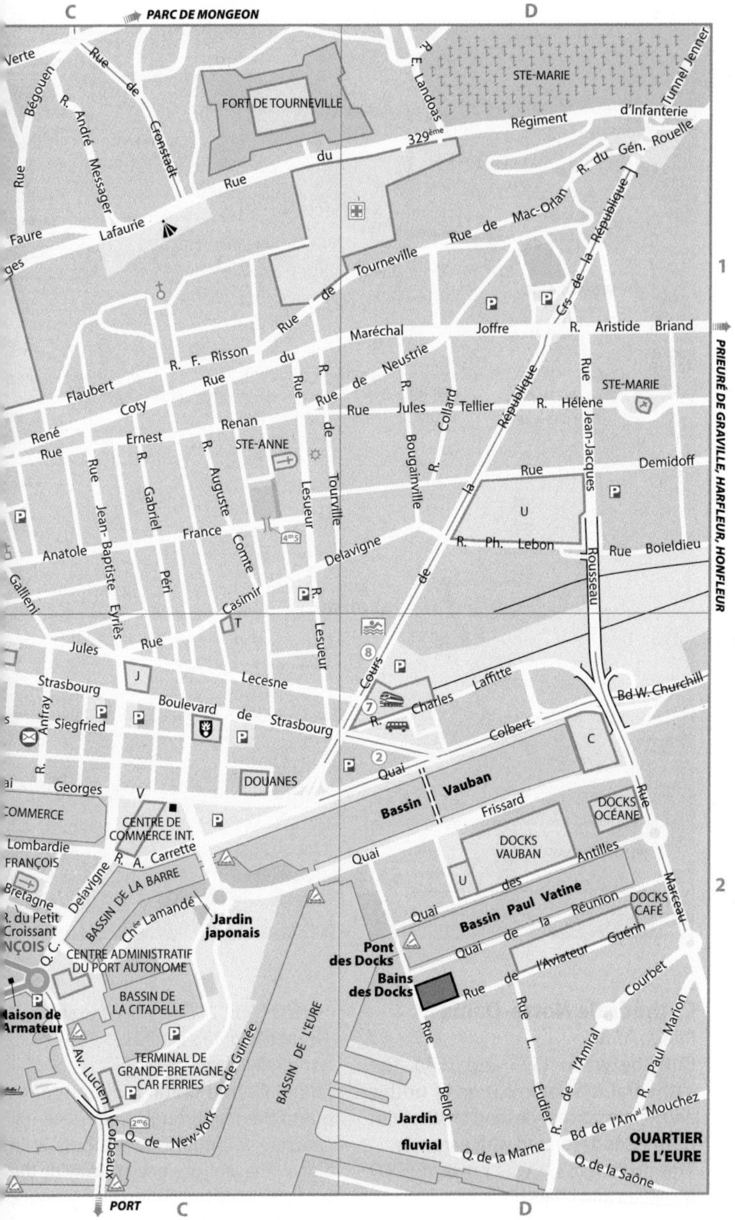

WHERE TO EAT

Auberge (La petite)........ ③

Odyssée (L')........ ⑦

Wilson (Le)........ ⑨

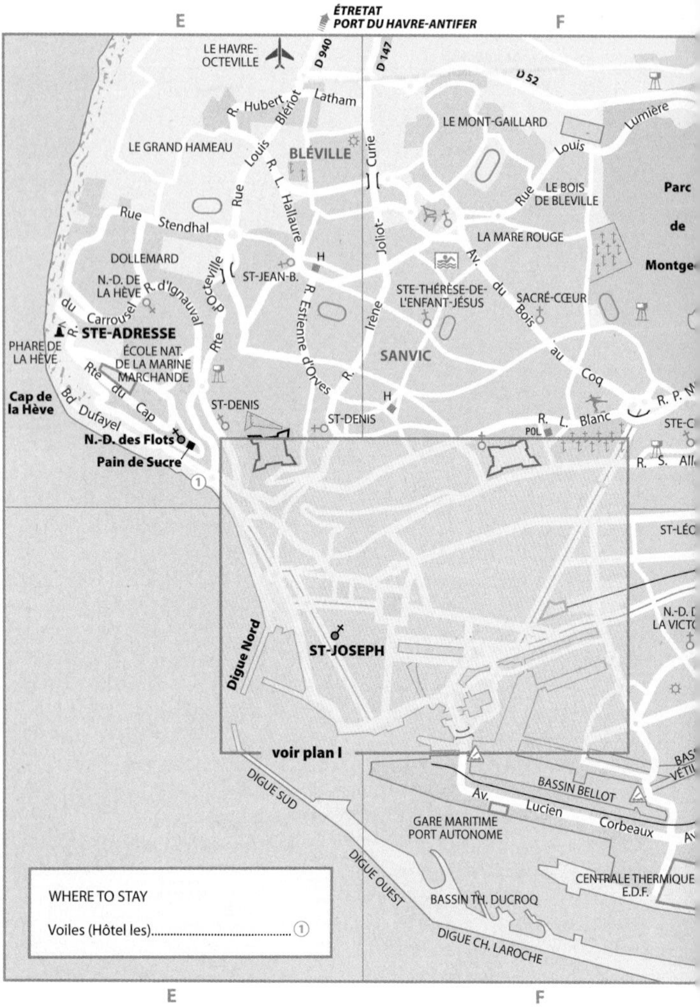

Cathédrale Notre-Dame

Rue de Paris.

Built between 1575 and 1630, the cathedral is a combination of Gothic and Renaissance styles and bristles with buttresses decorated with gargoyles. The organ (1637) was presented by Richelieu and bears his arms.

SIGHTS

Musée des Beaux-Arts André-Malraux★

2 bd Clemenceau. Open Wed–Fri and Mon 11am–6pm, Sat–Sun 11am–7pm. Closed 1 Jan, 1 May, 14 Jul, 11 Nov, 25 Dec. 5€ (no charge 1st Sat of month). 02 35 19 62 62. www.ville-lehavre.fr.

The glass and metal building looks out to the sea through a monumental concrete sculpture known locally as Le Signal. The roof, designed to provide the best possible light to the galleries inside, consists of six sheets of glass covered by an aluminium sun blind.

The museum presents a fine **collection**★ of works by **Raoul Dufy** (1877–1953), who was born in Le Havre, and **Eugène Boudin** (1824–98), a native of Honfleur.

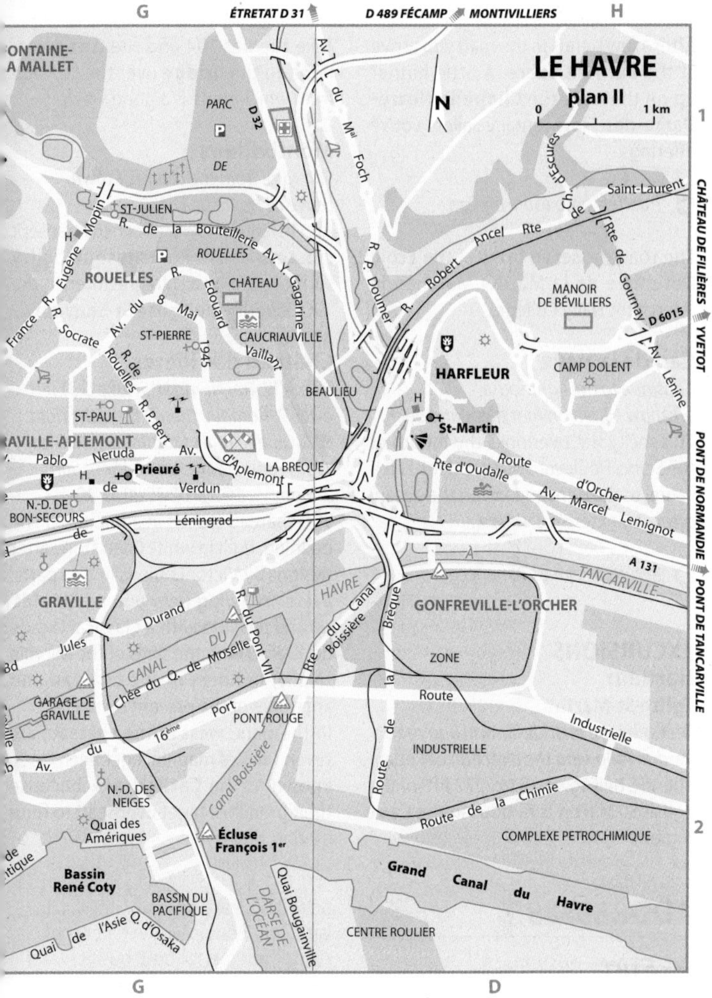

Muséum d'histoire naturelle

Place du Vieux-Marché. Open Tue–Wed and Fri–Sun 9.30am–noon, 2–6pm, Thu 2–6pm. Closed 1 Jan, 1 May, 14 Jul, 11 Nov, 25 Dec. No charge. 02 35 54 75 85. http://museum.ville-lehavre.fr.

The Natural History Museum is housed in the old 18C law courts. One of the rooms displays works by the naturalist painter **Charles-Alexandre Lesueur** (1778–1846).

SAINTE-ADRESSE★

Allow 1hr.

This a pleasant district extends from the edge of Le Havre towards the Hève Cape and consists of a seaside resort and the old town of Ste-Adresse.

Boulevard Albert-1er runs alongside the beach to place Clemenceau and the statue of Albert I, King of the Belgians from 1909 to 1934.

Follow the signs for Pain de Sucre and Notre-Dame-des-Flots.

After a few bends in the road you arrive at the **Pain de Sucre**. A little higher up on the right the **Chapelle Notre-Dame-des-Flots** contains sailors' votive offerings.

▶ *Turn left onto route du Cap.*

The road passes in front of the École Nationale de la Marine Marchande (Merchant Navy College).

Cap de la Hève
Continue to the lighthouse.
🔲 *Allow 15min on foot there and back.*
This rocky site overlooks the mouth of the Seine. Boulevard du Président-Félix-Faure, to the right and facing the ocean, offers an extensive **view**★.

▶ *Return to place Clemenceau.*

EXCURSIONS
Harfleur
Église St-Martin
Access by rue Aristide-Briand and rue de Verdun following the direction of Rouen.
The 15C bell-tower (83m/272.4ft) of the Église St-Martin is famous in the Caux region.

Take rue des 104 and rue Gambetta, right, to the **bridge** over the Lézarde from which there is a good view.

Montivilliers
8km/5mi from the centre of town.
Leave Le Havre on D 489.
An 11C lantern tower above the transept crossing and a Romanesque belfry surmounted by a spire (restored in the 19C) identify the **Église St-Sauveur**★.

Château de Filières
20km/12.4mi NE via N15; take D 31 left after St-Romain, then D 80 to the right.
💬 *Guided tours (30min) Jul–Aug daily 11am–6pm; May–Jun and Sept Sun 2–6pm. ◉6€. ℘02 35 20 53 30.*
The château stands in a fine park. The building, built in white Caen stone after designs by Victor Louis, is in two parts: a late-16C wing *(left)* and a plain 18C central pavilion with a Classical façade decorated with the arms of the Mirville family, builders of the château and ancestors of the present owners
In the park, west of the château, are seven rows of magnificent beech trees, known as the **Cathedral**★ because their branches meet overhead to form a living vault.

ADDRESSES

🏠 STAY

☞ **Hôtel Le Richelieu** – *132 r. de Paris. ℘02 35 42 38 71. www.hotel-lerichelieu-76.com. 19 rooms. ⚌6.50€.*
Located on a celebrated shopping street with many boutiques. Pleasant lobby in ocean colours. Restful, well-kept rooms, including family rooms and a suite.

☞☞☞ **Best Western Art Hôtel** – *147 r. Louis-Brindeau. ℘02 35 22 69 44. www.bestwestern.fr/arthotel. 31 rooms. ⚌13€.*
Centrally located by the harbour, this place has functional rooms and a bar.

☞☞☞ **Citôtel Le Marly** – *121 r. de Paris. ℘02 35 41 72 48. www.hotellemarly.com. 37 rooms. ⚌12€.* Located along the boulevard leading to the harbour, this somewhat austere-looking hotel is

quite practical. The rooms are suitably large, well equipped and functional. A good address for both business and tourism.

☞☞☞ **Inter-Hôtel Terminus** – *23 cours de la République. ℘02 35 25 42 48. www.grand-hotel-terminus.fr. Closed 22 Dec–1 Jan. 44 rooms. ⚌8€. Restaurant☞☞.* Just opposite the train station, this hotel has excellent soundproofing. Ask for one of the renovated rooms, which have bright colours and modern furniture. Buffet breakfast.

☞☞☞ **Hôtel Novotel** – *20 cours Lafayette. ℘02 35 19 23 23. 134 rooms. ⚌13€. Restaurant☞☞.* A modern hotell lon the banks of the Vauban lake, not far from the station. Providing spacious and well-equipped rooms. The restaurant has a designer décor and bay windows opening out onto the inner garden. Traditional cuisine.

⊜⊜⊜⊜ **Hôtel Restaurant les Voiles** – *3 pl.Clemenceau, 76310 Ste-Adresse. ℘02 35 54 68 90. 16 rooms. ☕12€. Restaurant*⊜⊜⊜. Overlooking the sea, this hotel calls its rooms "cabins". With a sea view, the terrace is a great place to enjoy a meal or drink from the hotel's restaurant or bar.

EAT

⊜⊜ **Le Wilson** – *98 r. Prés-Wilson. ℘02 35 41 18 26. Closed 3–20 Jul, Sun eve, Tue eve, Wed.* A bistro atmosphere and lively activity characterise this little restaurant on a small square in a commercial district. In fine weather, sit on the terrace. Traditional cuisine.

⊜⊜ **La Petite Auberge** – *32 r. Ste-Adresse. ℘02 35 46 27 32. Closed 20 Feb–1 Mar, 1–24 Aug, Sat lunch, Sun eve, Mon.* Not far from Ste-Adresse, this small restaurant with its dapper façade offers a menu based on regional recipes and fresh market produce with desserts to die for.

⊜⊜ **Le Bistrot du Chef...en Gare** – *28 cours de la République, train station. ℘02 35 26 54 33. Closed Aug, Sat lunch, Sun and Mon eve.* This attractive retro-style dining room is right at the train station. Daily specials based on fresh produce.

⊜⊜⊜ **L'Odysée**– *41 r. du Gén. Faidherbe. ℘02 35 21 32 42. Closed 18 Apr–2 May and 7–27 Aug.* As the name suggests, the menu as well as the interior decoration at this friendly restaurant in the lively François I neighbourhood is inspired by Poseidon. Fish, shellfish and langoustines fresh from the local markets.

NIGHTLIFE

Les Trois Pics – *Sente Alphonse-Karr, 76310 Ste-Adresse. ℘02 35 48 20 60. Closed Mon.* Whether you sit on the terrace overlooking the sea in summer or behind the large picture windows in winter, you can enjoy fish and seafood or choose something from the café-tearoom while admiring the exceptional panoramic view of the bay.

SHOPPING

Les Gobelines – *r. du Prés.-Wilson. Closed Tue, Thue, Sat–Sun.* This market is not very large, but it has the advantage of a central location, on a wide street near the town hall. Locals come here to buy fresh fruit and vegetables, meat and fish.

Les Halles Centrales – *Mon–Sat except public holidays.* This major marketplace is spread out, so stalls have plenty of room. Many of the most prestigious of the town's shopkeepers have stalls here, including some 30 that sell food.

LEISURE

Le Havre Station Nautique – *125 bd Clemenceau. ℘02 35 441 43 60. www.lehavretourisme.com.* Boat trips, tours, sail boats, kayaking and general water sports activities in Le Havre.

Club Le Havre Ocean Kayak – *58, rue de l'Artois. ℘02 35 44 33 29. http://site.voila.fr/kho.* Rental of kayaks and windsurfers. They also run activities such as canoeing.

Aéro-club du Havre – Jean-Maridor – *r. Louis-Blériot, Le Havre-Octeville Airport. ℘02 35 48 35 91. http://acbjm.free.fr/acjm/index.php. Closed Sun pm.* First flights and beginners' flights lasting 30min! Short, but intense. On board a 2- or 4-seat aircraft, you'll fly along the coast to Étretat, then return via the countryside and the Normandy Bridge before going round Le Havre over the estuary.

CALENDAR

The tourist office publishes a monthly newspaper, *Agenda*, that gives a schedule of events as well as arrivals of all the big cruise ships.

Abbaye de Jumièges★★★

Jumièges is one of the most impressive ruins in France, occupying a splendid site on the Lower Seine. The history, galleries, south aisle, the nave roof, the transept crossing, the chancel apse and the roofless cloisters are described below.

- **Michelin Map:** 304: E-5.
- **Info:** Rue Guillaume-le-Conquérant. ☎02 35 37 28 97. www.jumieges.fr.
- **Location:** Jumièges is located on a graceful meander of the Seine, between the villages of Duclair and Trait, 28km/17.4mi W of Rouen.
- **Don't Miss:** Not far from Jumièges, in Mesnils sous Jumièges *(5km/3mi SE via the D 65)* sits the 13C manor where the lovely and astute Agnès Sorel, mistress of Charles VII, died in 1450.
- **Timing:** You may wish to spend time admiring the view and strolling near the Seine.

A BIT OF HISTORY

Jumièges Almshouse – In the 10C Duke William Longsword rebuilt Jumièges on the ruins of the 7C abbey destroyed by the Vikings. The new Benedictine abbey soon became known as the Jumièges Almshouse as well as a centre of learning. The abbey church was consecrated in 1067 in the presence of William the Conqueror.

The last monks dispersed at the Revolution, and in 1793 the abbey was bought by a timber merchant who intended to turn it into a stone quarry and used explosives to bring down the church lantern. A new proprietor in 1852 set about saving the ruins, which now belong to the nation. Many consider these to be the most beautiful ruins in France.

Abbaye de Jumièges

A. de Valroger/MICHELIN

Jumièges is a ruin and not covered in places. Consider this an outdoor venue, and dress accordingly.

The Abbey★★★

Rue Guillaume-le-Conquérant. Open daily Jul–Aug 9.30am–6.30pm; mid-Apr–Jun and 1st half Sept 9.30am–1pm, 2.30–6.30pm; 2nd half Sept–mid-Apr 9.30am–1pm, 2.30–5.30pm (last entry 30min before closing). Closed 1 Jan, 1 May, 1, 11 Nov, 25 Dec. 3€. ☎02 35 37 24 02.

Église Notre-Dame

The projecting porch is flanked by twin towers (43m/141ft high),whose spires were visible until 1830.

The entire nave (27m/88.6ft high) still stands, together with part of the transept and the chancel. At the west end there is a deep gallery overlooking the nave, which is articulated by strong square pillars, quartered by columns, alternating with more slender clusters of columns; the aisles are covered by rib vaulting. Most of the transept was demolished in the 19C. Only the west side of the lantern has survived, resting on an arch which is impressive for its

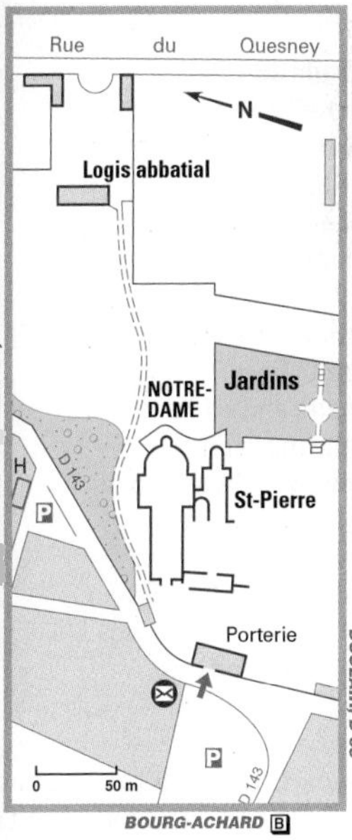

ABBAYE DE JUMIÈGES

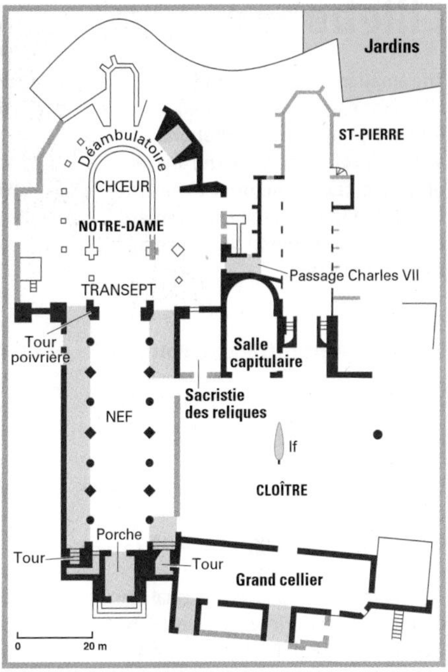

height and reach. A slim, pepper-pot turret is attached to the NW corner.

Passage Charles-VII

The passage leading to St Peter's Church was named for the visit of King Charles VII (1403–1461) to Jumièges.

Église St-Pierre

The porch and first bays of the nave are Norman Carolingian (oculi and twinned arcades) the remaining ruins date from the 13C and 14C. The arched entrance porch is flanked by two small doors with stairs to the gallery towers behind. The first two bays of the nave are a rare example of 10C Norman architecture.

Chapter house

Between the abbey and St Peter's, the 12C chapter house opens off the cloisters. The square body and apse were covered with some of the earliest ogival vaulting known to have existed.

Cloisters

In the middle of the cloisters grows an ancient yew tree. The four galleries once consisted of 26 bays. The refectory was on the south side.

Storeroom

The great cellar dates to the late-12C.

Gardens

Beyond a fence, a 17C set of steps leads to a broad terrace and the gardens.

Abbot's Lodging

Beyond the lawn rises the former abbot's lodging, a majestic 17C rectangular building.

Église paroissiale St-Valentin

Open Jul–Aug Wed–Mon 2–6pm.
02 35 37 28 97.
The parish church, which dominates the village, has an 11C–12C nave and a 16C chancel and ambulatory; inside, altarpieces and 15C–16C stained-glass windows in ambulatory chapels escaped pillaging in the Revolution.

Lillebonne

The small industrial town of Lillebonne was once a Roman military camp named Juliobona, after Julius Caesar. With the arrival of several textile factories towards the end of the 19C, the Lillebonne-Bolbec valley came to be known as the Golden Valley.

- **Population:** 9 651.
- **Michelin Map:** 304: D-4.
- **Info:** Rue Victor-Hugo. 02 35 38 08 45.
- **Location:** Lillebone is 67km/41.6mi W of Rouen and 37km/23mi E of Le Havre via D 982.
- **Don't Miss:** The Roman theatre and artefacts at the museum.
- **Timing:** Although some sights are closed for renovation, you can admire them from the outside while enjoying their surroundings.

SIGHTS

Théâtre-Amphithéâtre romain

Under renovation for an undetermined length of time. Guided tours by reservation. Enquiries: 02 35 15 69 11.

From place de l'Hôtel-de-Ville it is possible to see the general layout of this Roman amphitheatre, built in the 1C and 2C.

The central arena follows the usual plan of amphitheatres in north-west Gaul, where all kinds of spectacles were held (mythological scenes, gladiator fights, performing animals, hunts with small game). The crowd watched on from the **cave★**, a series of stands probably made of wood.

Château

Access by 46 r. Césarine. Closed for visits.

Little remains of the fortress (rebuilt in the 12C and 13C), where William the Conqueror assembled his barons before invading England: one wall of an octagonal tower and, on the left, a round three-storey keep.

Église Notre-Dame

Rue Sadi-Carnot.

This 16C church has a sweeping spire (55m/181ft) rising above a square tower. Inside, a stained-glass window tells the story of John the Baptist. The stalls were originally from the Abbaye du Valasse.

Musée municipal

pl. Félix-Faure, across from Roman theatre. Open May–Sept 10am–noon, 2–6pm; Oct–Apr Wed–Mon 2–6pm. Closed 1 Jan, 25 Dec. 1.50€. 02 32 84 02 07.

The museum is devoted to popular art and traditions. The basement houses archaeological finds from local excavations (cremation tombs, pottery and ironwork from the 1C to the 3C).

EXCURSIONS

Le Mesnil-sous-Lillebonne

2km/1mi S. Church open Jun–Sept 2–6pm 1.50€. 02 32 84 02 07.

The extremely ancient parish **church** has recently been restored. It presents a display of religious art and a collection of fossils and minerals.

L'Abbaye du Valasse at Le Parc Eana

6km/3.7mi NW by D 173. Open Jul–Aug daily 10am–7pm; Sept Wed–Sun 10am–6pm; Oct Sat–Sun and school holidays except Christmas 10am–6pm. Closed 19 Dec–1 Jan (except restaurants). 9€ (children 7.50€). 02 35 38 08 45. www.eana.fr/parc/labbaye.php.

Since 2009, the site has operated as a **leisure park**, with access to the abbey, gardens and park.

The foundation of the abbey resulted from two vows, one made by Waleran de Meulan for escaping a shipwreck, and one made by Empress Matilda, William the Conqueror's granddaughter, for surviving the struggle for the

throne of England against her cousin Stephen of Blois. The abbey, consecrated in 1181, prospered until the 14C, when the Hundred Years' War and the Wars of Religion brought ruin. The building was sold at the Revolution, converted into a château, then sold to a dairy; in 1984 it was bought by the municipality of Gruchet-le-Valasse.
The main façade is an elegant 18C pedimented composition with two return wings.
The central pediment bears the arms of Empress Matilda: three Normandy leopards (from William the Conqueror) and

Neufchâtel-en-Bray

The former capital of the Pays de Bray is today the capital of "bondon", a cylinder-shaped cheese. The other local stars are the "petit-suisse", invented near Gournay-en-Bray, and the ***fromage de Neufchâtel*****, a farm cheese produced in several shapes.**

- **Population:** 4 946.
- **Michelin Map:** 304: I-3.
- **Info:** 6 place Notre-Dame. ✆02 35 93 22 96. www.neufchatel-en-bray.com.
- **Location:** This village is 45km/28mi SW of Dieppe, 50km/31mi NE of Rouen.
- **Don't Miss:** Église St-Pierre -et-St-Paul (in Aumale).
- **Timing:** Count on a good half-day to see Neufchâtel and its pretty countryside.

VISIT

Église Notre-Dame

pl. Notre-Dame.

The doorway dates from the end of the 15C; the early-16C nave contains Renaissance capitals.
The eight windows in the aisles depict local saints: St Radegonde, St Vincent, St Anthony. In the 13C chancel round columns support the pointed vaulting; against a pillar is a gilt wood Virgin crowned.

DRIVING TOUR

Northern Pays de Bray

46km/28mi – 1hr30min

Leave Neufchâtel on D1314 to the north.

From the road, which runs north through the so-called Bray Buttonhole formation, there are extensive views of the Béthune Valley *(left)* and Hellet Forest *(north)*.

Turn left on D 56.

The road crosses through Hellet Forest. From Croixdalle, D 77 *(turn left)* goes down the Béthune Valley as far as Osmoy-St-Valery, where it climbs the southwest slope, and passes through a gap. The view is of Nappes Forest.

Fromage de Neufchâtel

G. Targat/ MICHELIN

The Bray Buttonhole

The movement of the earth's crust during the Tertiary era (64–1.8 million years ago), which brought about the raising of the Alps some 12 million years ago had repercussions as far as the Paris basin. The shocks formed wide, deep undulations in a southeast/northwest direction and subsequently, in the area we call Bray, one of these swelled into a large dome with a steep northeast face.

Erosion relentlessly ate into the limestone surface of the dome, exposing clay laid down in the upper Jurassic Period some 160 million years ago. This elliptical cut, with its clearly defined rim, is known to geologists as a buttonhole, hence the term Bray Buttonhole (*see FORGES-LES-EAUX, p347*). Continued erosion has given the area irregular, varied landscapes of marshes, *bocage* country, cultivated fields, orchards and great forests.

As you leave the Mesnil-Follemprise Valley the bell-tower of Bures-en-Bray appears, along with the Hellet Forest and the Château of Mesnières.

Château de Mesnières
Institution Saint Joseph, 76270 Mesnières-en-Bray. Open mid-Mar–mid-Nov Sat–Sun 2–6pm. 4€. 02 35 93 10 04. www.seinemaritime.net. The château, occupied by a private agricultural school, was damaged in a 2004 fire, but is being restored.
This majestic Renaissance château, begun in the late 15C on the site of a medieval castle, lies at a strategic crossing of two royal roads, Paris-Dieppe and Abbeville-Rouen. The beautiful park was designed by Le Nôtre.

Bures-en-Bray
Church. Guided tours on request from M. Daniel Longin. 02 35 93 09 48.

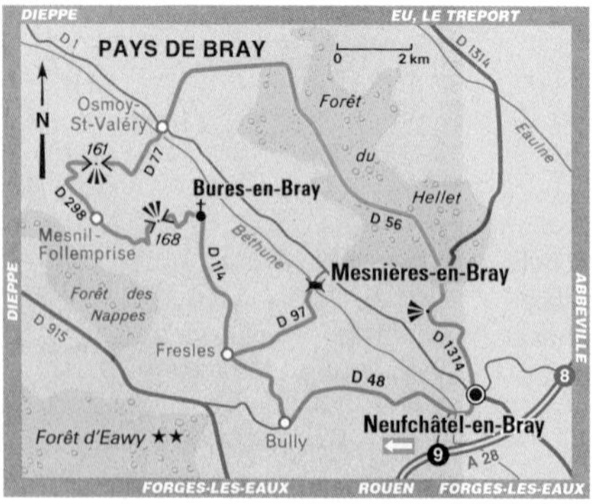

The **church**, partly 12C, has a modern brick façade with porch and a bold twisted wooden spire. In the north transept are an Entombment, a 16C stone altarpiece and a 14C Virgin and Child.

Uphill after the church take the first road, D 114, left near the café-tobacconist.

The road follows a terrace at the foot of the southwest face on which the villages have been built.

At Fresle turn left onto D 97.

Aumale
The **Église de St-Pierre-et-St-Paul** displays both the Flamboyant and the Renaissance styles. The south portal, attributed to Jean Goujon (1510–66), has been damaged.

Take N 29 towards Neufchâtel, turn immediately right onto D 920.

Foucarmont
The squat impression given by the concrete **church** (rebuilt 1959–64) is somewhat alleviated by the wonderful irregular stained-glass windows and by the precious stones inlaid in the walls.

N 28 leads back to Neufchâtel.

Rouen★★★

Rouen, capital of Upper Normandy, has undergone a remarkable campaign of restoration that has given new life to the old city's network of narrow, winding streets lined with magnificent half-timbered houses. In addition, Rouen is a city of first-rate museums – the Musée de Beaux-Arts alone is worth the trip – and possesses one of the most sumptuous Gothic cathedrals in France. Rouen sits in a lovely valley surrounded by high hills, from which there are extensive views over the city and the Seine.

- **Population:** 107 904.
- **Michelin Map:** 304: G-5.
- **Info:** 25 pl.de la Cathédrale. 02 32 08 32 40. www.rouentourisme.com.
- **Location:** Some 130km/81mi NW of Paris, Rouen spreads out along both banks of the Seine.
- **Parking:** Car parks are found on: place du Général-de-Gaulle (Hôtel de Ville), Square Verdrel, Palais, Vieux-Marché, La Pucelle, Charrettes, la Bourse (rue du Général-Leclerc), la Haute-Vielle-Tour, St-Marc, 39e RI and St-Vivien. There are free car parks on the lower quays of the left bank and at Boulingrin, near the train station.
- **Don't Miss:** The Gothic splendour of the cathedral and of the churches of St-Maclou and St-Ouen; the lovely half-timbered houses of Old Rouen; the Musée des Beaux-Arts.
- **Timing:** Spend at least one day here: the morning exploring the old streets, reserving the afternoon for museums.
- **Kids:** Musée Flaubert; Musée d'Histoire de la Médecine; Musée Maritime, Fluvial and Portuaire.

A BIT OF HISTORY

Rollo the Forerunner – After the **Treaty of St-Clair-sur-Epte** in the year 911, Rollo, the Viking chief and first Duke of Normandy, was baptised at Rouen, the capital of the new duchy, and took the name Robert. He proved to be a far-sighted planner: he narrowed and deepened the river bed, built up unused marshlands, linked the downstream islands to the mainland and reinforced the banks with quays. His works lasted until the 19C, unrivalled for their efficiency.

Goddons – Rouen was hard hit during the Hundred Years' War: in 1418 Henry V of England besieged the town, which was starved into capitulation after six months.

Revolts and plots followed against the Goddons – the nickname for the English derived from their common blasphemous phrase, "God damn". Hope was reborn by the exploits of Joan of Arc and the coronation of Charles VII, then Joan was taken prisoner at Compiègne by the Burgundians. The English threatened the Duke of Burgundy with economic sanctions and through the mediation of Pierre Cauchon, Bishop of Beauvais, Joan was handed over to the English. On Christmas Day 1430 she was imprisoned in the Tower of the Fields in the castle built in the 13C by Philippe Auguste. A strong military presence under Lord Warwick deterred any uprisings.

Golden Century – The period between the French reconquest (1449) and the Wars of Religion (1562–98) was a golden century for all Normandy and particularly for the city of Rouen. Local dignitaries built sumptuous stone mansions and carved woodwork adorned the façade of burgesses' houses.

Joan of Arc

Trial of Joan of Arc – Bishop Cauchon promised a fair trial and opened the first session on 21 February 1431. An amazing dialogue began between Joan and her judges: the Maid replied to all the tricks and subtleties of the churchmen and lawyers.

On 24 May, in the cemetery of the Abbey of St-Ouen, tied to a scaffold, Joan was pressed to recant; she finally gave in, was granted her life but condemned to life imprisonment.

The English were furious and threatened the judges; Cauchon replied, "We will get her yet." On Trinity Sunday the guards took away Joan's women's clothes which she had promised to wear, and gave her men's clothing instead. At noon "for the necessities of the body, she was constrained to go out and indulge in the said habit". She was thus said to have broken her promise and was condemned to the stake. On 30 May she was burned alive in place du Vieux-Marché.

In 1449 Charles VII entered Rouen; in 1456 Joan was rehabilitated and in 1920 she was canonised and made **Patron Saint of France**.

Rouen merchants in cooperation with Dieppe navigators traded along all the main maritime routes.

Industrial Upsurge – Industrialisation, launched by textile manufacturing, called for changes in the port: in the 19C docks were constructed, the railway was built; the old city on the right bank spread to the tributary valleys and hillsides.

Modern City – Industrial expansion accelerated at the beginning of the 20C. During World War II, the old districts close to the Seine and the industrial zone on the south bank were destroyed. On the right (N) bank, a series of arching boulevards define the city centre, its old residential districts and historic centre. On the left (S) bank are administrative offices, the Préfecture, modern residential and business districts, and the industrial zone.
Lacroix Island, formerly industrial, has become residential with parks and open spaces.

THE PORT

Bd Émile-Duchemin, Hangar 13 (on the road to Le Havre from the Pont Guillaume-le-Conquérant.

Rouen is France's fifth-busiest port after Marseilles, Le Havre, Dunkerque and Nantes-St-Nazaire, and the third-biggest river port. Its location between Paris and the sea is a great advantage.
Owing to improved maritime access, modernisation of port equipment and facilities, and the building of silos and new terminals, the growth of the port has been constant. It now stretches from Rouen to Tancarville on the right bank of the Seine and from Rouen to Honfleur on the left bank. For displays recounting a great many riverside and maritime adventures, visit the **Musée Maritime, Fluvial et Portuaire** on Quai Émile-Duchemin, Hangar 13 (follow the directions for Le Havre from the Guillaume-le-Conquérant bridge) *Open Wed–Fri and Mon 10am–12.30pm, 2–6pm (5pm Nov–Feb), Sat–Sun and public holidays 2–6pm (5pm Nov–Feb). Closed 1 Jan, 1 May, 24, 25 and 31 Dec. 4.50€. 02 32 10 15 51. www.musee-maritime-rouen.asso.fr.*

Cathédrale Notre-Dame★★★

Allow 1hr30min

Tactile map and brochures in braille available. Open daily except Mon morning. Guided tour (1hr30min) including the baptistry, the Chapel of the Virgin and the crypt, usually closed to the public, Sat–Sun at 2.30pm (daily during school holidays). Closed 1 Jan, 1 May, 8 May 11 Nov. No charge. 02 35 71 71 60.

The cathedral of Rouen is one of the most beautiful examples of French Gothic architecture. Construction began in the 12C but after a devastating fire in 1200 the building was reconstructed in the 13C. The cathedral took on its final appearance in the 15C under the master builder Guillaume Pontifs and in the 16C under Roulland le Roux. In the 19C it was crowned with the present cast-iron spire. Badly damaged during World War II, the cathedral is open but the enormous restoration work started over 50 years ago continues.

Exterior

The attraction of Rouen Cathedral lies in its infinite variety, including an immense façade bristling with openwork pinnacles and framed by two totally different towers: the Tour St-Romain on the left and the Tour de Beurre on the right.

West front

This imposing façade was used in a series of paintings by Monet to study the effects of lighting at different times of the day on the same subject. Dating from the 12C, the **Portail St-Jean** *(left)* and the **Portail St-Étienne** *(right)* doorways each have a delicately carved semicircular arch crowned by a small colonnade. The two tympana are 13C. The lattice-work window gallery (1370–1420) above the two portals is in the Flamboyant style; the niches decorated with statues and topped by openwork gables are 14C and 15C.

The **central doorway** (early 16C) is flanked by two powerful pyramid buttresses decorated with statues of the Prophets and Apostles. The tympanum is decorated with a Tree of Jesse, destroyed by the Huguenots and restored in 1626.

The **Tour St-Romain**, to the left, is the oldest tower (12C), and in the Early Gothic style. The sumptuous **Tour de Beurre** (Butter Tower) was thus named in the 17C when it was believed that it had been paid for by dispensations granted to those didn't fast during Lent. It never received a spire but was

South doorway of Cathédrale Notre-Dame

S. Sauvignier/MICHELIN

surmounted by an octagonal crown. Inside is a carillon of 56 bells.

South side

The **central lantern tower** with its spire is the tallest in France (151m/495.5ft) and the glory of Rouen. It was started in the 13C and was raised in the 16C. The present spire, in cast iron, replaced in 1876 the wooden spire covered in gilded lead, which dated from 1544. The **Portail de la Calende** (Calende doorway), which opens between two 13C square towers, is a 14C masterpiece.

North side

On skirting the **Cour d'Albane** (Albane Court), closed to the east by the cloister gallery, one can see the north side, the lantern tower and spire and the upper section of the Booksellers' transept.

A little further on the **Cour des Libraires** (Booksellers' Court) is closed by a magnificent stone gateway in the Flamboyant style. At the end of the court is the **Portail des Libraires** (Booksellers' Doorway) (*see Introduction: Religious architecture, p62*), which opens on to the north side aisle.

The tympanum (late-13C) is decorated by a Last Judgement depicted in terrifying detail.

Return to the parvis to enter the cathedral by the main door.

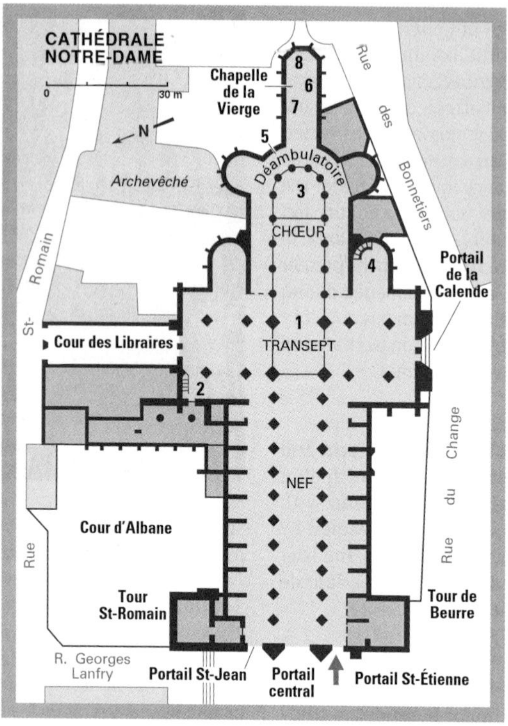

Nave

In the early Gothic style, the nave is made up of 11 bays four storeys high. Dominating the transept crossing is the **lantern tower** rising with incredible boldness 51m/167.3ft on enormous piles which sweep upwards.

Transept

In the north arm is the famous Escalier de la Librairie (Booksellers' Stairway); from a charming little balcony rise the two flights of the staircase (the first is 15C, the second 18C).

Chancel

The choir of finest 13C style is the most noble part of the cathedral on account of its simple lines and the lightness of its construction. The high altar is made of a marble slab from the Valle d'Aosta, and dominated by a Christ in gilded lead (18C). Opening off the south arm is the apsidal chapel dedicated to Joan of Arc and embellished with modern stained-glass windows by Max Ingrand.

Crypt, Ambulatory, Lady Chapel

♿ *Guided tours (1hr30min). For conditions, see Cathédrale Notre-Dame.*

The 11C ring-shaped **crypt** preserves its altar and its curb stone well (5m/16.4ft deep). The heart of Charles V is preserved in a coffer embedded in the east end wall.

The **ambulatory** *(access south arm – exit north)*, which is made up of three apsidal chapels, holds the recumbent figures of Rollo, Richard Lionheart (late 13C), Henry (second son of Henry II of England) the Young King (13C), and William Longsword, Duke of Normandy and son of Rollo (14C). Also shown are five 13C **stained-glass windows**★, the bottom one of which, depicting St Julian the Hospitaller, was presented by the Fishmongers' Guild and inspired Flaubert to write a tale.

The **Lady Chapel** (14C) contains two admirable 16C tombs. To the right, the **tomb of the Cardinals of Amboise**★★ of the Early Renaissance (1515–25) was carved after drawings by Roulland le

Roux. The two cardinals – Georges d'Amboise *(left)*, minister under Louis XII and Archbishop of Rouen, and his nephew, also Georges *(right)* – are shown kneeling.
On the left, stuck on the recess of the Gothic tomb of Pierre de Brézé (15C) is the **tomb of Louis de Brézé**★, Seneschal of Normandy and husband of Diane de Poitiers, who became the mistress of Henri II after her husband's death. It was built between 1535 and 1544.
In addition, the chapel possesses 14C stained-glass windows representing the Archbishop of Rouen and a fine picture by Philippe de Champaigne, *The Adoration of the Shepherds*, framed in a rich altarpiece of 1643.

WALKING TOURS

OLD ROUEN★★★

Allow about 30min.

Depart from place de la Cathédrale.

Place de la Cathédrale

Opposite the cathedral on the corner of rue du Petit-Salut stands the former **Bureau des Finances** (House of the Exchequer – tourist office), an elegant Renaissance building (1510).

Rue St-Romain★★

One of Rouen's most fascinating streets with its beautiful 15C–18C half-timbered houses and at the end the spire of the Église St-Maclou. Note no 74, a Gothic house with 15C bay windows.

Archevêché

Closed for tours.

Next to the Booksellers' Court stands the 15C Archbishop's Palace (altered in the 18C). A gable pierced by the remains of a window is all that is left of the chapel where the trial of Joan of Arc ended on 29 May 1431, and where her rehabilitation was proclaimed in 1456.
Cross rue de la République to reach **place Barthélemy** bordered with picturesque half-timbered houses where St Maclou's Church stands.

Rue Martainville★

The street has kept some marvellous 15C–18C half-timbered houses. On the northwest corner of St Maclou's Church is a lovely Renaissance fountain.

Aître St-Maclou★★

184–186 r. Martainville.

This 16C ensemble is one of the last examples of a medieval plague cemetery. The half-timbered buildings which surround the yard were built from 1526 to 1533; the south side was built in 1640 and never served as a charnel house.
The ground floor of these buildings is made up of galleries which were once open – as in a cloister. On the column shafts (formerly door frames) are carved figures (damaged) portraying the Dance of Death.
Above the ground floor, the attic was used as a charnel house until the 18C.
These buildings now house the School of Fine Arts (École des Beaux-Arts).

Return to the west end of St-Maclou and turn right.

Rue Damiette★

The street is lined by half-timbered houses and offers a nice vista of the central tower of St Ouen's Church. Note on the right the picturesque blind alley of the Hauts-Mariages.
In place du Lieutenant-Aubert bear left onto rue d'Amiens to the 17C **Hôtel d'Étancourt** and admire its façade embellished with large statues.

Return to place du Lieutenant-Aubert; turn left onto rue des Boucheries-St-Ouen; turn right onto rue Eau-de-Robec.

Rue Eau-de-Robec

In this street, lined with old houses boasting recently restored timber framing, flows a little stream, spanned by a series of footbridges. Several of these tall buildings have workshop-attics, where drapers would leave their skeins of cotton and sheets of fabric out to dry.

Musée national de l'Éducation★

185 r. Eau-de-Robec. Open Mon and Wed–Fri 10am–12.30pm, 1.30–6pm, Sat–Sun 2–6pm; school holidays Wed–Mon 2–6pm. Closed public holidays. 3€ (children no charge). 02 35 07 66 61. www.inrp.fr/musee.

The National Museum of Education is housed in a handsome 15C residence known as the **Maison des Quatre Fils Aymon**★. It was once a notorious trysting spot referred to as the House of Marriages on account of the many casual encounters that took place there.

The museum evokes school life from the 16C up to the present day. A 19C classroom has been reconstituted.

On the corner of rue du Ruissel, note the **Pavillon des Vertus**, a fine 16C mansion decorated with statues of women symbolising the cardinal virtues.

Return to rue des Boucheries-St-Ouen, take rue de l'Hôpital left in front of **St-Ouen Church**★★ *(see entry, p366).*

At the corner of rue des Carmes stands the attractive Gothic Crosse fountain (restored), and further on at the corner of rue Beauvoisine and rue Ganterie is a handsome half-timbered house.

Palais de Justice

S. Sauvignier/MICHELIN

Turn right onto rue Beauvoisine, which crosses rue Jean Lecanuet, one of Rouen's most commercial streets.

In rue Beauvoisine note no 55, a carved half-timbered house with courtyard: no 57 is a Renaissance house. Turn left onto rue Belfroy, bordered at the beginning by 15C–16C half-timbered houses, to reach place St-Godard *(the* **church of St-Godard**★ *is described on p366).*

Across rue Thiers and square Verdrel, allée Eugène-Delacroix leads to the charming **rue Ganterie**★, lined with old half-timbered houses. In the other direction, towards place Cauchois, this street is **rue des Bons-Enfants**, where several 15C houses still stand; on no 22, notice the sculpted figures.

Take rue des Carmes to the right, then turn right again on rue aux Juifs, which runs alongside the Palais de Justice.

Palais de Justice★★

This splendid 15C and early 16C Renaissance building was built to house the Exchequer of Normandy (law courts). Renovated in the 19C, it was badly damaged in August 1944.

The **main court** – excavations have revealed a 12C Jewish place of worship – is flanked by two wings, the **façade**★★ (1508–26) of which is exquisite.

The decoration of the façade, is typical of the Renaissance: the base is quite plain but the ornamentation increases on each floor so that the roof line is a forest of chiselled stone with pinnacles, turrets, gables and flying buttresses.

The left-wing stone staircase leads to the **Salle des Procureurs** (Prosecutors' Room). This large room has a splendid modern panelled ceiling.

Place du Vieux-Marché★

In the Middle Ages the square was the scene of public mockery and executions. On the north, the foundations of the pillories have been excavated, and on the South, an outline marks the tribune from where the judges of **Joan of Arc** watched her execution. A cross has

St Romain and the Gargoyle

In the 7C, St Romain was the Bishop of Rouen, and at the time, a terrible monster known as the Gargoyle was terrorising the city. To rid Rouen of this horrible beast, St Romain needed help. A man who had been condemned to death was the only person brave enough to come forward. Together they set out to confront the dragon. The bishop managed to wrap his stole around the dragon's neck and they led the beast back into town, where it was killed. The courageous prisoner was freed. From the 12C and until the Revolution, one prisoner was chosen by the canons of the church every year to present the reliquary holding the holy remains of St Romain to the crowd from the top of the Haute-Vieille Tower. In return, he would be freed. Nowadays, the legendary event is recalled in the annual fun fair held in the month of October.

been erected at the spot where she was burned at the stake on 30 May 1431.

Rue du Gros-Horloge★★

Connecting place du Vieux-Marché to the cathedral is the abbreviated rue du Gros, a busy commercial street during the Middle Ages and the seat of local government from the 13C to the 18C. With its large cobblestones and attractive 15C–17C half-timbered houses, rue du Gros-Horloge is nowadays one of the city centre's major tourist attractions.

Gros-Horloge

The most popular monument in Rouen. The clock, formerly placed in the **belfry** (*see below*), was moved to its present location in 1527 when the arch was specially constructed to receive it.

In addition to the single hand which gives the hours, there is the central section telling the phases of the moon and the lower inset indicating the weeks.

Belfry

Audio-guided tours (45min) Apr–Oct Tue–Sun 10am–1pm, 2–7pm; Nov–Mar Tue–Sun 2–6pm (last entry 1hr before closing). Closed 1 Jan, 25 Dec. 6€. 02 32 08 01 90.

This small tower is topped by a dome added in the 18C to replace the one removed by Charles VI in 1382 to punish the citizens of Rouen, who had organised a tax revolt, known as La Harelle.

Within there is a spiral staircase (1457). Inside are the two bells (13C) which gave the signal for the Harelle uprising: on the right the Rouvel (not operated since 1903); on the left, the Cache-Ribaud, which sounds the curfew every night at 9pm. From the top of the belfry there is a majestic **vista**★★ of the city, its port and the surrounding countryside.

Next to the belfry is the Renaissance loggia, where the Great Clock keeper used to stand, as well as a beautiful 18C fountain.

On the corner of rue du Gros-Horloge and rue Thouret stands the old town hall (1607).

Rue du Gros-Horloge leads back to place de la Cathédrale.

After this long walk around town, you will want to relax in one of the outdoor cafés set up around the square.

From place de la Calende, rue de l'Épicerie leads to the Fierté St-Romain and the Halle aux Toiles.

Fierté St-Romain

This charming Renaissance building is crowned by a stone lantern that used to contain the relics of St Romanus.

The building adjoins the **Halle aux Toiles** (Linen Hall), with exhibit, conference and banquet rooms.

CHURCHES

Église St-Maclou★★

3 r. du Gén.-Sarrail. Open Apr–Oct Mon and Fri–Sun 10am–noon, 2–6pm; Nov–Mar to 5.30pm. Closed 1 Jan, 25 Dec. 02 35 71 85 65.

ROUEN

0 100 m

WHERE TO STAY

- Brithotel Versan ... (2)
- Cardinal (Hôtel le) ... (4)
- Carmes (Hôtel des) ... (6)
- Cathédrale (Hôtel de la) ... (8)
- Dandy (Hôtel) ... (10)
- Dieppe (Hôtel de) ... (12)
- Ferme du Coquetot (Chambre d'hôte la) ... (14)
- Muette (Chambre d'hôte la) ... (16)
- Vieux Carré (Hôtel le) ... (18)

WHERE TO EAT

- Bistrot des Halettes (Chez l' Gros) ... (4)
- Bistrot du Siècle (Le) ... (6)
- Bois Chenu (Au) ... (8)
- Couronne (La) ... (10)
- Gourmand du Sud-Ouest (Le) ... (12)
- Guinguette Chez Dédé ... (14)
- Maraîchers (Les) ... (16)
- Marmite (La) ... (20)
- Pascaline ... (22)
- P'tits Parapluies (Les) ... (23)
- Réverbère (Le) ... (25)
- Toque d'Or (La) ... (27)

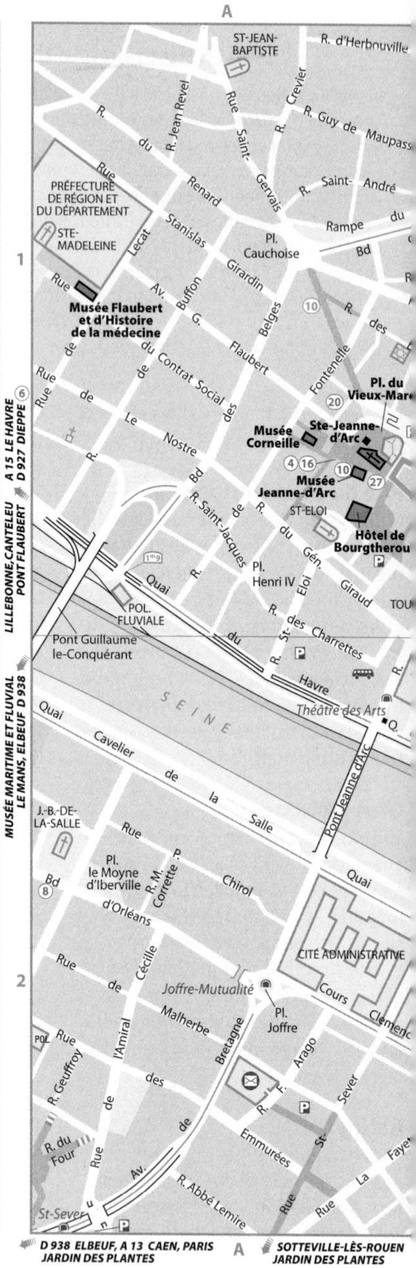

This beautiful church of Gothic-Flamboyant style, built between 1437 and 1517, is remarkable for its homogeneity, despite being finished during the heyday of the Renaissance. Only the spire of the belfry is modern.

The west façade, the finest part of this building, is preceded by a large five-panelled porch set like a fan. Two of the three doorways, the central one and that on the left, are celebrated for their Renaissance **panels★★**.

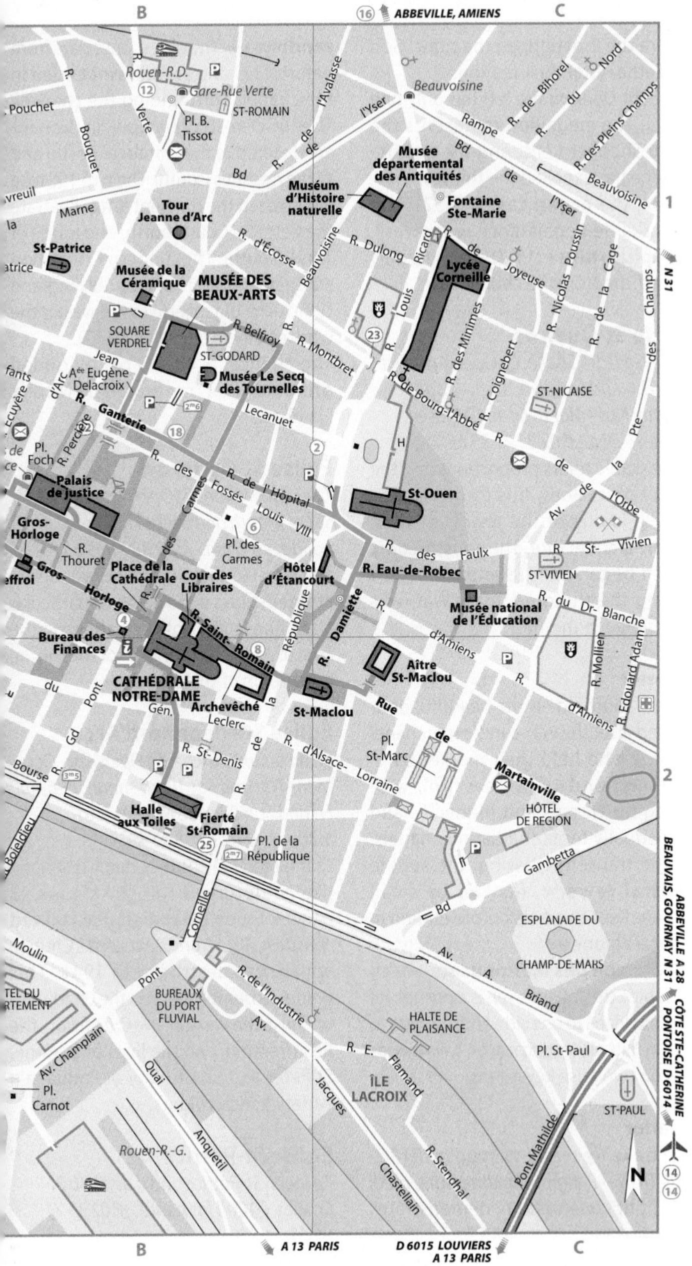

These panels are divided into two parts: the leaf of the door has charming little bronze heads of lions and other animals and designs in semi-relief of pagan inspiration, whereas the upper panel, which is a little heavy, has a carved medallion. The medallions on the central door represent the Circumcision on the left and the Baptism of Christ on the right; the upper part of the door represents on the left God the Father

before the Creation; on the right, God the Father after the Creation.
The Font Door on the left has only one panel. The medallion represents the Good Shepherd entering the pasture after he has expelled the thieves.
Inside, the **organ case★** (1521) has remarkable Renaissance woodwork. The **spiral stairs★** (1517), magnificently carved, are from the choir screen.

Église St-Ouen★★

pl. du Gén-de-Gaulle. Open Apr–Oct Tue–Thu and Sat–Sun 10am–noon, 2–6pm; Nov–Mar to 5pm. Closed 1 Jan, 25 Dec. 02 35 71 85 65.
Remarkable for its proportions and the purity of its lines, this former abbey church is one of the jewels of High Gothic architecture. The construction, which began in 1318 and slackened during the Hundred Years War, was completed in the 16C.

Exterior

On the south side is the beautiful door named after the wax candle merchants *(ciriers)* who held their market here. The **east end★★** is beautiful, with flying buttresses and pinnacles and individually roofed radiating chapels. At the transept crossing, the square **central tower★**, flanked by small towers, rises two tiers before ending in a ducal coronet.
The **Porche des Marmousets**, which occupies the lower level, is unusual: its arching leans to one side and appears to end in mid-air, resting not on colonnades but on two false keystones.

Interior

The **nave** (*see illustration in INTRODUCTION – Religious architecture, p63*), of a light construction, demonstrates elegance and harmonious proportions. Such perfection could be explained by the golden mean, which in this particular case would be a ratio of 1 to 3: the piers are each separated by 11m/36ft and the vaults reach a height of 33m/108.3ft.
This slender structure is further enhanced by the warm, radiant light that filters through the large **stained-glass windows★★**. The oldest ones date from before 1339 and are still embedded in the chapels surrounding the chancel. The 16C clerestory windows in the nave are devoted to the Patriarch (north) and to the Apostles (south). The two 15C rose windows in the transept arms illustrate the Celestial Court (north) and a Tree of Jesse (south). The modern Crucifixion adorning the axial bay is by Max Ingrand (1960). The big rosette to the west is the work of Guy le Chevalier (1992).
The chancel is closed off by gilded **grilles★★** (1747) executed by Nicolas Flambart.

Église St-Godard★

r. Jacques-Villon. Open 1st and 3rd Sat of month and eves of religious holidays 3–7pm. 02 35 71 85 65.
This late-15C church contains wonderful **stained-glass windows★**, in particular a 16C one on the right side showing the Tree of Jesse. The window of the Virgin, is made up of six 16C panels.

Église Ste-Jeanne-d'Arc

pl. du Vieux-Marché. Open Apr–Oct Mon–Thu and Sat 10am–noon, 2–6pm, Fri and Sun 2–6pm; Nov–Mar to 5.30pm. 02 32 08 32 40.
Completed in 1979, the church is shaped like an upturned ship. Inside are 13 panels of superb **Renaissance stained glass★★** (16C) from St Vincent's Church, which was destroyed in 1944. This unique ensemble depicts the Childhood of Christ, the Passion, the Crucifixion, the Resurrection, and the lives of St Anne, St Peter and St Anthony of Padua in a variety of rich colours.

Église St-Patrice

Corner r. St-Patrice and r. de l'Abbé-Cochet. Call for hours. 02 35 71 85 65.
This Gothic church is remarkable for its **stained-glass windows★** made between 1538 and 1625. The windows on the north side of the chancel depict the Triumph of Christ; in the adjoining chapels are St Faron, St Fiacre, St Louis and St Eustache, and an Annunciation in Italian Renaissance style as well as

View of Rouen (1892) by Claude Monet, Musée des Beaux-Arts de Rouen

Catherine Lancien et Carole Loisel/Musée des Beaux-Arts de Rouen

a Nativity scene. In the north aisle are the stories of St Barbara and St Patrick and Job. An 18C gilt baldaquin crowns the altar.

Église St-Romain

r. de la Rouchefoucauld. Call for hours. 02 35 71 42 64.
The former 17C Carmelite chapel, restored in the 19C and again in 1969, contains interesting Renaissance **stained glass**.

MUSEUMS AND MONUMENTS

A ticket for 5.35€ gives entry to three major museums: Beaux-Arts, Céramique and Le Secq des Tournelles. Purchase at participating museums.

Musée des Beaux-Arts★★★

espl. Marcel-Duchamp. Open Wed–Mon 10am–6pm (south wing closed 1–2pm) (last entry 1hr before closing). Closed public holidays. 3€. 02 35 71 28 40. www.rouen-musees.com
The 19C Museum of Fine Arts, restored between 1989 and 1994, has recovered its original harmonious proportions and gained modern exhibition areas.

A plan handed out at the entrance shows the layout of the museum. For a chronological visit, start with the south wing, to the right of the reception area.

15C–17C Painting

One of the most striking canvases is an oil painting on wood, *The Virgin among the Virgins*, by Gérard David (c. 1460–1523), one of the masterpieces of Flemish Primitive painting.
Besides the Italian Primitives, you can admire works by Guerchin, Giordano, Bronzino and especially Veronese *(St Barnabus Healing the Sick)* and Caravaggio *(The Flagellation of Christ)*. Spanish masters include Velásquez and Ribera; Dutch art is represented by Martin de Vos, Van de Velde, N Berchem and Rubens *(The Adoration of the Shepherds)*. French painters include François Clouet *(Diane Bathing)*, Louis de Boullogne *(Ceres or Summer)*, Poussin (*Venus Arming Aeneas* and *The Storm*), Simon Vouet and Jouvenet.

18C Painting

Second floor of the south wing. The most noteworthy painters are Lancret *(The Bathers)*, Fragonard *(The Washerwomen)*, Van Loo *(Virgin with Child)* and Traversi *(The Music Lesson)*.

19C Painting

This section is the highlight of the museum, in terms of both its size and the high standard of its collection. Europe's main artistic movements are represented – **Neoclassicism**, **Impressionism** or **Symbolism** – as well as great masters: Ingres, Monet,

David, Géricault, Degas, Caillebotte, Corot, Chassériau, Millet, Moreau, Sisley, Renoir and many others.
In the Salle du Jubé (Rood Screen Room), **Romanticism** is represented by five sculptures by David d'Angers along with *Justice of Trajan* by Delacroix and *Les Énervés de Jumièges*, a hyper-realist painting by Vital-Luminais.

20C Painting

Contemporary painters include Modigliani, Dufy *(The Seine River)*, the Duchamps brothers, Dubuffet, Nemours and others.

Musée de la Céramique★★

1 r. Faucon or 94 r. Jeanne-d'Arc. Open Wed–Mon 10am–1pm, 2–6pm (last entry 5.30pm). Closed public holidays. 2.30€. 02 35 07 31 74. www.rouen-musees.com.

The 17C Hôtel d'Hocqueville houses the Ceramics Museum, which presents an outstanding collection of 16C to 18C Rouen faïence.
The work of Masséot Abaquesne, Rouen's first faïence maker, who plied his trade around 1550, is represented by paving flags and portrait vases.
After a lull, production resumed with Louis Poterat (1644–1725), whose workshop produced dishes and tiles enhanced with a blue and white décor. The colour red made its first appearance around 1670.
Faïence was to enjoy a surge of popularity in the early 18C. Decors featuring five colours (starch or yellow ochre ground) appeared. In the room devoted to polychrome decoration, note the **celestial globe** by Pierre Chapelle, a masterpiece of faïence making. After 1721, motifs became more varied. Subsequently, around the mid-18C, the Rococo style came into fashion, embellished with varied floral motifs.

Musée Le Secq des Tournelles★★

r. Jacques-Villon. Open Wed–Mon 10am–1pm, 2–6pm (last entry 40min before closing). Closed public holidays. 2.30€. 02 35 88 42 92. www.rouen-musees.com.

The Wrought Ironwork Museum is housed in old Église St-Laurent, a fine Flamboyant building, and is exceptionally rich (3C–20C).
The nave and transept contain large items, such as balconies, signs, railings, etc., and in the display cabinets, locks, door knockers and keys. Note their evolution from Gallo-Roman times.
The north aisle includes displays of locks, belts and buckles from the 15C to 19C. The south aisle exhibits a large variety of domestic utensils and tools.
The north gallery on the first floor is devoted to accessories such as jewels, clasps, combs, and smoking requisites. A rare 16C–19C collection of professional tools is housed in the south gallery.

Musée Jeanne-d'Arc

33 pl. du Vieux-Marché. Open mid-Apr–mid-Sept 9.30am–1pm, 1.30–7pm; mid-Sept–Mar 10am–noon, 2–6.30pm. Closed 1 Jan, 25 Dec. 4€. 02 35 88 02 70. www.jeanne-darc.com.

Exhibits include a wax museum and a vaulted cellar with a model of the castle where Joan of Arc was imprisoned.

Hôtel de Bourgtheroulde

15 pl. de la Pucelle, behind the place du Vieux-Marché. Open Mon–Fri 8.30am–5.30pm, Sat–Sun 10am–6pm. No charge.

This famous early 16C mansion (pronounced Boortrood), inspired both by Gothic and early Renaissance styles, was built by Guillaume le Roux, Lord Bourgtheroulde. Once a bank, it recently became a luxury hotel.
Stand back a little to look at the façade and then enter the inner court.
The end building is pure Flamboyant, with a hexagonal staircase tower. The left gallery is entirely Renaissance with six wide basket-handle arches. It is surrounded by friezes: the upper one, disfigured, shows the Triumphs of Petrarch, the lower, the famous meeting of Henry VIII and François II on the Field of the Cloth of Gold (1520).

Rouen Faïence

The word ceramics covers all aspects of terracotta (baked clay), whereas faience is a type of ceramic made of compound clay covered with a tin-based enamel. White in colour, faïence can be decorated. Two types of earth went into the making of Rouen faïence: St-Aubin (from the Boos Plateau), clayey and bright red, and earth from Quatre-Mares (between Sotteville and St-Étienne-du-Rouvray), a light, sandy alluvial soil. Mixed in the right proportions, the result was ground, washed, dried, powdered, sifted and placed in decantation containers. When sufficiently consistent, the mixture was placed near an oven to finish the evaporation process, and then trodden to extract fermentation gases. Sand was then added to form a ceramic compound. Finally there were the different processes of shaping, casting, glazing, painting and curing.

Musée Pierre Corneille

4 r. de la Pie. Guided tours (30min) Jul–Aug Wed–Sun and public holidays 2–6pm; Sept–Jun Sat–Sun and public holidays 2–6pm (last entry 30min before closing). Closed 1 Jan, 25 Dec. No charge. 02 35 71 28 82.

The French playwright **Pierre Corneille** (1606–84) was born and lived here for 56 years. Considered the father of French Classical tragedy he wrote, among others, *Mélite* (1629; first performed in Rouen), *Le Cid*, *Horace* and *Cinna*.

Musée Flaubert et d'Histoire de la Médecine

51 r. de Lecat. Open Tue 10am–6pm, Wed–Sat 10am–noon, 2–6pm. Closed public holidays. 3€. 02 35 15 59 95. www.chu-rouen.fr/museeflaubert,

The Hôtel-Dieu (17C–18C) has a Classical façade. This museum devoted to the history of medicine is set in the home where **Gustave Flaubert** (1821–80) was born. His father worked as a surgeon. Souvenirs of Flaubert are on display.

Tour Jeanne-d'Arc

r. du Donjon. Open Apr–Sept Mon and Wed–Sat 10am–12.30pm, 2–6pm, Sun 2–6pm; Oct–Mar to 5pm. Closed 1 Jan, 1 May, 1 and 11 Nov, 25 Dec. 1.50€ 02 35 88 02 70.

This is the former keep in Philippe Auguste's 13C castle, where Joan was tortured on 9 May 1431. The second floor is devoted to the life of Joan of Arc.

Musée des Antiquités de la Seine-Maritime★★

198 r. Beauvoisine. Open Mon and Wed–Sat 10am–12.15pm, 1.30–5.30pm, Sun 2–6pm. Closed 1 Jan, 1 May, 1 and 11 Nov, 25 Dec. 3€. 02 35 98 55 10.

A 17C convent houses this museum which displays objects from prehistory to the 19C. From the Middle Ages and the Renaissance are items including stunning religious gold and silver plate (12C Valasse Cross), 12C–13C **enamels**★, 5C–16C **ivories**★ (a 14C seated Virgin) as well as a collection of arms and Moorish and Italian majolica. In a long gallery are Gothic and Renaissance **carved façades**★ from half-timbered houses in old Rouen. A separate gallery contains the 15C **Winged Deer tapestry**★★ and Renaissance furnishings.

The **Gallo-Roman collection**★, famed for its bronzes and glassware, includes the **Lillebonne mosaic**★★ (4C, restored 19C), the largest signed and illuminated Roman mosaic in France.

Near the museum gardens stands the large **Fontaine Ste-Marie** by Falguière.

Lycée Corneille

16 r. Maulévrier. Closed for visits.

This former 17C–18C Jesuit college was attended by Corneille as well as by Corot, Flaubert, Maupassant and Maurois.

EXCURSIONS

Jardin des Plantes★

2.5km/1.5mi. Leave Rouen by avenue de Bretagne, or take bus route no 12 and get off at Dufay or Jardin des Plantes. Open daily 8.30am–8pm in summer 8am until dark in winter. Greenhouses open 9–11am, 1.30–4.30pm. No charge. 02 32 18 21 30.

This beautiful 10ha/25-acre park, originally designed in the 17C, contains around 3 000 plant species inside the conservatories and **tropical hothouses** and a further 5 000 out in the open air. A star attractions is the **Victoria Regia**, a giant water lily from the Amazon, whose large, flat leaves can reach a diameter of 1m/3.3ft in summer. Its flowers bloom, change colour and die the same day.

Centre Universitaire

5km/3mi. Leave Rouen by rue Chasselièvre NW.

From the road, which ends on the Mont-aux-Malades plateau where the university lies, there is a good **panorama**★★ of the city, the port and the curve in the river.

Manoir Pierre-Corneille

In Petit-Couronne, 8km/5mi. From Rouen take avenue de Bretagne, on the map; turn right by the first houses of Petit-Couronne onto rue Pierre-Corneille. Leave the car before no 502. Open Apr–Sept Wed–Mon 10am–12.30pm, 2–6pm, public holidays 2–6pm; Oct–Mar Wed–Mon 10am–12.30pm, 2–5.30pm, public holidays 2–5.30pm. Closed 1 Jan, 1 May, 1 and 11 Nov, 25 Dec. 3€. 02 35 68 13 89.

The Norman "house in the fields" was bought in 1608 by the poet's father, who died in 1639, leaving it to Corneille. The museum evokes the writer's family life with 17C furniture.

Musée industriel de la Corderie Vallois

8km/5mi NW. Leave Rouen by quai Gaston-Boulet and proceed towards Dieppe; follow N 27 until you reach Notre-Dame-de-Bondeville. Guided tour (1hr30min) daily 1.30–6pm. Machines are run every hour, with commentary by a mechanic. Closed 1 Jan, 1 May, 1 and 11 Nov, 25 Dec. 3€. 02 35 74 35 35.

Recently restored, this old factory has retained 19C rope-making machinery in working order. A huge paddle wheel drives the whole complex mechanism.

Forêt Verte

23km/14.3mi – Allow about 1hr. Leave Rouen by rue Bouquet.

The road passes through the forest, a favourite spot with the Rouennais.

Barentin

17km/10.5mi NW. Leave Rouen by A 15 or N 15.

Visitors entering Barentin from Mesnil-Roux are greeted by a 13.5/44.3ft polystyrene Statue of Liberty, made for the French film *Le Cerveau (The Brain)*. The town boasts works by sculptors such as Rodin, Janniot, Bourdelle and Gromaire. On the place de la Libération is a 17C fountain by Nicolas Coustou. The brick railway viaduct, 505m/1 657ft long, which carries the Paris-Le Havre railway line across the Austreberthe Valley, stands in Barentin.

The 19C **church** (*open Mon–Tue and Thu–Sat 9am–5pm; closed public holidays; 02 35 91 21 35*) has modern windows depicting the lives of St Martin, St Helier and St Austreberthe.

DRIVING TOURS

The Corniche★★★

10km/6mi – plus 15min sightseeing, preferably at sunset.

Starting from place St-Paul, drive along rue Henri-Rivière and its continuation, rue du Mont-Gargan. Branch right onto rue Annie-de-Pène.

The road climbs to the top of Ste-Catherine Hill, a chalk spur separating the Robec and Seine valleys.

Côte Ste-Catherine★★★
Leave the car on a terrace in a sharp bend to the left.
There is a strikingly beautiful **panorama** *(viewing table)* over the river bend and the town with all its belfries.

Continue along D 95, which meets N 14 by a school. Turn left; after 200m/219yd turn right before the Café de la Mairie.

Bonsecours★★
The neo-Gothic basilica of Bonsecours (1840), which crowns the Mount Thuringe spur, is an excellent belvedere from which to see the shipping on the river and industrial Rouen. From the monument to Joan of Arc the **view** includes Rouen and the Seine Valley. From the foot of the Calvary *(viewing table)* there is a **panorama** downstream: the port and the bridges (*left bank*) and the cathedral *(right bank)*.

Continue on N 14 towards Paris; turn right onto N 14 to return to Rouen.

Croisset; Canteleu★
9km/5.6mi – plus 15min sightseeing.

Leave Rouen by quai Gaston-Boulet, towards Duclair. Turn left onto D 51 towards Croisset.

Croisset
Pavillon Flaubert, 18 quai Gustave-Flaubert, Dieppedale-Croisset. Guided tours (15min) Jul–Aug Wed–Sun 2–6pm; Sept–Jun Sat–Sun and holidays 2–6pm. Closed 1 Jan, 1 May and 25 Dec. No charge. 02 35 71 28 82.
The **Pavillon Flaubert**, now a museum, is where Gustave Flaubert wrote *Madame Bovary* and *Salammbô*.

Return to D 982 and continue west to Canteleu.

Canteleu★
There is an interesting but limited view of the port and part of the town from the church terrace.

LOWER SEINE VALLEY TOURS★★★

From Rouen to Le Havre
109km/68mi – allow about 4hr30min.
The route provides a variety of views of the meanderings of the Lower Seine.

From Rouen take D 982.

A **view★** of Rouen can be glimpsed to the east through a small valley.

Canteleu★
See above.
The road *(D 982)* crosses the Forêt de Roumare before emerging near St-Martin-de-Boscherville with a view of the Seine Valley and the old abbey church in the foreground.

St-Martin-de-Boscherville★★
See ST-MARTIN-DE-BOSCHERVILLE, p376
The road between La Fontaine and Mesnil-sous-Jumièges follows the outer side of the bend for several miles between the river bank and the cliff.

Duclair
From place de la Libération, you can watch the passage of large cargo vessels, incongruous in such a rural setting.
Eglise St-Denis (*to visit, ask at tourist office; 227 av. du Prés-Coty; 02 35 37 38 29*), restored in the 19C, has retained its 12C belfry surmounted by a 16C spire.

West of Duclair bear left onto D 65.

This road across the end of the Jumièges Promontory is on the **Route des Fruits**, where blackcurrants, redcurrants, cherries, etc. are sold to the public.

Le Mesnil-sous-Jumièges
It was in the 13C manor house at Mesnil that Agnès Sorel, the favourite of Charles VII, died in 1450.
The road runs past the **country park** and **open-air leisure centre**, part of the Brotonne Regional Nature Park.

Abbaye de Jumièges★★★
See Abbaye de JUMIÈGES

Yainville
The square church tower and nave are 11C. The goldsmiths Christofle set up a factory in the town in 1971.

Le Trait
The 16C **parish church** of this industrial district includes some delightful alabasters (*Adoration of the Magi* and *Coronation of the Virgin*) beneath the statues surrounding the altar.

Head NW on D 982, then right onto D 22.

St-Wandrille★
See Abbaye de ST-WANDRILLE.

Return to D 982 and continue west.

Caudebec-en-Caux
See CAUDEBEC-EN-CAUX.

From Caudebec-en-Caux take D 81 and D 281 south and west.

West of Caudebec-en-Caux, the woodland gives way to the alluvial lowland along the estuary and industrial sites.

Villequier★
See CAUDEBEC-EN-CAUX.

Château d'Ételan★
Open mid-Jun–Sept Sat–Tue and public holidays 11am–1pm (park and chapel only) 3–7pm (park, chapel and château) (last entry 1hr before closing). 3€ morning, 5€ afternoon. 02 35 39 91 27.
This remarkable Flamboyant Gothic building dating from 1494, which occupies the site of an old fortress, dominates the valley.
An elegant, nine-bay staircase turret heralds the Early Normandy Renaissance. The terrace provides a superb **view** (foreground) of the St-Maurice-d'Ételan and Norville marshes and (background) of Brotonne Forest. The boats on the Seine appear to be gliding through the field.

Notre-Dame-de-Gravenchon
Interesting modern church with a lead and copper composition on the façade of St George slaying the dragon.

Lillebonne
See LILLEBONNE.

The whitish cliffs around Tancarville emerge in the distance; the road bridge comes clearly into view.

Tancarville
The last chalk cliff on the north bank of the Seine provides a fine view of the river estuary.
The **Pont de Tancarville**★ (1954–59) is one of the largest suspension bridges in Europe (length 1 400m/4 943ft). Before its construction, all cross-river traffic on the Lower Seine was carried by ferries. From the bridge *(leave your car at one end)* there is a lovely **view**★ of the Seine estuary and Tancarville Canal in the foreground; in the far distance you can glimpse the Pont de Normandie downstream.
The only part of the feudal 10C château to survive intact is the Tour de l'Aigle (Eagle Tower) built in the 15C.

West of Tancarville the road (D 982) passes under the north end of the bridge (view of the bridge) and skirts the cliff as far as Le Hode.

There is a good view of the south bank of the estuary and of the industrial zone south of the Tancarville Canal.

St-Jean-d'Abbetot
The **church**, which dates from the first half of the 11C, is decorated with frescoes (12C, 13C, 16C); the **finest frescoes**★ are in the crypt.

Continue west to Le Havre.

ADDRESSES

STAY

Chambre d'hôte La Ferme du Coquetot – *46 r. du Coq, 27380 Bourg-Beaudouin, 18km/11mi NE of Rouen via N 14. 02 32 49 09 91. http://fermeducoquetot.free.fr. 3 rooms and one cottage. . Meal.* This red brick house sits on the grounds of an abandoned château, now a working farm. The rooms are simple and pretty. The cottage is in an old dovecote, with lots of charm. Friendly reception.

Brit Hôtel Versan – *3 r. Jean-Lecanuet. 02 35 07 77 07. www.rouen-hotel-versan.com. 34 rooms. .* A practical address on a busy boulevard not far from the town hall. The rooms are all similar, functional and well equipped. Efficient soundproofing.

Chambre d'hôte La Muette – *1057 r. des Bosquets, 76230 Isneauville, 10km/6mi NE. 02 35 60 57 69. www.charmance-lamuette.com. Closed mid-Dec–mid-Mar. 5 rooms. .* Spacious, cosy rooms in themed rooms are found in this stunning 18C Norman building. Breakfast room overlooking the park.

Hôtel des Carmes – *33 pl. des Carmes. 02 35 71 92 31. www.hoteldescarmes.com. 12 rooms. .* Situated in the town centre, not far from the cathedral, this hotel is appealing. The delightfully decorated reception area hints of artistic tendencies, and the clutter-free bedrooms are charming and well fittet out. A very good address for budget-conscious travellers.

Hôtel Le Cardinal – *1 pl. de la Cathédrale. 02 35 70 24 42. www.cardinal-hotel.fr. Closed 18 Dec–14 Jan. 20 rooms. 8€.* Near the Notre Dame Cathedral, this family hotel with a distinctive red façade offers moderate-sized guest rooms with modern furnishings. Summer, breakfast on the terrace.

Hôtel Le Vieux Carré – *34 r. Ganterie. 02 35 71 67 70. www vieux-carre.fr. 13 rooms. 7€.* This charming, half-timbered property (1715) has modern rooms with free-standing wardrobes.

Hôtel de la Cathédrale – *12 r. St-Romain. 02 35 71 57 95. www.hotel-de-la-cathedrale.fr. 26 rooms. 8.50€.* Beautiful 17C building in a pretty, pedestrianised street near the cathedral. Rooms are comfy and the atmosphere delightful. Lovely patio.

Hôtel Dandy – *93 bis. r. Cauchoise. 02 35 07 32 00. www.hotels-rouen.net. Closed 26 Dec–2 Jan. 18 rooms. 11€.* Near place du Vieux-Marché, this hotel with tearoom and bar is quite charming. Rooms are refined and the breakfast room pretty.

Hôtel de Dieppe – *pl. Bernard Tissot (oppoite train station) 02 35 71 96 00. www.hotel-dieppe.fr. 41 rooms. 11€.* This hotel has been run by the same family since 1880. It offers guests neat bedrooms with customised decoration. Rouen duck is this restaurant's speciality; duck drawings and objects enhance the dining room's elegant décor.

EAT

Les Maraîchers – *37 pl. du Vieux-Marché. 02 35 71 57 73. www.les-maraichers.fr.* A restaurant with Parisian bistro airs in a half-timbered house. Banquettes, a bar, close-set tables, old advertising plaques, hat and jug collections – nothing's missing! Improvised cuisine. Norman-style second dining room on the ground floor.

Le Bistrot du Siècle – *75 r. Jules Ferry, 76480 Duclair, 20km/12.4mi NW. 02 35 37 62 36. Closed 25 Dec–1 Jan, Sun and Mon.* This little bistro has a fine local reputation. Conviviality reigns in its two dining rooms: one is decorated with old posters; the other is on the veranda. Cuisine with an accent on meat flame-grilled on a wood fire. A few dishes from Reunion Island.

Le Gourmand du Sud-Ouest – *24 r. Rollon. 02 35 07 36 08. Closed 15 Jul–15 Aug, Sun and Mon. Reservations advised.* Here, the entire Tessal family bustles about to ensure you're well fed according to the culinary precepts of southwestern France. The cassoulet of course is highly placed on a menu featuring solid, nourishing dishes. Friendly atmosphere.

€€ **Guinguette Chez Dédé** – *40 Les Écluses, 27380 Amfreville-sous-les-Monts. ℘02 32 49 80 06. Closed Mon.* Afternoons and evenings, the accordion plays for dances featuring waltzes and tangos. A vast terrace overlooks the Seine. Traditional cuisine: mussels with French-fries, fried fish, etc.

€€ **La Marmite** – *3 r.de Florence. ℘02 35 71 75 55. http://lamarmiterouen.unblog.fr.* Delicious odours waft from the cooking pot *(marmite)* situated near place du Vieux-Marché. Push open the door to enjoy a delicately flavoured cuisine, prepared with fresh products and presented with care. Dining room freshly renovated.

€€ **Les P'tits Parapluies** – *pl. Rougemare. ℘02 35 88 55 26. Closed 3–19 Aug, 2–8 Jan, Sat lunch, Sun eve, Mon.* The building is from the 16C and formerly housed an umbrella factory (hence its name, meaning "umbrellas"). Pleasant, modern atmosphere, lovely exposed period beams and modern cuisine with a personal touch.

€€ **Pascaline** – *5 r. de la Poterne. ℘02 35 89 67 44. www.pascaline.fr. Reservations advised.* Located next to the courthouse, this restaurant with a bistro façade is very pleasant. Brasserie décor with handsome wood counters, long seats and yellow walls. Choice of attractive fixed-price menus. Book ahead – it's often full.

€€ **Reverbère** – *5 pl. de la République. ℘02 35 07 03 14. Closed 28 Apr–4 May, 28 Jul–17 Aug, Sun, public holidays.* A discreet glass front, overlooking a small square, near the river bank. Modern dining room, extended by a small, low-key lounge and wooden staircase leading to a rustic lounge.

€€ **La Toque d'Or** – *11 pl. du Vieux-Marché. ℘02 35 71 46 29. www.toquedor.fr.* Well-placed opposite place du Vieux-Marché, this pretty half-timbered house holds two different restaurants: on the ground floor, a large elegant room offers refined fare (the ***tête de veau*** is remarkable), while upstairs, a more relaxed menu features grilled meat served at a faster pace.

€€–€€€ **Au Bois Chenou** – *23 pl. de la Pucelle-d'Orléans. ℘02 35 71 19 54. Closed Sun eve from Sept–mid-Jun, Tue eve and Wed.* On the ground floor of a 17C half-timbered building. Inside, the furnishings are modern and the food very agreeable.

€€–€€€ **Bistrot des Halettes (Chez L'Gros)** – *43 pl. du Vieux-Marché. ℘02 35 71 05 06. Closed 25 Dec–1 Jan, Sun and Mon. Reservations recommended.* Traditional cuisine influenced by seasonal ingredients is served in this bistro with its friendly atmosphere. Superb terrace.

€€€ **La Beffroy** – *15 r. Beffroy. ℘02 35 71 55 27. Closed Sun eve, Tue. Reservations required.* In this 16C, typical half-timbered Norman house you'll find a very pleasing dining room. A good place for generous portions of high-quality cuisine using good quality produce.

€€€ **Restaurant La Couronne** – *31 pl. du Vieux-Marché. ℘02 35 71 40 90. www.lacouronne.com.fr.* This building, constructed in 1345, is one of the oldest inns in France and has a great atmosphere with high quality food and a good wine list.

Dame Cakes– *70 r. St-Romain, Cathedral district. ℘02 35 07 49 31. Closed Sun.* This tea room occupies the former workshop of the famed ironsmith Ferdinand Marrou. Magnificent old ornamental ironwork, including a balcony. The owner has a taste for cakes "that Grannie used to make": chocolate cake, vegetable crumble, a variety of cakes both sweet and salty. The menu changes every month.

NIGHTLIFE

Famed as the spot where Joan of Arc met her end, the place du Vieux-Marché is today a lively centre of evening activity, with lots of bars and restaurants, many with terraces. Check *The Viking*, a free brochure distributed locally, for more information.

Bar de la Crosse – *53 r. de l'Hôpital. ℘02 35 70 16 68. Closed Sun, 1st half Aug, public holidays.* This small bar has gained its popularity from the relaxed and friendly atmosphere you find here. Concerts and exhibitions.

Le Bateau Ivre – *17 r. des Sapins. ℘02 35 70 09 05. http://bateauivre.rouen.free.fr. Closed Sun–Mon, Aug.* Ever on the lookout for new talent, this bar has been livening up Rouen night life for the past 20 years. Concerts Fridays and Saturdays, ballads and poetry Thursdays, café-theatre or French songs Tuesday evenings. A few programmes are available at the tourist office.

Taverne St-Amand – *11 r. St-Amand. ℘02 35 88 51 34. Closed Sun and 3 weeks in Aug.* Set up as a restaurant-bar for 32 years, this 17C house has welcomed painters, writers, actors and other artistic habitués.

PERFORMING ARTS

Théâtre de l'Écharde – *16 r. Flahaut. ℘02 35 15 33 05. Tickets also sold at theatre before performance.* Theatre with 100 seats where the troupe's performances and shows for young theatre-goers are performed.

Théâtre des Deux Rives – *48 r. Louis Ricard. ℘02 35 70 22 82. www.cdr2rives.com.* Classical and modern theatre, with an emphasis on living playwrights.

Théâtre des Arts – *7 r. du Dr-Rambert, Vieux-Marché. ℘02 35 71 41 36. www.operaderouen.com.* A whole host of concerts, plays and operas shown.

SHOPPING

Faïencerie Augy-Carpentier – *26 r. St-Romain. ℘02 35 88 77 47. www.fayencerie-augy.com. Closed Sun–Mon. Tour of the workshop by appointment.* The last hand-made and hand-decorated earthenware workshop in Rouen offers copies of many traditional motifs from blue monochrome to multicoloured, and from lambrequin to cornucopia.

Chocolatier Auzou – *163 r. du Gros-Horloge. ℘02 35 70 59 31. www.auzou-chocolat.fr. Closed Sun Jul–Aug, 1 Jan, 1 May.* Located in a half-timbered house, this renowned chocolatier will tempt you with ***les Larmes de Jeanne d'Arc*** (Joan of Arc's Tears: lightly roasted almonds covered with nougatine and chocolate) or ***l'Agneau Rouennais*** (a sort of sponge cake) and candied apples.

Hardy–*22 pl. du Vieux-Marché. ℘02 35 71 81 55. Closed Sun.* This delicatessen occupies a suberb half-timbered house on one of the liveliest squares in Rouen. Specialities include sheep's foot ***à la rouennaise***, ***andouilles*** with hot peppers and Caen tripe cooked in Calvados and cider. In the afternoons, you can eat in the establishment's restaurant.

ANTIQUES MARKET

Place St-Marc Sun 8am–1.30pm

TRADITIONAL MARKETS –

Place St-Marc– Tue and Fri–Sun.

Place des Emmurées – Tue and Sat.

Place du Vieux-Marché – Tue–Sun.

LEISURE

The tourist office distributes two useful brochures: *L'Agenda rouennais* (3-weekly) and the *Rouen magazine* (bi-monthly).

Audio-guided Tours in 6 languages are available, along with **horse-and-carriage tours**, **group tours** and **little train tours** through the city.

CULTURAL EVENTS

Evening light shows – *℘02 32 08 32 40 (Rouen tourist office). Open early Jun–late Sept from about 10pm.* A dozen cathedral pictures inspired by Monet are projected onto the façade of Rouen Cathedral, creating strange forms and colours.

St-Martin-de Boscherville★★

The Benedictine abbey was founded in 1144 by William of Tancarville on the site of a collegiate church built around 1050 by his father, Raoul, Grand Chamberlain to William the Conqueror. The monks were driven out during the Revolution.

- **Population:** 1 453.
- **Michelin Map:** 304: F-5.
- **Info:** 227 av. du Président-Coty, 76480 Duclair. ☏02 35 37 38 29. www.duclair.fr.
- **Location:** St-Martin, on the western edge of the Forêt de Roumare, is W of Rouen via D 982, then the D 67.
- **Don't Miss:** Local tourist offices offer maps of circuits you can take in the Forêt de Roumare.
- **Timing:** The abbey can be visited in an hour.

Abbaye St-Georges★★

Abbey Church

The building, which was constructed from 1080 to 1125, apart from the vaulting in the nave and transept which is 13C, possesses a striking unity of style and harmony of proportion.

The façade is plain: the ornaments on the main door archivolts are geometric, in typical Norman Romanesque style. The nave of eight bays has Gothic vaulting. The monumental confessional in the south transept is 18C. The remarkable acoustics have inspired concerts organized each June and September *(enquire at tourist office)*.

Abbey Buildings

Open daily Apr–Oct 9am–6.30pm; Nov–Mar 2–5pm. Guided tours Sun and public holidays Apr–Sept 4pm; Oct–Mar 3.30pm. Closed 1 Jan, 25 Dec. Apr–Oct 5.50€; Nov–Mar 5€. ☏02 35 32 10 82. www.abbaye-saint-georges.com.

Chapter house

The 12C chapter house is surmounted by a 17C building. Inside, a fine frieze of Hispano-Moorish inspiration runs above the place where the monks' stalls once stood. Excavations have uncovered vestiges of Gaulish and Gallo-Roman temples and a Merovingian funerary church.

Conventual outbuilding

Erected by the Maurists in 1690 and partly demolished during the French Revolution, it was restored in 1994.

Chapelle des Chambellans

It was built in the late 13C to serve the Chambellans of Tancarville.

Park

This formal French garden designed in the tradition of the great landscape architect André Le Nôtre (1680) has recently been restored.

ADDRESSES

STAY

Chambre d'hôte Les Hauts du Catel – *282 chemin du Panorama Le Catel, 76480 Duclair, 8km/5mi NW. ☏02 35 37 68 84. Closed Nov–Feb school holidays. 4 rooms.* The views from this 1930s villa are simply breathtaking: the meanders of the Seine stretch out below you. The colourful rooms are pleasant; two are located under the roof. Panoramic breakfast room.

Abbaye de St-Wandrille★

St-Wandrille Abbey, like Le Bec-Hellouin, is a moving testimony to the continuity of the Benedictine Order in Normandy. Today, the monks earn their living mainly from the manufacture of furniture polish and household products.

- **Population:** 1 179.
- **Michelin Map:** 304: E-4.
- **Info:** 15 rue des Caiettes, 76490 Saint-Wandrille-Rançon. ℘02 35 96 10 89. www.saint-wandrille-rançon.fr.
- **Location:** The village and abbey lie on D 982, 4km/2.5mi E of Caudebec and 51km/32mi W of Rouen.
- **Don't Miss:** The cloister, the only part of the abbey still intact.
- **Timing:** Visit on Sunday morning or, on other days, in the afternoon.

A BIT OF HISTORY

God's Athlete (7C) – King Dagobert's court was celebrating the marriage of Count Wandrille, who seemed destined to a brilliant career, when, to general surprise, the bride entered a convent and Wandrille joined a group of hermits. The king ordered Wandrille to return to court but, enlightened by a miracle, accepted the choice. Wandrille's saintliness and magnificent physique earned him the nickname of God's Athlete.

Valley of the Saints (7C–9C) – In 649 Wandrille founded Fontanelle monastery, "where saints flourish like rose trees in a greenhouse".

Benedictine Continuity – In the 10C monks began to rebuild the abbey, destroyed by Vikings. It survived the Wars of Religion, but the Revolution scattered the monks and the buildings fell into ruin. In 1931, the Benedictines returned permanently.

Abbaye★

Allow 45min.

The entrance to the abbey is through a 15C door surmounted by a symbolic pelican. The porter's lodge and its twin are 18C. The imposing 18C Porte de Jarente leads to the main courtyard, accessible on guided tours only. The only parts of the abbey church still standing are the tall columns.

Cloisters★

Open daily 5.15am–1pm, 2–9.15pm. Guided tours (1hr) Easter–Oct Wed–Sat and Mon 3.30pm, Sun and public holidays 11.30am, 3.30pm; Nov–Easter Sat 3.30pm, Sun and public holidays 11.30am, 3.30pm. Closed Easter, 25 Dec. 3.50€. ℘02 35 96 23 11. www.st-wandrille.com.

The 14C south gallery *(only one open to the public)*, parallel with the nave, was linked to it by a door surmounted by a now mutilated tympanum illustrating the Coronation of the Virgin. A niche in the 13C church wall contains the graceful 14C statue of Our Lady of Fontenelle.

Èglise

Mass (with Gregorian chant) Mon–Sat 9.45am, Sun and public holidays 10am. Vespers Mon–Wed and Fri–Sat 5.30pm, Thu 6.45pm, Sun and public holidays 5pm. No visits during services.

The church is an old 13C tithe barn, the Canteloup Barn, which was transported in 1969 from La Neuville-du-Bosc in the Eure and re-erected at St-Wandrille.

Chapelle St-Saturnin

Closed to the public. By car, follow the signs; on foot about 45min there and back. Leave the abbey and take the path downhill (right); note the 16C Entombment in a niche. Skirt the wall for 150m/164yd; go around a field and take the path beside the abbey wall.

This small 10C oratory was probably built on Merovingian foundations. The façade was remodelled in the 16C.

Le Tréport

Le Tréport, a small fishing port at the mouth of the Bresle near the border with Picardy, is a seaside resort which is all the more popular for its close proximity to Paris. During the summer lively crowds round the harbour turn the town into a fair. The long shingle beach, backed by tall cliffs, is packed with visitors on weekends. Mers-les-Bains, on the right bank of the Bresle, is less commercial than Le Tréport and has many devotees, as has Ault, a beach further north.

- **Population:** 5 698.
- **Michelin Map:** 304: I-1.
- **Info:** Quai Sadi-Carnot. 02 35 86 05 69. www.ville-le-treport.fr.
- **Location:** Le Tréport is 93km/57.8mi from Rouen and 30km/18.5mi NE of Dieppe by D 925, on the border of Picardy.
- **Don't Miss:** The view from the Calvaire des Terrasses.
- **Timing:** Spend the morning in Le Tréport, then see the pretty resort of Mers-les-Bains.

SIGHTS

Calvaire des Terrasses★

Allow 30min round-trip on foot. Access by car via rue de Paris, rue St-Michel and boulevard du Calvaire.

A flight of stairs *(378 steps)* leads up from the town hall to the Calvary on the clifftop. From the terrace, there is a **view**★ over the town, extending north beyond the Caux cliffs to Hourdel Point, the Somme estuary and inland, along the Lower Bresle Valley to Eu and the lower town's slate roofs, beach and harbour.

Église St-Jacques

The church, which stands halfway up the hill, dates from the latter half of the 16C, but was extensively restored in the 19C. The modern porch shelters a Renaissance doorway. Inside, at the far end of the church, stands a fine statue of the Virgin of Tréport. The chapel of Notre-Dame-de-la-Pitié (Our Lady of Mercy) holds a 16C Piéta. A low relief over the altar shows a Virgin surrounded by Biblical emblems.

ADDRESSES

STAY

Golf Hôtel – *102 rte de Dieppe. 02 27 28 01 52. www.treport-hotels.com. Closed 17–26 Dec. Reservations advised weekends. 10 rooms.* Turn left at the entrance to the campsite, where a tree-lined alley leads to a fine 19C timber-framed house. A small, charming hotel at reasonable prices.

Chambre d'hôte Le Prieuré Sainte-Croix – *2km/1mi E via D 925 (Abbeville-Dieppe road), access through the roundabout. 02 35 86 14 77. http://prieuresaintecroix.free.fr. Closed for part of Dec and Jan. 3 rooms.* This 19C house was formerly on the grounds of Château d'Eu. Total calm, pretty garden, country views.

EAT

La Matelote – *34 quai François-1er. Le Tréport. 02 35 86 01 13. Reservations advised summer and weekends.* The chef bases his inventive cuisine on the day's catch. The upstairs dining room has a view of the port and the cliffs of Mers-les-Bains.

Le St-Louis – *43 quai François-1er. 02 35 86 20 70. Closed 15 Nov–18 Dec.* A seafood restaurant with a view of the fishing docks. Brasserie-style décor, beneath a coloured glass roof. Covered veranda in front.

Varengeville-sur-Mer★

The resort consists of a series of hamlets in a charming landscape of hedges and half-timbered houses. The church stands on an attractive site★ overlooking the sea. The stained-glass window in the south aisle depicting the Tree of Jesse is by 20C abstract artist Georges Braque, who is buried in the graveyard.

- **Population:** 1 071.
- **Michelin Map:** 304: F-2.
- **Info:** 6 place du Village, 76740 Le-Bourg-Dun. 02 35 97 63 05.
- **Location:** The pretty coastal road D 75 leads to Varengeville, which is 4km/2.5mi W of Dieppe, between Pourville-sur-Mer and Vasterival.
- **Don't Miss:** The beautiful view from the church; the garden at the Bois des Moustiers, designed by Gertrude Jekyll.
- **Timing:** Take 1hr to see the garden.

SIGHTS

Parc floral du Bois des Moustiers★

Open mid-Mar–mid-Nov daily 10am–noon, 2–6pm, public holidays 10am–9pm. 7€. 02 35 85 10 02.

In a valley facing the sea, this English-style garden (9ha/22 acres) has a profusion of flowering plants and giant rhododendrons. The **house** (1898) was designed by the renowned Sir Edwin Luytens and the **garden** by his frequent collaborator, Gertrude Jekyll.

Chapelle St-Dominique

On the outskirts of Varengeville, on the left side of the road to Dieppe. Open Jun–mid-Sept daily 9am–5.30pm. 02 35 85 12 14.

There is more **stained glass** by Braque as well as a painting by 20C artist Maurice Denis.

EXCURSIONS

Phare d'Ailly★

1km/0.6mi on D 75A off D 75. Guided tour (15min) on request 1 week before, mid-Apr–mid-Sept Mon–Fri 10am–noon, 2–4.30pm. 02 35 85 11 19.

A modern lighthouse has replaced the two older ones (18C–19C), destroyed in 1944.

Manoir d'Ango

Follow the signs from D 75 onto a little road, and turn right a bit further on; a drive bordered with beech trees leads to the parking area. Open May–Sept daily 10am–12.30pm, 2–6pm; Apr and Oct Sat–Sun and school holidays 10am–12.30pm, 2–6pm. 5€.

This lovely Renaissance home, built between 1535 and 1545 by Italian artists, was the home of **Jean Ango**, the great 16C navigator, fleet-owner, governor of Dieppe and naval adviser to François I. The building is designed around a large inner courtyard. The southern part opens on the ground floor into an Italian-style **loggia**. The mullion windows are set in walls of sandstone and flint. The décor is typically Renaissance, with many sculpted ornaments forming the shapes of foliage, seashells and medallions.

ADDRESSES

EAT

La Buissonnière – *Rte du Phare d'Ailly, 76119 Ste-Marguerite-sur-Mer, 2km/1mi NW of Varengeville via D 75. 02 35 83 17 13. Closed Jan–Feb, Sun eve and Mon. Reservations required weekends.* Early-20C house set in an exquisite garden. Inventive cuisine, three small dining areas and a charming terrace.

LA SUISSE NORMANDE

This extraordinary name denotes an area in Normandy which straddles the Orne *(see pp264–299)* **and Calvados** *(see pp80–151)* **regions. It has neither mountains nor lakes in the Swiss sense and does not even include Normandy's highest points, but nevertheless draws tourists to its attractive landscape. The River Orne, as it cuts its way through the ancient rocks of the Armorican Massif, produces a kind of hollow relief through which flows a pleasantly winding river course bordered by steep banks surmounted by rock escarpments.**

Located in the midst of Calvados *bocage* country some 30km/18.5mi south of Caen and extending into the Orne *département*, the Suisse Normande lies between the towns of Condé-sur-Noireau, Thury-Harcourt and **Putanges**; some extend the range eastwards to Falaise and the rugged Ante Valley. Besides the valley of the Orne, the area takes in several small tributary rivers including the Noireau, the Vère, the Rouvre and the Baize. Deeply eroded valleys and escarpments appear in stark contrast with the flat plain around Caen. The curious name Suisse Normande was coined by tourism promoters in the 19C, as the train, followed by an improved road, brought city-dwellers into the area. Switzerland, then as now, evoked images of inspiring scenery, clean air, vigorous sports and healthy living. The branding was not too far-fetched, as the rivers and canyons still attract canoeists, hikers and anglers, as well as people who enjoy soaring off cliffs on the Route des Crêtes aided by gliders and delta planes. At the Rochers des Parcs, near Clécy, you can observe climbers clinging to the cliffs. Clubs in **Pont-d'Ouilly**, Clécy and Thury-Harcourt offer opportunities to canoe and kayak along the Orne. On a reservoir at **Rabodanges**, you can enjoy water sports and a lakeside café. Pont-d'Ouilly and Notre Dame du Rocher offer opportunities for horseback rides.

The many craggy promentories provide good views for hikers: the most renowned is the **Roche d'Oëtre**, near Pont-d'Ouilly, which achieves almost Alpine grandeur; others are the Pain de Sucre at Clécy and Mont Pinçon at Thury-Harcourt.

The local Armorican granite, as in Brittany, figures in much local construction. Tourists subtracted, the Suisse Normande is resolutely rural, with pastures for horses and cattle, fields of rapeseed, winding roads between ancient hedgerows, swathes of forest and picturesque little villages. Near Clécy lies a 16C château that can be visited, while the gardens of the old château of Harcourt are open to the public.

For more information on sights in and around La Suisse Normande, see Orne and Calvados sections of this guide.

La Suisse Normande, Vallée de l'Orne

La Suisse Normande★★

DRIVING TOUR

Vallée de l'Orne★★

From Thury-Harcourt to Putanges

99km/61.5mi – Allow 3hr. Nearly all sights require a short walk. Be sure to wear suitable shoes.

Thury-Harcourt

See THURY-HARCOURT, p147.

From Thury-Harcourt take D 562 south.

The road drops down into the valley. Ahead is the small Chapelle de la Bonne-Nouvelle, perched on a hillock, followed immediately by Caumont with its abandoned sandstone quarry (left) and St-Rémy and its mining installations.

St-Rémy – Fosses d'Enfer

The St-Rémy iron mines, the most productive in Normandy, were worked from 1875 to 1967; surface mining had taken place since medieval times. About 700m/.5mi off the D562 an 11C Romanesque **church,** renovated in the 19C, stands under an enormous yew tree on a promentory; the **view** over the Orne valley from the cemetery is pretty. The Château de la Maroisière *(closed to the public)* dates to the 18C.

Maison des Ressources Géologiques de Normandie

Open Jul–Aug daily 10am–12.30pm (last entry noon), 2.30–6pm (last entry 5pm); May–Jun and Sept Wed–Mon 2–6pm; Apr and Oct Wed–Mon 2–5.30pm. 4.60€ (children 2.30€). 02 31 69 67 77.

An educational museum on the site of the former mine describes the formation of earth and the geological basis of all sorts of mineral extraction, especially of energy resources. A footpath takes you past the geological site, the mine, and the miners' lodgings.

Michelin Map: 303: J-6 to K-7.

Info: Place du Tripot, Clécy. 02 31 69 79 95. www.ot-suisse-normande.com.

Location: The Suisse Normande takes in the Orne River Valley as well as the Noireau, the Vère, the Rouvre and the Baize.

Don't Miss: The remarkable view of the gorge of the Rouvre river from the belvedere of the Roche d'Oëtre.

Timing: Tour the area in your car before deciding on which of the many hikes to try.

Clécy★

See CLÉCY, p115.

Leave Clécy along D 562 south. In Le Fresne turn left onto D 1.

The road follows the crest of the ridge separating the valleys of the Orne and Noireau and then joins up with the Béron crest. East of the Rendez-vous des Chasseurs (500m/547yd) there is a view north of the Orne Valle, and of the Rochers des Parcs. The downhill stretch offers a view (right) of the Oëtre Rock before reaching Chapelle St-Roch, a 16C pilgrimage chapel where a *pardon*

La Suisse Normande

S. Sauvignier/MICHELIN

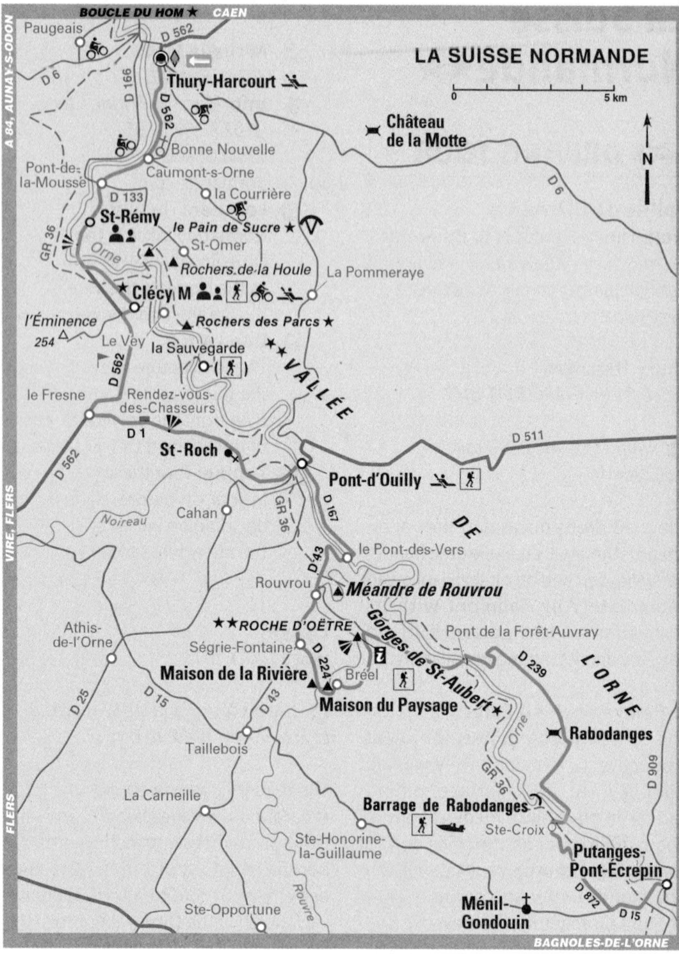

is held on the Sunday after 15 August. Continue on to **Pont-d'Ouilly**, a busy tourist centre at the confluence of the River Orne and River Noireau.

Take D 167 southeast along the Orne to Pont-des-Vers.Turn right onto D 43.

Ségrie-Fontaine

Maison de la rivière et du paysage

Open Apr–Sept Mon–Fri 9.30am–5.30pm (Jul–Aug 6pm), Sat–Sun 2–7pm; rest of the year Mon–Fri 9.30am–5.30pm. 02 33 62 34 65. www.cpie–collines normandes.org.

This educational nature centre includes four walks along the river and its gorge.

Return to Rouvrou, take the road signposted Site de Saint-Jean, then turn right after the cemetery.

Méandre de Rouvrou

Allow 15min round-trip on foot from the war memorial.

This is the best point from which to view the bend in the river at the narrowest part of the rock ridge.

Return to the car and follow the signs to **Roche d'Oëtre★★**.

The rock is in a grandiose **setting** dominating the **Gorge de la Rouvre** with its steep escarpment.
East of the Roche d'Oëtre the road runs along the the valley; the last viewpoint is the bridge in La Forêt-Auvray.
At this point on its course, north of the Argentan region, the Orne flows through a succession of narrow defiles, known as the **Gorges de St-Aubert**★, which are accessible only on foot.

Rabodanges
The 17C moated castle *(closed to the public)* is set in a park overlooking the Orne Valley. Further on, at the Barrage de Rabodanges, the road follows the shoreline of the 95ha/235-acre lake. There are fine views of Rabodanges Lake from the road and also from the bridge in Ste-Croix.

In Ste-Croix turn left onto D 872 just before the war memorial.

S. Sauvignier/MICHELIN

Putanges-Pont-Écrepin
This little town on the Orne is a starting point for visiting the **Gorges de St-Aubert** – accessible only on foot. Take the D 121 to the dam. From the car park, a steep path leads to the trail head, to the right.

ADDRESSES

STAY

Chambre d'hôte La Ferme du Vey – *14570 Le Vey. 02 31 69 71 02. www.ogites.com/ferme-du-vey. 3 rooms.* This working farm with 80 head of cattle offers 3 comfortable and tidy rooms in an outbuilding. The sociable proprietor is delighted to talk about his farm.

EAT

Au Poisson Vivant – *Pont-Érambourg, t-Pierre-du-Regard, 9km/5.6mi W of Pont-d'Ouilly via D 511 dir. Caen, then Pont-Érambourg. 02 31 69 01 58. Closed 2–16 Jan, Mon–Tue. Reservations advised at weekends.* This former dance hall has a small dining room lengthened by a veranda and decorated in 1930s style.

Auberge Saint-Christophe – *Pont-d'Ouilly, 12km/7.4mi SE of Clécy. 02 31 69 81 23. Closed Feb and Nov holidays, 19 Aug–3 Sept, Sun eve, Mon.* This old house, covered in Virginia creeper, sits on a quiet country road. Rustic dining room, regional cuisine. Some rooms available.

LEISURE

With so many rivers, the Suisse-Normand will thrill water sports enthusiasts. Many sites offer rental of equipment for water sports. At Clécy, look for Au fil de l'eau, le Beau Rivage and Lionel Terray; at Thury-Harcourt, La Roc qui Beu and the Kayak Club; at Pont-d'Ouilly, the Base de Plein Air.

DISCOVERING THE CHANNEL ISLANDS

South Coast Cliffs, Guernsey
© VisitGuernsey

The Bailiwicks

The nine Channel Islands are divided into the Bailiwick of Jersey, which includes two rocky islets – the Minquiers and the Ecréhous – and the Bailiwick of Guernsey, which includes Alderney, Sark and Brecqhou, Herm and Jethou. All the islands encourage tourism, maintaining marinas to attract sailors, ensuring clean beaches for surfers and swimmers, and conserving the countryside to the delight of birdwatchers, walkers and cyclists. The islands are served by ferry service from France and England, and by flights to Jersey, Guernsey and Alderney. Scheduled ferries also run among the islands.

GEOGRAPHY

Owing to their situation and the Gulf Stream, the islands enjoy a mild climate that nurtures spring flowers and semi-tropical plants. Long sandy beaches contrast with rugged cliffs; quiet country lanes meander between traditional granite houses. Tidal currents in the islands are among the strongest in the world; at low tide, when the sea may retreat as much as 12m/39.5ft, huge areas of rocky reefs are exposed, greatly increasing the land mass and making it possible to walk seaward (up to 3km/2mi).

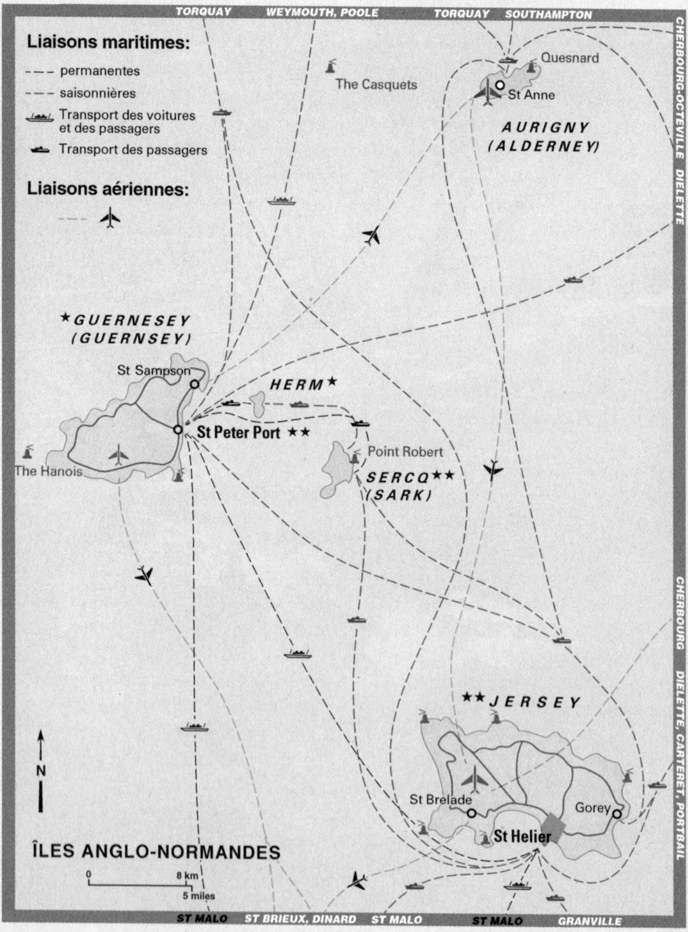

Wrecks and Lighthouses

The Channel Islands are surrounded by extensive offshore reefs and rocky islets which, together with strong tides, treacherous currents and fog, make these seas some of the most hazardous in Britain. Among documented shipwrecks are a Roman galley that sank off St Peter Port; the *White Ship* carrying the heir to the English throne which foundered on the Casquets in 1119; *HMS Victory*, which went down on the Casquets in 1774 with the loss of 1 000 men; the *Liverpool*, which ran aground off Corblets Bay due to fog in 1902; the *Briseis*, which struck a reef off Vazon Bay in 1937 with 7 000 casks of wine on board; the *Orion*, an oil rig mounted on an ocean-going barge, which ran aground off Grand Rocques in Guernsey in 1978. There are now four lighthouses owned by Trinity House in the Channel Islands.

The earliest to be built was the one marking the **Casquets** (1723); then followed the three towers, known as St Peter, St Thomas and Donjon (9m/29.5ft high), which were lit by coal fires. In 1770 oil lamps were introduced, and in 1818 revolving lights. The main light (37m/121.4ft above sea level) has a range of 27km/17mi in clear weather.

The **Hanois Lighthouse** was built in 1862 on the treacherous Hanois Reef. **Quesnard Light** (1912) on Alderney and **Point Robert** (1913) on Sark are sited on land and can be visited.

A BIT OF HISTORY

Although the Channel Islands have been associated with the English crown since the Norman conquest, they lie much nearer to the French coast and were largely French-speaking until the 20C. English is now the universal language of the islands; the native tongue, a dialect of Norman French, the language of William the Conqueror, is rarely spoken. Beneath their apparent Englishness lie 1 000 years of Norman tradition and sturdy independence.

The original Norman laws and systems were enshrined in the first charters granted by King John in the 13C; modifications were introduced in 1949 to separate the judiciary from the legislature. In 2006 Sark introduced a democratic constitution.

Alderney

The island (5.6km/3.5mi long by 2.4km/1.5mi wide) slopes gently from a plateau in the southwest, to a tongue of low-lying land in the northeast. There is one main settlement, St Anne, also known as The Town. Alderney is a haven for nature lovers: flora includes wild broom, thrift, sea campion, ox-eye daisies, wild orchids and the bastard toadflax *(thesium humifusum)***; among the fauna are black rabbits and blonde hedgehogs. Birdwatchers can spy hoopoes and golden orioles, birds of prey and the occasional white stork or purple heron. Seabirds include fulmars, guillemots and kittiwakes, as well as colonies of gannets and puffins.**

- **Population:** 2 294.
- **Michelin Map:** 503.
- **Info:** States of Alderney, PO Box 1, GY9 3AA Alderney. 01481 8211. www.alderney.net.
- **Location:** Alderney is the most northerly of the Channel Islands and lies 12km/7.5mi W of the Cherbourg Peninsula, separated from the Cap de la Hague headland by the treacherous tidal current known as the Alderney Race.
- **Don't Miss:** The best beaches are in the bays of Braye, Clonque and Telegraph. Also try the cliff walk from Haize to Giffoine.

A BIT OF HISTORY

Owing to its key position, nearest to England, France and the Channel shipping lanes, Alderney has frequently been fortified. The Romans seem to have used it as a naval base; there are traces of a late-Roman fort at the Convent. The first English fortifications were initiated by Henry VIII on the hill south of Longis Bay. In the Napoleonic period, the British strengthened existing defences and sent a garrison of 300.

Between 1847 and 1858, alarmed by the development of a French naval base at Cherbourg, the British Government created a safe harbour at Braye by constructing a huge breakwater and built a chain of ten forts along the north coast.

In June 1940 almost all the population left the island and the livestock was evacuated to Guernsey. During their five-year occupation, the Germans re-fortified most of the Victorian forts and built masses of ugly concrete fortifications. When the islanders began to return late in 1945 they found their possessions gone and their houses derelict or destroyed. It took ten years and substantial government aid to make good the damage.

Constitution

Alderney is part of the Bailiwick of Guernsey. Since the introduction of the new constitution on 1 January 1949, the budget and other financial matters have to be approved by the States of Guernsey. Otherwise all island business is decided by the Committees of the States of Alderney, which consists of ten elected members and an elected President, who serve for four years. The court consists of six Jurats under a chairman, all of whom are appointed by the Home Office.

ST ANNE

St Anne, with its cobbled streets and smart whitewashed granite houses, lies about half a mile from the north coast on the edge of the best agricultural land, known as La Blaye.

The original medieval settlement was centred on **Marais Square**. As in ancient times, narrow lanes or *venelles* lead out to the un-enclosed fields divided into *riages*, each consisting of a number of strips: Alderney is one of the few places in Britain still to use this archaic system of managing open agricultural land.

Another settlement grew up at **Le Huret**, where the people assembled to decide when to gather the seaweed *(vraic)* used to fertilise the land. In the 15C more houses were built to the east of the square and the Blaye was extended to support a population of 700. In the 18C the huge profits made from privateering led to a building boom; thatch was replaced by tiles, the first Court House was built and the governor improved the communal buildings as well as his own residence. The northern part of the town – **Queen Elizabeth II Street**, **Victoria Street**, **Ollivier Street** – developed in the early Victorian era. Workmen's cottages were built at Newtown and elsewhere. Many attractive houses and gardens line the green lanes, such as La Vallée, which run from St Anne down to the north coast.

St Anne's Church

Consecrated in 1850, this church was designed by Sir Gilbert Scott in the transitional style from Norman to Early English cruciform.

English was then replacing Norman French as the local language; the lectern holds two Bibles, and the texts in the apse and near the door appear in both languages.

During the war the church was used as a store and the bells were removed; two were recovered on the island and the

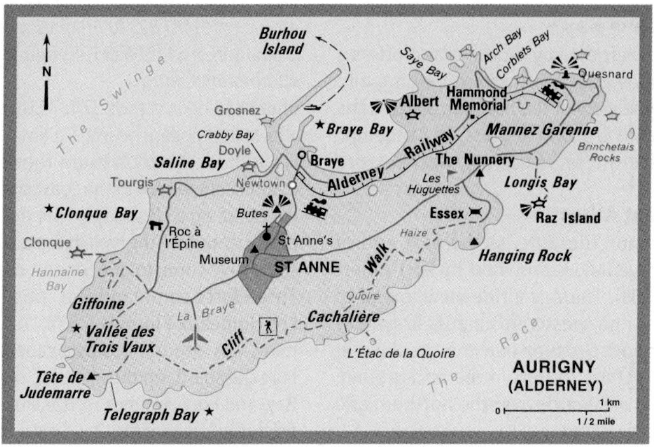

other four were found in Cherbourg. The churchyard gates in Victoria Street, erected as a memorial to Prince Albert, were removed by the Germans but replaced by a local resident.

Museum

Open Apr–Oct Mon–Fri 10am–noon, 2–4pm, Sat–Sun 10am–noon. £2. 01481 823 222. www.alderney society.org.

The Alderney Society's museum, installed in a former school founded in 1790 by Jean Le Mesurier, governor of the island, presents island geology; flora and fauna; archaeology, particularly finds from the Iron Age settlement at Les Huguettes; domestic and military history, including the Victorian fortifications and the German Occupation.

The **Clock Tower** (1767) standing nearby is all that remains of the old church, which was pulled down when the present one was built.

The elegant Royal Connaught Square, renamed in 1905 after a visit by the Duke of Connaught, third son of Queen Victoria, was the town centre in the 18C.

Island Hall *(north side)*, a handsome granite building which is now a community centre and library, was enlarged in 1763 by Governor John Le Mesurier to become Government House. Mouriaux House was completed in 1779 by the governor as his private residence.

Courthouse

Guided tours Mon–Fri 9.30am–12.30pm, 2–5pm. Ask at Court Office. 01481 822 817.

The present building in Queen Elizabeth II Street dates from 1850. Both the court and the States of Alderney hold their sessions in the first-floor courtroom.

The name of Victoria Street, the main shopping street, was changed from rue du Grosnez to celebrate Queen Victoria's visit in 1854.

The Butes recreation ground provides fine views of Braye Bay *(northeast)*, across Crabby Bay and the Swinge to the Casquets *(northwest)* and the English Channel.

TOUR OF THE ISLAND

14km/8.5mi. Allow one day.

It is possible to walk round the island following the clifftop footpath or to drive around.

Braye

The harbour is protected by Fort Grosnez (1853) which was built at the same time as the massive **breakwater** (914m/1 000yd long plus another 548.5m/600yd submerged).

The first quay, the Old Jetty, was built in 1736 by the governor to provide a safe landing-stage for the privateers and smugglers he protected. The modern concrete jetty dates from the turn of the 20C.

Braye Bay★

The largest bay on the island offers a sandy beach with good bathing and a fine view of the harbour. Skirting the beach is a strip of grass, Le Banquage, where the seaweed *(vraic)* was left to dry.

Fort Albert

Mount Touraille, at the east end of Braye Bay, is crowned by Fort Albert (1853). There is a fine view inland to St Anne, westwards across Braye Bay to Fort Grosnez and the breakwater with Fort Tourgis in the background, and eastwards over the northern end of the island.

Hammond Memorial

At the fork in the road E of Fort Albert.

Labourers of the Todt Organisation – paid volunteers from Vichy France, political refugees from Franco's Spain, Ukraine, Russia and North Africa who worked under duress during the Nazi Occupation – are recalled by plaques inscribed in their languages. Three camps on Alderney each held 1 500 men.

North Coast

Three excellent sandy bathing bays cluster round the most northerly headland beneath the walls of Fort Château à l'Étoc (1854), now converted into private flats: **Saye Bay**, nearly symmetrical in shape; **Arch Bay**, named after the tunnel through which the carts collecting seaweed reached the shore; **Corblets Bay**, overlooked by Fort Corblets (1855), now a private house with a splendid view.

Mannez Garenne

The low-lying northern end of the island, known as Mannez Garenne (Warren), is dominated by the remains of a German observation tower.

Quesnard Lighthouse

Guided tour (weather permitting) Easter–Sept Sat–Sun and bank holidays. £2. Steep steps; children under 1m/3.3ft in height are not permitted to ascend. 01481 823 077 (lighthouse attendant) or 01481 823 737 (Tourist Information Centre).

Built in 1912, it stands 37m/121ft high and casts its beam nearly 27.5km/17mi. From the lantern platform there is a magnificent **view**★ of the coast and the Race and, on a clear day, of the nuclear power station on the French coast. Many ships have come to grief on this coast. Three forts command the coastline: Les Homeaux Florains (1858), now in ruins, was approached by a causeway; Fort Quesnard, on the east side of Cats Bay, and Fort Houmet Herbe, another offshore fort reached by a causeway, were built in 1853.

Longis Bay

The retreating tide reveals a broad stretch of sand backed by a German tank trap which provides excellent shelter for sunbathing. The shallow bay was the island's natural harbour from prehistoric times until it silted up early in the 18C. Traces of an Iron Age settlement were discovered at **Les Huguettes** in 1968; the finds are displayed in the Alderney Society's Museum. Various relics indicate the existence of a Roman naval base protected by a fort (c. 2C–4C AD).

Raz Island

A causeway, which is covered at high tide, runs out to Raz Island in the centre of Longis Bay. The fort (1853) has been partially restored and there is a fine **view** of Essex Castle and Hanging Rock *(to the southwest)*.

The Nunnery

This building, parts of which date to the 4C and which is thought to be the oldest on the island, stands on a rectangular site enclosed within a 5m/16ft wall. John Chamberlain converted it to his use when he became governor in 1584. It was named by British soldiers garrisoned there in the late 18C. It is now private dwellings owned by the States of Alderney.

Essex Castle
The first fort on Essex Hill overlooking Longis Bay was begun in 1546 by Henry VIII but abandoned in 1553. It was razed in 1840, when the present structure was built, to be used first as a barracks and then as a military hospital; it is now private property. Governor John Le Mesurier started a farm to feed the garrison at the Nunnery and called it Essex Farm; the name ascended the hill to the castle.

Hanging Rock
The tilt of the 15m/49ft column projecting from the cliff face is said to have been caused by the people of Guernsey trying to tow Alderney away.

Cliff Walk
From Haize around to Giffoine there is a magnificent walk served by frequent paths running inland back to St Anne. The view of the steep cliffs plunging into the rock-strewn sea is spectacular.

Cachalière
A path leads down past the old quarry to an abandoned pier. From here the rocks of **L'Étac de la Quoire** can be reached at low water.

Telegraph Bay★
Access to the tower is by a path and steps, which are not recommended as they are steep and difficult. Beware being cut off from the base of the steps by the rising tide.

The Telegraph Tower (1811), which provided communication with Jersey and Guernsey, has given its name to the bay below. Except at high tide, there is excellent bathing, sheltered from all but a south wind, and a fine view of La Nache and Fourquie rocks.

Tête de Judemarre
The headland provides a fine **view** of the rock-bound coast and of the islands of Guernsey, Herm and Sark.

Vallée des Trois Vaux★
This deep cleft is in fact three valleys meeting on a shingle beach.

Giffoine
From the cliff it is possible to see the birds on their nests in the gannet colony on Les Étacs. The remains of a German coastal battery crown the headland above Hannaine Bay, where sandy spits between the rocks provide reasonable bathing. Fine **view** of Burhou, Ortac and the Casquets *(north)*.

Clonque Bay★
A path descends the gorse and heather-clad slope above the attractive sweep of the bay. A causeway runs out to Fort Clonque (1855), now flats. Two causeways enabled the *vraicing* carts to descend to the beds of seaweed.

Just south of Fort Tourgis (1855), at the northern end of the bay, is the best-preserved burial chamber on the island, **Roc à l'Épine**, which consists of a capstone supported by two upright stones. Alnerney once had many such megaliths, which seem to have been destroyed when the Victorian fortifications were built.

Saline Bay
The shore, exposed to heavy seas so that bathing can be hazardous, is commanded by Fort Doyle, now a youth centre; beyond lies **Crabby Bay** in the lee of Fort Grosnez.

Burhou Island
For permission to spend the night, contact the Harbour Office. 01481 822 620. £20 per night; bring water. Closed 15 Mar–Jul (breeding season). A tour boat makes trips around the island and reefs daily. McAllister's Wet Fish Shop, Victoria St. 01481 823 666.

The island, which lies northwest across The Swinge (about 2km/1mi), is riddled with rabbit warrens and supports large colonies of puffins, razorbills, gannets and storm petrels as well as other seabirds. A hut provides simple accommodation for an overnight stay for bird watching.

Guernsey★

Less sophisticated than Jersey, its larger neighbour, Guernsey has its own particular charm: a slower tempo, the Regency elegance of the capital St Peter Port, the proximity of other islands – Sark, Herm and Jethou. Since World War II its main sources of income have been tourism, offshore finance, insurance and tomatoes.

- **Population:** 61 029.
- **Michelin Map:** 503.
- **Info:** North Esplanade, St Peter Port, GY1 2LQ Guernsey. ☎01481 723 552. www.visitguernsey.com.
- **Location:** Guernsey is the second largest of the Channel Islands (63sq km/24sq mi). The south coast, higher, rocky and ragged, contrasts with the sandy bays of the rest of the coast.
- **Don't Miss:** A stroll down the streets of St Peter Port, a swim in Côbo Bay, and the panoramic view from Icart Point in the south.
- **Timing:** You'll need a half-day at St Peter Port, plus a day or two to tour the island by car or bicycle, with time for swimming, of course.
- **Kids:** The Folk Museum; the Aquarium has tortoises and tropical fish.

VICTOR HUGO'S EXILE

Hauteville House★

38 Hauteville. Guided tours (1hr) May–Sept Mon–Sat 10am–4pm; Apr noon–4pm. £4. ☎01481 721 911.

Victor Hugo was exiled from his native France for political reasons in 1851. After time in Brussels and Jersey, he bought this great white house in 1856.

During his 14 years' residence Hugo redecorated the interior, doing much of the work himself. The result is certainly eccentric: mirrors are placed so as to enhance the effect of various features. Hugo used to work on his poems and novels standing at a small table in the **Glass Room** on the third floor overlooking the sea. From the **Look-out** where he sometimes slept, he could see the house up the road *(La Fallue at 1 Beauregard Lane)* into which his faithful mistress, Juliette Drouot, settled in November 1856. In April 1864 she moved down the road *(no 20 Hauteville)*.

Candie Gardens

Splendid gardens laid out in 1898 and recently renovated extend below the museum and the Priaulx Library.

ST PETER PORT★★

The island capital is built on the east coast overlooking an anchorage protected from high seas by Herm and Sark. The medieval town by the shore was rebuilt after bombardment during the Civil War (1642–46).

Profits from privateering in the late 18C produced a delightful Regency town. Guernsey's popularity as a tourist destination was assured when Queen Victoria visited in 1846.

As you walk up Market Street, to the right is the covered market, comprising Les Halles with the Assembly Rooms above, completed in 1782. Opposite is the Doric-style meat market (1822). Les Arcades, 1830 *(on the left)*, is very handsome despite the loss of the final bay. The Fish Market was finished in 1877. Finally, the Vegetable Market was constructed in 1879.

The large modern harbour bustles with car and passenger ferries, fishing

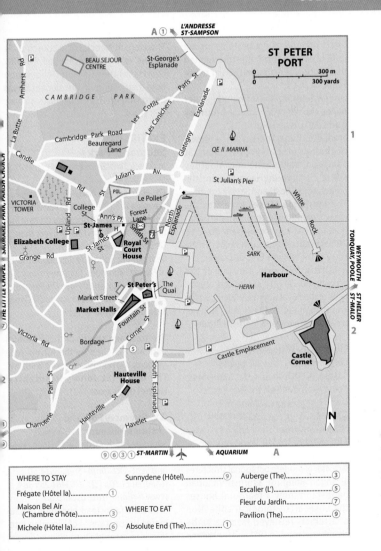

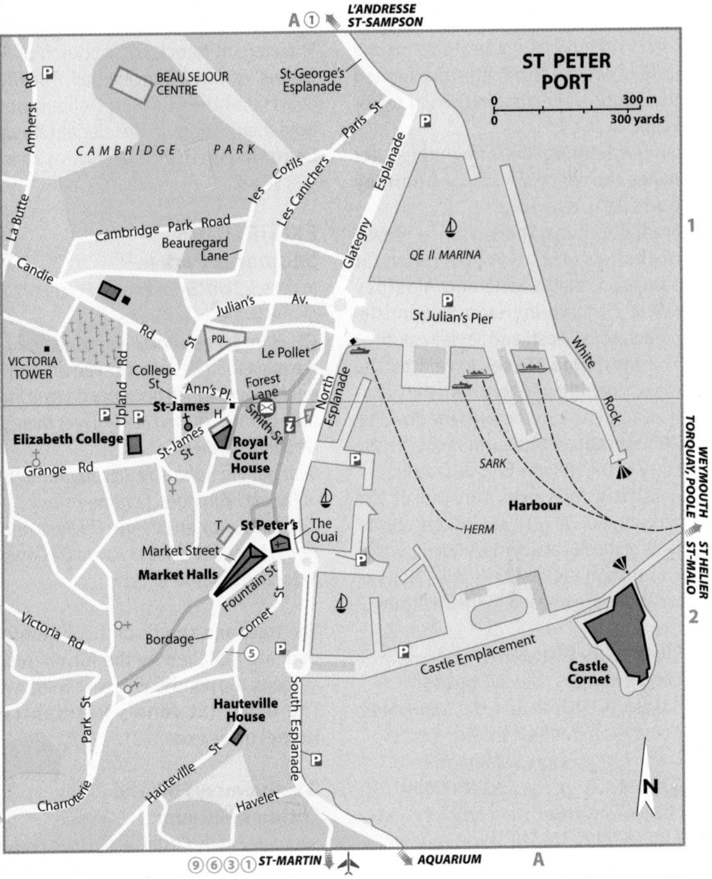

WHERE TO STAY
Frégate (Hôtel la)........①
Maison Bel Air (Chambre d'hôte)........③
Michele (Hôtel la)........⑥
Sunnydene (Hôtel)........⑨

WHERE TO EAT
Absolute End (The)........①
Auberge (The)........③
Escalier (L')........⑤
Fleur du Jardin........⑦
Pavilion (The)........⑨

boats and private yachts. Stroll out to White Rock or visit the castle for a fine **view** of the town, the harbour and the neighbouring islands.

The Town Church, as **St Peter's**★ is known, was begun by William the Conqueror in 1048, and completed around 1475. The nave and west door are part of the original Norman structure, which doubled as a fort.

Elizabeth College was founded in 1563 by Elizabeth I. The Mock Tudor-style building dates from 1826–29.

SIGHTS

Castle Cornet★

Allow 2hr. Open Apr–Oct daily 10am–5pm (the 4 museums have staggered hours). £7.25; joint ticket with Guernsey Museum and Fort Grey: £10; entry after 4pm £1. Nearby. 01481 721 657 (castle); 01481 726 518 (Guernsey Museum). www.museums.guernsey.net.

An exhibition in the Main Guard relates the **Story of Castle Cornet** from prehistoric to present times. The original castle (c. 1206) was reinforced under Elizabeth I and again under Victoria. The castle suffered its greatest misfortune in 1672 when a lightning strike ignited the gunpowder store in the old tower keep.

On the Saluting Platform in the outer bailey the ceremony of the **noonday gun** takes place daily.

From the citadel there is a fine **view**★ of the harbour and town *(west)*, St Sampson, Vale Castle and Alderney *(35km/21.7mi north)*, Herm, Sark and the French coast *(east)* and Jersey *(south)*.

The **Maritime Museum** relates the island's maritime history from the Gallo-Roman period to the present day. The **201 Squadron Museum** recounts the story of the island's RAF squadron.

A **Militia Museum**, housed in the hospital building (1746), contains artefacts of the Royal Guernsey Militia, which was disbanded in 1939. Collections of weapons are housed in the **Armoury**.

Guernsey Museum

Candie Gardens, late-19C pleasure garden. Open Apr–Oct 10am–5pm; Nov–Dec and Feb–Mar 10am–4pm. Living history show 11.15am Thu. Closed 25–26 Dec. £4.50; joint ticket with Castle Cornet and Fort Grey £10. 01481 726 518. www.museum.guernsey.net.

A cluster of modern octagonal structures arranged alongside a former Victorian bandstand (now a tearoom) houses the Lukis archaeological collection of artefacts retrieved from La Varde chambered tomb in 1811 and the Wilfred Carey Collection of paintings, prints and ceramics.

St James' Concert and Assembly Hall

College St. Consult website for programmes. Box office: 01481 711 361. www.stjames.gg.

Royal Court House

Open Sept–Jul Mon–Fri 9.30am–12.30pm, 2.30–4.30pm. Parliament: debates last Wed and Thu of month (except Dec, when 2nd Wed of month). Details of debates available from the Greffe. No charge. 01481 725 277.

The elegant Neoclassical church of **St James'** is now a concert hall. The law courts and the States of Deliberation hold their sittings in the elegant **Royal Court House** (1792); its archives go back 400 years.

EXCURSIONS

Saumarez Park★

In Castel, 3km/2mi NW of St Peter Port.

From St Peter Port head west along the main road (St Julian's Avenue). Stay on this road, which becomes College St then Grange Rd then Les Gravees then De Beauvoir then Rohais.
Bear right at Rohais de Bas, slightly left at Rue des Varendes. Continue along L'Aumone, stay on La Haye Du Puits as it turns right, take a left at Route De Côbo to to reach Saumarez Park.

The trees and shrubs of this beautiful park are matched by the formal rose gardens; the pond is alive with wildfowl. The house **(St John's Residential Home)** dates from 1721.

Guernsey Folk and Costume Museum

Saumarez Park, Castel. Open daily May–Aug 9.30am–5.30pm, Mar–Apr and Sept–Oct 10am–5pm. £4.50 (children £1.50). P. 01481 255 384. www.national trust-gsy.org.gg.

Inside the farmstead buildings of Saumarez House a series of Victorian interiors is re-created. Outbuildings display items from the **Langlois Collection of Agricultural Implements**.

Parish Church

From St Peter Port take the main road (St Julian's Avenue) uphill opposite the harbour; continue straight past the St Pierre Park Hotel on the left, and turn left down Castle Hill/Les Rohais de Haut. The church is on the right before the crossroads.

Early documents list the castle's 12C church of St Mary (**Ste-Marie-du-Castel** or Our Lady of Deliverance) as belonging to the abbey of Mont-St-Michel in 1155;

before then, the site may have had a pre-Christian sanctuary and Roman fort.
Fine **views** extend to the coast and across to Vale Church.

St Andrew

From St Peter Port take the main road (St Julian's Avenue) uphill opposite the harbour; bear left onto Queen's Road and continue straight onto Mount Row/Le Vauquiedor/Mauxmarquis Road, after passing the church (left) turn left to the German Underground Hospital (sign).

German Underground Hospital and Ammunition Store

La Vassalerie Rd. Allow 20min. Open Apr–Oct 10am–noon, 2–4pm (last entry 1hr before closing). Limited opening Mar and Nov, check with Information Centre. £4 (children £2). 01481 238 205.
The hospital took nearly three and a half years to build and consists of a series of tunnels excavated down into the granite bedrock. Today the miles of hollow corridors and interlocking wards are eerily vacant, with some departments (operating room, store, etc.) open.

Return to the main road, turn left and drive west; as the road descends, turn right (sign) to the Little Chapel and Guernsey Clockmakers.

Little Chapel★

Les Vauxbelets, 1km/0.6mi from Underground Hospital. Allow 20min.
The Unknown Little Jewel is a model of the grotto and shrine at Lourdes built in 1925 by Brother Deodat, a Salesian monk from Les Vauxbelets College.

DRIVING TOURS

1 CLOS DU VALLE: ST PETER PORT TO VALE CHURCH

8km/5mi – allow half a day.

Until 1806 the northern part of Guernsey, known as Clos du Valle, was cut off by the Braye du Valle – a tidal channel of mudflats and salt-marsh. The channel was filled in and the reclaimed land (121ha/300 acres) is now covered with glasshouses.

Leave St Peter Port by the coast road (Glategny Esplanade) north towards St Sampson. Turn left in Belle Grève Bay onto Le Grand Bouet and then take the second right.

The ruined medieval **Château des Marais** crowns a low knoll: it was first used in the Bronze Age, protected by the surrounding marshy ground. The castle was refortified in the 18C.
Guernsey's second port, St Sampson, lies at the eastern end of the Braye du Valle.
St Sampson, the oldest church in Guernsey, was allegedly built where the saint came ashore (c. 550), either from Llantwit Major in South Wales or from Dol in Brittany. Its churchyard overlooks the disused Longue Hougue Quarry.

From the bridge take Vale Avenue north and bear left onto the main road (Route du Braye). Oatlands Craft Centre is located opposite a garden centre on Gigandis Road.

Oatlands Craft Centre

Braye Rd, St Sampson. Open daily 9.30am–5pm. . 01481 244 282.
An old brick farmstead and its thatched outbuildings arranged around a courtyard house a craft centre.

Vale Castle★

The medieval castle, now in ruins, was built on the site of an Iron Age hillfort (c. 600 BC) on the only high point in Clos du Valle. There is a fine **view** inland, along the east coast and out to sea to the reef, Alderney *(north)*, Herm and Sark *(west)*, and Jersey *(south)*.
Bordeaux Harbour provides mooring for fishing boats and the only safe swimming in the area.

Follow the main road north; as it curves gently left, turn right onto the minor road; bear left; park by the

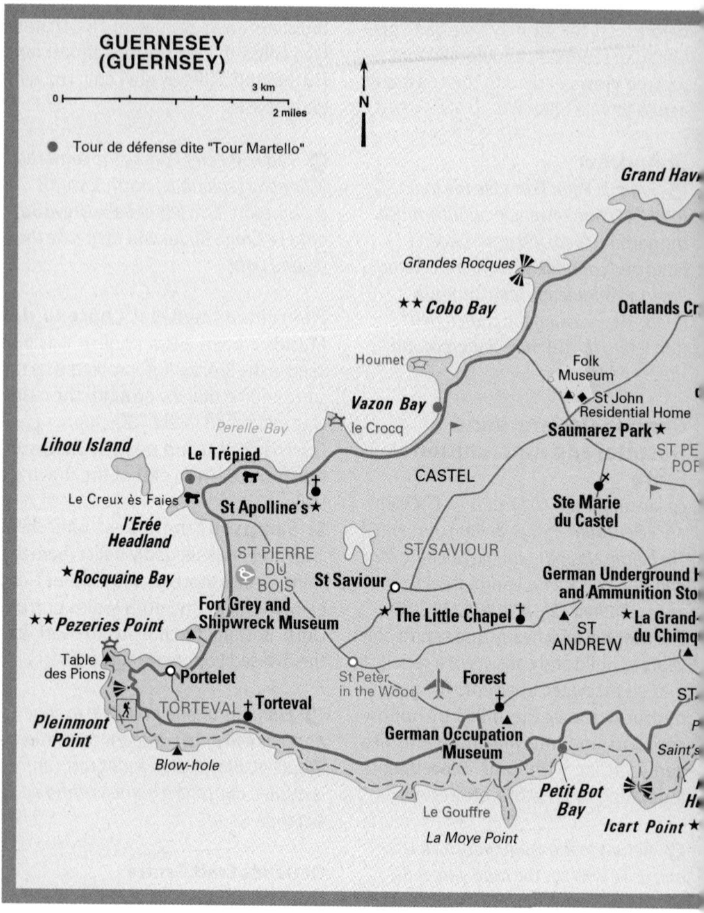

dilapidated glasshouses (right) opposite the passage tomb.

Dehus Dolmen

Open daily sunrise–sunset. Light switch on the left as you enter.

This passage grave has four side chambers covered by seven capstones: crouch down to see Le Gardien du Tombeau, the figure of an archer *(switch for spotlight)*.

Several minor roads meander north to the coast.

The Beaucette Quarry Marina was created by a well-placed blast in an old quarry, opening a breach to the sea.

From Fort Doyle there is a **view★** of the Casquets reef and Alderney *(north)*, the French coast, Herm and Sark *(west)*.

Fort Le Marchant is the most northerly point in Guernsey. It offers a fine view, particularly of L'Ancresse Common, the only extensive open space on the island, used for recreation, and of L'Ancresse Bay, popular for bathing and surfing.

La Varde Dolmen is the largest passage grave in Guernsey. **Les Fouaillages** burial ground is 7 000 years old.

St-Michel-du-Valle Church was consecrated in 1117 on the site of an earlier chapel dedicated to St Magloire, who with St Sampson brought Christianity to Guernsey in the 6C.

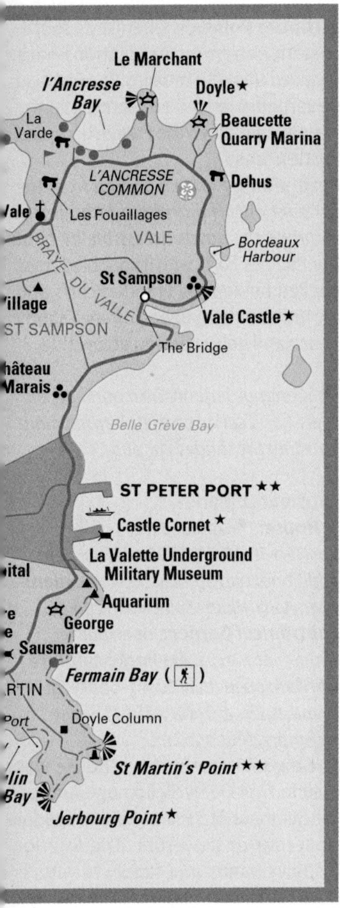

2 WEST COAST: LE GRAND HAVRE TO PEZERIES POINT

11km/7mi – allow about half a day.

The **Grand Havre**, an ample inlet at the west end of the Braye du Valle, is best admired from the Rousse headland with its tower and jetty. A more extensive horizon is visible from the German gun battery on the granite headland, the **Grandes Rocques**.

Côbo Bay★★ is a charming combination of sand and rocks. *Swimming is safe.* The huge beach between Fort Houmet *(north)* and Fort le Crocq *(south)* at Vazon Bay is excellent for swimming.

St Apolline's Chapel★ in the Grande-Rue at Perelle received its charter in 1394. It is decorated with a **fresco** *(light switch)* of *The Last Supper*. The original dedication to Ste Marie de la Perelle was changed in 1452 to St Apolline, a popular saint at the time.

Le Trépied Dolmen burial chamber at Le Cationoc was excavated in 1840 by Frederic Lukis, whose finds are in the Guernsey Museum. In past centuries the site was used for witches' Sabbaths.

The tall defensive tower on the L'Erée Headland is called Fort Saumarez. To the south stands **Le Creux ès Faies Dolmen**, a passage grave. Excavation has produced items dating from 2000 BC to 1800 BC.

In 1114 a priory was founded on Lihou Island and dedicated to Our Lady of the Rock (now in ruins). On the west coast a 30m/98.5ft rock pool provides excellent bathing *(acessible by causeway at low tide; check tide tables before setting out and take note of the time for returning to the main island)*.

The grand sweep of **Rocquaine Bay**★ is interrupted by the Cup and Saucer, originally a medieval fort. It is painted white as a navigation mark.

Fort Grey Maritime Museum

Open Apr–Oct daily 10am–5pm. £3. 01481 265 036. www.museums.guernsey.net.

A small museum is dedicated to the many shipwrecks in Guernsey waters.

The picturesque harbour of Portelet, full of fishing boats, is backed by the houses of the Hanois Lighthouse keepers. Nearby is the **Table des Pions**, where the *pions* or footmen of the Chevauchée de St Michel ate their lunch sitting at the grass table with their feet in a trench.

Pezeries Point★★ is the most westerly point in all the Channel Islands, a remote and unfrequented place. The fort was built in the Napoleonic era.

3 SOUTHERN CLIFFS: PLEINMONT POINT TO ST PETER PORT

26km/16mi – allow half a day.

These cliffs along the south coast and round to St Peter Port provide some of the most wild and dramatic scenery in the island (*beware the cliff face, which can be unstable and dangerous*); a footpath runs from the western end to the town.

The headland at **Pleinmont Point** provides an extensive **view**: along the southern cliffs *(east)*, out to the Hanois Lighthouse and its reefs *(west)*, across Rocquaine Bay to Lihou Island *(north)*.

A footpath stretches all along the clifftops, past all the watch houses before coming out by the Aquarium in St Peter Port. **La Moye Point**, the smallest of the three promontories on the south coast, is wild and beautiful.

German Occupation Museum

In the parish of Forest, south of the church. Allow 1hr. Open daily Apr–Oct 10am–5pm (last entry 4pm). £4. P. *01481 238 205.*

The museum displays artefacts from the Nazi occupation: weaponry, uniforms, vehicles, personal effects, etc.

Petit Bot Bay, which has good bathing and sand at low tide, lies at the foot of a green valley guarded by a defensive tower (1780).

Return uphill to the main road; turn right down rue de la Villette, which turns inland to rejoin the valley leading down to Moulin Huet Bay.

Icart Point★★ is the highest and most southerly headland with very fine **views** of the coast. On the east side is **Saint's Bay**, a favourite mooring for fishermen. A water lane runs down the valley, one of the most beautiful in Guernsey, to Moulin Huet Bay, where the stream plunges down the cliff face to the sea. Both this bay and its eastern neighbour are good for bathing but **Petit Port** is superior.

St Martin parish in southeast Guernsey and is principally residential. Near the car park at **St Martin's Point★★** there is a magnificent view down to the lighthouse on the point, north up the coast to St Peter Port and seaward to the other islands.

Follow the path along the cliff.

Jerbourg Point★ is Guernsey's south-eastern extremity: excavations have revealed Neolithic remains. The Château de Jerbourg protected islanders in the Middle Ages when the French occupied Castle Cornet.

Fermain Bay *(access on foot from the car park or cliff path from Jerbourg; in summer, the bay is accessible by boat from St Peter Port)*, with its pebbled cove, backed by densely wooded cliffs and an 18C defensive tower, offers a sandy beach and good bathing at low tide.

Continue east on the main road; on a left-hand curve, turn left beyond main gate into the shaded car park.

Sausmarez Manor

House: *guided tours daily Apr–Oct 10.30am, 11.30am; Jun–Sept additional tour 2pm. £6.90.* ***Garden:*** *open daily 10am–5pm. No charge.* ***Subtropical Garden::*** *open daily 10am–5pm. £5.* ***Art Park Sculpture Garden:*** *open daily 10am–5pm year round. £5. 01481 235 571. www.sausmarezmanor.co.uk.*

The elegant Queen Anne house was built in 1714–18 by Sir Edmund Andros, the Seigneur of Sausmarez and former Governor of New York. The interior displays handsome family furniture, portraits and mementoes of the family's 750 years on the island.

The wooded **grounds** are planted with tall bamboo and camellias and include a **sculpture park**.

A modern luxury housing estate occupies the site of Fort George, built from 1782 to 1812 and, used bythe Luftwaffe as an early warning service, destroyed by Allied bombers the day before D-Day.

At the gate into St Martin's churchyard stands a Stone Age menhir, **La Grand'mère du Chimquière★** carved to represent a female figure. The church itself dates from 1225 to 1250; the south porch was added in the 1520s.

Return to the main road; turn right to Jerbourg.

La Valette Underground Military Museum
Open Mar–mid-Nov daily 10am–5pm. £4.50. 01481 722 300.
The museum occupies five tunnels that were excavated to hold fuel tanks for refuelling U-boats and displays apparel belonging to the Guernsey Militia, German artefacts and mementoes of the Occupation.

Guernsey Aquarium
Open daily 10am–6pm (Sun and bank holidays 5.30pm). Closed 1 Jan, 25–26 Dec. £4.50 (children £3.50). 01481 723 301.
Installed in a disused tunnel is a series of water tanks housing a variety of aquatic creatures.

ADDRESSES

Coin ranges for the Channel Islands are derived from approximate conversions of the euro coin ranges on the cover flap into Pound Sterling (£).

STAY

Zest – *Lefebvre St. 01481 723 052. Closed 2 weekends Jan, Sat.* Nestled in the town centre with simple décor and intimate alcoves, this place has a good selection of modern cuisine.

Hôtel La Frégate – *Les Cotils. 01481 724 624. www.lafregatehotel.com. 22 rooms. . Restaurant.* Enjoy a panoramic view over the port and St Peter at this high-end boutique hotel. Peaceful site and friendly welcome.

ST-MARTINS

Hôtel La Michèle – *Les Hubits. 01481 238 065. www.lamichelehotel.com. Closed late autumn–early spring. 16 rooms. . Restaurant (no lunch).* Near Fermain Bay, comfortable, well-equipped rooms. Relaxing lounge, garden, terrace and swimming pool.

Sunnydene Country Hotel – *r. des Marettes. 01481 236 870. www.sunnydenecountryhotel.co.uk. Closed Oct–Easter. 20 rooms. .* Comfortable family lounge, swimming pool and pretty green space. Rooms in the main house or in an outbuilding set in the park.

FOREST

Chambre d'hôte Maison Bel Air – *Le Chêne, 9.6km/6mi W. 01481 238 503. www.maisonbelair.com. Closed Dec–Feb. 6 rooms. .* This smart Victorian guesthouse overlooks Petit Bot Bay. Spacious rooms.

EAT

The Absolute End – *Longstore, St Peter Port, GY1 2BG, N. 01481 723 822. Closed Jan and Sun.* A favourite with locals for its excellent seafood. Comfortable bar upstairs.

L'Escalier – *6 Tower Hill. 01481 710088. www.lafregatehotel.com. 22 rooms. . Restaurant.* This intimate, Anglo-French restaurant is just a short walk from the town centre. Ice cream, bread and pasta are made on the premises. Worth a detour.

CASTEL

Fleur du Jardin – *GY5 7JT Kings Mills. 01481 257 996. www.fleurdujardin.com.* This award-winning restaurant in a 15C house serves contemporary cuisine at reasonable prices. 15 bedrooms.

ST SAVIOUR

The Pavilion – *Le Gron. 01481 264 165. Closed Jan, Mon, Christmas.* This restaurant serves. delicious seafood.

ST MARTINS

The Auberge – *Jerbourg Rd. 01481 238 485. www.theauberge.gg. Closed 24–26, 31 Dec.* From the garden and the terrace, enjoy a splendid view over the sea and the neighbouring islands. Modern cuisine.

TRANSPORT

By car – Guernsey's roads are often very narrow. Behind the tourist office, **Economy Cars** rents tiny cars well suited to Guernsey's roads (£30 a day).
By bus – www.buses.gg
By bike – www.guernseyhire.co.uk

Herm

The broad sandy beaches on Herm's north coast contrast with the steep cliffs at the southern end of the island. Herm has neither roads nor cars, and walkers enjoy a profusion of wild flowers, dunes, trees and cliffs. The deep fringe of rocks offshore is most impressive at low tide. South-west, across a narrow channel, the islet of Jethou (private property leased from the British Crown) rises like a hillock in the sea, home of seabirds.

- **Population:** 97.
- **Michelin Map:** 503.
- **Info:** Administration Office, Herm Island, Guernsey GY1 3HR. ☎01481 722 377. www.herm-island.com.
- **Location:** Herm (2.4km/1.5mi long by 0.8km/0.5mi wide) lies halfway between Guernsey and Sark.
- **Don't Miss:** The countryside from the Grand Monceau.
- **Timing:** You need one day to enjoy the island.

A BIT OF HISTORY

Prehistoric tombs made of granite slabs found in the north of the island are evidence of human settlement in 2000 BC. In the 6C Christianity was introduced by St Magloire, who founded monasteries in Sark and Jersey. In the 17C pirates used the island as a base but

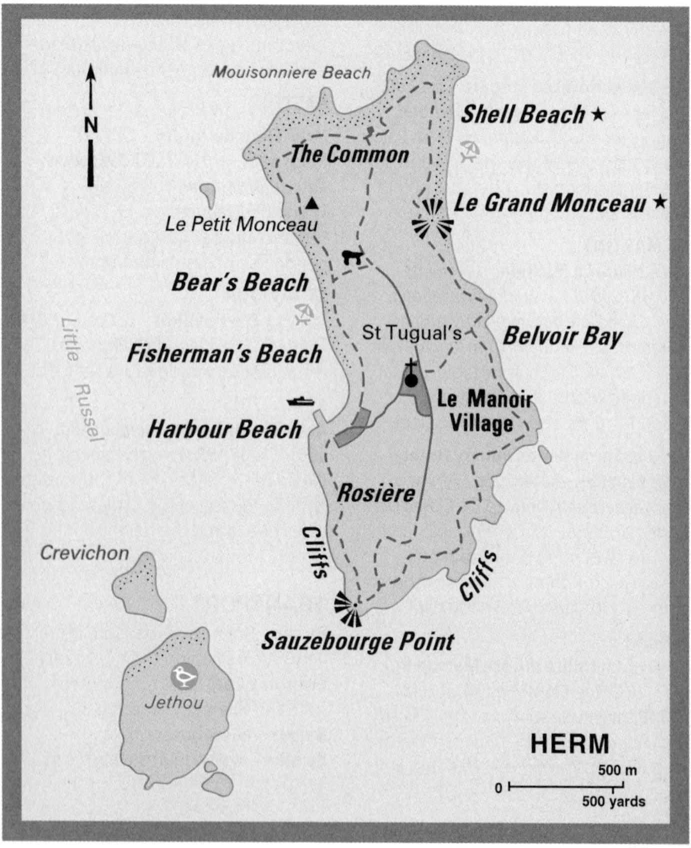

it remained largely deserted. In 1947 the Crown sold Herm to Guernsey and in 1949 Major Peter Wood and his wife became tenant. In 1987 the lease was transferred to their family company. The island has been developed for tourism, maintaining its great natural beauty.

VISIT

Le Manoir Village

A surfaced road climbs up to the tiny hamlet next to the 18C manor house with its square tower. **St Tugual's Chapel** was built in the 11C.

The northern end of the island is composed of sand dunes, known as The Common, covered by prickly vegetation and fringed by sandy beaches popular in summer (Bear's Beach, Mouisonnière Beach, **Shell Beach** so called because it is composed of millions of shells deposited by the Gulf Stream). From the hillock of **Le Grand Monceau★** there is a splendid panoramic view of the sands, the rocks and the islands. North on the horizon lies Alderney; to the east the French coast. **Le Petit Monceau** beyond is a smaller hillock, overlooking the Bear's Beach.

The southern end of the island is composed of steep granite cliffs dropping sheer into the sea. In **Belvoir Bay** nestles a small sheltered bathing beach. The southern headland, Sauzebourge Point, provides a view of Jethou (southwest) with Guernsey in the background (west) and Sark (southeast).

ADDRESSES

STAY

The White House Hotel – *GY1 3HR Herm. ℘01481 722 159. www.herm-island.com/hotels. Closed Oct–Mar. 40 rooms.*
Splendid views of the island's harbour and beach. Choice of rooms in the main house or in the cottages, and of formal or informal dining. Garden with a summer swimming pool.

Jersey★★

In addition to the delights of the beaches and the countryside, visitors to Jersey can enjoy a wide range of more sophisticated pleasures – theatre and cinema, cabaret and floor shows, discotheques and disco-bars.

Victor Hugo, who spent three years in Jersey (1852–55) before moving to Guernsey, was enchanted: "It possesses a unique and exquisite beauty. It is a garden of flowers cradled by the sea. Woods, meadows and gardens seem to mingle with the rocks and reefs in the sea."

- **Population:** 87 186.
- **Michelin Map:** 503.
- **Info:** Liberation Square, St Helier, Jersey JE1 1BB. ℘01534 448 800. www.jersey.com.
- **Location:** Jersey,the largest of the Channel Islands (116sq km/44.7sq mi), lies 19km/12mi W off France's Cotentin Peninsula.
- **Don't Miss:** The walking paths along the north and east coasts.
- **Kids:** The Jersey Zoo; Living Legend recreation park.

A BIT OF HISTORY

The tombs and prehistoric monuments found on the island indicate human habitation between 7 500 and 2 500 BC. The Roman presence was brief, and in the 6C St Helier arrived and established Christianity. The dominant influence is that of the Normans who invaded in the 10C and left a rich heritage of customs and traditions.

After 1204, when King John was forced to cede mainland Normandy to France, the French made repeated attempts to recover the Channel Islands: the last attempt occurred in 1781 when Baron de Rullecourt, a soldier of fortune, landed by night in St Clement's Bay. Under Major Peirson, a young man of 24, the militia and British forces defeated the enemy in the main square in what came to be known as the **Battle of Jersey**; both leaders were mortally wounded.

Famous Sons and Daughters

The most famous name connected with Jersey is **Lillie Langtry** (1853–1929): the Jersey Lily who became an actress and a close friend of Edward VII and captivated British high society with her beauty; she is buried in St Saviour's churchyard.

The fashionable 19C painter, **Sir John Everett Millais** (1829–96), who won acclaim with his painting entitled *Bubbles*, grew up in Jersey and belonged to an old island family. So too did **Elinor Glyn** (1864–1943), who became a novelist and Hollywood scriptwriter.

The well-known French firm which makes Martell brandy was started by **Jean Martell** from St Brelade.

Constitution

Jersey is divided into 12 parishes, which together with two groups of islets, the Minquiers to the south and the Ecréhous to the northeast, make up the Bailiwick of Jersey. The Parliament, known as the States of Jersey, with 53 elected members, is presided over by the Bailiff, who is appointed by the Crown. The three other officers and the Dean of Jersey, an Anglican clergyman, also Crown appointees, may speak in the assembly, but only the 12 Senators, 12 Constables and 29 Deputies, elected to serve for a period of three to six years, may vote.

Economy

Agriculture has long sustained the islanders: wheat and rye, turnips and parsnips, four-horned sheep supplying wool for the famous Jersey stockings and knitwear (17C), apples for cider (18C), table grapes grown under glass and famous Doyenne de Comice pears. The mild climate continues to favour the cultivation of flowers (daffodils, freesias, carnations and lavender) and vegetables for export. Some crops are grown in the open fields, others under glass. Unique to Jersey is the giant cabbage *(Brassica oleracea longata)*, which grows up to 3m/9.84ft tall.

In recent years, lucrative businesses have developed in tourism and financial services, industries driven by competitive young residents who have benefited from excellent local education.

ST HELIER

St Helier is a lively town, the main commercial centre on Jersey and the seat of government, situated in a sheltered position on the south side of the island. The shops in the pedestrian precinct formed by **King and Queen Streets** are a popular attraction for

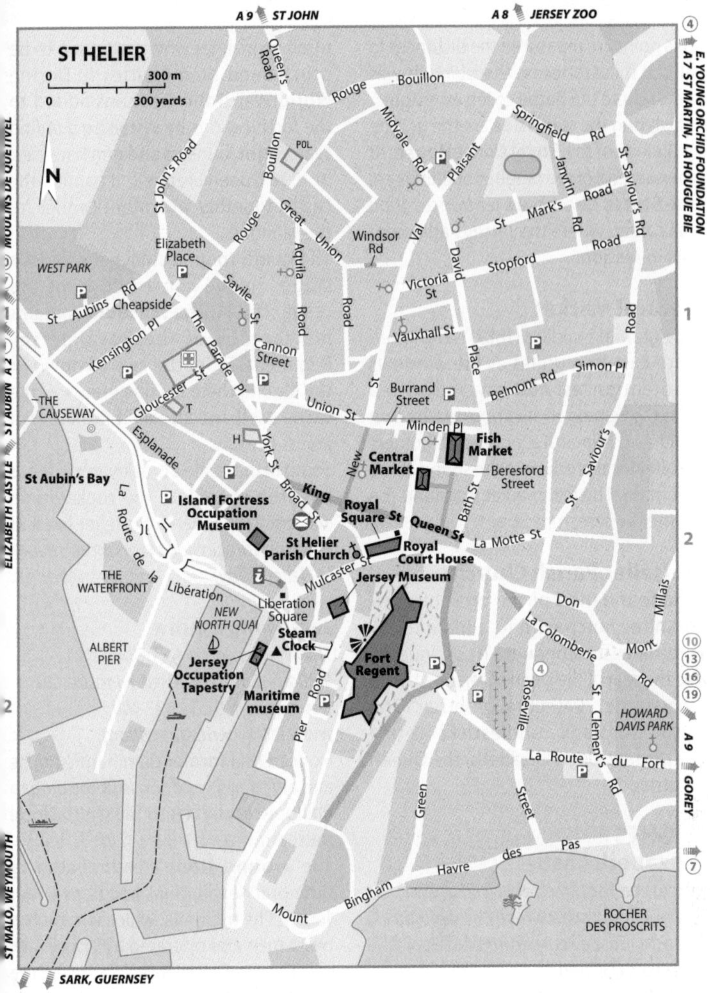

WHERE TO STAY		WHERE TO EAT			
Bonne Vie (Chambre d'hôte la)	4	Bistro Soleil	1	Suma's	13
Caprice (Chambre d'hôte au)	7	Frère (Le)	4	The Jersey Pottery (Garden Restaurant)	16
Moorings (Hôtel)	10	Green Island	7	Village Bistro	19
		Old Court House Inn	10		

visitors to the island. The town is named after St Helier, one of the first Christian missionaries to land in Jersey, who was murdered by pirates after living as a hermit there for 15 years (c. 555). The scant local population was swelled by refugees fleeing the St Bartholomew Day Massacre (1572) and the Revolution (1789) in France.

Royal Square

Royal Court House. Open Sept–Jul: for hours, contact the Visitor Service Centre on Liberation Square. 01534 44880. www.gov.je.

The gilded-lead statue of George II, dressed as a Roman emperor, looks down on this charming small square with its spreading chestnut trees; from this point are measured the distances to all the milestones on the island. It was here where the Battle of Jersey erupted. Bordering the south side are the granite buildings of the **Royal Court House**. At the east end of the range of buildings are the **States Chambers** *(entrance round the corner)* where the Jersey Parliament sits in session.

Central Market

The granite building (1882) is furnished with cast-iron grilles at the windows and entrances, and covered with a glass (perspex) roof supported by iron columns. Beneath it open-stall holders proffer local produce to the sound of the fountain. The fish market is around the corner in Beresford Street.

St Helier Parish Church

The foundation of the present pink-granite church with its square tower pre-dates the Conquest. It continues to be the seat of the Dean of Jersey – hence the epithet "Cathedral of Jersey". The altar cross and candlesticks were a gift from Queen Elizabeth, the Queen Mother.

SIGHTS

Elizabeth Castle

Access on foot by a causeway at low tide (30min); otherwise by amphibious vehicle (Castle Ferry) from West Park Slipway. Open Apr–Oct daily 10am–6pm (last admission 5pm). £8–£10. Guided tour (1hr). 01534 723 971 (Castle). www.jerseyheritagetrust.org.

In the 12C William Fitz-Hamon, one of Henry II's courtiers, founded an abbey on St Helier's Isle in St Aubin's Bay. The castle buildings were completed shortly before Sir Walter Raleigh was appointed governor (1600) and called Fort Isabella Bellissima in honour of Queen Elizabeth I. It was considerably reinforced during the Civil War (1642–1646) while occupied by Royalists who, after resisting the repeated assaults from Parliamentary forces on the island, surrendered after a 50-day siege. The young Prince of Wales stayed here when fleeing from England in 1646, and again three years later when returning to be proclaimed King Charles II. During World War II the Germans added to the fortifications by installing a roving searchlight, bunkers and gun batteries. In 1996 Queen Elizabeth II handed the castle, together with Mont Orgueil, to the islanders.

The guard room displays the various stages in the construction of the castle. The **Militia Museum** contains mementoes of the Royal Jersey Regiment. From the keep, known as the Mount, there is a fine **view**★ of the castle itself and also of St Aubin's Fort across the bay.

South of the castle a breakwater extends past the chapel on the rock where, according to legend, St Helier lived as a hermit *(procession on or about 16 July, St Helier's Day)*.

Jersey Museum★

The Weighbridge. Open daily 9.30am–5pm. Closed 1 Jan, 24–26 Dec. £7. 01534 633 300. www.jerseyheritagetrust.org.

Housed in a former merchant's house and adjoining warehouse belonging to Philippe Nicolle (1769–1835) is the local museum.

The **ground-floor** area is shared by temporary exhibitions and films about Jersey. The treadmill, which was turned by 12 men and operated a pepper mill, was used in St Helier prison during the 19C. By the stairs is displayed a number of silver toilet articles from the set which accompanied Lillie Langtry on her travels.

On the **first floor**, the history of the island from the Stone Age to the present is unfurled as a series of tableaux.

The **second floor** displays the Barreau-Le Maistre collection of fine art with paintings, drawings and watercolours by local artists or of topographical interest: Sir John Everett Millais PRA (1829–96), PJ Ouless (1817–85), "the Jersey Turner" J Le Capelain (1812–48) and the illustrator Edmund Blampied (1886–1966). Works by **Sir Francis Cook** (1907–78) bequeathed to the Jersey Heritage Trust are on permanent display in their own

gallery, a converted Methodist Chapel, in Augrès *(A 8, Route de Trinité).*
The **third-floor** rooms re-create domestic interiors (1861) typical of a middle-class Jersey family.

New North Quay

The most prominent landmark is the world's largest **steam clock** (11m/36ft tall), modelled on a traditional paddle steamer of a type that once shuttled between the islands and Southampton. It was inaugurated in August 1997 as part of the development of the St Helier waterfront.

Maritime Museum and Jersey Occupation Tapestry

New North Quay. Open daily 9.30am–5pm. Closed 1 Jan, 24-26 Dec. £7.50. 01534 633 372. www.jerseyheritagetrust.org.
Installed in converted 19C warehouses, the Jersey **Maritime Museum** has changing displays relating to the fishing, shipbuilding and trading industries and to piracy.
The **Jersey Occupation Tapestry** comprises 12 panels (2x1m/6x3ft) illustrating the story of the Occupation of Jersey from the outbreak of war to the Liberation: each scene, based on archive photographs and contemporary film footage, has been embroidered by a separate Parish.

Fort Regent

Access by escalators in Pier Road. Open summer Mon–Fri 6.30am–9.30pm (hours vary for facilities), Sat–Sun 8.15am–5pm, bank holidays 10am–5pm; for winter hours, contact Visitor Services Centre. P. Prices depend on activity. Closed 1 Jan, 25–26 Dec. 01534 449 600. www.gov.je.
The massive fortifications of Fort Regent were built to protect Jersey from invasion by Napoleon. Within, topped by a shallow white dome, is a modern leisure centre operated by the government and providing a variety of sports facilities and entertainment: swimming pool, badminton, squash, table tennis, snooker, play area for children, puppet theatre, exhibitions, aquarium, and audio-visual shows on the history and culture of the island. It is also home to the Jersey Signal Station. The rampart walk provides splendid **views★** of the town and St Aubin's Bay (west).

Jersey Pass

2-, 4- and 6-day passes give you free entry to 11 of the most popular museums and attractions for £32–£59. www.jerseypass.com.

EXCURSIONS

Jersey Zoo★★

From St Helier take A 8 N to Mont de la Trinité; at rue Asplet turn right onto B 31 towards Trinity Church; this road soon becomes rue des Picots passing in front of the zoo (right). Open daily summer 9.30am–6pm; winter 9.30am–5pm (last entry 1hr before closing). Closed 25 Dec. £12.90. Guided tour (1hr, until 3pm) by arrangement. P. 01534 860 000. www.durrellwildlife.org.
The Durrell Wildlife Conservation Trust, with its headquarters at Jersey Zoo (Les Augrès Manor), was founded by the naturalist **Gerald Durrell** (1925–95) in 1963 as a unique centre for research and breeding of rare and endangered species. The undulating park (10ha/25acres) provides compatible environments for some 1 000 animals. Exotic species of plants provide the animals with both food and natural cover.
Residents include babirusas from Indonesia, spectacled bears from the forest uplands of Bolivia and Peru (the only bear indigenous to South America), snow leopards and cheetahs, and a long list of birds.
The most popular animals, however, are probably the primates: a dynasty of lowland gorillas descended from the silverback Jambo (1961–92), orangutans from Sumatra and lemurs from Madagascar, marmosets and tamarins

from Brazil, some of which roam freely in the thick shrubbery.

Tortoises, terrapins, snakes, frogs, toads and lizards, happy to lounge in their warmed enclosures among sprigs of flowering orchids, thrive in the **Gaherty Reptile Breeding Centre**.

Eric Young Orchid Foundation★

Victoria Village, Trinity. Even with signs in Victoria village, the Orchid Foundation is difficult to find. Open Wed–Sat 10am–4pm. Closed 1 Jan, 25–26 Dec. £3.50. 01534 861 963. www.ericyoungorchidfoundation.co.uk.

A fabulous show of prize orchids is presented here in a display house. Displays are regularly reorganised to ensure constant shows of species, the groups arranged to allow close study of their distinctive blooms.

Jersey War Tunnels★

5km/3mi W. Les Charrières Malorey, Saint Lawrence, Saint Helier, JE3 1FU. Leave St Helier on St Aubin's Road, at Bel Royal, turn right. Open Feb–Nov daily 10am–6pm (last entry 4.30pm). Closes at 2pm 9 May, 13 Aug, 10 Sept (last entry 12.30pm). £9.85. 01534 860 808. www.jerseywartunnels.com.

This large complex of tunnels is kept as a compelling memorial to the forced labourers (Spaniards, Moroccans, Alsatian Jews, Poles, Frenchmen, Russians) who worked on its construction for three and a half years under the severest conditions. Note that some visitors may find the visit rather harrowing, others may suffer from claustrophobia.

Hohlgangsanlagen 8 was intended as a secure, bomb-proof artillery barracks. In January 1944, still incomplete, it was converted into a hospital equipped with an operating theatre, five 100-bed wards, X-ray room, mortuary, stores, kitchen, staff quarters, etc. Wartime films, archive photographs, newspaper cuttings, letters and memorabilia document the personal suffering and trauma of those caught up in the events.

The **Occupation Walk** opposite the complex leads to an area fortified by anti-aircraft gun positions, crawl trenches, barbed wire entanglements and personnel shelters (leaflet available from the Visitor Centre).

Moulin de Quétivel

Open May–mid-Sept Sat 10am–4pm. £2.50. P. 01534 483 193. www.nationaltrustjersey.org.je.

The **mill** (pre-1309), on a bend in St Peter's Valley, is one of several powered by the rushing water of streams until steam power made them obsolete. During the German Occupation the machinery was restored before being largely destroyed by fire (1969). Since 1979, re-equipped with parts from other disused Jersey mills, Quétivel has ground locally grown grain and produced stone-ground flour for sale.

Living Legend

Take the A 11, St Peter's Valley Road, to the C 112, then follow posted signs. Open Apr–Oct daily 9.30am–5pm, Mar and Nov Sat–Wed 9.30am–5pm. £7.50 (children £5). 01534 485 496. www.jerseyslivinglegend.co.je.

Inside the granite buildings unfurls the entertaining multi-sensory experience that relates the history and myths of Jersey. The time travellers explore a labyrinth of mysterious chambers, make their way through castle towers and across the decks of a Victorian paddle steamer to discover the lives of past islanders and stories told of heroes and villains.

St Peter's Village

On the square is an underground bunker built by the German Organisation Todt in 1942, strategically placed so as to keep surveillance over the airport and access roads to the west of the island.

St Peter's Church

The parish church has a remarkable steeple (37.8m/124ft high); at its apex is a red navigation light used by aircraft coming in to land at the airport nearby. Behind the altar is a reredos by George Tinworth, commissioned in the 1880s from Royal Doulton.

La Hougue Bie★

From St Helier take either A 6 (Route Bagatelle) or A 7 (St Saviour's Hill) NW; at Five Oaks take A 7 (Princes Tower Road) to the entrance to La Hougue Bie (left).

La Hougue Bie Museums

Open 6 Apr–Oct daily 10am–5pm (last entry 4pm). £6.70. P. 01534 633 373. www.jerseyheritagetrust.org.

The tiny park, encircled by trees, is dominated by a high circular mound. Its name may be derived from the old Norse word *haugr* (meaning barrow) and *bie*, a shorthand for Hambye, a Norman lord who in the Middle Ages came to rid Jersey of a dragon that stalked St Lawrence marsh.

During the German occupation, the site was heavily fortified, as it provides an excellent **view** over outlying countryside. *All the following sites are at Hougue Bie.*

Archaeology and Geology Museum

Open mid-Mar–Oct daily 10am–5pm. £5.25. 01534 853 823.

Artefacts displayed were brought to light by local excavations – notably from La Cotte de St Brelade, a sea cave in the Ouaisné headland and the Belle Hougue caves on the north coast: remains of mammoths, objects belonging to Neolithic farmers and hunters, Bronze Age metal objects found in St Lawrence, etc. The geology section presents samples of the various rocks and minerals found on the island.

Neolithic Tomb★

The cruciform passage burial chamber, excavated in 1924, dates from 3500 BC. Similar tombs have been discovered in England and Brittany.

The grave was originally built above ground with upright stones and roofed with granite slabs before being covered by a mound of earth and rubble (12m/40ft). A passage (10m/33ft long) leads to the funeral chamber (3x9m/10x30ft), which is covered with huge capstones (the heaviest weighing 25t). The central granite pillar is a modern addition to support the large capstones which were found to be cracked.

Chapels

The mound is surmounted by two medieval chapels: the **Chapel of Our Lady of the Dawn** (Notre-Dame-de-la-Clarté) dates from the 12C; the altar (late medieval) came from Mont-Orgueil Castle. The abutting **Jerusalem Chapel** was built in 1520 by Dean Richard Mabon after a pilgrimage to Jerusalem. The interior bears traces of frescoes of two archangels.

German Occupation Museum

A German bunker, built in 1942 as a communications centre, houses radio equipment, weapons, medals, original documents (orders and propaganda) and photographs of the period.

DRIVING TOURS

1 FROM ST HELIER TO CORBIÈRE

18km/11mi – allow about 2hr.

From St Helier take A 1 (Route de St Aubin) west.

Millbrook

The Villa Millbrook was once home to Sir Jesse Boot, first Baron Trent of Nottingham, founder of Boots the Chemists, who is buried at St Brelade.

St Matthew's Church

Open Sun–Fri 9am–6pm. P. 01534 502 864.

The **Glass Church**, as it is also known, was unexceptional until 1934 when **René Lalique** (1860–1945), the French specialist in moulded glass, was invited by Lord Trent's widow to redecorate the interior with distinctive **glasswork**★: the entrance doors are made of panels presenting a row of four angels. The flowering lily appears in the windows, screens and in the Lady Chapel. The luminescent, ethereal quality is most apparent at dusk when the lights are switched on.

Follow the main road (Route de La Haule) and then A 1 (Route de La Neuve).

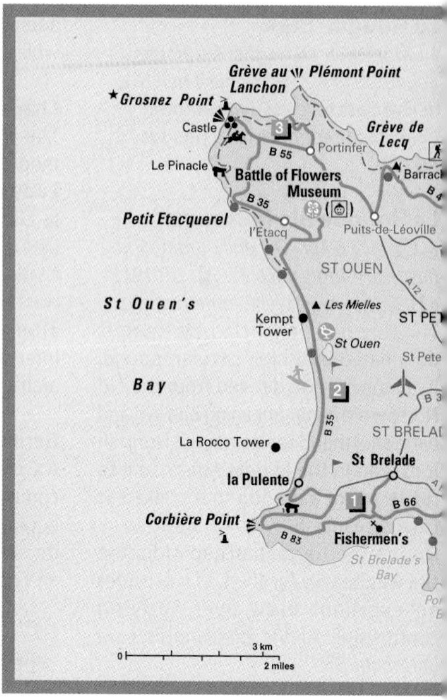

St Aubin

The little town, which faces east across St Aubin's Bay, is particularly picturesque with its long sandy beach, fishermen's cottages and tall granite merchants' houses lining steep, narrow streets or clinging to the cliffs along the shore. St Aubin was invoked as protector against pirates. The local church (1892) has a fine stained-glass window made by William Morris & Co. **St Aubin's Fort** on the island *(access at low tide)* was built in the reign of Henry VIII, 1509–47.

The Corbière Walk from St Helier to Corbière follows the line of the old **Jersey Railway**, which opened in 1870.

Turn left off the main road onto B 57 (Route de Noirmont) for access to the promontory and Portelet Bay.

Noirmont Point★

Command Bunker. Open Apr–Sept Sun 11am–4.30pm. Also some Sat 10am–1pm. Consult Channel Island Occupation Society www.ciosjersey.org.uk. £1.50. P.

The local saying warns of the onset of gales from the southwest:

> *Quand Nièrmont met san bonnet,*
> *Ch'est signe de plyie*
>
> ("When Noirmont (Black Hill) dons his cap, It is a sign of rain").

Beyond the pebble beach nestling in **Belcroute** stretches the headland, still scarred by the remains of substantial German fortifications (1941 and 1943-44) including the **Command Bunker**. The most advanced bastion gives fine views of the rocks immediately below and round westwards to the Île au Guerdain.

Return to the main road A 13 (Route des Genets) and then fork left down B 66 (Mont Sohier).

St Brelade

This favourite seaside resort is situated in a sheltered bay; its sandy beaches and usually safe waters (*certain areas can be tricky)* are ideal for swimming and water-skiing. **Winston Churchill Memorial Park** backs the bay.

At the western end of the beach, behind a screen of trees, the parish church and detached medieval chapel are surrounded by a graveyard.

Parish Church

Light switch inside on the left of the entrance.

The cherished church of St Brelade is built of granite from the cliffs of La Moye. The chancel, nave and belfry date from the 11C. In the 12C the church became cruciform with the addition of a transept; the aisles were added later.

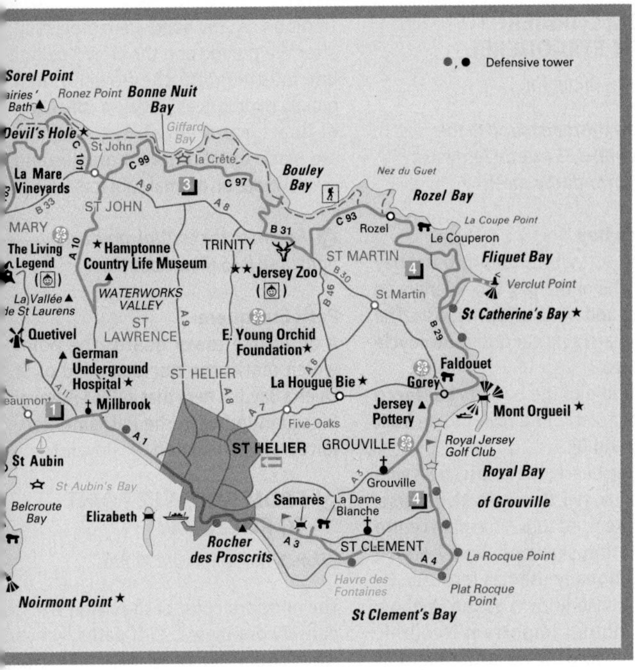

The altar is a solid slab of stone, marked with five crosses representing the five wounds of the Crucifixion. The 15C font is made of granite from the Chausey Islands, which lie south of Jersey and belong to France.

Fishermen's Chapel

Light switch inside on the left of the entrance.

The family chapel, which is built of the same granite as the church, is decorated in the interior with delicate medieval **frescoes**★.

At the east end is an Annunciation dated as c 1375; the other paintings are from a second phase of work c 1425: the south wall (right of the altar) shows *Adam and Eve* followed by *The Annunciation* and *The Adoration of the Magi*; the west wall bears *The Last Judgement*; on the north wall fragments have been deciphered as scenes from *The Passion*.

The paintings survived because from c. 1550 to the mid-19C the chapel was used as an armoury and as a carpenter's shop.

Behind the chapel a short flight of steps leads to a path through the churchyard to the beach; this is the only surviving example of a *perquage*: once commonplace in medieval Europe, these paths were escape routes from a church, traditionally a place of sanctuary, to the shore and away out to sea.

Continue along the road back into town; turn left onto A 13 (Route Orange); bear left down B 83 (Route du Sud) to Corbière.

Corbière

All that remains of the terminus of the Jersey Railway is the concrete platform. As the road descends, a magnificent view is steadily revealed of the rock-strewn point and the white lighthouse rising from its islet: a good place to watch the sun set over the Atlantic. Before the lighthouse *(access on foot at low tide but closed to the public)* was built in 1874, this was a perilous stretch of water where a number of ships foundered; in clear weather the electric beam carries 28km/17.4mi.

2 FROM CORBIÈRE TO PETIT ÉTACQUEREL

13km/8mi – allow 1hr.

Follow the road round to the junction with B 35 (rue de Sergente); turn left towards the coast.

St Ouen's Bay

The deep surf which rolls into the bay makes it a favourite spot for experienced surfboard and windsurf enthusiasts. The firm sand attracts car and motorcycle racing fans.

In the middle of the bay sits **La Rocco Tower**, the last round tower to be built in Jersey (1800).

Beyond the beach, the landscape is wild and uncultivated, the vegetation sparse. **La Pulente** used to be the main centre for gathering seaweed *(vraic)*, which was traditionally used as fertiliser. La Sergenté, also known as the Beehive Hut, is another important Neolithic tomb near to which a large hoard of coins from Brittany was found. The **St Ouen Pond** on the right of the road is a haven for birds and wild flowers, notably the Jersey or lax-flowered orchid. The three upright stones, Les Trois Rocques, are presumed to be part of a dolmen.

Kempt Tower

Open May–Sept daily 2–5pm. £2. P. 01534 483 651.

This defensive tower has been converted into an interpretation centre for a nature reserve called **Les Mielles** (the Jersey dialect word for sand dunes), set up to monitor and protect indigenous plants, birds and butterflies.

Follow B 35 (Route des Laveurs); turn left onto C 114 (Mont des Corvées).

Battle of Flowers Museum

Open Easter–Oct daily 10am–5pm (last entry 4.30pm). £4.50 (children £2). P. 01534 482 408.

The **Battle of Flowers**, held on the second Thursday in August along Victoria Avenue in St Helier, was started in 1902 to celebrate the coronation of Edward VII. Traditionally, the floats were broken up after the parade and the crowd pelted one another with the flowers, then mostly hydrangeas. Today, a collection of floats is presented. The tableaux are made up of different grasses and concentrate on animal subjects.

Return to the coastal road; bear right onto B 35 (Route de l'Étacq).

Petit Étacquerel

A defensive tower guards the point which marks the northern end of St Ouen's Bay. It is here that in 1651 Admiral Blake landed with the Parliamentary forces which defeated the Royalists.

3 FROM GROSNEZ POINT TO ROZEL BAY

27km/17mi – allow 2hr30min.

The northern coast of the island is less densely populated. Cliff paths, which stretch from Plémont Bay to Sorel Point and beyond, provide spectacular views of the uneven coastline and the open sea to France, Guernsey and Alderney.

Continue north by bearing left onto B 55 (Route de l'Ouest): bear left again to reach the car park and look-out point at Grosnez.

Grosnez Point★

An area of desolate heathland, covered with gorse and heather and known as Les Landes, extends from Étacquerel to Grosnez Point. Southwest of the race-course sits **Le Pinacle**, an impressive rock associated with pagan rituals since Neolithic, Bronze Age, Iron Age, even Roman times. Little remains of **Grosnez Castle** (c. 1373–1540); it enjoys magnificent views out to sea, of Sark and the other islands (northwest).

Return to B 55; in Portinfer turn left onto C 105 (Route de Plémont); fork left to Grève au Lançon; eventually the road skirts the holiday village to end in a car park from where a footpath runs along the coast to Grève de Lecq.

Steep cliffs containing caves shelter this attractive small bay, **Grève au Lançon**, which has a sandy beach at low tide. The rocky promontory **Plémont Point** projects into the sea giving a fine view of the cliffs.

Return along C 105 (Route de Plémont); turn left onto B 55 (Route de Vinchelez) from Grosnez, which leads to Léoville in the parish of St Mary. Turn left onto B 65 (Mont de la Grève de Lecq).

Grève de Lecq

Barracks (North Coast Visitor Centre). Open May–Sept Wed–Sat 10am–5pm, Sun 1–5pm. Donations welcome. 01534 482 238. www.nationaltrustjersey.org.je.

The defensive tower on a charming sandy bay with its stream and mill was built in 1780; the conical hill behind is from an Iron Age fortification.

The **barracks** were built between 1810 and 1815 to accommodate the 150 British soldiers who manned the gun batteries on the slopes around the bay. In spring and early summer the area is abloom with wild flowers: gorse, daffodils, bluebells, foxgloves.

The water's edge is broken by jagged rocks locally known as **Paternoster Rocks** after the many prayers uttered by passing fishermen, remembering colleagues who perished there. Far out to sea is the French coast.

From Grève de Lecq continue along B 40 (Mont de Ste-Marie); turn left onto B 33 (La Verte Rue) and left again before the West View Hotel onto C 103.

La Mare Vineyards

Open 6 Apr–Oct daily 10am–5pm. Guided tours Mon–Fri 10.45am–3.30pm (subject to change). £5.50. P. 01534 481 178. www.lamarevineyards.com.

The estate of an 18C farmhouse has been planted with the only vineyards and cider orchard in Jersey.

You can tour the winery and learn about the process. German-style white wines are produced and may be tasted: Clos de la Mare, Clos de Seyval and Blayney Special Reserve.

Continue along C 103 to the Priory Inn.

Devil's Hole★

Park by the inn and take the concrete path down to the cliff.

The blow hole is an impressive sight dramatised by the amplified thunder of the sea entering the cave below. The name is thought to derive from the old French term *creux de vis* meaning screwhole.

Minor roads run east to St John's Parish and north to the coast.

Sorel Point

The section of road named **Route du Nord** is dedicated to the islanders who suffered during the German Occupation (stone marker in the car park). It runs from Sorel Point where a mysterious pool (7.3m/24ft wide by 4.6m/15ft deep) known as the Fairies' Bath (Lavoir des Dames) is revealed in the rocks at low tide. To the east is Ronez Point, a headland scarred by granite quarries.

Hamptonne Country Life Museum★

Open daily 6 Apr–Oct 10am–5pm. £6.70 (child £4.20). P. 01534 863 955. www.jerseyheritagetrust.org.

Jersey's rural heritage is brought alive in farm buildings with the help of talkative, costumed characters.

Drive through St John; turn left onto A 9 (Route des Issues); after the Jersey Pearl Centre fork left again onto B 67 (Route de Mont Mado). Turn left onto C 99, a minor road to Bonne Nuit Bay and Giffard Bay.

Bonne Nuit Bay

This bay, haunted by smugglers and pirates in the past, is a favourite place for swimming and sailing. Charles II is supposed to have returned from exile to England from this attractive bay.

The fort, La Crête, at the east end was built in 1835.

From here a footpath follows the coast to Bouley Bay; to reach Bouley Bay by car, take C 98, B 63, C 97 (rue des Platons).

Bouley Bay

This deep sandy bay protected by a jetty and backed by high granite cliffs is a safe, popular place for swimming.

Return towards Trinity; turn left onto B 31 (rue ès Picots) past Jersey Zoo before turning sharp left onto C 93 (rue du Rocquier) to Rozel Bay.

Rozel Bay

Part of the bay is taken up with a fishing port where the boats go aground at low tide. Above the bay, at the northern end, traces of a great earth rampart survive from the Castel de Rozel, an Iron Age settlement. At the opposite end sits Le Couperon, a Neolithic passage grave (2500 BC).

4 FROM ROZEL BAY TO ST HELIER

13km/8mi – 1hr30min

The road turns inland before returning to the coast above Fliquet Bay and finally meandering down to the water line. **Fliquet Bay** is a rocky bay between La Coupe and Verclut points: an ideal place for deciphering the volcanic evolution of the island.

Either follow the road to St Martin or make a detour to explore the country roads – B 38 (Grande Route de Rozel), B 91 (rue des Pelles), B 91 (Route du Villot), B 29 (Mont des Ormes) to Verclut Point (left) and to Gorey Harbour (right).

St Catherine's Bay★

From the lighthouse at the end there is a magnificent **view★★** of sandy bays alternating with rocky promontories along the coast southwards. Out to sea lie the Ecréhou islets, once a favoured trading bank for smugglers and now a popular spot for a Sunday picnic.

Bear right off the coast road (Route d'Anne Port).

Faldouet Dolmen

A tree-lined path leads to this dolmen, which is 15m/49ft long and dates from 2500 BC. Excavation has revealed a number of vases, stone pendants and polished stone axes.

Gorey

This little port at the northern end of Grouville Bay is dominated by the proud walls of Mont Orgueil Castle on its rocky spur. Attractive old houses line the quay where yachts add colour to the scene in summer.

Mont-Orgueil Castle★

Open mid-Mar–Nov daily 10am–6pm (last entry 5pm); Dec–mid-Mar Fri–Sun 10am to dusk. £9.50. 01534 853 292. www.jerseyheritagetrust.org.

Gorey Castle received its present name in the early 15C from Henry V's brother, Thomas, Duke of Clarence, who was so impressed by the castle's position and its defensive strength that he called it Mount Pride (Mont Orgueil in French). Over the centuries the castle has served as a residence to the lords and governors of the island, including **Sir Walter Raleigh** (1600–03), a prison for English political prisoners, and a refuge for a spy network during the French Revolution. The earliest buildings date back to the early 13C when King John lost control of Normandy and built a castle to defend the island from invasion. In 1996 Queen Elizabeth II handed the castle over to the islanders.

The **view★★** from the top is extensive: down into Port Gorey, south over the broad sweep of Grouville Bay, north to the rocks of Petit Portelet and west to the French coast.

A series of waxwork tableaux in the rooms of the castle illustrates significant events in the history of Mont Orgueil.

Take A 3 along the waterfront.

Royal Bay of Grouville

Grouville is graced with Jersey's finest bay, a magnificent crescent of sand stretching from Gorey harbour to La Rocque Point. The Seymour and Icho Martello towers (1811) may be reached on foot at low tide.

Grouville Church

Originally dedicated to St Martin of Tours, the church has an unusual 15C granite font.

Jersey Pottery★

Open Mon–Sat 9am–5.30pm, Sun 10am–5.30pm. Closed 1 Jan, 25 Dec. No charge. P. 01534 850 850. www.jerseypottery.com.

A paved garden, hung with baskets of flowers and refreshed by fountains, surrounds the workshops where the distinctive pottery is produced. You can watch the craftsmen at work, and the show room displays the full range of products for sale.

Royal Jersey Golf Club

The local golf course enjoys a particularly picturesque position; founded in 1878, it was granted its Royal Charter by Queen Victoria.

St Clement

St Clement is Jersey's smallest parish, named after the church dedicated to Clement I, the third Pope (AD 68–78); it was here that Victor Hugo wrote two volumes of poetry, *Les Châtiments* and *Les Contemplations*, before departing to Guernsey in 1855.

The dolmen at Mont Ubé, the 3.4m/11ft menhir known as **La Dame Blanche**, and a tall granite outcrop called Rocqueberg suggest that this section of the island was inhabited by Neolithic man.

The oldest extant parts of the present church date from the 12C; the wall paintings from the 15C (*St Michael Slaying the Dragon*; *The Legend of the Three Living* and *Three Dead Kings*).

St Clement's Bay

This sandy bay stretches from Plat Rocque Point, past Le Hocq Point, marked by a defensive tower, to Le Nez Point (3km/2mi). Out to sea strong tides sweep through, churning the water.

From A 4 (Grande Route de St Clement) turn onto B 48 (rue du Pontille), which leads onto A 5 (St Clement's Road), to reach Samarès Manor (right).

Samarès Manor

Open Apr–mid-Oct daily 9.30am–5pm. Gardens and manor £6.50. ***Manor house:*** *guided tour (40min) Mon–Sat. £3.50. P. 01534 870 551. www.samaresmanor.com.*

The name Samarès is probably derived from the Norman *salse marais*, the salt pans which provided the lord of the manor with a significant part of his revenue. In the 11C William Rufus, son of William the Conqueror and King of England, granted the Samarès fief to Rodolph of St Hilaire. In the 17C Philippe Dumaresq drained the marsh by building a canal to St Helier and imported trees and vines from France. The gardens were landscaped and replanted by Sir James Knott who acquired the property in 1924. On the grounds is a rare 11C dovecote; in the house there is the Norman undercroft or manor chapel crypt and the wood-panelled dining room.

Continue west on the coast road.

Le Rocher des Proscrits

Small plaque facing the road.

On the east side of the White Horse Inn, a slipway descends to the beach and a group of rocks, Le Rocher des Proscrits (The Rock of the Exiles), where **Victor Hugo** used to meet regularly with fellow exiles.

ADDRESSES

STAY

ST HELIER

Chambre d'hôte La Bonne Vie – *Roseville St, St Helier JE2 4PL. ℘01534 735 955. www.labonnevie-guesthouse-jersey.com. 10 rooms.* Situated close to the beach and the town centre, this flower-decked Victorian house is meticulously looked after. Warm welcome and rather sweet guestrooms with their flowery cushions, curtains, and eiderdowns.

LA HOULE

Chambre d'hôte Au Caprice – *Route de la Houle, La Houle, JE3 8BA. ℘01534 722 083. www.aucapricejersey.com. Closed Nov–Mar. 12 rooms.* White, luminous and airy, with large doors and windows, this house offers comfortable rooms at a reasonable price. Near a long sandy beach.

ROZEL BAY

Hôtel Beau Couperon – *Rozel Bay, JE3 6AN. ℘01534 865 522. 33 rooms. Restaurant*. This fortress from the Napoleonic era, near the Jersey Zoo, offers a splendid view of Rozel Bay. Most of the spacious rooms have balconies. The dining room windows open onto the sea.

GOREY

The Moorings Hotel – *Gorey Pier, JE3 6EW. ℘01534 853 633. www.themooringshotel.com. 15 rooms.* The location of this small, unpretentious hotel, just below Mont-Orgueil Castle and facing the harbour, will certainly appeal to you. The rooms are well fitted, and you will receive a cordial welcome.

EAT

BEAUMONT

Bistro Soleil – *rte de la Haule, JE3 7BA Beaumont. ℘01534 720 249. Closed Sat eve and Mon.* A series of rooms opening into each other, with views over St Aubin Bay. Minimalist style, just a few modern paintings. Audacious menus with a Mediterranean touch.

ST AUBIN

Old Court House Inn – *St Aubin's Harbour, St Aubin, JE3 8AB. ℘01534 746 433. www.oldcourthousejersey.com. Closed 25 Dec.* This 15C inn specialises in seafood dishes. One room is a former tribunal, another the reconstructed stern of a galleon. Terrace overlooking the harbour. Spacious guestrooms.

GOREY

Jersey Pottery Garden Restaurant – *Gorey Village, JE3 9EP. ℘01534 850850. www.jerseypottery.com. Closed Mon.* Adjacent to a pottery workshop, this restaurant is a veritable garden: green plants and vines are throughout the dining room. The local seafood is very good and there is a good selection of sandwiches, salads and desserts.

Suma's – *Gorey Hill, JE3 6ET. ℘01534 853 291. www.sumasrestaurant.com. Closed 23 Dec–Jan. Reservations required.* This elegant restaurant is a favourite of locals and tourists alike. The bright interior displays works by local artists. From the terrace, views of Mont-Orgueil Castle and the harbour.

Village Bistro – *Main Road, Gorey Village, JE3 9EP. ℘01534 853 429. Closed 2 weeks in Nov, Sun eve, Mon. Reservations required.* A family cottage with a relaxed atmosphere. Specialities include prawn-and-mushroom risotto and orange-flavoured crème brûlée. Lunch menu at an attractive price.

ROZEL BAY

Le Frère – *Le Mont de Rozel, Rozel Bay, JG3 6AN. ℘01534 861 000. Closed Sun eve and Mon.* This *frère* (brother) is very much in demand! His secret? A menu to satisfy every taste, reasonable prices and a splendid terrace with a view of the sea and, in fine weather, the French coast.

ST CLEMENT

Green Island – *St Clement, JE2 GLS. ℘01534 857 787. Closed Sun eve and Mon.* This place is very popular with both locals and tourists attracted by its menu based on the local catch and provisions fresh from the market. Relaxed atmosphere in a nautically themed dining room.

LEISURE

Beaches and Swimming – Jersey offers some 30 beaches and bays suitable for swimming; they are among the cleanest in Europe. During summer months, this is generally the hottest place in Great Britain and precautions such as sun screen are recommended.

Biking and Walking – Jersey has networks of footpaths, bike trails and green lanes for non-motorised traffic.

Nightlife – Jersey has 11 discotheques and discobars, and many hotels offer dancing and cabarets. In addition, the island abounds in pubs, many of which also offer meals. Check to be sure children are allowed.

Sark★★

Sark, the last feudal fief in Europe and also the smallest independent state in the Commonwealth, offers peace and tranquillity and a traditional way of life without cars. Its two parts – Great Sark and Little Sark – are linked by La Coupée, a high narrow neck of land which inspired Turner and Swinburne. The island consists of a green plateau bounded by high granite cliffs dropping sheer into the sea or flanking sheltered bays and sandy beaches. Sark is a haven for wildlife – marine creatures in the rock pools and caves; a wide range of bird species; wild flowers in spring and summer.

- **Population:** 600.
- **Michelin Map:** 503.
- **Location:** Sark is located at the very heart of the Channel Islands, 12km/7.5mi E of Guernsey, 30.4km/19mi S of Alderney, 19km/12mi NW of Jersey. The island is 5.6km/3.5mi long by 2.4km/1.5mi wide.
- **Don't Miss:** The magnificent view from the heights of La Coupée.

A BIT OF HISTORY

In the middle of the 6C St Magloire, the nephew of St Sampson, landed in Sark from Brittany with 62 companions and founded a monastery. Little is known of the island's history before it became part of the Duchy of Normandy. In 1042 Sark was given to the abbey of Mont-St-Michel by William the Conqueror, Duke of Normandy. After centuries of intermittent invasions and lawlessness, during which the monks fled, Sark finally returned to English control in the 16C. In 1565 Elizabeth I granted Sark to Helier de Carteret, Lord of the Manor of St Ouen in Jersey, on condition that he establish a colony of 40 settlers prepared to defend the island. He divided the land into 40 holdings, attributing one to each of the 40 families who had accompanied him from Jersey. Half of the island population traces descent to these colonists.

The island of Brecqhou (just off the west coast across the Gouliot Passage), a dependent of the fiefdom of Sark since 1565, was acquired in 1993 by the reclusive multi-millionaire British twins Sir David and Sir Frederick Barclay, who have built a massive neo-Gothic mansion, which they rarely visit.

Constitution

At its head is the hereditary Lord (seigneur) who holds the fief of Sark; the present holder is Michael Beaumont, grandson of Sybil Hathaway, the Dame of Sark, who reigned from 1927 to 1974.

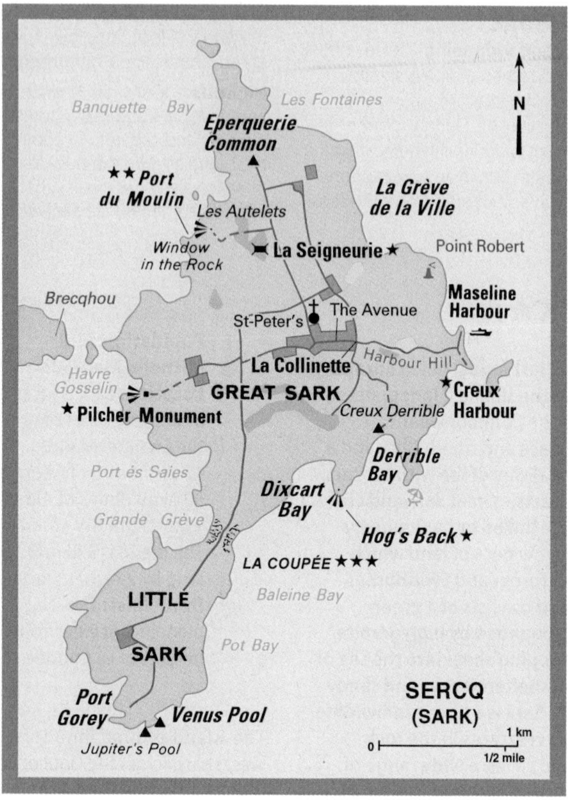

Sark's Parliament, the Chief Pleas, was for 443 years composed of the 40 Tenants plus 12 Deputies elected for three years. In 2006, however, influenced by the Barclay twins, the Chief Pleas voted to install a democratically elected legislature; elections held 10 December 2008 returned 28 elected members, plus two unelected. Candidates backed by the Barclays, however, lost.

EXCURSION

Allow one day.

Great Sark

Maseline Harbour

The lighthouse (1912) looks over the harbour from the cliffs on Point Robert.

Creux Harbour★

Opposite the tunnel to Maseline Harbour is a second tunnel to Creux Harbour, dry at low tide.

La Collinette

A short tunnel leads to Harbour Hill (0.8km/0.5mi); at the top is the crossroads called La Collinette.

Straight ahead stretches **The Avenue**, the main street lined with shops. The small barrel-roofed building on the left at the far end is the two-cell island prison built in 1856. Beyond is **Le Manoir**, built by the first Seigneur and bearing the De Carteret arms. **St Peter's Church** dates from the 19C. The embroidered hassocks are the work of the island women.

La Seigneurie★
La Seigneurie Gardens – ♿ ⏲ Open Easter–Sept Mon–Sat 10am–5pm. £1.80. ☏ 01481 832 345 (Sark Tourism). www.sark.info.
The residence of the Seigneur of Sark stands on the site of St Magloire's 6C monastery. Begun in 1565, it was considerably enlarged in 1730. The square tower, built in 1860, provides a splendid view of the island.
The house is sheltered from the wind by a screen of trees and high walls. The gardens are luxuriant with flowers and shrubs.

Port du Moulin★★
A road along the north side of the Seigneurie grounds becomes a path along the clifftop. Follow the Window and Bay sign to the **Window in the Rock**, which the Rev William Collings, then Lord of Sark, had made in the 1850s to provide an impressive **view** of Port du Moulin.

Return to the fork in the path and take the other branch to Port du Moulin.

The bay, popular with bathers, is flanked by stark rocks in strange shapes. On the right stand **Les Autelets**, three granite columns accessible as the sea retreats.

Derrible Bay
At Petit Dixcart turn left onto a stony path, then right onto a path beside a field; a left fork leads down through the trees to Derrible Bay, which at low tide has a large sandy beach.
Part way down, a turning to the right leads to the **Creux Derrible**, an enormous hole in the granite cliffs (*take care in poor light*).
Return to the first fork and bear left; at the seaward end of the ridge known as the **Hog's Back★** stands an ancient cannon, where a magnificent **view** includes, left, Derrible Bay and Derrible Point, right, Dixcart Bay with La Coupée and Little Sark in the background.

La Coupée★★★
On either side of the narrow isthmus joining Great Sark and Little Sark steep cliffs drop into the sea. The view is magnificent: Brecqhou, Jethou, Herm and Guernsey to the right; the coast of Jersey and the French coast to the left Grande Grève Bay is a good place for bathing.

Little Sark
On the southern headland lie abandoned 19C silver mines. A footpath to the left of the old mine chimney runs down to Venus Pool, visible at low tide, when visitors (*to avoid being stranded, check the time of high tide*) can walk from the Venus Pool westward round the headland via Jupiter's Pool, several caves and the rocks in Plat Rue Bay, to Port Gorey, which served the silver mines.
The clifftop path, always open, provides a fine view down into Port Gorey.

ADDRESSES

STAY
Dixcart – *Dixcart Lane, GY9 0SD. ☏ 01481 832 015. www.dixcartbayhotel.com. 15 rooms.* This is the oldest hotel on the island, housed in a 16C farm. Exposed beams, antique furniture, fireplaces and stone walls add to the warmth of the place, ideal for a restful stay in the bay area.

EAT
La Sablonnerie – *Little Sark, GY9 0SD. ☏ 01481 832 061. Closed mid-Oct–Easter.* A country lane leads to this restaurant located in a beautifully renovated 16C farm. The wood furniture and the fireplace contribute to the rural atmosphere. Spacious guest rooms.

INDEX

A

B

D

E

F

G

H

I

J

K

L

STAY

EAT

MAPS AND PLANS

THEMATIC MAPS

MONUMENTS

LOCAL MAPS FOR TOURING

LOCATOR MAPS

TOWN PLANS

	Sight	*Seaside resort*	*Winter sports resort*	*Spa*
Highly recommended	★★★		✻✻✻	
Recommended	★★		✻✻	
Interesting	★		✻	

Selected monuments and sights

- Tour - Departure point
- Catholic church
- Protestant church, other temple
- Synagogue - Mosque
- Building
- Statue, small building
- Calvary, wayside cross
- Fountain
- Rampart - Tower - Gate
- Château, castle, historic house
- Ruins
- Dam
- Factory, power plant
- Fort
- Cave
- Troglodyte dwelling
- Prehistoric site
- Viewing table
- Viewpoint
- Other place of interest

Sports and recreation

- Racecourse
- Skating rink
- Outdoor, indoor swimming pool
- Multiplex Cinema
- Marina, sailing centre
- Trail refuge hut
- Cable cars, gondolas
- Funicular, rack railway
- Tourist train
- Recreation area, park
- Theme, amusement park
- Wildlife park, zoo
- Gardens, park, arboretum
- Bird sanctuary, aviary
- Walking tour, footpath
- Of special interest to children

Special symbol

- Beach

Abbreviations

A	Agricultural office (Chambre d'agriculture)
C	Chamber of Commerce (Chambre de commerce)
H	Town hall (Hôtel de ville)
J	Law courts (Palais de justice)
M	Museum (Musée)
P	Local authority offices (Préfecture, sous-préfecture)
POL.	Police station (Police)
	Police station (Gendarmerie)
T	Theatre (Théâtre)
U	University (Université)

Additional symbols

- Tourist information
- Motorway or other primary route
- Junction: complete, limited
- Pedestrian street
- Unsuitable for traffic, street subject to restrictions
- Steps – Footpath
- Train station – Auto-train station
- Coach (bus) station
- Tram
- Metro, underground
- Park-and-Ride
- Access for the disabled
- Post office
- Telephone
- Covered market
- Barracks
- Drawbridge
- Quarry
- Mine
- Car ferry (river or lake)
- Ferry service: cars and passengers
- Foot passengers only
- Access route number common to Michelin maps and town plans
- Bert (R.)... Main shopping street
- **AZ B** Map co-ordinates

REGIONAL AND LOCAL MAPS

To make the most of your journey, travel with Michelin maps at a scale of 1:200 000: **Regional maps nos 512 and 518** and the new local maps, which are illustrated on the map of France below. And remember to travel with the latest edition of the **map of France no 721** (1:1 000 000), also available in atlas format: spiral bound, hard back, and the new mini-atlas – perfect for your glove compartment.

Michelin is pleased to offer a route-planning service on the Internet: **www. ViaMichelin. com**. Choose the shortest route, a route without tolls, or the Michelin recommended route to your destination; you can also access information about hotels and restaurants from *The Red Guide*, and tourist sites from *The Green Guide*.

Bon voyage!

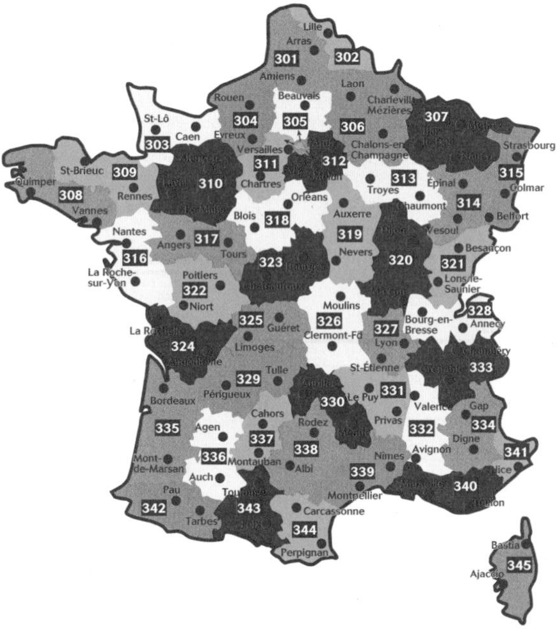

Michelin Apa Publications Ltd

A joint venture between Michelin and Langenscheidt

58 Borough High Street, London SE1 1XF, United Kingdom

ISBN 978-1-906261-87-0
Printed: November 2009
Printed and bound in Germany

Driving Tours

For descriptions of these tours, turn to the Practical Information section following.

- Roman ruins
- Aquarium
- Battle site
- Religious building
- Château, castle or historic house
- Tourist train
- Outstanding natural feature
- Regional specialities
- Fortifications
- Garden, park
- Historic site
- Museum, art gallery
- Viewpoint
- Wildlife park, zoo
- Bird sanctuary, aviary
- Industrial heritage
- Boat trips
- Seaside resort
- Outstanding site
- Spa
- Old town
- Picturesque village